SECOND EDITION

PSYCHOLOGY
EXPLORING OUR UNIVERSE WITHIN

EDITED BY PATRICIA ALEXANDER AND DEBORAH YAKEL

Custom Publishing

New York   Boston   San Francisco
London   Toronto   Sydney   Tokyo   Singapore   Madrid
Mexico City   Munich   Paris   Cape Town   Hong Kong   Montreal

Printed in the United States of America

10 9 8 7 6 5 4 3 2 1

2007500195

CO/RH

Pearson
Custom Publishing
is a division of

www.pearsonhighered.com

ISBN 10: 0-536-53182-X
ISBN 13: 978-0-536-53182-7

Contents

Chapter **1** **Exploring Psychology**
by Boris Vukov, MA   1

Chapter **2** **Research Methods**
by Christopher M. Hakala, PhD,
and Patricia Alexander, PhD   31

Chapter **3** **Biopsychology**
by Robert W. Flint, Jr., PhD   63

Chapter **4** **Sensation and Perception**
by Elizabeth Shobe, PhD, and
Robert W. Flint, Jr., PhD   93

Chapter **5** **States of Consciousness**
by Janice E. Jones, PhD   133

Chapter **6** **Motivation and Emotion**
by Marc W. Patry, PhD, and
Deborah Yakel, PhD   165

Chapter **7** **Learning**
by Brian L. Thomas, PhD   195

Chapter **8** **Memory**
by Vanda Wark, EdD, and Deborah Yakel, PhD   229

Chapter **9** **Thinking, Language, Intelligence, and Creativity**
by Deborah Yakel, PhD 261

Chapter **10** **Gender and Sexuality**
by Amy Sweetman, MA, and Patricia Alexander, PhD 299

Chapter **11** **Social Psychology**
by Christopher Hayashi, MA 341

Chapter **12** **Developmental Psychology**
by Elizabeth Shobe, PhD 377

Chapter **13** **Personality**
by William July, PhD, and Patricia Alexander, PhD 409

Chapter **14** **Psychological Disorders**
by Patricia Alexander, PhD 447

Chapter **15** **Therapies**
by Binh Nguyen, MA 483

Chapter **16** **Health and Stress**
by Robert Flome, MA, MFT, DAPA 511

References 541

Glossary 591

Index 643

Chapter 1

Exploring Psychology

by Boris Vukov, MA

An unexamined life is not worth living.

—SOCRATES

What Is Psychology?

FIGURE 1.1 *A travel through the universe within.*

Few would argue that our universe is filled with wonder and awe, but our inner universe is perhaps even more wondrous, awesome, and mysterious. If you've ever pondered where your thoughts and behaviors come from, you have probably realized that you are attempting to navigate a vast and expansive realm—a universe within. All those thoughts passing through your head . . . sometimes they seem like those of a genius, but other times they don't seem to make any sense at all. Sometimes it even seems like you have no control over what pops into your mind. The more you try not to think about some disturbing memories, the more they haunt you. You have an ability to imagine all sorts of things, right? How do you create those images? Where do they come from? And dreams? Have you ever tried to analyze your dreams in the morning? Why are they so difficult to remember?

Isn't there music you like and music you dislike? Why do you have that preference? What is your favorite painting? *Starry Night* by van Gogh? Perhaps something by Dalí? Why? What kind of emotions, thoughts, or needs does it evoke in you? How did it feel when you realized you loved someone and that love was not returned? How about when the feeling was mutual? How intense is your sexual need? What about your need for realizing your ultimate goals? Have you thought about your need for respect from others?

These questions are just a tiny portion of what makes you, *you*. You are much more than just the thoughts, feelings, and actions that you are aware of on a daily basis. It is not an exaggeration to think about all that is within us as an entire

1

universe. When you complete this book, you will realize that you are much more complex than you could have ever imagined. You will see that it is not just a metaphor to say you have an infinite, vast realm inside you. This book is really like a doorway to the universe within you. Psychology examines that inner world.

What Is Psychology?

Psychology is the scientific study of mental processes, behavior, and physiological reactions. Mental processes are feeling, thinking, sensing, imagining, dreaming, learning language, memory, problem solving, and intelligence. Collectively, mental processes are called the mind. In the word "psychology," "psyche" and "**logos**" derive from Greek. "Psyche" refers to the mind, and "logos" translates as a study; therefore, psychology is truly a study of the mind.

In terms of behavior, psychologists can study reflexes, tremors (rhythmic and uncontrollable shaking of body parts), drug use, walking, talking, intercourse, and so forth. Any behavior that one can think of can be investigated by psychologists. They often investigate behaviors to make inferences about mental processes. We have to make these inferences because we can't directly observe mental processes. In other words, we have yet to invent a mindoscope—a machine that can peek into one's mind and identify very specifically what a person is thinking, feeling, and desiring. Since we can't directly observe mental states, we rely on behaviors to infer what is happening in a person's mind. For example, you are in a store and you see a woman in the makeup aisle. As she looks at the variety of cosmetics, she positions her finger as indicated in Figure 1.2. This behavior suggests to you that she is experiencing a dilemma, so you infer that she can't decide on what makeup to buy.

FIGURE 1.2 *Nonverbal behavior.*

Types of Behavior

Behaviors can be voluntary (happening at will), like deciding to go to school, or involuntary (happening without our will), like reflexes. Behavior can also be verbal and nonverbal. **Verbal behavior** is any behavior that involves producing meaningful sounds, like sighs and moans, and words, such as when writing a letter or telling someone about your current mood. **Nonverbal behavior** refers to actions that involve neither sounds nor words. Some examples of nonverbal behavior are facial grimacing, posture, eye contact, hand gestures, touch, and personal-space habits (Brehm, Kassin, & Fine, 2005).

Same Behaviors in Different Cultures

There is a great deal of continuity across cultures for some nonverbal behaviors such as facial expressions. For example, a smiling face conveys happiness; a frowning face suggests sadness (Ekman & Rosenberg, 2005). However, it is

FIGURE 1.3 *Invasion of personal space can freak one out in some cultures.*

important to know that some similar nonverbal behaviors in different cultures might convey messages about completely different mental processes. For example, shaking your head left and right in the United States means no, but in Bulgaria the same nonverbal behavior means yes. Be careful if you want to say "great" in Germany or Brazil, because if you form a circle with your thumb and forefinger as we do in the United States, you will be making an obscene gesture (Axtell, 1993).

When I visited New Zealand for the first time, a tall, muscular Maori man with tattoos all over his face approached me. In fact, he came so close to me, it appeared he was reaching for my mouth with his. I was shocked! I couldn't move, as I perceived (as a person coming from the U.S. culture) that my personal space was being totally invaded by a stranger with homosexual tendencies. But he didn't kiss me—he just rubbed his nose against mine in the traditional, accepted Maori form of greeting. Once again, we need to be cautious when interpreting behaviors in different cultures.

Sometimes the same *verbal* behaviors mean completely different things in different cultures. My native tongue is Serbian—"da" in Serbian means "yes" in English. When you say "da (duh)" in English, however, it means "stupid."

Physiological Reactions and Psychology

Psychologists also explore **physiological reactions**, which are bodily processes. Examples of physiological reactions are heart rate, breathing, sweating, brain activity, cellular activity, and so on. To study most of these processes you must have special equipment; however, some internal processes can be determined by simply observing the individual. For example, the pupil will dilate in response to emotional arousal. This finding was demonstrated in the movie *Blade Runner*. In the movie, Harrison Ford plays detective Rick Deckard, whose job it is to capture human replicas called replicants. These replicants are without emotions, making them extremely dangerous. Deckard tests them to determine whether they have emotions by asking them questions that can elicit an emotional response. He then watches the reaction of the replicants' pupils, as pupils usually automatically dilate when a person experiences an intense emotion (Partala, Jokiniemi, & Surakka, 2000; Siegle, Granholm, & Ingram, 2001). When he doesn't see a dilated pupil, he knows the subject is a replicant, and thus Deckard "retires" the replicant.

Another example illustrates why psychologists are interested in physiological reactions. A study was conducted that looked at the level of stress women and men experience when they imagine their partner being disloyal to them. Two kinds of disloyalty were investigated: (1) when a partner develops romantic feelings for another person (let's call this emotional disloyalty), and (2) when a partner is physically intimate with another person without emotional connection to that person (physical disloyalty). Researchers asked the study participants (men and women) to imagine first the physical disloyalty of their partner. Participants' physiological reactions, such as heart rate, muscular tension, and sweating response, were measured with a machine, since increased heart rate, more muscular tension, and more sweating suggest more stress. It turned out that males were under more stress than females when physical disloyalty was imagined. However, when participants imagined emotional disloyalty, women were more stressed (Buss, Larsen, Westen, & Semmelroth, 1992).

Psychology Through Time

The psychologist Herman Ebbinghaus (1850–1909) correctly observed that psychology has a long past but only a short history. By this he meant that although people thought about topics of psychology from the earliest times, the history of psychology didn't officially begin until psychology began to emerge as a scientific field, in 1879. This was the year that Wilhelm Wundt (1832–1920), of Germany, founded the first psychology laboratory. Throughout time, people have been curious about the subject matter of psychology and have reflected on attention, thinking, feeling, memory, dreaming, needs, consciousness, verbal and nonverbal behavior, and so on. Wundt, however, wanted to overcome mere opinions about the mind and behavior and create a scientific field collecting evidence to test his views about the mind and behavior. A view that can be scientifically tested is called a **hypothesis** (Thorne & Henley, 2001).

Ancient (3500 BC–AD 500) Views on the Mind and Behavior

There are numerous documents showing ancient people's reflections toward the mind and behavior, but these reflections are opinions and are not based on scientific studies. Most of these opinions came from ancient religions, ancient philosophy, and ancient physiology; hence, we can consider religion, philosophy, and physiology as the roots of psychology. For example, the Egyptians believed that one's soul (modern psychology uses the terms "mind" and "personality" to refer to the soul) resides in one's heart. After the individual's death, the god Anubis put the deceased person's heart on one part of the scale and the feather of truth on the other. If the feather was lighter than the heart, that meant the person was immoral, and the entire mind of that person was devoured by a ferocious beast. If the heart balanced with the feather, however, the god Osiris granted eternal life in paradise to the mind of the deceased individual. Thus the Egyptians believed that one's sense of morality resides in one's heart (Brummet et al., 2003). However, modern science clearly points out that one's morality resides elsewhere—in one's brain. For example, when a person has a bad heart and receives a new heart from a donor, this person does not become any different in terms of his or her mental processes, including the sense of morality. When people suffer brain damage, however, their behaviors may change. There have been cases where someone who was a criminal prior to the brain damage became an upstanding and honest person after the brain damage (Giles, 2004), and there have also been cases of ethical people becoming unethical after brain damage (Damasio, 2005).

FIGURE 1.4 *The Egyptians believed that morality resides in one's heart. Science suggests otherwise.*

Various ancient philosophers offered their opinions on the subject of psychology, but those reflections were not tested scientifically. The ancient Greek philosopher Aristotle (384–322 BC) shared the

Egyptians' belief that the brain is not important for the soul (the mind). Instead, he too believed that the heart is the seat of the mind. This belief was due to an observation that anger and fear produce sensations in the chest (Laver, 1972). Aristotle offered many views on perceiving the world through the senses, thinking, memory, and dreams. For example, he believed that repetition improves our ability to recall something, and that dreams during sleep are similar to hallucinations during wakefulness (Sahakian, 1968). Aristotle believed that the mind of a newborn is a "tabula rasa" (blank slate) so that the mental and behavioral repertoires are learned through one's experience (Schacter, Gilbert, & Wegner, 2007). The idea that experience shapes our mind and behavior has been extensively researched by psychologists.

Another ancient Greek philosopher, Plato (427–347 BC), believed that certain thoughts are inborn, like the ideas of goodness, justice, courage, wisdom, beauty, redness, and roundness (Soccio, 2004). According to Plato, through our everyday experience we are actually learning to uncover these ideas that already exist deep in our minds (Thorne & Henley, 2001). Psychologists today continue to scientifically explore the notion that certain aspects of our minds are innate.

Roman philosophers Cicero (106–43 BC), Seneca (4 BC–AD 65), and Marcus Aurelius (AD 121–180) believed that people have the power to tame their feelings of anger, fear, hatred, and joy, and that conquering these feelings can lead to an ultimate accomplishment—a feeling of serenity or peace of mind. These philosophers, however, did not conduct a scientific study to verify their beliefs (Soccio, 2004).

Chinese philosopher Laozi (6th or 5th century BC) believed that happiness could be obtained by withdrawing from society, living in harmony with nature, breathing properly, eating well, and involving oneself in sexual practices. Confucius, another Chinese philosopher, believed that happiness could be obtained by being a moral person, showing empathy toward others, having a desire to grow as a person, and helping others do the same. Neither Laozi nor Confucius, however, tested their views by collecting research evidence (Brummet et al., 2003; Soccio, 2004). Modern psychologists scientifically study happiness. In one such study, psychologists designed certain exercises that were given to people in order to improve their positive emotions. The participants were instructed to (1) compose a letter of gratitude to someone to whom they were grateful but had never thanked, and read that letter to the person by phone or in a face-to-face meeting, and (2) each evening write down three good things that happened and explain why they thought these things happened. The study showed that engaging in these exercises for just one week helped people feel happier. The positive effect of exercise #2 lasted for six months (Seligman, Rashid, & Parks, 2006).

Modern psychology originates, in part, from ancient physiological views. Physiology is the study of how the body works. This field explores the functioning of the body by investigating its electrical and chemical processes, cells, tissues, organs, and bodily systems. These include the skeleton, the muscles, the nervous system, the senses, the system of blood vessels and blood, the lymphatic system, the immune system, the respiratory system, the urinary system, the digestive system, the system of glands and hormones, the reproductive system, and the skin (Martini et al., 2004; Sherwood, 2004). Reflections on the relationship between the bodily functions and the mind and behavior are apparent in the writings of the ancient Greek Hippocrates (5th century BC). He saw the importance of proper nutrition and exercise as a means of introducing balance to the bodily fluids, which in turn contributes to mental health (Magner, 1992). He properly believed that the brain creates sorrow, pain, grief, thoughts, a sense of beauty, and the sense of morality (Breedlove, Rosenzweig, & Watson, 2007). However, he erroneously believed that mental disorders are caused by a wandering uterus. In some mental disturbances, he believed that the uterus was lodged behind the woman's eyes. To remedy this problem, he prescribed pregnancy. While Hippocrates' contemporaries believed that epilepsy was caused by the gods stealing the victim's mind, Hippocrates believed that the illness resulted from an imbalance of four body fluids: black bile, yellow bile, blood, and phlegm. We know today that epilepsy results from an imbalance in the brain chemicals called neurotransmitters. Although Hippocrates did not test his views and although his views were often incorrect, he did posit correctly that there is a connection between the mind and the workings of the body.

How Did the Renaissance (AD 1300s–1600s) Influence Psychology?

FIGURE 1.5 *The Renaissance influenced the emergence of science, which was suppressed by the Dark Ages.*

Many scientific accomplishments, including Wundt's establishment of the first psychology lab, were influenced by the progressive developments of the Renaissance (AD 1300s–1600s), a period within the medieval era (AD 500–1600s). The medieval period also contains the Dark Ages (AD 500–1300s), named in such a way due to rare attempts to question established views dictated by the church. For example, the **Malleus Malleficarum** (or The Witch Hammer) was a religious text used by church authorities (in AD 1400s) to identify and punish witches. The book stated that females are sexually insatiable. Due to their extreme sexual desire, the book viewed women as easy prey for the devil, who could seduce them. The only relevant desire was the desire to worship God.

Whereas the Dark Ages confined human curiosity within the dark walls of its views that were not to be challenged, the Renaissance opened the doors to freedom of exploration. It is important to mention the factors that facilitated this different **zeitgeist**, or spirit of the time (Thorne & Henley, 2001). The development of cities was one of those important factors. Independent from rulers, growing cities allowed companies and technology to expand, which led to a development of ships that in turn opened the exchange of ideas. Also, there were no slaves in the cities. Thus the Renaissance was the right environment for unconstrained thinking to happen (Leahey, 2004).

Another factor was the invention of printing, which took place in the fourteenth century. Before printing was invented, books were written manually, which slowed down their distribution as well as the generation of new ideas. With the new process, however, books could spread much faster through the masses of common people (not just the clergy), who could now more easily afford them. Also, the time saved by mechanical book production could now be used to explore new ideas and develop new knowledge. Printed books became more accessible to the people now that they were written in their native languages; formerly they had been published in Latin, a language comprehensible only to the clergy (Thorne & Henley, 2001).

In addition, Martin Luther (AD 1483–1546), the founder of Protestantism, convinced many laypeople that the clergy were, in many respects, thinking and behaving in a manner counter to their preaching about justice and compassion. Luther pointed especially to the practice of selling **indulgences**—papers stating that one's sins were forgiven. This act seriously undermined the church's authority and opened the door for exploration. The emphasis on exploration was no longer on God but on the human mind and behavior. This view that the exploration of humans rather than God should be the primary focus is called **humanism** (Thorne & Henley, 2001).

Renaissance astronomers conducted rigorous scientific calculations to verify the church's views about the universe. They realized that it was not the earth that was the center of the universe, as the church wanted them to think, but rather the sun that was the center of our galaxy and the earth revolved around it, just like any other planet of the system. This revolutionary discovery is called a **paradigm shift**, a major change in the standard way of thinking, and it opened even wider the doors to explorations beyond dogma (Thorne & Henley, 2001). All these factors facilitated much broader-minded thinking than during the earlier years of the medieval period.

Physiological advancements of the Renaissance were also important for psychology. Leonardo da Vinci (1452–1519) was one of the first artists to produce drawings of the bodies he dissected. His representations of anatomical structures were important for researchers to visualize the internal complexities of the body (Breedlove et al., 2007) and to later refine da Vinci's drawings. Leonardo's focus on humans stimulated other researchers to focus their explorations on humans too—a dramatic change from the preceding medieval era, which almost exclusively concentrated on the teachings of God and his relationship with humans.

In considering the dissection of the human body, philosopher René Descartes (1596–1650) noticed that the body is composed of various fibers, organs, and fluids, which reminded him of machines at the time. Adopting the view that the human body is machinelike, he proposed the idea of a reflex that involves several steps. For example, when a person touches fire, a stimulus from the environment (heat, for example) causes the movement of the fluid through the fibers of one's arm. This fluid travels to the brain and back to the arm so that the person automatically withdraws his or her arm (responds reflexively) from the stimulus. While the details of Descartes' view on reflexes are incorrect, he nevertheless stimulated researchers of the time to think of human behavior in terms of the bodily processes occurring in anatomical structures that can all be scientifically studied. He also proposed the idea that the human mind causes behavior of the body and that the mind interacts with the brain (specifically, in the pineal gland of the brain stem) to affect behavior. While many aspects of his views are incorrect, Descartes saw a relationship between the brain and the mind and behavior—a relationship that subsequent researchers have explored scientifically (Breedlove et al., 2007). In 1600, physician William Gilbert

(1540–1603) published one of the first papers on electricity, a force that later proved to be extremely important for understanding how the brain gives rise to the mind and behavior (Thorne & Henley, 2001).

Modern-Age (1600s–Present) Views on the Mind and Behavior

The Renaissance was a springboard for the modern age (1600s–present day) to develop. This new epoch was characterized by much more unconstrained thinking than the medieval period. This improved thinking was obvious in **empiricism**—a philosophical school of thought from the seventeenth century that argues that human knowledge derives from our experience and observation. Some famous empiricists were John Locke (1632–1704), David Hume (1711–1776), and George Berkeley (1685–1753). Empiricism significantly influenced psychology, as one of the essential elements of psychology is an understanding that knowledge has to derive from collected evidence and that the evidence can be obtained through observation and measurement (Thorne & Henley, 2001).

Biological discoveries of the modern age (eighteenth and nineteenth centuries) were especially important for psychology. People accepted the notion that the mind and behavior are produced by the nervous system. Researcher Luigi Galvani (1737–1798) demonstrated that the nervous system conducts electricity, and other researchers showed that electrical stimulation of the nervous system results in changes in mental processes and behaviors. For example, Roberts Bartholow (1831–1904) elicited a visual and auditory experience in patients whose brains he stimulated with an electrical current (Thorne & Henley, 2001). The importance of the nervous system for the mind and behavior also became clear in discoveries pertaining to brain damage. Researchers demonstrated that damage to the nervous system affects aspects of the mind and behavior. Moreover, damage to different brain regions causes different problems in the mental processes and behaviors. For example, Paul Broca (1824–1880) discovered that if a patient suffers an injury to a specific brain area, the patient will have serious problems producing speech sounds. Carl Wernicke (1848–1904), however, noticed that when a different brain area was injured, the patient could speak but the language was incomprehensible (Thorne & Henley, 2001).

Science of the Mind and Behavior

Even though the empiricists advocated for the collection of evidence, and advancements in the field of biology (modern age especially) were based on the collection of evidence, we cannot say that the above-mentioned investigators clearly intended to create a scientific field such as psychology. Wilhelm Wundt, however, is credited for intentionally developing psychology as a separate field.

The year 1879 is usually taken as the date when psychology officially became a science. At that time Wundt was a professor at the University of Leipzig in Germany. In his laboratory, he launched a completely new field, psychology, and the objective was very clear—a scientific investigation of the mind and behavior. Wundt moved psychology from the realm of speculation to his lab, where he could perform serious studies with research design, research participants, instruments, data collection, and measurements. Wundt created the first psychological journal dedicated to experimental research, and he supervised numerous graduate students in psychology, many of whom later became influential psychology figures (Thorne & Henley, 2001).

Historical Approaches

Voluntarism

Wundt's goal was to scientifically explore the human consciousness by examining his research participants' behavior. More specifically, his interest was in how people experience the world primarily through their vision and hearing. His focus was the study of the structure of consciousness, such as the experience of quality (e.g., is an object yellow or blue, round or rectangular?) and of intensity (e.g., how bright is the yellow object?). In one experiment Wundt studied people's reaction times to light by measuring how long it took them to release a button they held down. Then he measured how much longer it took them to release the button when they had to determine the color of light (Bernstein, Penner, Clarke-Stewart, & Roy, 2008).

FIGURE 1.6 *The roots of psychology are religion, philosophy, and physiology.*

FIGURE 1.7 *I was thinking here, "Did you also get in the photo that mountain behind me?" Introspection is reporting your subjective experience.*

Wundt also investigated the **span of attention**, or how many stimuli (words, letters, numbers, etc.) can be held with clarity in one's consciousness with a single exposure. In his experiment, stimuli were flashed on a screen, and subjects were asked to recall them. Wundt saw human attention as a process that we can direct at will to the stimuli that enter our experience. Wundt called this view—that we can choose what we experience—**voluntarism** (Thorne & Henley, 2001). He also investigated human feelings, concluding that the basic aspects are pleasure, displeasure, tension, relaxation, and excitement. Wundt pioneered the technique of **introspection**—research participants reporting their subjective experience (Bernstein et al., 2008). He was criticized by his colleague Hermann Ebbinghaus for relying too much on introspection, because people can be biased and erroneously report their subjective experience. Also, Ebbinghaus pointed out that Wundt's research on human consciousness was limited since he focused almost exclusively on sensation and perception but didn't explore learning and memory, which are also important mental processes (Bernstein et al., 2008).

Structuralism

Edward Titchener (1867–1927), one of Wundt's students, was influenced by Wundt to study the structure of the human consciousness. By exploring participants' introspection and employing similar machines that Wundt used in his experiments, Titchener also explored the elements of the consciousness, such as sensations (hearing, vision, etc.), images, and feelings. He also explored the features of these elements, such as quality, intensity, duration, clarity, and so on. Titchener was primarily interested in the basic structural elements of the consciousness; thus, he called his system **structuralism**. To illustrate a distinction, consider the following: Titchener saw attention as a mere term that we ascribe to the clarity of our experience, while Wundt saw attention as an act of our will, which is capable of selecting our experience. Another major difference between these two individuals was that Wundt didn't believe that psychology could scientifically explore mental processes such as language, memory, and thinking. Titchener disagreed with this view. He graduated from Oxford in 1890 (Leahey, 2004) and later moved to the United States, where he created a psychology laboratory at Cornell University (Thorne & Henley, 2001).

Gestalt

German psychologists Kurt Koffka (1886–1941), Wolfgang Kohler (1887–1967), and Max Wertheimer (1880–1943) believed that Wundt and Titchener were not doing justice to psychology by breaking the human mind into its elements or parts. They argued that the whole (or **Gestalt**, in German) of experience is more than the mere sum of its parts. In other words, just adding together the elements of experience doesn't produce the totality of experience.

For example, in one of his famous experiments, Wertheimer presented two lights that flashed rapidly in succession on a screen. When the time between the flashes was set for one-fifth of a second, the research participants saw the flashes as two separate lights flashing one after the other. However, when Wertheimer reduced the time between flashes to about one-twentieth of a second, the participants saw a single flash moving back and forth. Since the lights were so rapidly presented, the participants couldn't see the individual flashes and they falsely interpreted the flashes as a single, moving flash. Thus, the experience of individual flashes combined into a whole (a single moving flash). Wertheimer termed this illusion of movement the "phi phenomenon" (Schacter et al., 2007).

This phenomenon is similar to a blinking traffic signal indicating that the right lane will close and that we should move into the left lane. We see the blinking lightbulbs on the sign and it appears as though the arrows are moving. In reality, the lightbulbs aren't moving; rather, the pattern of the blinking lights creates this apparent motion in our mind. According to Gestalt psychologists, our experience of the apparent motion is more than just the experience of

FIGURE 1.8 *You don't see individual details on the dancer's dress (although they do exist), but a unified, round whole.*

the individual lights flashing in a particular sequence; this phenomenon is an experience of individual stimuli combined into a whole. Gestalt psychologists discovered various principles that are still used today to explain human perception (Bernstein et al., 2008).

Functionalism

FIGURE 1.9 *What is the function of the human consciousness in a harsh environment?*

Like the Gestalt psychologists, William James (1842–1910) argued that Wundt's and Titchener's approaches to the study of the human experience were too simplistic, and that exploring the mind by breaking it down into its elements was like studying a house by looking at its bricks. Rather than study the bricks (elements) of the house (the mind), James (1890) wanted to know what the function of the "house" was. Thus, James's approach, called **functionalism**, was to study the functions of the mental processes. The function of consciousness, according to James, is to help one adapt to the environment so that he or she can survive and progress. For example, consider Figure 1.9. In this scenario, the function of the consciousness is to identify the threat, which is coldness. This awareness helps the person decide to wear warm clothing (Thorne & Henley, 2001). James is also credited for creating the first psychology laboratory in the United States, at Harvard University in the late 1870s. This lab, however, was primarily designed for demonstration purposes to educate students, not for research.

Modern Contributions

Freud and Psychoanalysis

Another influential figure in psychology is Sigmund Freud (1856–1939), who heavily emphasized the unconscious mental processes (the ones that we are not consciously aware of) as primary forces in shaping human behavior. Freud was especially interested in helping mentally disturbed individuals overcome their problems, and he used a therapy he termed psychoanalysis. The goal of **psychoanalysis** was to bring to the patient's awareness all conflicts among the patient's impulses, rational decisions, and moral attitudes. Freud believed that these conflicts exist in the patient's unconscious, and by employing psychoanalysis, the patient could "unearth" the conflicts and face them in a mature way, which would in turn cure that person. Freud proposed some additional revolutionary ideas, such as childhood sexuality, as well as an idea that the development of personality is influenced by the development of sexuality. Freud is an important figure in the history of psychology, as he offered numerous novel ideas, many of which have inspired the process of their scientific verification through research studies that still go on today. Many psychoanalysts today are influenced by Freud's notions, and they are often successful in helping people feel better when they are disturbed (Bernstein et al., 2008; Schultz & Schultz, 2005).

Behaviorism

John Watson (1878–1958), who taught psychology at Johns Hopkins University, held that the focus of psychology should be an examination of observable behaviors in humans and animals. Only the observable, according to Watson, can be objectively measured and studied; thus the mind (which is subjective) cannot. While Watson believed that the human mind does exist, he thought, however, that the mind should not be an object of scientific investigation. This focus on the observable, measurable behavior is called **behaviorism**. His emphasis was the study of learning and how learning affects the development of human and animal behavior. From 1920 until the 1960s, behaviorism was a dominant approach in psychology. During this time, the study of consciousness was not nearly as attractive for psychologists as behaviorism. Consciousness, however, became attractive to scientists of the 1970s and continues to be explored today (Bernstein et al., 2008).

Gender and Ethnic Diversity in Psychology

Margaret Floy Washburn (1871–1939) was the first woman to obtain a PhD in psychology, in 1908 at Cornell University (Plotnik, 2005). Her supervisor was Titchener (who also supervised other PhD students, one-third of which were women). Later, she published *The Animal Mind,* the first book about animal psychology in the United States. In the book she focuses on the findings (at the time) of perception, memory, and learning across different animal species. She also maintains that animals, like humans, have conscious experience (Scarborough & Furumoto, 1987). She was the president of the American Psychological Association in 1921, and, like Titchener, she was a structuralist. She also taught psychology at several colleges and universities (Thorne & Henley, 2001).

Another well-known early female psychologist was Mary Whiton Calkins (1863–1930). When she was a student at Harvard, her psychology teacher, Hugo Munstenberg (1863–1916), recommended her as a PhD candidate. However, Harvard (unlike Cornell University) did not grant women PhD degrees until 1963, so she was rejected as a candidate. Meanwhile, Radcliff College had offered Calkins a PhD in psychology, but she refused the offer since she saw in it a way for Harvard to continue its discrimination against women. This setback did not stop Calkins from teaching psychology at Wellesley College and from publishing over 100 papers and 4 books. Her most important contributions to psychology are in the field of memory research and the concept of self. For example, she was the first to identify the **primacy versus recency effect**, which refers to an observation that we are most likely to remember information that was most recently presented to us as well as information that was presented to us first (Madigan & O'Hara, 1992). She also stressed the importance of the exploration of the concept of self and its relationship to others (Wentworth, 1999). In 1903 she was ranked as one of the most important American psychologists, and in 1905 she was elected the first female president of the American Psychological Association (Thorne & Henley, 2001).

One of the first well-known psychologists of Mexican ancestry was George Sanchez (1906–1972). He obtained his PhD at the University of California, Berkeley. His research disproved the view that Mexican children are racially inferior to Caucasian children. His evidence demonstrated that reading scores and intelligence scores of Mexican children can be significantly improved when the tests are accurately translated into the Spanish language, and when they reflect the culture of the children. Sanchez's work was well known in the 1930s in the United States, and it continues to stimulate contemporary psychologists to argue for adjustment of tests to the ethnic context to which the tested individual is familiar. Sanchez is considered to be the father of Chicano psychology (Padilla, 1988).

Francis Sumner (1895–1954), who attended Clark University, was the first African American student to obtain a PhD in psychology in the United States, in 1920 (Schacter et al., 2007). One of his major contributions was the development of an undergraduate program at Howard University, which graduated more African American psychologists than any other university at the time. In 1933 Beverly Prossor (1897–1934) earned a PhD in psychology from the University of Cincinnati, and she became the first African American female psychologist. The first African American president of the American Psychological Association (in 1971) was Kenneth Clark (1914–2005). His research focused on the negative self-image of African American children (Schacter et al., 2007). One of his major contributions in the field of social psychology was research that found that African American preschool children preferred White dolls to Black dolls (Thorne & Henley, 2001). Clark's studies pointed out that segregation of the races creates psychological harm for African American children, and his research influenced the Supreme Court to outlaw racial segregation in public schools in 1954 (Schacter et al., 2007).

Modern Perspectives in Psychology

Psychology is a broad-minded field, as it attempts to understand a phenomenon from various angles or perspectives. We will take an example of human behavior and try to understand it from these different angles, addressing the following perspectives: psychodynamic, cross-cultural, learning, cognitive, biological, humanistic, and evolutionary. It is important to understand that these perspectives are often not exclusive; in other words, you can try to understand a phenomenon by having an eclectic perspective—consisting of several or all perspectives complementing one another.

Why Did Anakin Skywalker Kill the Tuscan Raiders?

Our example deals with *Star Wars: Episode II—Attack of the Clones*. In a scene from the movie, a virtuous Jedi knight in training, Anakin Skywalker, finds out that his mother is a prisoner in a camp of dangerous humanlike creatures called Tuscan Raiders. Finding her seconds before she dies, he becomes enraged and kills everyone in the camp—even his enemies' babies. Why did Anakin do this when a Jedi kills only in self-defense? You will see that different psychological perspectives offer different explanations (these explanations are not mutually exclusive, though).

Psychodynamic Perspective

The **psychodynamic perspective** argues that mental processes and behaviors result from conflicting interactions among three mental structures: the **id** (one's impulses), the **ego** (one's reasoning and planning), and the **superego** (one's sense of morality). The founder of this perspective was Sigmund Freud (1856–1939).

TABLE 1.1	Some important individuals who influenced psychology.	
3500 BC–AD 500, Ancient Period		
3100–332 BC	Egyptians	Egypt
6th and 5th century BC	Confucius	China
6th and 5th century BC	Laozi	China
5th century BC	Hippocrates	Greece
106–43 BC	Cicero	Rome
4 BC–AD 65	Seneca	Rome
427–347 BC	Plato	Greece
384–322 BC	Aristotle	Greece
AD 500–1600s, Medieval Period/Dark Ages		
AD 1300s–1600s, Medieval Period/Renaissance		
AD 1600s–Present, Modern Age		
1737–1798	Luigi Galvani	Italy
1824–1880	Paul Broca	France
1832–1920	Wilhelm Wundt	Germany
1842–1910	William James	United States
1848–1904	Carl Wernicke	Germany
1856–1939	Sigmund Freud	Austria
1863–1930	Mary Whiton Calkins	United States
1867–1927	Edward Titchener	England
1871–1939	Margaret Floy Washburn	United States
1878–1958	John Watson	United States
1880–1943	Max Wertheimer	Germany
1886–1941	Kurt Koffka	Germany
1887–1967	Wolfgang Kohler	Germany
1895–1954	Francis Sumner	United States
1897–1934	Beverly Prossor	United States
1914–2005	Kenneth Clark	United States

Returning to the example, Anakin's aggressive impulses (his id) completely overwhelmed him, and he acted to satisfy these impulses. Due to this surge of id, Anakin's ego (rational/practical aspect of one's mind) was prevented from functioning properly. Otherwise, the rational/practical ego would have stopped Anakin, telling him, "Hey, stop! You are going against the Jedi code.

FIGURE 1.10 *Shadow.*

If you obey your aggressive impulses, you will suffer negative consequences—you will be punished by the Jedi council." When Anakin later reflects on what he did, his superego (sense of morality) judges his aggressive impulses as morally unacceptable, and his ego evaluates his behavior as senseless—acting in a way opposite from what a Jedi would do. Anakin's id, however, still feels hatred toward the Tuscan Raiders, and he is anxious due to the conflict between his superego and ego on one side, and his id on the other (Schultz & Schultz, 2005).

Carl Jung (1875–1961) was another important contributor to psychodynamic perspective. He would have posited that Anakin killed the Tuscan Raiders because he was influenced by the human tendency to be impulsively destructive. Jung called this tendency/aspect of the mind the **shadow**. He also called it an **archetype**—a very old, primeval tendency passed genetically from parents to their offspring. Later remorseful, Anakin tells his fiancée what he has done to the Tuscan Raiders; he expresses his genuine compassion for them, or his **Anima archetype**—a male's feminine tendencies. According to Jung, archetypes exist in the human **collective unconscious**—a realm of the mind we share with our ancestors, and the realm of which we are not consciously aware (Crowne, 2007).

Cross-Cultural Perspective

The **cross-cultural perspective** places an emphasis on the human mind and behavior as largely influenced by the culture in which an individual is raised (Shweder & Sullivan, 1993). According to this perspective, Anakin must have been raised in a culture in which he witnessed a lot of aggression and where it was normal to use force to solve problems. As you may recall from the movie, Anakin was indeed raised on a planet where killing and confrontation were everyday occurrences. Also, slavery was the norm on this planet, and Anakin and his mother were slaves of a rude, heartless slave owner. The atrocity Anakin committed was a product of his upbringing. If, however, Anakin were raised in a different culture, a peaceful one, his behavior could have been very different.

Learning Perspective

Explore **learning** in Chapter 7, p. 212

Influenced extensively by Edward Thorndike (1874–1949) and B. F. Skinner (1904–1990), the **learning perspective** views behavior as a product of its consequences. If a behavior's consequences are positive, the behavior will probably be repeated (or learned). If the consequences are negative, the behavior will probably not be repeated (Galef, 1998; Skinner, 1938; Thorndike, 1898).

According to this perspective, Anakin killed the Tuscan Raiders because his aggressive behavior had been *rewarded* in the past, and for that reason he repeated it. Recall in *Episode I—The Phantom Menace* when Anakin is in the spaceship and engages in a shootout with robots in a hangar. After he destroys the machines, he is considered a hero. According to this learning perspective, if his aggressive acts had not been rewarded in the past, then he probably would not have committed such violent acts later on.

Ivan Pavlov (1849–1936) and John Watson (1878–1958) belonged to a different learning school of thought, providing some striking evidence that behavior does not have to be learned only through its consequences (Fancher, 1979). According to this school of thought, it is possible that in the past, Anakin witnessed an anger-provoking event—the slave owner shouting at Anakin's mother, for example. Feeling angry, Anakin left his home and went to the desert, to be alone. But he was not alone, since the Tuscan Raiders lived in the desert, and Anakin noted their presence. Frequently when the slave owner was rude to his mother, Anakin would go to the desert, always observing the Tuscan Raiders. Later, even in the *absence* of the slave owner's rudeness, when Anakin saw the Tuscan Raiders, he felt angry *at them*. How is this possible? The image of the Tuscan Raiders was associated with his anger (when his mother was treated badly), so that whenever he saw them, his anger was evoked. Anakin learned to be angry at the Tuscan Raiders. This particular school of thought would argue that Anakin killed the Tuscan Raiders because he learned to associate his anger with them.

Cognitive Perspective

Explore
cognition
in Chapter 9, p. 262

The term "cognition" means "thinking." **Cognitive perspective** suggests that mental processes and behaviors are motivated by the thinking aspects such as language, expectations, memory, problem solving, and decision making (Neisser, 1967). Anakin was facing a problem—should he kill the Tuscan Raiders or spare them? When he approached them, he didn't understand what they were shouting (they spoke a different language), yet he expected that they perceived him as their enemy. He interpreted the words they shouted as obscenities directed toward him. Because of his negative expectation and his inability to comprehend their language, he didn't feel any connection or empathy toward them. He recalled the vivid, painful memory of his mother's suffering in captivity, and this memory influenced his decision to kill them. His act was justified by his reasoning: the fewer of these creatures in the world, the fewer the problems in the world.

Biological Perspective

Donald Hebb (1904–1985), Roger Sperry (1913–1994), and Karl Lashley (1890–1958) were important contributors to the **biological perspective**. The biological perspective views behavior and mental processes as resulting from genes, hormones, anatomical structures, and the physiological process of the body (Kolb & Whishaw, 2003). This view would explain Anakin's behavior by pointing to biological processes in his body that are responsible for what he experienced and did. He felt anger, and he became aggressive due to a surge of activity in his **amygdala**—the area of the brain associated with aggression. He couldn't inhibit the aggressive impulse coming from the amygdala, since the frontal lobe (rational part of the brain) was overwhelmed with the activity of the emotional part of the brain (amygdala).

Why was Anakin unable to inhibit his amygdala when his Jedi mentor, Obi-Wan Kenobi, would surely inhibit his amygdala in the same situation? Biological perspective might discuss genetics, specifically that Anakin's *genes* created a more active amygdala in his brain and a less active frontal lobe. Biological perspective might also say that Anakin's blood contained more testosterone—the hormone linked with aggression—than Obi-Wan's blood.

Humanistic Perspective

According to the **humanistic perspective**, a human being is someone who has the potential for the entire range of experience and behaviors (for example, sadness, joy, good deeds, and bad deeds) and strives to fulfill his or her potential. Abraham Maslow (1908–1970) and Carl Rogers (1902–1987) represent this perspective. A person's mind and behavior are influenced by needs such as food, shelter, friends, having a certain social status, and realizing one's ultimate dreams and talents. A person is free to make choices about his or her life (Maslow, 1970; Rogers, 1961).

This perspective would say that Anakin killed the Tuscan Raiders in a moment of weakness. His strong need for belonging, for family, and for his living mother influenced the surge of his rage and his choice to kill. Even though he did not do the right thing, this doesn't mean that he won't ever regret what he did. Since Anakin, like anyone else, has the potential for good and bad, the time might come when Anakin will "awaken" and choose the right behavior. In fact, this is exactly what you see in *Episode 6—Return of the Jedi*. In this final episode, Anakin chooses goodness, since only that path can satisfy his need to become a person of virtue.

FIGURE 1.11 *We have the potential to be destructive and constructive. It's up to us to choose what aspect will predominate.*

Evolutionary Perspective

Charles Darwin (1809–1882) was one of the major contributors to the view of evolutionary perspective. According to the **evolutionary perspective**, there are mental processes (e.g., sexual desire) and behaviors (e.g., intercourse) that are motivated by survival. Organisms may need to change their behavior to adapt to a changing environment; otherwise, the organism may eventually die. This process of mental and behavioral change that allows adaptation is called evolution. Mental processes and behaviors that are important for survival are passed down from ancestors to their offspring through their genes (Buss, 1999).

Returning to Anakin, his ancestors were able to survive by utilizing anger (mental process) and by fighting (behavior) their enemies. Anakin's ancestors passed down to him their anger and their fighting skills. Anakin started his Jedi training as a very talented pilot, but his skill was not refined enough to cope with an increasingly hostile environment where only an expert warrior could survive. Anakin's fighting skills (piloting and the use of the lightsaber) tremendously improved over the years, and he became a superb warrior. His anger and his improved fighting skills allowed him to kill his enemies—the Tuscan Raiders. By killing their children, he completely eliminated the Raiders' chances of survival and maximized his own. The improvements in his fighting skills and the persistence of his anger enabled him to adapt to the hostile environment.

Careers in Psychology

By now you probably have a pretty good understanding of what psychology is and how it has developed over time. Therefore, we will now discuss the careers available to those who have a degree in psychology. Generally speaking, a person with a degree in psychology can be involved in research, clinical practice, teaching, or any combination of these. Researchers design studies to gain knowledge about phenomena of interest to them, and practitioners apply that knowledge to everyday situations. Let's look at these career options more specifically (O'Hara, 2005).

Clinical Psychologists deal with assessment, treatment, and prevention of psychological disturbances. For example, they help a patient deal with physical pain, the crisis of a divorce, or the death of a loved one. They also help the patient to overcome mental health issues such as panic attacks, depression, schizophrenia, and substance abuse. Some clinical psychologists specialize in specific populations such as gays and lesbians, minority groups, and the elderly. Clinical psychologists work in clinics, hospitals, rehabilitation centers, counseling centers, universities, medical schools, and independent and group practices (O'Hara, 2005).

Counseling Psychologists interview and test people to advise them in dealing with life changes or making changes in their lives. In comparison to clinical psychologists, counseling psychologists deal mostly with issues related to marriage, family, and career. For example, counseling psychologists conduct vocational and career assessment and guidance, help students adjust to college, and help people with marital problems. They may also advise on overeating and drug abuse. They work at university counseling centers, individual or group practices, and hospitals (O'Hara, 2005).

Positive Psychologists study the strengths and virtues that help people and communities to thrive. Some of the human strengths that these psychologists investigate are our capacity for love, courage, compassion, resilience, creativity, curiosity, self-knowledge, moderation, self-control, wisdom, responsibility, parenting, justice, work ethic, leadership, teamwork, and tolerance. Positive psychologists seek to provide people with the knowledge of how to build families and schools that allow children to flourish, how to create workplaces that have satisfied and productive employees, and how to establish communities that encourage people to identify issues of public concern and to act to improve their societies (Compton, 2005).

Cognitive Psychologists research cognition, specifically perception, learning, memory, creativity, reasoning, intelligence, decision making, problem solving, and language. Cognitive psychologists are interested in the steps of the creative process, ways for memorizing information, animals' ability to learn language, and artificial intelligence (computers) as models of human thinking (O'Hara, 2005).

Developmental Psychologists research psychological development throughout people's life spans. These psychologists investigate when and how a person becomes aware of oneself, when and how a person is most vulnerable to the influences of social factors (like peers, family, school, and the media) and to the influence of biological factors (like genes, hormones), the development of moral reasoning and speech, and age differences in the perception of death (American Psychological Association [APA], 2003; O'Hara, 2005).

Educational Psychologists research the factors that facilitate human learning at all ages. Being aware of these factors, educational psychologists develop teaching tools and methods so that optimal learning can happen in an academic and work environment (APA, 2003; O'Hara, 2005).

School Psychologists actively interact with public and private schools, where they conduct assessments and counsel students, consult parents and school staff, and implement interventions when students need them (e.g., teaching them to improve study skills). They are also involved in developing programs that educate children with special needs (APA, 2003; O'Hara, 2005).

Engineering Psychologists research ways of improving human interaction with machines. They are concerned with issues such as what type of airplane interior is the most relaxing for people who fear traveling in airplanes, and what type of computer design best prevents eye strain. These psychologists work mostly in industry settings (APA, 2003; O'Hara, 2005).

Experimental Psychologists research motivation, attention, learning, memory, emotion, sensation, and perception in human participants and animal subjects. Experimental psychologists are interested in questions such as the following: Why do we fear snakes? What is stronger, a need for food or a need for attachment with a parent? What are the consequences of sleep deprivation? These psychologists work mostly in academic settings, private research settings, and in business, nonprofit, and government organizations (APA, 2003; O'Hara, 2005).

Forensic Psychologists apply psychology to the law. They are important in court because they are often asked to evaluate a defendant's mental competence to stand trial or to determine which parent should get custody of a child. These psychologists are also interested in the accuracy of eyewitness testimony (APA, 2003; O'Hara, 2005).

Health Psychologists study how psychological factors influence the development, prevention, and treatment of illnesses. For example, they are interested in how one's expectations of recovery from illness affect that person's actual recovery, and why some patients don't comply with their medications. They develop programs to prevent teenage pregnancy, substance abuse, risky sexual behaviors, poor diet, and lack of exercise and sleep. They also educate people about the optimal doctor-patient relationship. These psychologists work mostly in hospitals and in private practice (APA, 2003; O'Hara, 2005; Straub, 2002).

Industrial/Organizational Psychologists apply their knowledge of psychology to the workplace. Their objective is to improve the quality of work experience and productivity. For example, they are interested in the colors and the type of lighting that can influence job satisfaction and optimal work output, and how to avoid crowding employees in too small of a workspace. These psychologists are often asked to suggest improvements for marketing plans. They are also important in selecting the optimal employees for certain jobs and for training new employees (APA, 2003; O'Hara, 2005).

Neuropsychologists research the relationship between the nervous system and the mind and behavior. For example, they are interested in the biological processes that are the bases for love, fear, learning, memory, and drug addiction. Clinical neuropsychologists can also assess and treat people with psychological problems (APA, 2003; O'Hara, 2005).

Quantitative/Measurement Psychologists participate in research design, analyze collected data, and evaluate the quality and fairness of psychological tests (APA, 2003; O'Hara, 2005).

Psychometrists construct, administer, and interpret psychological tests. From these tests, psychometrists are able to assess people's skills and abilities and predict their performance in career and academic settings (APA, 2003; O'Hara, 2005).

Social Psychologists research how other people influence one's mind and behavior. For example, they are interested in how others such as our parents or peer group influence our attitudes toward people from different ethnic groups and our actions toward them. They address questions such as why and to what extent do we obey authorities, what types of leaders influence our actions the most, what makes a romantic relationship last, and what strategies do people use to persuade us. These psychologists work mostly in academic settings, advertising agencies, business organizations, and government (APA, 2003; O'Hara, 2005).

Sports Psychologists work with athletes to help them learn to concentrate, build self-confidence, set and achieve goals for themselves and their teams, maximize their time and organize themselves, utilize relaxation in coping with anxiety, develop imagery skills to attain their goals, reduce aggression on the court and deal with fan violence, build team cohesion, be more motivated, and deal with failure and injuries (APA, 2003; O'Hara, 2005).

The Job Outlook

What can you do with your degree in psychology? This is an important question, of course, and the answer depends on the type of degree you have. With a bachelor's degree, for example, you can be an assistant in rehabilitation, mental health, or correctional centers, or you can be a research assistant. You may also be able to teach psychology in high school if you meet state certification requirements. Most graduates with bachelor's degrees have jobs in administrative support, public affairs, education, sales, business, health, biological sciences, or computer programming. They work as correction counselor trainees, interviewers, probation officers, writers, personnel analysts, and employment counselors (APA, 2003; O'Hara, 2005).

With a master's degree, you can work in clinical, counseling, and school psychology. You can also be a psychometrist or work in the field of quantitative psychology. You can be involved in research and data collection and analysis at universities, private companies, and the government. Individuals with master's degrees in psychology hold industry and government jobs in compensation, data analysis, personnel issues, and training. You can also teach psychology at community colleges and high schools (APA, 2003; O'Hara, 2005).

If you are a doctoral graduate, the greatest range of jobs and the highest-paying jobs are available to you. Many doctoral graduates pursue research and teaching jobs in the academic environment. Most doctoral graduates have jobs in the fields of clinical, counseling, and school psychology, as well as industrial/organizational psychology (APA, 2003; O'Hara, 2005).

When considering employment, it is useful to know which areas offer the most jobs. Statistics show that 25% of psychologists work in colleges, universities, and professional schools—doing research and writing; 18% in mental health facilities (such as clinics, hospitals, and counseling centers)—conducting testing and therapies for disturbed children and adults; 40% in private practice, consulting businesses, and other organizations—testing and treating disturbed children and adults; 6% in business and government—assessing job satisfaction of employees, testing potential employees, improving leadership skills, identifying conflicts and resolving them, offering stress management, and improving equipment design for better productivity; 4% in schools (including schools for developmentally disabled and emotionally disturbed children)—testing mental abilities, consulting with parents, creating programs to improve academic performance, and identifying problematic children; 8% in other fields—conducting research on military personnel and research in private organizations, teaching prison inmates, and advising lawmakers on public policies and educational issues (APA, 2006).

Chapter Summary

In this chapter you learned that psychology is a scientific study of mental processes, behaviors, and physiological reactions. Psychologists make inferences about mental processes by examining behaviors and physiological reactions. Behaviors can be verbal or nonverbal, voluntary or involuntary. Physiological reactions are bodily processes that reflect mental processes such as emotional reactions and the experience of stress.

People have reflected on the subject matter of psychology since ancient times. These reflections are evident in religious and philosophical writings. However, the conclusions of the ancient thinkers were not obtained through the scientific method; thus many of these opinions were incorrect. The Egyptians believed that one's soul resides in one's heart, not recognizing the importance of the brain for the mind and behavior. The ancient Greek philosopher Aristotle offered many views on sensing, thinking, memory, dreams, and how human knowledge derives from experience. Plato, another ancient Greek, believed that ideas are inborn, like the concepts of goodness, justice, courage, wisdom, and beauty.

Ancient Chinese thinkers such as Laozi and Confucius offered their opinions about what constitutes happiness.

The Renaissance period was especially important for the emergence of psychology since it offered a new kind of thinking beyond the view of the church. Leonardo da Vinci began drawing human anatomical structures that stimulated researchers to look into the human body and explore it. This kind of exploration was not at all the focus of the medieval era, which emphasized the need for understanding God and his bond with humans. Another Renaissance thinker, René Descartes, saw a relationship between the brain and the mind and behavior. William Gilbert published one of the first papers on electricity in the brain, a force that was later more thoroughly explored and proved to be extremely important for understanding that the electricity of the brain influences the emergence of the mind and behavior.

Some additional factors during the Renaissance contributed to the emergence of psychology: technological advances that led to the development of ships that in turn opened the exchange of ideas; the invention of book printing, which facilitated the spread of ideas among common people; the Protestant revolution, which publicly exposed the clergy's views and practices that were designed to manipulate the people; and astronomers' mathematical calculations and observations that pointed to the inaccurate beliefs of the church.

Biological discoveries of the eighteenth and nineteenth centuries convinced researchers that the mind and behavior have biological foundations. All these advancements influenced the emergence of the new science of psychology in the late 1870s. Wilhelm Wundt created this new science, and his goal was to conduct scientific research to collect data about the mind and behavior. He created the first psychology lab, at the University of Leipzig in Germany. During the early history of psychology, researchers adopted different approaches to their psychological endeavors. For example, structuralists like Wundt and Titchener were interested in the basic structure of the mind, such as sensations and their characteristics. William James, however, felt that the structuralists were reducing the mind to its bare elements without taking into account the functions of the mind; thus he proposed his functionalist view of the mind.

Women were not able to earn PhD degrees from some educational institutions, while at the same time men were granted these degrees. However, female psychologists actively participated in the development of the field of psychology from its very beginning. African American psychologists also made early contributions, starting with Francis Sumner, who was the first African American student to obtain a PhD in psychology in the United States, in 1920. In 1933 Beverly Prossor earned a PhD in psychology from the University of Cincinnati, and she became the first African American female psychologist. One of the first well-known psychologists of Mexican ancestry was George Sanchez, whose evidence demonstrated that reading scores and intelligence scores of Mexican children can be significantly improved when the tests are accurately translated into the Spanish language and when they reflect the culture of the children.

Today psychology explores its subject matter by employing various perspectives—the most famous ones being psychodynamic, cross-cultural, learning, cognitive, biological, humanistic, evolutionary, and eclectic. Psychodynamic perspective identifies the conflicts among the id, the ego, and the superego as the main force that motivates our mind and behavior. Cross-cultural perspective places an emphasis on the human mind and behavior as largely influenced by the culture in which an individual is raised. Learning perspective views behavior as a product of its consequences. Positive consequences lead to the behavior being repeated, and negative consequences reduce and eventually eliminate the behavior. Learning perspective also argues that behavior does not have to be learned through consequences but through association. Cognitive perspective suggests that mental processes and behaviors are motivated or governed by the thinking aspects such as language, expectations, memory, problem solving, and decision making. The biological perspective views behavior and mental processes as resulting from genes, hormones, anatomical structures, and the physiological process of our body. According to humanistic perspective, a human being is someone who has the potential for the entire range of experience and behaviors and strives to fulfill his or her potential. According to the evolutionary perspective, there are mental processes (e.g., sexual desire) and behaviors (e.g., intercourse) that are motivated by survival. The organism must be able to adapt to a changing environment or it will not survive. An eclectic perspective incorporates all these perspectives into a complementing whole.

Finally, you have a good idea of what careers are available in psychology, in case you are considering it as your profession. We hope that you will consider psychology after reading this book, and that you will recognize yourself in some of the career fields described in the chapter: counseling psychology, positive psychology, cognitive psychology, developmental psychology, educational psychology, school psychology, engineering psychology, experimental psychology, forensic psychology, health psychology, industrial/organizational psychology, neuropsychology, quantitative/measurement psychology, psychometry, social psychology, and sports psychology.

Knowledge Builder

RELATE TO YOURSELF

1. Imagine that you hold a degree in psychology. What career in psychology would you choose (clinical psychologist, neuropsychologist, etc.) and why?

   I would also like in cognitive
   psychologist because I am ? would
   ly ... people ... I remember

2. A friend of yours who has never taken a psychology class tells you that taking such a course is a waste of time since psychology is just opinionated mumbo-jumbo about how people think. Do you agree with your friend? If not, why not?

   _____

   _____

   _____

   _____

3. Try to put yourself in the mind of Wilhelm Wundt. It is the nineteenth century, and you have an urge to create a psychology lab. Can you explain why you have such an urge?

   _____

   _____

   _____

   _____

4. You are a psychologist who has a humanistic orientation/perspective. You are invited to present your argument about whether the death penalty for murderers should exist. What would be your argument?

   _____

   _____

   _____

   _____

CHAPTER REVIEW QUESTIONS

1. Translated from Greek, the term "logos" means "the brain." **T or F?**

2. According to Freud, we cannot have a mental process that we are not aware of. **T or F?**

3. Three types of behavior are verbal, nonverbal, and paraverbal. **T or F?**

4. Psychology explores thinking, memory, dreams, and consciousness, but the study of positive emotions is not a concern of psychology. **T or F?**

5. The founder of the field of psychology is Gottfried Wilhelm Leibnitz. **T or F?**

6. Dogma is _____ .

    (a) a hypothesis   **(b)** a type of mindoscope

    (c) the same as karma   **(d)** a set of religious beliefs accepted without question

7. _____ research cognition, specifically perception, learning, memory, creativity, reasoning, decision making, problem solving, and language.

    (a) Engineering psychologists   **(b)** Clinical psychologists

    (c) Cognitive psychologists   **(d)** Neuropsychologists

8. The _____ perspective argues that Anakin Skywalker was overwhelmed with id when he killed the Tuscan Raiders.

    (a) psychodynamic   **(b)** Ptolemaic

    (c) humanistic   **(d)** learning

9. Watson's psychological approach that focuses on the observable, measurable behavior is called _____ .

    (a) behaviorism   **(b)** functionalism

    (c) structuralism   **(d)** existentialism

10. You are a student of Kurt Koffka's, and you have just presented a lecture titled "The Demise of Structuralism and the Rise of Gestalt." Judging by the audience's standing ovation (including Kurt, who was in the audience), your lecture and demonstration completely impressed the listeners. Explain how you won over the audience and what kind of message you presented.

    _____

    _____

    _____

    _____

11. *Consider the following scenario:* Pretend that you are John Watson, and, as Watson, you are deeply concerned that Freud's ideas about the mental processes are inaccurate. You know they are inaccurate because you are convinced that there is a fundamental problem in *how* Freud explores the mind. What can you say to the scientific community in order to persuade them that a paradigm shift is badly needed in *how* evidence is collected in psychology?

_____

_____

_____

_____

12. *Consider the following scenario:* An international competition titled *Psychology Meets Art* awards $1 million to the painting that best captures the artist's message. To enter the competition, you must create a painting titled the *Roots of Psychology.* Describe your painting and what it represents (for artistic expression you can use any style, such as realism, surrealism, cubism, impressionism, etc.). The judges will determine how well the artistic images capture your message.

_____

_____

_____

_____

13. How did the Renaissance influence the emergence of psychology, and how did the Dark Ages affect the progress of psychology?

_____

_____

_____

_____

USEFUL WEB SITES

AMERICAN PSYCHOLOGICAL ASSOCIATION (APA)

www.apa.org

The APA is a major global psychological organization. This is an excellent site to find out about advancements in the field of psychology, internships or employment possibilities, conferences, and the benefits of APA membership.

PSI CHI, THE NATIONAL HONOR SOCIETY IN PSYCHOLOGY

www.psichi.org

This site introduces you to Psi Chi—one of the most active psychology organizations on campuses. This honor society organizes research competitions, holds conferences, publishes a magazine, and provides about $225,000 annually in awards and grants.

PSI BETA, NATIONAL HONOR SOCIETY IN PSYCHOLOGY

www.psibeta.org

Psi Beta is primarily for students at two-year colleges. In other respects it is very similar to Psi Chi.

THE AMERICAN BOARD OF PROFESSIONAL PSYCHOLOGY (CERTIFICATION)

www.abpp.org

This site explains the process that certifies psychologists.

BOOK BY SHELLEY O'HARA: *WHAT CAN YOU DO WITH A MAJOR IN PSYCHOLOGY?: REAL PEOPLE, REAL JOBS, REAL REWARDS*

www.wiley.com

This book gives you an excellent understanding of your options if you pursue psychology as a career, along with the steps you will need to complete to obtain your degree(s) in psychology.

Chapter 2

Research Methods

by Christopher M. Hakala, PhD, and Patricia Alexander, PhD

No amount of experimentation can ever prove me right; a single experiment can prove me wrong.

—ALBERT EINSTEIN

Psychological Science

Psychology is a science. Researchers in this field have many of the same goals as scientists in other fields and, in fact, use many of the same approaches implemented in other forms of science. When investigating a phenomenon, psychologists employ the **scientific method,** which refers to a series of techniques and attitudes that speak to the way we try to answer questions about the world. For example, let's say you are interested in understanding how studying in college influences students' grades. You could answer this question by simply asking your friends how they study and what their grade point average (GPA) is. However, this approach may not yield an accurate answer, because your friends might not tell you the truth or they may inadvertently mislead you because they don't know how they study, having never thought about it. Also, your friends might not be like the majority of other people, so their responses won't tell you what is true for most people. A better way to investigate the matter is to follow the scientific method. Specifically, you should have as objective a method as possible when studying an issue that interests you. Try to eliminate bias when asking the question by gathering information in such a way as to give an accurate picture of the behavior you want to know about, without the influence of the problems that can occur when you simply ask your friends. This chapter introduces you to the scientific method, used by psychologists to help answer difficult questions about human behavior.

Research is essential in psychology because it helps psychologists accomplish their goals. This chapter will help you understand more specifically the role that research plays in psychology. You will learn about not only the techniques used to gather information about the phenomena in question but also the manner in which psychologists use statistics to help them understand the meaning of the information they have gathered.

The Scientific Method

The scientific method begins with making observations of phenomena. This step refers to the systematic noting of and recording events. Once observations are made, they must be measured to determine the dimensions of the event. Typically, in the field of psychology this involves finding a way to quantify human characteristics or behaviors. For instance, if you want to know about anxiety in human beings, you can talk to a group of people about what makes them anxious. You might then summarize the variety of things the group has indicated that make them anxious. Or, you might decide to list all the different anxiety-provoking stimuli that were brought up. At this point, you have begun to quantify the content of your discussion. Another way to understand the anxiety of this same group would be to give each person an anxiety assessment tool, such as a paper-and-pencil instrument like the Taylor Manifest Anxiety Scale. After each assessment is scored, you could discuss with the group members their scores as compared with the average score for the group, so that each person could see whether he or she is less anxious, about the same, or more anxious than his or her fellow students. The benefit of quantifying the level of anxiety experienced by people is that you can make comparisons among individuals and between groups of people.

Once a phenomenon has been observed and measured, the next step in the scientific method is to develop a tentative explanation about the observed events. This is known as constructing a theory. Theories aren't of much use, however, unless they are tested. To assess whether a theory is accurate, a testable hypothesis should be developed. A **hypothesis** is a predictive statement that proposes a relationship (usually cause-and-effect) between two or more variables. After the hypothesis is constructed, the next step is to conduct an experiment to test the hypothesis; at the same time, the theory from which the hypothesis was generated is tested. Data are collected, which means that more observations are made, and then analyzed. The data either support the hypothesis or fail to support it. Thus, the original theory is given either more credence or less. The last stage of the scientific method is to publish the results. This allows other researchers in the field to scrutinize the methodology used and to ensure that the researchers followed the rules of the scientific method, so that their findings can be trusted. Publication also helps prevent useless repetitions of the same research. Of course, some attempts to replicate the results will need to be made, because research findings are of no use if they cannot be verified by the work of others. However, once a sufficient number of replications

TABLE 2.1 **Steps of the scientific method.**
Make observations
Measure the observed phenomenon
Construct a theory to explain the phenomenon
Propose a hypothesis to test the theory
Conduct an experiment to test the hypothesis
Analyze the data collected during the experiment
Publish the results to make the findings public

have been done, the results should be trusted and the researcher should move on to the next step in a given research area. In this way, scientists build on the research of others to form a reliable body of knowledge about some subject matter.

The Goals of Psychology

Psychologists typically have goals that they try to accomplish in order to understand human behavior. These goals are to describe, explain, predict, and control behavior. The goals of psychology follow the steps of the scientific method, but they also apply to the process that a psychotherapist goes through when attempting to help people suffering with difficulties in their lives. Clinical psychologists work to help people overcome their problems, whereas experimental psychologists try to provide answers to questions about why people do what they do.

Suppose that you have a friend who is an elementary school teacher. She complains that a child in her fourth-grade class is "incorrigible." You want to help your friend, so you plunge in and ask her what the child is doing that is so upsetting. She tells you that this young boy, Jose, wads up paper and throws it around the classroom. He also talks when his teacher is giving instructions or teaching a lesson. In addition, Jose touches his classmates in ways that provoke them to slap him back. You have just obtained a detailed *description* of this boy's behavior. What else should you know in order to fully understand the situation? Well, what do the teacher and the other kids do when Jose engages in these behaviors? Let's suppose that sometimes the other kids laugh at Jose, and other times they slap him when he touches them. As Jose's teacher, your friend tends to stop her lesson to talk to Jose about his behavior in order to try to get him to stop what he is doing.

Have you developed a tentative *explanation* about why Jose acts the way he does? You might think that he is seeking and getting attention as a result of what he is doing. There are other possible explanations, of course, and we won't know which is correct until we check them out. One way to find out what is really going on is to test the possible explanations, one by one. If we can make a prediction based on the tentative idea that Jose is seeking and receiving attention, we might be able to determine whether we are on the right track.

Prediction of a behavior means that we can anticipate under what circumstances the behavior will occur in the future, and how the behavior will manifest itself under certain circumstances. What makes the scientific method superior to relying on common sense is that the former strategy predicts what people are likely to do, whereas commonsense explanations tend to be applied after the fact. When predictions turn out to be true, the theory upon which the predictions were based is strengthened. If, however, the predictions don't pan out, then the theory (or tentative explanation) is called into question.

The fourth goal of psychological science is *control*. Control refers to altering conditions that affect behavior. Psychologists attempt to control behavior for humane reasons. For example, if Jose's behavior in his fourth-grade classroom can be controlled, then he will learn better, the other students' ability to learn will also be improved, and the teacher will be more likely to enjoy her job. Similarly, if a clinical psychologist helps his client overcome a serious depression, control is involved. Whenever psychologists are able to predict behaviors, they have uncovered an accurate enough explanation for the things that they have observed to allow them to exert some control over the situation.

Beginning the Research

Explore
interpersonal attraction
in Chapter 11, p. 361

Research in psychology begins with an interest in a particular topic. Naturally that interest stimulates the formulation of a research question. Let's assume that you are interested in understanding why two people become friends. You notice that sometimes people who are friends have very different personalities. Then, in other cases, people who are friends have similar interests and experiences. Is it the case that "opposites attract" or is it that "birds of a feather flock together"?

In order to become testable, a research question must be transformed into a hypothesis. In the case of our current example, a hypothesis might be that people who are similar will be more attracted to each other than people who are dissimilar. The researcher will need to decide how to measure both similarities among people and attraction. Then the researcher will select a particular technique for gathering the appropriate data. Obtaining data is essential in order to confirm or disconfirm a hypothesis.

Defining Variables

Before we even begin to make observations, we need to make sure that we have clearly and concisely defined our variables. A **variable** is any observable phenomenon that can take on more than one value in any given study. Examples of variables that may be of interest to psychologists are income, number of courses taken in psychology, IQ, handedness, level of depression, and memory scores. A problem that psychologists often have is that although there are many variables that are of interest to the discipline, many of them are not easily defined or measured (quantified). Consider the difference between measuring behavior and measuring other aspects of the natural world. In the natural world, we might measure the number of one-celled animals in a particular drop of water or the luminescence of the sun at noon. These variables are clearly defined and easily measured (assuming we have the proper instruments). Many of the variables that are of interest to psychologists (friendship, for example) are not so easily quantified. To alleviate the difficulty that this problem creates, psychologists create **operational definitions** for their variables. To operationalize a variable, psychologists define it in such a way that the variable in question can actually be measured by using some form of reliable instrument.

As was mentioned earlier, a psychologist might be interested in friendship. Friendship is a variable that is not easily measured directly, as there really is no way to establish any completely objective definition of this concept. In fact, there have been a plethora of studies done on friendship, and in each, psychologists used their own definition of the term. This situation contrasts a great deal with some of the natural sciences. For example, in biology we can clearly define most of our variables because we are working with directly observable phenomena. However, in psychological science we often work with variables that aren't directly observable, so we need to make some accommodations. Thus, researchers must state how they intend to measure a variable such as friendship and what behaviors they plan to use as a proxy for the concept of friendship. A researcher interested in friendship might operationally define it as the number of times a person talks to another person or the number of times a participant refers to that person in a conversation. Alternatively, among elementary school children, friendship might be defined as those with whom the child plays at recess or with whom the child sits during lunch. In such a way, the researcher states in clear terms what he or she is going to use as a means of identifying the concept of friendship. This definition of the concept may not coincide with a definition that you would develop in your own research, but as long as the researcher clearly states an operational definition of the variable, he or she can convey to others how friendship has been measured and understood in the research study.

Research Techniques

Psychology relies on a variety of well-established research techniques to collect data. Some research techniques are clearly observational in nature, and we will turn to those techniques first. Later in the chapter we'll look at experimentation, which is the most sophisticated research tool available to psychologists.

Observational Techniques

When psychology began as a separate discipline from philosophy in 1879, the main point of distinction between the two was that psychology relied on **empirical evidence** (data gathered through direct sensory experience) rather than on intuitive speculation. Throughout most of the early history of the discipline, psychologists worked diligently to establish psychology as a scientific enterprise. The rise of psychological science really began to take shape when behavioral psychology emerged as a dominant perspective through the work of many of the early American psychologists, including John B. Watson (1878–1958), B. F. Skinner (1904–1990), and Margaret F. Washburn (1871–1939). According to their scientific perspective, observation is essential in psychology. We cannot know the causes of behavior without first describing them, and we cannot describe a behavior without first observing it in a controlled (carefully monitored) setting. Much of the work of mid-twentieth-century psychology is predicated on this simple assumption.

Although the methods of doing observation have changed over the years, observation still remains the essential component of research in psychology, as in all sciences. Studying a problem in psychology involves carefully constructing observations of the phenomenon under different (carefully controlled) conditions.

FIGURE 2.1 *Nonparticipant observation—knowing that we are being observed can change our behavior, so concealment may be desirable.*

For example, psychologists are often interested in questions about behavior in specific contexts. Consider a psychologist who wants to understand how children in elementary school learn to read. To answer questions about how children learn this essential skill, we could observe children under a variety of teaching strategies in the classroom and attempt to determine which strategy is most effective. Such a technique is called **naturalistic observation**, and psychologists often use this method of investigation. Naturalistic observation involves going to the actual location where the behavior of interest occurs and observing it as it happens. This can occur with some form of participation (such as actually taking part in the situation being observed, which is called **participant observation**) or without intervention (such as observing from a separate location, which is called **nonparticipant observation**).

Both strategies have positive and negative aspects. If we participate in the situation, we might get caught up in what is happening and cause a change in the behavior we are interested in observing. Even without active participation, an obvious observer can alter the behavior of those being observed. Consider a situation in which you were being observed by a teacher. The mere act of being observed may change your behavior so that you are not doing what you would normally do. Or, consider being at a party with an acquaintance who doesn't normally associate with you and your friends. You may act differently because that person is present. Under both observational situations, the behavior in question and the results that are obtained from observing these actions may not be representative of what typically happens in these situations. On the other hand, it may be difficult to make observations while concealed from the view of our subjects.

Survey

FIGURE 2.2 *Survey data may be collected over the phone.*

One research technique that has proved important in psychology is the **survey method**. It is a procedure for collecting data from participants, which consists of a series of questions designed to help understand a particular group's attitude or actions on some topic. Surveys can be administered through paper-and-pencil forms, telephone interviews, face-to-face interviews, or by computer. There are several important benefits to using surveys: You can gather a great deal of information at one time, you can ask questions about what people *might* do in a given situation without having to put them into the actual situation, and you can collect data from a large number of people in a short amount of time. However, there are drawbacks to using surveys. First, participants do not have to reply to questions on surveys if they choose not to. If the survey is administered in a classroom, students could potentially respond in a way that others around them might respond, by looking at what others are putting on their surveys and following suit. Second, participants could simply not answer the questions honestly, because they want to present themselves to the researchers in a favorable light. These problems need to be considered when using surveys for research purposes. It must also be understood that the majority of people asked to participate will decline, which means that the sample will probably be biased. For instance, those who have a vested interest in the outcome of the survey are more likely to participate than those who do not. This and many other situations can bias the survey responses.

Case Study

Another research technique that psychologists can employ is the case study. A **case study** is an intensive examination of an individual with characteristics or abilities that the researcher wishes to study. For example, we might study someone who demonstrates a high degree of memory ability or someone who has had an accident that makes him or her unique. Phineas Gage (1823–1860) is a famous case study. He was a railroad worker who was initially a popular mine supervisor and a rational and emotionally balanced man. Phineas suffered a devastating brain injury when a mining charge detonated accidentally, sending a metal rod through his brain that severed the connections between his frontal lobe (a brain area that supports rational thinking) and the limbic region (which mediates the experience of emotions). Amazingly, Gage survived, but he seemed to be a different person after the accident. As a consequence of this terrible injury, Phineas's personality radically changed—he became irrational, powerless to tame his frequent mood swings. Many of the case studies that have been done in psychology involve people who have suffered unfortunate circumstances, and they provide a unique glimpse into the varieties of human behavior that we wouldn't otherwise observe.

Explore
the biology of personality
in Chapter 13, p. 433

It is important to realize that all that can be determined from a case study is what happened to a particular individual in a given situation. That is, we cannot use the results from the study of a single individual to judge whether the results would be the same for other people. In general, a case study provides us with a very detailed description of a phenomenon, and this phenomenon may or may not generalize to others we are interested in knowing about.

Limitations of Nonexperimental Research Techniques

The previously mentioned research techniques are common in psychology and are important in the study of mental processes and behavior. However, from the research strategies using the previously mentioned nonexperimental techniques, we cannot draw conclusions concerning cause and effect. This is because, by using these techniques, we may get a very detailed *description* of a phenomenon, but we don't have the ability to say that we know that something caused a mental process or behavior to occur. So far we have examined descriptive techniques that are forms of nonexperimental research. They help us accomplish the first goal of psychology—description—but cannot help us explain or predict or control behavior.

Experimental Designs

As mentioned previously, nonexperimental techniques are good for helping researchers gain insight into a particular phenomenon. However, nonexperimental techniques do not allow us to explain, predict, and control behavior and mental processes—the other goals of psychology— since they only allow descriptions of behaviors and mental processes. The lack of control one has over the variables of interest makes it difficult to draw conclusions about data. Therefore, researchers will often attempt to answer research questions by controlling or manipulating variables, using an **experiment**. The essential elements of an experiment are independent and dependent variables, to which we turn next.

Independent and Dependent Variables

An **independent variable** is the variable in an experiment that is the presumed cause of some effect, and it is the variable that is *manipulated* (i.e., changed from one group to another) by the experimenter. In a typical experiment we might try to understand the effects of the drug caffeine on human behavior. Thus, we would have caffeine be the independent variable. We would divide our sample of subjects into two groups, an experimental group and a control group. The **experimental group** would be given the caffeine, and the mood and behavior of the subjects in this group would be monitored. The **control group** subjects would not be given caffeine; they would either receive nothing or receive an inactive substance that looks like caffeine but does not influence behavior. For example, in many drug studies, participants are given a **placebo** (an inert substance, such as a sugar pill) to use as a basis of comparison with the experimental condition. The purpose of giving a placebo is to disguise which group has been given the active ingredient.

We then measure our experimental result (the consequence of giving caffeine versus a placebo to the subjects) by observing the dependent variable. The **dependent variable** is our outcome variable, that is, what happened to the subjects when we manipulated the independent variable. How the subjects did on the dependent variable is expected to *depend* on whether they were given the active substance (caffeine) or the placebo.

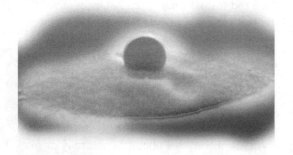

FIGURE 2.3 *Placebo—tablet with sugar inside.*

Experiment Example #1: Does Teaching Style Influence Student Grades?

Suppose we are interested in understanding the effect of a particular teaching strategy on the ability to learn the information presented in an introductory psychology course. We could take two classes of introductory psychology and provide one group of students with one form of teaching (say, teaching with a heavy emphasis on discussion) and provide the second group with a more standard form of teaching (say, a straight lecture format). For the entire course, both instructors would teach the exact same material from the same book. At the end of the semester, we would give both classes the same final exam and then compare them on their performance. In this experiment, the different teaching styles are the independent variable, with the lecture format being the control condition and the discussion method being the experimental condition. The grades on the common final exam represent the dependent variable (since grades are the outcome of interest).

Experiment Example #2: Does the Number of People in a Room Influence Anxiety During a Presentation?

Let's assume we are interested in determining whether the number of people in a room has an impact on the degree of anxiety a student feels while making an oral presentation. To test this, we have three levels of the independent variable (number of people in the room): the student could give the presentation in a room alone (control condition), the student could give the presentation in a room with 5 people (experimental condition), and the student could give the presentation in a room with 40 people (the second experimental condition). We would continuously measure the student's anxiety during the presentation, since the dependent variable is anxiety. We can measure anxiety by looking at heart rate or skin conductance (these are our operational definitions of anxiety).

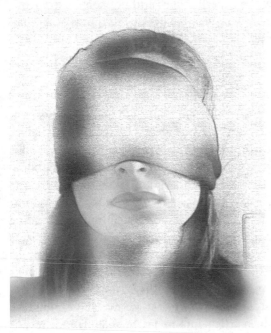

FIGURE 2.4 *Preventing people from knowing—a "blind" study.*

Experiment Example #3: Does Drinking Caffeine Cause Students to Sleep Less?

Our third example contains a slight variation, something in addition to what you have already learned about an experiment. Suppose we want to learn whether drinking caffeine causes students to sleep less. We could have two groups. The experimental group would be given soda to drink (containing a measured amount of caffeine). The control group would also be given soda to drink; however, the participants in this group would drink caffeine-free soda (the placebo). Neither group would know whether the soda they were drinking contained caffeine. In such an experiment, we can determine the impact of caffeine on sleeping behavior. If, however, one group knew that it drank soda with caffeine and the other group knew that it drank caffeine-free soda, we wouldn't be able to tell whether any changes in sleeping behavior were due to the caffeine or due to the participants' belief about what they drank. A mere belief in drinking caffeine can energize people's behavior, making them stay awake. In other words, it can create the effect of actually drinking a caffeinated beverage. In this study, belief is a confounding variable because the increased arousal level could either be due to consuming caffeine (the independent variable) or be due to the belief that one will be revived from drinking a caffeinated beverage. Preventing people from knowing what they drank can control that confounding variable.

In psychology, these types of experiments are common. To have a complete description of an experimental design, we need to better understand the role of *control* in the development of experimental procedures. To establish cause-and-effect relationships, we need to manipulate variables in such a way that we have control over other factors in the environment that could influence the behavior of interest, and thus operate as a confounding variable. The following paragraphs will help you understand this important concept of experimental control.

Experimental Control

To conduct an effective experiment in psychology, we must first understand the notion of experimental control. As described earlier, when we conduct an experiment we manipulate one variable and measure the effect of that variable in multiple conditions. Experimental control refers to ensuring that the only thing influencing participants' performance on the dependent variable is the independent variable selected by the experimenter, and not some extraneous variable. In this section, we will review results that are due to things other than those intended by the experimenter.

Extraneous Variables

To do experiments well, we need to eliminate (or control for) **extraneous variables**. These are variables that interfere with our ability to determine whether the independent variable has had an important effect on the dependent variable. Extraneous variables can be divided into nuisance variables and confounding variables. Both types of extraneous variables impact our ability to interpret the results of our experiments. A nuisance variable causes unsystematic (or random) variation in our data. For example, assume we are interested in understanding memory. We set up two conditions. In the first condition, a group of students is given a word list to memorize while listening to music. In the second condition, a group of students attempts to learn the list in silence. We then test their memory by having the students recall the list of words. If the students do not all participate in the experiment at the same time of day, we may have a nuisance variable. For example, assume some participants are tested at 8:00 in the morning, while they are still sleepy, and others are tested at noon, when they are hungry. If there is no systematic control over time of day (in other words, there is no fixed time when all participants must show up), then time of day might become the nuisance variable. In this case, the problem is that the participants' ability to perform the task may be unsystematically influenced by the time of day that the participants run through the experiment. To control for this, all participants should be run through the experiment at the same time of day.

Confounding Variables

A study can be even more flawed if there is an extraneous variable that functions as a confounding variable. A **confounding variable** changes systematically along with the independent variable in an experiment, so that any difference between the experimental group and the control group on the dependent variable could have been caused either by the independent variable or by the confounding variable. For example, assume the memory study from the previous paragraph is designed so that all the participants who study with music are run at 8:00 in the morning, and all the students who study without music are run at noon. If we find that the students who learned the material without music did substantially better, it could either be due to learning the information without music or be due to the time of day that they were run through the experiment. Since there is no way to determine which potential cause created the difference between the groups on the dependent variable, the results of such a study are not informative. The research will have to be conducted again, this time controlling for any potential confounding variables (such as the time of day). In this case the experimenters would control for the confounding variable either by requiring participants to show up at the same time of day or by running half of the experimental group and half of the control group at 8:00 am and running the other halves of the two groups at noon.

The key to doing good experimental research is to control variables that might influence the study's results but are not the variable of interest in this particular research. That is, to run good experiments, we must work hard to ensure that we set them up in such a way that there really is no other explanation for differences between the experimental and control groups other than the manipulation of the independent variable. This is, of course, easier said than done. Careful planning and preparation are essential.

Additional Control Strategies

FIGURE 2.5 *Random selection is analogous to picking names out of a hat.*

In addition to issues involved with the way an experiment is conducted, the selection of participants remains an issue that must be considered as a means of control. In any experiment, the researchers must obtain a sample from the population in order to examine the issue they are interested in. One of the first issues to consider is how the sample is to be obtained. In an ideal world, we would have a sample drawn from the population we are interested in by **random selection**. This procedure involves ensuring that each member of the population has an equal chance of being included in the sample. Some strategies that are used for random selection are drawing names or numbers out of a hat or using a table of random numbers to guide the selection of a representative sample.

Using random selection to draw a representative sample of the population we are interested in knowing about is the ideal, but in practice it is actually very difficult to do. For example, most of the research done in psychology is conducted at colleges and universities. A convenient sample to use consists of students enrolled in college-level psychology courses. Now, many colleges (perhaps your own) ask introductory psychology students to participate in experiments during the semester, although they must provide students with the option of participating in an alternative experience in case they don't wish to become research subjects. This practice enables researchers to have a pool of participants from which to conduct their experiments and allows students to have a firsthand opportunity to see what psychological research is like. However, this method of recruiting research subjects does not constitute random selection. For one thing, the students in the participant pool are already interested in psychology (they have chosen to take a psychology course), they are potentially interested in the area of research (oftentimes, students select from several studies the one they want to take part in), and they are motivated to do well (their grades may be influenced by participating). Thus, the research participants drawn from introductory psychology courses may be unlike other people in the overall population of college students, or people in general.

Another common approach is to utilize **random assignment**, a control procedure in which the participants involved in the experiment are assigned to different conditions within the experiment on a random basis. This control procedure does not accomplish a representative sample as does random selection, but it does provide the best opportunity to begin the experiment with equal groups, so that if the groups end up being different after the experimental group receives the treatment, then the difference observed would seem to be due to one group being exposed to the independent variable while the other (control) group was not.

Experimenter bias has sometimes been implicated as influencing the outcome of an experiment. Experimenter bias occurs when the researcher knowingly or unwittingly influences the outcome of a study through selection of participants, assignment of participants to groups, or by interacting differently with the groups of participants. For example, suppose we are interested in determining whether in colleges and universities there is a difference between men and women in attitudes toward women. We could sample students from different classes and administer a survey to assess their attitudes. Suppose the experimenter samples students from a class on the psychology of women. This might lead to a bias in our results since students in a psychology of women class might be more sensitive to the issue of attitudes toward women than students enrolled in classes that don't discuss these issues. The point is that by selecting that class, the experimenters may be slanting their results toward an answer that may not be representative of the population as a whole.

Specialized Research Techniques

Research Methods in Developmental Psychology

Some disciplines require unique methodological approaches. Such is the case with developmental psychology. Developmental psychologists are interested in examining change in people over time. Characteristics that might be of interest to developmental psychologists are personality, perceptual skills, language skills, and other aspects of both physical and psychological maturation. To study these characteristics, developmental psychologists use one of three research techniques appropriate for investigating these matters: cross-sectional, longitudinal, or sequential designs.

In a **cross-sectional design**, an experimenter measures the behavior of interest in people of different ages. For example, a developmental psychologist interested in language development might study a group of 1-year-olds, 5-year-olds, and 10-year-olds to see what the differences are in whatever aspect of language development he or she is interested. Alternatively, perhaps a personality psychologist is interested in understanding how altruism (giving to others without expectation of reciprocity) changes over time. She or he might measure giving behavior among 25-year-olds, 50-year-olds, and 75-year-olds. The results of the study would provide evidence that the differences obtained are due to aging. However, any differences found among participants of different age groups could also be attributed to other variables such as individual differences or **history effects**, which are events that happen in the outside world that alter the behavior of the people who lived through the event. To understand this concept, think of how the events of 9/11 affected the U.S. population and, to a lesser extent, people around the world. Thus, one group may differ from another due to differences in ages or due to events experienced by those in one age cohort but not in another. When two causal elements are possible, the actual cause of the behavior being studied cannot be determined.

The cross-sectional design allows researchers to look at the differences between age groups. Because it has the advantages of speed and relatively low cost, it is the most frequently used design when studying development. The speed advantage refers to the fact that researchers do not need to wait for individuals to change over time. And cost is reduced by not having to track participants down years later. However, this strategy does not allow researchers to observe the change process or to be sure that any differences found between groups of participants are due to the variable thought to be the causal agent.

An alternative way to study how people differ because of age is to take the same individuals and measure their behavior over time, with a **longitudinal design**. With this research design, the individuals or groups of subjects act as their own control group; thus, individual differences do not play as great a role in the results of the study. However, due to the nature of a longitudinal design, time has to pass, which makes this an expensive process that requires patience and a painstaking follow-up to track down participants. For example, the 9/11 study would require too much of a time commitment for it to be a viable project for most researchers, although there have been a small number of studies that have actually tracked and monitored participants throughout their lives.

When using a longitudinal design, researchers must dedicate many years to a single project. The dropout rate of the subjects, called **subject mortality**, tends to be high, as people move, change their names, or become weary of participating due to the intrusiveness of being observed. The sample that is left in the later years of a long-term study might be systematically different from the larger group that was studied in the earlier phases, which limits the researchers' conclusions about changes over time.

The problems of confounding involved in the cross-sectional and longitudinal designs can be resolved through use of a sequential design (Schaie, 1965). By combining features of longitudinal and cross-sectional designs, the researcher may assess the relative contributions of age, **cohort**, and time in one study and discover what differences between groups are due to these factors. In addition, a sequential design allows the sources of difference to be determined in a relatively short period of time. Basically, a **sequential design** involves the remeasurement of a cross-sectional sample of people following a fixed interval of time. This design calls for obtaining repeated measures from each of the cohort groups included in a given cross-sectional sample (Lerner, 2001). For instance, a researcher may begin with a group of 4-year-olds, 8-year-olds, 12-year-olds, and 16 year-olds and repeatedly measure them every six months over a period of five years. This would enable a detailed observation of ages 4–20. As in the longitudinal design, this design can capture changes in individuals, but it also benefits from the speed of cross-sectional designs because fewer years are invested (5 years versus 12 years, as shown in this example). The reduction in invested time lessens the cost as compared to a traditional longitudinal design.

Which method to choose depends on the researcher, who must consider the goals of the research as well as the constraints under which the study will be conducted. Researchers tend to choose designs based on their research questions and their available resources.

Research Methods in Biopsychology

Methods of research in biopsychology, such as neuroimaging techniques and electrophysiological techniques, examine the relationships between people's physical states and their psychological states. Animal research is often used in lieu of human experimentation mainly due to ethical issues involved in research using people as subjects.

Animals rather than human subjects are used in research that involves inflicting pain and even death, because this type of research would not be considered ethical on human subjects. Animals are similar to human beings; thus they serve as useful models that enable the findings from animal studies to be cautiously generalized to human beings.

According to researcher Michael Domjan (2003), animals are important research subjects for three reasons. First, they are simple, in that they lack some of the complexities that exist in human beings that make it difficult to isolate the physical or psychological processes of interest. For example, the axons of banana slugs and giant squid are large enough to be observed without the aid of a microscope and have thus helped researchers study how neurons operate. Second, the use of animals allows for a greater degree of experimental control in the research. Animals such as mice and rats can be bred to have virtually identical genes, which makes it much easier to start an experiment with equal groups of subjects. Researchers can also control every aspect of an animal subject's environment. Suppose an experimenter wants to study cocaine addiction through administering specific doses to animals and then recording their nervous system changes through electrodes implanted in the animals' brains. It would hardly be ethical to administer illegal substances to human subjects, get them addicted, and then monitor the effects of the substance through implanted electrodes. Domjan's third advantage of working with animal subjects is that they are less expensive to work with than human subjects. One of the authors recently attended a Cal Tech lecture at which the presenter explained that he studied mice and fruit flies in order to look at emotional expression and mating practices in these species in order to extrapolate the findings to human beings (Anderson, 2007). He stated that although fruit flies are much less like people than are mice, they are cheaper to house and they reproduce much more quickly than do mice. Thus, the expense of research projects must also be considered.

A crucial consideration in selecting nonhuman models is that the model must have a relevant feature or relevant function similar to that found in human beings (Flint, 2006). In the example of using a giant squid, this animal was a relevant model because its neurons functions in a manner similar to that of the neurons that make up the human nervous system.

Animal studies allow researchers to conduct controlled experiments when only correlational studies would be ethical with human participants. There are, however, guidelines for the use of animals in research, which means that scientists cannot feel free to do what they like with nonhuman subjects. Proposed studies are scrutinized by institutional animal care and use committees (IACUCs), whose job it is to ensure that researchers comply with federal laws regulating the use of animals in research. The proposed research must have potential benefit to human welfare in order to justify any pain to animals or sacrifice of them that is required by the process. In addition, alternatives to animal research (such as computer simulation or cellular level research) must be considered and rejected before animal research can move forward.

The advancement of brain-imaging techniques over the last few decades has made it possible to study the workings of the brain without the need for surgery. One of the most common noninvasive methods is the electroencephalograph (EEG), which records the electrical activity of the brain. The EEG detects minute amounts of electrical activity in the brain, or brain waves, that are conducted between electrodes. Certain brain-wave patterns are associated with mental states such as relaxation and the different stages of sleep. The EEG is used to examine brain-wave patterns associated with brain damage and mental disorders such as schizophrenia. The EEG is also used by medical personnel to reveal brain abnormalities such as tumors. Use of the EEG does not provide details about activity in specific brain structures, but it does give an overall picture of activity in any given region of the brain.

Brain-imaging techniques generate images that reflect the structure and functioning of the brain. In a computed tomography (CT) scan, a narrow X-ray beam is aimed at the head. The radiation that passes through is measured from multiple angles. The CT scan—also called a CAT (computerized axial tomography) scan—reveals abnormalities in shape and structure that may be suggestive of lesions, blood clots, or tumors. Use of the computer enables scientists to integrate the measurements into a three-dimensional picture of the brain, and it reveals structural abnormalities in the brain that may be implicated in various patterns of abnormal behavior. Furthermore, evidence of brain damage that was once detectable only by surgery may now be displayed on a monitor.

Another imaging method, the positron emission tomography (PET) scan, is used to study the functioning of various parts of the brain. In this method, a small amount of a radioactive compound is mixed with glucose and injected into the bloodstream. When it reaches the brain, patterns of neural activity are revealed by measurement of the positrons—positively charged particles—emitted by the tracer. The glucose metabolized by parts of the brain generates a computer image of neural activity. Areas of great activity metabolize more glucose. The PET scan has been used to learn which parts of the brain are most active (metabolize more glucose) when people listen to music, solve math problems, or use language. It can also be used to reveal abnormalities in brain activity in people with schizophrenia, obsessive-compulsive disorder, or certain other mental disorders.

A third imaging technique is magnetic resonance imaging (MRI). In order to take an MRI, the person is placed in a machine that generates a strong magnetic field. Radio waves of certain frequencies are then directed at the head. As a result, the brain emits signals that can be measured from several angles. As with the CT scan, the signals are integrated into a computer-generated image of the brain, which can reveal brain abnormalities associated with mental disorders.

One type of MRI, called functional magnetic resonance imaging (fMRI), is used to identify parts of the brain that become active when people engage in particular tasks, such as those involving vision, memory, or use of speech (Carpenter, 2000; Ingram & Siegle, 2001; Stern & Silbersweig, 2001). The fMRI detects blood flow to specific areas of the brain as a person makes different movements or engages his or her memory. Through a series of complex computerized calculations, a 3-D image of the brain is created that provides a detailed picture of the active brain regions.

Brain electrical activity mapping (BEAM), a sophisticated type of EEG, uses the computer to analyze brain-wave patterns and reveal areas of relative activity or activity in which the subject is performing mental or behavioral tasks (Duffy, 1994; Silberstein et al., 1998). Information about brain activity is fed into a computer from approximately 20 electrodes attached to the scalp. The computer analyzes the signals and displays the pattern of brain activity on a color monitor, providing a vivid image of the electrical activity of the working brain. BEAM can be helpful in studying the brain activity of people with schizophrenia and children with attention deficit/ hyperactivity disorder, among other physical and psychological disorders.

In addition to the techniques already discussed, there are some invasive electrophysiological methods that are almost always reserved for research on nonhuman subjects. Single-unit recordings include both intracellular and extracellular recording methods. For these techniques, extremely tiny electrodes are inserted into the intracellular or extracellular fluid of neurons, where they may be used to record the electrical activity in the microscopic area. Single-unit recording is commonly done on anesthetized animals, in which an electrode is surgically inserted into the brain of a live animal. An alternative technique is a slice preparation, a procedure in which nervous system tissue is removed from the animal and kept alive in a petri dish. In one instance, by examining tissue from the hippocampus that was kept alive while electrodes were inserted into it, researchers were able to develop a model of how memories are formed in the brain (Flint, 2006).

Small N Designs

Several areas of psychology do not do research as described previously. Sometimes psychologists study one animal (or human) at a time and draw conclusions about behavior in this manner. For example, behavior analysts often utilize a **small N design** ("N" stands for number of participants) to answer questions about behavior. In this design just one or a few subjects are used. Typically, the experimenter collects baseline data to see how the subject behaves before the application of the independent variable. Then, the treatment is applied and any change in the dependent variable is noted. In some cases, the independent variable is then removed in order to see whether the subject's behavior returns to the baseline rate. The treatment is then applied a second time. If the changes in the dependent variable are altered both times by the treatment, then it is clear that the treatment is affecting the dependent variable.

Small *N* designs are useful when we are interested in understanding the influence of a manipulation of the independent variable on the behavior of a single organism. For example, suppose you want to know what kinds of rewards (independent variable) will increase sitting behavior (dependent variable) in your dog. You would use one organism (your dog) and train him in a controlled setting.

As another example, suppose we are interested in determining the influence of a drug (independent variable) on motivation. To study this in a single-subject design, we would first probably do an animal study. Suppose we decide to use a single rat to study motivation. We could train the rat to push a bar to obtain food. The rat could then be given the drug, and we could measure the response rate of the rat under the influence of the drug. The dependent variable would be the change in the rat's response rate due to the administration of the drug. In such a way, we could clearly plot the response rate and see any changes there might be.

Single-subject designs are useful for seeing an individual's change in behavior. Rather than grouping participants, we are able to note the influence of an intervention on an outcome measure within a single organism. The disadvantage of single-subject designs is that the results might not generalize to a larger group of organisms.

Statistics

Once we have gathered data about a particular phenomenon we must utilize a variety of procedures to translate into numerical information the human characteristics we are interested in studying. This quantification of data allows us to make comparisons across different groups of people. When we want to know whether the experimental group is significantly different from the control group due to exposure to the independent variable, we use statistics. Statistics traditionally fall into two categories: descriptive statistics and inferential statistics.

Descriptive Statistics

Descriptive statistics are those used to describe a sample. For instance, if we have a set of data, such as scores on an exam (80, 80, 90, 95, 100), we can describe these scores in a variety of ways. First, we can tell what the most common score is (80). This is the **mode**. Second, we can tell which score is in the middle of the distribution (90). This is the **median** (like a median strip divides the highway, the median score divides the distribution into two parts). Finally, we can take the numbers, add them up, and divide by the number of scores, to obtain a value of 89. This is the **mean**, and it is the most commonly used and useful measure of central tendency because it lends itself to the greatest number of mathematical operations. Another important descriptive statistic is the **standard deviation**, which is the amount, on average, that each score departs from the mean. Thus, the standard deviation tells us about how much the scores tend to differ from the average score. The bigger the standard deviation, the more spread out the scores are in the distribution. Another measure of variability besides the standard deviation is the **range**. The range is the difference between the highest and lowest scores in a group of scores. There are other descriptive statistics, but they are beyond the scope of this chapter.

Let's say your psychology class takes an exam, and the scores are 90, 88, 90, 87, 77, 65, 80, 99, and 100. A good way to describe this sample is to calculate some statistics on the scores. We might choose to calculate the mean, as this will give us an idea of how well the typical student did. In this case the mean is 86.22, the mode is 90, and the median is 88. Thus, each measure of central tendency tells us something different about the sample. In addition, we often use what we know about measures of dispersion, such as the standard deviation and the range, to describe samples. The sample that is drawn can determine where a score falls in the distribution. Calculation of the standard deviation is beyond the scope of this book, but it is 10.5 in this example. The range of scores in our example is 35 (the lowest score, 65, was subtracted from the highest score, 100).

When we measure a population on many variables in which psychologists are interested, such as IQ, speed of processing information, or aggression, we find that when we collect a large enough sample, the scores that people obtain on these variables are often normally distributed. The **normal curve** (or bell curve, as it is often called) is a distribution of scores that looks like Figure 2.6. We often use the normal curve because we know so much about it. We know, for example, that if we randomly select a single score from the distribution, it is most likely to be a score that falls between -1 and $+1$ standard deviations from the mean. Essentially, we can predict that there is a 68% chance of getting a score from that portion of the distribution, since more than two-thirds of the scores fall within this range. This information is enormously helpful when it comes to another type of statistics, called inferential statistics.

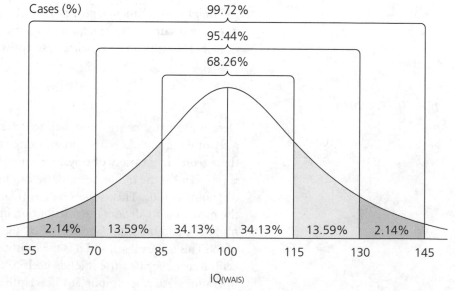

FIGURE 2.6 *Bell curve.*

Inferential Statistics

In order to really understand inferential statistics, students must be familiar with the concept of probability. Probability is essentially a theory that suggests that things will sometimes happen by chance. For instance, if you flipped a coin 10 times, there is a small chance that it will be heads all 10 times, but it is more likely that it will be heads 5 times. One of the goals of using probability in psychology is to determine the likelihood that a result happened by chance rather than as the result of a planned experimental manipulation. Inferential statistics are concerned with the question of how likely it is that the results we obtained from our research are due to chance or to our actual manipulation of the independent variable.

Let's go back to the memory study described earlier in this chapter, in which the experimental group studied the material while listening to music and the control group studied the same material in silence. After we collect our data, let's say we find that these two groups of participants differ in memory performance (on a 10-point test) by about 3 points. Specifically, we find that the subjects who studied without background music answered an average of three more questions correctly than did people who were exposed to music. We can use statistics to evaluate whether this three-point difference is meaningful (due to our manipulation of the independent variable) or is instead likely to be due to chance. When results are not due to chance, we say that they have **statistical significance**. By this we mean that we are seeing whether we could expect a difference of three points by chance or if it is something that is not likely to be due to chance.

Correlation

It is often the case that once a descriptive study has been completed, researchers need to work with what they have found so that they can truly understand what it means. For example, if a researcher uses a survey to gather information concerning the relationship between income and college GPA, he or she might then do a **correlational study** to understand the relationship between the two variables. A correlational analysis is a type of inferential statistical procedure that allows psychologists to understand the degree to which two variables are related. A **correlation coefficient** is calculated using an inferential statistical procedure and the number ranges from -1.00 to $+1.00$. The correlation coefficient provides us with two pieces of information concerning the relationship between the variables. The *sign* tells the researcher the direction of the relationship—that is, whether the relationship is one in which the numbers vary together (as one increases or decreases, the other does the same) or one in which the variables vary inversely (as one increases, the other decreases; and as one decreases, the other increases). The *number* tells the researcher the strength of the relationship. The closer the number is to either 1 or −1, the stronger the relationship. For example, let's assume we are interested in determining the correlation

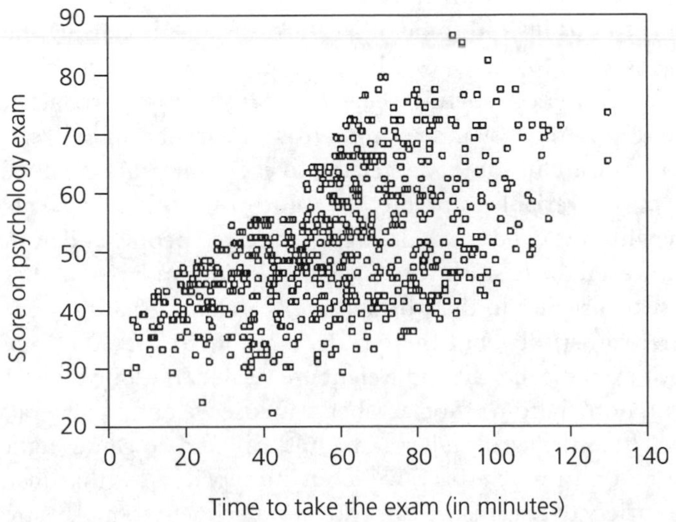

FIGURE 2.7 *Scatterplot.*

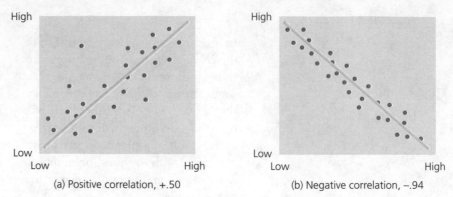

(a) Positive correlation, +.50   (b) Negative correlation, −.94

FIGURE 2.8 *Positive and negative correlations. Courtesy of Wood et al.,* World of Psychology, *6th edition, 2008.*

between income and college GPA. We first collect survey data from a group of people so that we can study their college GPA and their current income. Then, we compute the correlation coefficient between the income and GPA variables. If GPA and income are related such that the higher the GPA the higher the income, the correlation would be positive (say, +.75). If the relationship is inverse—that is, as GPA increases, income decreases—the correlation would be negative (say, −.60). A third alternative would be a zero correlation, indicating that there is no relationship between college GPA and income.

The correlation between two variables is often depicted by a scatterplot, which plots one score against another. The scatterplot in Figure 2.7 shows that the more time that students have available to complete an exam, the better their score. When variables (like exam score and time to complete the exam) vary in the same direction, it is called a positive correlation.

Correlation Does Not Imply Causation

The correlational analysis gives us some understanding of how two variables relate. It does not enable us to know which variable is the causal agent, whether either is the causal agent, or instead some other third variable is causing the two variables being studied to correlate. Thus, we cannot draw cause-and-effect relationship claims after conducting a correlational analysis. Correlation does not imply causation. All we can determine from a correlation between two variables is that they are in some way related to each other, and that we can use knowledge of one variable to predict the value of the other. Students sometimes struggle with this concept, as do highly educated people and even medical doctors. However, the best way to consider this is to understand that when we measure two variables in the world, there is a chance that they are related to each other statistically, but there really is no way to say that one caused the other. For example, height and weight are related, but one doesn't cause the other—you don't become shorter when you lose weight. In general, children do gain weight as they grow taller, but adults can and do gain weight without becoming taller. In psychology, we often study variables that *look* causative, but for a variety of reasons we can't do an experiment to make sure that they are. Therefore, a correlational study is the best we can do. Indeed, the variables may have a causal relationship, but we can't show this with a correlational analysis.

Consider the following example. Suppose we find that there is a strong correlation between smoking cigarettes and lung cancer. In fact, the relationship is so strong that there is a correlation of about +0.65, suggesting that these two variables (smoking and lung cancer) often coincide. However, this does not indicate that smoking causes lung cancer, since, in fact, a correlation cannot demonstrate this. Remember, correlation can only show a relationship among variables, so that one variable can predict what will happen to the other. When we want to make a cause-and-effect statement in science, we have to actually make that relationship occur in the world (or in an experiment). In this case, we didn't really do that. Rather, we measured smoking and we measured lung cancer. Both were found to occur together, but they might have occurred together for some unknown reason. Therefore, we can say that smoking and lung cancer are correlated, but we cannot say that one definitely causes the other. To do that, we would need to run an experiment in which we manipulated participants' amount of smoking and then measured their lung cancer rates. This, of course, is neither possible nor ethical. However, experimental studies have been done with laboratory animals, so we are now able to say that there is a causal relationship between smoking and lung cancer.

Knowing that two variables are correlated does not tell which variable is the cause and which is the effect. This dilemma is known as the directionality problem. It is possible that neither of the two variables is causing the other to occur. Both of the correlated variables may also be related to a third variable, which is the actual causal factor. This is the third variable problem. For example, in 2004, a positive correlation between fatal breast cancer and antibiotics was established. However, it's not clear whether (1) antibiotics are a cause of breast cancer, for example, by killing stomach bacteria, (2) the condition that required antibiotics causes breast cancer, or (3) that women have poor immune system functioning (a possible third variable), which prompts the need for frequent antibiotics and makes women vulnerable to cancer.

So far we have discussed correlational studies in which the relationship between two variables is measured. Correlational research can handle more than two variables, however. In fact, multivariate designs can handle as many as 50 or more variables, although this type of research is a bit unusual.

The *t*-Test and the Analysis of Variance

Several inferential statistical procedures are common in psychology. The correlational analysis was already explained as one of the common procedures used in nonexperimental research. In experimental research, two common procedures are the *t*-test and the analysis of variance. Both tests allow us to evaluate the probability of a particular outcome occurring by chance. The *t*-test is used when there are only two groups of participants or two different conditions (control and experimental) being compared. In contrast, the analysis of variance may be used when more than two groups of participants or conditions are to be compared. The value yielded by a *t*-test or an analysis of variance (ANOVA) is then compared to what we know about probability to determine whether the obtained result is one that we should expect by chance.

Ethics in Psychology

Human Participants

Since psychology deals with living organisms, we need to be ethical about how we do research. Contrary to popular belief, psychologists do not torture animals (or humans) or purposefully create situations that give rise to emotional or psychological harm in experimental participants. In fact, psychologists are guided by ethical principles set forth by the American Psychological Association to ensure that they follow the rules of decorum when running experiments. For research involving human beings, participants are entitled to informed consent before the study commences if they are to be put at risk by participating in the study. If subjects are determined to be at minimal risk by participating, and deception is deemed necessary, a full **debriefing** must follow the experiment. Being at minimal risk means that the subject's likelihood of being harmed while participating is not greater than the subject's risk of being harmed during ordinary life activities. Debriefing is a necessary follow-up procedure implemented when deception has been used in a research study, in which immediately following the conclusion of the study, participants are informed as to the true nature and purpose of the study. The participants may not be coerced into taking part in an experiment and should know that they can leave at any time. In addition, all proposals that involve experiments are typically reviewed for ethical standards by an Institutional Review Board (IRB) prior to the beginning of the study. The IRB at the institution doing the research ensures that the research will not cause the participants any undue harm.

In many cases in psychology, researchers have to judge the benefits of the project. They operate on a cost-benefit analysis. If the benefits of the research outweigh the costs, and the human participants will not suffer, an argument can be made for the ethical nature of the research. If deception must be used, the participants need to be debriefed immediately following the study and given the opportunity to discuss their participation in the research. Any deception that is used cannot be of a type that would have caused the subjects to refuse to participate in the study had they known its true nature. Finally, data should be collected anonymously, and the participants' identities should be confidential.

Animals as Research Subjects

FIGURE 2.9 *Rules of ethics guide the use of animals in research. Courtesy of Debbie Whitaker.*

Most psychological research involves human participants, but sometimes animal subjects are used in place of human beings. The federal regulations and ethical restrictions on human research, along with the cost of human studies, the inability to establish experimental control, and the complexity of the human nervous system, make it necessary to pursue some avenues of research using animals as subjects. Favorite animal research subjects are monkeys (very similar to humans), rats, mice, crayfish, fruit flies (cheap to keep and fast reproducers), pigeons, quail, giant squid, and sea slugs (both have large neurons that can be seen without the aid of a microscope).

Research of this type is carefully regulated by laws and ethics codes. If animals are to be used, the researchers are responsible for ensuring their proper care: the temperature must be controlled, the animals must be fed (unless refraining from feeding them is an aspect of the experiment), cages must be cleaned, and the animal rooms need to be secured. A minimum number of animals should be used to achieve interpretable results, and if the animals are to be sacrificed, this should be done humanely without the subjects experiencing pain (usually by being anesthetized to the point of dying).

Animal research has benefited both human beings and other animals. In medical research, animals are used to test new medications, surgical procedures, and methods for relieving pain. Psychological experiments with animals have led directly to benefits in the treatment of such diverse psychological problems as bedwetting, phobias, obsessive-compulsive disorders, anorexia nervosa, and depression (Miller, 1985). Animal research on learning has led to the development of programmed learning materials, and teaching sign language to chimps and gorillas has enabled researchers to better understand the structure of human language. Studying animals has advanced our knowledge of human behavior in the areas of perception, conditioning, memory, and stress (Domjan & Purdy, 1995). Work with animals has demonstrated experimentally the link between psychological stress and physical health. Psychological research has led to the development of more natural environments for zoo animals, more successful breeding techniques for endangered species, and more effective training for pets and wild animals in captivity.

Chapter Summary

Psychology is considered a science because it relies on empirical evidence to support its theories. Researchers employ the scientific method in order to gain a reliable body of evidence about human beings. The steps in the scientific method are to make observations, measure the observed phenomenon, develop a tentative theory, generate a testable hypothesis based on the theory, conduct an experiment to test the hypothesis, and publicize the results of the experiment. The scientific method parallels the four goals of psychology: describe, explain, predict, and control human behavior.

Two types of research strategies are used in psychological research, nonexperimental and experimental research. Nonexperimental research provides descriptions of data. Some nonexperimental techniques are observational in nature, such as naturalistic observation, surveys, case studies, and correlational studies. Naturalistic observation refers to describing the behavior of human beings or animals as they live in their normal habitats. Surveys may be done over the phone, in person, over the Internet, or through the mail, and ask respondents to answer a series of questions about their behaviors, attitudes, beliefs, and the like. Case studies involve an intensive investigation of a single individual. Correlational studies investigate whether variables are related to one another or function independently. No cause-and-effect conclusions may be drawn when these nonexperimental research strategies are used. This is an important limitation, since determining what causes people and animals to behave as they do enables us to predict their behavior. This is one of the goals of psychological science.

Researchers can obtain cause-and-effect relationships by having people and animals participate in experiments. In an experiment, the researcher manipulates the independent variable as a way to ascertain its influence on the dependent variable. A variable is some characteristic in which people or animals in the study have different scores, such as sex or the number of college units completed. The independent variable is the presumed cause of some effect, and that effect is referred to as the dependent variable.

A third type of variable that may exist in a research study is an extraneous variable. Experimenters attempt to eliminate or control potential extraneous variables to keep them from interfering with an appropriate test of the research hypothesis. Extraneous variables may simply be a nuisance variable or may function as a confounding variable. A nuisance variable simply makes it more difficult to notice the effect of the independent variable on the dependent variable. A confounding variable poses a more serious problem because it varies systematically along with the independent variable, and thus the researcher does not know whether the independent variable or the confounding variable had the observed effect on the dependent variable. There are several ways to anticipate and control extraneous variables in order to isolate the independent variable as the only possible cause of the effect on the dependent variable.

Random selection and random assignment are two methods for establishing control of extraneous variables. Random selection of research participants is one procedure for establishing experimental control. It requires that each member of the population of interest to the experimenter have an equal chance of being selected for the sample to be studied. The resulting representative sample of the population allows researchers to generalize the results of the findings with the sample back to the population as a whole. Random assignment refers to participants in a study being assigned to the experimental or control group in a nonbiased fashion, so that each subject has an equal chance of being assigned to each group. If the sample size is adequate, this procedure enables researchers to assume that individual differences among the subjects have been balanced across conditions so that the groups start out as equal. If the groups end up being different on the dependent variable after the treatment has been applied to the experimental group, then researchers may conclude that the difference was brought about by the independent variable.

The subfields of developmental psychology and biopsychology have specialized research methods. Developmental researchers may use either cross-sectional research designs, longitudinal designs, or sequential designs. Biopsychologists use neuroimaging techniques and electrophysiological methods.

Descriptive and inferential statistics are used in psychological research. Descriptive statistics refer to measures of central tendency (mean, median, and mode) as well as measures of variability such as the range and the standard deviation. Inferential statistics are used to determine whether the effect the independent variable had on the dependent variable was "significant." Inferential statistics covered in this chapter were a correlational analysis, the t-test, and the ANOVA.

When psychologists conduct research, they must follow the laws and ethical guidelines that apply to the use of human beings as subjects and separate guidelines for the use of animals as subjects. There are committees that oversee research with both human and animal subjects. These committees weigh the benefits of the research against any harm that might come to the subjects as a result of their participation. In the rare cases when human subjects are put at risk due to their participation, they must give informed consent.

Knowledge Builder

RELATE TO YOURSELF

1. How would you design a study to understand why you wake up really tired on some mornings but not on others?

_____

_____

_____

_____

2. Describe a situation in which you thought that one thing caused something to happen, but later discovered that the causal element was something else.

_____

_____

_____

_____

3. The subject of psychology was probably represented differently in this chapter from what you had previously learned about it from other contexts (TV, friends). What have you learned from reading this chapter that has given you a different point of view of what psychologists do?

_____

_____

_____

_____

4. Why do psychologists use statistics? What are the limitations as to what we can learn from a statistical analysis of research data, such as a correlational study?

_____

_____

_____

_____

CHAPTER REVIEW QUESTIONS

1. A nuisance extraneous variable is a variable that completely explains our results but that is not the independent variable. **T or F?**

2. If we want to describe the typical responses of subjects in a given sample, we would use the standard deviation. **T or F?**

3. A *t*-test is used when we want to compare two groups or conditions. **T or F?**

4. The APA takes the position that it is ethically justified to use animals in psychological research if appropriate conditions are met. **T or F?**

5. The correlational study can show that one variable causes another. **T or F?**

6. The most commonly used measure of central tendency is called the
   _____ .

   (a) median   (b) mean

   (c) standard deviation   (d) mode

7. The _____ is the variable that is used to measure the outcome of an experiment.

   (a) independent variable   (b) moderator variable

   (c) nuisance variable   (d) dependent variable

8. Assume that you have an experiment in which a second, unexpected and uncontrolled variable can completely explain your results. That unexpected variable is called a _____.

   (a) confounding variable   (b) dependent variable

   (c) moderator variable   (d) nuisance variable

9. Which of the following correlation coefficients indicates a weak, inverse relationship between two variables?

   (a) 0.0   (b) +.15

   (c) −.15   (d) −.90

10. *Consider the following scenario:* You are an experimental psychologist trying to understand how language develops in children. You can't, of course, isolate children to determine what factors contribute to their language acquisition. Rather, you need to rely on a completely different technique. What would you do? What kind of statistics would you use once you did your study?

_____

_____

_____

_____

11. *Consider the following scenario:* You are in an introductory psychology course (not hard to imagine) and you are asked to develop an experiment. Below, list the problem you are interested in, your hypothesis, the independent and dependent variables, the variables you would attempt to control, and how you would actually control them.

_____

_____

_____

_____

_____

_____

12. Is it better to do a correlational study or an experiment if you are trying to determine cause and effect? Why?

_____

_____

_____

13. What do you think is the best measure of central tendency? Why?

_____

_____

_____

_____

14. Let's say I do a study that looks at the rate of smoking and how it relates to lung cancer in human beings. To do this, I survey numerous individuals and identify those with cancer and those who smoke. Is this an experiment? Why or why not?

_____

_____

_____

_____

15. How would I set up a study that examines the variables that contribute to language development? Is this an experiment? Why or why not?

_____

_____

_____

_____

USEFUL WEB SITES

AMERICAN PSYCHOLOGICAL ASSOCIATION

http://www.apa.org

This Web site has a great deal of information on current issues in psychology as well as important information on ethics in research.

AMERICAN PSYCHOLOGICAL SOCIETY

http://www.psychologicalscience.org

The Web site of the American Psychological Society presents a great deal of information on the science of psychology, including how to do good, quality research along with terrific examples of high-quality research studies.

SOCIAL PSYCHOLOGY NETWORK RESEARCH METHODS PAGE

http://www.socialpsychology.org/methods.htm

This page is hosted by Wesleyan University and provides links to a variety of research methods and statistics pages on the Web. It is useful for finding out the vast array of topics studied by psychologists and how they study them.

SOCIETY FOR THE TEACHING OF PSYCHOLOGY

http://www.teachpsych.org

A useful Web site for lots of ideas on how to teach (and learn) psychology.

Chapter 3

Biopsychology

by Robert W. Flint, Jr., PhD

> *The adult human brain weighs about three pounds and consists of about 100 billion nerve cells or neurons . . . And if we concentrate on the number of possible connections . . . we get an even more astounding number: 10 followed by a million zeros.*
>
> —RICHARD RESTAK

Biological Basis of Behavior

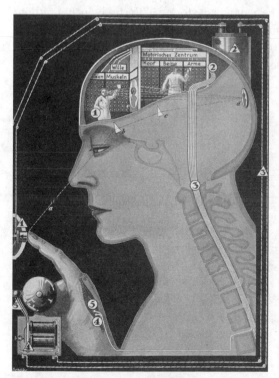

FIGURE 3.1 *The nervous system here is visually compared to an electronic signaling system; the brain is an office where messages are sorted. Stuttgart, 1926. Relief halftone. National Library of Medicine.*

Imagine the following scenario: As you pull into an intersection you register a brief flash to your left just prior to a large impact. You awaken in the hospital, and a doctor calling herself a neuropsychologist tells you that you have been in an automobile accident that has left you with brain damage. Her job, as she explains, will be to administer a variety of tests in order to determine the extent of your current abilities and to work with other doctors to reach a conclusion regarding your status. This is an unfortunate event, no doubt, but an all too common one. Thousands of people experience brain damage every year, and millions suffer from disorders and diseases that influence the normal functioning of their nervous systems.

The field of **biopsychology** is the study of relationships between the brain and behavior (see Figure 3.1). Biopsychologists want to understand the contributions of different neurobiological substrates (components) to behavior and mental processes, whether they are considered normal aspects of human behavior or abnormal ones. These substrates include the roles of various regions of neural tissue, the biochemical functioning of neurons, and the influence of hormones on the brain and behavior. Issues of interest may include head trauma, Alzheimer's disease, brain tumors, and chronic pain, as well as cardiovascular disease, AIDS, drug addiction, and aggression. The field of psychology is diverse, but despite this diversity, few subdisciplines within psychology can escape the contributions of biology to our understanding of behavior and mental processes.

As technology has advanced, so too has the field of biopsychology. Many scientists with interests in the connections between brain and behavior now refer to themselves as behavioral or cognitive neuroscientists. In 2008, the Society for Neuroscience boasted that membership in 2007 had reached 38,677, many of whom have earned PhDs in psychology. The explosion of interest in biopsychology has been coupled with an equally large and interesting number of discoveries on how the biology of the body is related to the functioning of the mind.

As you work your way through this chapter, you will be presented with a very basic introduction to the structure and function of the nervous system. A number of neurological and psychiatric conditions will be presented that will demonstrate the contribution of certain neurobiological substrates to behavior and mental processes. This will help you understand the organization of the nervous system, the functions of many areas of the brain, the electrical and biochemical properties of neuronal communication (activity within and between cells in the nervous system), and the contributions of the endocrine system to biopsychology.

The Nervous System

The **nervous system** contains all the neural tissue found in the body, including both the central and peripheral nervous systems (see Figure 3.2). The **peripheral nervous system (PNS)** is composed of the neurological tissue found outside the brain and spinal cord. Its primary responsibility is to transmit information to and from

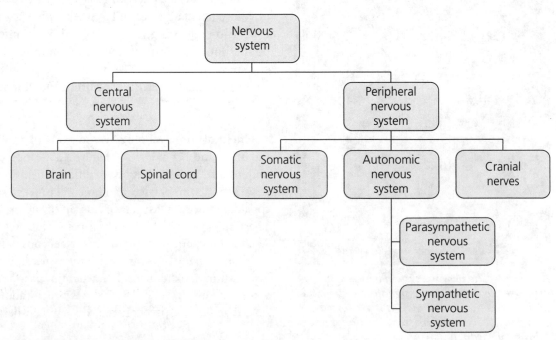

FIGURE 3.2 *Major components of the nervous system.*

the **central nervous system** (CNS; brain and spinal cord). For example, as you sit here reading this text, the images of these words are reflected from the page onto the retina in the back of your eye (see Figure 4.3 in Chapter 4). Special sensory receptor cells in the retina turn the image into neural impulses and transmit the information out the back of the eye through a part of the PNS called the optic nerve. You may recall seeing a horror or science fiction movie where an eye is removed, leaving a stringlike structure hanging off the back of it. This is the optic nerve. Once the optic nerve reaches your brain, the neural signals are transmitted to various brain regions where the information can be processed and transformed into a conscious visual perception of that image. You can probably also feel the chair you are sitting on, taste the drink or snack you are consuming, and move your hand to turn the page or highlight a section of text. All these sensory and motor functions involve your PNS sending information to and from your CNS.

PNS

Somatic Nervous System

The PNS is separated into the somatic nervous system and the autonomic nervous system. The **somatic nervous system (SNS)** is the portion of the PNS responsible for transmitting neural information to and from the CNS. This information involves the skin senses (e.g., touch, pain, and temperature), body position, and voluntary muscle movement such as raising your hand in class. Within the SNS is a special set of 12 nerves, known as the **cranial nerves** (see Table 3.1), that emanate from the base of the brain (Rosenzweig, Breedlove, & Watson, 2005). The majority of these nerves connect to areas in the head and neck and are responsible for sensory and motor functions such as vision, taste, smell, hearing, and facial movements. One of the major responsibilities of the SNS is **somatosensation** (skin senses), or our ability to experience different types of touch stimuli. This information is largely conducted through **spinal nerves** that extend from the spinal cord to various segments of the body. When a mosquito lands on your arm, you are often able to swat it away before it bites you. This is because the mosquito lands with enough force to stimulate some sensory neurons in your skin. These neurons send signals to your brain, which you interpret as something on your arm. You may have looked at your arm, seen the mosquito, and sent motor signals from your brain to your opposite arm instructing it to swat the mosquito. This scenario describes an interaction between the SNS and the CNS. Sometimes, however, we may engage in a behavioral response to a stimulus in our environment before the information about that stimulus has actually been received by the brain. Reflexes are one such type of behavior.

TABLE 3.1	**The number, name, and general function of the 12 cranial nerves.**	
Number	**Name**	**Function(s)**
I	Olfactory	Smell
II	Optic	Vision
III	Oculomotor	Eye movement
IV	Trochlear	Eye movement
V	Trigeminal	Jaw movement; facial sensation
VI	Abducens	Eye movement
VII	Facial	Facial sensation; facial movement
VIII	Vestibulocochlear	Hearing, balance
IX	Glossopharyngeal	Taste; tongue and pharynx movement
X	Vagus	Movement and sensation of heart; viscera, lungs
XI	Spinal accessory	Neck movement
XII	Hypoglossal	Tongue movement

Reflexes in the SNS

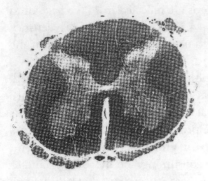

FIGURE 3.3 *A cross-section of the spinal cord as seen through a microscope. The dark outer areas primarily carry information to and from the brain, while cells in the lighter center area (shaped like an "H") send information to and receive information from areas of the body. Picture courtesy of R. W. Flint.*

Biopsychologists have been interested in **reflexes** for a long time due to their simplicity. The reflex primarily involves the SNS, although signals are routed through the spinal cord (see Figure 3.3). During your last physical, your doctor most likely checked your reflexes by gently tapping the tendon in your knee with a triangular rubber mallet as you sat on the edge of the examining table. As a result, the lower part of your leg moved forward as though you were lightly kicking a soccer ball. The difference between this reflexive response and kicking a soccer ball is that you voluntarily choose to kick a ball. In this case, your brain did not send the signals to your leg, and you did not voluntarily move it. If you examine the nervous system components of the reflex, you will find that the sensory stimulus (mallet) was detected and sent to the spinal cord. The signal passes directly across the spinal cord and out through motor neurons. These fibers that exit the spinal cord are responsible for the motor signals that move your leg. The idea that the brain is not directly involved in this movement is sometimes difficult to comprehend. Consider the last time you touched something hot or sharp. Did you reflexively respond by moving your hand away from the stimulus and then say ouch as you began to perceive the pain? This is because the information reached the brain after the reflex arc had been activated (Toates, 2007) (see Figure 3.4).

Autonomic Nervous System

The **autonomic nervous system (ANS)** contains the remaining portions of the PNS, which connect with glands and organs throughout the body, some of which play an important role in the involuntary movements of the heart and lungs. The ANS is concerned with the involuntary regulation of arousal and relaxation. The ANS may be subdivided into sympathetic and parasympathetic divisions that work in concert to maintain **homeostasis**, a certain degree of physiological balance within our systems. An example of homeostatic balance is your ability to maintain your body temperature at 98.6°. When your temperature rises above or drops below 98.6°, your body reacts by attempting to return the temperature to its homeostatic balance. The **parasympathetic division** is generally responsible for conserving energy. Activation of this division causes the blood vessels in some organs to dilate, increases stomach secretions, constricts bronchioles in the lungs, and decreases heart rate. The **sympathetic division** is responsible for arousal and generally prepares the body for expending energy. Blood flow is routed away from many of the internal organs and sent to the muscles; adrenaline is released from the adrenal glands, on top of the kidneys; heart rate increases; and the bronchioles in the lungs dilate. One way to conceptualize the sympathetic and parasympathetic divisions is to recall the last time you were sufficiently scared or aroused, possibly as a result of a fight or some road rage. At the time, you likely felt shaky, overly alert, and excited, and you probably even broke into a sweat. Thankfully, this

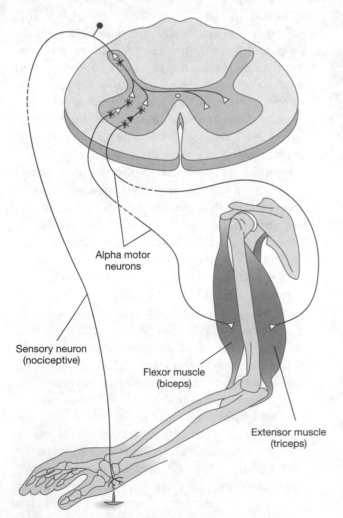

Alpha motor neurons

Sensory neuron (nociceptive)

Flexor muscle (biceps)

Extensor muscle (triceps)

FIGURE 3.4 *The nociceptive reflex. Courtesy of Guyton,* Textbook of Medical Physiology, *1991.*

state of arousal does not typically last for an extended period of time. The parasympathetic division kicks in and helps return your body's physiology to its normal homeostatic level.

Some people find that activation of the sympathetic division actually provides a positive and reinforcing experience (Gondola & Tuckman, 1982). You may know people who engage in extreme sports or who might be considered "adrenaline junkies." These people may spend their free time surfing dangerous waves, racing cars or motorcycles, snowboarding in avalanche zones, or skydiving. It is interesting to note that one can get addicted to the adrenaline rush that occurs. As with most addictions, the more frequently you expose yourself to the "drug," the less effective it becomes. For this reason, those who pursue extreme sports often increase the danger or lethality of the sport in order to reach a greater adrenaline high.

Navigating the CNS

In this section we will explore some of the different views and directional terms used to examine the CNS. To a novice, understanding where neuroanatomical structures are located in the CNS and being able to accurately describe the specific site of damage or neuronal activation can be difficult. These difficulties usually come from an unfamiliarity with both the terminology and the CNS. It is important to have a firm understanding of these terms and concepts, as they will help you formulate a broader understanding of the brain/behavior relationships discussed later.

Within the small confines of your skull you hold billions of cells separated into different regions of the brain. This section will help you describe the location of an abnormal cell group in epilepsy, understand where the damage is when you hear of a friend who suffered a stroke, and know which view of the brain best allows you to examine a particular structure.

Examine the pictures of human and monkey brains in Figure 3.5 and consider trying to describe to someone the location of the star in each picture. While a general understanding of neuroanatomy would undoubtedly be helpful, it is still

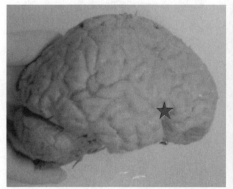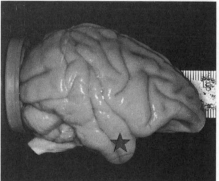

FIGURE 3.5 *Human (left) and rhesus monkey (right) brains, viewed from the lateral surface of the right hemisphere. Note: The pictures are not on the same scale. Pictures courtesy of R. W. Flint.*

challenging to accurately describe the location of the star. To complete this task, you must first learn a new set of terms that are used by many biopsychologists, neuropsychologists, and neuroscientists. These terms provide scientists with consistent ways to describe orientations and directions within the CNS.

Orientations and Directions

There are six major terms that are utilized when navigating through the CNS. Figure 3.6 displays images of the human brain from different orientations. The top surface of the brain is referred to as the **dorsal** surface. This might seem odd at first, since the term "dorsal" likely brings to mind the image of a dorsal fin cutting through the water to the ominous tune from *Jaws*. Human beings are different from most mammals in that we walk upright. If you were to crouch down on all fours and look straight ahead, you would notice that the dorsal surface of your brain is in the same plane as your back—the location of a dorsal fin, if you had one. So, when you stand upright, your back and the top of your head are no longer in the same plane, but both are referred to as the dorsal surface of your brain and spinal cord, respectively. The bottom or base of the brain is referred to as the **ventral** surface (bottom), the front is the **anterior** surface, and the back is the **posterior** surface. When looking at the side

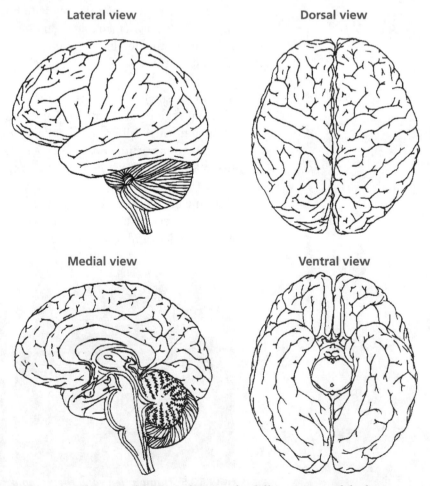

Lateral view   **Dorsal view**

Medial view   **Ventral view**

FIGURE 3.6 *Schematic diagrams showing the different views of the human brain. Brain images courtesy of Amy Vatanakul.*

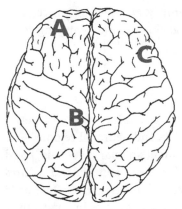

FIGURE 3.7 *Dorsal view of the human brain. Brain image courtesy of Amy Vatanakul.*

of the brain, you are viewing the **lateral** surface, and if the two hemispheres are separated, you can then view the **medial**, or middle, surface.

In our discussion thus far we have used some new terms in reference to various surface areas of the brain, but they are much more versatile than this. Using Figure 3.7, describe the spatial relationship between areas A and B of the human brain. If we use area A as our starting point we might say that area B is medial (closer to the middle of the brain) and posterior (closer to the back of the brain) to area A. Thus, we can use these terms to help us locate neuroanatomical regions and discuss their spatial locations in the brain in reference to other structures. Can you describe the location of area C in relation to area A as your starting point? Remember, area C is in a different hemisphere. (Answer: Area C is located in the right hemisphere and is posterior to and slightly more lateral to area A as it would appear in the right hemisphere.)

Functional Neuroanatomy

Understanding the functions of different brain regions is a major interest of biopsychologists. The best way to understand functional neuroanatomy is to break the brain down into functional parts. This section describes many of the major regions of the brain along with their primary functions. The main connection between the two hemispheres of the brain is called the **corpus callosum**. It is through the corpus callosum that most of the information passes from one hemisphere to the other. Closer inspection of this region in Figure 3.8 reveals that it is a different color (**white matter**) than much of the tissue along the surrounding edges of the brain (**gray matter**). The same thing may be seen in the spinal cord (Figure 3.3), where the white matter (stained dark) appears on the outside of the cord and the gray matter makes up the "H" or "X" shape in the center of the cord. This color difference occurs because particular regions in the brain are primarily made up of axons coated with a fatty substance called myelin, which gives the tissue a whitish appearance.

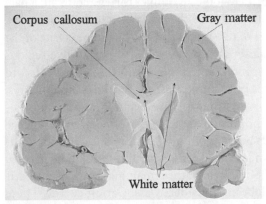

FIGURE 3.8 *Coronal section of human brain showing the corpus callosum and regions of white and gray matter. Picture courtesy of R. W. Flint.*

The result of severing the corpus callosum was extensively studied by the scientist Roger Sperry and is sometimes called a **split-brain** procedure. Sperry's work on the effects of disconnecting the two hemispheres led to his Nobel Prize in 1981. While severing the corpus callosum may seem extreme, the split-brain procedure is sometimes utilized in situations with individuals who suffer from **epilepsy** (abnormal discharge of electrical activity in the brain, which produces seizures) and are unresponsive to antiepileptic pharmacological treatments, thus experiencing a very poor quality of life. By performing a split-brain procedure, the abnormal seizure activity in one hemisphere of the brain is prevented from spreading to the opposite hemisphere. Studies of patients who have received split-brain surgery have revealed that each hemisphere functions independently even though it is functionally isolated from the other (Kandel, Schwartz, & Jessell, 1991). These authors also suggest that both hemispheres are capable of engaging in basic tasks including learning, memory, and sensory processing. However, the right hemisphere is limited in engaging in tasks requiring complex reasoning or analysis.

Lobes of the Cerebral Cortex

The **cerebral cortex** is the wrinkled surface of the brain. It is approximately 6 mm thick and contains a number of cellular layers and neuronal regions. The indentations on the surface are referred to as **sulci** (singular is "sulcus") and **fissures**, and the ridges between sulci and fissures are referred to as **gyri** (singular is "gyrus"). Normally sulci are more shallow and shorter in length than fissures. The location of major sulci and gyri helps doctors and scientists determine the location and function of many cortical regions.

The cerebral cortex in each hemisphere of the brain may be divided into four lobes using some of the sulci and fissures (see Figure 3.9). Looking at the lateral surface of the brain, the **frontal lobes** may be identified as the portion toward the front in each hemisphere. The frontal lobes are the largest lobes of the brain and contain the **primary motor cortex**. Given the size of the frontal lobes, they are involved in numerous functions, including short-term memory, problem solving, language, and movement. These regions of cortex are probably the most highly evolved lobes of the cerebral cortex. Just behind the frontal lobes on the dorsal/lateral surface of each hemisphere are the **parietal lobes**. These lobes house the **somatosensory cortex**, responsible for our skin senses involved in touch. Both the somatosensory cortex and the primary motor cortex are arranged as maps of the human body. Figure 3.10 displays the primary motor cortex and indicates that the amount of cortex allotted to a particular region of the body is associated with the degree of fine motor control. The same is true of the somatosensory system. The more sensitive regions of our skin have more brain tissue dedicated to them. For example, the resulting humanoid figures, known as a motor homunculus and a somatosensory homunculus, have disproportionately large hands because of our exceptional fine-motor abilities and detailed sensory abilities with these parts of our body. Much of the remaining cortex of the parietal lobes is considered association cortex. These areas are involved in integrating various sensory (e.g., vision) and motor functions (e.g., reaching for an object or moving your eyes to gaze at something), which help you interact with your environment. On

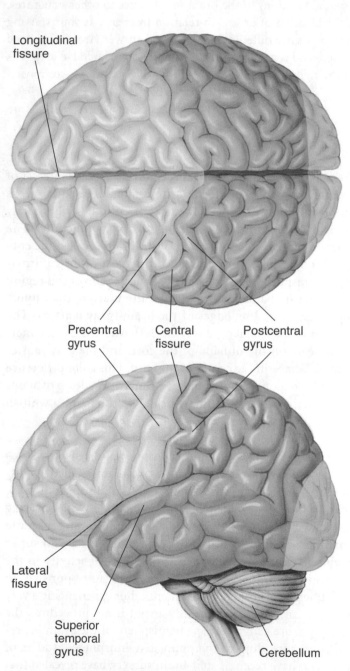

FIGURE 3.9 *Dorsal and lateral views of the human brain showing the location of the frontal, parietal, temporal, and occipital lobes. Image courtesy of J.P.J. Pinel,* Biopsychology, *6th edition, 2006.*

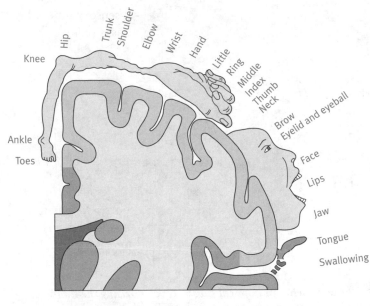

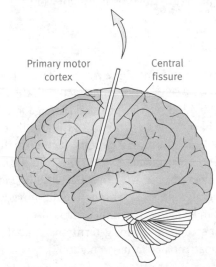

FIGURE 3.10 *Topographic representation of the human motor cortex. Courtesy of Pinel,* Biopsychology, *1997.*

the lateral and ventral surfaces of the brain, below portions of the frontal and parietal lobes, are the **temporal lobes**. These regions of cortex are important for visual recognition, memory, and hearing, as they contain the **primary auditory cortex**. The fourth set of lobes, the **occipital lobes**, are found on the posterior surface of the brain and contain the **primary visual cortex**, involved in processing visual information.

Basal Ganglia Motor System

The **basal ganglia motor system** is composed of a group of interconnected brain structures, primarily subcortical, that are responsible for controlling movement (Takakusaki, Saitoh, Harada, & Kashiwayanagi, 2004; Tisch, Silberstein, Limousin-Dowsey, & Jahanshahi, 2004). The importance of these structures to motor movement is revealed in individuals with disorders such as Parkinson's disease and Huntington's disease. **Parkinson's disease** is the selective loss of dopamine neurons in part of the basal ganglia motor system called the substantia nigra. Individuals with this disease, such as the actor Michael J. Fox, suffer from tremors, immobility, and muscle rigidity because of the degeneration of these cells. **Huntington's disease** is associated with damage to other regions of basal ganglia and causes major motor impairments such as involuntary movements and difficulties with speaking and swallowing. An added complication of this genetic disorder is the development of cognitive impairments such as significant changes in mood and memory. Because of the strong genetic inheritance of Huntington's disease, a large debate exists in the medical community about whether people with relatives suffering from Huntington's should be screened for the disorder and counseled about the risks of passing it on through reproduction.

Limbic System

The **limbic system** is similar to the basal ganglia motor system in that it is a group of interconnected neurological structures (see Figure 3.11). This system includes the olfactory bulbs, the amygdala, the hippocampus, the fornix, the cingulate cortex, the thalamus, and the hypothalamus. As a system, these structures are involved in memory and emotion (Buchanan, 2007; Joseph, 1992; Morgane & Mokler, 2006; Pruessner et al., 2008). Individually, they make different contributions to these general abilities. The **amygdala**, a Latin term that means "almond," is a small, oval-shaped structure located within the temporal

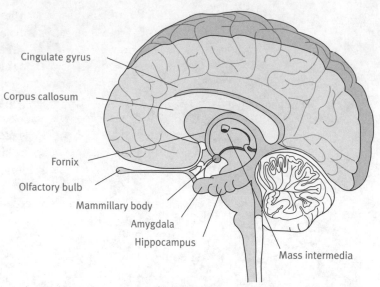

Cingulate gyrus

Corpus callosum

Fornix

Olfactory bulb

Mammillary body

Amygdala

Hippocampus

Mass intermedia

FIGURE 3.11 *Major neuroanatomical substrates comprising the limbic system and their location. Courtesy of Carlson,* Physiology of Behavior, *2004.*

lobe that has been shown to significantly contribute to a person's experience of fear and aggression (Murray, 2007; Phelps, 2006). **Urbach-Wiethe disease** is a very rare condition in which individuals suffer bilateral damage to the amygdala. One study examined 10 Urbach-Wiethe patients and found that bilateral amygdala damage produced profound emotional deficits, including the loss of the ability to determine an emotion from facial expressions and to remember emotionally arousing pictures (Siebert, Markowitsch, & Bartel, 2003). From this evidence we can discern that bilateral brain lesions limited to the amygdala result in a variety of emotional deficits in humans. The amygdala is also connected to the **hippocampus**, an important structure for long-term and spatial memory (Neves, Cooke, & Bliss, 2008; Wagatsuma & Yamaguchi, 2007).

The amygdala's connection with the hippocampus is important, as it seems to modulate memories, especially those associated with highly emotional situations. For example, the amygdala is likely to be involved with the enhanced memories for traumatic events such as those that occur in acute stress disorder and post-traumatic stress disorder (PTSD) (Adami, Konig, Vetter, Hausmann, & Conca, 2006; McNally, 2006). PTSD may develop following exposure to a devastating event such as rape, war, a tornado, and terrorism, and is characterized by intense flashbacks of the event accompanied by physiological arousal. Similarly, the amygdala may be involved in a special form of amnesia (memory loss) known as "red-outs," which have reportedly occurred when an individual commits a violent act but has no recollection of it (Swihart, Yuille, & Porter, 1999). The fornix is a set of connections between the hippocampus and other structures of the limbic system (Gaffan, 2001). If these fibers are severed, memory impairments may sometimes result (Spiers, Maguire, & Burgess, 2001). The cingulate cortex is visible on the medial surface of each hemisphere above the corpus callosum. This gyrus houses important regions for emotion, and it is unique because it is not considered part of any one lobe of cerebral cortex (Vogt, 2005). The limbic system also includes the thalamus and the hypothalamus.

The **thalamus** and the hypothalamus may be subdivided into a variety of smaller structures called nuclei (not to be confused with the nucleus of an individual cell). These nuclei are clusters of neurons that share the same function. The thalamus is commonly referred to as the sensory relay station of the brain (Miyata, 2007). Sensory information is sent through this structure on its way to the primary cortex of the brain, where the initial processing of that sensory information will occur. The one exception to this is the olfactory system, which sends information directly to regions of the temporal lobe involved in processing emotion and memory. This is likely the reason why you often have such vivid and powerful memories associated with particular odors (Herz & Cupchik, 1995). You can probably think of at least one occasion where you caught a whiff of a certain odor that immediately caused you to recall a particular memory that was likely associated with some degree of emotional arousal.

The **hypothalamus**, also part of the limbic system, has been comically referred to by some as playing a major role in the four F's: feeding, fighting, fleeing, and "sex." These complex yet basic behaviors involve a variety of emotional, motivational, and memory components. In a review of four case studies of hypothalamic disorders, researchers reported that patients suffered from a range of problems including depression, memory loss, anorexia, excessive eating, drowsiness, and inability to maintain core body temperature (Martin & Riskind, 1992). The hypothalamus is also considered part of the endocrine system and is the brain region responsible for controlling the pituitary gland (see "Endocrine System," pp. 83–85).

Since the limbic system is involved in both memory and emotion, it is home to a number of neuropsychological disorders such as Alzheimer's disease. **Alzheimer's disease** is a widespread neurological disease that affects primarily elderly individuals. There are, however, rare cases of early-onset Alzheimer's that may occur in middle-aged individuals (Filley et al., 2007). Regardless of the age of onset, approximately 4.5 million Americans have Alzheimer's, a number predicted to increase significantly over the next 50 years, according to a press release from the Alzheimer's Association in 2003. The disease is a progressive disorder, normally beginning with memory impairments that appear as increased forgetfulness (Gabrieli, 1998; Mayeux, 2003; von Gunten, Bouras, Kovari, Giannakopoulos, & Hof, 2006). As time passes and the disease progresses, the memory impairments become more profound and the individual may experience confusion, agitation, language impairments, delusions, and hallucinations. Eventually the individual becomes completely dependent on a caregiver and may suffer from seizures and incontinence before ultimately dying. The disease is characterized by the development of abnormal masses of protein called **neurofibrillary tangles** inside the neurons and **amyloid plaques** in the spaces outside the neurons. Many of these abnormal proteins are concentrated in areas such as the temporal lobe, the amygdala, and the hippocampus—regions important for memory and emotion. As the disease progresses, the tangles and plaques spread through the cortex and subcortical areas of the brain. Unfortunately, there is no definitive diagnosis for Alzheimer's other than through brain biopsy. At this time there is also no cure, although many pharmaceutical companies are focusing on developing drugs that will help alleviate the severe memory impairments associated with this disease.

Explore
Alzheimer's disease
in Chapter 8, p. 250

Research on Alzheimer's disease, head-trauma patients, and neurological diseases is very useful in helping scientists understand the cause and progression of these disorders. The hope is that this better understanding will lead to an eventual cure. In many of these conditions the damage to the brain is widespread or at least may affect a number of different regions. Rarely is the damage **bilateral**, or equivalent in size, shape, and location in both hemispheres. From a biopsychological perspective, conditions such as these make it difficult to determine the relationship between a specific brain structure and a specific behavioral or cognitive impairment. Rare occurrences of selective brain damage provide unique insights into brain/behavior relationships and emphasize the value of case study research.

The Brain Stem

The **pons** plays an important role in sleep, arousal, and some motor and sensory function (see Figure 3.12). Thus, individuals who suffer damage to their pons may display impairments in motor movements, posture, and REM sleep (stage of sleep characterized by rapid eye movements and the stage during which most dreaming occurs).

The **reticular formation** is a long structure buried within the tissue of the brain stem and midbrain regions that is shaped somewhat like a hotdog. The reticular formation is the primary structure contributing to the reticular activating system (RAS), involved in CNS arousal. Given the role of the RAS, it makes sense

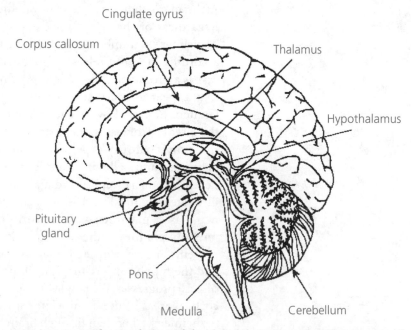

FIGURE 3.12 *Midsagittal view of the right hemisphere identifying some of the major structures. Image courtesy of Amy Vatanakul.*

that it is close to structures like the pons and the medulla. The **medulla** plays a very important role in basic life functions such as heart rate and respiration. In a recent case study, a young woman who reported suffering from breathing and motor difficulties was found to have a tumor in the dorsal region of her medulla (Kobayashi, Sawamura, & Ikeda, 2005).

The **cerebellum**, or "little brain," sometimes appears to be a small brain in itself that has been attached to the brain stem (see Figure 3.12). Damage to the cerebellum may induce profound impairments in one's ability to coordinate motor movements and may impair some forms of learning. Damage to the cerebellum sometimes happens as a result of severe frontal head trauma (I hope you are scratching your head right now, wondering why severe frontal head injury would damage a structure located on the back surface of the brain). The reason for this, simply put, is ricochet. When the front of your head strikes something very hard when moving at a high velocity, your brain shifts forward and hits the inner front surface of your skull. The injury that results to the frontal lobe region is called a **coup injury**. Unfortunately, your brain is likely to then ricochet backward and hit the inner back surface of the skull. This results in damage to regions of the brain such as the occipital lobe and the cerebellum. In situations such as this, the damage opposite the coup injury is referred to as the **contrecoup injury**.

Anatomy of the Neuron

Different brain regions are responsible for different functions associated with behavior and mental processes. Each region we have discussed so far is made up of small cells called neurons. **Neurons** are the primary functional cells of the nervous system and are responsible for receiving and passing on neural signals. It was once believed that the adult brain was rather solidified in its structure and neuronal organization and that it remained relatively unchanged over time once adolescence had been reached. Evidence now shows the brain to be quite **plastic**, or malleable, which may be the mechanism through which experience-dependent changes occur (e.g., establishment of new memories). There are different types of neurons in the nervous system, but the majority are similar with respect to their primary anatomical composition.

Soma and Dendrites

The most common type of neuron in the CNS is the multipolar neuron (see Figures 3.13 and 3.14). The cell body, or **soma**, of the multipolar neuron is the center of metabolic activity and houses many of the intracellular organelles commonly found inside cells (e.g., nucleus, endoplasmic reticulum, and mitochondria). Emanating from the soma are numerous branchlike structures called **dendrites**, which are covered with small bumps called **dendritic spines** (see Figure 3.14). The dendrites serve as the primary input pathways through which the neuron receives signals from other neurons, a process that will be described in more detail in the next few sections. Signals are received through

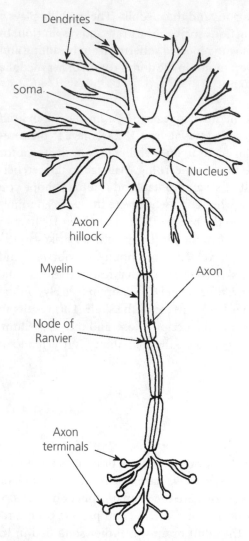

FIGURE 3.13 *Multipolar neuron. Image courtesy of Amy Vatanakul.*

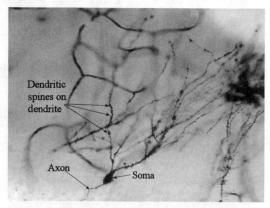

FIGURE 3.14 *A pyramidal neuron found in the dentate gyrus, a region of the hippocampal formation. Tissue was sectioned at 200 microns on a vibratome and stained with the Golgi-Cox stain. Magnification is 250×. Picture courtesy of Russ Brown, East Tennessee State University.*

the dendritic spines and may result in a change in the electrical potential (charge) of the cell.

Axon and Axon Terminals

Also emanating from the soma is a larger branch known as the **axon**. The junction between the soma and the axon is known as the **axon hillock**, which is the region where signals coming in from the dendrites are added together to influence the bioelectrical status of the cell. The neuron's axon is the primary output pathway through which a signal is delivered to one or more cells. Some axons in the PNS and the CNS are coated by specialized cells. These cells provide a sheath of support and protection to the axon, referred to as the **myelin sheath**, and increase the speed of the electrical signal that travels down these **myelinated axons**. Not all neurons have a myelin sheath (**unmyelinated axons**), but the presence of the myelin is what gives the white matter in the brain and spinal cord its whitish appearance. Since the myelin sheath is made up of specialized cells, a small gap in the coverage of the axon is created between them. These open spaces in the myelin sheath are called **nodes of Ranvier**, and they are important for maintaining the electrical signal sent down an axon. The importance of these nodes will be discussed in more detail later in the section "Neural Conduction."

A number of problems can arise with neurons that will disrupt their ability to function normally. One such example is **multiple sclerosis (MS)**, a neurodegenerative disorder in which the myelin, and sometimes axons in the CNS, is damaged or destroyed (Trapp, 2004). The loss of myelin on axons is commonly referred to as **demyelination**. As a result of demyelination, individuals who suffer from MS may experience motor deficits, cognitive impairments, respiratory problems, and blindness. The cause of MS is unclear, although many believe that it is an **autoimmune disease**, in which one's own immune system identifies the myelin as foreign and attacks.

The axon splits into a number of **terminal branches**, and at the end of each branch is a bulbous-shaped structure called the **axon terminal**. Within the axon terminal are **synaptic vesicles**, which are small spheres filled with a chemical called **neurotransmitter**. Axon terminals often release the neurotransmitter into the surrounding space, called the **synaptic cleft**, where it may bind with receptors found in the membrane of nearby cells (e.g., on the dendritic spines from other neurons). The axon terminal does not physically touch the dendritic spine of the next cell, and the small space between it and the dendritic spine creates the synaptic cleft. This raises the question of how an electrical signal might be transferred from one neuron to another. As an analogy, you might ask yourself if you could receive an electric shock by placing your hand on top of an electrical outlet. You are safe, of course, unless you actually stick your fingers or an object into the socket and make contact with the terminals inside. By placing your hand on the surface of the outlet plate, a space still remains between your hand and the contacts within the socket. Thus, when the neurotransmitter is released it travels across the synaptic cleft and produces the change in the next cell.

Ions and the Resting Membrane Potential

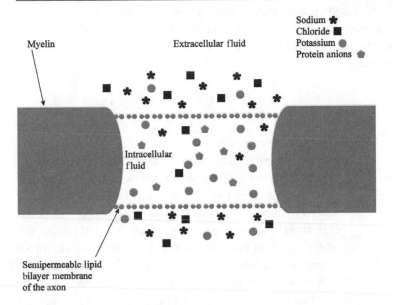

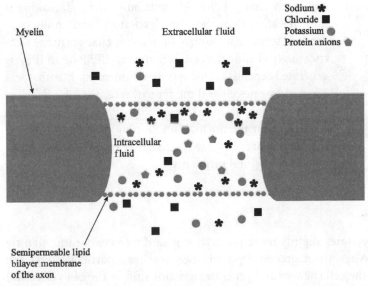

FIGURE 3.15 *Node of Ranvier when neuron is at rest (top panel) and during synaptic transmission (bottom panel) showing the influx of sodium ions causing depolarization of this localized region of the axon. Images courtesy of R. W. Flint.*

When a neuron is inactive or at rest, it maintains an internal electrical charge of approximately −70 mV. The maintenance of this charge, known as the **resting membrane potential**, is due to a number of factors. The membrane of a neuron is semipermeable, meaning that it prevents the free passage of many molecules across the membrane. However, the membrane also contains specialized proteins that create channels. These channels, when open, may allow certain molecular **ions** (positively or negatively charged particles) to pass back and forth across the membrane. Thus, the channels are called ion channels. There are many different ions found in the human body, and some of the most important ones for the CNS include **sodium** (Na^+), **potassium** (K^+), **calcium** (Ca^{++}), and **chloride** (Cl^-). Additionally, there are larger protein molecules found primarily inside the cell, called **anions**, which have a negative charge. In resting (inactive) neurons, ions are distributed so that there is a greater positive charge outside the neuron and a greater negative charge inside the neuron (see Figure 3.15). The maintenance of this distribution establishes the resting membrane potential.

Sodium, chloride, and calcium ions are normally found in higher concentrations outside the cell, while potassium and protein anions are found in greater concentrations inside the cell. When a neuron receives a signal, some of the ion channels open and allow some of these ions to move from the inside to the outside of the cell, or vice versa.

Neural Conduction

Neurons communicate with one another through both electrical and chemical means, a requirement due in part to the presence of the synaptic cleft, discussed earlier. **Neural conduction** is concerned with the signal generated inside a neuron and the conduction of that signal to the synaptic terminals. Within a neuron, an electrical signal is commonly received through the dendritic spines and may reach the soma. Since a single multipolar neuron has many dendrites covered with dendritic spines, each of which has the potential to receive signals from many other neurons, the electrical potential of a single neuron is the result of all the signals it is receiving at a given moment in time, a concept known as **summation**. If the received signal is positive and of sufficient strength, a new output signal may be generated at the axon hillock and sent down the axon to the synaptic terminals.

Post-Synaptic Potentials

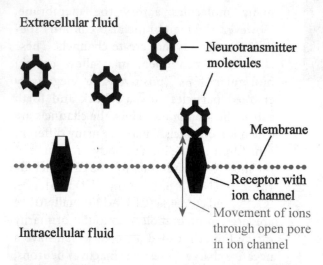

Extracellular fluid

Neurotransmitter molecules

Membrane

Receptor with ion channel

Movement of ions through open pore in ion channel

Intracellular fluid

FIGURE 3.16 *Diagram of a neurotransmitter molecule binding to and opening a post-synaptic receptor containing an ion channel. This will allow ions of a particular type to move into or out of the cell depending on the type of receptor. The passage of ions will produce an EPSP or an IPSP. Image courtesy of R. W. Flint.*

The signal received at a dendritic spine is called a **post-synaptic potential**. The term "post-synaptic" is used to indicate that we are talking about the receiving cell on the other side of the synaptic cleft, and the term "potential" is used to indicate that an electrical change is involved. An **excitatory post-synaptic potential (EPSP)** causes the receiving cell to become slightly more positive. The EPSP is commonly caused by the movement of positively charged sodium ions into the receiving cells through ion channels (see Figure 3.16). An **inhibitory post-synaptic potential (IPSP)** may be generated when chloride channels open and negatively charged chloride ions enter the cell, making it more negative. Thus, the terms "excitatory" and "inhibitory" are used to indicate positive or negative changes in the electrical status inside the cell. Whether an EPSP or an IPSP is generated depends on the type of neurotransmitter that was released by one cell and the type of receptor it binds to on the receiving cell. Regardless, both IPSPs and EPSPs are important for the normal functioning of the nervous system; imbalances in these systems may result in severe mental and behavioral problems.

Action Potentials

When a cell becomes slightly more positive, it is said to have become slightly **depolarized**. When the degree of depolarization reaches a particular level, the membrane of the cell changes and generates a major shift in the cell's electrical potential. This shift is known as an **action potential** (i.e., the cell becomes activated; see Figure 3.17). Neurons must become depolarized by a specific amount in order to reach the **threshold of excitation**, or the minimum electrical potential necessary to generate an action potential. The **all-or-nothing law** concep-

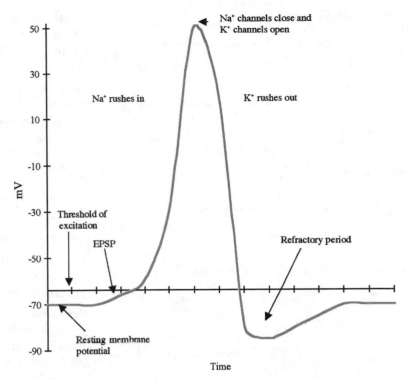

FIGURE 3.17 *Graphic representation of an action potential. Image courtesy of R. W. Flint.*

tualizes this effect and states that a neuron's response is not dependent upon the strength of the signals it receives; rather, an action potential will be generated as soon as the threshold of excitation is reached. Depolarization of a neuron that does not reach the threshold of excitation will not produce an action potential. Once the threshold is reached, a biochemical change occurs that generates the action potential.

You might consider the act of pushing a broken-down car as an analogy. A certain amount of force is required to get the car moving. If too little force is applied, the car will not budge. However, once the amount of force reaches the threshold and causes the wheels to rotate, the car will begin moving forward. It doesn't matter if you push more than the minimum threshold; the car will begin to move with any force at or above the minimum threshold.

When the cell becomes depolarized to the threshold of excitation, special ion channels called **voltage-dependent sodium channels** open in a small section of the cell membrane at the axon hillock. This process allows sodium to rush into the cell, depolarizing that segment of the axon and activating the voltage-gated sodium channels in the *next* section of the axon. The sodium channels close shortly after opening, and **voltage-dependent potassium channels** open, allowing potassium to exit the cell in the process of returning that segment of the axon to its resting membrane potential. This produces a cascading effect in which the action potential (rush of sodium ions into the cell) is carried down the axon to the synaptic terminal (see Figure 3.18).

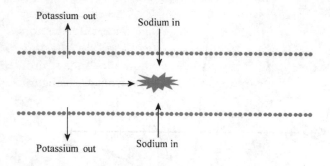

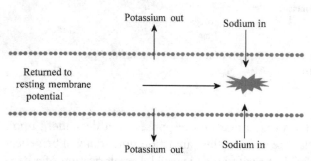

FIGURE 3.18 *Schematic diagram of a segment of unmyelinated axon demonstrating the passage of the action potential toward the synaptic terminal. Image courtesy of R. W. Flint.*

In neurons with myelinated axons, the myelin sheath covers large portions of the axon, effectively preventing the movement of ions across the neuron's membrane. As a result, the neuronal signal jumps quickly through the myelinated sections and is regenerated at the node of Ranvier, where the voltage-dependent channels may permit the movement of ions into the cell, and vice versa.

Synaptic Transmission

Synaptic transmission is a process in which the electrical signal traveling down the axon is transmitted biochemically across the synaptic cleft to the next cell. When the action potential reaches the axon terminal (see Figure 3.19) it causes **voltage-dependent calcium channels** to open, allowing calcium ions to rush into the cell of the axon terminal. When calcium enters the cell, it causes the synaptic vesicles to fuse with the membrane of the axon terminal, dumping the neurotransmitter into the synaptic cleft. The neurotransmitter is now available to bind with receptors on the dendritic spines of other neurons. Once it binds with a receptor, it will open ion channels on the dendrites and the process will start over. The relationship between the neurotransmitter and the post-synaptic receptor is analogous to the relationship between a key and a lock in that specific keys open specific locks. When the neurotransmitter binds with the receptor, it activates it, often causing the opening of an ion channel.

Neurotransmitter Systems

A large number of molecules act as neurotransmitter substances in our nervous systems, some of which include acetylcholine, GABA, glutamate, dopamine, serotonin, norepinephrine, and endorphins. The normal release of these chemicals allows us to engage in the behaviors and mental activities that make us who we are. Joy, sadness, fantasy, memory, verbal and nonverbal behaviors—none of these could exist without neurotransmitters. Disruptions in these neurotransmitter systems are responsible for a wide variety of neurological disorders as well as sought-after psychological effects (e.g., legal and illegal drug use).

The neurotransmitter is also subject to a number of processes that reduce its effectiveness. One such pro-

FIGURE 3.19 *Synaptic terminal demonstrating the influx of calcium ions and subsequent release of neurotransmitter substance into the synaptic cleft. Image courtesy of R. W. Flint.*

cess is **enzymatic degradation**, where enzymes present in the synaptic cleft break down and thus inactivate the neurotransmitter molecules. The longer the neurotransmitter remains in this area, the greater the chance that it will be destroyed. Some neurotransmitter substance may be inactivated because it is reabsorbed into the synaptic terminal, a process called **reuptake**. When a neurotransmitter is reabsorbed, it may be recycled for future use. The reabsorption process reduces the effectiveness of the neurotransmitter by reducing the amount of time the chemical is present in the synaptic cleft and able to bind with receptors on the dendritic spines. In addition to activating the post-synaptic receptors on the next cell, the neurotransmitter may also activate special receptors found on the axon terminal called **autoreceptors**. When these autoreceptors are activated, they signal the synaptic terminal to cease the release of neurotransmitter substance. This feedback through autoreceptors allows the neuron to regulate the release of neurotransmitter and prevent it from releasing too much or too little.

Acetylcholine

The neurotransmitter **acetylcholine (ACH)** plays an important role in a variety of places in the CNS and the PNS. One of its major peripheral roles is in the control of muscles throughout our bodies. Acetylcholine released at the neuromuscular junction causes muscle movement. This neurotransmitter also plays an important role in a number of cognitive processes, including attention and memory. Large numbers of acetylcholine receptors are found in the hippocampus and the basal forebrain region. Given the role of acetylcholine in memory, you should not be surprised to learn that the acetylcholine system is significantly disrupted in individuals who suffer from Alzheimer's disease. Some people like to take advantage of the arousal-related properties associated with acetylcholine by self-administering drugs containing nicotine, which increases the release of acetylcholine and other neurotransmitters (Julien, 2003).

GABA

GABA, or **gamma-aminobutyric acid**, is the primary inhibitory neurotransmitter found in the nervous system. Its release from synaptic terminals produces inhibitory effects in the dendrites of the receiving neurons. Zwanzger and Rupprecht (2005) found that drugs that enhance GABA have antianxiety effects and that they largely reduce panic-related symptoms such as accelerated heart rate, sweating, and choking. Research such as this is promising and may lead to treatments for those who suffer from anxiety and panic disorders.

Glutamate

Glutamate is one of the nervous system's primary excitatory neurotransmitters. Release of glutamate into the synaptic cleft excites the receiving neuron, increasing the likelihood of generating an action potential. Glutamate plays an important role in epilepsy, schizophrenia, memory, and even **ischaemic stroke** (Kew & Kemp, 2005). An ischaemic stroke occurs when something (e.g., a blood clot) blocks blood flow to a particular region of the brain. The deprived region begins to release excessive amounts of glutamate, which overstimulates the receiving cells and causes those cells to also release glutamate, subsequently exciting the connected neurons, and so on. This overstimulation has an excitotoxic (overly excites the subsequent neurons to a detrimental degree) effect that eventually kills the cells. So while glutamate is important for a number of functions, excessive release can be very problematic.

Dopamine

The neurotransmitter dopamine was mentioned earlier in our discussion of the substantia nigra and Parkinson's disease. In addition to its role in motor movement, dopamine is also important for providing you with the pleasure you experience when you have sex or eat and drink foods you enjoy. Dopamine also provides the pleasure associated with many illegal drugs, such as cocaine, and is responsible for the reinforcement involved in many forms of learning. One interesting aspect of the pleasing and reinforcing properties of dopamine is that it all seems to take place in the same region of the brain. In other words, eating chocolate, snorting cocaine, and having sex all stimulate the release of dopamine in the same place in the brain—the **nucleus accumbens**. The repeated release of dopamine in the nucleus accumbens when these behaviors are performed is linked with the addictive nature of these activities. The interaction of these behaviors also suggests that we all have a centralized pleasure center in the brain. As a final note on dopamine, it is worth pointing out its role in schizophrenia. The dopamine theory of schizophrenia continues to sustain considerable interest as an explanation for many of the positive symptoms of this disorder (Jones & Pilowsky, 2002). According to this theory, there is a hyperactivity of certain dopamine receptors responsible for many of the effects of schizophrenia (Pinel, 2006; Snyder, 1978).

Explore **the dopamine theory of schizophrenia** in Chapter 14, p. 470

Serotonin

In psychiatry, a popular class of drugs called **selective serotonin reuptake inhibitors (SSRIs)** has been developed as treatments for depression. This class of drugs acts by inhibiting the reuptake process that normally reabsorbs the neurotransmitter **serotonin** after it has been released. By inhibiting this process, serotonin remains in the synaptic cleft for a longer period of time, where it is able to continue to bind with and activate post-synaptic receptors. A reduction in the level of serotonin has been associated with depression, and an increase in the level of serotonin with the reduction of depression. Serotonin also plays an important role in mental processes including emotion, sleep, and appetite (Schloss & Williams, 1998). Scientists are concerned about the effectiveness and safety of SSRIs and other antidepressant drugs for children and adolescents suffering from depression (Whittington, Kendall, & Pilling, 2005). While controversy over the psychopharmacological treatment of minors with depression continues, other scientists have discovered that manipulations in the serotonergic system may provide important information about autism (Whitaker-Azmitia, 2005), alcohol addiction (Addolorato, Leggio, Abenavoli, & Gasbarrini, 2005), and obsessive-compulsive disorder (Hollander, 2005).

Norepinephrine

Norepinephrine is a stress hormone and neurotransmitter that is released from the adrenal glands as well as from neurons in the nervous system. Historically, norepinephrine has been considered to play a major role in nervous system arousal, although more recent evidence suggests a complex role in behavior as well (Aston-Jones & Cohen, 2005). Studies examining the role of norepinephrine in psychological disorders have found that it is involved in attention deficit/hyperactivity disorder (Chamberlain et al., 2007) and depression (Preston, O'Neal, & Talaga, 2005). Beyond these broad effects, norepinephrine has also been shown to play an important role in learning tasks that involve the cerebellum (Cartford, Gould, & Bickford, 2004) and dementia (Herrmann, Lanctot, & Khan, 2004).

Endorphins

The last neurotransmitter we will discuss is actually a class of neurotransmitters called **endorphins**. These neurotransmitters are natural painkillers released by our bodies when we sustain injury. As such, endorphins have been implicated in developmental disorders that involve self-injurious behaviors, either because the release of endorphins following pain is pleasurable and addictive, or because endorphins reduce pain perception and self-injurious behaviors occur as a form of self-stimulation (Sandman & Hetrick, 1995). Endorphins are also known to be involved in drug addiction because of the euphoric effects they produce (Ratsma, Van Der Stelt, & Gunning, 2002; Topel, 1988) and in altering our moods in response to acute bouts of exercise (Yeung, 1996). Some have suggested that the latter effect may contribute to the phenomenon called the "runner's high," where long-distance runners reach a point of euphoric rush (Franklin, 1987).

Endocrine System

The **endocrine system** is the hormonal regulatory system of the body. Because the brain, specifically the hypothalamus, controls the endocrine system and because hormones have a wide variety of effects on the brain and behavior, it is important to understand some of the basics of this system. Figure 3.20 presents

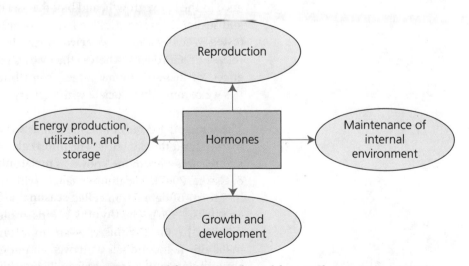

FIGURE 3.20 *Major hormonal functions. Adapted from Wilson & Foster (1992).*

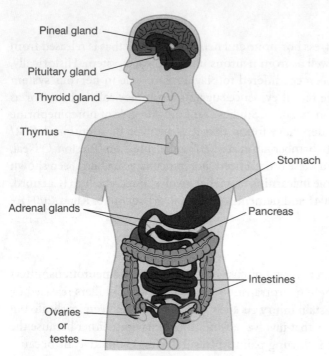

FIGURE 3.21 *Location of the major endocrine glands.*
Courtesy of Toates, Biological Psychology, *Second Edition, 2007.*

an overview of the endocrine system and its primary functions. You may recall that the hypothalamus is involved in many motivational and emotional behaviors, such as feeding, fighting, fleeing, and sex. Adrenaline, also called epinephrine, acts as both a hormone and a neurotransmitter and is involved in both fighting and fleeing behavior. Insulin from the pancreas is involved in hunger, and sex hormones are involved in sexual behaviors and characteristics associated with sex differences. Figure 3.21 presents the general location of the major endocrine glands.

When it comes to the endocrine system, the hypothalamus is involved in regulating your overall hormonal state. It is connected with the pituitary gland through both the nervous and circulatory systems. These connections allow the hypothalamus to receive information about the hormone levels in the body from the circulatory system and then "command" the pituitary gland to release or stop releasing hormones. Thus, the chemicals released from the hypothalamus are often referred to as **releasing** and **inhibiting hormones** because of their effects on the pituitary gland.

The **pituitary gland** is sometimes referred to as the "master gland" because many of the chemicals it releases directly affect specific endocrine glands in the body, stimulating the release of certain hormones from them. The **adrenal glands** are activated under times of stress and emotional arousal. In addition to the release of **glucocorticoids** (e.g., cortisol), they are also responsible for releasing **epinephrine**. The release of these hormones helps us prepare for the expenditure of energy and, in a manner of speaking, may facilitate coping behaviors that help us manage the stress.

Because the pituitary gland regulates other endocrine glands, it is involved in a wide variety of functions, including uterine contractions, milk release, water balance in the body, growth, and blood vessel constriction. Reproductive behavior and sexual characteristics are largely associated with hormones released by the **testes** in males and the **ovaries** in females. The testes are responsible for the release of androgens, whereas the ovaries release estrogens and progestins. The effects of these hormones largely contribute to the secondary sex characteristics we commonly associate with puberty.

The remaining three endocrine glands we will review are the pineal gland, the thymus, and the pancreas. The **pineal gland** is located at the base of the brain and releases a hormone known as **melatonin**, which is involved in sleep (Sajith & Clarke, 2007). Melatonin changes with the seasons and has been implicated in a form of depression called **seasonal affective disorder** (Dalgleish, Rosen, & Marks, 1996). The **thymus** glands are located in the neck. The hormones released by the thymus play an important role in the body's growth and metabolism. Individuals with over- or underactive thymus glands often exhibit abnormal growth or weight gain. Finally, the **pancreas** is responsible for managing **glucose** (blood sugar) levels through the release of hormones such as insulin. Blood sugar disorders such as diabetes are often associated with abnormalities in the pancreas.

Chapter Summary

The field of biopsychology is broadly interested in understanding the relationships between the biology of an organism and its behavioral and mental processes. Within this field, scientists may examine the importance of specific neural structures in the brain for language, study the role of certain neurotransmitter systems in depression, determine the contributions of reproductive hormones to sexual activity, or attempt to discern the underlying neural damage contributing to the deficits in individuals suffering from a stroke or head trauma. In this chapter you were introduced to topics such as the components of the nervous system, functional neuroanatomy, anatomy of the neuron, ions and the resting membrane potential, neural conduction, synaptic transmission, neurotransmitter systems, and the endocrine system.

Our nervous system may be divided into the central nervous system (brain and spinal cord) and the peripheral nervous system (somatic and autonomic). Subsequently, the autonomic nervous system may be divided into sympathetic and parasympathetic divisions. Together, these regions are made up primarily of neurons that communicate with one another through both bioelectrical and biochemical processes. At the bioelectrical end, the movement of ions across the cell membrane of the neuron alters the electrical charge within the cell. Upon the generation of an action potential, this signal is transmitted to the axon terminals of a neuron, where the neurotransmitter substance is released. This biochemical result may produce a bioelectrical change in the receiving neuron, thus creating the potential for the generation of an action potential in the neuron. The effect of a neurotransmitter on a cell depends heavily on the type of neurotransmitter that has been released and the type of receptor that it binds to on the receiving cell. There are many types of neurotransmitters and receptors, and new ones are being discovered all the time. Massed together, the ongoing activity within our nervous system is responsible for our every reflex, thought, sensation, memory, and movement.

The neurons in the brain are arranged and organized into different functional regions, although they communicate with a diverse number of other brain areas. The neurons of the cerebral cortex house many functions and are divided into the frontal lobes, parietal lobes, occipital lobes, and temporal lobes—one in each hemisphere connected by the corpus callosum. Beneath the cerebral cortex exist a number of subcortical structures, some of which are linked together to form major systems such as the basal ganglia motor system and the limbic system, which is important for emotion and memory. Regions of the brain stem such as the pons, medulla, reticular formation, and cerebellum play important roles in many basic life functions and motor coordination.

Although some suggest that we are driven by our hormones, at least in certain circumstances, we know that the hypothalamus in the brain is responsible for commanding the endocrine system via the pituitary gland. Having received signals from the hypothalamus, the pituitary releases chemicals that subsequently direct the release of hormones from other endocrine glands such as the thymus, pancreas, adrenal glands, and reproductive glands. The resulting release of hormones has the capacity to influence the body, behavior, and/or the mental state of the organism.

This basic understanding of biopsychology will help you as you proceed through the subsequent chapters in this textbook. Maybe this chapter will even provide you with some unique topics of conversation at social gatherings. Well, maybe that's wishful thinking, but you should have at least gained some winning terms for the next time you play Scrabble.

Knowledge Builder

1. Consider the variety of neuroanatomical regions you read about. If you were to select one on which to conduct a biopsychological study, which one would you choose and why?

   _____

   _____

   _____

   _____

2. Having now selected that neuroanatomical region to study, what biopsychological method(s) discussed in Chapter 2, "Research Methods," would you use? Is there one method or technique that would provide more definitive results than another?

   _____

   _____

   _____

   _____

3. Describe a recent situation where your sympathetic nervous system was activated. How did you feel? What biochemical changes are likely to have been responsible for those feelings?

   _____

   _____

   _____

   _____

CHAPTER REVIEW QUESTIONS

1. Dendrites are the primary input pathways of neurons. **T or F?**

2. The hippocampus is an important structure for motor movement. **T or F?**

3. An excitatory post-synaptic potential (EPSP) occurs because sodium enters the cell. **T or F?**

4. The neurotransmitter dopamine is released in the context of pleasurable or rewarding stimuli. **T or F?**

5. Alzheimer's disease is associated with the neurotransmitter serotonin. **T or F?**

6. The occipital lobes receive information for the visual system. **T or F?**

7. A lesion of the amygdala will likely impair _____ in a rat.

   (a) reproductive behaviors   (b) eating

   (c) motor abilities   (d) fear

8. A stroke often produces neurological damage because of the excitotoxic effects of the neurotransmitter _____.

   (a) dopamine   (b) acetylcholine

   (c) glutamate   (d) norepinephrine

9. A neuron must be depolarized enough to reach the _____ before an action potential will be produced.

   (a) synaptic terminal   (b) threshold of excitation

   (c) neurotransmitter   (d) IPSP

10. Damage to the thalamus may result in problems associated with _____.

   (a) vision   (b) touch

   (c) taste   (d) all of the above

11. The _____ coats many axons in the central nervous system and is destroyed by multiple sclerosis.

   (a) myelin   (b) axon hillock

   (c) post-synaptic membrane   (d) dendritic spine

12. *Consider the following scenario:* Your roommate is taking a fencing class and is practicing while you sit at your desk studying. You turn around and lean toward him to ask a question just as he makes a jab toward your head. The fencing foil enters your nostril and goes deep into your brain. As a result, you now suffer from severe amnesia. Based on your knowledge of the central nervous system, what structures might have been damaged by the fencing foil? (Note: This scenario is based in part on a true story.)

_____

_____

_____

_____

13. *Consider the following scenario:* You've just received a call from a concerned friend who just found out that her father has Alzheimer's disease. What can you tell her about some of the behavioral, cognitive, and neuroanatomical characteristics of this disease?

_____

_____

_____

_____

14. How are white matter and gray matter generally different? Identify one area of the brain comprised primarily of each type of matter.

_____

_____

_____

_____

15. Explain what an action potential is and why it is important. Include a step-by-step explanation of what occurs with sodium and potassium ions that accounts for the occurrence of the action potential.

_____

_____

_____

_____

USEFUL WEB SITES

THE WHOLE BRAIN ATLAS

http://www.med.harvard.edu/AANLIB/home.html

The Whole Brain Atlas site provides a review of imaging technology and brain images from normal brains and the brains of individuals suffering from a variety of neurological conditions including strokes, tumors, Alzheimer's disease, and AIDS.

NEUROSCIENCE FOR KIDS

http://faculty.washington.edu/chudler/neurok.html

This Web page provides many links to exercises, resources, and information for people of all ages.

COMPARATIVE MAMMALIAN BRAIN COLLECTIONS

http://www.brainmuseum.org

This is a wonderful collection of brain images from more than 175 species for anyone interested in comparative neuroscience topics.

JOURNAL FOR UNDERGRADUATE NEUROSCIENCE EDUCATION

http://www.funjournal.org/

The Journal for Undergraduate Neuroscience Education *is a full-text, peer-reviewed online journal dedicated to promoting undergraduate neuroscience education. Faculty and students will find descriptions of useful classroom and laboratory exercises, editorials, and reviews of new print and multimedia materials.*

THE SOCIETY FOR NEUROSCIENCE

http://web.sfn.org/

The Society for Neuroscience is an international organization of neuroscientists. The Web page provide useful links to and timely information from the field of neuroscience as well as the monthly newsletter, Brain Briefings.

Chapter 4

Sensation and Perception

by Elizabeth Shobe, PhD, and Robert W. Flint, Jr., PhD

> *Moral qualities rule the world, but at short distances the senses are despotic.*
>
> —RALPH WALDO EMERSON

Introduction

As Emerson suggests in the quote above, we are ruled by and subject to our senses, but it is their interpretation that really determines our world. Sensation and perception are two distinct but related phenomena. Each has its own role in how we make sense of the world around us. **Sensation** means that we are using our eyes, ears, mouth, nose, and skin to see, hear, taste, smell, and touch physical stimuli in our environment. It is through our senses that we are able to experience the world. **Perception** is how we organize, select, and interpret sensations so that we can understand what is going on around us. Perception includes the mental and neurological processes used to extract meaning from the physical information received by the senses. We can readily appreciate the many differences among the five senses or **sensory modalities**, but less obvious is that the senses have many aspects in common. We will discuss these commonalities first, followed by discussions of the unique contribution of each sensory modality to the human experience. Because these six commonalities are repeated throughout the chapter, identifying them as you read will help you study.

Six Things Your Senses Have in Common

1. *The senses receive physical stimulation from the external world.* Information that we take in from the outside world is received by a variety of specialized cells called **receptors**. Sensory receptors are part of the peripheral nervous system and are located within the sense organs. The eyes, ears, tongue, nose, and skin each contain sensory receptors. Sensory receptors respond to physical stimulation (measurable, observable entities that follow laws of physics) and transform this into something the brain can understand—namely, patterns of electrical and chemical cell responses.

Johannes Muller (early 1800s) first described this process in his **law of specific nerve energies**, which states that we are aware of objects only through signals or energies transmitted through our nerves, and that different kinds of nerves transmit different signals. It is important to understand that once stimulated, a nerve fiber sends its modality-specific message. The source of the stimulation is less important, and there are times when we sense something that isn't even there. For example, some people sneeze in response to bright sunlight. One explanation of this is that the optic nerve from the eye travels to the brain in proximity to the trigeminal nerve from the face. The very bright light over the whole visual field vigorously stimulates the optic nerve, and just by means of close contact, the trigeminal nerve is also stimulated and a sneeze results. The sneeze is not really a response to the nasal irritants of sunlight; rather, it is a trigeminal nerve response to coincidental stimulation by the optic nerve. While recognizing the insight of Muller, nowadays we refer to these "energies" or "signals" as physical stimuli acting on different kinds of receptor cells, which in turn send their message along nerve fibers to the central nervous system.

2. *Receptors respond differently to different stimuli.* Sensory receptors are unique because they respond differently than the neurons you learned about in Chapter 3. Rather than the all-or-none responding characterized by typical neurons, **receptor potentials** are **graded**. That is, their response rate (how fast they send impulses) varies with the intensity of stimulation and/or the type of stimulation received. For example, increasing the pressure on the skin results in an increased firing rate of the receptors located there, and the levels of brightness result in corresponding response rates for visual receptors. Additionally, some receptors may respond maximally to the color red but exhibit much less responding to orange or yellow, and not at all to blue. This rate of responding begins to decline until the receptors cease to respond, even if the physical stimulus itself has not ceased or declined in intensity. This is a process referred to as **adaptation**. Receptors may adapt slowly, enabling prolonged sensation, or they may adapt rapidly, enabling only an initial sensation. Adaptation illustrates that sensory receptors respond best to changes in stimulation, which is crucial to our understanding of perception. Because the purpose of sensation and perception is to help the organism by identifying features of the environment important to survival, if something is constant, there are no physical changes to the environment and all potentially relevant features have already been identified and processed. Thus, perception is not always a faithful interpretation of sensation, and sensation is not always faithful to the physical environment. This can give rise to some interesting sensory illusions that we will discuss later in the chapter, but it is important to realize that much of our perception is based on receptor responding, which may or may not reflect what is actually going on in our environment.

3. *Sensation and perception are based on combinations of cell responses.* While receptors tend to have a "best response" or stimulus to which they are maximally responsive, they typically respond in varying degrees to a range of stimuli (remember, receptors have graded responses). For

example, a given visual receptor may respond best to pure green, but it will also respond with a reduced rate to orange. Another visual receptor may respond maximally to red, but it will also respond to orange, and with greater intensity than the receptors responding to green. These overlapping responses are present in each sensory system and illustrate that sensations and perceptions are achieved through patterns of activity among different cells within each modality. For example, with color, it is not enough to know that one kind of receptor is responding; the brain must also know how many of the others are responding before a color can be perceived. These kinds of patterns of responding are also found with odor, taste, hearing, and touch.

4. *The specific location of receptors is important.* The senses of touch, vision, hearing, and, to a lesser extent, smell maintain what's referred to as **sensory maps**. Sensory maps are the location, or topography, of receptors within a modality. The location of the receptors provides us with additional clues about the environment. The location of receptors may correspond to a specific location in physical space, as in vision and touch, or it may reflect a particular quality of the stimulus, as in hearing and smell. For example, different locations in visual space stimulate different receptors in the eye, and adjacent areas in space are adjacent in the eye. Thus, an entire visual scene can be constructed because receptors that respond to one location in space are different from those responding to a different location. Touch operates the same way: Specific "cold" receptors on your feet signal the specific location on your body that is cold, and you respond by putting on socks, but not gloves or a jacket. With hearing, different tones stimulate different receptors, and similar sounds stimulate adjacent receptors. Smells also stimulate different cells, the location of which distinguishes different smells. The locations of receptors, organized as maps, provide the brain with more information about where and/or what is in the physical environment.

5. *The amount of stimulation is important.* **Sensory threshold** is a concept used to explain the levels of intensity or how much stimulation is necessary to trigger a sensory response. This concept can be understood more easily if you think of the volume control on a radio. We can decrease the volume to make the sounds very quiet, almost inaudible; we can increase the volume to make the sounds just right; and we can increase the volume even more to make the sounds much too loud for us to listen comfortably. The **absolute threshold** is the lowest level at which a stimulus can be detected. In this example, the volume control would be set at the quietest point at which we can detect the sounds. The **difference threshold** is the minimal increase in intensity required to detect a difference. In keeping with the radio example, it would be the difference between the loudness detected for one volume setting and the amount the control needs to be adjusted to detect a change (softer or louder).

6. *The thalamus is a relay station.* The nerves or fibers carry the information from the sensory organs to the brain (sensations outside the head first enter the spinal cord and then ascend to the brain). Once in the brain, and with the exception of smell, information from each sense is received by the thalamus. The thalamus (midbrain) is segregated into

different areas that connect or synapse with the different sensory fibers. Actually, not much processing and analysis goes on in the thalamus. It primarily serves as a connection between higher brain centers and the sense organs, and it is frequently referred to as a relay station or gateway. The nuclei in the thalamus project to the different lobes of the cortex. Visual information goes to the occipital lobe, some vision and auditory information goes to the temporal lobe, and sensations from the skin go to the parietal lobe. Mostly, perception occurs in the sensory pathways after the thalamus, but exactly where and how this occurs has perplexed scientists for generations.

From Sensation to Perception

From the preceding points, it is clear that the sensory systems are very good at keeping different kinds of information separate, even within the same modality. However, this is not what we consciously experience. Our experience is unified and coherent because we integrate all the information from each sense and all the senses. For example, you would be able to tell that a big brown object with a foul smell and a loud roar that was moving toward you was a bear even though this information was sent to the brain via completely different channels. At some point, these channels must all come together to form the unified percept, and the **superior colliculus** (midbrain) and the **superior temporal gyrus** (top of the temporal lobe) may be just two of the many structures that accomplish this. Scientists have only begun to understand how we integrate the information from each sense into a unified perception, which is known as the **binding problem**.

We do know, however, that several factors are important for binding or unifying information from different modalities. One such factor is timing. The different sensations from one source arrive in the brain at roughly the same time and can be assumed to belong together. Intensity is another factor, keeping in mind that the purpose of sensation is to get the attention of the organism so that it can react appropriately. A stimulus that produces a high-intensity response in one modality may not become united with the others, because one intense experience is sufficient to initiate your response. If you've ever experienced several people yelling at once, it is not clear who is saying what. This is because you've oriented toward the sounds, which have not combined with the faces or the voices. On the other hand, lower-intensity stimuli can benefit more from unification of senses because they enhance one another, resulting in a clearer perception. It is harder to hear someone talking at a low volume if you can't also see that person. A third important factor for integrating the sensory modalities is their location in space. For example, if I see something land on my arm and I feel something painful, I could perceive that I have just been stung by a bee because there is overlap in the locations of the visual and touch receptors in their respective sensory maps. Therefore, the visual and touch sensations must belong to the same stimulus. At this point, though, it must be said that we are still quite puzzled over the brain pathways involved and how they connect with the psychological experience of perception.

Touch

Sensations and perceptions from the skin, joints and muscles, and organs are collectively referred to as the **somatosenses** and provide information to the brain about touch, temperature, pain, movement, body position, and internal organs. They include receptors, the fibers that extend from the receptors to the brain (**afferent fibers**), and the central nervous system pathways and structures that relay information about the body. The somatosenses include cutaneous, kinesthetic, and organic senses. The **cutaneous** sense provides information from the skin about touch, temperature, and pain. The **kinesthetic** sense provides information from the muscles, joints, and other organs about body position and movement. Our knowledge of the kinesthetic sense has improved in recent years, but it is still very much incomplete. The **organic** sense provides information about the states of internal organs such as the stomach, heart, kidneys, and lungs. We know almost nothing about the organic sense. This section presents an overview of the cutaneous sense, which has been studied the most, but our knowledge to date is still markedly incomplete.

The Cutaneous Sense

The skin is divided into two layers: an outer layer called the **epidermis** and an inner layer called the **dermis**. Even though the skin is the largest organ of the body, it is difficult to study for three reasons. First, the receptors of the skin are responsive to several kinds of stimuli, including temperature, pressure, vibration, and pain. Second, the sensitivities or thresholds of many skin receptors change depending on the combination of stimuli that are present. For example, objects feel heavier when cold than when they're warm (Hensel & Witt, 1959; Weber, 1846), blurring the distinction between pressure and temperature. Third, the skin receptors themselves may be difficult to pinpoint because they are located in different layers of the skin, they can be extremely small, and their connections to the rest of the nervous system can be somewhat intricate and elusive. Indeed, scientists sometimes prefer to describe the anatomy of cutaneous sensations in terms of their axons or fibers instead of receptors because we are often unsure of which endings go with which fibers.

Anatomy of Touch

Skin Receptors

The receptors of the skin are categorized by the types of stimulation they detect. Figure 4.1 shows the distribution of receptors in the skin. **Mechanoreceptors** respond to pressure (indentation) on the skin, such as touch, vibration, and a cool breeze. Mechanoreceptors are characterized by how quickly they adapt to continuous pressure and by the size of their receptive field. Some receptors (e.g., **Merkel's discs** and **Ruffini cylinders**) adapt slowly and allow you to feel sustained pressure, such as holding something in your hands for an extended time without losing the sensation of the object. Other receptors rapidly adapt (e.g., **Pacinian corpuscles** and **Meissner corpuscles**) and, therefore, mostly respond to change but not to continuous pressure. Because of rapidly adapting receptors, you have no sensation of the continuous contact of your clothing on your

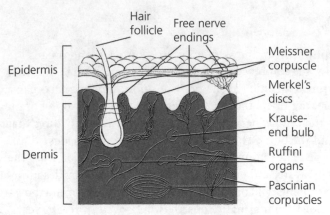

FIGURE 4.1 *Cross-section of skin showing different receptor types.*

body unless you shift positions. Size of the receptive field, which refers to the area of skin to which a given receptor responds, is also important in the cutaneous sense. The fingertips have rapidly adapting receptors with small receptive fields and low thresholds, enabling for fine discrimination—such as that required for reading the tightly clustered raised dots of Braille (LaMotte & Mountcastle, 1975; Werner & Mountcastle, 1965).

Thermoreceptors respond to changes in temperature, which is why you feel so cold when you first get into a swimming pool, or why the water in a bathtub feels hot when you first get in but then becomes more temperature neutral. Thermoreceptors convey information through firing rate (rapidity of receptor potentials) and respond to either a cold change or a warm change but not both. Thus, they are often labeled "cold receptors" (or "**cold fibers**") or "warm receptors" (or "**warm fibers**"). Cold fibers respond to temperatures between 59°F and 104°F, and warm fibers respond to temperatures between 86°F and 122°F. For both kinds of fibers, their rates of responding are the lowest at the high and low temperatures in their range. Notice that there is a range of temperatures in which their responding overlaps. This is the range of normal temperatures for the human body, known as **physiological zero**. Temperatures in this range result in very low rates of responding in both cold and warm fibers, illustrating that the thermoreceptors respond mostly to change and are less concerned with the status quo.

Each thermoreceptor is responsive to temperature changes that occur on a small patch of skin, about 1 mm in diameter, and most of the skin is not responsive to temperature changes at all. Mostly, the brain determines skin temperature by combining the input from cold and warm spots across the skin. You can locate "cold receptors" on your skin by gently dotting the tip of a ball point pen on the back of your hand in a haphazard manner. You will notice that every so often the pen feels cold, but mostly it feels temperature neutral. Where the pen feels cold, you've stimulated cold receptors. Even though your entire hand may sometimes feel very cold or very warm, it is only the temperature-sensitive spots that are actually responding. The density or number of thermoreceptors in an area of skin determines the ability to detect changes in temperature. The most sensitive areas are the forehead and the cheek, and the least sensitive areas are the calf and the thigh. The individual thermoreceptors, however, are very precise in their detection of temperature change, detecting even .003°C of change (Hardy & Oppel, 1937).

Nociceptors are free nerve endings that respond to excesses that are potentially damaging to the skin, such as excess cold, excess heat, excess pressure, excess electrical stimulation, and excess chemical stimulation. They are the reason why closing your hand in a door (excess pressure) hurts (nociceptor response). These receptors are located throughout the epidermis and dermis layers of the skin. The characteristic that sets them apart from other receptors is their very high thresholds, thus requiring intense stimulation to initiate a response. Like other skin receptors, their firing rate also indicates intensity of the stimulation. Different nociceptors respond to excess pressure or to excess temperature, and many respond to pressure, temperature, and/or harmful chemicals. Chemicals that stimulate nociceptors can be from an external source (exogenous) or from chemicals produced when cells are damaged (endogenous). Histamine and prostaglandin are examples of chemicals that are released when cells are damaged. Allergy sufferers are familiar with the discomfort associated with the release of histamine, and those who suffer menstrual cramps are familiar with the pain caused by the release of prostaglandin (Soderquist, 2002). Nociceptors responding to these chemicals signal the presence of a damaging or potentially damaging stimulus, which interprets this as pain, motivating the individual to change his or her situation (move to different environs or take an aspirin) to avoid injury.

Central Nervous System Touch Pathways

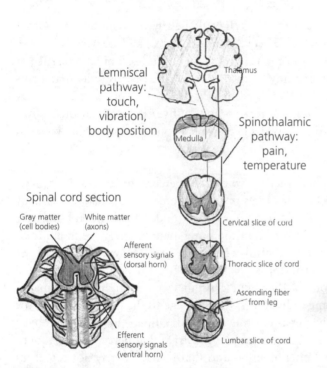

FIGURE 4.2 *Drawing of spinothalamic and lemniscal pathways.*

The fibers that carry information from the skin synapse with **dorsal horn** cells located within the spinal cord at the point of entry. Once in the spinal cord, the fibers do two things: (1) reflexively withdraw a limb in response to pain or a harmful stimulation (termed the **flexor reflex**), and (2) become part of a pathway to the thalamus and brain. There are two pathways to the brain within the spinal cord. The **spinothalamic pathway** carries information about pain, temperature, and some touch to the brain. The **lemniscal pathway** (or **dorsal column pathway**) carries information about touch, vibration, and body position to the brain. Figure 4.2 illustrates these pathways. Both the spinothalamic and the lemniscal pathways, along with the fibers from the face (trigeminal nerve), synapse with neurons in the thalamus. Within the thalamus, the neurons are organized in a **somatotopic** manner; that is, the layout of these neurons mirrors the layout of the body, with adjacent neurons representing information relayed by adjacent body parts. Interestingly, the pain and temperature pathway (spinothalamic) has several offshoots at the brain stem level (before the thalamus) that connect to the reticular formation, important for arousal and consciousness (Shepherd, 1994). Pain and temperature changes arouse us and make us take notice, and these connections are why.

Explore **the homunculus** in Chapter 3, p. 71

As in the other senses, the thalamus serves as a relay station or gateway to the cortex. Cells from the thalamus project to the **somatosensory cortex**. The somatotopic organization in the thalamus is preserved in the cortex. The amount of cortical space dedicated to areas of skin is determined by the number of receptors located there and the size of the receptive fields. More space is dedicated to areas that have many densely packed receptors with small receptive fields, such as the fingers, lips, face, tongue, and foot. Conversely, the elbow, hip, shoulder, wrist, and neck have very small representations in the cortex. If we actually looked the way the cortex represents us, we would be rather distorted, with huge hands, lips, and face, and tiny legs, torso, and arms. This distorted figure has become known as the **homunculus**, or "little man."

Perception of Touch

The interpretation of touch has been studied largely in terms of sensitivity. Here, sensitivity is defined by the size of the surface area represented by a single receptor (**receptive field**) and also how close the receptors are to each other (**density**). Studies of this kind of sensitivity have used a method of **two point discrimination**. The two point discrimination method requires the simultaneous placement of two points on the skin. We know that different receptors are responding to the pressure when the participant can perceive that there are in fact two points. When participants perceive the two points as only one, then only one receptor is responding. Some receptors have very large receptive fields, and so fine discriminations are not possible. Large receptive fields are responsible for the sometimes impossible and frustrating task of pinpointing an itch, as we often experience with our backs and calves. A receptor is responding, but it's covering a large area, and the source of the itch could be anywhere in that area. Other receptors, such as those on the lips, cover very small areas and are densely packed. This makes it possible to do some very fine two point discriminations, such as pinpointing the location of a tiny crumb. It is this kind of sensitivity that forms the homunculus. It is important to realize that your perception of touch may not reflect reality. If two points (or three or four or five) are simultaneously stimulating a single receptive field, you'd perceive it as one thing touching you, but you would be incorrect.

Consider the alternate phenomenon, where you perceive touch that isn't there. The **Rubber Hand Illusion** illustrates this sensation. In this illusion, a visually seen rubber hand was believed to be one's own hidden hand when both were being stroked, say, by a paintbrush, in the same manner and were in approximately the same posture (Constantini & Haggard, 2007). However, when a laser light was used instead of a paintbrush on the rubber hand, participants reported that they felt the heat from the laser light (Durgin, Evans, Dunphy, Klostermann, & Simmons, 2007). Some individuals with damage to the parietal lobe of the right hemisphere feel the persistent touch (called **palinaesthesia**) of an object after it has been removed. These examples illustrate that perception is a mental, neurologically based phenomenon and that it may or may not represent actual sensations.

Perception of Temperature

As you learned earlier, the sensation of temperature change is precise, but some interesting phenomena show us that its interpretation and localization can be rather inaccurate. For example, if a very hot stimulus is applied to a single cold patch, the thermoreceptor located there responds with a sensation of cold, called **paradoxical cold**; additionally, a very cold stimulus applied to a warm spot results in **paradoxical warm**. Paradoxical cold or warm occurs because thermoreceptors respond to *any* intense stimulation. Another example of inaccuracy is **synthetic heat**, which is the perception of painful heat if warm and cold patches that are close together are alternately stimulated. Synthetic heat may be caused by the brain's adoption of a "better safe than sorry" strategy. In a situation where the brain is receiving confusing messages, the environment is ambiguous. Interpreting the ambiguous information as painful heat is a safety precaution that motivates the individual to change something (retract the limb, move away) and return to a position the brain can recognize.

Localization of temperature change on the body may also be highly inaccurate. In one study, participants had difficulty distinguishing between stimuli presented to the front of the torso and stimuli presented to the back of the torso (Cain, 1973). This may be because the brain understands temperature change by taking into account thermoreceptor activity over large areas of skin; thus, the precise localization of temperature change may be relatively unimportant (Weisenberger, 2001). Beyond this, very little is known about how the brain perceives temperature. Interestingly, the perception of temperature can be altered by cortical processes such as thought and emotion. For example, using methods of biofeedback, individuals are able to raise or lower the temperature of their hands by simply using thought processes aimed at matching their physical state with a visually (or aurally) displayed criterion. L. P. Ince (personal communication, April 24, 2006), one of the pioneers in the field of biofeedback, recalled a case where this method was used to help a young girl with nerve damage feel warm so she could go swimming.

Perception of Pain

The perception of pain has been studied for decades. Scientists have developed many techniques for relieving pain, yet its explanation remains elusive. This is partly because one must operationally define something before it can be studied, and pain is difficult to define because it is a physiological response with significant emotional and cognitive components that vary from one person to the next. Individuals who have experienced minimal insult may perceive unbearable pain, and individuals who have experienced great insult may experience minimal pain. Further, there is not a simple, straightforward relationship between the intensity of the physical stimulation and the degree of perceived pain. The longer one is in pain, the more important the psychological and/or emotional factors become in its perception. People sometimes feel pain in a limb when there is no stimulation at all, as is the case with phantom limbs. **Phantom limb** pain is the common perception of severe pain, or "pins and needles," in the missing limb of amputees. This perception can be temporary or persist for many years. Scientists are unsure if phantom limb pain is a creation of the brain or if there is a dysfunctional mass of residual fibers at the point of amputation. Even different combinations of physical stimulation interact to affect pain perception. Multiple painful stimulations in proximity can have an additive effect, intensifying the perception of pain even though just the number of stimulations has increased and not the actual physical intensity. Conversely, pain can be reduced by a simultaneous painful stimulation in a more distant part of the body (Rollman, 1991). Scientists have had difficulty measuring and identifying pain, which is why a valid definition has yet to be found. We are sure of one thing: Pain is a primitive response that serves to protect and preserve the organism. Although unpleasant when we feel it, pain makes us stop and take notice that something is wrong; without it, we surely would not have survived toddlerhood.

One of the more popular accounts for pain perception is the **gate control theory** (Melzack & Wall, 1965; Wall & Melzack, 1994). This theory suggests that pain perception is dependent on the activity among a specific circuitry of cells located in the spinal cord, and the release of the neurotransmitter Substance P. The nociceptors scattered throughout the skin all over the body are the free nerve endings of **C fibers** and **A-delta fibers**. C fibers are slow traveling, slow adapting, and have higher thresholds. A-delta fibers are fast traveling (they are myelinated), rapidly adapting, and have comparatively low thresholds. Both C and A-delta fibers synapse with the pain circuitry in the spinal cord. If this circuitry is excited (by C fibers), the "gate" opens and a message of pain is sent to the brain. If this circuitry is inhibited (by A-delta fibers), the "gate" is closed and a message of pain is not sent via the spinal cord. Interestingly, the A-delta fibers also have an additional, direct connection to the thalamus that circumvents this circuit. Because the messages travel quickly along A-delta fibers directly to the thalamus, we feel an initial sharp pain when we are injured. The sharpness of the pain quickly subsides, however, because these fibers are fast adapting. The slower C fibers eventually arrive at the spinal cord and excite the pain circuit, sending a pain message to the brain. By this time, the A-deltas have stopped responding, so the continued throbbing pain we feel is due to the activity of the slowly adapting C fibers' interaction at the pain circuit of the spinal cord. The two fiber types acting in concert is why we first feel the sharp pain, followed by the duller throbbing pain. Further, because of their relative thresholds, you'd need to take a hard hit to experience the throbbing caused by the C fibers (such as stubbing your toe). However, a pin prick is likely to be just a sharp pain that quickly subsides. It's enough to stimulate A-deltas but not enough to stimulate the C fibers.

The pain will eventually subside due to activity among the brain and pain circuit cells in the spinal cord, a process known as **analgesia**. The pain can be reduced by messages from the frontal lobes that travel down the spinal cord. Some of those messages inhibit the pain circuitry, and others inhibit just the C fibers. Pain also subsides when the skin is stimulated by rubbing, tickling, brushing with a feather, using electrical means, or using acupuncture. These actions stimulate the more sensitive A-delta fibers to close the gate, but they are not intense enough to stimulate the C fibers or the A-deltas to send a message to the thalamus. **Opiates** such as morphine and heroin also close the gate at the spinal cord, inhibit parts of the thalamus, and reduce the activity of C fibers and substance P. **Cryotherapy**, or the cooling of inflamed areas immediately following an injury to tissue (such as muscle spasms, tendonitis, or rheumatoid arthritis), serves to decrease the speed of transmission along the nociceptor fibers, reducing the perception of pain. Methods to cool the inflamed area include applying ice packs, immersing the area in ice, fanning the skin, or applying a cooling substance such as a spray or cream to the area.

The perception of pain is not always directly related to the intensity of stimulation received by the nociceptors. For example, **primary hyperalgesia** occurs when we become more sensitive to less stimulation following exposure to a painful stimulus. So, under ordinary conditions, if someone gently bumped your knee, you'd hardly notice it. But if you had just experienced a painful bump to the knee, a subsequent gentle bump would hurt. This sensitization is partially due to the extra responsiveness of C fibers. Related to this is **causalgesia**, which is pain that follows the path of a partially damaged peripheral nerve. This pain is present only during the healing process, and intense pain is triggered by even the slightest movement. Additionally, **thalamic pain** occurs from damage to the thalamus, but there is no actual injury to the body. Thalamic pain is unrelenting and frequently migrates to a region of the body opposite the lesion. Cortical lesions can result in the perception of pain where the cortical representation is greatest, such as the hands, face, and lips. Pain in an area that has not had an injury is often an indicator of a brain lesion.

Lastly, the perception of pain is also strongly affected by emotional and cognitive factors. This is particularly true in cases of **chronic pain**, which is pain that is present for more than six months. Because an individual in pain can find it very difficult to concentrate on anything else (recall your last headache), chronic pain can be quite debilitating, taking over the person's life. It can result in the loss of jobs, friends, and stability, which can lead to problems with anxiety and depression. Therefore, it is important to use treatments for the nonphysical components of pain that are aimed at altering the perception of pain. Some of these techniques include relaxation methods, hypnosis, biofeedback, operant conditioning, and meditation.

Vision

The visual sense far exceeds the other senses in the depth and breadth in which it has been studied. Vision is the process of receiving and interpreting light reflected from objects in the environment. It is important to realize that objects themselves do not emit light but instead reflect it, an idea first described by **Johannes Keppler**. Our visual system cannot sense objects that do not reflect light. Our ability to see so many different objects under so many different conditions is due to a visual system that transforms reflected light into pattern, shape, color, and movement.

But what is light? Owing largely to the work of Isaac Newton, Thomas Young, Albert Einstein, and James Clerk Maxwell, we understand light to consist of tiny particles of energy, called **photons**, which travel through space in waves. These waves are part of an enormous range of electromagnetic radiation, all traveling at a rate of 186,000 miles per second (commonly referred to as the speed of light). The movement of charged particles creates electromagnetic radiation. This can be accomplished through heat (**incandescent light**) or by colliding and exciting electrons that emit light when they return to their normal state (**luminescent light**). Incandescent light is emitted by the sun, a regular lightbulb, and fire. Luminescent light is emitted by fluorescent bulbs, televisions, and lasers. Just like all waves, energy or light waves consist of alternating highs (peaks) and lows (troughs) that differ in distance from trough to trough (or peak to peak). This distance is known as **wavelength**. In order for us to see photons, they must travel in waves that range in length between 370 and 730 nanometers (billionths of a meter, which is pretty tiny). In the following sections you will learn how the eye receives these waves, how they are transformed into cell responses for the nervous system to interpret, and what the nervous system interprets these signals to be.

Anatomy of Vision

The Eye

The eye contains the visual receptors, and it is where the processing of a visual scene begins. Note in Figure 4.3 the structures of the iris, pupil, ciliary muscles, and lens. The **iris** is your eye color, but more importantly it consists of two rings of muscles that form the pupil. The **pupil** is the opening in the eye that lets in light, and its size is determined mostly by lighting conditions. In dim light, the dilator muscles of the iris contract, causing the pupil to become larger. In bright light, the sphincter muscles of the iris contract, causing it to become smaller. Ingesting certain chemicals, such as those found in the mandrake or belladonna plants, blocks acetylcholine and inhibits the sphincter muscle, causing pupil dilation. The **ciliary muscles** are connected to, and alter, the shape of the lens. The **lens** serves to focus or direct light onto the retina, which is located on the inner lining of the eye. The ciliary muscles can pull the lens into a flat shape to focus the reflected light of distant objects onto the retina, or release their pull so the lens assumes a rounded shape for focusing the reflected light of nearby objects onto the retina. This is a process known as **accommodation**.

The **retina** is a thin (only 5 cell layers deep), transparent structure in the eye that connects the outside and the inner world. Sometimes the cells in the retina are referred to as a mosaic: Each piece contributes a small part to the whole image, becoming apparent by the resulting pattern. Like a mosaic, the cells of the retina respond to different parts of the visual scene, and the total pattern of activity among those cells portrays the whole image. The retina contains the visual receptors (**photoreceptors**) and also the cells that synapse directly with the brain (**gan-**

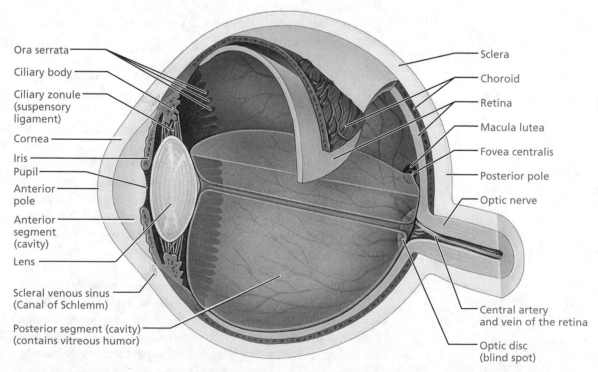

FIGURE 4.3 *Parts of the eye. From Marieb and Hoehn,* Anatomy and Physiology, *Third Edition (Benjamin Cummings, 2008).*

glion cells). The photoreceptors (literally, "light receivers") make up the last layer of the retina, so light must pass through the other cell layers to reach them; the ganglion cells that communicate with the brain occupy the first layer of the retina, and their axons must cross the retina (at the optic disc) to head back to the brain. The optic disc produces a blind spot in the retina, where there are no receptors. The photoreceptors are wired up to **bipolar cells** that are wired up to ganglion cells, with horizontal cells and amacrine cells serving as relays among the photoreceptor, bipolar, and ganglion cell layers. There are two kinds of photoreceptors, **rods** and **cones**, and both contain chemicals, called **photopigments**, that absorb light. The absorption of light breaks apart the chemical composition of the photopigment, resulting in a receptor potential. There are only four kinds of photopigments, and each absorbs a different range of wavelengths. The photopigment in rods is called **rhodopsin**, and rods respond best to wavelengths of 500 nm. The three kinds of photopigments in cones absorb relatively long wavelengths (560 nm), medium wavelengths (530 nm), or short wavelengths (420 nm) and are often referred to as red, green, and blue cones because of the visible colors of light at those wavelengths. As illustrated in Figure 4.4, all the photoreceptors have a range of wavelengths to which they respond with decreasing sensitivity as the wavelengths increase and decrease from that point. Because cones respond to different wavelengths, cones are responsible for color vision, and their range of sensitivities will be important in our discussion of color perception. All rods respond to wavelengths in exactly the same manner, but they are more sensitive to light than are cones. This means that they require fewer photons for stimulation than do cones and can therefore respond in much dimmer light. Rods do not respond to wavelengths in well-lit conditions, because there is too much light, and their photopigment has been broken down. Only when it becomes dark can new photopigment molecules be created, and this takes a certain amount of time. You may have noticed that when the lights go out, you are totally blind. This occurs because the cones can't respond to the limited number of photons, and the rods have not yet recovered enough photopigment to absorb the photons. It takes about 10–15 minutes for the rods to recover, a process known as **dark adaptation**.

The photoreceptors are not evenly distributed along the retina. Referring to Figure 4.3, the center portion of the retina in the direct path of gaze is known as the fovea. The fovea contains no rods, so light at the center of gaze is processed by cones only. Here, the cones are densely packed and have small receptive fields. This means that each cone responds to a very tiny portion of space, and its density makes it so that small details don't get lost. When we want to see fine details (such as letters) we must shift our gaze to use foveal vision. In contrast, rods are located to the sides and are responsible for vision in the periphery. **Visual acuity** (ability to see fine detail) drops dramatically outside the fovea. This acuity is also determined by the connections of the rods and cones to the bipolar and ganglion cells. Each bipolar and ganglion cell for cones receives information from only one cone, so the message remains intact.

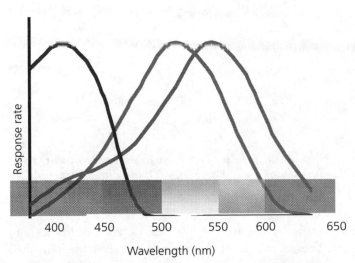

FIGURE 4.4 *Response rates of three cone types to various wavelengths.*

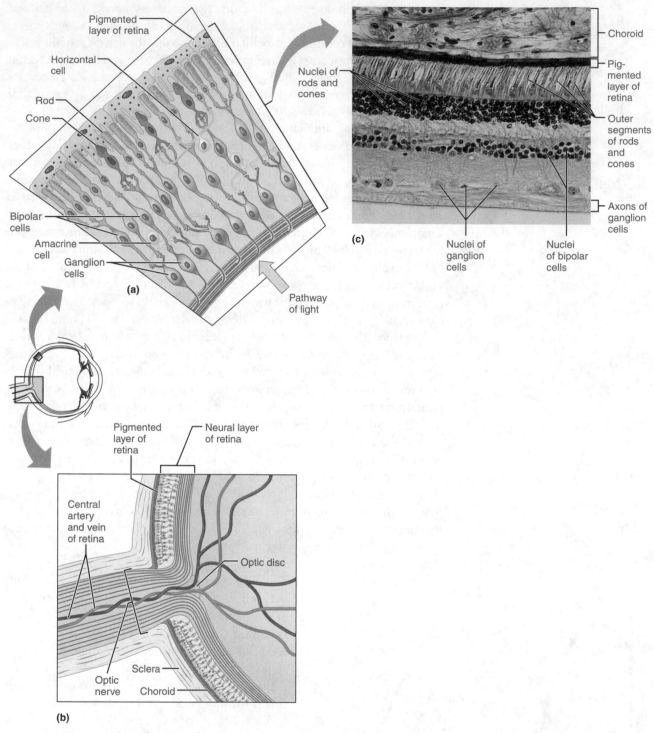

FIGURE 4.5 *Cross section of retina. The patterned ovals at the top illustrate the size of receptive fields for the bipolar and ganglion cells as a result of convergence. From Marieb and Hoehn,* Anatomy and Physiology, *Third Edition (Benjamin Cummings, 2008).*

However, many rods converge onto a single bipolar cell, and several bipolars onto a single ganglion cell. This means that at the ganglion cell level, the individual messages from rods about their particular part of space have all been combined, and it is impossible to distinguish precise locations of details in peripheral vision. Figure 4.5 illustrates convergence of cells in the retina.

The different sensitivities and locations of the rods and cones explain some interesting experiences. On a clear night, if you focus your eyes on a particular location, you will see some stars in your periphery (the right or left side of your fixed gaze) that seem to disappear when you shift your eyes to look directly at them. If you move your eyes back, the stars reappear in your peripheral vision. You can do this several times, and you will find that some stars are bright enough to be detected by the rods in your peripheral vision but too dim to be detected by the cones in your foveal vision. This is why the stars seem to disappear and reappear with shifts in gaze. You can accomplish the same effect with any object that glows in the dark and gradually fades. There will be a point where the object is reflecting enough light to be seen in the periphery, but it will disappear if you look at it directly. Similarly, we do not see colors in the dark; objects appear in shades of gray because, in darkness, there is enough reflected light (it only takes a few photons) to affect the rods but not enough to affect the cones. This is also why you see only general forms and not fine details in the dark.

Central Nervous System Pathway for Vision

The axons of the ganglion cells form the optic nerve and synapse with cells in the pretectum (receives brightness information for constriction and dilation of the iris), the superior colliculus (important for hearing, aids in visually locating the source of a sound), or a part of the thalamus known as the **lateral geniculate nucleus (LGN)** (Shepherd, 1994). The synapses with the LGN are the beginnings of two neurally and functionally distinct visual systems: the "What" and "Where" systems. The **"What" system** processes information from the cones in the fovea and is therefore responsible for color and detail vision (includes object and face recognition) and stimulus identification. The **"Where" system** processes information from the peripheral photoreceptors and is responsible for perceptions of depth, motion, spatial layout, and general shapes; it is primarily involved with stimulus location. Only primates have the "What" system, whereas all mammals have the "Where" system, which is why dogs and cats are color-blind. The "Where" and "What" divisions are organized in a **retinotopic** manner, meaning that not only do the cells within each division convey specific kinds of information, they do so about specific locations on the retina.

What is the significance of having these two separate systems? To survive, predators need to be quite good at locating prey, and prey need to be ever vigilant to avoid being eaten. To predators, anything that moves is a potential meal, so its general shape, movements, distance, and precise location must be determined. This enables the animal to determine whether the object is something edible, like an antelope, or inedible, like a truck, and if it is close enough to catch. Similarly, prey must be able to notice even the slightest movements in their entire visual fields, but they can't just run off at anything, or they'd soon be exhausted from constant motion. They, too, need to determine distance and basic shape. As primates evolved, so did the "What" system. This system allows us to determine whether some whiteness on a piece of meat is fat or maggots, and we can easily distinguish the faces of friends from those of foes.

These divisions and their retinotopic organization continue within the LGN and then move on to the **primary visual cortex (striate cortex)**, located in the occipital lobe. The visual cortex is arranged by columns of cells. Cells within the columns respond similarly, are associated with either the "What" or "Where" system, and contain specialized cells that are responsive only to a particular feature in the environment, such as horizontal lines. These specialized cells are called **feature detectors**. Hubel and Wiesel discovered these cells, earning them the Nobel Prize in 1981. More recent discoveries suggest that there are even feature detectors for more complex stimuli such as the face or the hands. Indeed, it appears as though there are many different kinds of feature detectors, including those that respond to color, near objects, far objects, locations of objects, edges, textures, and lines of every orientation. The arrangement of adjacent columns is retinotopic. The amount of cortex dedicated to each part of space is somewhat distorted by acuity, and the fovea is represented by a larger area than the periphery. The columns in the primary visual cortex have projections to the visual association cortex (circumstriate cortex). The "Where" system then projects to the parietal and temporal lobes; the "What" system projects to the temporal lobe.

Perception of Color

How does light become color? White light (such as that from the sun) is the integration of all colors in the visible spectrum (range of visible light). Newton cleverly illustrated this process. He observed that white light passing through a prism was effectively bent and separated into its color components. Each color is a different wavelength, so white light is actually a combination of different wavelengths, and the prism divides the wavelengths. Objects appear colored because their chemical and/or physical makeup absorbs some of the wavelengths but reflects others. We see the reflected wavelengths of light, and coloring an object is a matter of applying a chemical compound that reflects some wavelengths better than others to render the desired appearance.

The perception of color is accomplished through different processes. At the photoreceptor level, color is determined by the relative activity of three kinds of cones, known as the **trichromatic theory**. If a pure ray of light, one that contains only wavelengths of 530 nm, is shone into the eye, only the photopigments that respond to those wavelengths will respond, and the other two kinds will not. Referring back to Figure 4.4, note that wavelengths of 570 nm would result in activity in both the medium (green) and long (red) wavelength cones, with slightly more activity in the red, and no response in the short (blue) cones. This pattern of activity signifies yellow. Observe the activity among the three cones at the left side for purple. The highest activity is in the short (blue) cones, with lower levels for the long (red), and even lower for the medium (green) cones. Using the information from just these three cone types, humans can detect approximately 7 million colors. Each color is represented by a unique pattern of activity among the three cone types.

The trichromatic theory of these three types of cones—"red," "green," and "blue"—cannot, however, account for the experience of **afterimages**. An afterimage is the complementary color you see after staring at a colored object. For example, if you stare at something red for about 60 seconds, when you look away you will see an afterimage of green. If you stare at a green object, you'll get an afterimage of red. If you stare at blue, you'll get an afterimage of yellow, and if you stare at yellow, you'll get an afterimage of blue. The same opponent colors occur for black-and-white afterimages. Because these colors occur in pairs, Ewald Hering developed the **opponent process theory**, which states that patterns among cells that respond to pairs of colors are responsible for color vision. Bipolar, ganglion, and thalamus cells contribute to the opponent process system for coding of color. Opponent process cells respond with either excitation or inhibition to two opponent colors. For example, "red-on green-off" cells will be excited by red and inhibited by green, whereas "red-off green-on" cells will be inhibited by red and excited by green. This same pattern occurs for blue-yellow cells. You can try this by staring at any single color for about 60 seconds and then shifting your gaze to a white space. You will experience the afterimage of the opponent color.

Both the trichromatic theory and the opponent process theory are accepted as explanations of color processing at different levels, but they do not tell the whole story. For example, neither theory explains the phenomenon of **color constancy**, which states that we perceive the same color under different levels of illumination or that we sometimes perceive the same reflected light as being different colors (see Figure 4.6). For example, in a brightly lit room you may perceive a lemon as yellow, and a cherry as red. In a dim room, the same objects would appear to be the same as they were in the brightly lit room: yellow and red. However, neither object reflects the same light in both conditions. It is only their color relative to each other that enables you to perceive them as unchanged under different lighting conditions. Color constancy is explained by the **retinex theory**, which states that the cerebral cortex compares the information received from the retina and that the resulting color pattern represents relative activity, not absolute. So, while the activity of cells in the retina changes from one lighting condition to another, their relative pattern stays the same, and colors are perceived as constant. By the way, if you don't have bright and dim conditions to compare (in front of you or from memory), the color constancy effect is diminished.

FIGURE 4.6 *The colors appear the same in both bright and dim conditions, due to color constancy. Courtesy of BigFoto.com.*

Perception of Objects and Forms

Perceptions of objects and forms occur from bottom-up and top-down processes. **Bottom-up processes** reduce an object into elemental features. **Feature detection theory** suggests that letters and numbers are made up of simple features, such as lines of different orientations and arcs, and that to perceive a letter or number we must identify the features that compose it and how those features come together (Geyer & Dewald, 1973; Gibson, 1969). For example, it is not enough to know that the letter "X" is composed of one forward and one backward oblique line, because a "V" has the same features. To distinguish "X" from "V" also requires recognition of the configuration. Some of the support for this theory comes from the observations of feature detector cells in the visual cortex (Hubel & Wiesel, 1962, 1963, 1979). To account for object recognition, the **recognition by components theory (RBC)** suggests that elemental components and their configurations must be identified, but these components are geometric shapes, not simple lines (Biederman, 1993). Both the feature detection and the RBC theories require that a form be reduced to basic features, and then your knowledge of which forms have which features in what configuration builds the perception from the bottom up. While there is good evidence for both theories, they do not tell the whole story. Perception is also driven by **top-down processes**, which are those that use your knowledge and experiences from higher cortical centers to determine the meaning of lower-level percepts. For example, in the string "A B C D " the second letter is perceived as "B," but in the string "12 B 14 15" the second letter is perceived as "13," even though both are identical. It is your knowledge of what should appear in those contexts that makes you perceive these identical forms as different (Biederman, Rabinowitz, Glass, & Stacy, 1974).

Before you even begin to identify the features of an object, you must first determine which features or parts must go together to form the whole object. When viewing a room, features are organized into overall patterns, which enable you to see a table and a chair as separate objects. A group of German scientists, now referred to as the **Gestalt Psychologists** ("Gestalt" means "whole"), argued that an object is not perceived as just the sum of its parts, but that perception is driven by rules or laws of organization that determine overall patterns (the whole). These laws of organization are shown in Figure 4.7. Each rule states what your initial perception should be, but with extra effort (beyond perception) you can see alternative patterns.

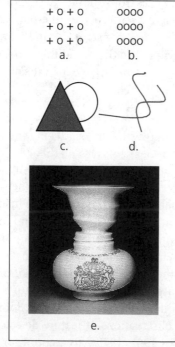

```
+ o + o      oooo
+ o + o      oooo
+ o + o      oooo
   a.          b.

   c.          d.

        e.
```

a. **Similarity:** Features that are similar are grouped together. You organize this pattern into 2 columns of '+' and 2 of 'o'

b. **Proximity:** Features that are close together, go together. You organize the 'o's into 3 rows.

c. **Good Form or Simplicity:** Objects are perceived as simply as possible. You see a circle behind a triangle, when really, the part you do not see can be anything

c. **Closure:** Objects are seen as having clear boundaries, even when you don't see them. You assume the shape behind the triangle is a closed circle.

d. **Continuity:** Points connect in a straight or smoothly flowing line. You see two curvy lines that spiral.

e. **Figure-Ground:** Objects (figure) are distinguished from their background (ground). This ambiguous image enables one to easily switch figure and ground. You can see the vase as the figure or the profiles as figure and the vase as ground. *Vase picture from Illusion works, LLC.*

FIGURE 4.7 *Gestalt laws of perceptual organization.*

Perception of Depth and Size

Perception of depth or distance is based on binocular (both eyes) and monocular (one eye) cues. **Binocular cues** take into account the images on the retinas of both eyes. Because your left and right eyes are in different locations, an image appears in different locations on their retinas. You can quickly demonstrate this by locating an object in your environment (you can even use your nose) and alternate closing your left and right eyes while looking at the object. The object appears to shift because it is reflecting onto different locations in each retina. **Stereopsis** is the process of reconciling these retinal disparities to determine depth and distance. Depth perception can be poor with one eye closed, where stereopsis cannot be used, and it is why you should not drive with one eye closed (or both eyes closed, but for different reasons). **Convergence** is another binocular cue that indicates depth or distance, but it only works within 10 feet. Convergence is the feeling of your eyes moving inward when both focus on an object. If the object is close, there is much more convergence, and if the object is farther away, there is less convergence. You can readily demonstrate this by holding a pencil vertically so that it touches the tip of your nose. When you look at the pencil, there is high convergence, the ciliary muscles feel strained, and your eyes appear "crossed." Move the pencil farther away, and you can feel your eyes move outward.

Monocular cues enable depth perception with only one eye. One cue heavily relied upon to determine depth is **luminance** (perceived brightness). In the three-dimensional world and the two dimensions of art, this is communicated through light and shading. This is why a barrel appears deeper than a dinner plate, and **these letters** appear thicker than *these letters*. Colors of equal luminance in a picture show no depth, because there are no brightness cues for the "Where" system to use, and the "What" system, which detects the color difference, does not code depth. For centuries, artists have played with the effects of luminance to achieve different depth perceptions. Another monocular cue is the **motion parallax**. As we move, we pass nearby objects much more quickly than more distant objects. The difference in how quickly we pass near and far objects is the motion parallax. While driving you may experience nearby trees or buildings pass by very quickly, but a distant mountain range or building doesn't seem to have moved at all. If you've ever had the feeling that the moon is following you in your long-distance travels, it isn't. It's just so far away that you are not passing it in the distances that you travel. Similarly, using the cue of **atmospheric perspective**, distant objects appear fuzzier and less detailed due to a greater amount of air and particles between us and the object. There are several other monocular cues that are easier to understand with a corresponding picture (see Figure 4.8). **Interposition** is a depth cue where objects that are in front of others appear to be closer.

Perception of size is determined by **visual angle** and depth perception. If you extend lines from your pupil to the top and bottom of an object being viewed, the angle between those lines is called the visual angle (see Figure 4.9). A smaller object has a smaller visual angle, and as an object moves away from you, its visual angle decreases. You can tell the size of an object at different distances from you because of depth cues. Also, an object that moves farther away from you appears smaller, but you do not perceive the object itself as shrinking. That is, your

Atmospheric perspective:
Closer objects appear sharper.
Courtesy of BigFoto.com.

Detail:
The ability to see details diminishes as
distance increases. Courtesy of BigFoto.com.

Interposition:
Objects, such as these wheels, that occlude
other objects are closer. Courtesy of
BigFoto.com.

Height:
More distant objects are higher in the
visual field. Courtesy of BigFoto.com.

Relative size:
The pairs of nuns are the same size. Nuns in
the foreground appear tiny relative to nuns
in the background because of their identical visual angle. Courtesy of BigFoto.com.

Linear perspective:
Although the path is straight, the edges
seem to converge toward an unseen point.
Courtesy of BigFoto.com.

Texture gradient:
Objects appear to cluster together as their
distance increases, as seen in the lines of trees.

FIGURE 4.8 *Various monocular cues.*

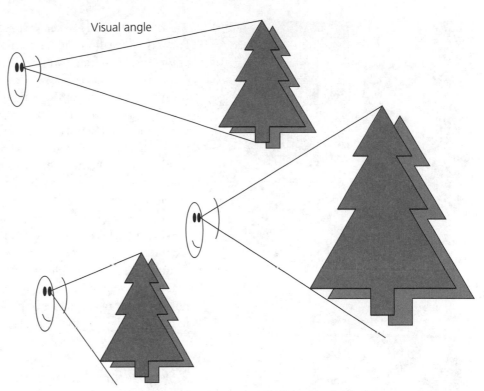

Visual angle

FIGURE 4.9 *Visual angle is larger for the closer tree than for the farther tree of the same size. The visual angle is larger for the larger tree than for the smaller tree at the same distance.*

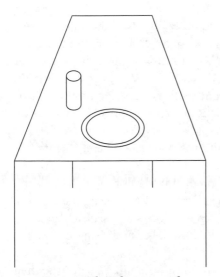

FIGURE 4.10 *What shapes are the table and the plate? Because of depth cues, we see the table as a rectangle and the plate as a circle, which is consistent with our knowledge of these shapes. If you look at the shapes without the legs of the table, they look flat; the table becomes a trapezoid, and the plate becomes an oval.*

knowledge of the size of an object relative to surrounding objects and depth cues achieves **size constancy**. When you do not have depth cues, an object moving toward or away from you appears to grow or shrink because you are solely dependent on visual angle. Depth cues are also responsible for **shape constancy**. An object appears to have the same shape when viewed at different depths, even though the visual angle has, in fact, been altered (see Figure 4.10).

The relationship between visual angle and depth can also be illustrated by some well-known illusions. The **Ames Room** produces the illusion that people of equal sizes are different sizes. This is achieved by its special construction, where there appears to be two far corners of a room, but in reality, one corner is far and the other is actually much nearer. The difference in size is purely because one person is farther away than the other, but because the true depth cues are eliminated, they look equally far away, giving you the perception of small people on one side and giant people on the other (see Figure 4.11).

The **Ponzo** or **Railroad Illusion** is illustrated in Figure 4.12. The top horizontal line appears longer than the bottom line, but they are exactly the same length with the exact same visual angle. This illusion occurs because we perceive the picture as having depth (due to **linear perspective**), and higher points in a picture are assumed to be farther away. Therefore, the higher horizontal line appears farther away, and because it has an identical visual angle to the lower line, we assume it to be bigger. That is, we perceive something to be bigger if it has the same visual angle as something else that appears closer.

FIGURE 4.11 *The Ames Room Illusion. Courtesy of Illusion Works, L.L.C.*

FIGURE 4.12 *The Ponzo Illusion. Courtesy of BigFoto.com.*

The **Moon Illusion** is when we think the moon at its horizon is much larger than the moon at its zenith (high in the sky). It appears larger at the horizon because we can compare the size of the moon to the sizes of other objects in the terrain. At its zenith, there are no other comparison stimuli, so we do not perceive a **relative size**. The Moon Illusion is similar to the Ponzo Illusion in that the actual visual angles of the moon at the horizon and at its zenith are identical, so people who judge the horizon moon to be bigger assume that it is farther away. But it is not; the moon does not noticeably change its distance from the earth as it moves through the sky. Sometimes people who are closer to the horizon judge the horizon moon to be closer. If you don't believe that the horizon and zenith moons are identical in size (have identical visual angles), make a hole in a piece of paper using a standard hole puncher, hold it at arms' length, and view the moon through the hole at the horizon and then at its zenith. You will see that they are identical in size. If you don't believe that the moon does not physically move farther or closer when it is in different positions in the sky, ask you physics professor.

Perception of Movement

Motion detection requires responses in cortical cells called **movement detectors**, which receive input from a succession of retinal cell responses to an image moving across it. Also taken into consideration are the movements of the eye as it follows a moving object. Even if you move, you can tell that an object has not moved, because it has not changed its relation to other objects. If the object moves, its relationship to other objects changes. Determining movement through comparisons among object relationships is called **relative motion**. However, sometimes we perceive motion when there is none. One example of this is **apparent motion**. Apparent motion occurs when two separate points of light that are illuminated in succession (separated by about 60 milliseconds of darkness) result in the perception of the first light moving to the position of the second light. One type of apparent motion is the **phi phenomenon**, which requires a period of darkness between 60 ms and 200 ms. In this phenomenon, individuals believe that one dot has moved to the location of the other, but they admit not seeing the motion. This occurs even when the two points are different colors, such as red and green—in which case, participants believe that the dot has moved and changed colors.

Another illusion of apparent motion is **induced movement**. This occurs when a stationary object appears to move, because its surroundings move. If you've ever looked out the window while sitting on a plane, you may suddenly brace yourself because you think your plane is moving when, in fact, it was a neighboring plane that was moving. Similarly, when pigeons walk, it appears as though their heads are jutting back and forth, but they are not. Instead, the pigeon moves its head forward, which then remains stationary, and then its body moves so that its breast juts out farther than the head. Even though the movement is in the body, it appears as though the head is moving to and fro. The head's perceived backward motion is induced movement.

Vision Disorders

Color Blindness

Color blindness is typically due to missing or abnormal red or green cones, and causes an inability to distinguish among red, green, and other colors that rely heavily on the combined activity of red and green cones. Red-green color blindness is more common in males than in females, where it is rare. This is because the genes for red and green cones are carried on the X chromosome. Because females have two X chromosomes, the second can compensate if there is a problem with the first; males, however, are at a loss because they have only one X chromosome. Another kind of color blindness, **achromatopsia**, is caused by damage to the visual association cortex. Individuals with achromatopsia are completely color blind, seeing the world in shades of gray. One such patient is described by well-known neurologist and author Oliver Sacks (1996), in his book *An Anthropologist on Mars: Seven Paradoxical Tales*. The patient was a painter (ironically) who sustained a brain injury in a car accident. The patient complained mostly that everything seemed so drab, especially his food. Indeed, his diet became very limited because gray food looked so unappetizing that he couldn't eat it.

Visual Agnosia

"Agnosia" means "inability to recognize." Individuals who suffer from **visual agnosia** have perception deficits, but their sensations are intact. **Object agnosia** can be quite specific, affecting only some kinds of objects but not others. For example, some agnosics can recognize different kinds of motor vehicles but not different kinds of cars (Damasio, Damasio, & Van Hoesen, 1982). There are even instances of people being unable to recognize nonliving things but still able to recognize living things. These are specific perceptual deficits to the "What" system, resulting from damage to the cerebral cortex. Individuals who experience a combination of agnosias either have widespread damage and should show many other deficits as well, or have damage to structures earlier in the perceptual process. Other agnosics exhibit **prosopagnosia**. Prosopagnosics are unable to recognize faces but can discriminate details of objects and nonhuman faces. Neuroimaging studies indicate that the areas of the brain specialized for face processing are the fusiform gyrus and the anterior temporal lobe of the right hemisphere (Damasio, Grabowski, Tranel, Hichwa, & Damasio, 1996; Sergent & Signoret, 1992). Damage to both hemispheres of the parietal lobe can lead to an unusual kind of agnosia called **simultanagnosia**. Simultanagnosia is the inability to recognize more than one object at a time, and simultanagnosics cannot perceive a complex visual scene or associate different parts of a scene as being related (Humphreys, 1998).

Auditory System

Humans are capable of detecting a wide range of sounds, but this range is still far from being inclusive. For example, many animals such as dogs have a much more keen auditory sense and are able to detect sounds that fall outside the human range of hearing.

Properties of Sound

Sound is experienced when **sound waves**, vibrations or compressions of air molecules, travel through the air around us and are received by our auditory system. Sound waves differ from one another on a number of physical dimensions, which are responsible for producing different psychological or perceptual dimensions. Examining the physical characteristics of a simple sound wave will help provide a more clear understanding of these phenomena (Goldstein, 2002). For example, in Figure 4.13, the height of the sound wave is known as the **amplitude** and is primarily responsible for the perceptual experience of **loudness**. The higher the amplitude of the sound wave, the louder the sound, which is commonly measured in **decibels** (dB). Notice, too, that the sound wave repeats itself, so you could actually count the number of times it occurs in a specified period of time. In Figure 4.13 the sound wave repeats itself four times. The number of repetitions of the sound wave is referred to as the sound wave's **frequency**. The frequency of a sound wave translates into the perceptual dimension called **pitch**. High-pitched sounds are associated with high-frequency sound waves, while low-pitched sounds are associated with low-frequency sound waves. Sound wave frequencies are commonly measured in **hertz** (Hz).

The final physical dimension of sound waves is a bit more complex and is not commonly discussed, at least among the nonmusically inclined. In reality, most sounds are composed of a number of sound waves that, when added together, produce the sound that you hear. The final sound wave produced by all these other sound waves may share the same frequency and the same amplitude as another sound wave, but perceptually may be very different. Physically, this is the **complexity** of the sound wave, and the perceptual dimension is referred to as the **timbre** (Handel, 1995). For example, you could ask two musicians, a pianist and a guitarist, to play the same note on their instrument. The two sounds share the same frequency or pitch and share the same amplitude or loudness, yet you can clearly tell that one sound came from a piano and the other from a guitar. This difference is associated with the complexity of the sound waves that make up the final sound wave you receive.

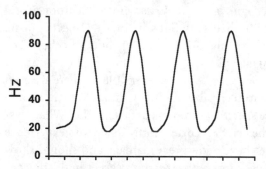

FIGURE 4.13 *Schematic representation of an auditory sound wave. The height of the wave is the amplitude, and the number of peaks within a given period of time is the frequency.*

Anatomy of the Auditory System

Ears come in all shapes and sizes, but the inner workings of the auditory system (see Figure 4.14) are quite similar across mammalian species. The **external ear**, or **pinna**, a common region for jewelry, has a number of small ridges and curves that help funnel sound waves into our auditory system and may serve to resonate the sound waves we receive. While some of us may be able to wiggle our ears a bit, we lack the proficiency to angle our pinna to facilitate the reception of sound waves. Other mammals such as cats, dogs, and horses can physically move their pinna so that the sound waves may be caught more effectively and funneled into their auditory system. As humans, we

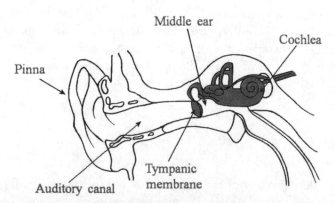

FIGURE 4.14 *Schematic diagram of the external, middle, and inner ear regions. Courtesy of Amy Vatanakul.*

might find ourselves cupping our ears with our hands to hear faint sounds or turning our heads so that one pinna is in a direct "line of sight" with the source from which the sound wave is being emitted. Once the sound wave reaches the pinna it is funneled into the **auditory canal**, the tube that runs into our head. At the end of the auditory canal is a delicate piece of tissue called the **tympanic membrane (ear drum)**. When sound waves reach the tympanic membrane, they cause it to vibrate. The strength of this vibration depends on the physical properties of the sound wave. For example, someone whispering in your ear will vibrate the tympanic membrane slightly, whereas sitting in the front row at a concert, where you can physically feel the sound waves from the speakers vibrating your skin, will vibrate your tympanic membrane much more vigorously, and it is likely to lead to permanent damage in your auditory system as well.

The sound wave has now been converted into physical movement within the auditory system. On the other side of the tympanic membrane is a region called the middle ear, where we find a set of small bones called the **ossicles**. These three connected bones—the **malleus** (hammer), the **incus** (anvil), and the **stapes** (stirrup)—are the smallest bones in the body. The malleus is connected to the tympanic membrane, so it will move when a sound wave vibrates the tympanic membrane. The incus is connected to the malleus, and the stapes is connected to the incus; thus the sound wave–induced vibrations are transferred through this series of small bones. As you might have experienced, a cold that moves into your "ear" often makes it difficult to hear. This is because fluid has built up in the middle ear region and the ossicles are no longer able to move freely and conduct the energy from the sound wave.

The last of the ossicles, the stapes, comes into contact with a small membrane that covers an opening (**oval window**) in a large bony structure called the **cochlea** (Kellaway, 1945). The cochlea has the appearance of a snail shell and contains the **organ of corti**, which is the organ for the auditory system. Within the organ of corti are the **basilar** and **tectorial membranes**, which have small neurons called **hair cells** protruding from or attaching to them. Auditory hair cells may be divided into inner or outer hair cells. Inner hair cells are responsible for transmitting the vast majority of auditory information to the brain, whereas outer hair cells are primarily involved in carrying signals from the brain to the organ of corti. The purpose of this feedback from the brain through the outer hair cells is not yet entirely clear. Together these hair cells and membranes make up the organ of corti, which is enveloped in fluid as it curves around within the snail-like cochlea. The hair cells serve as the sensory receptor cells for the auditory system. When a sound wave produces vibration in the tympanic membrane, it is transmitted through the ossicles and onto the oval window. Since the cochlea is filled with fluid, the vibration of the oval window produces a small wave to be generated within the cochlea. As the wave flows through the cochlea, the hair cells in the basilar membrane bend, producing action potentials that are sent to the brain through the **auditory nerve**. These signals are transmitted through a number of brain regions before reaching the primary auditory cortex (see Figure 4.15; Recanzone & Sutter, 2008). Thus, transduction occurs in the hair cells.

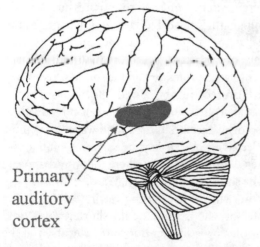

Primary auditory cortex

FIGURE 4.15 *Schematic diagram of the human brain showing the general location of the primary auditory cortex. Courtesy of Amy Vatanakul.*

Theories of Auditory Pitch Perception

In an attempt to understand how vibrations of air molecules bend hair cells and influence our ability to hear, scientists have developed a number of theories. Many of these theories concentrate on our perception of pitch (Tramo, Cariani, Koh, Makris, & Braida, 2005). The first of these theories is referred to as **place theory**, which argues that the location on the basilar membrane that vibrates the most will produce the greatest amount of stimulation of the hair cells in that location (Warren, 1984). It is the specific location or place along the basilar membrane that corresponds with our perception of pitch. According to the place theory, hair cells on the basilar membrane that are close to the oval window respond best to high-frequency tones, while hair cells located farther down the basilar membrane respond best to low frequencies. The second theory is called the **frequency theory**, which argues that the location of hair cell stimulation along the basilar membrane is not as important as the rate of firing in the hair cells themselves. In other words, a hair cell that responds at a higher rate will simply be interpreted by our brains as a higher-pitch tone. Finally, the **volley principle** argues that it is the pattern of firing, or "volley" of neural signals, created in a group of hair cells that is crucial for determining pitch. In reality, it is likely that our auditory systems make use of each principle underlying these theories to account for the range of our pitch perception.

Sound Localization

Sound localization refers to your ability to find the source of a sound in your environment. Consider standing facing forward in the center of a classroom with your professor (who is six feet tall in this example) standing in front of you to your left. When your professor speaks, you can detect approximately where he or she is located in the classroom, even with your eyes closed. To accurately locate the sound source, you must use three coordinate systems. The first is called the **azimuth** and is associated with your ability to locate sound on a horizontal (left/right) plane. A major source of information for the azimuth comes from **interaural differences**, or the difference in the time and sound pressure received by each ear (Colburn, Shinn-Cunningham, Kidd, & Durlach, 2006). In our example, you are facing the front of the classroom and you hear your professor speaking in front of you to the left. When your professor speaks, the sound is received by your left ear first, since it is closer to your professor and the sound waves travel directly to that ear. Your right ear also receives the sound information, but in addition to receiving it a moment later, the sound waves do not directly enter your right ear. Because your head blocks the path of the sound waves, they must travel around your head and be reflected off objects in your environment in order to enter your right ear. This creates a **sound shadow**, where the sound appears louder in the ear that is closest to the sound source (Coren, Ward, & Enns, 1999). The second coordinate is **elevation**, which refers to the vertical plane. If you replace your professor with a professor who is substantially shorter, you would likely be able to tell that the new professor is shorter due to the elevation of the sound source. The last coordinate is the distance of the sound source. A variety of cues give us the ability to detect the distance of a sound source, including the frequency and amplitude of the sound. Together, azimuth, elevation, and distance enable us to accurately localize sounds in our environments.

Disorders of the Auditory System

According to Goldstein (2002), auditory handicaps may be produced by a variety of sources that fall into two general categories: conductive hearing losses and sensorineural hearing losses. **Conductive hearing losses** may result from problems in the outer ear, namely, the auditory canal and the tympanic membrane, or from problems within the middle ear region. In his review, Goldstein indicates that obstructions in the outer ear region, such as objects, excessive buildup of ear wax, infection-induced swelling, congenital malformation, and ruptured tympanic membranes, induce conductive hearing loss. Within the middle ear, bacterial infections and abnormal bony growths on or around the ossicles may also produce conductive hearing loss. **Sensorineural hearing losses** are generally associated with the sensory receptor cells or the neurons responsible for transmitting sound-induced neural signals through the brain. Goldstein indicates that this may be a natural occurrence associated with hair cell degeneration in aging (**presbycusis**), exposure to very loud sounds that damage hair cells, disease that produces excessive fluid buildup in regions of the inner ear (**Meniere's disease**), or damage to neural pathways in the brain that transmit auditory information. Individuals who repeatedly expose themselves to very loud noise may develop a condition called **tinnitus**, which is a constant ringing in the ears. Unfortunately, there does not appear to be an effective treatment for this problem.

Vestibular System

The **vestibular system** is responsible for our sense of balance and comprises a series of tubes and sacks found above the middle ear region (see Figure 4.16). A closer examination of these tubes reveals that they are positioned in different planes—horizontal, vertical, and lateral—which allows them to respond to movements of the body in any direction. The movement of our bodies creates the stimulus for the vestibular system. The stimulus is the movement of fluid within the semicircular canals that displaces hair cells (receptors). This transduction creates a cascade of electrochemical messages that travel to the brain, where they are interpreted as our experience of balance. It is important to note that the vestibular system depends heavily on gravitational effects. For this reason, when we find ourselves without other sensory stimuli and under a great deal of pressure (that would negate the effects of gravity), as might occur in deep sea diving, it can be difficult to determine which way is up and which way is down. Some individuals also suffer from a vestibular disorder called **vertigo**. Vertigo is dizziness often associated with spinning, and may be caused by a variety of conditions ranging from the flu or colds to more serious conditions such as strokes (Perennou & Bronstein, 2005; Sedlaczek et al., 2005).

FIGURE 4.16 *Schematic diagram showing the semicircular canals of the vestibular system and the cochlea. Courtesy of Amy Vatanakul.*

Olfactory System

The olfactory system is one of two chemical sensory systems, and it is considered to be one of the oldest or most primitive sensory systems we have. Our ability to receive airborne molecules and detect them depends on the attachment of these molecules to specialized regions in our nose.

Anatomy of the Olfactory System

The anatomy of the **olfactory system** (see Figure 4.17) begins with the nose, as you might expect. When we inhale through our nose, airborne molecules called **odorants** are pulled into the **olfactory cavity** and become attached to a specialized patch of mucous membrane at the top of our nasal cavity called the **olfactory epithelium** (Mombaerts, 1999). Within this olfactory epithelium are the olfactory sensory neurons. These neurons have small cilia with receptors to which odorant molecules may bind and activate the neuron. The receptor neuron expresses the odorant molecules in terms of an electrochemical message that travels to the brain. Just above the olfactory epithelium is a bone called the **cribiform plate**. There are small holes in the cribiform plate through which the axons of the olfactory sensory neurons pass as they make their way to a region of the brain called the **olfactory bulb**. While many of our sensory systems pathways are crossed—for example, touch sensations on our left hand are processed in the right hemisphere of our brain—the olfactory system's connections between the nostrils and the brain remain primarily on the same side. In other words, odorant molecules that enter the right nostril are largely processed by the right hemisphere, and those that enter the left nostril are processed by the left hemisphere. At this point it is important to remember that all sensory systems relay their neural signals through the thalamus of the brain prior to processing, with the exception of the olfactory system. Neural signals carrying olfactory information leave the olfactory bulb, eventually split, and pass through a series of structures including either the orbitofrontal cortex or the amygdala and hippocampus.

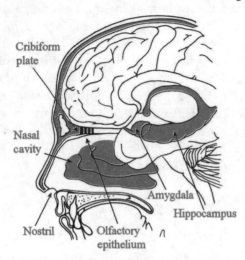

FIGURE 4.17 *Schematic diagram of the human olfactory system. Courtesy of Amy Vatanakul.*

Properties of Olfaction

Olfactory signals to the orbitofrontal cortex region of the brain are believed to be largely involved in processing information associated with the conscious perception of odors, whereas those connections with the amygdala and hippocampus are believed to be associated with the affective or emotional characteristics of odors. In other words, your ability to recognize and name a smell likely involves your orbitofrontal cortex, while any links between the smell and emotion likely involve your amygdala and hippocampus. Indeed, many people commonly report very strong emotional memories in association with specific olfactory cues (Richardson & Zucco, 1989).

Herz, McCall, and Cahill (1999) reported the results of a study where individuals were presented with a series of pleasant odors to one nostril at a time and were asked to name each odor and rate it in terms of pleasantness and arousal. The authors found that odors received by the left nostril were more likely to be named correctly, whereas odors received by the right nostril were rated as being more pleasant. These results are consistent with the evidence that there are differences between the hemispheres in processing emotion and language—namely, the right hemisphere is dominant for emotion, and the left hemisphere is dominant for language.

Vomeronasal Organ and Pheromones

The **vomeronasal organ** is a small structure found in the nasal cavity of many mammals, although its presence in adult humans is controversial (Doty, 2001). In one review, Levin (2004) reported that scientists found the vomeronasal organ present in between 8% and 80% of human adults. In nonhuman mammals this structure appears to play an important role in the detection of **pheromones**, chemical signals that are likely involved in attraction and sexual behavior. The reviews by Doty and Levin clearly indicate that considerable debate exists over whether the vomeronasal organ in humans is functionally receptive to pheromones, and even if it is, it is not clear whether these signals are associated with sexual behavior.

Gustatory System

Why is it that some people like spicy foods and others prefer salty foods and still others prefer sweet foods? Why are some people able to detect and name every little ingredient in a dish, while others can't seem to say much beyond their personal satisfaction or dissatisfaction with the dish? There is a wide range of variation with respect to our sensitivities and abilities within our sensory systems as you are, no doubt, already learning. The **gustatory system** is no different.

Anatomy of the Gustatory System

The gustatory system is largely responsible for our sense of taste. Small bumps and ridges on our tongue, particularly around the tip, sides, and back surface, are called **papillae** (see Figure 4.18). There are three main forms of papillae associated with our sense of taste: **Circumvallate papillae** are found on the back of the tongue, **foliate papillae** are found along the sides of the tongue, and **fungiform papillae** are found on the front tip of the tongue. Around these papillae are grooves called **taste pores**, which extend down into the surface of the tongue. Molecules from the foods we eat and the drinks we consume fall into these pores, where they interact with clusters of small cilia that extend into the pore. These small cilia are part of **taste receptor cells**, which are grouped together in small bunches in the walls of the taste pores called **taste buds**. Thus, it is a myth that you can see the taste buds on your tongue. The small bumps that you can see are actually the papillae. The taste buds are much smaller and are located along the sides of the taste pores in the tongue. The axons from the taste receptor cells in the taste buds come together to form two cranial nerves. Information is carried through these nerves to the brain stem, up through the thalamus, and to regions of the brain where the taste information is processed.

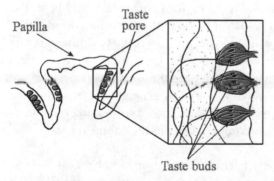

FIGURE 4.18 *Schematic diagram of a papilla (left). The taste pore and taste buds are made up of individual taste cells (right). Courtesy of Amy Vatanakul.*

Basic Tastes

Historically there have been four basic tastes: sweet, sour, salty, and bitter. Scientists believed that certain areas of the tongue housed taste receptors for certain tastes. We now know that the taste receptor cells responsible for detecting each of these basic tastes are located throughout the taste-sensitive regions of the tongue, although some regions of the tongue have more of one particular taste receptor than other receptors. In addition to these four basic tastes, there is now good evidence for a fifth taste, called **umami**, which has been described as a meaty or savory experience that is associated with monosodium glutamate (Bellisle, 1999; Yamaguchi, 1991).

The Ice Cream Headache

The ice cream headache, often referred to as brain freeze, is a severe headache induced by the consumption of very cold beverages or ice cream. This headache has been reported to be the most common cause of head pain, affecting approximately one-third of the population (Hulihan, 1997). Contrary to popular belief, its cause is not associated with the freezing of tissue or neurons; rather, it is associated with the dilation of blood vessels in the brain. In his review of ice cream headaches, Hulihan indicated that this dilation of blood vessels in the brain associated with ice cream headaches is similar to those of migraine headaches, and thus the ice cream headache may serve as a good model to study the devastating effects of migraines.

FIGURE 4.19 *Brain freeze! Courtesy of Amy Vatanakul.*

Factors Influencing Taste/Food Preference

Many factors profoundly influence both the short-term and long-term consumption of foods. Some of the most common are associated with the appearance of the food we are considering consuming. The manner in which both the smell and the appearance of foods influence our preferences is often rooted in cultural norms and prior experiences. For example, in the United States, delicacies to some of us, such as steak tartar and scrapple (leftover fried pork scraps formed into a loaf with cornmeal), may be just as strange as foods in other countries, such as blood pudding or sheep head. While the latter two may sound unappealing to you, are they really any different from a corndog—a hot dog shoved on a stick, dipped in corn meal, and deep fried? Interestingly, children often seem to be immune to the aversions associated with the appearance of foods that deviate from the cultural norm. In fact, some food manufacturing companies have even tried adding food coloring to certain products to produce strange-colored food to cater to the young at heart.

Explore
learning and association
in Chapter 7, p. 197

Sensory specific satiety is another common factor that influences food preference and is associated with the frequency with which that food has been recently consumed. In other words, a food that has been eaten repeatedly across days or in a large amount at a single meal may be deemed as less preferable. Consider the last time you gorged on pizza. You may have consumed three, four, or more slices before announcing that you were completely stuffed and couldn't eat another piece. But then a friend showed up with dessert, and you happily helped yourself to a serving. In this circumstance, you had become satiated on pizza. This suggests that humans like variety, but variety may create problematic situations with food consumption.

The cafeteria diet is associated with the broad selection of foods often found in cafeterias. Under these circumstances, people often find themselves sampling a variety of foods and thus consuming a greater amount of food than if there were only a few choices. This frequently leads to an increase in body weight, and on college campuses it's referred to as the "freshman 15."

Chapter Summary

In this chapter we discussed the different sensory modalities and our perceptions of the physical world. We rely on our sensations for different aspects of our daily experiences, but it is their combinations that provide us with a coherent, unified perception of the world. We use our perceptions of the world to guide our behaviors, and sometimes it seems that we do surprisingly well for how little we get and the distortions we create in our minds. We receive, process, and interpret precisely what we need to survive, so things that get misinterpreted or simply missed do not seem to have much bearing on our survival, however interesting the effects are that we observe in our labs. The unusual effects we observe help us understand how parts of the sensory systems work and how they come together, but much work remains to be done. Hopefully one day you will be inspired to discover something and shed some more light on how we sense and perceive the world.

Knowledge Builder

RELATE TO YOURSELF

1. Examine your tongue. Now that you know the different types of papillae, can you find them and see the differences?

_____

_____

_____

_____

2. Can you think of and describe an odor that is associated with a personal memory?

_____

_____

_____

_____

3. Using a math compass at its lowest setting as an instrument for two point discrimination, create a homunculus or somatosensory map of your hand (or any body part you choose). Which areas have large receptive fields and which have small? How do these different sensitivities affect your daily activities?

_____

_____

_____

_____

4. Use the gate control theory to describe the pain you would feel from closing your hand in a car door. What behaviors could you use to stop the pain?

_____

_____

_____

_____

5. Look down a long hallway. Explain all the depth cues that are present.

_____

_____

_____

_____

CHAPTER REVIEW QUESTIONS

1. Pitch perception is associated with sound wave amplitude. **T or F?**

2. Umami are the sensory receptor cells for the olfactory system. **T or F?**

3. Our sense of smell has separate pathways for conscious perception and emotional aspects of odors. **T or F?**

4. Sensory receptors use firing rate to indicate the characteristics of a stimulus. **T or F?**

5. Each sensory modality represents the location of a stimulus in the environment using maps. **T or F?**

6. Brightness is an important depth cue. **T or F?**

7. The part of the eye where most cones are located is called the _____.

   (a) lens   (b) fovea

   (c) iris   (d) periphery

8. Which of the following is NOT a somatosensory receptor?

   (a) mechanoreceptor   (b) nociceptor

   (c) photoreceptor   (d) Pacinian corpuscle

9. Where are feature detectors?

   (a) primary visual cortex   (b) association of circumstriate cortex

   (c) ventral posterior nucleus (d) parietal lobe

10. The bony structure that contains the organ of corti is called the _____.

    (a) ear   (b) cribiform plate

    (c) ossicles   (d) cochlea

11. The constant ringing in the ears following repeated exposure to very loud sounds is called _____.

    (a) presbycusis   (b) tinnitus

    (c) a hallucination   (d) anosmia

12. One of the important contributing factors to our feelings of hunger around "meal time" is _____.

    (a) sensory specific satiety   (b) classical conditioning

    (c) food appearance   (d) anosmia

13. *Consider the following scenario:* Last night you were at a concert, and on the way home you had the music in your car turned up pretty loud. This morning you jump in your car, turn it on, and the music practically blasts you right out of your seat. Assuming that you simply forgot to turn the music off last night and that no one else has used your car, explain why the stereo seems so much louder this morning.

_____

_____

_____

_____

14. *Consider the following:* In *The Man Who Mistook His Wife for a Hat,* Dr. Sacks recounts the case of a patient, Dr. P, for whom the book is titled. Dr. P had trouble recognizing objects—in one instance he mistook the hand of his wife for his hat. His visual sense was intact, and he could easily describe details of things he was shown—describing a rose as, "About six inches in length . . . A convoluted red form with a linear green attachment." He eventually deduced the object, "I think this could be an inflorescence or flower." It is clear that Dr. P did not have a problem with his eyesight, his ability to detect features, or his use of language and verbal labels. However, his problem was purely visual because he immediately identified the object as a rose when he was able to smell it. In addition to being unable to recognize objects, Dr. P could no longer recognize faces. He had been a rather talented artist, and much of his art throughout the years was displayed on his wall. Dr. Sacks observed Dr. P's earlier work to be quite realistic, with fine details of objects, whereas his later work became less brightly colored, abstract, geometrical or cubist, and finally just blotches of paint. Dr. P was also a music teacher, and his abilities here were intact, with the exception that he could not recognize his students while they were sitting still but could recognize them when they moved by their characteristic movements. As it turns out, Dr. P had a massive brain tumor. From the information given here, what was damaged by the tumor?

_____

_____

_____

_____

15. *Consider the following:* It has been suggested that the immune system be considered as another sensory modality. The evidence is that it has specialized cells (antigens) for responding to physical stimuli (germs). These specialized cells communicate with antigen-specific white blood cells, there are direct nerve pathways from immune system structures (e.g., lymph nodes) to the brain, there are corresponding firing rates of neurons in the hypothalamus to the intensity of antibody response, and there is also a corresponding change in behavior that serves to protect the animal, such as fever, sleep, and reduced activity. Given this information, do you think the immune system qualifies as a sensory modality?

_____

_____

_____

_____

USEFUL WEB SITES

PRESS RELEASE FROM THE NOBEL ASSEMBLY ABOUT THE
2004 NOBEL PRIZE FOR WORK ON THE OLFACTORY SYSTEM

http://nobelprize.org/medicine/laureates/2004/press.html

THE QUESTION OF TASTE

http://www.brainconnection.com/topics/?main=fa/question

This Web site presents an article reviewing a variety of unique characteristics of taste.

CLASSROOM LAB ACTIVITIES FOR TASTE PERCEPTION

http://staff.washington.edu/chudler/pdf/tastetg.pdf

This document reviews a couple of useful classroom activities for taste perception.

BASIC SOMATOSENSORY INFORMATION

http://faculty.washington.edu/chudler/brainsize.html

VISUAL ILLUSIONS

http://www.moillusions.com

http://www.Illusion-optical.com

VISION RESEARCH

http://www.visionscience.com/

VISUAL SYSTEM IN DETAIL

http://webvision.med.utah.edu/

VISION AND ART

http://webexhibits.org/colorart/about.html

VARIOUS RESOURCES ON SENSATION AND PERCEPTION

http://psych.athabascau.ca/html/aupr/sensation.shtml

Chapter **5**

States of Consciousness

by Janice E. Jones, PhD

Inside the doors are sealed to love,

Inside my heart is sleeping,

Outside the world's still burning,

Outside the drums are calling.

—STING

What Is Consciousness?

One of the most interesting yet demanding aspects of psychology to examine is consciousness. "Awareness of internal and external stimuli" sounds like a simple definition of consciousness, yet we are referring to a complex mental process. The complexity of consciousness is reflected in the fact that there are different states or levels of this mental process.

Some people imagine that consciousness is "continuous," just like a stream, but this is a false impression due to the array of states a person can experience even over a short time. In this chapter we will examine different states of consciousness: wakefulness and sleep, hypnotic trance (or hypnotic state of mind) and meditation, and how the use of psychoactive (or mind-altering) drugs completely alters our consciousness. Altered states of consciousness are induced with certain tools, techniques, or agents (like drugs, for example), whereas regular states of consciousness happen naturally.

Studying Consciousness

Psychology has at its roots the study of consciousness. It was in the last century that psychologists stopped defining their work as the study of consciousness and instead chose to define it as the study of behavior and mental

FIGURE 5.1 *Consciousness isn't continuous like a stream. Photograph by Ivan Maric.*

processes, one of which is consciousness. This important shift in thinking has affected the work we do now and the research focus of many important scholars of our time.

As we reached the 1970s, technology had improved enough that advances in neuroscience made it easier for psychologists to study brain activity and link that activity to different mental states/processes, including consciousness. As technology continued to improve, so did the research being done on various forms of consciousness. Researchers began to study, for example, the effects of psychoactive drugs on consciousness. The advent of technology and research methods recently allowed an old legend to be verified and confirmed. According to the legend, in ancient Greece there was a priestess named Pythia living in the temple of Delphi. Ancient observers had claimed that Pythia was inhaling certain vapors that gave her the ability to prophesize. As Pythia prophesized, an altered state of mind was reflected in her strange behavior, which included screaming, sweating, and throwing punches while she responded to people's inquiries. Scientists collected a sample of water from below the temple, and the sophisticated analysis showed that the water contained the drug ethylene. Subsequent studies have shown that ethylene can alter the consciousness of research participants in ways similar to Pythia's unusual state of consciousness (Hale, Zeillinga, Chanton, & Spiller, 2003).

The image of a brain on a computer screen is certainly not anything we could have seen 50 years ago. With modern technology (see Chapter 3), we can see inside the brain to determine abnormalities or whether the brain is functioning normally or abnormally. These technological advancements allow us to see what regions of the brain are active while people are experiencing a hypnotic state of mind, while they are experiencing the effects of drugs, or while they are meditating. Also, this modern technology aids us in understanding the brain structures that facilitate states of consciousness. Even though we are familiar with some of the structures that support consciousness (like protomesencephalon of the brain stem), the search for the remaining structures continues (Kalat, 2003).

Levels of Consciousness

Consciousness is what allows us to carry on the normal functions of everyday life. If we were not conscious, we would not be able to get to work, participate in sports, or do any of the other things we do each day. Without consciousness we wouldn't be able to function at all. However, in certain situations we don't need much consciousness to function. In fact, the awareness that we have of our daily activities varies depending on the amount of *concentration* we need to complete the task. We have all had the experience of not knowing how we got where we are. Perhaps because, as we traveled to get there, our mind was on the homework we needed to complete or the chores we needed to do when we got home. How is this possible? The level to which we learned a certain activity is the answer to this question. We know that as we practice something and learn it well, we are able to pay less attention to what we are doing, and our attention is free to wander to other tasks. Recall the quote from Sting at the beginning of the chapter. If we saw him live in concert, we would notice that he can sing and play bass guitar at the same time, since he learned to do both well. Mothers become especially good at performing a multitude of tasks while paying attention to their children's activities. One of our strengths as humans is our ability to learn automatic behaviors so that our conscious awareness can be focused elsewhere. Many of us have had the experience of driving a car and ending up where we wanted to go, but our minds were focused on the day's activities and we were not aware that we were driving.

The Circadian Rhythm

Sleep is one of the most perplexing mysteries of human existence. Psychologists are trying to understand what those mental and biological processes involve. Why is sleep elusive for many people, something they struggle to achieve? Why do others find it difficult to stay asleep after they have fallen asleep? Through technological advances we are able to record and observe their brain waves (or patterns of electrical activity in the brain) and other psychological processes during sleep. Through these observations we have determined the cyclical pattern of our sleep (as we will understand more fully later).

Our bodies cycle through a 24-hour sleep-wake cycle called a **circadian rhythm**. Researchers discovered this cycle by studying how humans respond when they are deprived of light. One researcher spent six months in a cave to study how his body responded to the lack of light (Moore, 1997). "Circadian" is a Latin word that roughly translates to "about a day." Scientists have discovered that we are at our sharpest thinking and memory when we are at the peak of our circadian arousal. For some people, such as older adults, this is early morning, and for others, such as college-aged students, it is later in the day (May & Hasher, 1998).

Jet lag—waking up too early and going to bed too early—is a term used to describe what we experience when we fly overseas. Jet lag happens because we have disrupted our natural circadian rhythm. Researchers have found that if we spend the first day outdoors, absorbing natural sunlight, we will feel better and reduce the amount of jet lag we experience (Oren & Terman, 1998). Most airlines recognize this and provide overnight flights to Europe so that their passengers can arrive in the morning at their destination feeling refreshed.

We can alter our circadian rhythms by altering our sleep schedules. We have become attuned to staying up later on weekends because we can sleep longer on weekend mornings. Almost everyone has experienced the Monday-morning "blahs"—the feeling we get when we have altered our sleep schedule by partying late at night or sleeping in late on Saturday and Sunday mornings. When we disrupt our circadian rhythms, it is hard to readjust our bodies to the routine workweek.

Wakefulness and Sleep

What triggers our experience of sleepiness? When light hits the retina of our eye, it causes a neural center in the hypothalamus (or the suprachiasmatic nucleus) to produce certain proteins. These proteins accumulate during the day, and by

FIGURE 5.2 *Sleep. Photograph by Debbie Whittaker.*

evening they have sufficiently built up to induce sleepiness. People who have problems producing these important proteins fall asleep and wake up much earlier than normal. Another important trigger of sleepiness is the hormone melatonin. In the evening, the same neural center in the hypothalamus stimulates the nearby pineal gland to release melatonin, further inducing sleepiness. People with pineal gland impairment have problems falling asleep. In the morning, the amount of the mentioned proteins and melatonin is low, causing the individual to awaken (Kalat, 2003).

Researching Stages of Sleep

Our bodies cycle through five distinct sleep stages. To research the cycles of sleep, researchers conduct sleep studies. An individual participating in a sleep study enters a sleep lab late in the day. Electrodes are attached to the individual's head as he or she prepares to go to sleep in a laboratory. A video camera records the person's movements, and an **electroencephalograph (EEG)**, a machine displaying the recording from the electrodes picking up the gross electrical brain activity, is also used. Laboratory assistants normally watch from an adjoining room to monitor the brain-wave activity the individual exhibits. These technicians observe the individual and monitor his or her behavior through a special one-way mirror. In addition to the electrodes on the scalp, electrodes are also placed next to the eyes to detect eye movement and on the chin to detect muscle tension. Often there is a device used to detect heart rate and respiration rate. One might ask why all these things are being monitored when we are interested in just those five stages of sleep. The answer is that one can differentiate one stage of sleep from another through different patterns of brain activity, heart rate, respiration (breathing), muscular activity, and eye movement (Roth, 2004).

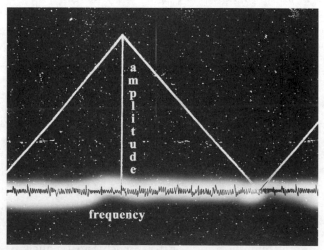

FIGURE 5.3 *Amplitude and frequency of brain waves characteristic of sleep and wakefulness.*

Stages of Sleep and Brain Waves

During each stage of sleep, the EEG shows different patterns of brain waves. The amplitude (height) of the brain wave tells us the **synchrony** of the brain cells, which is the extent that the cells are active as a unit versus working independently from one another. Larger amplitude suggests more synchrony of brain cell activity; smaller amplitude suggests less synchrony. As we go from stage 1 to stage 4, we see that the amplitude becomes larger—cells show more synchronous firing. The reason for this is that in each subsequent stage of a deeper sleep, we are less and less responsive to the environment. This also means that stimuli from the environment are unable to stimulate our brain cells as much as they do when we are awake. This is not to say

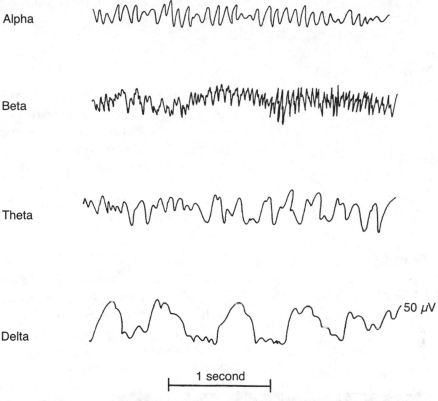

FIGURE 5.4 *Brain waves associated with the various stages of sleep. Courtesy of Pearson Custom Publishing.*

that the cells are not working. The cells are indeed working, since there are some internal mechanisms—certain brain regions that stimulate the cells to be active—and these several regions stimulate the cells more uniformly than the information from a variety of sources from the environment.

In addition to their amplitude, brain waves have another important characteristic—the frequency or speed by which they occur. When a wave occurs with more frequency, this suggests more cellular activity. Less frequency suggests less cellular activity. In the earlier stages we see more cellular activity and therefore more frequency. In later stages we see less frequency. More frequency suggests a shallower sleep, and less frequency a deeper sleep.

Additional Bodily Changes During Stages of Sleep

As mentioned earlier, there are other bodily changes that happen during sleep; the pattern of brain waves is just one aspect that changes from stage to stage. Muscular activity also changes from stage to stage—muscles become more and more relaxed as we go from stage 1 to subsequent stages of sleep. Breathing and heart rate also become slower as we go from stage 1 to the subsequent stages. While our bodies are resting, our body temperature also lowers during the sleep-wake cycle.

Non-REM Sleep

Stages 1 through 4 are called **non-REM sleep,** since rapid eye movements (REM) do not happen during these stages. REM sleep usually indicates the beginning of a dream. About 80% of the time a person will remember a dream if awoken during REM sleep. However, dreams sometimes occur during non-REM sleep too. We probably experience more than 1,500 dreams a year (Roth, 2004).

Wakefulness is characterized by **beta waves. Alpha waves** are the electrical brain waves that occur during presleep, meditation, and hypnosis (Roth, 2004).

Stage 1

Stage 1 is usually considered to be a transitional stage from wakefulness to deeper sleep. **Theta waves** are slower in frequency and can be found in stage 1. It is very easy to be awakened from this stage, and the person usually experiences unusual images, drifting thoughts, and feelings of floating called **hypnogogic hallucinations.** When we wake up in the morning, it is almost impossible to remember images from stage 1. Salvador Dalí, the famous Spanish painter, utilized this stage of sleep in his work. He constructed a method of capturing these unusual experiences. Dalí used to relax in a chair on his balcony, having a cup on a coffee table next to him. Above the cup he would hold a metal spoon. Then, his hypnogogic images would soon overwhelm him as he transitioned from wakefulness to sleep. Before he would lose those hallucinations to stage 2 of sleep, though, his spoon would hit the cup and wake him, allowing him to remember his recent hallucinations. Dalí is known for his world-famous surrealistic paintings, which are composed of unusual images (Dalí, 2007). We usually spend about five minutes in stage 1 sleep before we fall into stage 2 sleep.

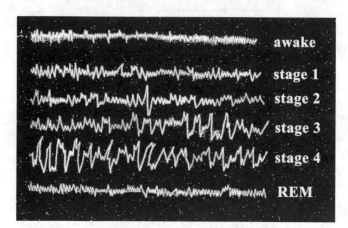

FIGURE 5.5 *Stages of sleep.*

Stage 2

The brain waves of stage 2 sleep occasionally have bursts of very high-frequency waves called **sleep spindles. K-complexes,** which occur during this stage, can be seen by looking at stage 2 of Figure 5.5 and noticing the spikes in the brain waves. It is interesting that individuals with mental retardation show a higher amount of sleep spindles in their stage 2 sleep than do healthy individuals. In this stage we might sleep talk or talk in ways that are not understandable to anyone listening, although people can sleep talk in any stage (Mahowald & Ettinger, 1990). Stage 2 sleep lasts about 20 minutes.

Stages 3 & 4

Stage 3 sleep is often referred to as transitional sleep as we go through this stage and into stage 4, which is a deep sleep. Stages 3 and 4 are characterized by **delta**

waves, which are larger brain waves. The difference between stage 3 and stage 4 is that in stage 3, less than 50% of the brain waves are delta waves, and in stage 4 more than 50% of the brain waves are delta waves (Mahowald & Ettinger, 1990). It is thus difficult to awaken someone from this stage of sleep.

Stage 4 sleep is associated with the production of growth hormone, which stimulates cellular processes throughout the body, influencing physical growth, brain development, and production of immune cells. During this phase, children often wet the bed or sleepwalk. It is most difficult to awaken someone from this stage of sleep.

FIGURE 5.6 *Rapid eye movement (REM).*
Photograph by Debbie Whittaker.

During **REM sleep**, sleep muscles in the body, especially the neck muscles, are extremely relaxed/paralyzed (**postural muscle paralysis**), yet some muscles of the face and of the fingers and toes are very active. Among the facial muscles are those that move our eyeballs left and right. About every 30 seconds our eyes dart around under our closed eyelids.

Even though most muscles throughout the body are very much relaxed during REM sleep, the beta brain waves look just like the brain waves of a person who is fully awake. This is called **paradoxical sleep**. REM sleep differs from other stages in that the heart rate and breathing have more irregular patterns (increasing of heart rate and breathing alternates with decreasing of these processes) than those in stages 1–4. This irregularity is also seen during wakefulness. REM sleep is where we dream, and muscle paralysis keeps us from moving when we dream. During this sleep stage our bodies are almost paralyzed because our brain stem is blocking any messages for movement (Mahowald & Ettinger, 1990).

Sleep Cycles

As mentioned earlier, sleep is divided into non-REM and REM sleep. We spend about 20% of our time in REM sleep and 80% in non-REM sleep. REM and non-REM sleep occur in stages or sessions, and it is false to assume that we cycle through the stages in this way: stage 1, stage 2, stage 3, stage 4, REM, stage 1, stage 2, and so on. Our sleep cycles repeat themselves about every 90 minutes. We spend about 90–120 minutes in REM sleep each night, 15–60 minutes per REM session. There are several sessions of REM sleep each night. Also, REM sessions last longer toward the morning. We spend about 15–60 minutes in each non-REM sleep stage (Mahowald & Ettinger, 1990).

Why Do We Sleep?

Sleep is very important to our well-being. We spend about one-third of our life sleeping. As newborns, we slept about 16 hours a day, and as we reach adulthood, we will feel lucky to achieve 8 hours of uninterrupted sleep a night. As we get even older, our sleep patterns will change again. Some of us will need only 5 hours of sleep a night, while others will take short naps during the day, making our sleep total reach up to 12 hours a day. It is normal to have sleep patterns different from those of our friends and even our relatives. It is also normal to have different sleep patterns across our lifespan (Jacobs, 1999).

All of us have experienced sleep deprivation at some point in our lives. **Sleep deprivation** is not getting the amount of sleep needed in order to sustain our health. For some of us, this happens during exam time at school, during the holiday season, when we may be at work longer or attending more parties, or during especially stressful periods in our lives. Oftentimes during sleep deprivation our bodies are physically exhausted and we are emotionally taxed to the point that we become crabby and irritable (Jacobs, 1999).

When we are sleep deprived, we are more vulnerable to accidents, more prone to mistakes, and more likely to have difficulty studying or completing our daily routine. We may also experience symptoms of depression. In a typical research lab, a participant can experience sleep deprivation by not being allowed to fall asleep. Studies show that sleep-deprived humans have a reduced amount of immune cells (which fight invading microorganisms) and thus are more vulnerable to infections. When we have an infection, we tend to sleep more, which naturally allows our bodies to produce more immune cells. In some cases, people who were sleep deprived displayed hallucinations. Some individuals have been found in the snow in the morning (thinking it was a warm bed), and to others, snow appeared to be a hot shower (Berger & Oswald, 1962). Clouded thinking and moodiness are usual effects of sleep deprivation. Scientists studying traffic accidents have noticed that after the seasonal spring time change there tends to be more accidents, which could be a result of individuals being sleep deprived from losing an hour of sleep. Sleep deprivation has also been linked to obesity and other problems (Spiegel, Leproult, & Van Cauter, 1999).

REM Sleep Deprivation

When deprived of REM sleep, an individual will spend more time in REM sleep the next time he or she sleeps. Contrary to some people's beliefs, REM sleep deprivation does not cause memory problems; in fact, it even improves memory slightly. Studies show that lack of REM sleep affects cognitive performance on tasks and affects mood states negatively. People tend to be more irritable when they do not get enough sleep (Siegel, 1999). After we learn a piece of information, REM sleep deprivation does not interfere with our retention of that information. As an example, dolphins have little or no REM sleep, but they show impressive reasoning and learning. There is some evidence that REM sleep deprivation can help people who suffer from depression. In these individuals, this condition has been associated with a lower than normal amount of the neurotransmitter serotonin in their neuronal synapses. During REM sleep, the amount of serotonin production is reduced, and this healthy mechanism allows receptors to rest from absorption of the neurotransmitters. However, in people with depression, serotonin levels are already low, and REM sleep deprivation can actually be beneficial for some patients because it increases the amount of serotonin (Jacobs, 1999).

Preventing REM sleep in infant kittens usually leads to abnormalities of the kittens' visual systems. This and another finding led psychologists to believe that REM sleep has an important function in the development of the nervous system cells. A platypus, for example, spends a long time in REM sleep—about

8 hours per day. A newborn platypus is defenseless—it cannot regulate its temperature well or find food on its own, and it is attached to its mother for weeks (Siegel, 1999). On the other hand, at birth, dolphins can swim independently, avoid predators, find their own food, and regulate their temperature well. The dolphin's evidently well-developed nervous system at birth is probably why dolphins have very small amounts of REM sleep at birth and throughout their life span. Human infants, like the platypus, are born with a very underdeveloped brain in comparison to most mammals. A human baby sleeps about 17 hours per day, of which about 8.5 hours (50% of sleep) is spent in REM sleep. A 4-year-old child spends 20–30% of his or her sleep in REM. Human adolescents and adults sleep 7–8 hours per day. Psychologists believe that REM sleep stimulates the underdeveloped nervous system to optimally develop. Some researchers believe that we dream to stimulate our brain and that the increased brain activity helps develop and preserve our brain's neural pathways. Since we dream during REM sleep, this theory helps explain why babies spend so much time in REM sleep: Their neural pathways are growing and developing (Jacobs, 1999).

Non-REM Sleep Deprivation

Which sleeps longer, a cat or an elephant? You might say an elephant since it is bigger and needs more sleep to rest its huge body. It makes sense, but it's wrong. The correct answer is that cats sleep longer. Smaller animals have faster cellular processes (metabolism) than larger animals. A natural byproduct of these processes is free radicals, dangerous substances that damage cells. Thus, faster metabolism equals more damage. During non-REM sleep, however, certain proteins are more efficient in repairing the damaged cells. More non-REM sleep equals more repair of cells (Jacobs, 1999).

Disorders of Sleep

Sleepwalking

Sleepwalking usually occurs in sleep stages 3 and 4. The individual gets up and walks while asleep, sometimes with open eyes. The following behaviors have been documented in people who sleepwalk:

- Drawing knives from kitchen drawers
- Walking outside in the yard or street
- Physically and verbally attacking others
- Cooking and eating food
- Getting into a car
- Using the telephone
- Moving furniture
- Feeding pets
- Dressing
- Bathing

In addition, the person can even climb stairs, with poor coordination (clumsiness), but he or she is able to avoid objects. Cognitive functioning is impaired, and it is difficult to awaken this person. The best treatment is to take the individual by the hand and lead him or her back to bed. The condition peaks at 11 years of age, and it happens in 40% of children (*Sleepwalking,* n.d.).

Sleep Talking

While **sleep talking** is harmless and is not considered to be a sleep disturbance, it can interrupt normal functioning and disrupt others who are sleeping near the sleep talker. Sleep talking occurs in non-REM sleep, but it is most often associated with REM sleep. It is more common in children than in adults. Sometimes the talking is monotone, and sometimes it is loud and frightens those around the person sleeping (Watson & Vaughn, 2006).

Night Terrors

Night terrors occur during stages 3 and 4 of sleep. These terrors are characterized by waking in a panic, accompanied by screams, rapid breathing, and increased heart rate. Night terrors are not usually preceded by bad dreams or nightmares, as they do not occur during REM sleep. Usually, a person does not recall the night terror the next morning, and this experience affects mostly children ages 4–12 (3–7% of them). The condition usually disappears by adolescence (Burnham, Gaylor, & Anders, 2006).

Nightmares

Nightmares are frightening dreams that occur in REM sleep. An individual can usually describe the nightmare when he or she wakes up. The best way to cope with nightmares is to use anxiety-reducing techniques. Twenty-five to seventy percent of children and about 10% of adults experience nightmares. Nightmares are most prevalent in children three to six years of age (Burnham et al., 2006).

Explore
**anxiety-reducing
techniques**
in Chapter 15, p. 490

Narcolepsy

Narcolepsy is an inappropriate attack of sleep and/or an inappropriate attack of behaviors associated with healthy/normal sleep. The onset of this disorder is when people are 15 to 25 years of age. The attack can happen while an individual is driving a car, working, taking care of his or her children, or even while he or she is in the middle of an argument. While socially embarrassing, it is more of a safety concern, as it is easy to imagine a person getting injured if he or she falls asleep while driving or while using a dangerous instrument. Sleep attacks can occur at any time, normally lasting 2–5 minutes, but they can last up to 15 minutes. Boredom or intense emotions can trigger the onset of these attacks (Hockenbury & Hockenbury, 2006).

Narcolepsy can manifest itself in the form of cataplexy or **muscular paralysis** (loss of muscle tone), which can make one fall down on the floor while still awake. This loss of muscle tone is typical for REM sleep. During the attack of cataplexy the person is usually awake with eyelids open. People usually remember what is said and done around them. Cataplexy usually attacks at times of emotional excitement, so if emotions are under control, the attack might be prevented. Narcolepsy can also manifest itself as an attack of **sleep paralysis** (normal aspect of sleep), when this paralysis shouldn't happen. Specifically, when a person wakes up, he or she is still in a state of paralysis. Sleep paralysis is usually brief but can last up to 20 minutes. The paralyzed person can be stimulated to exit sleep paralysis by someone calling his or her name or by touch. This inappropriate sleep paralysis can be accompanied by hallucinations (visual, auditory, etc.) when a person is about to fall asleep or right after waking up. The person is aware of these hallucinations and of reality mixing with imagination. It is likely that these hallucinations are leftovers from one's dreaming mode. These hallucinations can also occur with cataplexy (Kolb & Whishaw, 2003).

Research has suggested that a lack of a sufficient amount of the neurotransmitter orexin is the reason for narcolepsy. Drugs that would increase orexin amounts are being developed. Drugs like pemoline (Cylert) and methylpenidate (Ritalin) are currently used to increase wakefulness (Kalat, 2003; Plotnik, 2002).

REM Behavior Disorder

While most people are inactive during REM sleep, experiencing muscular paralysis, some people are very active while they sleep. In fact, some are so active that they injure themselves and sometimes even the person they sleep next to. It seems that these people (most of them are 65 years of age and above) act out their dreams during their REM sleep; thus, this condition is called **REM behavior disorder**. When these people wake up, they don't remember their movements, but they do remember their dreams. Research in which the brain stems of cats were damaged showed that the cats chased imaginary mice while they slept (they were acting out their dreams). These studies indicate that there might be some abnormality in the brain stems of people with REM behavior disorder. Benzodiazepines, drugs that stimulate the GABA neurotransmitter and have a calming effect on the brain, are usually used to treat this condition.

Insomnia

Insomnia is the inability to fall asleep or stay asleep, and it refers to an inadequate amount of sleep. There are several simple, inexpensive methods for falling asleep. Avoid caffeine before bed; try a glass of milk instead. Milk seems to be an excellent sleep aid because it contains tryptophan. Oftentimes people try to artificially bring on sleep with sleeping pills or alcohol. Avoid these, as they can aggravate the problem. Sleeping pills and alcohol reduce our amount of REM sleep and make us feel lethargic and "out of it" the next day. It has also been demonstrated that exercise aids in regular sleep, as does relaxing before bed. Engaging in moderate evening exercise at least an hour before sleep can help people fall asleep more easily (Hockenbury & Hockenbury, 2006).

Sleep Apnea

Sleep apnea is a sleep disorder in which a person stops breathing while sleeping. It normally affects overweight men, and it is estimated that 1 in 20 men suffers from this disorder. Imagine how terrifying it would be to wake up gasping for breath. Now imagine that this happens all throughout the night, with as many as 400 awakenings each night. While this disorder is said to "normally" affect overweight men, women who sleep in the same room as these men report interrupted sleep, fear that their husband is going to die, and suffer anxiety over their husband's disorder. People who suffer from sleep apnea are prone to the same problems as people who don't get enough sleep: they have an increased chance of accidents, they feel tired, and they are irritable the next day. Causes of sleep apnea include a genetic predisposition, nonfunctional brain processes that are involved in breathing, and a compressed windpipe. Treatment usually consists of three different approaches that may be used separately or in combination. The first approach involves the patient losing weight, as extra weight presses on the air passages. The second involves the patient wearing a mask while sleeping that provides steady air inflow. The mask allows fresh air to pass into the airways and prevents sleep apnea from occurring. The third is a form of surgery that reduces the size of the tissue blocking the throat, and in some cases the airways are widened (Hockenbury & Hockenbury, 2006).

Dreams

The seemingly bizarre, loosely connected, surreal elements of dreams have often made people believe that there is, in fact, some hidden, deeper message. There is no consensus, however, about what dreams mean, and some researchers believe that dreams do not mean anything.

There are many views among those who believe in the meaning of dreams. The ancient Greeks, for example, thought that dreams contained messages about healing illnesses. They would travel to the famous island of Kas to reach a temple of Aesclepios—the god of healing. In this temple, sick people, upon falling asleep, would have sacred dreams in which they would see Aesclepios, who would diagnose their illness and educate them about a cure.

Alexander the Great, another famous Greek, also believed in the deeper meaning of dreams. He had a dream while trying to conquer the city of Tyros. In his dream, Satyros (a mythological creature) danced on his shield. Whenever Alexander tried to catch the creature, it escaped his grasp. When he finally caught the creature, he woke up. A dream interpreter explained that the dancing Satyros was not what it appeared to be. The word "Satyros" is composed of two words "tyros" and "sa," meaning "Tyros will become yours." Shortly after, Alexander conquered the city of Tyros, convinced that his dream was telling him that by being persistent, he would win.

Famous psychiatrist Sigmund Freud (1900/1913) published a book entitled *The Interpretation of Dreams,* which discusses the importance of the contents of our dreams. Freud reported that we have **manifest** and **latent content** in our dreams. Manifest content is the actual plot of our dreams, while latent content refers to the unconscious desires that our dreams symbolize. In other words, Freud believed there was a hidden message in our dreams that is often camouflaged in symbols; this theory is called the **Freudian dream theory**. Symbols need to be decoded so that one can arrive at the true meaning of a dream. Freud thought that most of our adult dreams could be traced back to sexual desires even though there were no sexual images in our dreams. For example, smoking a cigarette would suggest to Freud a desire for oral sex.

Consider a dream that Freud began having as a child. His mother is lying on a bed. Next to her are strange creatures resembling people with bird beaks. These creatures lower their beaks, touching the woman's stomach. In Freud's opinion, this dream is not about some strange creatures and his mother; instead, the dream symbolizes his own sexual desire for his mother, since the word "birds" in German is used not only to refer to birds but also to suggest having sex. According to Freud, our dreams use symbolism to hide impulses that we don't want to be associated with, yet we are still able to express those impulses within our dreams.

Some psychologists have a completely different view of dreams. According to these scientists, dreams are meaningless. This theory is called the **random activation synthesis theory**. These researchers noticed that during our dreams, the brain stem sends random electrical impulses stimulating random areas of the cortex. These cortical areas contain our memories. When these cortical areas are stimulated, they induce our visual, auditory, touch, and other sensory experiences. These random experiences are why our dreams are full of unpredictable, disconnected events (Kolb & Whishaw, 2006).

Other theorists suggest that dreams contain our ongoing problems and recent events. This theory is called the **extension of waking life theory**. Colors and emotions in dreams are often related to our experience during the waking period. Sixty four percent of dreams contain feelings of sadness, anger, and anxiety, and about 18% contain positive emotions. An individual is twice as likely to dream about an event in which he or she is threatened than a nonhostile event. Only about 1% of our dreams have sexual content. Most often we dream about enemies (people and animals), and some researchers believe that this dominance of negative content in our dreams (threats, pursuit, our negative emotions) is beneficial for us during wakefulness—dreams teach us to get used to and be prepared for dangers when we are awake, the dangers of the "real world" (Revensuo, 2000).

Hypnosis

We have seen "hypnotists" portrayed on television and in the movies. Perhaps they will swing a pocket watch in front of the "victim's" face and tell him or her, "You are getting sleepy." And the next thing we know, the "hypnotized" person is on stage in his or her underwear, quacking like a duck. In this chapter, however, we will learn about genuine hypnosis, its induction procedure, and its benefits and limitations.

Hypnosis refers to a technique used by a trained specialist to induce an altered state of consciousness called a hypnotic state. A person experiencing this state is very relaxed and highly suggestible. The word "hypnosis" comes from the Greek word "hypnos," who was the god of sleep. Hypnosis resembles sleep in that some hypnotized subjects have their eyes closed. When brain waves are monitored in a person in a hypnotic state of consciousness, the individual exhibits alpha waves, indicating a relaxed state of wakefulness.

Can Hypnosis Uncover Repressed Memories?

The recall of memories of past events has been extremely popular since the 1980s. During this time we saw an increase in people recalling past childhood sexual abuse, being abducted by aliens, or having lived a past life. It is a common misperception that people are able to accurately recall details of a crime or past events through hypnosis. When we read Chapter 8, "Memory," we will understand that such recall is almost impossible. Research points out that hypnosis is known to be unreliable in uncovering accurate memories from one's past. People may "remember" segments from their past, but these segments are often inaccurate (Bernstein, Penner, Clarke-Stewart, & Roy, 2006). Similarly, research shows that hypnosis can create false memories. For example, a hypnotist suggests to a person that he (the subject) was in Hawaii yesterday, when in reality he was in New York. After the session is over, the subject is convinced that he was in Hawaii yesterday, since "memory doesn't lie." Then he finds out that he was at work in his office in New York and that the pleasant trip to Hawaii is just a false memory. What often happens is that people construct false memories and then believe them to be accurate recollections of past events (Hockenbury & Hockenbury, 2006). One benefit of hypnosis for many patients seeking reconstruction of past events is the amount of relaxation that hypnosis produces. When people are relaxed, they may be able to reflect and recall better because of their relaxed state—as long as the hypnotist does not suggest any new information that might bias the recall of the memory.

Who Can Be Hypnotized?

Although hypnosis is sometimes associated with snake oil salesmen or quack medicine, it is a functional tool for those who believe in it and those who can be hypnotized. People who study hypnosis have found that the power of hypnosis is in the subject's willingness to suggestibility. In other words, a person who doesn't want to be hypnotized will not be hypnotized. About 15% of the population can be easily hypnotized, and about 10% are very difficult to hypnotize. People with vivid imaginations are good subjects for hypnosis. These people report having wonderful fantasy lives; that is, they are easily absorbed into the drama of a movie or book. Good subjects are also those who are open to cooperation, can better sustain attention, and have positive expectations of hypnosis. Children are more responsive to hypnosis than adults, and children as young as five can be hypnotized (Hockenbury & Hockenbury, 2006). In the Western world, individuals ages 8–12 years are the most susceptible to hypnosis, and in some non-Western societies, children's susceptibility to hypnosis does not diminish in adulthood. Gender is unrelated to susceptibility to hypnosis (Pastorino & Doyle-Portillo, 2006).

Benefits and Limitations of Hypnosis

There is some therapeutic benefit to hypnosis. After hypnosis, *some* people report that they have successfully changed their unwanted behavior. Hypnosis is proving to be a popular method for individuals wishing to combat overeating, nail biting, alcoholism, gambling, or smoking. Research shows that hypnosis is more successful than no treatment at all, but this is not to say that hypnosis can completely eliminate these behaviors (Pastorino & Doyle-Portillo, 2006). With hypnosis as the only therapy, the reduction of these behaviors is usually short-lived, especially for smoking (Hockenbury & Hockenbury, 2006). Studies show that hypnosis is as successful in reducing these behaviors as some other therapies (Pastorino & Doyle-Portillo, 2006). Research also shows that hypnosis coupled with cognitive behavior therapy is effective, specifically for weight loss (Hockenbury &Hockenbury, 2006). Other researchers reported that clients who participated in psychotherapy in addition to hypnosis reduced unwanted behaviors by as much as 70% (Kirsch, 1996; Kirsch & Lynn, 1998).

Hypnosis can be effective in blocking or reducing pain due to dental work, burns, abdominal surgery, childbirth, arthritis, and migraine headaches (Pastorino & Doyle-Portillo, 2006). Hypnosis can reduce nausea and vomiting due to chemotherapy, and it can help reduce surgical bleeding and postoperative recovery time (Bernstein et al., 2006). Many people who suffer from stress-related skin disorders, headaches, and asthma have found relief from **posthypnotic suggestion**, in which they received a suggestion during hypnosis that they were able to use after they were no longer hypnotized.

How Is the Hypnotic State Induced?

Franz Mesmer (1734–1815) was a physician from Vienna who was a very controversial individual. Although he was disliked by his colleagues for using nontraditional methods of treatment, he was loved by the public, since his unusual treatments sometimes worked. While other physicians of the time treated people by bloodletting, Mesmer used hypnosis. He didn't call his method "hypnosis" (this term shows up later, in 1842), but instead called it **mesmerism** (Hergenhahn, 2001).

Mesmer claimed that there is a force—which he called animal magnetism—that pervades everyone and everything. According to Mesmer, a person becomes physically or mentally ill from an imbalance in animal magnetism. He also believed that he knew the secrets of the force and could therefore restore its balance. He suggested to his patients that they would feel the force harmoniously flowing through their bodies and that they would feel better. His patients were suggestible, and thus they truly felt that if he told them they would feel better, then they would.

A typical session went something like this: He would talk to his patients, showing empathy for their problems and establishing their trust. Making sure that his patients were relaxed, he would then arrange them in a circle and ask them to hold magnetized rods (picture a rod with one end held by one person and the other end held by another person). Mesmer would then tell people to focus their attention on the rods. He would make suggestions such as, "Soon you will feel a powerful force passing through you. . . . It will completely overwhelm you and penetrate you." Suggestible people would begin to feel exactly what he was suggesting.

"The magnets will cure you. . . . You will feel your illness going away. . . . You are feeling much better now." Oftentimes people would feel better after a session with Mesmer, but those who didn't were probably not open to suggestion.

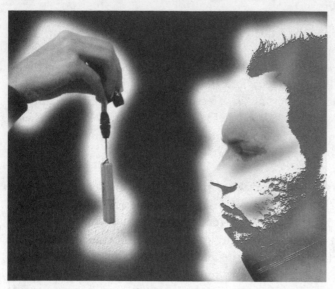

FIGURE 5.7 *Hypnotic induction.*

Mesmer used steps that are commonly used today in inducing the hypnotic state of mind. For an individual to be hypnotized, the following aspects need to happen:

♦ The participant should trust the hypnotist.

♦ The participant should be relaxed, which increases the likelihood of being open to suggestion.

♦ There should be a point of focus. It can be any sort of object or even the hypnotist's voice. This point of focus directs attention to the hypnotist and reduces other distractions in the environment competing for one's attention.

♦ The hypnotist suggests changes the participant will experience.

♦ The participant experiences the proposed changes.

Is There Really a Hypnotic State of Consciousness?

Some studies indicate that hypnosis is just role playing (Pastorino & Doyle-Portillo, 2006). Other studies, however, show that hypnosis doesn't entail this role playing. In fact, one can raise a skin blister when touched by something cool during hypnosis, if this individual believes that the cool object is a smoking cigarette. It doesn't seem that people can raise a blister if touched by something cool during regular wakefulness. Thus, it appears that some element of an altered state is involved in hypnosis. The "hypnotic state of mind" might really be a different mental state of heightened concentration, relaxation, and suggestibility (Flemons, 2005).

Meditation

Meditation is the age-old art of relaxation and altering consciousness. Oftentimes we will see a person meditating while seated on the floor, legs crossed, and palms upstretched and relaxed on the knees. Individuals may chant or repeat monosyllabic words such as "ooomm." Many people practice meditation as part of a daily prayer ritual (Longer, 1989).

The term "meditation" comes from the Latin word *meditatio,* meaning "contemplation." It also means physical and intellectual exercise. Meditation refers to a technique that can alter one's state of consciousness, and the resulting state of mind is characterized by the following experiences:

♦ Sense of timelessness

♦ Sense of inner peace and relaxation

♦ Awareness of the connection between an individual and the universe

♦ Heightened awareness of one's environment

♦ Increased attention

♦ Reduction in pain (Bernstein et al., 2006)

FIGURE 5.8 *Meditation is part of various religions. Photo by Debbie Whittaker.*

FIGURE 5.9 *Meditation produces a state of relaxation.*

Meditation is part of religions such as Taoism, Buddhism, Christianity, Hinduism, Islam, and Judaism. However, many people meditate for nonreligious reasons. A common method for inducing a meditative state of mind is to concentrate on one thing or one sound (one's breathing, for example), or a word or phase (a mantra) until one stops thinking about everything else and reaches pure awareness. By doing this, the practitioner allows distracting thoughts to fall away without actively trying to suppress them. The result of reaching pure awareness is that one becomes more fully aware of the present moment rather than being caught up in the past or future. This type of meditation is called concentrative meditation (Bernstein et al., 2006). Another method of meditating is called opening-up meditation or mindfulness meditation. Here, one does not focus on anything in particular; instead, one is aware of the present moment. This quiet type of meditation does not involve mental uttering of mantras.

Effects of Meditation

Research shows that meditation is often successful in reducing insomnia, anxiety, high blood pressure, headache, and back pain. In addition, evidence points out that meditation can increase one's social openness, self esteem, and attention. Most often a person learns meditation in an effort to reduce stress, to relax, and to ease pain.

Through various methods of visualizing physiological processes within the human body, we can see that during meditation an individual has decreased activity (blood flow) in the parietal lobe. This can explain the person's altered sense of time (sense of timelessness) and space (sense of connectedness with everyone and everything), since the parietal lobe is associated with our ability to do spatial and temporal tasks (Flemons, 2005). Studies show that the meditating person also has reduced breathing, reduced heart rate, reduced muscle tension, reduced blood pressure, and reduced oxygen consumption—processes that are associated with a reduction in anxiety and an increase in relaxation. Further, meditation increases blood flow to one's thalamus and frontal lobe, brain regions associated with attention. There is also an increase of dopamine production in the brain, which has been linked with the experience of pleasure. Brain waves during meditation are clearly alpha waves, indicating a state of relaxation (Bernstein et al., 2006).

Drugs and Consciousness

Psychoactive Drugs

Drugs affecting the mind and behavior are called **psychoactive drugs**. Aspects of the mind that are particularly affected are mood, sensations, perceptions, thinking, and consciousness. When a person's drug use occupies a very important role in his or her life, the individual is said to suffer from substance abuse. Drug addiction, however, is the next level of substance abuse; it is when a person who is abusing a substance develops drug dependence and drug tolerance. We will examine drug dependence and drug tolerance more closely.

Drug Dependence

One's extreme reliance on a drug is called **drug dependence**, and this dependence has different forms. **Physical dependence** is a condition in which one's body needs the drug to function; when the drug is not available, the person develops **withdrawal** symptoms. These symptoms include vomiting, shaking, diarrhea, sweating, physical pain, headaches, cramps, anxiety, convulsions, hallucinations, and even death. Withdrawal symptoms start several hours after the last use of the drug and can last for days until they subside (Franz & Koob, 2005).

Psychological dependence is somewhat different; it refers to needing a drug to function cognitively and emotionally. Psychological dependence can happen in the absence of physical dependence (no withdrawal symptoms), but even psychological dependence reflects drug addiction.

Drug Tolerance

Drug **tolerance** occurs when a person needs a greater amount of drug with every subsequent use. There are three types of tolerance: metabolic, cellular, and learned.

Metabolic tolerance occurs when certain enzymes break down the drug; thus the drug is absorbed by the body much more quickly than when a person has not developed drug tolerance. Cellular tolerance is different; here, brain cells adjust to the effects of the drug so that the behavioral signs of intoxication are low or not visible, despite a high blood level of the drug. Learned tolerance is when a person learns to cope with intoxication and no longer appears to be drunk (Pastorino & Doyle-Portillo, 2006; Kolb & Whishaw, 2006).

How Does Addiction Develop?

The following aspects are usually involved in the development of an addiction:

♦ The drug produces pleasure by stimulating the activity of dopamine in the brain.

♦ With repeated drug use, the brain cells react to the high dopamine levels by reducing their dopamine receptors. When there are fewer receptors, the amount of dopamine that can bind is decreased. Due to this decrease in dopamine system activity, pleasurable experience is reduced. More drug is now needed to produce the same effect as before (tolerance).

♦ Activities that were normally pleasurable are no longer pleasurable, since the experiences of pleasure are supported by dopamine activity, which is now diminished. Negative feelings become dominant.

♦ One now needs drugs to cope with these negative feelings.

♦ The desire for the drug is highest when one is experiencing drug-induced pleasure.

♦ This pleasure becomes associated with even the sight of the drug and the procedure of drug use; thus every subsequent sight and use of the drug reinforces the pleasurable image of the drug.

♦ One starts to collect objects that are reminiscent of the drug (e.g., pipe collecting by pipe smokers).

♦ One forms a habit of using the drug even though it is no longer pleasurable, but one still does it because it has become his or her lifestyle.

♦ The desire for the drug is less high when one goes through withdrawal symptoms. (Hockenbury & Hockenbury, 2006)

Types of Drugs

Depressants or Sedative-Hypnotic Drugs

Alcohol, barbiturates, and tranquilizers are named **depressants** since they depress the activity of the nervous system. They are also called "sedative" drugs because in low doses they have a calming effect on an individual, and they are termed "hypnotics" because in high doses they induce sleep. What these drugs have in common is that they increase the availability of GABA neurotransmitters, which reduces neuronal activity. This can create the effect of drowsiness and relaxation.

Alcohol and the Nervous System

Alcohol acts on GABA, dopamine, serotonin, endorphins, and glutamate neurotransmitters (Bernstein et al., 2006). Drugs such as naloxone and naltrexon, which block endorphins, are good at reducing alcohol cravings and decreasing the relapse rate of recovering alcoholics. Alcohol increases dopamine activity in nucleus accumbens, so dopamine agonists (drugs that mimic dopamine activity) reduce alcohol cravings and withdrawal effects. It stimulates GABA receptors, inducing inhibitory effects in the brain (Julien, 2003). Additionally, it acts on the endorphin system, increasing the effects of endorphins; this might be the reason for the "high" that people experience when they drink alcohol. Further, alcohol inhibits the hippocampus, impairing the formation of new memories and inhibiting the normal functioning of the cerebellum. Alcohol influences poor coordination and inhibits and depresses the activities of the hindbrain. In high doses, alcohol can be fatal (Bernstein et al., 2006).

Alcohol increases serotonin production, and selective serotonin reuptake inhibitor (SSRI) medications, which increase serotonin amounts, can reduce alcohol cravings (Julien, 2003). This may be due to an increase in positive mood, which decreases the desire to drink. Alcohol inhibits the activity of glutamate receptors (located on the glutamate-releasing neurons), so chronic users experience glutamate receptor proliferation, meaning that when the receptors are blocked, the cell reacts by growing more of them. With this increased amount of receptors, more neurotransmitters can bind and cause seizures (Julien, 2003). Because it lowers anxiety levels, alcohol is used by many people to self-medicate.

Effects of the Amount of Alcohol.   The amount of alcohol consumed can be measured by looking at how many grams of alcohol are present in 100 milliliters (mL) of the consumer's blood (Hockenbury & Hockenbury, 2006). One to three drinks per day seems to be positive for human health in reducing the risk of cardiovascular and cerebrovascular disease (disease affecting the blood vessels of the brain). Alcohol stimulates the production of the T-P enzyme, which breaks down clots and raises HDL cholesterol levels, keeping arteries free of buildup. One drink is defined as 1 ounce of whiskey, 4 ounces of wine, or 12 ounces of beer (Hockenbury & Hockenbury, 2006).

Excessive consumption of alcohol is also linked to liver damage, pancreatitis, peptic ulcers, and cancers of the oral cavity, stomach, and intestines. Another possible effect of chronic alcohol use is **Korsakoff's syndrome**. This condition is characterized by memory problems and dementia (Hockenbury & Hockenbury, 2006). Some other devastating effects of alcohol are evident in **fetal alcohol syndrome (FAS)**. FAS is a condition affecting the central nervous system of fetuses prenatally when they are exposed to alcohol through the mother's blood. Characteristics of FAS are lower intelligence, hyperactivity, difficulties in social interactions, slower growth, facial abnormalities, and a malformed heart and ears (Grilly, 2002).

Barbiturates

Barbiturates (Seconal, Nembutal) are known to reduce anxiety, promote sleep (very deep, with reduced REM stage), increase sedation, and promote euphoria. They also depress breathing centers in the brain as well as centers for wakefulness and arousal. In low doses, barbiturates promote relaxation, mild euphoria, and reduce inhibitions, and in large doses they induce loss of coordination, impair cognition, and induce depression, coma, and even death (Hockenbury & Hockenbury, 2006).

The effect of barbiturates becomes apparent in about 30 minutes. Barbiturates enhance GABA activity by keeping the GABA receptor stimulated longer than normal (Grilly, 2002). Barbiturates also increase dopamine activity and induce tolerance by induction of drug-metabolizing enzymes in the liver and adaptation of neurons to drug presence (Julien, 2003). These drugs produce physical and psychological dependence. Their withdrawal symptoms are irritability and nightmares when a person uses low doses; with higher doses, the withdrawal symptoms are hallucinations, disorientation, restlessness, and convulsions (Hockenbury & Hockenbury, 2006).

Tranquilizers

Tranquilizers (Xanax, Valium) are less powerful than barbiturates but have similar effects. Effects include increased muscle relaxation, increased sedation, reduced anxiety, and reduced likelihood of a seizure. These drugs stimulate GABA activity, especially in the limbic system. Tranquilizers are linked to a low incidence of psychological and physical dependence, but in some cases they can be addictive. Withdrawal symptoms consist of a return of anxiety, insomnia, restlessness, irritability, unpleasant dreams, hallucinations, and seizures. Symptoms subside after one to four weeks (Julien, 2003).

Stimulants

Stimulants (amphetamines, cocaine) speed up the nervous system activity. They also elevate mood, increase feelings of well-being, and increase alertness and energy. Stimulants often produce a feeling of euphoria in users by stimulating dopamine and increasing neurotransmitter activity within the brain.

Amphetamines.

Amphetamines (methamphetamine) reduce GABA activity in the brain. They also increase the release of norepinephrine and dopamine, and decrease the breakdown of these neurotransmitters, making them more abundant in the synapse. Typical effects of amphetamines are alertness, arousal, appetite suppression, reduced fatigue, euphoria, increased memory for verbal material, and increased attention and reaction time. When the effects wear off, the user crashes, usually suffering from low energy levels, paranoia, and depression. Overdose can lead to coma and death (Pastorino & Doyle-Portillo, 2006). Methamphetamine is the most popular form of amphetamines used today. It is more powerful, more addicting, and more harmful to the central nervous system than the amphetamines of the 1960s and 1970s. On the street, methamphetamine is referred to as "ice," "crystal meth," or "crank."

Amphetamines act on the central nervous system and on the sympathetic branch of the peripheral nervous system. By constricting blood vessels, they raise blood pressure and heart rate. These drugs induce pleasurable sensations due to their activation of the dopamine system by blocking the reuptake of the neurotransmitters and simultaneously releasing dopamine.

Continued use of amphetamines usually leads to anxiety, insomnia, heart problems, brain damage, movement disorder, confusion, paranoia, and uncontrollable speech. Psychological and physical dependence can develop. Withdrawal symptoms are fatigue, increase in appetite, deep sleep, depression, and cognitive impairment (Bernstein et al., 2006).

Studies document about a 10% tissue loss in the brain areas of reward and emotion. There also continues to be a loss of dopamine receptors for several months after the last use. Tissue loss has also been observed in the hippocampus, and it has been linked with poor performance on memory tasks (Hockenbury & Hockenbury, 2006).

Cocaine.

Cocaine is derived from the leaves of the South American coca tree. (This plant shouldn't be confused with the cacao plant, whose beans are a source of cocoa and chocolate.) Cocaine decreases GABA activity and acts on the serotonin, norepinephrine, and dopamine systems, increasing their activity (Bernstein et al., 2006). Specifically, cocaine blocks the reuptake of these neurotransmitters, increasing their availability and effects on the receptors. Users of cocaine display increased self-confidence, a sense of well-being, and optimism (Julien, 2003).

The effects of cocaine—decreased appetite and increased heart rate and blood pressure—last 10–30 minutes, but repeated use is common. After the effects wear off, the person crashes into a depressed mood and has decreased energy levels (Pastorino & Doyle-Portillo, 2006). Continued use of cocaine leads to nausea,

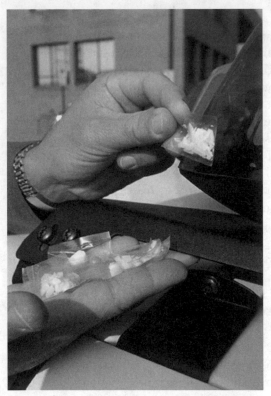

FIGURE 5.10 *Cocaine in street form—ready for sale. Courtesy of Larry Mulvehill/Image Works.*

insomnia, paranoia, depression, sexual dysfunctions, seizures, and hallucinations. An overdose can result in a fatal heart attack or stroke (Bernstein et al., 2006).

Prolonged use also includes respiratory and heart problems, spontaneous abortions, and miscarriages. Babies born to mothers who are cocaine addicts are also addicted to cocaine, as evidenced in these babies' displays of withdrawal symptoms similar to those of adults. As these babies grow up, they will be hyperactive at school and have disorganized thinking and delayed language learning (Pastorino & Doyle-Portillo, 2006). Finally, long-time users may also suffer from psychotic symptoms such as paranoid delusions and auditory hallucinations (hearing voices) (Hockenbury & Hockenbury, 2006).

Nicotine. Smoking kills more people than do AIDS, alcohol, motor vehicle accidents, drug overdoses, murders, and suicides *combined* (Pastorino & Doyle-Portillo, 2006). **Nicotine** activates acetylcholine receptors in the brain, elevates dopamine levels (Pastorino & Doyle-Portillo, 2006), and enhances glutamate activity (Bernstein et al., 2006). After providing a stimulating effect, nicotine blocks the same areas and provides a calming effect (Plotnik, 2002).

In low doses, nicotine increases attention, elevates mood, and improves memory, but in high doses it induces vomiting, diarrhea, sweating, and dizziness. Three out of four smokers attempt to quit smoking—2 out of 10 succeed. People make four to five attempts at quitting before they succeed (Pastorino & Doyle-Portillo, 2006). Nicotine has been linked to physical and psychological dependence. Withdrawal symptoms are cravings, anxiety, irritability, lowered heart rate, and weight gain (Bernstein et al., 2006).

Nicotine is linked to lung cancer, throat cancer, emphysema, and heart disease. Smoking during pregnancy may result in babies who are irritable, have respiratory problems, and have a lower birth weight (Hockenbury & Hockenbury, 2006).

Caffeine. Even a single cup of coffee has an effect on the brain, by stimulating the cortex. Caffeine increases mental alertness and wakefulness. Found in coffee, tea, and chocolate, caffeine has been found to be beneficial when taken in moderation. Antioxidants within these products have been found to help improve our cardiovascular function. Withdrawal symptoms are headaches, irritability, drowsiness, and fatigue. Symptoms may last for a week or more (Hockenbury & Hockenbury, 2006).

Caffeine blocks adenosine, which is known to slow down brain activity and induce sleepiness. In small doses, caffeine enhances problem solving and decreases reaction time. In high doses, caffeine induces insomnia, upset stomach, racing heartbeat, nervousness, and irritability. Excessive use can lead to high blood pressure and the development of fibroid cysts in female breasts. Pregnant women are advised not to use caffeine, as it has been linked to miscarriage and birth defects (Pastorino & Doyle-Portillo, 2006).

Opiates/Narcotics

Opiates (morphine, heroin, opium) are sleep-inducing and pain-relieving drugs. The drug opium is extracted from the poppy plant. Its active ingredient is morphine, which is often used for pain relief. Heroin is derived from morphine, and it is three times more powerful than morphine. These drugs stimulate the activity of glutamate. Opiates occupy endorphin receptors, mimicking endorphin activity. Opiates alter the brain's sensitivity to pain; they don't block pain locally (on the skin). When injected into the vein, heroin reaches the brain in seconds. The effects are a rush of euphoria, contentment, peacefulness, and warmth. Withdrawal symptoms are fever, chills, cramps, and gastrointestinal problems (Hockenbury & Hockenbury, 2006).

The effect of opiates is pleasure (e.g., floating on a cloud). When an individual takes opiates, the brain detects numerous endorphins and reduces their production. When the effects of opiates wear off, the user feels pain and an absence of pleasure. Tolerance can develop, and physical tolerance can develop within a few weeks. Withdrawal symptoms are hot and cold flashes, cramps, sweating, and shaking. These symptoms last four to seven days but are not life threatening. Overdose, however, is life threatening. The exact amount that leads to an overdose is difficult to predict, since bodily sensitivity to opiates fluctuates (Pastorino & Doyle-Portillo, 2006).

Psychedelic Drugs

The term "psychedelic" means "mind-manifesting" (affecting the mind). **Psychedelic drugs** produce perceptual distortions, alter mood, and affect thinking (Hockenbury & Hockenbury, 2006). These drugs are also called psychotomimetics, since they are known to mimic psychosis in some cases. The effects of psychedelics are distortions of body image (one may feel gigantic or tiny), loss of identity (confusion about who one really is), and dreamlike fantasies and hallucinations. Lysergic acid diethylamide (LSD) is a psychedelic drug that was synthesized from rye fungus in the 1930s. The effects of LSD are time distortion, sounds that cause visual sensations, and out-of-body experiences. LSD stimulates serotonin receptors in the brain, as LSD's chemical structure is very similar to serotonin. LSD is not addictive, but tolerance can develop. LSD's adverse effects are severe short-term memory loss, depression, paranoia, violent outbursts, nightmares, panic attacks, distortions in visual sensations (can remain for years after heavy use has ended), and flashbacks (in which a person returns to an LSD state of mind weeks or years after the drug use has stopped) (Bernstein et al., 2006). LSD is not associated with physical withdrawal symptoms (Hockenbury & Hockenbury, 2006).

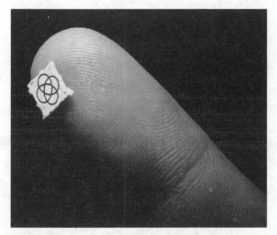

FIGURE 5.11 *LSD—a hallucinogenic drug. Courtesy of Custom Medical Stock Photo.*

MDMA/Ecstasy

Methylenedioxymethamphetamine (MDMA) is a synthetic drug similar to the stimulant methamphetamine and the hallucinogen mescaline. Street names for MDMA include **ecstasy**, XTC, hug, beans, and love drug. Ecstasy provides enhanced mood and energy levels, and a heightened sensory experience. Effects start 30 minutes after taking it, and last 3 to 6 hours. It can also induce depression, drug cravings, teeth clenching, insomnia, nausea, overeating, cardiac complications, kidney failure, stroke, seizures, and psychoses (Pastorino & Doyle-Portillo, 2006).

Ecstasy enhances the activity of the dopamine, norepinephrine, and serotonin systems. It has also been shown to damage serotonin and dopamine neurons (Pastorino & Doyle-Portillo, 2006). Ecstasy overstimulates serotonin release and blocks its reuptake (Hockenbury & Hockenbury, 2006). It has also been shown to kill neurons carrying the dopamine neurotransmitter, by overstimulating the release of dopamine in the axons (Bernstein et al., 2006).

The effects of ecstasy include a closeness to others, a release from one's inhibitions, and jaw muscle spasms (lockjaw) (Bernstein et al., 2006). The day after using ecstasy, the user likely experiences poor concentration, fatigue, and muscle aches. Continued use leads to increasingly more negative effects. Ecstasy impairs memory even after discontinuing use, and people may develop panic disorders (Bernstein et al., 2006).

Other effects of ecstasy are dehydration, rapid heartbeat, tremor, and hyperthermia (abnormally high body temperature). There is a risk of death due to hyperthermia and dehydration. Some studies show that memory and reasoning problems lasted for a year after the users stopped using ecstasy (Hockenbury & Hockenbury, 2006). Chronic use of this drug is associated with damage to the serotonin neurons in the brain. After long-term use, serotonin levels are severely depleted, resulting in depression. Chronic use is also associated with anhedonia—an inability to experience pleasure due to a loss of dopamine neurons (Biello & Dafters, 2001).

Marijuana

Marijuana is extracted from the Cannabis sativa plant. Its leaves, seeds, and flowers are dried and crushed. The mixture of these is marijuana. The active ingredient in marijuana is tetrahydrocannabinol (THC), which reaches the brain in 30 seconds. Hashish is made from Cannabis sativa's rosi. There is a brain chemical called anandimide, which reduces painful sensations, and it is involved in mood and memory. THC binds to anandimide receptors, as THC and anandimide are structurally similar. In low doses it induces a sense of well-being, mild euphoria, relaxation, more focused senses, more vivid sensations (taste, touch, and smell are more enhanced), and an altered perception of time.

In high doses, marijuana induces sensory distortions resembling mild psychedelic experiences. High doses of THC do not interfere with breathing and heartbeat, since there are very few THC receptors in the brain stem (depressants and opiates do affect breathing and heart rate since they bind to many receptors of the brain stem). Marijuana is not linked to tolerance or to physical or psychological dependence.

Chronic users of extremely high doses, however, can develop some tolerance and withdrawal symptoms, such as irritability, restlessness, insomnia, tremors, and decreased appetite. Marijuana is helpful in the treatment of pain, epilepsy,

FIGURE 5.12 *Marijuana cigarettes. Courtesy of Gary Hansen/PhototakeUSA.com.*

hypertension, nausea, glaucoma, and asthma; in cancer patients it prevents the nausea and vomiting that result from chemotherapy. Marijuana interferes with muscle coordination and with learning, memory, and cognitive function (Hockenbury & Hockenbury, 2006).

It is difficult to classify marijuana since it has the effects of several drug types. It has the effects of a depressant (drowsiness and lethargy) and a narcotic (it's a weak painkiller). In low doses it creates a mild euphoria (as with stimulants); in moderate doses it intensifies sensory experience and induces distortions of time (as with psychedelics); and in high doses it induces hallucinations, delusions, and distortions of body image (also as with psychedelics).

PCP/Angel Dust

In low doses **phencyclidine** (PCP) is like a stimulant—it increases blood pressure, heart rate, and breathing. In moderate doses, it numbs limbs and induces out-of-body experiences and sensations of walking on spongy surfaces, as with psychedelics. In high doses, PCP is like a depressant—it decreases blood pressure, pulse, and respiration. PCP users experience nausea, vomiting, blurred vision, dizziness, hallucinations, paranoia, garbled speech, disoriented thinking, violence, suicidal behavior, seizure, coma, and even death (Pastorino & Doyle-Portillo, 2006).

Chapter Summary

In this chapter, we examined various states of consciousness. We began by looking at the sleep-wake cycle, called the circadian rhythm. Scientists have determined that even in the absence of light, our bodies follow a cyclical pattern of sleeping and waking that lasts approximately 24 hours. Various brain centers and chemicals are involved in triggering wakefulness and sleepiness. The suprachiasmatic nucleus is a cluster of neurons in the hypothalamus that trigger wakefulness. An important trigger for sleepiness is the release of the hormone melatonin.

During sleep, our brains cycle through five distinct stages. In presleep, the brain produces alpha waves, which create a relaxed state. In stage 1 sleep, brain-wave activity decreases even more, producing theta waves. It is easy to be awakened from this stage, and the person can experience hypnogogic hallucinations. During stage 2, the brain produces bursts of very high-frequency waves called sleep spindles and high-amplitude spikes called K-complexes. Stages 3 and 4 are called deep sleep and are characterized by delta waves. After cycling through these stages and returning to stage 1, the individual then enters the first REM stage of sleep. REM sleep is characterized by beta waves, rapid eye movement, and dreaming.

Sleep is very important to our well-being. When someone does not get the amount of sleep needed, sleep deprivation may result. REM sleep deprivation appears to affect cognitive performance on tasks and affects mood states negatively.

Non-REM sleep deprivation appears to produce physical exhaustion and decreases the ability of the immune system to fight infections.

We also discussed several sleep disorders. Sleepwalking occurs when an individual gets up and walks around while sleeping. Sleep talking is generally harmless and occurs in non-REM sleep. Night terrors occur during deep sleep and are characterized by waking in a fearful panic, while nightmares occur during dream sleep and are really just frightening dreams. Narcolepsy is a sleep disorder in which a person suddenly falls asleep during the day. REM behavior disorder causes a person to act out his or her dreams while asleep. One of the most common sleep disorders is insomnia, the inability to fall asleep or stay asleep. An individual with sleep apnea stops breathing while sleeping.

We explored many theories about what dreams represent. Early philosophers thought that dreams were insights into the spiritual realm. Freud, however, felt that dreams were sequences of symbols that represent the hidden desires and motives of the unconscious mind. The random activation synthesis theory states that during dreams, the pons sends random impulses to the brain, causing neurons to fire, and then the brain organizes them into meaningless sequences. The extension of waking life theory suggests that dreams are a continuation of events and emotions that occur while we are awake.

This chapter also covered the states of consciousness that occur during hypnosis and meditation. A person experiencing hypnosis is very relaxed and highly suggestible. Since people are highly suggestible during hypnosis, it is not very reliable in uncovering repressed memories. However, it appears to be somewhat effective as a form of therapy in changing unwanted behavior. During meditation, a person is also very relaxed, and this state of consciousness increases one's social openness, self-esteem, and attention. Meditation is also successful in reducing insomnia, anxiety, high blood pressure, headache, and back pain.

Finally, we explored the altered states of consciousness that can be experienced with various drugs. Depressants, such as alcohol, barbiturates, and tranquilizers, decrease the activity of the nervous system and tend to have a calming effect on the individual in low doses. Stimulants, such as amphetamines, cocaine, and caffeine, speed up the activity of the nervous system. They elevate mood and increase energy and feelings of well-being. Opiates, such as morphine, heroin, and opium, are sleep-inducing and pain-relieving drugs that alter the brain's sensitivity to pain and create feelings of euphoria. Psychedelic drugs, such as LSD, produce perceptual distortions, alter mood, and affect thinking. Drugs such as ecstasy, marijuana, and PCP are combinations of stimulants, hallucinogens, and/or depressants.

Knowledge Builder

RELATE TO YOURSELF

1. Determine if you are a "morning" or "evening" person. What time of day do you feel the most energized? What time of day do you go to sleep? What time of day do you wake up?

_____

_____

_____

_____

2. What would happen to your pet if you deprived it of sleep?

_____

_____

_____

3. Why do we sleep? Before you read this chapter, why did you think you sleep? Now that you've read this chapter, why do you think you sleep?

_____

_____

_____

_____

4. Explain what it means when someone says he or she has "consciousness," that he or she is a "conscious person."

_____

_____

_____

_____

CHAPTER REVIEW QUESTIONS

1. There are six stages of sleep: stages 1 through 5 and the REM stage. **T or F?**

2. Salvador Dalí utilized stage 3 of sleep for harvesting his hypnogogic images for his paintings. **T or F?**

3. An individual's daily cycles of consciousness, alertness, and sleep are referred to as the sleep cycle. **T or F?**

4. The levels of melatonin in the bloodstream rise until late into the night. **T or F?**

5. Another name for paradoxical sleep is _____.

   (a) hypnosis   (b) REM sleep

   (c) consciousness   (d) circadian rhythm

6. The _____ is a small cluster of neurons in the hypothalamus that respond to levels of sunlight.

   (a) SCN   (b) REM

   (c) RAS   (d) NREM

7. The _____ produces melatonin in response to signals from the suprachiasmatic nucleus.

   (a) thyroid gland   (b) hypothalamus

   (c) pineal gland   (d) RAS

8. *Consider the following scenario:* You work in the emergency room of a hospital, and you have just begun your shift. You have just admitted a young man who is obviously under the influence of alcohol. His family has arrived at the hospital to help him. His mother, crying and distraught, turns to you and asks for any information you can provide about the effects of alcohol. What do you say to her?

   _____

   _____

   _____

   _____

9. *Consider the following scenario:* You are a new mother, and you have been up night after night with your baby, who cries at night and sleeps during the day. Normally, you work 40+ hours each week, maintain a clean, lovely home, and are always impeccably dressed. But now, with your baby, your circadian rhythm has changed. What does this mean, and how does this change impact your life?

_____

_____

_____

_____

10. *CRITICAL THINKING EXERCISE.* Identify the similarities and differences between stage 4 of sleep and paradoxical sleep.

_____

_____

_____

_____

USEFUL WEB SITES

NATIONAL CENTER ON SLEEP DISORDERS

http://rover.nhlbi.nih.gov/about/ncsdr/

Affiliated with the National Institutes of Health, this informative site presents the latest scientific research on sleep-related disorders and difficulties.

SLEEPNET

http://www.sleepnet.com

Sleepnet is a noncommercial site with abundant information on the science of sleep and sleep hygiene.

UNIVERSITY OF ARIZONA CENTER FOR CONSCIOUSNESS STUDIES

http://www.consciousness.arizona.edu/

This site offers a variety of scientific and philosophical viewpoints and studies on the nature of consciousness.

THE ASSOCIATION FOR THE STUDY OF DREAMS

http://www.asdreams.org/

This is the main Web site of a multidisciplinary association for the study of dreams and the processes of dreaming.

NATIONAL INSTITUTE ON DRUG ABUSE

http://www.nida.nih.gov/

This is the home page of a leading governmental organization dedicated to education on all legal and illegal drugs of abuse, prevention, and treatment of substance-related disorders.

VAULTS OF EROWID

http://www.erowid.org/index.shtml

This Web site provides a great deal of information about psychoactive substances, exploring the cultural and historical aspects of substance use and abuse.

STUDENTS AGAINST DRUNK DRIVERS

http://www.sadd.org/

This Web site is packed with information for students who wish to help other students avoid driving drunk.

A note to the reader: Always be careful when researching alcohol and drugs online, and never buy medications online.

Chapter 6

Motivation and Emotion

by Marc W. Patry, PhD, and Deborah Yakel, PhD

Desire is the key to motivation, but it's determination and commitment to an unrelenting pursuit of your goal—a commitment to excellence—that will enable you to attain the success you seek.

—MARIO ANDRETTI

What Are Motivation and Emotion?

Why do we get hungry? What makes us find ways to make money? Why do some people push themselves to accomplish incredible feats such as running a marathon? Where do our emotions come from, and why do we have them? If you have ever wondered about such things, you have wondered about motivation and emotion.

Motivation refers generally to the factors that stimulate us to behave in certain ways, such as hunger and thirst, and it is the process by which we are moved to action and guided in our actions; psychologists refer to these processes as the activation and direction of behavior. In a sense, motives are some of the most basic building blocks that make up one's personality (Mayer, 2005). There are two classes of motives: biological and social.

FIGURE 6.1 *Strawberry shortcake (yum!).*

Biological motives are innate motives (motives we are born with) and are often referred to as drives. These motives are also referred to as deficiency motives because they motivate the individual to fill a physiological deficit. Usually biological motives, such as hunger, thirst, the need for sleep, and sex drive, serve to ensure survival. The biological need for sex differs slightly in that it is not necessary for an individual to satisfy it in order to survive. However, a species would soon be extinct if its members did not reproduce.

So, biological drives may be necessary for the survival of the individual or the survival of the species.

Social motives are generally **learned motives** and serve to satisfy needs that are not directly tied to bodily requirements. Social motives are often called **abundancy motives** because they encourage the individual to attain greater satisfaction and stimulation. Learned motives are often linked with biological drives. For example, the motivation to achieve social status is often viewed as a derivative of the sex drive. Social motives are generally not considered innate motives, because they vary considerably between individuals and cultures. However, some psychologists argue that there are innate social motives, in spite of the variance among individuals. They suggest that these are universal motives and that we just vary in the degree to which they serve to motivate our behavior. For example, affiliation, achievement, and power motivate all individuals, and so they are commonly believed to be universal and innate. The manner and frequency of expression of these motives, however, will vary between individuals and will be determined by a person's past experiences, culture, and immediate social context. For example, someone with a strong power motive may seek power and wealth in order to dominate others, whereas another person with a strong power motive may seek to satisfy their needs by taking leadership roles that allow them to aid and support others. Our ability to satisfy our motives in a variety of ways is not surprising, given human adaptability and flexibility. While this may aid in our survival, it makes it more difficult to determine which of our motives are innate and universal (O'Neil, 1994).

Emotions, or feelings, are another very basic cause of human behavior. Happiness, sadness, fear, excitement, dread, and disgust are just a few of the many examples. In many ways, our feelings and motives are intertwined. For example, think about the last time you missed a meal. Did you get angry or have any other intense feelings? What kinds of emotions come into play when you are working toward accomplishing a goal, such as a high mark on your psychology exam? Since motivation and emotion are so closely related, psychologists often consider them together as interrelated causes of human behavior. In this chapter, we will explore the major theories and research findings in the areas of motivation and emotion.

Theories of Motivation

There are several major theories of motivation. In this chapter, we will focus on four major perspectives on what motivates human behavior: the evolutionary and instinct theory, the incentive and cognitive theory, the arousal theory, and the drive-reduction theory. We will also explore implicit and self-attributed motivation, goal setting, sensation-seeking motivation, achievement motivation, connectedness motivation, and power motivation.

Evolutionary and Instinct Theories of Motivation

According to Charles Darwin (1874), human beings have developed in such a way that makes us likely to survive and reproduce. From an evolutionary perspective, survival and reproduction are key motives for behavior: We are

FIGURE 6.2 *The family members in this picture help one another.*

motivated to behave in ways that will keep us alive and help us pass on our genes. Behaviors such as aggression against competitors and help offered to family members serve the general evolutionary motives of survival and reproduction.

From an evolutionary perspective, we are motivated to help our family members so that our genes will survive. Kin selection is a recent iteration of evolutionary psychology, which extends Herbert Spencer's (1882) original "survival of the fittest" idea. **Kin selection** holds that, even if we individuals do not survive, we seek to perpetuate our genetic material through those who are closely related to us. Basically, this perspective asserts that we are evolutionarily programmed to seek continuation of our genetic material through our own survival or the survival of those closely related to us, since they share much of the same genetic material. So, by helping family members, we increase the likelihood of their survival and therefore the survival of our shared genetic material. Research findings show support for kin selection. Data show that we are more likely to help those who are genetically related to us. We can recognize kin from an early age, and new mothers can detect their children by sight and smell. We are also more likely to help others who are similar to us, which is arguably an indicator of genetic relatedness (Fiske, 2004).

Some of our behaviors are involuntary, genetically programmed reflexive responses known as **instincts**. William James was the first psychologist to formulate a theory of motivation based on instincts (Reeve, 1997), a theory that was based on Charles Darwin's theory of evolution. James's theory cataloged 17 human instincts, which included imitation, fear, parental love, cleanliness, and curiosity. James defined instincts as tendencies to behave in specific ways that move us toward achieving some kind of goal.

Psychologists disagree about exactly which behaviors can be categorized as truly instinctual, but they generally agree that there are some behaviors that are genetically "hard wired" into our systems. For example, infants will turn their heads toward potential food sources and suckle. Other neurological pathways relevant to motivation may be learned after birth, a flexible capability of our central nervous system (CNS) called neural plasticity (Lang, 1995).

We know that biological systems in the CNS are clearly at work when factors in the environment cause us to be motivated or "primed" for certain reactions. For example, researchers have clearly shown that the amygdala is a key element of our reactions to negative situations, such as those that result in fear of danger to our well-being (Lang, 1995). One may have a variety of reactions to a given dangerous situation, but they can generally be characterized as (1) being oriented toward some kind of defensive action or (2) becoming acutely aware of one's surroundings—for example, freezing—in order to monitor the situation carefully and determine whether action will be required in the future (Lang, 1995).

Incentive and Cognitive Theories of Motivation

Psychologists recognize two different general categories of incentive motives: extrinsic and intrinsic. **Extrinsic motivations** are those that have to do with forces outside our own inner desires, such as the need to earn money in order to purchase food and shelter. On the other hand, **intrinsic motivations** are those that come from within us. Consider your motives or reasons for enrolling in this psychology course. Are you motivated primarily by extrinsic factors, such as the desire to complete a degree program in order to obtain desirable employment or gain admission to graduate school? Or are you motivated intrinsically, such as by curiosity about human nature and the causes of human behavior, or an internal desire for knowledge? You can probably see that there are some elements of both intrinsic and extrinsic motives in your decision to take a course in introductory psychology. However, you can probably identify either extrinsic or intrinsic motives as being the primary category of forces that led you to enroll in this course.

FIGURE 6.3 *Skydiving illustrates a high need for arousal.*

Arousal Theory of Motivation

Arousal refers to physiological activity in the nervous system and in muscles and glands. According to **arousal theory**, we seek to maintain an optimal level of arousal at all times.

Why do some people voluntarily jump out of airplanes? According to the arousal theory of motivation, these individuals may seek a very high level of arousal that they can achieve only through extreme behaviors such as skydiving.

Have you ever woken up from a deep sleep and discovered that you had little time to attend to an important task? Did you try to wake yourself up by splashing cold water on your face or by drinking coffee or some other caffeinated drink? If so, you were actively trying to stimulate your arousal level. When you wake up to an important task (like your psychology class), you probably won't be at your best performance unless you are more awake; that is, you need to stimulate your arousal level in order to have peak task performance.

Now consider situations where you tried to complete important tasks when you were overstimulated. Did you find it difficult to concentrate in class after having too many cups of coffee, or have a hard time talking with a friend when you were stressed about an upcoming exam? In these situations your task performance was likely less than ideal because your arousal level was too high.

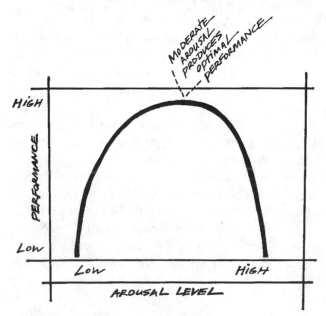

FIGURE 6.4 *The Yerkes-Dodson Law.*

So what level of arousal is best? According to the **Yerkes-Dodson Law**, task performance is at its peak for moderate levels of arousal. According to this principle, your

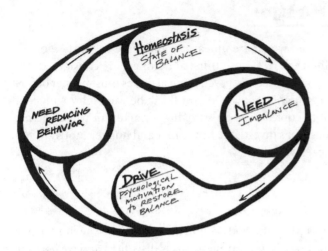

FIGURE 6.5 *Drive-reduction theory.*

performance will suffer when you are under- or over-stimulated. Another facet of this principle is that optimal arousal varies depending on the difficulty of the task: high arousal for simple tasks, moderate arousal for intermediate tasks, and low arousal for difficult tasks.

Drive-Reduction Theory of Motivation

According to the **drive-reduction theory**, we are motivated to behave in ways that help fulfill our needs. In a very basic sense, motivation comes from our physiological needs. **Needs** are the most basic necessities for human survival. Our biological needs are driven in part by **homeostasis**, our natural tendency to seek inner balance. When we are out of balance—a condition psychologists refer to as "being in a state of need"—we are motivated to do something to restore balance. This motivation to restore balance is referred to as a **drive**. Drives are internal states of arousal that lead us to behave in need-reduction behaviors. Needs are considered to be physiological deficits, and drives are psychological desires to satisfy needs and return to a state of balance.

It is important to note that drive-reduction theory is more about what motivates us to act, and less about exactly how we act. People may respond in different ways to needs, but we will generally repeat behaviors that have the effect of reducing our needs and returning us to homeostatic balance.

Maslow's Hierarchy of Needs

Abraham Maslow used the concept of needs in a comprehensive theory of the self. Maslow organized human needs in a progressive format that he called the **hierarchy of needs**. In Maslow's hierarchy, physiological needs are at the bottom of the pyramid. According to Maslow, we cannot progress to the higher-level needs without having met our physiological needs. Next in the hierarchy come safety needs, followed by love and belongingness, and then self-esteem. At the top of his hierarchy of needs, Maslow defined a concept called self-actualization, an ongoing process of fulfilling one's human potential. According to Maslow, most people never reach self-actualization, because they spend their entire lives working to fulfill needs at lower levels of the hierarchy. According to Maslow, if you experience a sudden problem in meeting the needs of a lower level of the pyramid, you will "regress" to that level until the lower need is satisfied, and then you can begin to progress up the pyramid again.

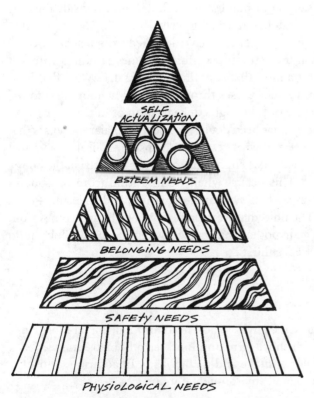

FIGURE 6.6 *Maslow's hierarchy of needs.*

Two Primary Drives: Thirst and Hunger

Usually, psychological drives, which are unlearned and serve to satisfy biological needs, are called **primary drives**. Both thirst and hunger are considered primary drives. According to Maslow, basic psychological drives must be met before we can consider satisfying higher goals. Do you think he was right? Consider how difficult you find it to concentrate on studying for an exam when you are racked with hunger pangs. Let's investigate how thirst and hunger motivate you from a basic physiological level.

Thirst

Thirst is a drive that arises when the body requires water. When the fluid inside or outside the cells in the body is low, homeostasis is disrupted and we become thirsty. Thirst is the psychological manifestation of our body's need for water, which is triggered by the hypothalamus. What do we do when we are thirsty? We drink fluids that are generally composed mostly of water. Shortly thereafter, our body tells us that we are all set, that we no longer require water. At that point, we have returned to a state of homeostasis, and our thirst goes away. Thus, we have traveled from a state of homeostatic balance to a state of a physiological need for water, which results in a psychological drive (called thirst) to satisfy that need for water, which leads to the need-reducing behavior of drinking fluid, which addresses the need and returns us to homeostasis.

Researchers have demonstrated that there are two kinds of thirst, both of which relate to the amount of salt in our bodies. Intracellular fluid is inside the cells in the body, and extracellular fluid is outside the cells. **Intracellular thirst** occurs when the body's cells have lost water and have departed from a state of equilibrium. This occurs when the extracellular fluid becomes saturated with salt (for example, after you eat a meal that contains a lot of salt). When that happens, water from within the cells passes through the cell membrane into the extracellular fluid to balance out the high concentration of salt. So, the intracellular fluid (inside the cells) has been depleted. The hypothalamus senses that the intracellular fluid is low, and what results is the psychological drive called thirst. **Extracellular thirst** occurs when the fluid becomes depleted in the body's tissue (Robertson, 1983). This occurs when we lose fluid from our bodies through various processes such as sweating, urinating, and sneezing—even bleeding and vomiting. The fluid that we excrete from our bodies comes from the extracellular fluid. The hypothalamus detects when the extracellular fluid is low, and then we experience thirst.

Hunger

Hunger, our drive to reduce the physiological need for food, is a bit more complex. Hunger involves both short-term and long-term homeostatic feedback loops, which relate to caloric intake and metabolism. In addition, hunger is affected by social, cognitive, and environmental influences.

Central Cues to Hunger

Central cues are hunger triggers coming from the central nervous system (CNS), which consists of the brain and the spinal cord. From a biological perspective, hunger is regulated by two areas of the brain, located specifically in the hypothalamus. The first of these, the **lateral hypothalamus (LH)**, stimulates hunger and causes us to start eating. Electrically stimulating the feeding center in the LH causes rats to eat even if they are full. And when the LH is destroyed, rats will initially refuse to eat. After being force-fed they will regain the ability to eat, but never to a normal degree (Anand & Brobeck, 1951).

The second, the **ventromedial hypothalamus (VMH)**, signals satiety and tells us to stop eating (Hernandez & Hoebel, 1989; Steffens, Scheurink, & Luiten, 1988). Researchers have demonstrated the importance of the VMH in studies with rats. Rats whose VMH has been electrically stimulated will stop eating (Duggan & Booth, 1986). Lesions to the VMH produce excessive eating. A rat with a lesioned VMH will become extraordinarily obese because its brain lacks a mechanism to tell it to stop eating (Hetherington & Ranson, 1940; Parkinson & Weingarten, 1990). A rat in one of these studies weighed six times as much as a typical rat. Interestingly, a rat whose VMH is damaged will eventually stop overeating. In addition, damage to the VMH makes rats less willing to press a lever for their food and more particular about the types of food that they are willing to eat. This makes it difficult to determine the precise role that the VMH plays in obesity.

Several neurotransmitters released by the hypothalamus also serve as central cues that regulate our eating patterns. When we consume low levels of carbohydrates in our diet, the brain releases **norepinephrine**, which causes us to crave carbohydrates. Norepinephrine is an adrenaline-type neurotransmitter that is released in high quantities when we are stressed. This explains why we often crave carbohydrates when we are under stress. Chronic consumption of low levels of fat causes the hypothalamus to produce more galanin. **Galanin** stimulates us to eat more fat in our diet. If you go on an extremely low-fat diet, galanin will eventually sabotage your efforts and stimulate you to eat more fat.

Peripheral Cues to Hunger

Peripheral cues are hunger triggers that occur in areas of the body outside the brain and spinal cord. One of these areas is the muscles of the stomach. A classic study by Cannon and Washburn (1912) illustrates some of the mechanisms in the hunger feedback system. Their study helped illustrate exactly what physiological changes outside the brain are associated with the psychological sensation of hunger, and some changes that are associated with a reduction in hunger. Specifically, they examined the importance of hunger pangs to see if they are what they seem to be (contractions of the stomach muscles).

Washburn swallowed a balloon that was attached to a tube leading up and out of his mouth. The balloon was filled with air and attached to a device that measured the contraction of his stomach muscles. Their findings showed that feelings of hunger were associated with contractions of stomach muscles. What the researchers did not know was whether the stomach contractions were actually the *cause* of the hunger pangs. Other research has shown that the psychological drive of hunger occurs in circumstances where it is literally impossible that stomach contractions were the cause, such as when patients have had their stomachs removed.

What makes us stop eating? Research has demonstrated that the stretch receptors in the stomach fire and signal satiety when the stomach is full, regardless of whether it is filled with food or water (Plotnik, 1998). **Satiety** is a term used by psychologists to refer to factors that relate to ending our food intake. Thus, the commonsense notion is correct that sensing the stomach is full is a satiety cue.

There is also evidence that our bodies can sense the amount of energy in the food we consume (calories) and that we adjust our food intake accordingly (Deckers, 2001). One chemical satiety cue is stimulated when the gastrointestinal tract begins to digest the food coming from the stomach. A hormone called **cholecystokinin** (**CCK**) is secreted when the food moves from the stomach into the intestinal tract. We know from the research in this area that the presence of CCK in the brain is an important satiety signal. For example, some research has shown that when the receptor sites for CCK are blocked with a synthetic chemical, animals will eat larger meals compared to similar animals that have not had their CCK receptor sites blocked. Similarly, animals that receive CCK prior to a meal will eat less food than animals that did not receive CCK. Plus, there is a negative relationship between the presence of CCK and food consumption: The more CCK an animal is given prior to a meal, the less it will eat (Strubbe & Woods, 2004).

The hormone **ghrelin** is secreted by an empty stomach and appears to serve to increase appetite. Obese patients undergoing gastric bypass surgery have part of their stomach sealed off. The remaining stomach then produces much less ghrelin, and their appetites decrease (Lemonick, 2002).

Additional research has shown that low blood sugar (glucose) levels are related to feelings of hunger. **Insulin** is a hormone secreted by the pancreas that converts glucose into energy. The role of insulin is to get glucose into the cells for energy. When the level of insulin in the bloodstream is high, we are likely to feel hungry and to crave sweet foods high in sugar (Deckers, 2001). When individuals continually eat refined carbohydrates, which absorb quickly into the bloodstream, they experience highs and lows in blood sugar levels. The individual may become insulin resistant. In insulin-resistant individuals, the glucose cannot get into the cells easily and so is stored as fat rather than being used by the cells for energy.

Another peripheral cue that contributes to controlling eating is our fat cells. When an individual reaches a certain level of body fat, his or her fat cells secrete a hormone called **leptin**, which signals a person to stop eating. Due to genetic mutations in mice, researchers have been able to understand the role of leptin in inhibiting eating. Mice with a mutant obese gene produce extremely low levels of leptin. They eat more and convert calories to fat more easily, and they typically weigh up to three times as much as a typical mouse (Coleman, 1979).

However, research shows that very few humans have the obese gene or produce low levels of leptin. Moreover, injections of leptin have not reliably reduced the body fat of obese individuals (Heymsfield et al., 1999).

Set Point Theory and Energy Reservoir Theory

Body temperature is another factor that may serve as a satiety cue. Research has shown that body temperature decreases as energy levels drop following a lengthy period without food. The process of eating and digesting food heats up the body, reversing the temperature decline and signaling satiety (Strubbe & Woods, 2004).

Long-term weight regulation is also related to biological factors. When there is excess energy in our system, our bodies store that energy (mostly) in our fat cells. That energy is then broken down and used by the body when we are low on fuel. The amount of fat stored in our bodies is one of several interrelated factors that contribute to variations in our body weight. Two major theories on weight regulation are the set point theory and the energy reservoir theory (Deckers, 2001).

According to **set point theory**, our body weight is set at a specific value. The value of the set point differs across individuals but remains constant over time. We may gain or lose weight in the short term, but our bodies will adjust our consumption of energy in response to weight loss or gain so that we are more likely to return to the set point. Proponents of set point theory state that under extraordinary circumstances it is possible to change one's set point. Set point theorists also argue that our set points can fluctuate during the course of our life span. Opponents of the theory argue that these exceptions to the "rule" of one's set point illustrate that the theory is not valid (Deckers, 2001).

The **energy reservoir theory** of long-term weight regulation holds that our bodies' long-term storage levels dictate the levels at which we consume stored energy and store new energy (Deckers, 2001). When a great deal of energy (food) enters the system, a good deal of energy can be stored for the long term in the form of fat deposits. When energy consumption exceeds the amount of incoming new energy, we begin to use up our stored energy (fat). According to the energy reservoir theory, when we begin to use up our fat reservoir, our bodies slow down in terms of energy consumption out of a desire to avoid depleting our stored fat reserves too quickly. In this way, our fat reserves function like a water reservoir: When we begin to use up the reservoir, we begin to conserve so as not to deplete our reserves too quickly.

But biology only gets us so far in explaining hunger. If hunger simply revolves around a biological feedback mechanism, does this mean there is something wrong with the biology of every person who is over or under their ideal weight? The answer is no. Most people who are over- or underweight do not suffer from biological irregularities (though some of them do). There are additional factors at work in the regulation of hunger. Our thoughts play an important role in hunger regulation, as do social and environmental forces.

The environment provides many **external cues** related to eating. Sight and smell are two senses that are closely related to our eating behavior. Do you remember the picture of strawberry shortcake at the beginning of the chapter? Did seeing that picture make you want to eat, even for a moment? Have you ever felt hungry when you smelled good food cooking? Have you ever wanted something to eat when you saw other people eating? These are examples of environmental cues, including our social environment, which can stimulate hunger.

Social Motivation

Researchers have devoted their attention to the importance of goal setting as it relates to human motivation. Four major types of goals that researchers have studied are goals of sensation seeking, achievement, connectedness to others, and striving for power over others. Sensation-seeking motivation explains why we seek new experiences. Achievement motivation refers to one's interest in accomplishments. Connectedness motivation helps explain our tendencies to associate with other people for reasons other than sexual reproduction. Power motivation varies across individuals and helps explain why some people are highly motivated to achieve positions of social or personal power.

Implicit and Self-Attributed Motivation

Some researchers distinguish between implicit motives and self-attributed motives (Larsen & Buss, 2005). This distinction arose mainly as researchers tried to defend a projective test of motives called the **Thematic Apperception Test**, or TAT. **Implicit motives** include those aspects of our motives of which we are not consciously aware, but which can be measured by gauging people's thoughts and fantasies, such as in projective tests. **Self-attributed motives**, on the other hand, are those motives about which we are consciously aware. According to this theoretical distinction, there are some elements of our motives about which we are directly aware, or about which we *think* we are aware, while our *true* motives may be unconscious.

Explore **projective tests** in Chapter 13, p. 411

Let's take achievement motivation as an example. People are likely to express some level of achievement motivation, which is self-attributed motivation. One person might say, "I am willing to work very hard, and I will do just about anything in order to achieve a high-status position in the student association," while another person might say, "I'm interested in achieving a position with the student association, but only if I can enjoy myself along the way." According to the theory of implicit and self-attributed motives, these self-attributed statements about achievement motivation might not reveal the individuals' *true* achievement motivation. The theory states that in order to discover an individual's achievement motivation, psychologists would need to carefully examine the person's thoughts, feelings, and behaviors. By doing so, we can determine someone's level of achievement motivation based on their responses to a more general type of stimulus. Keep reading for more information on achievement motivation.

Goals

One theory of motivation revolves around the manner in which we set our goals and the strategies we use to accomplish them (Funder, 2004). We can think about both short-term, specific goals and long-term, general goals. Psychologists distinguish between **ideographic goals**, which are specific to individual people, and **nomothetic goals**, which are common to all people. Examples of ideographic goals (person-specific) are finishing up a paper for class or keeping weekend plans with your friends. Examples of nomothetic goals (universal) would be something that most people strive to achieve in a more general sense, such as trying to have a successful career or trying to get along with others.

Sensation-Seeking Motivation

Studies show that both humans and animals seek sensory stimulation, even if there is no obvious goal in mind. **Sensation seeking** is the tendency to seek novel, varied, complex, and intense sensations and experiences. A few of the motives identified in sensation seeking are the curiosity motive, the change motive, and the manipulation motive. The **curiosity motive** stimulates individuals to explore new places in order to gain new information. The **change motive** occurs because animals and people tend to prefer complex and changing stimuli. The **manipulation motive** is our desire to handle things in our environment. Sensation-seeking behavior can affect vocational preferences, job satisfaction, social relationships, premarital and marital relationships, eating habits and food preferences, media and art preferences, humor, fantasy, creativity, and social attitudes (Zuckerman, 1994). In some situations, individuals may even take risks for the sake of sensory experiences. Examples of various types of risky sensation-seeking behavior are gambling, taking financial risks, using drugs, engaging in promiscuous sexual behavior, and participating in extreme sports.

Achievement Motivation

Take a good look at the women in Figure 6.7. They are in the middle of a grueling five-day bicycle tour during an intense summer heat wave. Why are they putting themselves through this miserable ordeal when they could be home eating chocolate chip cookies?

One perspective on human motivation revolves around our individual drive for achievement, which psychologists refer to as **achievement motivation**. According to this theory, individuals differ in terms of their need to achieve. For someone who is high in achievement motivation, hard work and suffering are worthwhile in order to pursue some distant goal. For others who are low in achievement motivation, putting themselves through a difficult ordeal is not likely to seem worth it. Those who are low in achievement motivation generally do not set lofty goals for themselves; they are satisfied with more moderate achievements that require less effort.

FIGURE 6.7 *Achievement motivation.*

Who is to say whether a five-day bicycle tour in the heat of summer is worthwhile? According to the theory of achievement motivation, this is a matter of the individual's level of motivation to achieve.

Connectedness or Affiliation Motivation

FIGURE 6.8 *Connectedness motivation.*

The people in Figure 6.8 seem to be happy in one anothers' company. Why do we seek out and maintain relationships with others when the outcome of those relationships is clearly not to reproduce? According to the **connectedness theory**, we seek out and maintain relationships with others because it is a basic human need that we feel connected to others. Evolutionary theory suggests that this tendency for social connections developed because it benefits our physical and mental well-being (Townsend & McWhirter, 2005).

The theory of connectedness might even explain why some people like to have house pets. Do you know anyone who has a special sense of connectedness with an animal? Have you ever wondered why many people have pets?

Power Motivation

Some humans have a need to achieve power over others (Winter, 1988). This motivation for power differs across individuals—some are high in power motivation, others are less oriented toward power. **Power motivation** is associated with various behaviors, including seeking positions of leadership and status. Research suggests that men and women are equally motivated to seek power, but the motivation for power may sometimes manifest itself differently for women as compared to men. According to Winter (1988), these sex differences in the expression of power motivation result from differences in childhood training. For example, in men, power motivation is associated with excessive alcohol use, aggressive behavior, and a higher likelihood of taking sexual advantage of others. Women are trained to behave responsibly, whereas men receive less responsibility training and therefore sometimes express their need for power in irresponsible, destructive ways. However, when men are trained, they are also able to satisfy their need for power in more productive ways.

Theories of Emotion

What, exactly, are emotions, and where do our emotions come from? Psychologists differ in their opinions in terms of how we define emotion and in the causes of emotion. For example, there is some debate about whether fear is an emotion or a reflexive response to stimuli in the environment (Buck, 1985). How are emotions related to motivation? Almost all psychologists working in areas related to motivation and emotion would agree that our emotions and motivations are intertwined. One view, which is supported by research, is that emotions are a mechanism for expressing our motivations: Motivation is the underlying basis of emotion (Buck, 1985). For example, if we are motivated to get a job, we will experience a positive emotion, such as joy, when we get one. If we do not want a job and someone gives us one, then we will more likely experience frustration or some other negative emotion.

Psychologists have studied emotion for decades. They sometimes disagree about the causes of emotions (Reeve, 1997), but they generally agree that there are three major components to emotion: the physiological, the behavioral, and the cognitive. This next section explores these three components and how they are explained in the four major theories of emotion.

When you are walking alone on a deserted street late at night and a loud sound surprises you, how do you react? Most people would say that their initial reaction would be to feel startled or afraid. When we experience fear, there are clear physiological changes in our bodies that go along with that emotion. The physiological component of an emotion relates to the physiological arousal associated with that emotion. When we feel happy, or sad, or scared, or sexually aroused, the reaction of our bodies is an important part of that emotion. Heart rate and blood pressure, body temperature, perspiration, and pupil dilation are just a few of the physiological variables that can change when we experience a particular emotion. The **physiological component** of emotion involves immediate physiological reactions (changes in the body) that occur as a result of various situations or thoughts that we experience. There are many theories about the physiology of emotion, but psychologists agree that all people share a few basic emotions, and these emotions have evolutionary physiological underpinnings (Reeve, 1997). A great deal of research has tied certain emotional reactions to activity in specific regions of the brain. As noted earlier, we know that the right hemisphere of the brain plays an important role in terms of recognizing and expressing emotions. Research has also shown that the limbic system and related brain structures are substantially involved in processing emotions. Specifically, the amygdala, hypothalamus, thalamus, hippocampus, and a small grouping of cells in the brain stem (called the ascending reticular activation system) have been linked to our emotions (Buck, 1985).

The **cognitive component** of emotion has to do with our thought processes, specifically what we are thinking when we experience a particular emotion. Whatever emotion you happen to be experiencing, it has a cognitive component to it. For example, when you are happy, you are thinking about certain elements of whatever is making you happy. More specifically, if you are happy because you just learned that you did very well on your most recent psychology exam, you might be thinking about all the time and effort that you put into your studies, or how your friends and relatives will react to the news, or how your overall course grade will be affected by your most recent mark, or how you pushed yourself harder than you ever had before in order to obtain that high mark.

The **behavioral component** of emotion is your outward expression of the emotion. The behavior corresponding to a particular emotion might be something as obvious as jumping for joy to something as subtle as frowning or sitting up a bit more in your chair.

Common-Sense/Affectiveness-Primacy Theory of Emotion

Original theories of emotion revolved around the idea that common sense tells us that an event or stimulus excites a mental process called emotion, and this mental state gives rise to the physiological arousal that occurs with each emotion. This is sometimes referred to as the **common-sense theory** or the **affectiveness-primacy theory**. It suggests that we experience an emotion before we experience any physiological arousal. In fact, the common-sense theory implies that the mental experience of the emotion triggers the physiological arousal. We are attacked by a thief, we feel afraid, and then our body begins to produce adrenaline so that we can fight or run. In our natural way of thinking, the stimulus triggers the mental event (or *feeling*) of the emotion, and then our body reacts to correspond to the emotion (James, 1884).

James-Lange Theory of Emotion

William James, who is widely regarded as the father of American psychology, suggested that the order of sequence in the common-sense theory was incorrect (James, 1884). His theory is referred to as the James-Lange theory of emotion because a similar idea was proposed independently by a Danish physiologist named Carl Lange at about the same time (Lang, 1994; 1995). According to the **James-Lange theory** of emotion, our bodies react to situational stimuli by creating physiological arousal; we then arrive at the mental experience that we experience as emotion based on our perceptions of the physiological changes that have occurred in our bodies. James suggested that without the physiological manifestations occurring in our body in reaction to stimuli, the mental event would be purely cognitive in form and lack any emotional warmth. Therefore, we might see the thief approaching us, intending to attack us, and decide it is best to run, but we could not actually feel afraid unless we experienced physiological arousal. Not all psychologists agree with the James-Lange theory, and a number of theories were developed in reaction to it. One biological perspective on emotion that stems from the James-Lange theory is the facial feedback hypothesis. The **facial feedback hypothesis** holds that our facial muscles respond to stimuli. Our brains interpret those facial muscle movements and trigger an appropriate emotional reaction (Tomkins, 1962).

One specific example of research on facial feedback involves participants contorting their faces in ways that mimic facial muscle movements associated with common emotions. For example, if you hold a pencil horizontally between your teeth, your facial muscles will be in a similar position as when you naturally smile. Research using this technique has shown that participants holding a pencil in this way find cartoons to be funnier than do other participants who are not holding a pencil in their mouths (Strack, Martin, & Stepper, 1988). These findings and other findings along these lines are cited by researchers as supporting the facial feedback hypothesis.

Cannon-Bard Theory of Emotion

Walter Cannon (1927) developed a theory of emotion in reaction to the James-Lange theory. Philip Bard (1934) later extended this theory. The central idea of

TABLE 6.1	**Theories of emotion.**	
Theory	**Summary**	**Example**
Common-sense Affectiveness-primacy	The mental event of emotion occurs first in response to a stimulus. Then the body responds by changing the state of physiological arousal.	Someone unexpectedly startles you in the parking lot late at night. You experience fear, and your body reacts by changing its physiological arousal to match your state of fear.
James-Lange	Emotional reactions occur first in the body (biological component). We then mentally process (cognitive component) the information about our state of physiological arousal.	Someone unexpectedly startles you in the parking lot late at night. Your heart pounds, and an instant later you experience the feeling of fear.
Cannon-Bard	Information from the environment is simultaneously relayed from our senses to our thalamus, which coordinates the physiological aspect of emotion (biological component), and to the cerebral cortex, which results in our mental experience of emotion (cognitive component).	Someone unexpectedly startles you in the parking lot late at night. Your heart pounds and at the same time you experience the feeling of fear (information from the senses relayed simultaneously to the body and the mind).
Schacter-Singer	Our bodies respond to situational stimuli by becoming aroused (biological component). Physiological arousal does not differ qualitatively depending on emotions. Our subjective experience of emotion is a cognitive interpretation of situational stimuli (cognitive component).	On your first date with a potential romantic partner, you ride a roller coaster. Your body reacts to the stimulation of riding on the roller coaster. You mistakenly interpret the physiological arousal from the roller coaster as being related to your date, and you find yourself more attracted to this person than you were before your roller coaster ride.
Lazarus	Emotions are initially processed in the brain (cognitive component), sometimes very quickly and sometimes outside our awareness. Signals about emotion are then relayed to our bodies (physiological component).	Someone unexpectedly startles you in the parking lot late at night. Your heart pounds and you experience the feeling of fear simultaneously (brief cognitive processing preceded the biological changes).

the **Cannon-Bard theory** of emotion is that information from our senses is relayed simultaneously to the body and mind. This theory directly competes with the James-Lange theory because it holds that the physiological component of emotion occurs at the same time as the cognitive component, and that the cognitive component is independent of the physiological component. According to the Cannon-Bard theory, sensory information is relayed simultaneously to the thalamus, which coordinates the biological component of emotion, and to the cerebral cortex, home to the cognitive component of emotion.

Cognitive Interpretation of Physiology: The Schacter-Singer Theory

Evidence clearly shows that the right hemisphere of the brain serves important functions in terms of understanding and expressing our emotions (Buck, 1985). Schacter and Singer proposed a model of emotion based on the theory that cognitive processes are critical to understanding emotion. The **Schacter-Singer theory** states that the emotions we experience are based on our *interpretations* of physiological responses to situational stimuli. According to this model, we interpret the physical sensations in our bodies differently, resulting in different emotions. Imagine two people riding next to each other on a roller coaster. One person enjoys the ride; the other experiences fear. According to the Schacter-Singer theory, the physical reactions of both of these individuals are identical, but their interpretations of those sensations are different and thus lead to very different emotions.

Schacter and Singer tested their theory in a classic experiment (1962). In their study, participants were injected with what they were told was a "vitamin supplement." This injection actually contained either a placebo or the drug epinephrine (also known as adrenaline), which has a powerful stimulant effect. Next, participants were told to wait in another room for the next part of the study to begin.

While they were waiting, participants were exposed to another person who was also supposedly waiting but was actually a confederate working with the researchers. The confederate acted in either a happy manner (e.g., throwing paper airplanes) or a grouchy manner (e.g., grumbling about the wait). When the researchers measured the emotions of the participants, they found that the people who had had the adrenaline injections showed more pronounced emotions (either happy or angry, depending on the condition they were in) than those who had not received the injections. This seems to be strong evidence that there is some interpretation of physiological information that is involved in our experience of emotion.

In another classic illustration of this theory, Dutton and Aron (1974) examined male sexual arousal as a function of fear. In the **shaky-bridge study**, Dutton and Aron had an attractive female research assistant approach males on a scary 400-foot-long suspension bridge over a 230-foot drop above a river. The research assistant asked the participants to complete a questionnaire that included a projective test designed to show their unconscious thoughts. When the participants completed the questionnaire, the research assistant wrote down her phone number on a piece of paper and handed it to the participants, telling them to call her if they had any questions. The researchers repeated this procedure, using the same attractive female research assistant, with males who had crossed a solid wooden bridge just over 10 feet above the ground.

FIGURE 6.9 *Interpretation of arousal.*

The researchers' basic hypothesis was that the participants' physiological arousal, associated with fear from being on the scary suspension bridge, would be reinterpreted as sexual attraction when they were approached by an attractive woman (the female research assistant). The researchers coded the responses to the projective tests for sexual content, and they also collected data on the number of participants who called the research assistant (they assumed that phone calls to the research assistant would be a measure of sexual interest). Sure enough, the projective tests of the participants on the shaky bridge had significantly more sexual content as compared to participants who had crossed the stable bridge (and were therefore not aroused by fear). Furthermore, the participants who were on the shaky bridge made significantly more telephone calls to the attractive female research assistant. In summary, the Dutton and Aron study provides additional evidence for the theory that emotion can result from a cognitive interpretation of physiological arousal.

The man in Figure 6.9 climbs high in the trees. He works with a powerful and potentially dangerous power tool while he is suspended hundreds of feet in the air. He enjoys his work. While many people might find this sort of experience terrifying, others interpret similar physiological sensations as pleasurable or enjoyable.

Lazarus's Cognitive Theory of Emotion

Lazarus (1991) developed a theory of emotion in which he held that cognition is an essential element in the experience of emotion. According to **Lazarus's cognitive theory** of emotion, we cannot experience emotion without first having some cognitive interpretation of the stimuli that cause us to feel one way or another. Lazarus distinguished between two types of cognition: knowledge (which can be impersonal, cold, and unemotional) and appraisal, which involves evaluating environmental stimuli in terms of positive or negative personal importance. Appraisal can be conscious or unconscious, meaning that we may be aware of our appraisal or it may occur outside our awareness. There is substantial evidence for both of these levels of cognitive processing. All emotion involves prior cognitive appraisal, and cognitive activity (knowledge or appraisal) is enough to stimulate emotion.

This theory states that in order for an emotion to occur, we must first have some sense of how a situation or other stimulus is relevant to our personal well-being (Lazarus, 1991). According to Lazarus, emotion may stem from a variety of sources, including physiological causes within the body (e.g., drug effects), but all causes of emotion must first be recognized and evaluated in the mind. So, according to this model, drugs and other physiological effects, such as hunger, cannot directly cause emotions, but they can cause emotions after first being cognitively processed in order to evaluate the importance in terms of our well-being (appraisal).

Evolutionary Aspects of Emotion

Darwin (1979) suggested that emotions are inherited traits that are passed down from one generation to the next because they serve as powerful survival aids. He speculated that the ability to express emotion allowed our ancestors to convey messages that helped them survive before they were able to communicate with words. Facial expressions could convey threats or submission, allowing humans to avoid or escape a dangerous situation. Some of the facial movements involved in emotional expression may also have aided us in adapting to the environment. When we express disgust, the nose wrinkles, decreasing the ability of the foul odor to enter the nasal cavity. When we are surprised, our eyes widen, allowing us to take in more visual information.

This Darwinian approach has led psychologists to focus largely on negative emotions like fear, sadness, disgust, and anger and the way in which they aid us by alerting us to danger (Peterson, 2006). Psychologists who categorize basic emotions usually include one or two positive emotions, such as joy, and surprise or curiosity. However, from an evolutionary perspective, there are several ways in which positive emotions differ from negative emotions. Most negative emotions are linked to a specific action tendency. This means that emotions that are usually negative produce a very specific behavioral response—for example, fear makes us want to run, and anger makes us want to attack. Positive emotions, like joy, may cause us to act, but usually in more varied ways. Negative emotions are also usually experienced in threatening situations, whereas positive emotions are not. This makes it difficult to see the evolutionary payoff for positive emotions, because it is not immediate (Nesse, 1990).

Fredrickson (2001) suggests that positive emotions create a more long-term payoff by broadening and building our potential. Her **broaden-and-build theory** suggests that positive emotions aid us in enhancing creativity, increasing motivation, and developing insights. They lead us to engage in behaviors that increase our cognitive and behavioral skills and lead to an evolutionary payoff in the future. A final dissimilarity with respect to negative and positive emotions is their underlying physiological mechanisms. Typically, negative emotions are associated with specific physiological patterns within the right hemisphere. Although most positive emotions seem to activate the left hemisphere, it has been extremely difficult to identify specific physiological patterns among positive emotions (Tomkins, 1962, 1963, 1982). One of the most interesting physiological findings of positive emotions is their ability to undo the physiological effects of negative emotions. It appears that areas for positive emotion are generally not active at the same time as areas for negative emotions, leading researchers to conclude that they generally do not occur simultaneously. For example, positive emotion has been linked to activation in the left prefrontal cortex, an underactive area in depressed and OCD patients (Fredrickson & Levenson, 1998; Tugade & Fredrickson, 2004).

Plutchik's theory of emotion (1980) states that the purpose of emotion is adaptation to the environment, and that emotions are activated to aid in survival. He believed that emotions were not just a feeling state but could be better understood as a chain reaction of stimulus, event, cognition, feeling, and behavior related to survival. He did not believe that the physiological arousal associated with emotions was relevant to a theory of emotions, because the physiological arousal was similar in many situations involving different emotions. Plutchik proposed in his functional theory of emotions that there are eight basic emotions. Plutchik's emotion model represents the relations among emotions and compares them to the analogous colors on a color wheel (see Figure 6.10). The eight sections represent the eight primary emotions arranged in four pairs of opposites. The circles represent the degree of similarity among the emotions, and the cones' vertical dimension represents the intensity of the emotion, with the darker colors indicating the greatest intensity of the emotional continuum. The emotions in the blank spaces between the color sections are emotions that are a mixture of the two adjacent emotions.

Plutchik's (1980) functional theory of emotions consists of 10 postulates:

1. The concept of emotion is applicable to all evolutionary levels and applies to animals as well as to humans.

2. Emotions have an evolutionary history and have evolved in various forms of expression in different species.

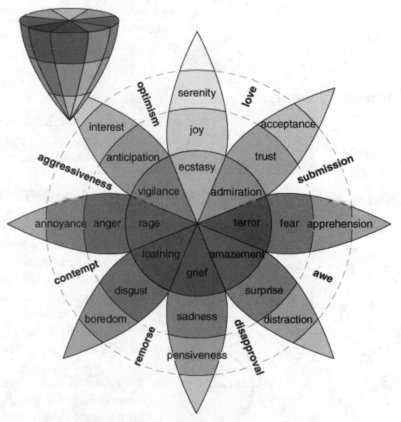

FIGURE 6.10 *Plutchik's (1980) emotion model.*

3. Emotions serve an adaptive role in helping organisms deal with key survival issues posed by the environment.

4. Despite different forms of expression of emotions in different species, there are certain common elements, or prototype patterns, that can be identified.

5. There is a small number of basic, primary, or prototypical emotions.

6. All other emotions occur as combinations, mixtures, or compounds of the primary emotions.

7. Primary emotions are hypothetical constructs or idealized states whose properties and characteristics can only be inferred from various kinds of evidence.

8. Primary emotions can be conceptualized in terms of pairs of polar opposites.

9. All emotions vary in their degree of similarity to one another.

10. Each emotion can exist in varying degrees of intensity or levels of arousal.

Social Functions of Emotion

Emotions have a clear social component. There is some evidence that we are far more likely to experience strong emotions when we are engaged in social interactions as compared to when we are alone (Reeve, 1997). Facial expressions of emotions serve clear social functions: They communicate our emotions to others.

Culture and Emotion

Just as there are cross-cultural similarities in terms of facial expressions of emotion and corresponding recognition of facial expressions, there are also cross-cultural differences in terms of how we express emotions. For example, in one study, Friesen (as cited in Ekman et al., 1987) showed film clips to Japanese and American participants. These films depicted either gruesome bodily mutilation scenes or neutral nature scenes. The researchers videotaped participants' facial expressions with a hidden video camera, and the participants viewed the videos either alone or with a researcher present. The researchers found that the Japanese and American participants had similar facial expressions of emotion when they viewed the films alone. When they were in the presence of a researcher, however, the Japanese participants masked facial expressions of negative emotions (e.g., disgust when viewing the mutilation scenes) with smiles, whereas American participants did not alter their facial expressions of negative emotions.

Researchers have demonstrated that some basic emotions are clearly distinguishable across cultures. In several studies, people in different cultures were shown photographs of individuals creating different emotional expressions and then asked to identify the emotion expressed in the photograph (Ekman & Friesen 1975; Izard, 1977,

FIGURE 6.11 *Universal emotions.*

1994). They discovered that people were very accurate in identifying six basic emotions, regardless of culture. The **six primary emotions** (see Figure 6.11) that were easily identified across cultures and languages were joy, anger, fear, sadness, surprise, and disgust (Ekman et al., 1987). The ability of individuals to universally recognize these basic emotions has led some psychologists to conclude that the ability to produce and recognize basic emotions is innate or inborn. This theory is supported by research demonstrating that blind infants, who have never seen another face produce an emotional expression, still display the ability to spontaneously exhibit these common emotional facial expressions (Eibl-Eibesfeldt, 1971; Galati, Scherer, & Ricci-Bitti, 1997).

Researchers use the term **display rules** to refer to types of culture-specific norms for how and when we express different emotions. According to Paul Ekman (1993), a leading researcher on facial expression of emotion, there are universal emotions that are common across cultures. However, expression of these universal emotions differs across cultures because we have display rules, which limit and dictate our expression of emotions to fit with cultural norms.

Emotion in the Workplace

Display rules are not only applicable to different cultures; the term also applies to the expression of emotion in specific circumstances within a culture, such as the workplace. There has been a good deal of recent research on workplace display rules and the importance of emotion in the workplace (Diefendorff & Richard, 2003). Specifically, researchers have focused their attention on a skill they call **emotional labor**, which is the act of controlling one's emotions in workplace settings to conform to workplace-specific display rules. The data suggest that for people who are very committed to workplace display rules regarding expression of emotion, these rules can have a strong influence in terms of worker behavior (Gosserand & Diefendorff, 2005).

Chapter Summary

In this chapter we discussed motivation and emotion. Motivation refers to the factors that stimulate us to behave in certain ways—factors that prepare us to act and guide our actions. Emotions are feelings that are closely linked to motivation.

There are several major theories of motivation: the evolutionary and instinct theory, the incentive and cognitive theory, the arousal theory, and the drive-reduction theory. The evolutionary and instinct theory of motivation explains behavior in terms of our innate tendencies to do things that will likely result in our survival and the survival of our offspring. The incentive and cognitive theory suggests that there are external and internal factors that motivate our behavior. Extrinsic motivation refers to factors outside oneself that stimulate behaviors, such as the need for money in contemporary Western cultures. Intrinsic motivation refers to factors within us that cause our behavior, such as interest and pleasure. According to the arousal theory, we seek out activities that will help us maintain an optimal level of arousal. The drive-reduction theory of motivation explains behavior in terms of maintaining homeostasis through a system of needs and need-reducing behavior. According to Maslow, some needs take priority over others. He suggests that we move progressively toward self-actualization by first fulfilling basic physiological needs, then safety needs, then belonging needs, then esteem needs.

Two of the most primary physiological drives are thirst and hunger. When the fluid inside or outside the cells in the body is low, homeostasis is disrupted and we become thirsty. Cues from the central nervous system and the peripheral areas of the body may trigger feelings of hunger or satiety. Two areas of the brain, the lateral hypothalamus and the ventromedial hypothalamus, are instrumental in inhibiting eating and initiating eating. Neurotransmitters also play a role in stimulating cravings of particular types of foods. Galanin causes us to crave fat, whereas norepinephrine stimulates the craving of carbohydrates.

Other peripheral cues, such as hormones, also play a role in triggering feelings of hunger or satiety. A hormone called cholecystokinin (CCK) is secreted when food moves from the stomach into the intestinal tract and is an important satiety signal. The hormone ghrelin is secreted by an empty stomach and appears to serve to increase appetite. Insulin is a hormone secreted by the pancreas that converts glucose into energy. When the insulin level in the bloodstream is high, we are likely to feel hungry. Our fat cells secrete a hormone called leptin, which signals a person to stop eating.

Long-term weight regulation is related to biological factors, among other things. Two major theories on weight regulation are the set point theory and the energy reservoir theory. According to set point theory, our body weight is set at a specific value. The value of the set point differs across individuals but remains constant over time. The energy reservoir theory of long-term weight regulation holds that our bodies' long-term storage levels dictate the levels at which we consume stored energy and store new energy.

Researchers have devoted their attention to the importance of social interaction as it relates to human motivation. Social motivations include goal setting, sensation seeking, achievement, connectedness to others, and striving for power over others. Sensation seeking is the tendency to seek novel, varied, complex, and intense sensations and experiences. Achievement motivation refers to one's interest in accomplishments. Connectedness motivation helps explain our tendencies to associate with other people for reasons other than sexual reproduction. Power motivation varies across individuals and helps explain why some people are highly motivated to achieve positions of social or personal power.

Emotion is the result of a complex set of interrelated factors: physiological, cognitive, and behavioral. There are several major theories of emotion. The common-sense theory suggests that we mentally experience an emotion in response to a stimulus before we experience any physiological arousal. The James-Lange theory holds that the physiological component of emotion precedes our cognitive experience of emotion. The Cannon-Bard theory, on the other hand, states that the physiological and cognitive components of emotion happen simultaneously. The Schacter-Singer theory of emotion is similar to the James-Lange theory in that it states that biological arousal precedes cognitive activity in the experience of emotion. However, unlike the James-Lange theory, the Schacter-Singer theory states that the physiological changes for all emotions are similar, and that we interpret the emotion from analyzing the situation. Lazarus's cognitive theory of emotion states that all emotions start with some level of cognitive processing of stimuli, and that sometimes the initial cognitive activity occurs outside our awareness.

There also appears to be an evolutionary and social aspect to emotions. Darwin suggested that emotions are inherited traits that are passed down from one generation to the next because they serve as powerful survival aids. Facial expressions can convey threats or submission, allowing humans to avoid or escape a threatening situation. Positive emotions also seem to create a more long-term payoff by broadening and building our potential repertoire of skills. Plutchik proposed that the purpose of emotion is adaptation to the environment. Studies suggest that we are far more likely to experience strong emotions when we are engaged in social interactions, as compared to when we are alone. Researchers have demonstrated that some basic emotions, such as joy, anger, fear, sadness, surprise, and disgust, are clearly distinguishable across cultures. However, expression of these universal emotions differs across cultures because societies have display rules, which limit and dictate the expression of emotions to fit with cultural norms.

Knowledge Builder

RELATE TO YOURSELF

1. Explain how positive emotions aid in the survival of human beings.

   _____

   _____

   _____

   _____

2. Describe which hunger cues stimulated you to eat your last meal.

   _____

   _____

   _____

   _____

3. Explain the arousal theory of motivation and give an example from your own life.

   _____

   _____

   _____

   _____

4. Give an example of a time when you had difficulty accomplishing a task. How does the Yerkes-Dodson law help explain your task performance?

   _____

   _____

   _____

   _____

CHAPTER REVIEW QUESTIONS

1. In Maslow's hierarchy of needs, self-actualization is the first step. **T or F?**

2. Our desire to study in order to get a good grade on an exam is an example of intrinsic motivation. **T or F?**

3. The facial feedback hypothesis states that we figure out how we are feeling based on interpreting how the muscles in our faces react to situations. **T or F?**

4. Which of the following is the neurotransmitter responsible for stimulating cravings for fat?

    (a) galanin   (b) insulin

    (c) norepinephrine   (d) ghrelin

5. The main idea in _____ theory is that we developed emotions in order to aid our survival.

    (a) James-Lange's   (b) the common-sense

    (c) Plutchik's   (d) Cannon-Bard's

6. The _____ theory of long-term weight regulation holds that our bodies' long-term storage levels dictate the levels at which we consume stored energy and store new energy.

    (a) homeostasis   (b) energy reservoir

    (c) set point   (d) broaden and build

7. Which theory suggests that positive emotions aid us in enhancing creativity, increasing motivation, and developing insights?

    (a) the broaden-and-build theory   (b) the incentive theory

    (c) the creativity theory   (d) the functional theory

8. Which of the following views suggests that organisms are motivated to behave in certain ways based on internal or external rewards?

    (a) arousal theory   (b) instinct theory

    (c) drive-reduction theory   (d) incentive theory

9. *Consider the following scenario:* You are standing on the edge of a cliff. The ground begins to crumble beneath you. You experience an emotion. What are some physiological changes that you would feel in your body? (e.g., heart rate increases).

_____

_____

_____

_____

What emotion would you experience in this situation?

_____

Now, consider another scenario: Your friend has just introduced you to someone new and you are very attracted to him or her. What are some physiological changes that you might feel in your body? (e.g., fast breathing).

_____

_____

_____

_____

What emotion are you experiencing?

_____

Now analyze the similarities and differences in your responses between the two different scenarios. Did you list similar physiological responses but different emotions or different physiological responses and different emotions? Which theory of emotion could best explain your responses? Why?

_____

_____

_____

_____

USEFUL WEB SITES

POSITIVE PSYCHOLOGY CENTER

http://www.ppc.sas.upenn.edu/index.html

This site has information on positive emotions and is founded on the belief that people want to lead meaningful and fulfilling lives, to cultivate what is best within them, and to enhance their experiences of love, work, and play.

AMERICAN POLYGRAPH ASSOCIATION

http://www.polygraph.org

This Web site has a wealth of information and FAQs about polygraphs.

NEBRASKA SYMPOSIUM ON MOTIVATION

http://www.unl.edu/psypage/symposium/

This Web site has up-to-date historical information on the Nebraska Symposium on Motivation, where leading motivation researchers have gathered every year since 1953 to share research findings and discuss current and future research directions.

NIMH CENTER FOR THE STUDY OF EMOTION AND ATTENTION

http://csea.phhp.ufl.edu/

This is the official Web site of a group of leading researchers in motivation and emotion. The site has a variety of information, including summaries of ongoing cutting-edge research in this area.

THE SWISS CENTER FOR AFFECTIVE SCIENCES

http://affect.unige.ch/

This Web site for some of the leading Swiss emotion researchers has useful information on graduate-level educational opportunities.

UNIVERSITY OF WISCONSIN–MADISON RESEARCH CENTERS

http://www.news.wisc.edu/packages/emotion/ &
http://www.healthemotions.org/

The Brain and Emotions Research site includes a variety of specific nontechnical content articles written for lay audiences. The Health Emotions Web site also has a variety of current and archived content articles.

Chapter 7

Learning

by Brian L. Thomas, PhD

The purpose of learning is growth, and our minds, unlike our bodies, can continue growing as long as we live.

—Mortimer Adler

What Is Learning?

FIGURE 7.1 *Practice drills are structured activities designed to maximize learning. Courtesy of Ron Linek.*

Learning is what you are (hopefully) doing right now as you begin to read this chapter. As a reasonable person, you might be asking yourself, "What can I learn about learning that I do not already know?" Well, here's your first test. Stop reading and try to define learning. If your first experience is anything like mine, trying to define learning is sort of like trying to define thinking or feeling. You have been learning for so long that you find it difficult to characterize.

Learning refers to a set of processes that occur within the nervous system that are activated either by **exteroceptive** stimuli (stimuli in the environment) or **interoceptive** stimuli (stimuli that originate from within the body). It is inferred that some type of learning process has been activated when an organism's behavior changes as a consequence of the experiences it has had (Mazur, 2002).

For example, as a high school student, you might have been a member of a varsity sports team or the school band. In either case, you probably spent many hours practicing the skills required to perform at a high level of competence. How does practice relate to learning? The goal of practice is to produce a change in behavior as a consequence of a deliberately structured type of experience (e.g., a practice drill). As you became a better athlete or musician, you most likely attributed the improvements to learning without worrying too much about the underlying process or the nature of the changes that were taking place in your nervous system. Good news! In this chapter, you get to worry about those things!

Antecedents and Consequences

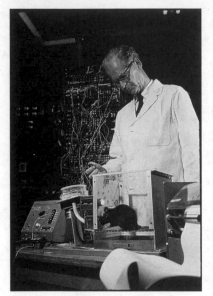

FIGURE 7.2 *Burrhus Frederic Skinner (1904–1990). Courtesy of Nina Leem/Time Life Pictures.*

Antecedents are stimuli that are present before a behavior occurs, and they activate the learning process. **Consequences** are stimuli that follow a behavior, and they help determine how the learning process will influence future behavior under similar circumstances. As mentioned earlier, antecedent stimuli may be exteroceptive or interoceptive. For example, you might be motivated to prepare your lunch as a result of an enticing television commercial (exteroceptive) or because of sensations originating in your stomach (interoceptive). Similarly, you might feel compelled to sleep in a class where the professor's voice is soft or monotonous (exteroceptive) or because of sensations of fatigue originating in your muscles or eyes (interoceptive). Consequences can be classified as reinforcers or punishers. **Reinforcers** are stimuli that increase the likelihood that a behavior will reoccur under similar circumstances. In contrast, **punishers** are stimuli that decrease the likelihood that a behavior will be repeated under similar circumstances (Schwartz, 1989).

Prominent behaviorist Burrhus Frederic (B. F.) Skinner argued that psychologists should concentrate their investigations on understanding the relationships among *observable* antecedents, behaviors, and consequences (ABCs). For example, in a laboratory setting, one could present a discrete antecedent stimulus—a light—wait for the subject to make an overt response to the light, and then study how different consequences influenced the likelihood that the response would reoccur. In 1938 Skinner demonstrated how effective this approach to understanding behavior could be in a classic book entitled *The Behavior of Organisms*.

Learning and Performance

From a Skinnerian point of view, learning is reflected in the rate of performance of a particular response. For example, if an experimenter arranges a situation or **contingency** where a rat is given the opportunity to press a lever for a sweet reinforcer, the rate of pressing is used as an indicator of the underlying, covert learning process. At first, the rat is unlikely to press the lever with any regularity. However, each time the lever press is followed by a reinforcer, the probability of future lever presses increases. Learning and the lever pressing rate increase to a maximum rate or **asymptotic level** where additional experience does not result in further learning (Skinner, 1966).

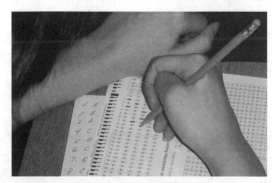

FIGURE 7.3 *Cheating is another reason that performance may not reflect learning.*

The assumption that learning is accurately reflected in performance is commonplace in the study of learning, but it should be apparent to you that sometimes your performance does not accurately indicate what you have learned. Unfortunately, in the animal laboratory or in the college classroom there is an implicit assumption that what you can do (on the exam) is a valid measurement of what you know (about the material). Take a moment to think about reasons why your performance might not reflect what you have learned. Hopefully you reasoned that overt behavior depends on a large number of factors, including emotionality, attentiveness, motivation, and fatigue. You might have learned the material required for the test, but if you are too tired, too stressed, distracted, or ambivalent, it is likely that your performance will suffer even if all the information is retained and can be expressed at some time after the exam. This highlights the importance of understanding that learning and performance are distinct processes and that laboratory investigations into learning should attempt to include multiple measures of performance and control for factors that might influence a subject's performance at the time of testing (Cory-Slechta, O'Mara, & Brockel, 1999).

Types of Learning

Learning processes come in a variety of forms. One distinction that has been made is between nonassociative and associative learning processes (Mackintosh, 1974). **Nonassociative learning** processes produce temporary changes in the intensity of reflexive behaviors. For example, if you arrive home to find a construction crew working outside your home, your perception of the noisiness of the work is likely to change over time. For some, the intensity of the noise will decrease to a point where it may become imperceptible. For others, the intensity of the noise will seem to increase. The key is that nonassociative changes are temporary in nature. If the construction crew quits for the day and returns the next morning, one's perception of the noisiness will return to the point where it started the previous day. In **associative learning**, it is assumed that an **association**, or a strengthened neural connection, is made between neurons that normally respond to the individual events. For example, if you noticed that your roommate read the textbook and reviewed class notes before an exam, you would expect the same behavior before other exams. Associations are connections between two or more stimuli that allow an organism to predict when or where an event will take place. It should be clear that one adaptive characteristic of associative learning is that it allows an organism to anticipate events. Indeed, one prominent theory of learning holds that we learn only when we are surprised (Rescorla & Wagner, 1972).

Within the categories of associative and nonassociative learning processes, additional distinctions have been made (Domjan, 2006). Associative learning processes may be described as either classical or operant conditioning. Nonassociative learning processes may be described as either habituation or sensitization (see Figure 7.4). Each of these types of learning will be discussed in detail in this chapter.

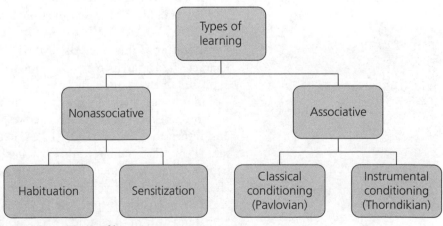

FIGURE 7.4 *Types of learning processes.*

Nonassociative Learning Processes

Have you ever noticed that your *perception* of a stimulus changes over time even if the stimulus itself is unchanged? For example, when you moved into the dormitory for the first time, were you shocked at the size of the room? Did you think it would be impossible for two people to live in such close proximity? What happened to your perception of the space after you had lived in it for a while? If you are like most, you adapted to the room and most of the original discomfort declined. **Habituation** is a nonassociative learning process that allows you to adapt to a stimulus or situation that initially elicits a strong reaction and that is for the most part unchanging. It is considered nonassociative because it can be easily undone and it does not appear to result in the long-lasting neurological changes that characterize associative types of learning. Now, what happened when you went home for your first long holiday and then returned to your dorm room? Did the original sense of discomfort return for a time? The habituation that occurred earlier may have decayed in the absence of the situational stimuli, resulting in a recovery of the original discomfort. **Spontaneous recovery** is a phenomenon where a habituated response reappears after a period of time away from the situation. Again, it is this temporary nature of habituation that places it in the category of nonassociative processes.

FIGURE 7.5 *Do you think you would ever habituate to the beauty of Big Sur? Courtesy of pdphoto.com.*

One could reasonably question the value of habituation given its temporary nature. However, habituation allows an organism to redirect its attention away from an unchanging stimulus (i.e., something familiar or predictable) toward other stimuli that are novel or changing and that may be less well understood. Focusing attention on stimuli that are new or that change periodically could facilitate learning about relationships that involve these stimuli. For example, suppose you are taking a class in an unfamiliar lecture hall with beautiful stained glass windows and high vaulted ceilings. During the first class period, your attention might be drawn toward the stimuli associated with the architecture of the classroom. However, it is clearly in your best interest to shift your attention from these "distracting" stimuli to the course material. While these distracting stimuli may be beautiful, they are nevertheless unchanging and predictable, so it follows that you should habituate to them. In contrast, the class material, which is novel and constantly changing, should not activate the habituation process, and you should find it easier to sustain your attention.

Sensitization is the other, opposite, nonassociative learning process, and it is characterized by an increase in the intensity of a reflexive behavior with repeated exposure to an emotionally arousing stimulus. Much like habituation, sensitization is maintained only if exposure to the stimulus is chronic. In the absence of stimulus exposure, the heightened response will undergo **spontaneous decay** and return to a baseline level (Lutz, 2000). For example, suppose that you are taking your first exam in your psychology course. The woman sitting next to you begins to tap her pencil. Does your perception of the intensity of the sound change over time? If you are like most people, the intensity of the sound will seem to increase over time (along with your frustration). In all likelihood, the actual intensity of the sound in decibels is unchanged. Like the effects of habituation, sensitization effects are temporary. If you allow the tapping to continue, you will probably begin to habituate to it. However, a few weeks later on the next exam, you are likely to experience sensitization once again.

How is a temporary sensitization to a stimulus beneficial? Stimuli that are perceived to be more intense command a greater part of our attention than stimuli that appear less intense. Since it follows that attention plays an important role in associative learning, it is reasonable to suppose that sensitization should facilitate learning about these intense stimuli at the expense of the less intense stimuli. For example, it is likely that you will form an association between the woman tapping the pencil and the frustration that you felt during the exam. If this association allows you to anticipate frustration on future exams, you might act preemptively to prevent it from happening (i.e., before the exam begins, you might ask the woman not to tap her pencil).

What determines if a person will habituate or become sensitized to a stimulus? Davis (1974) designed an important experiment with rats to help answer this question. Rats were divided into two conditions. In the first condition, they were placed in a chamber with 60 dB of background white noise. In the second condition, they were placed in a chamber with 80 dB of white noise. In both conditions, rats received frequent exposures to a 70 dB tone stimulus, and the magnitude of their startle behavior (how much they jumped in response to the tone) was recorded. Given that both conditions involved a 70 dB tone, one might predict that startle behavior would be similar across conditions. Interestingly, rats exposed to the 70 dB tone in the setting with 80 dB of white noise became sensitized to the tone, as indicated by an increase in the intensity of their startle behavior. In contrast, rats exposed to the same 70 dB tone in the setting with 60 dB of white noise became habituated to the tone, as indicated by a decrease in the size of their startle behavior (see Figure 7.6). Davis concluded that an

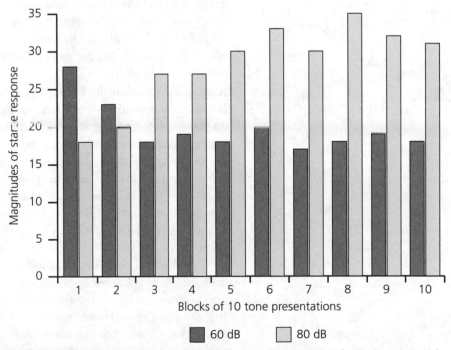

FIGURE 7.6 *Magnitude of the startle reflex to a 70 dB tone stimulus in contexts with 60 dB or 80 dB of background white noise. Adapted with permission from Davis, 1974,* Journal of Comparative and Physiological Psychology, 87, *pp. 571–581.*

organism may become either habituated or sensitized to the same stimulus depending on its level of arousal. He reasoned that the 80 dB white noise was more arousing than the 60 dB white noise and that it was this difference in general arousal that determined whether a rat would habituate or sensitize to the tone. Let's return to the pencil-tapping example. While you may have become sensitized to the pencil tapping as your level of arousal increased, you may also have noticed that others in the class seemed less affected by the noise. One way of explaining this difference is to assume that the noise was less bothersome (i.e., less arousing) to others and that they were able to habituate more readily than you were. The practical lesson you might take from Davis's study is that the key to overcoming a frustrating or arousing stimulus in the short run is to relax yourself and keep your arousal level at a minimum.

Associative Learning: Classical Conditioning

FIGURE 7.7 *Ivan Petrovich Pavlov (1849–1936). Courtesy of Bettmann/Corbis.*

Pavlovian or **classical conditioning** refers to an associative learning process that Russian physiologist Ivan P. Pavlov discovered at the turn of the twentieth century. In 1897, Pavlov directed one of his students, S. G. Vul'fson, to test the hypothesis that the type of food a dog ingested determined the quantity and composition of saliva that was produced. For example, Pavlov reasoned that dogs given a moist food like raw meat should produce less saliva than dogs given a dry food like bread. As expected, salivation in response to bread was greater than salivation with meat. Moreover, the chemical composition (e.g., types of digestive enzymes) of the saliva differed as well. Despite these interesting and predicted results, it was an unanticipated finding that would make Pavlov internationally famous in the burgeoning field of psychology. Vul'fson observed that after some amount of experience with the experimental protocol, dogs began to salivate *before* the test food item could be placed in their mouths. This result was surprising because at that time it was believed that salivation was a purely reflexive response to the contact of food in the mouth (like a knee-jerk response to a tap on the patellar tendon). Yet, the dogs seemed to be responding in anticipation of the upcoming meal. What was eliciting the salivary response, if not some sort of expectation?

In 1927, Pavlov published his unexpected findings in the book *Conditioned Reflexes*. The book describes a large number of studies including those involving the salivary response as well as studies on motor reflexes. In each study, the research methodology followed a basic plan. First, the investigator selected a reflexive behavior (**unconditioned response** [UR]) that could be reliably elicited by a particular stimulus (**unconditioned stimulus** [US]) under the control of the investigator. Each time the investigator presented the subject with the US, it responded reflexively with the UR because this behavior pattern was innate to the animal. Next, a second stimulus (**neutral stimulus** [NS]) was selected that did not elicit the UR. The investigator provided the NS just moments prior to the US on several occasions, and the subject's response to the NS was carefully recorded. An NS that was paired with a US came to elicit a specific (anticipatory) behavior on its own (**conditioned response** [CR]) and was assigned a new label, the **conditioned stimulus**, or CS. Changes in responding to the NS or the CS over time were interpreted as reflections of the underlying learning process that is now called classical conditioning. Figure 7.8 illustrates the process for salivary conditioning.

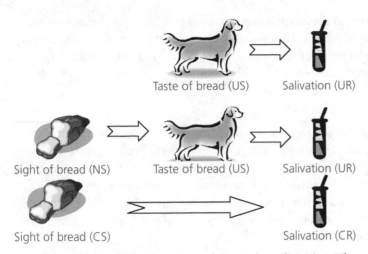

FIGURE 7.8 *The basic methodology of classical conditioning. The taste of bread always elicits reflexive salivation. The sight of food is paired repeatedly with the taste. The sight of food comes to elicit a conditioned salivary reflex.*

In 1924, John B. Watson published the book *Behaviorism*. The book summarizes his results from a series of studies on learning in infants. Watson observed that the number of different types of stimuli that elicit reflexes in infancy was significantly less than the number in adulthood. Moreover, he did not believe that the behavioral repertoire of adults was any richer than that of infants. Therefore, he reasoned that the increase in the complexity of behavior in adulthood could only reflect the formation and integration of either newly learned Pavlovian reflexes or instrumentally conditioned habits (described later). Using Pavlov's initial findings with dogs, Watson hypothesized that as we develop from infancy to adulthood, we discover relationships between innocuous stimuli and more important stimuli. With experience, the once-innocuous or neutral stimulus comes to evoke preparatory, reflexive behavior that allows us to predict the more important events of life. Watson called the CS a **substitute** for the US because it warned that something meaningful was forthcoming.

Watson's most enduring contribution to the study of learning was his discovery of the **conditioned emotional reflex** in human infants. Watson believed that three emotional unconditioned reflexes were present at birth: fear, rage, and love. Fear was expressed by a startle response, a pause in respiration followed by an increase in breathing, eye closure, clutching of the hands, and puckering of the lips. Fear could be induced by the surprise of a loud noise or the perceived loss of support (i.e., being dropped). Rage was characterized by slashing and flailing of the limbs, holding one's breath, and tightening of the muscles. It could be elicited by physical restraint of the arms, legs, or head. Finally, love was observed in smiles, movement of the arms or legs during laughter, and general cooing sounds. These responses were elicited by stimulation of the erogenous zones of the body. Watson reasoned that these unconditioned emotional responses could become associated with additional neutral stimuli provided that the neutral stimuli reliably preceded one or more of the unconditioned stimuli.

In a classic demonstration of this process, Watson and his student (and future wife) Rosalie Rayner established a conditioned fear reflex in an infant named Albert B., or "**Little Albert**" as he has come to be known. Albert was first exposed to a number of different neutral stimuli to be certain they did not elicit the fear reflex. Examples included a white rat, a monkey, a rabbit, and a Santa Claus mask. Next, Albert was presented with the rabbit on six occasions, and each time, Watson struck a metal bar with a hammer to produce the US (i.e., the surprising loud noise). Albert expressed the unconditioned behaviors associated with fear each time the loud noise occurred. Finally, Albert was once again presented with the rabbit, and, importantly, it elicited anticipatory fear responses in the absence of the loud noise US. In Watson's terms, the NS of the rabbit had become a substitute for the loud noise stimulus. Interestingly, the rat, the monkey, and the Santa Claus mask also elicited fearful behavior to different degrees, indicating that some of the conditioning to the rabbit had generalized to other stimuli that were never actually paired with the US. Watson had demonstrated in a controlled laboratory situation how most human fears might originate, and even today his findings provide the foundation for research into the treatment of phobias in humans.

Acquisition of a CR

A conditioned reflex is rarely expressed fully after a single pairing of the NS and the US. Instead, the magnitude of the conditioned reflex grows gradually over successive pairings until it reaches an asymptotic level (this process is called **acquisition**). Figure 7.9 illustrates a typical acquisition curve for a CR. Notice that the greatest amount of learning occurs during the initial pairings, followed by increasingly smaller changes. Shortly thereafter it reaches a maximum point and then levels off.

Characteristics of the CS

The CS plays an important part in the acquisition of the CR. A "good" CS has several features. First, it should be intense enough that it is easily detected in any setting. For example, if you want an alarm to act as a CS for an approaching tornado, it is critical that the alarm be loud enough to be heard by people at different distances from the loudspeaker and in spite of different levels of noise interference (e.g., inside a car with the radio on). If you think back to the section on nonassociative learning, you might suspect that a very loud stimulus is likely to activate the sensitization process, which should then facilitate the initial learning about the relationship between the alarm and the danger as well as arouse you for heightened reactivity to the stimulus once it has become meaningful. Second, a CS should be **salient**. Saliency refers to the attention-getting quality of a stimulus. A loud stimulus may initially be very salient, but you know that with repeated exposure, it is possible to become habituated to virtually any stimulus (e.g., loud trains or airplanes). Saliency is influenced by

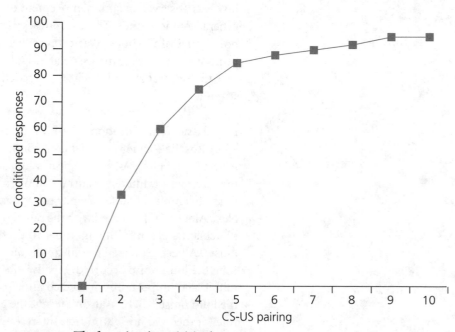

FIGURE 7.9 *The learning (acquisition) curve.*

FIGURE 7.10 *Is the moon the most salient stimulus because it is intensely bright or because other stimuli are not competing for your attention? Courtesy of pdphoto.com.*

intensity but also by novelty and by your own likes, dislikes, or ambivalence. For example, the sight of an attractive classmate for the first time should make him or her a very salient stimulus independent of whether he or she makes himself or herself intense by engaging in attention-seeking behaviors. Finally, a CS should "fit" the US it is being paired with. Martin Seligman (1971) suggested that organisms are more biologically prepared to associate some CSs with a US than others. He called this factor **biological preparedness**. For example, imagine that you are asked to participate in a psychology experiment where pictures of objects are presented to you and your salivation response is recorded. The first photo is of a couple sitting on a blanket with a small, closed picnic basket between them. The second photo is of a beautiful sports car parked underneath the marquee for Rick's Bar and Grill. The final photo is of a large plate of rotting meat with maggots crawling on it. Each of these stimuli should fail to elicit much salivation during the initial presentation. Next, each stimulus is again presented, and you are asked to take a bite of a very dry cookie while studying the photo. You go through the series of photos several times, and then each photo is tested to see how much salivation it elicits. Do you think that these stimuli would become CSs for a conditioned salivary reflex equally well (i.e., at the same rate and to the same asymptote)? In all likelihood, you would be contraprepared to associate rotting meat with the cookie in spite of the fact that it is very intense and salient. In fact, it is the only photo that explicitly depicts a food item. Take a minute to think about why rotting meat might not easily become a CS for the salivary reflex (hint: think about the function of salivation). Hopefully you concluded that salivation is a preparatory response for eating food. Indeed, one of the main functions of saliva is to lubricate the food and the throat to help reduce the risk of choking. If your psychology is tuned to avoid rotting meat, as opposed to eating it, you are probably contraprepared to learn an association between it and other more palatable foods. Does this mean that a picture of rotting meat cannot become associated with another US? Thankfully, the answer is no. In fact, if you were asked to take a drink of a liquid intended to produce a mild nausea (instead of eating a cookie), the photo of rotting meat might be expected to produce the strongest conditioned nausea of all the photos.

In a classic demonstration of preparedness, John Garcia and Robert Koelling (1966) presented rats with a compound stimulus followed by one of four different USs to test the idea that elements of the compound stimulus would differentially associate with each US. A **compound stimulus** is created by presenting two or more neutral stimuli simultaneously. Garcia and Koelling created a compound stimulus made up a flavor element and an audiovisual element. Rats drank a flavored solution while also experiencing an audiovisual stimulus (imagine drinking punch at a homecoming dance). The rats were then given one of the following as the US: radiation, a lithium chloride injection, an immediate foot shock, or a delayed foot shock. Both radiation and lithium chloride unconditionally produce sickness, whereas foot shock produces pain. The results of the study indicated that rats associated their sickness mostly with the flavor element of the compound stimulus and

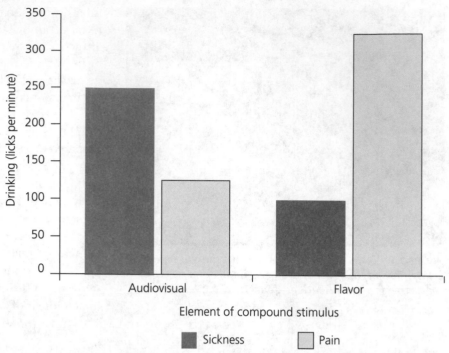

FIGURE 7.11 *When a compound stimulus is paired with a US that induces sickness or pain, some elements of the compound are more readily associated with the US than others. Learning is reflected by an interruption in drinking when the element is presented. Adapted from Garcia and Koelling, 1966,* **Psychonomic Science, 4, 121–122.**

associated the shock mostly with the audiovisual element in spite of the fact that each element was an equally reliable predictor of the US (see Figure 7.11). Thus, Garcia and Koelling demonstrated under controlled laboratory conditions that stimuli differ in how easily they may become CSs for a particular US. To summarize, effective CSs are stimuli that are intense, salient, and that fit well an organism's predispositions for learning.

Characteristics of the US

The US also plays an important role in the acquisition of a CR. In fact, the same characteristics that make for an effective CS often determine how effective a US will be. For example, an intense CS, such as a loud noise, can effectively warn us that something important is about to happen. However, if the US that follows the loud noise turns out to be of minor or no importance, one might correctly suspect that learning should not take place. Indeed, one of the best-studied aspects of the US is how its intensity influences the acquisition of the CR. As you might expect, we learn most readily about USs that are larger, of better quality, or of greater intensity.

Kenneth Spence and John Platt (1966) summarized several of the early investigations on the importance of US intensity in classical conditioning. The studies used an **eyeblink conditioning** paradigm in which human participants were presented with an NS (a tone) followed by the delivery of an airpuff US that elicited a reflexive eyeblink UR. The purpose of these studies was to examine how variations in the intensity of the airpuff influenced the rate of acquisition of an eyeblink CR.

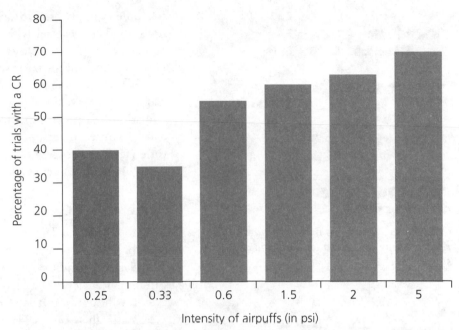

FIGURE 7.12 *Percentage of CS presentations that elicited an anticipatory eyeblink as a function of airpuff intensity in pounds per square inch (psi). Adapted from Spence and Platt, 1966*, Psychological Bulletin, 65, *1–10.*

The results supported the position that stronger airpuffs resulted in faster learning than weaker airpuffs. More specifically, participants who received stronger airpuffs made an anticipatory eyeblink on a greater percentage of CS presentations than participants who received weaker airpuffs (see Figure 7.12). Moreover, participants who received the weakest-intensity airpuffs frequently failed to make any anticipatory responses even though the tone was an effective stimulus.

Timing of the CS and the US

Another important factor that influences the acquisition of a CR is the timing of the CS and the US. The temporal relationship between the CS and the US can vary significantly from one situation to another, and certain relationships have been shown to produce more rapid acquisition than others. The schedule that produces the fastest and most reliable acquisition is called **forward** or **delayed conditioning**. In this schedule, the CS is presented for a short time, then the US is delivered, and finally the two stimuli end simultaneously. Another schedule, called **trace conditioning**, resembles forward conditioning except that the CS ends prior to the delivery of the US, resulting in a trace interval where neither the CS nor the US is present. Interestingly, trace intervals just a few seconds in length have been shown to disrupt acquisition in a variety of learning paradigms (Bolles, Collier, Bouton, & Marlin, 1978). **Backward conditioning** is simply the opposite of forward conditioning. The US is delivered first and lasts through the CS until both stimuli end simultaneously. Surprisingly, backward pairings have been shown to produce acquisition of a CS-US association when only a few trials were provided. If additional trials are given, the association weakens and diminution of the CR occurs (Cole & Miller, 1999). Lastly, **simultaneous conditioning** involves presentation of the CS and the US at the same time, and the stimuli end simultaneously. This

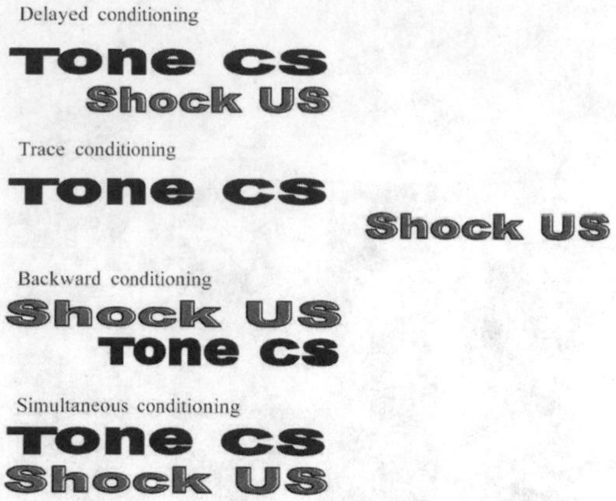

Delayed conditioning

Tone cs
Shock US

Trace conditioning

Tone cs   **Shock US**

Backward conditioning

Shock US
Tone cs

Simultaneous conditioning

Tone cs
Shock US

FIGURE 7.13 *Variations in the temporal relationships between a tone CS and a shock US.*

schedule typically produces poor acquisition because the CS does not provide the learner with any information that can be used to anticipate the US (since the US is already occurring). Figure 7.13 illustrates each of the basic schedules. As a final point, it is worth noting that learning is generally facilitated when the to-be-associated stimuli are contiguous. **Contiguity** refers to how closely two stimuli occur in time or space. For example, you may associate bacon with eggs because you often eat them at the same time (temporal contiguity) and you see them together on the same plate (spatial contiguity).

Higher Order Conditioning

Now that you have learned about many of the factors that influence the process of classical conditioning, you might have concluded that classical conditioning is limited to cases where a stimulus (a CS) signals an impending event that has some real importance to the learner (a US). However, it is important to recognize that associations can also form between two CSs. When this occurs, it is called higher order conditioning, and the assumption is that one of the two CSs has previously achieved significance as a result of its relationship with some US. For example, as a toddler, you were probably not overly excited when you received money in a birthday card (or with the card itself). At that point, money had not become associated with commerce, so its value was limited to whatever imaginative functions you might have created for it. However, as you repeatedly witnessed the exchange of money (CS) for tangible goods (US), some of the reinforcing aspects of the goods became associated with the once-neutral, green paper. In Watson's terms, the CS became a substitute for the US. Once this process of stimulus substitution was completed, you probably began to associate other cues with the availability of money through the process of higher order conditioning. For example, the once-neutral birthday card (a secondary CS) may have come to elicit excitement in the teenage years because it predicted the delivery of money (primary CS), which then signaled the opportunity to purchase some US. Analogous situations have been studied in the laboratory.

For example, Holland and Rescorla (1975) studied higher order conditioning in rats. Three groups of rats were first exposed to a flashing light stimulus (primary CS) and a food US. Groups PP and PU experienced pairings of these stimuli, and Group UP received the stimuli unpaired. Group UP acted as a control group. Since the stimuli were unpaired, it was not expected that the CS would become meaningful, and that was expected to make higher order conditioning impossible. In the second phase, the light CS was paired with a clicking sound (secondary CS) in Groups PP and UP, and responding to the clicking over trials was used to assess the progress of higher order conditioning. Group PU received the flashing light and clicking sound unpaired and acted as a second control group. Thus, the only condition favorable for higher order conditioning was Group PP. As expected, the results indicated that higher order conditioning occurred in Group PP, but not in either of the control conditions (see Figure 7.14). Higher order conditioning greatly expands the complexity of the associative network that must exist in all of us. Instead of simple connections between various CSs and USs, it should now be clear that classical conditioning can result in associations between virtually any pair of stimuli that provide infor-

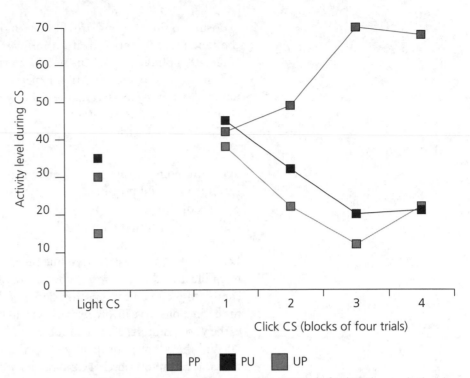

FIGURE 7.14 *Higher order conditioning of a noise (CS2)-light (CS1) association in rats. Increases in activity level were taken as evidence of learning. Adapted from Holland and Rescorla (1975),* Journal of Comparative & Physiological Psychology, 88, *459–467.*

mation useful to an organism capable of anticipation and of adjusting its behavior in productive ways.

Generalization and Discrimination

Another important feature of classical conditioning is called generalization. **Generalization** occurs when responding to a CS carries over to other neutral stimuli that resemble the CS. For example, if you have had the unfortunate experience of being pulled over by a police officer, you are likely to associate the flashing lights and siren (CSs) with the discomfort of the situation (US). The resulting association between the flashing lights/sound of the siren and the punishment is likely to result in reflexive braking in response to a variety of flashing lights and sirens (e.g., those of an ambulance or a fire engine). Conditioned responding generalizes across stimuli as a function of their similarity and the amount of direct experience that an organism has had with the stimuli. To a novice, sirens from police cars, fire engines, and ambulances probably sound very similar. They are very loud, high pitched, and variable. However, with a little practice, the average person could learn to differentiate among these three auditory signals, a process called **discrimination**, and reflexive braking would become a CR only to the police siren. Discrimination learning requires practice with both the stimulus to be associated with the US (the S^D, pronounced "S-dee") and the stimuli not to be associated with the US (the S^Δ, pronounced "S-delta"). Intermingled pairings of the S^D and the US along with

FIGURE 7.15 *The face side of the US $20 bill has 15 different features designed to facilitate the discrimination of legitimate currency from counterfeit. With training, you could learn to make this discrimination.*

exposure to the S△ alone provides an opportunity for a subject to overcome the tendency for generalization in favor of a tendency for discrimination (Pierce & Epling, 1995). This necessary and common experience is the basis on which we measure expertise. Experts typically make much finer discriminations than nonexperts, and their ability to do so depends on extensive experience with the various stimuli.

Extinction

Up to this point, coverage has been limited to those factors that determine how readily one might acquire a CR. In this section, the emphasis will shift to the process of **extinction**, where an established CR, and possibly its underlying CS-US association, is eliminated.

The Extinction Curve.

While the acquisition curve most often takes the form illustrated in Figure 7.9, the nature of the extinction curve varies significantly from one case to another. Some of the most important determinants of the extinction curve involve elements from the acquisition training that occurred earlier. For example, when two subjects are given pairings of a tone with a food US and the quantity or quality of food differs between them, they may reach the same asymptotic level of conditioned responding, and their acquisition curves may also look fairly similar. During extinction, when the tone is repeatedly presented in the absence of food, the rate at which the CR decreases is very likely to differ. More specifically, extinction of the CR is likely to occur most rapidly in the subject that received the larger or better quality food item during acquisition (Hill & Wallace, 1967). Other factors known to influence extinction rate include how reliably the food was delivered after the tone, variability in the quality or quantity of the food, and how the food delivered in acquisition compared with other foods the subject had experience with.

Pearce, Redhead, and Aydin (1997) reported on the effects of acquisition training on the extinction rate. In their study, rats were given acquisition training that involved a 10-second noise CS followed by the delivery of a food US. As rats learned the relationship between the noise and the food, they increasingly responded to the noise by searching the food magazine, and this behavior served as the measure for learning. Four different groups were trained (but only two are described here). Group P received food following 50% of the noise presentations but did not receive anything on the remaining 50%. Group C-24 received the same number of noise presentations, but food was delivered 100% of the time. In extinction, both groups received the same presentations of the noise alone, and the extinction rates for behavior directed at the food magazine were compared. The results clearly showed that the rats trained with the more reliable noise stimulus (Group C-24) extinguished faster (i.e., stopped searching the food magazine) than the rats trained with a less reliable CS (see Figure 7.16). This phenomenon is called the **partial reinforcement extinction effect** (PREE), and it is observed whenever resistance to extinction is weaker after training with a reliable stimulus than with a less reliable CS.

Spontaneous Recovery and Renewal of a CR.

When a CR has been extinguished, one should not assume that the underlying CS-US association has also been eliminated. Pavlov (1927) first demonstrated that a learned reflex

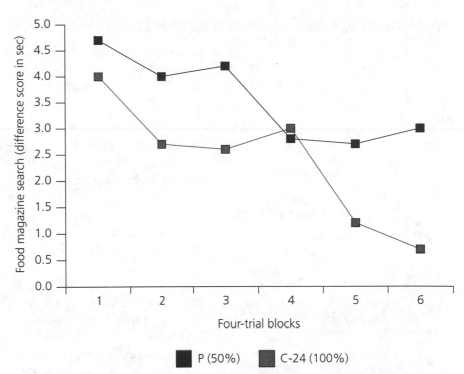

FIGURE 7.16 *Extinction of food search behavior as a function of the probability of food delivery during acquisition. Group P received food in 50% of the acquisition trials, and Group C-24 received food in 100% of the trials. Adapted from Pearce, Redhead, & Aydin (1997),* **The Quarterly Journal of Experimental Psychology,** *50B, 273–294.*

that had undergone extinction could regain strength with the passage of time and in the absence of additional CS-US pairings. He called this process spontaneous recovery. If a CR can be extinguished at one time and then be expressed at a later time without new opportunities to rebuild the CS-US association, the simplest explanation is that the weakened CR was not a reflection of a weakened CS-US association. Alternatively, Pavlov believed that extinction was an expression of the growth of a newly learned competing association. Specifically, during extinction, a subject was expected to learn a CS-no US association that interfered with the CR to the still-intact CS-US association (see Figure 7.17). This new type of CS-no US association results from a process now called **conditioned inhibition**, and Pavlov believed that extinction and conditioned inhibition were essentially the same process.

More recently, Bouton and Bolles (1979) discovered that an extinguished CR can regain strength immediately when tested in a setting different from that used during extinction. They called this new phenomenon the **renewal effect**. Whereas spontaneous recovery depends on the passage of time, renewal requires only that the CR be tested in a place different from the extinction setting. If one assumes that changes to the setting naturally occur over time, it might be that spontaneous recovery and renewal represent the same basic process.

Conditioned excitation

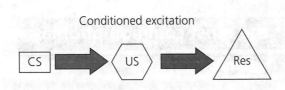

Conditioned inhibition

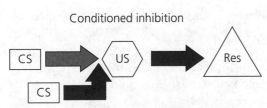

FIGURE 7.17 *Conditioned excitation results in a CS-US association (in orange). Conditioned inhibition produces a second CS-no US association (in black) that blocks the former association from being expressed in a response. Extinction of the CR may reflect the strengthening of the CS-no US association or the weakening of the original CS-US association.*

Applications of Classical Conditioning Principles

With increased understanding of the basic principles of classical conditioning, many researchers have turned their attention to potential applications of this knowledge. This section describes a sample of the applications currently being explored.

Phobias

Explore **phobias** in Chapter 14, p. 459

As Watson clearly demonstrated in his work with Little Albert, fear of an NS can be conditioned by pairing the stimulus with a fear-eliciting US. People who suffer from **phobias** have an irrational fear that most likely originated from a chance pairing of the feared stimulus and some frightening situation (imagined or real). Once the NS is associated with the physiological and emotional responses that characterize fear, anticipatory fear reflexes begin to occur at the mere sight or thought of the CS.

These anticipatory responses promote active avoidance of the stimulus, but they can be terribly inconvenient to the person. For example, a man with an irrational fear of closed spaces, **claustrophobia**, may react to the anticipatory fear by avoiding elevators, thus spending extra time and energy climbing stairs. If he works in a high-rise building, this could increase tardiness or prevent him from taking lunch outside the office. Moreover, he might quit his job to avoid the situation altogether. Research on the extinction of conditioned fears has provided and will continue to provide important insights for the development of treatments for human phobias (see Table 7.1).

Conditioned Taste or Odor Aversion

One of the fastest forms of classical conditioning involves learning about the tastes and smells of foods that have produced sickness. For example, when you eat a relatively novel food and become nauseated as a result, you are likely to

TABLE 7.1 A sample of the most common phobias.

Phobia	Description
Arachnophobia	Fear of spiders
Social phobia	Fear of being judged negatively by others
Aerophobia	Fear of flying
Agoraphobia	Fear of places not easily escaped or where help is unavailable or unlikely
Claustrophobia	Fear of being trapped in a small space
Acrophobia	Fear of heights
Emetophobia	Fear of vomit
Carcinophobia	Fear of cancer
Brontophobia	Fear of thunderstorms
Necrophobia	Fear of death or dead matter

form a strong association between the sight, smell, and taste of the food and the sickness in just a single experience. Garcia and his associates spent considerable time investigating the factors that contribute to the formation of **conditioned taste aversions**, and the findings have more recently been applied in the areas of radiation and chemotherapy (Arwas, Rolnick, & Lubow, 1989). It is not uncommon for cancer patients to form conditioned taste aversions, because for most, the treatment induces nausea. One goal for researchers in this area is to determine how to best extinguish taste aversions in cases where the relationship between a food item and sickness is only coincidental. Given the rapidity with which conditioned taste aversions are acquired, you should not be surprised to learn that they can be very difficult to extinguish.

Associative Learning: Operant Conditioning

The second type of associative learning process is known as instrumental or operant conditioning. As you now know, classical conditioning allows an organism to learn about relationships between a predictive stimulus and a particular outcome (a **stimulus-outcome association**). It is noteworthy that classical conditioning can occur even if the learner does not engage in any behavior related to the outcome. For example, when you are at a crosswalk, you can learn a great deal by simply watching the events that occur. You will notice that a red traffic light (the S^D) reliably predicts that cars will slow down and then stop. Moreover, you will notice that a green traffic signal (the S^Δ) predicts that cars will not slow down or stop. These associations allow you to anticipate the behavior of drivers and behave accordingly.

In comparison, **operant conditioning** allows an organism to learn how its own behavior can influence the nature of the outcome (a **stimulus-response-outcome** association). Operant learning is commonly called trial-and-error learning because the process is characterized by a series of exploratory or test behaviors, some of which lead to success (i.e., reinforcement) and some to failure (i.e., punishment). Both of these outcomes help the learner determine how to produce a desired consequence in the future.

For example, in some parts of the country, pedestrians are permitted to cross a street outside the crosswalk, and drivers are expected to yield the right of way. This results in a rather unfortunate pattern of behavior where residents occasionally cross the street seemingly without concern for oncoming traffic. Of course, like most relationships, this one is not 100% reliable, and people are injured or killed each year after walking out in front of a car. On most college campuses, students learn that pressing a walk button at a crosswalk causes the traffic light to change sooner, saving a few (sometimes precious) minutes that would otherwise be spent waiting for the light to change at the scheduled time. This illustrates the adaptive value of operant conditioning that is separate from classical conditioning. Classical conditioning allows one to understand relationships in the world that exist independently of one's behavior. Through operant conditioning, an organism learns how to shape its world through selective action (see Figure 7.18).

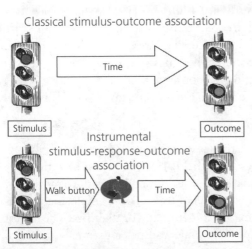

FIGURE 7.18 *Comparison of classical and operant conditioning processes.*

From 1897 to 1902, Edward L. Thorndike conducted the first programmatic investigation of instrumental learning in nonhuman animals

including cats, dogs, chicks, fish, and monkeys. He published his findings in the classic book *Animal Intelligence* (1911), and in doing so, he established animal research as a valid and productive approach to understanding human learning.

As a pioneer in this area, Thorndike had to develop his own apparatus and procedures for studying learning. One of the most famous tools that he created is called the **puzzle box** (see Figure 7.20). The puzzle box resembles a crate that has been modified to have a door on one side. An animal was placed inside the box and was required to make a particular behavior, or sequence of behaviors, to open the door. For example, in one version of the puzzle box, cats were required to reach through the slats near the door to turn a small piece of wood that held the door upright. Opening the door was a positive consequence for two reasons. First, most of the animals appeared agitated by the confinement of the box, making escape one favorable consequence. Second, Thorndike left a piece of fish just outside the door, and for a hungry cat, this provided an additional incentive to learn. Thorndike carefully measured how long it took the cats to solve the puzzle over trials, and he observed a gradual reduction in completion time. This reduction was assumed to reflect the buildup of the stimulus-response (S-R) association. Thorndike suggested that the strengthening or weakening of the S-R association depends entirely on the nature of the consequence that follows any given response. More specifically, positive consequences strengthened the S-R association, and negative consequences weakened the S-R association. Given that behavior presumably reflected the underlying association, Thorndike proposed the **law of effect**. The law of effect states that behaviors followed by positive consequences are likely to reoccur under similar conditions in the future. Conversely, behaviors followed by negative consequences are unlikely to reoccur under similar circumstances in the future. This simple law has proved to be a fundamental piece of the instrumental learning puzzle. However, learning is a complex process, and it should not surprise you to learn that the law of effect fails to account for a number of important learning phenomena.

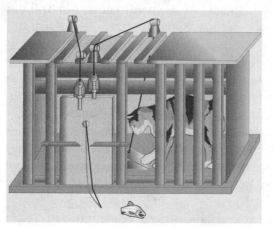

Acquisition of an Operant Response

As in classical conditioning, a number of factors influence how quickly or how well new stimulus-response associations are acquired. However, before addressing those factors, it is important to understand more generally how new responses are selected. In an important article entitled "Selection by Consequences," B. F. Skinner (1981) argued that there are two selective forces that determine how an organism will behave in a particular situation.

The first selective force is natural selection as Charles Darwin and Alfred Russell Wallace defined it in the mid-1800s (Whitfield, 1993). **Natural selection** is a process whereby some individuals in a species survive and reproduce more than others as a result of a particularly adaptive set of traits. For example, male gorillas differ in their opportunities for mating as a function of their size. The largest male silverback is typically the dominate male and has a greater number of mating opportunities than his smaller competition. Over generations, one

FIGURE 7.21 *Male gorilla (silverback) at the Cincinnati Zoo. Courtesy of morguefile.com.*

would expect the genes responsible for large body size to flourish and those for smaller body size to diminish as a result of selective mating, and this has indeed happened.

Skinner's second selective force is called **selection by consequences,** and it refers to the impact that consequences have on learning and behavior. Whereas natural selection has operated over eons, selection by consequence helps determine behavior in the present. In the case of the silverback, it is not enough for it to be large; it must also adjust its behavior to the immediate demands of its life. It must learn how to defend its high status, how to provide resources for its group, and how to navigate through jungle terrain. None of this knowledge is a birthright. Instead, the behavior that gets selected is the one that leads to positive consequences, and those behaviors that are not successful are not selected.

Positive and Negative Reinforcement

FIGURE 7.22 *Facial expressions are one important indicator that reinforcement is occurring.*

There are many factors that affect the process of selection by consequence. Reinforcers are stimuli that produce pleasurable consequences, and they act to increase the probability that a behavior will be selected in similar circumstances in the future. **Reinforcement** is the learning process that strengthens the underlying association. There are two different processes of reinforcement. **Positive reinforcement** occurs when a desirable stimulus is provided to the learner. For example, young children find inexpensive plastic toys very appealing, and behaviors that are followed by an opportunity to play with a toy increase in frequency over time. Similarly, adults find praise and social status highly reinforcing and will work very hard to acquire them. In contrast, **negative reinforcement** occurs when an undesirable stimulus is alleviated. For example, parents often succumb to a child's tantrums in order to avoid embarrassment or frustration. A simple analysis of the situation quickly reveals that both parties are likely to continue this pattern of behavior because both are under the influence of reinforcement. The child is receiving the stimulus that he or she desires (positive reinforcement), and the parent is alleviating an undesirable stimulus (negative reinforcement). Many people confuse negative reinforcement with punishment. Just remember that reinforcement always increases the likelihood that a behavior will be repeated. On the other hand, effective punishment is always intended to decrease the likelihood that a behavior will be repeated.

Positive and Negative Punishment

Stimuli that produce aversive consequences are called punishers, and they decrease the likelihood that an organism will repeat a behavior that yielded such unpleasant results. **Punishment** refers to the process that weakens the underlying association (or builds a new association to inhibit the older one). As with reinforcement, there are two types of punishment. **Positive punishment,** like positive reinforcement, involves the presentation of a stimulus—in this case, a stimulus that is painful, illness-inducing, frightening, and so forth. For example, many parents rely on spanking as a technique for reducing unwanted behaviors. Spanking exposes the child to a painful and frightening stimulus intended to prevent further unwanted behavior. **Negative punishment,** like negative reinforcement, involves the removal of a stimulus—in this case, a stimulus that is wanted. As an alternative to spanking, some parents employ the time-out technique. The logic of the time-out technique is that the child has experienced a response cost and that the loss of opportunity to engage in some more enjoyable activity should reduce the likelihood of further misbehavior. As in classical conditioning, higher order conditioning occurs with reinforcement and punishment. For example, a parent with a threatening look just prior to spanking a child may establish the look as a secondary punisher capable of suppressing behavior in the absence of further spanking.

In order to maximize the chances that a punisher has its intended result, it is important that several guidelines be followed. First, punishment is most effective when delivered immediately after the unwanted behavior. As with reinforcement, a delay between the response and the consequence allows for other behaviors to intervene, and it is those intervening behaviors that are most likely to be affected by the consequence. For example, when a parent withholds punishment in public only to deliver it in private some time later, the parent should understand that the best opportunity for learning has passed. At a minimum, the parent should preface the punishment by explaining to the child why the punishment is warranted. As you might expect, this is exceedingly difficult with younger children who are preverbal or minimally capable of processing old behaviors with new consequences (i.e., a tantrum in the morning at the grocery store with a scolding from dad in the afternoon). Moreover, if the child is in the midst of engaging in some positive behavior, it is possible that the punishment will be associated with that current behavior rather than the intended misbehavior. The second guideline is to provide a clear explanation about the contingency between a specific behavior and a specific consequence. This leads to an additional guideline: Punishment is most effective when it is used with consistency and when the intensity of the punishment is at the appropriate level. Once a contingency has been described, parents should not undermine it by failing to provide the punishment every time the targeted response is made. Moreover, parents must decide on the optimal intensity level for their child, which leads to the final guideline. Punishment is most effective when it is combined with reinforcement. Punishment only indicates which behaviors should not be performed. However, one can typically identify a behavior that would be a more appropriate substitute. Combining punishment of the unwanted behavior with reinforcement of an alternative provides two explicit contingencies that should facilitate the instrumental learning process.

Schedules of Reinforcement

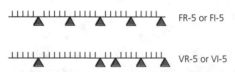

FIGURE 7.23 *Each tick represents one completed response or one second elapsed. Orange triangles indicate the delivery of a reinforcer.*

One of the best-studied areas of instrumental conditioning concerns the effects that different schedules of reinforcement have on behavior. A **schedule of reinforcement** is a set of guidelines that determine when and how a reinforcer may be earned. B. F. Skinner was a pioneer in this area of research. In 1957, Ferster and Skinner summarized the results of numerous studies in the classic book *Schedules of Reinforcement*. While the number of possible reinforcement schedules is quite large, four of the most fundamental schedules are the variable ratio (VR), fixed ratio (FR), variable interval (VI), and fixed interval (FI) (see Figure 7.23). Ratio schedules specify that reinforcers may be earned after the same response has been completed a number of times. In a **fixed ratio schedule**, the number of responses required is always the same. For example, in a fixed ratio-6 schedule, a reinforcer is earned after every sixth response is completed, and then the response counter is set back to zero. In a **variable ratio schedule**, the number of required responses changes each time the counter is reset. On a variable ratio-6 schedule, the number of required responses varies around an average of 6 responses. As you might expect, ratio schedules produce high rates of behavior because only completed responses move the subject closer to earning a reinforcer.

In contrast, interval schedules specify the amount of time that must pass between consecutive reinforcers. The behavior that a subject engages in during the waiting period does not affect the reinforcer. On a **fixed interval schedule**, a reinforcer is delivered for the first response performed after the timer has elapsed. For example, on a fixed interval-6 schedule, a subject receives a reinforcer for the first response made after six seconds have passed. Once the reinforcer is delivered, the timer is reset to zero. On a **variable interval schedule** (e.g., VI-6), the waiting time changes after each reinforcer, with the average being six seconds. Given that interval schedules require only that a subject wait a sufficient amount of time between responses, it will not surprise you to learn that interval schedules produce lower rates of behavior than ratio schedules. When graphed, this pattern of behavior yields a scalloping effect. The scallop is the result of two factors. First, immediately after a reinforcer, behavior is at its lowest rate (called the post-reinforcement pause). Behavior remains limited until the time nearly expires, and then it increases rapidly until the reinforcer is acquired and the post-reinforcement pause reoccurs. Scalloping is an exclusive feature of FI schedules, but the post-reinforcement pause is not. On FR schedules, where the ratio requirement is large, it is not uncommon to observe a similar post-reinforcement pause after a subject has completed a ratio and earned the reinforcer. For this reason, the schedule that generates the greatest amount of behavior is the VR schedule, where waiting does not contribute to the next reinforcer and the size of the ratio requirement is constantly changing (see Figure 7.24).

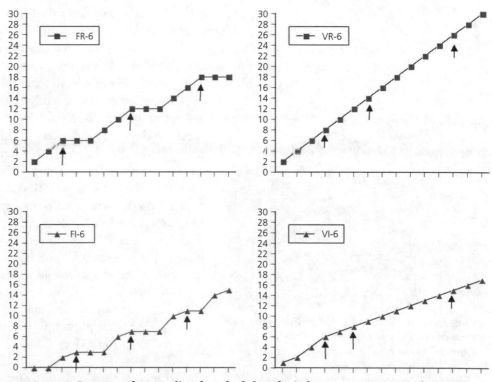

FIGURE 7.24 *Patterns of responding for schedules of reinforcement. Arrows indicate the delivery of a reinforcer.*

Applications of Operant Conditioning Principles

Operant learning principles explain how new habits are added to our behavioral repertoires through trial and error. American psychologist William James argued in the classic *The Principles of Psychology* (1890) that habits are the single most adaptive types of acquired behavior that animals engage in. Habits allow an organism to respond with minimal effort and attention to the task. This allows for other, novel behaviors to be explored until they also become habitual or are discarded. In this way, humans are able to engage in **multitasking**. Consider a concert musician who must concentrate on the musical score while at the same time playing an instrument. How can this remarkably complex set of behaviors ever happen? Through practice, the actual muscular responses become habitual. If the person reads the score, it signals to the muscles which habit to activate, and the musician must trust that the habit has been conditioned well. Failure to trust in the habit can cause a musician to think about the muscular responses, and doing so can actually interfere with the performance. In this section on operant learning, several applications of operant conditioning are described.

Token Economies

Token economies are carefully constructed systems of exchange that are used in a number of settings where behavior modification is desired. In a token economy, tokens are contingent upon the performance of certain desirable behaviors and also upon the inhibition of unwanted behaviors. Tokens can be earned for following the behavioral guidelines and can also be lost for misbehavior. At predetermined times, tokens (which are secondary reinforcers) can be exchanged for primary reinforcers that might include snacks, toys, or time to engage in some typically restricted behavior (e.g., watching television).

One well-known token economy was called Achievement Place. Developed by Elery Phillips and his associates during the 1960s in Kansas, Achievement Place aimed to rehabilitate boys who had been identified as at-risk for future juvenile delinquency. An elaborate token economy was developed in which identified specific behaviors earned points (e.g., watching the news, reading a newspaper, or getting good grades) and other behaviors cost points (e.g., using aggressive language, being late, lying, or cheating). Live-in teaching parents monitored behavior and completed a daily report card. The report card indicated points that were earned, points lost, and the amount available for spending. Points were spent once per week. Typical reinforcers were activities or consumable reinforcers. As the boys adjusted to the token economy, they were permitted to self-monitor for longer periods each day, and they were trusted to honestly determine when points should be credited or lost. In the final stage of the program, the points system was eliminated, and reinforcers were freely available as long as acceptable forms of behavior were maintained. Failure to do so resulted in reinstatement of the token economy. Achievement Place became a model for several hundred other programs, including the program now called Boys and Girls Town (Ivey, 2000).

FIGURE 7.25 *You have probably realized that our system of currency is very much like a token economy. Tokens have great reinforcing power because they can be exchanged for any number of different items or opportunities. Courtesy of morguefile.com.*

Unfortunately, the short-term successes documented within the group-home settings have not been shown to survive over the long term. For example, rates of criminal offenses are significantly higher in boys who have gone through token economy programs than the nationwide average (Wolf, Braukmann, & Ramp, 1987). Why might token economies result in behavior change during the course of the program, but fail to establish good habits that generalize beyond the group-home setting? One explanation relies on the fact that most boys return to the contexts and reinforcements that originally fostered misbehavior. Perhaps the artificiality of the group-home setting and the token economy increases the likelihood of context-specific learning.

Superstitious Behavior

Have you ever heard the old saying "When butter melts, calves die"? This is an example of a superstition. **Superstitions** are beliefs that two events are causally associated when, in fact, they occur together coincidentally or as a result of a third, unrecognized factor. Butter melting and calves dying are both most likely occurring under very hot temperatures and are otherwise completely unrelated phenomena. Examples of superstitious behavior are pervasive. Watch any sporting event on television and you will most likely observe superstitious behavior. From the batter who taps his cleats five times before entering the box, to the football player who touches a spot above the door on his way out to the field, to the basketball player who dribbles the ball four times before shooting a free throw, superstitions are normal, everyday occurrences.

Learning theorists attribute superstitions most often to adventitious reinforcement. **Adventitious reinforcement** occurs when a behavior is, by chance, followed closely in time by a reinforcer (Rudski, 2000). Of course, the reinforcer is certainly the result of some cause, but not the behavior that the person believes to have caused it. In basketball, dribbling the ball four times before shooting a successful free throw may have become a critical part of the habit that was developed during practice. Failure to include this component may result in a greater error rate, leading a person to suspect that dribbling the basketball four times causes it to go in the hoop. But in fact, dribbling is completely unrelated to the course taken by the ball once it is released. Gamblers who play the lottery, slot machines, or Bingo openly express their superstitions by selecting certain numbers that have meaning (e.g., birthdays or anniversaries), selecting slot machines in certain parts of the casino, or bringing items of "luck" to the Bingo hall. The examples described thus far have been mostly harmless, but occasionally, superstitious behavior results in much greater harm. For example, in Swaziland, Mozambique, and Botswana, a common superstition is that the disease AIDS can be cured if a man has sexual intercourse with a virginal female. This superstition has undoubtedly contributed to the spread of the disease (Hall, 2002).

FIGURE 7.26 *Why does the color of this cat's hair evoke fear in so many people? Courtesy of morguefile.com.*

Biofeedback

One final example of operant learning is a form of behavioral therapy called **biofeedback training**. In biofeedback, a person's physiological activity is displayed on a computer screen so that it becomes a source of feedback during the treatment session. After a few minutes of baseline recording, the person begins trial-and-error learning by making different behaviors (e.g., deep breathing, thinking of certain scenarios) and then watching to see how the behavior influences the physiology. Behaviors that result in positive changes in physiology are practiced until they become reliably associated with a particular physiological consequence. Behaviors that result in unwanted changes in physiology are avoided thereafter. In this way, a person learns a set of behaviors that can have particular effects on his or her physiology. For example, the most common types of psychological disorders are anxiety disorders. Anxiety is correlated with a variety of physiological responses (e.g., greater muscle tension, higher blood pressure). An electromyography (EMG) device can be used to quantify muscle tension, and this information can then be displayed as a number on a computer screen. Similarly, a simple blood pressure cuff can be used to display information about changes in blood pressure. If reduced anxiety is correlated with reductions in muscle tone and blood pressure, then the goal of therapy is to identify behaviors that achieve those outcomes through trial and error. Biofeedback training has been shown to provide significant and long-lasting benefits in cases involving asthma, epilepsy, hypertension, chronic migraine headache, neuromuscular disorders, and anxiety (Sarafino, 2001).

Cognition and Learning

FIGURE 7.27 *The personal computer is used as a metaphor for understanding human learning and memory in the information processing approach. Courtesy of morguefile.com.*

For the greater part of the twentieth century, the movement known as behaviorism dominated the study of the learning processes described in this chapter. Remember that the central argument of **behaviorism** was that the science of psychology should be limited to content that is observable and independently verifiable (i.e., overt behavior). This excluded a great deal of material from consideration because it occurred covertly (e.g., thinking, remembering, and decision making). However, in the 1960s, a movement to reintroduce these aspects of mental life arose, which became known as the **cognitive approach**. The cognitive approach allowed for the study of more covert learning processes.

Latent Learning

Edward Chase Tolman championed one of the earliest research programs that highlighted the role of cognitive processing. Tolman (1932) posited that behavior is not merely a reaction to a stimulus. Instead, he believed that a response is selected from a number of alternatives in order to achieve a specific goal or purpose. While it may seem obvious to you that animals of all types engage in decision making to some extent, this conclusion was not readily accepted in the 1930s, because it required the assumption that expectations determine behavior. Expectations are mental events (i.e., covert behaviors) that are not readily measurable or verifiable, as required by strict behaviorism.

Nevertheless, Tolman and his students continued to conduct research with the assumption that behavior reflects purpose. One of the most important

FIGURE 7.28 *As this child solves the maze, is he using trial and error, insight, or both types of learning? Courtesy of morguefile.com.*

discoveries from his laboratory was called latent learning. **Latent learning** refers to learning that is not expressed in behavior until the proper incentives are in place. In Tolman's lab, rats were trained in mazes, and the number of wrong turns was used as a measure of learning. More specifically, Tolman and Honzik (1930) trained three groups of rats in a maze that had 14 decision points. One group received a food reinforcer in each trial for finding a particular "goal" location. This group made fewer errors over trials throughout the study and revealed the typical learning curve for the maze. A second group did not receive food for exploring the maze; thus, these rats never learned to favor one place over another. The final group did not receive any food reinforcement during the first 10 days of the experiment, and these rats simply explored the maze. On Day 11, food was placed in the same location where it had been placed for the first group. Interestingly, on Day 12, rats that had received food from the beginning and rats that had received food only on the previous day made the same small number of errors. Tolman concluded that the rats that had explored the maze for 10 days had constructed **mental maps** of the maze in spite of the fact that they were not reinforced for doing so. Then, when an incentive (such as food) was provided, this mental map was revealed in the goal directedness of their behavior. This result was clear evidence that poor performance on a task might not indicate the failure of an established learning process and that associations between stimuli (in this case, the layout of the maze) can form even if a reinforcer is not available to "stamp in" the associations needed for a complete map.

Insight Learning

Recall that instrumental learning is also called trial-and-error learning because behavior is shaped over trials by the consequences that follow. In the book *The Mentality of Apes* (1927), Wolfgang Kohler describes a series of investigations that sought to demonstrate that new behaviors could arise as a result of insight rather than as a result of trial and error. **Insight** is the culmination of time spent thinking about a problem or goal and the tools available to satisfy the goal. Rather than reaching a solution by learning from one's mistakes (which could be costly), insight requires mental hypothesis testing that occasionally yields an experience commonly described as the **"ah-ha" experience.** Kohler claimed to have demonstrated insight in apes by having them perform a number of tasks.

For example, an ape named Sultan was shown some fruit suspended from a wire overhead. Several crates and a pole were scattered around the area. Kohler reported that Sultan, rather than trying a number of different solutions, first studied the problem, and in a single trial, stacked the crates, climbed them, and used the pole to retrieve the fruit. At that time, such a complex chain of behaviors would be expected to arise only through trial and error, yet Sultan seemed to utilize his private intellect to reach a solution.

Observational Learning

FIGURE 7.29 *Do violent video games, movies, and television programs promote imitation in real life?*

A final example of cognitive learning has been called vicarious trial-and-error (VTE), or observational learning. In **observational learning**, the learner watches a model behaving and notes the consequences of each action. In this way, the learner gets all the benefits that come from making mistakes without actually suffering through the errors. Learning seems to take place largely through mental practice and imagination (see Figure 7.29). Albert Bandura and his associates conducted some of the most systematic early research in this area in the 1960s. In one classic study (Bandura, Ross, & Ross, 1961), children were allowed to observe an adult interacting with a five-foot inflatable clown called a **Bobo doll**. One-third of the children observed an adult behaving aggressively with the doll (e.g., punching or verbally abusing it), one-third of the children watched an adult play with the doll in nonaggressive ways, and the final third did not watch a model play with the doll. Some time later, all the children were allowed a turn to play with the Bobo doll.

The results revealed three significant findings. First, children who observed an aggressive model behaved more aggressively with the doll than children who observed a nonaggressive model or who did not watch a model (these latter two conditions did not differ in how they behaved). Second, male children behaved more aggressively, physically, and verbally than female children in each of the three conditions. Finally, children were more likely to imitate the behavior of a model of the same sex than a model of the opposite sex. Bandura and his associates identified several factors that influenced the probability that a behavior would be successfully imitated. Imitation was most likely to occur when the observer paid careful attention to the model and to the consequences of an action, was capable of remembering well the behavior and its consequences, was capable of making the behavior, was properly motivated to perform the behavior, and was aware of when the behavior should and should not be made.

FIGURE 7.30 *Learning begins prenatally and transforms us in significant ways during childhood. Importantly, learning continues throughout the human life span as well.*

What Is Learning (Again)?

This chapter began with a simple question, "What is learning?" Unfortunately, while a definition of learning may seem difficult to come by, I think you will agree that an understanding of this complex set of processes is an even greater challenge. Psychologists who conduct research in this area continue to uncover new and exciting learning principles, and, in time, these principles should find their way out of the rat or pigeon lab and into the general knowledge base of teachers and learners alike. One final point that may not have been obvious to you as you read through the chapter, each of the five types of learning (nonassociative, classical, operant, insight, and observational) may take place simultaneously, and these learning processes surely impact one another. For example, you might be watching a friend attempt a behavior that results in a painful consequence (observational/operant learning). As a result of your friend's facial grimacing and moaning, you become aroused (sensitized) and form a conditioned fear of the most salient situational stimuli (classical conditioning). As in other areas, this chapter on learning was compartmentalized to highlight important distinctions and to simplify the material, but you should not fail to recognize that learning is a continuous, dynamic phenomenon that is a fundamental feature of life.

Chapter Summary

This chapter introduced several learning processes: habituation and sensation, classical conditioning, operant conditioning, and cognitive processes. Habituation and sensitization are nonassociative processes that allow the learner to ignore stimuli that are constant and predictable and to increase attention to novel, changing stimuli, respectively. Evidence that habituation and sensitization fail to produce durable neural associations comes from studies that have shown that people spontaneously recover from habituation and spontaneously decay from sensitization after a short rest period in the absence of the stimuli. Finally, a person's state of arousal at the time of stimulus presentation determines if he or she will become habituated or sensitized.

Classical conditioning is the process that accounts for associations between stimuli. Classical conditioning is influenced by a number of factors related to the intensity and saliency of the stimuli, the timing of the stimuli, and the preparedness of the learner to associate the events. Examples of phenomena that may be understood in terms of classical conditioning include phobias and drug tolerance. Operant conditioning is the process that accounts for associations among stimuli, responses, and consequences. Operant conditioning is influenced by some of the same factors as classical conditioning, but the schedule of reinforcement has been one of the most widely studied. Ratio schedules make a reinforcer dependent on a certain amount of behavior, whereas interval schedules require only that a certain amount of time pass since the last reinforcer. Additionally, reinforcing stimuli always increase the likelihood that a behavior will be repeated, and punishing stimuli have the opposite effect.

Applications of operant conditioning principles include token economies, where desirable behaviors are rewarded with tokens that can be exchanged for reinforcers; superstitious behaviors, where chance pairings of a behavior and reinforcer lead a person to believe incorrectly that the behavior actually caused the reinforcer; and biofeedback training, where a person utilizes physiological feedback to select behaviors that achieve a treatment goal (e.g., anxiety reduction).

The history of learning research is represented in great measure by the work of behaviorally oriented psychologists who limited their analyses of learning to overt stimulus and responses. Beginning in the 1960s, more cognitively oriented psychologists demonstrated that learning can occur in the absence of overt changes in behavior. Latent learning showed that learning can occur without reinforcement and can then be revealed when a proper incentive is provided. Insight learning suggested that organisms might test out some responses and discover solutions to problems in their minds before expressing their learning behaviorally. Finally, observational learning showed that an organism need not behave or experience consequences personally to learn from the trials and tribulations of others. By observing how others perform and the consequences that follow, the learner can adopt the most successful behaviors from the start.

Knowledge Builder

RELATE TO YOURSELF

1. The telephone rings, you answer it, and you hear someone's voice (an auditory stimulus). If the caller is a friend, you will quickly identify who he or she is just from the sounds of his or her voice. Use classical conditioning to explain how this occurs. Similarly, you turn on the radio and hear someone discussing the latest news. In your mind's eye, don't you create some version of what he or she looks like, even if you have never seen him or her? Where does that image come from and why?

    _____

    _____

    _____

    _____

2. William James argued that habits are useful adaptations because they allow a person to perform a behavior with minimal attention and effort. In modern society, multitasking has become a virtual requirement for success. What are some examples of habits that you have that allow you to multitask, and what do habits suggest about the necessity of free will and decision making?

    _____

    _____

    _____

    _____

3. The Rescorla-Wagner model is based on the premise that learning is facilitated when an event is unexpected. Unexpected events are generally more emotionally arousing than expected events. How could emotional arousal influence the durability of your memory? Hint: Think about some of the most memorable events in your life thus far and ask yourself if the situation was arousing.

    _____

    _____

    _____

    _____

4. Research on observational learning suggests that models of the same sex and age as the learner are often the most effective. Why would the similarity between the model and the observer be so important? What are some implications for parenting, teaching, or coaching? How could this fact be utilized in therapy with children?

_____

_____

_____

_____

CHAPTER REVIEW QUESTIONS

1. Reflexes cannot be modified by experience. **T or F?**

2. Classical and instrumental learning are associative processes. **T or F?**

3. Stimulus intensity is the sole determinant of whether a person will habituate or become sensitized to a stimulus. **T or F?**

4. A loud noise that produces a startle reflex the first time it is presented is a(n) _____.

   (a) conditioned stimulus   (b) unconditioned stimulus

   (c) conditioned response   (d) unconditioned response

5. Edward Thorndike discovered classical conditioning. **T or F?**

6. Classical conditioning occurs most readily with delayed conditioning. **T or F?**

7. The _____ was used by Thorndike to study trial-and-error learning.
   (a) Skinner box   (b) jumping stand

   (c) puzzle box   (d) water maze

8. A parent who spanks a child for misbehavior is utilizing _____.
   (a) positive punishment   (b) positive reinforcement

   (c) negative punishment   (d) negative reinforcement

9. This schedule of reinforcement requires that a certain, unchanging number of responses be completed before a reward is delivered.
   (a) variable interval   (b) variable ratio

   (c) fixed interval   (d) fixed ratio

10. *Consider the following scenario:* An adult male is afraid of heights and has recently passed up a great job opportunity because the employer resides on the 50th floor. How could classical conditioning processes have led to this unfortunate fear of heights?

    _____

    _____

    _____

    _____

11. *Consider the following scenario:* An employer would like to capitalize on the fact that variable ratio reinforcement schedules result in greater productivity than fixed interval schedules, but the employees want to get paid every Friday rather than be paid on a purely commission-based system. How could the employer incorporate a variable ratio component into a fixed interval pay schedule?

_____

_____

_____

_____

12. *Consider the following scenario:* A new parent utilizes spanking and scolding to stop misbehavior in a young child. What are the potential drawbacks to these techniques? Are there viable alternatives?

_____

_____

_____

_____

13. *Consider the following scenario:* A novice coach schedules a series of warm-up games with unqualified opponents to instill a sense of confidence in his players. What are the potential consequences for the players when the official season begins?

_____

_____

_____

_____

USEFUL WEB SITES

PROFESSOR FRANK PAJARES' SITE

http://www.des.emory.edu/mfp/james.html

This is a remarkable Web site dedicated to the work of William James. It includes his biography, photos, and full text articles.

THE WILLIAM JAMES SOCIETY

http://www.wjsociety.org/

The William James Society encourages the study of, and communication about, the life and work of William James and his ongoing influence in the many fields to which he contributed.

PSI CAFE

http://www.psy.pdx.edu/PsiCafe/KeyTheorists/Thorndike.htm

The Psi Cafe site provides biographical information on Thorndike as well as reviews of his papers and links to other sources of information.

MUSKINGHAM COLLEGE

http://www.muskingum.edu/~psych/psycweb/history/thorndike.htm

This site on Edward Thorndike includes a biography, a review of his theoretical ideas, a time line of his life, and a bibliography of his work.

THE MEMORIAL MUSEUM-ESTATE OF ACADEMICIAN PAVLOV I. P.

http://pavlov.amr-museum.ru/engl/e_nav.htm

This is the official Web site of the Pavlov museum in Russia. It has a wonderful collection of materials chronicling Pavlov's life and work.

NOBEL PRIZE

http://nobelprize.org/medicine/laureates/1904/pavlov-bio.html

This is the official Web site for the Nobel Prize (Pavlov won it in 1904). The site includes a biography, a review of Pavlov's award-winning research, and a transcript of his acceptance speech.

INSTITUTE OF EXPERIMENTAL MEDICINE (ST. PETERSBURG)

http://www.iemrams.spb.ru:8101/english/pavlov.htm

This site has a fine collection of photographs as well as some interesting information on Pavlov's early research into the digestive processes.

SCIENCE ODYSSEY

http://www.pbs.org/wgbh/aso/databank/entries/bhskin.html

This site includes a description of Skinner's education and his work. The video series includes a nice segment on Skinner as well.

B. F. SKINNER FOUNDATION

http://www.bfskinner.org/

This is the official Web site of the B. F. Skinner Foundation, whose mission it is to improve the understanding of human behavior through the science first proposed by B. F. Skinner.

Chapter **8**

Memory

by Vanda Wark, EdD, and Deborah Yakel, PhD

*When I was younger, I could remember anything,
whether it had happened or not.*

—MARK TWAIN

How Accurate Is Memory?

FIGURE 8.1 *Is memory as good as a photograph?*

How good is your memory? Many people take great pride in their memory. They believe that all the events they remember really happened. They believe that their memory is an unlimited, objective record of the events of their life. But is this truly the case? Memory is such an intimate part of who we are that it seems unlikely that we could be wrong about what we remember about our own lives.

But can we remember something that never happened? This is one of the most controversial questions asked in psychology today. It might be hard for students to believe that a seemingly dry topic such as the workings of memory could stimulate one of the most contentious debates currently being argued in the field (Ost, 2003). This topic has stirred up such an unpleasant debate among psychologists that it has been called the memory wars (Crews, 1995).

Beginnings of the Memory Debate

The memory debate seems to have begun with the McMartin Day Care scandal of the mid-1980s. The McMartin family members, who had owned and operated a day care center in Manhattan Beach, California, since the 1960s, were accused of sexually abusing the preschoolers in their charge. Other day care centers were also accused of sexual abuse, but the McMartin case was the most famous, so it serves as a good example of the tenor of the time.

229

FIGURE 8.2 *Can memories of satanic rituals be imagined?*

The children at the school told stories of having been sexually abused by the teachers at the school. They also reported being forced to participate in satanic rituals (Nathan & Snedeker, 2001). The thought of little children being treated so badly caused fear and anger around the country. When it was settled six years later, it became clear that none of these children had been abused. The hysteria was begun by one mother, who had been diagnosed with schizoaffective disorder, whose child may or may not have been sexually abused by his father (Nathan & Snedeker, 2001). Yet was it possible that all these children simply made up such terrible stories about their teachers? If so, why would they do this? Research suggests that their memories were influenced by the questions asked during the investigation.

False Memory of a Murder

In 1989 Eileen Franklin accused her father of murdering her eight-year-old friend, Susan, 20 years earlier. She said the memory returned in bits and pieces and was prompted by playing with her own young children. By the time she testified against her father, she completely recalled her father sexually violating Susan and then smashing Susan's head with a rock. George Franklin, Sr., was found guilty of murder and sentenced to life imprisonment primarily on the basis of his daughter's recovered memory. A conviction of this sort had never happened before (Loftus, 1993). His conviction was subsequently overturned, but prosecutors were going to retry him. They decided against this, however, when they discovered that Eileen Franklin had been hypnotized before giving her testimony ("Repressed-memory case," 1996). It has been found that hypnosis can create what has come to be known as false memories.

These apparent revelations seemed to force our society to come to terms with the reality of child sexual abuse. Women who had memories of being sexually abused as children began to come forward to accuse relatives of things that happened 20 or more years ago. Some wanted to take legal action against their perpetrators, but because of a statute of limitations, they were not able to do so in many states (Williams, 1996). A statute of limitation specifies the amount of time within which a criminal or civil action against someone must be taken. If the accuser does not act within that time period, she loses the right to take action. As more and more women came forth, the media became involved. Stories of women, and sometimes of men, who had been sexually abused as children were often heard on the nightly news and on TV talk shows (such as *The Oprah Winfrey Show*).

Many of the women coming forth had been in therapy when they recovered a memory of abuse (i.e., they had not remembered being sexually abused until going to therapy for some other reason). While in therapy, the women were engaged by their therapists in what is known as recovered memory therapy. **Recovered memory therapy** refers to any therapeutic procedure that attempts to uncover repressed memories, which may be interfering with current psychological functioning (Lindsay & Read, 1997). Techniques used include hypnosis,

FIGURE 8.3 *The U.S. Supreme Court hosted lawsuits based on recovered memories.*

guided imagery, and journaling (Working Party of the British Psychological Society, 1996).

The growing numbers of individuals claiming to have recovered memories of child sexual abuse caused the courts to look differently at the statutes of limitations for these cases (Brown, Scheflin, & Hammond, 1998). In many states the statutes were changed to allow adults who had recovered memories of sexual child abuse to sue the perpetrators 20 or 30 years later (Brown et al., 1998; Loftus, 1993; Underwager & Wakefield, 1998; Williams, 1996).

Many lawsuits based solely on recovered memories with no further corroborating evidence were filed against relatives. In reaction to these accusations, relatives who felt falsely accused of sexual abuse established the False Memory Syndrome Association, believing that recovered memories were really false memories (Loftus & Ketcham, 1994; Ost, 2003).

Questioning the Accuracy of Memory

Recovered memories of child abuse caused psychologists to question the accuracy of memory. Was it true that so many women had been abused and had repressed the abuse, only to have the memory recovered in therapy? Did memory work that way, they wondered? Were so many children really being abused at day care centers across the country? Could a child's memory for these events be trusted? Would a child make up horrible stories such as being forced to drink a rabbit's blood in a satanic ritual? (Nathan & Snedeker, 2001). Seeking answers to these questions, numerous researchers began taking a hard look at memory to understand how it really operated. Clinicians were forced to defend their "recovered memory therapy."

A Classic Study on False Memories

FIGURE 8.4 *Dr. Elizabeth Loftus.*

Dr. Elizabeth Loftus, a leading memory researcher, has conducted several studies that have tested whether it is possible to remember something that never happened. As far back as 1972, Loftus's research had indicated that people remember things that have never happened. In a number of studies, she found that it was indeed possible to get some people to recall memories for things that had never happened. In one of her studies, she implanted the memory into participants that they had been lost in a mall as a child for a period of time (Loftus & Pickerell, 1995). In that study, a close family relative of each participant provided the researchers with three real events that had occurred when the participant was a child. These events were written into a booklet, along with an event that had never occurred: getting lost in a shopping mall. The participants were to read each event and then write in the details. If the participant did not remember an event, he or she was told to write, "I don't remember."

When the participants had completed the booklets, they sent them to the researchers and an interview was scheduled. At the interview, the participants

FIGURE 8.5 *Getting lost.*

were asked to rate on a scale of 1–10 (10 being extremely clear) how clear their memory was for each event. Twenty-five percent of the participants had full or partial memory of the false event (being lost in a mall); however, their clarity rating for the false memory tended to be lower than for the true memories (Loftus & Pickerell, 1995). These results seem to indicate that it is possible to create memories for events that never happened in some people, but it may not be possible in many others. Seventy-five percent of the participants in this study did *not* remember the false event.

Research of this type generally finds that about one-fourth of the participants create false memories (Hyman, Husband, & Billings, 1995). However, when photographs are used along with the pseudoevents, the percentage of participants recalling the false memory goes up considerably. Wade, Garry, Read, and Lindsay (2002) followed a procedure similar to that used in the Loftus and Pickerell study, except that they added photographs. Three photographs were from real childhood events, and the other was a doctored photo of the participant between the ages of 4 and 8 in a hot air balloon. Although this event had never occurred, 50% of the sample reported recalling this memory. In a similar study, the number of participants recalling the false event went all the way up to 75% (Lindsay, Hagen, Read, Wade, & Garry, 2004).

False Memories of Events From TV

Many of us remember where we were when we heard the report that Princess Diana of England had been killed in a car crash. At the time there was a great deal of controversy over whether the paparazzi, who had been pursuing the car across Paris, had videotaped the car crash. Do you remember seeing the video of the actual crash? If you do, you have something in common with the 40% of participants in Britain who also remembered seeing this nonexistent video (Ost, Vrij, Costall, & Ball, 2002). In our own country, Pezdek (2003) found that 73% of the participants in her study reported that on September 11, 2001, they saw videotape of the first plane striking the World Trade Center tower; however, that video was not aired until September 12.

False Memories of a TV Star

Alan Alda, the TV and movie star, participated in two memory experiments with Dan Schacter, a noted memory expert. In one of the experiments, Alda watched a college-aged couple have a picnic for 10 minutes. As Alda watched the man and woman, Schacter told him to count how many times one of the young people stood up. After 10 minutes Alda was asked to leave. The young people had their picnic again, but this time a photographer took pictures. He also took pictures of things occurring at the picnic that Alda did not observe.

Two days later, Alda was shown 20 pictures of the picnic and was asked to rate each picture on a scale from 1 to 10 in terms of how well it was composed (i.e., he was to judge whether the subjects of the photograph were nicely centered and whether the resolution of the picture was sharp). Alda was fairly certain that Schacter was not really interested in his opinion about the composition of these photographs. He noticed that some of the pictures were of things that he had not witnessed. Schacter was attempting to create a false memory in Alda's mind for something that had never occurred at the picnic. After Alda rated all the pictures, Schacter read a list of objects. Alda was to say whether he had seen the object at the picnic. Even though Alda knew he was in a memory experiment, he incorrectly remembered two objects as being at the picnic that had only been in the photos. Obviously, his memory was influenced by the photographs.

This demonstrates that events that occur after the original memory can influence and even change the original memory. For example, take the memory from your birthday party when you turned six. This memory contains remnants from the original event, but it probably also contains elements from your parents' stories of that party and elements from photographs of that party and other birthday parties, including friends' parties. It could even have elements from Bart Simpson's birthday party.

Alda participated in a second experiment with Schacter in which Schacter read a list of words and Alda's task was to remember as many as he could. The list had a theme—that is, all the words had something to do with sleep, such as pillow, bed, and yawn—but the most obvious word, "sleep," was not on the list. When Alda was asked to read back the words that he could remember from the list, the first word he said was "sleep." Despite Alda's knowing that Schacter was trying to implant a false memory, he still couldn't prevent it. Twelve other participants took this test in Schacter's lab. One important difference in how the study was done in the lab was that the participants were given a PET scan while they read back the words. A **PET scan** (positron emission tomography) is a technique that doctors use to look inside the brain while it is working. A radioactive sugar is injected into the bloodstream and carried to the brain. As the radioactive blood sugar flows to active areas of the brain to provide energy, the scanner is able to detect the radioactivity and help psychologists view brain function (Pynes, 2005). In the study, Schacter found that when participants said the true memory of a word, the auditory cortex, a region in the brain, became more active. When participants reported a false memory, the auditory cortex did not become active. This attempt to distinguish true memories from false memories is very crude right now, but it may become more sophisticated in time (Scientific American Frontiers, n.d.).

Eyewitness Testimony

If memories are not as fixed as we might like, as indicated by the research studies we've discussed, then how can we know that the memories of an eyewitness to a crime are accurate? In the early stages of the sniper attacks in Washington, DC, which ultimately led to 10 deaths, some witnesses reported seeing a white truck or van leaving a number of the crime scenes. After later attacks had occurred, other witnesses also reported seeing a white vehicle. However, when the two snipers were captured, they were driving a blue car. How is it possible that so many people saw a white vehicle instead of a blue one?

Erroneous eyewitness identifications have caused more wrongful convictions than all other causes combined—a fact that most people are generally unaware of

(Loftus, 2002; Wells et al., 1998). Wells and colleagues (1998) examined 40 cases of incarcerated prisoners who were found to be innocent after a DNA analysis was done. Thirty-six (90%) had been convicted solely on the basis of eyewitness testimony. All these individuals had served time in prison, five on death row.

These types of studies indicate that we must be very cautious about convicting someone solely on the basis of **eyewitness testimony**. Juries tend to believe eyewitnesses, especially if they seem very confident. These studies have also found no correlation between eyewitness accuracy and the witness's level of confidence (Wells et al., 1998). An important lesson can be learned from the tragic experience of Jennifer Thompson and Ronald Cotton.

In 1984, a young college student, Jennifer Thompson, was raped by a man who broke into her home. While she was being raped, she intentionally attempted to memorize the man's face. She intended that he would go to prison and "rot." Later that day the police department had her work on a composite sketch of the man's face. She looked through hundreds of pictures of eyes, noses, and lips until they had a composite of the man who had raped her. Later that week she picked the man out of a lineup. She was "positive" she had the right man. Solely on the basis of Thompson's testimony, Ronald Cotton went to jail. Jennifer went on with her life. Eleven years later in 1995, Jennifer was asked to give a sample of blood for a DNA test. She willingly cooperated, knowing that it would simply be further evidence that Ronald Cotton had, indeed, raped her. She wrote in the *New York Times:* "I will never forget the day I learned about the DNA's results. I was standing in my kitchen when the detective and the district attorney visited. They were good and decent people who were trying to do their jobs—as I had done mine, as anyone would try to do the right thing. They told me: 'Ronald Cotton didn't rape you. It was Bobby Poole'" (Thompson, 2000).

FIGURE 8.6 *The effect of police questioning on memory.*

Loftus found that eyewitness accounts are vulnerable to the misinformation effect. The **misinformation effect** happens when a person is given new information after witnessing an event, and this new information changes what is remembered (Toland, Hoffman, & Loftus, 1991). Erroneous postevent information can influence one's memories in a number of ways. When we talk to others about an event, their ideas often get mixed in with our own, influencing what we recall. The media have their own ideas about events and thus influence our views of a situation. Even being questioned about an event in a suggestive manner can change our memory of the event (Loftus, 2003).

How Well Do We Remember Traffic Events?

In one study by Loftus, participants were shown a film of a car accident. After the film, they were divided into two groups and asked different questions according to their group assignment:

1. Did you see *the* broken headlight?

2. Did you see *a* broken headlight?

FIGURE 8.7 *Why was the yield sign a false memory?*

Can you hear the different implications of the two sentences? Those who were asked question one were more likely to answer that they had seen the broken headlight (Loftus & Zanni, 1975). This is a good example of postevent questioning changing an individual's memory of the event. How might the way an interrogator phrases a question affect what a witness remembers about an event?

In another study, Loftus (1978) showed study participants slides of a traffic accident. In the slides there was a stop sign but no yield sign. After viewing the slides, the participants were given a written summary of the slides. In one of the groups, the written summary mentioned a nonexistent yield sign. When these participants were questioned about what they had seen in the slides, many mentioned having seen a yield sign.

In an earlier study, Loftus (1975) showed a film segment of a car accident. After the film, the participants were asked, "Did you see the children getting on the bus in the film?" even though there was no bus in the film. After a week, the participants were asked, "Did you see a school bus in the film?" The participants saw a school bus three to four times more often than the control group, who were not asked about seeing the school bus immediately after the film. This demonstrates that the misinformation of the school bus affected the memories of some of the participants in the experimental group.

Stress and Memory Inaccuracies

Stress can also affect a witness's memory. In one study (Loftus & Burns, 1982), participants were shown a film of a holdup. At the end of the film, the experimental group saw a stressful event of a young boy getting shot in the face. Later, this group showed significantly poorer memory for 16 details that they were asked to recall, whereas the control group, who saw a nonviolent end, did not demonstrate these decrements in memory.

Child Testimony

Knowing what you do about eyewitness accounts, what would you expect to hear about children's testimonies in court? Before the mid-1980s, it was thought that children didn't understand reality well enough to give good testimony in court cases. But when the day care scandals began to occur, people were certain that children would not make up stories of sexual abuse. Society quickly went from not believing children's stories all the way to completely believing everything they said (Wade & Tavris, 2002).

Studies have shown that children's ability to recall autobiographical events can be highly accurate (Baker-Ward, Gordon, Ornstein, Larus, & Chubb, 1993). At the same time, there have been other studies that have shown different results—that children's reports about past autobiographical events can also be quite inaccurate. As you would expect, children, especially preschoolers, are more suggestible than adults. The accuracy of a child's testimony in court has much to do with the adults who are guiding the child. Children are especially influenced by suggestive interviewing techniques, which cause their memories to be susceptible to the misinformation effect. One of the biggest problems with police officers and court-appointed therapists is interviewer bias. **Interviewer bias** occurs when the adult thinks he or she already knows the answer to the question and uses subtle pressure, consciously or unconsciously, to get the child to change his or her view of an event (Bruck, Hembroke, & Ceci, 1997). This is what happened with the children at the McMartin Day Care Center. Adults "knew" the children had been abused, and so they applied subtle and not-so-subtle pressure to get the children to agree. (For an interesting fact-based dramatization of this case, see the HBO film *The Indictment.*)

Memory Under Hypnosis

FIGURE 8.8 *Hypnosis.*

As you learned in Chapter 5, "States of Consciousness," hypnosis is not some spooky thing that gives the hypnotist control over your mind. It's really just a heightened sense of relaxation that helps you be more open to suggestion, if you want to be (Baker, 1998). Hypnosis happens as a result of the client choosing to trust the hypnotist. Hypnosis is about accepting suggestions and being willing to engage in fantasy (Perry, n.d.). Knowing this, and knowing what you have already learned about memory, how helpful do you think hypnosis would be in remembering long-forgotten memories from your past?

It's a popular belief that hypnosis improves memory for things one couldn't recall prior to being hypnotized, but there is no evidence that this is true. Hypnotized people tend to produce more information, but this information may not be particularly accurate (Perry, n.d.). This is why evidence recalled through hypnosis is inadmissible in court in many states (Kihlstrom, 2003). Recall that earlier the prosecutors of George Franklin decided not to retry the case after learning that his daughter, Eileen Franklin, had been hypnotized before testifying during the first trial. Hypnosis makes confabulation more likely. **Confabulation** occurs when a person unwittingly invents information to fill in the gaps in his or her memory and comes to believe the invention to be a fact. Confabulation occurs to some extent with our everyday memories and can also occur with hypnosis and other similar techniques like guided imagery (Baker, 1998).

Memory of Space Alien Abduction

It all began back in 1961, when Barney and Betty Hill were driving toward Portsmouth, New Hampshire, from Canada after a short vacation. They were stopped by a flying object in the sky. It looked to be some type of bright star or an erratically moving planet. They got out of their car to get a better look at the object. They thought that perhaps it could be a plane, but since they couldn't really determine what it was, they continued on their journey home. They had expected to arrive home at 3 a.m., but much to their shock it was 5 a.m. when they got there. They had lost two hours! Over the following weeks, Betty began having nightmares of being examined by aliens while being held in an alien spacecraft. Barney became so nervous that the ulcer he already had grew worse. They sought the services of a well-known psychiatrist, Dr. Benjamin Simon. Over the course of six months, Dr. Simon used a technique called "regressive hypnosis." He took the Hills back in time through regression, in separate sessions, to the night they saw the object in the sky. From these sessions, Dr. Simon determined that the Hills had been abducted and examined by aliens during those two missing hours (*Abduction*, n.d.; *Betty and Barney Hill*, n.d.).

It is important to note that people who claim to have been abducted by space aliens do not exhibit signs of mental disturbance. Generally, they are mentally healthy adults who have experienced what is known as sleep paralysis. **Sleep paralysis** is a nonpathological experience that occurs when a person awakens while still in REM sleep. The individual is conscious that his or her body is paralyzed, which is normal during REM sleep. Along with this, many people experience what is called hypnopompic hallucinations. **Hypnopompic hallucinations** are vivid, dreamlike hallucinations that occur when one is waking up. The individual may feel an electrical tingling throughout his or her body, see flashing lights, or get the sensation of levitating out of bed. He or she might even have visual hallucinations of figures hovering over the bed. After a few seconds or minutes, the hallucinations vanish and the paralysis is gone. About 15% of the general population has had this experience, but not all of these individuals have interpreted their experience as having been visited by space aliens. The average "abductee" begins to feel like something happened after falling asleep, but before full awakening. Research has found that people holding this abduction belief have the same heightened physiological activity as someone who has been traumatized by war (McNally et al., 2004). Since researchers cannot determine the truth or falsity of a memory simply by the emotionality attached to it, these data cannot scientifically validate the abduction claims.

Hypnosis for "age regression" is also unlikely to lead to accurate memories of childhood. When adults are given the suggestion to regress to childhood, those who are highly hypnotizable will behave in ways that might be considered childlike. They say they feel like children. Still, research shows that these adults have not regressed in terms of their brain waves, thinking ability, or emotionality. Their age-regressed memories are also usually incorrect when checked against the facts of their early lives (Kihlstrom, 2003; Nash, 2001). Hypnosis is a valuable therapeutic tool for pain control, relaxation, and anxiety (Nash, 2001), but it isn't very helpful for bringing back accurate memories from the past.

Are Traumatic Memories Different From Other Types of Memory?

Explore
research ethics
in Chapter 2, p. 52

Some researchers believe that memory for trauma is different from other forms of memory—that after a traumatic experience, the memory is practically engraved on the brain (Terr, 1991). Indeed, it is not uncommon for those with post-traumatic stress disorder (PTSD) to experience intrusive memories of their traumatic experience (Schacter, 1996). Laboratory experiments, however, cannot ethically create the kind of trauma that victims of PTSD experience, so it becomes difficult to know whether traumatic memories are different from other memories that are vulnerable to distortion (van der Kolk & Fisher, 1995). Schacter (1996) notes that even when traumatic memories are distorted or decayed, the main portion of the event remains extremely accurate. You probably remember where you were and what you were doing on September 11, 2001. Some of that memory may be lost or distorted, but you probably remember that day better than you remember September 10, 2001.

Flashbulb Memories

FIGURE 8.9 *Can memories be like photos?*

Flashbulb memories are vivid, detailed memories caused by traumatic or memorable events that an individual remembers in great detail years later (Brown & Kulik, 1977). Or can you? You may have heard your grandparents or parents talk about remembering exactly where they were and with whom the day President John F. Kennedy was shot. They may have told you all the details they remembered from that day. Other vivid happenings have been experienced in this way—the shooting of Martin Luther King, Jr., the explosion of the space shuttle *Challenger* in the 1980s, the day the O. J. Simpson verdict was announced, and certainly the morning of 9/11. People remember these types of events as if a photograph were embedded in their brains.

During the O. J. Simpson trial, many people were so involved in watching this trial day after day that they dreaded the thought of this "show" ending. The day the verdict was to be delivered, people from all over the country huddled around their TV sets, breathless. Many people said they would never forget the details of hearing the verdict for the first time. However, when college students' responses 15 months after the trial were compared with the responses they gave 32 months later, there were many errors. Schmolk, Buffalo, and Squire (2000) found that after 32 months, more than 40% of the students' recollections contained distortions.

Even more dramatic was Talarico and Rubin's (2003) findings for the recall of September 11, 2001. The researchers recorded the memories of 54 Duke University students for the 9/11 terrorist attacks and for their autobiographical memories that occurred around the same time. The participants were divided into three groups. One group was tested after 1 week, another group was tested after 6 weeks, and the third group was tested after 32 weeks. What they found was that the participants' memories for the events of 9/11 were no more accurate than their memories for the ordinary autobiographical events of their lives. However, their *confidence* for their memories of 9/11 was greater than for the other events. Talarico and Rubin (2003) concluded that emotionally charged events that seem to drill themselves into our very brains may not be any more accurate than the ordinary dull things that happen to us every day, they just *feel* more accurate.

Research on Repressed Memory

Repressed memories refer to memories of which we are not consciously aware. Schacter (1996) tells a story of a college professor who went to a therapist because he felt vaguely discontented with his marriage and his job. Shortly after beginning therapy, he awoke from a dream that gradually turned into a recollection of having been abused by a camp counselor many years before. The professor was able to locate the former camp counselor by hiring a private detective. He confronted this man over the telephone, and the man admitted to abusing him; he had abused a number of boys at the camp, which led to his dismissal. This story alone provides evidence that it is possible to recover a long-buried memory of sexual abuse.

An interesting study also demonstrated that memories can be repressed. This longitudinal study, involving 129 women whose sexual abuse had been documented in the records of physicians and social service agencies, found that 38% could not recall their abuse when interviewed 17 years later (Williams, 1996). In another study it was found that out of 79 participants, 41% had experienced a time period when they had no memory or only a slight memory of their sexual abuse (Summers-Feldman & Pope, 1994). Of these 41% in the above survey, 38% percent were able to support their memory with evidence from another source besides their own testimony.

Many researchers have doubts about whether people can repress traumatic memories such as child sexual abuse and then 20 or 30 years later have the memories resurface *exactly* as they happened, with all the details accurate (Loftus, 1993; Schacter, 1996). One study compared women who had been raped with women who had not been raped. In this study, Schacter (1996) reported that rape victims rated their rape memory as more difficult to recall with clarity than non-rape victims rated their memories of other bad events.

Summing Up Both Sides of the Memory Debate

There are serious concerns on both sides of the memory controversy. Clinicians who work with clients often see traumatic experiences as being permanently embedded in the memory, and there may be some evidence for this. They believe that it is possible to revive these memories, and when they are revived, they will generally be accurate. As part of their patients' therapy, many clinicians have recommended that their clients confront their families with their recovered memories. The problem with this is that if the clinician is wrong and the memory is false, families will be needlessly destroyed. Some family members will be erroneously labeled as pedophiles and sometimes wrongly incarcerated without any corroborating evidence (Pendergast, 1996). Ray Buckey, the main defendant in the McMartin Case, spent five years in jail without ever being convicted of anything (Nathan & Snedeker, 2001).

Psychologists tend to see the majority of recovered memory cases from recovered memory therapy techniques such as hypnosis, journaling, and guided imagery as inducing false memories (Hyman, 2000; Working Party, 1996). However, this group needs to be careful not to go back to a time when people who were sexually abused were afraid to tell anyone. We don't want these people to be fearful that they will not be taken seriously by therapists and lawyers because of the prevalence of the false memory syndrome (Read & Lindsay, 1997; Shuman, 1997).

How Does Memory Work?

So far we have looked at how we are capable of remembering events that never happened and distorting those that did. We also looked at how some people can repress their memories and recall those memories years later. But how does memory actually work? Why do we remember some things better than others? How is it we remember the name of a former classmate we haven't seen in years by just

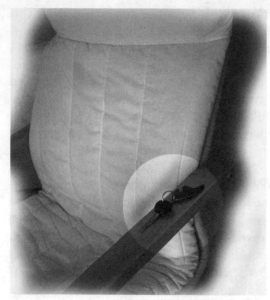

FIGURE 8.10 *Do you often ask yourself, "Where did I put my car keys?"*

looking at a photo, but we can't remember the name of the person we were just introduced to a moment ago? How is it we remember *yo tengo* means "I have" from an introductory Spanish class we took in ninth grade, but we can't remember where we put the car keys last night? All memory-making involves three basic processes.

1. Encoding—putting information into long-term memory

2. Storage—holding information in long-term memory

3. Retrieval—pulling information out of long-term memory

Levels of Processing

There are four models of memory; each looks at memory in a slightly different way. The **levels of processing model** states that the information we remember best is that which has been processed most fully when we receive it (Craik & Lockhart, 1972; Craik & Tulving, 1975). This model explains what you do when the information operator gives you a telephone number and you don't have a pen. You probably keep reviewing it in your mind or even saying it out loud until you can dial the number. What you've been doing is called **maintenance rehearsal**. Chances are, after you finish your phone call you no longer remember the number. There is, however, a more effective, deeper way to process information so that you have a more lasting memory (Jahnke & Nowaczyk, 1998). When you connect new material to what you already know, you are using **elaborative rehearsal**. It is easier to remember something that relates to something you already know. You've probably heard that if you want to improve your vocabulary, you need to first look the word up in a dictionary. Then, you should use it in your own sentence. In this way you are connecting the new word with ideas and concepts with which you are already familiar.

The Information Processing Memory Model

The **information processing model**, developed by Atkinson and Shiffrin (1968), is the oldest and most detailed model in the memory field (Roediger, 1990). This model divides the basic structure of memory into three parts: the sensory register, short-term memory, and long-term memory (Atkinson & Shiffrin, 1968; Izawa, 1999).

Sensory Register

Information from the external and/or internal world enters your senses. Each sense has its own **sensory register** and can store a large amount of information. For instance, your visual sense is picking up many sights, such as your bed, the lamp on your desk, maybe a bird that landed in a tree outside your window. While your visual sense is doing this, you are simply sitting in your bedroom studying. These sights are passed into your visual register. At the same time, your auditory register is also picking up many sounds, such as the radio playing in the background. These sounds are being passed along to your auditory register. These sights and sounds stay in their register for only a very short time. If there is no reason for you to pay attention to these impressions, they will be lost. Studies show that the sensory register can hold visual images for only a fraction of a second and sounds for about two seconds (Crowder, 1992; Klatsky, 1980).

But how much of the visual image or auditory information is stored in the registers? Researcher George Sperling (1960) conducted several experiments to test the limits of iconic memory. **Iconic memory** is what is stored in the visual sensory register. Sperling showed people three rows of letters simultaneously for about 1/20th of a second and then asked them to immediately report what they had seen. He found that participants recalled only about half of the letters. Was it because only half were recorded in the sensory register? Sperling cleverly uncovered the answer to this question by conducting partial recall tests. In the partial recall test, he showed participants the three rows of nine letters, as in the first experiment. But this time, he sounded a high, medium, or low tone immediately afterward. Each tone told them to report either the first row, the second row, or the third row. In the partial recall test, participants had almost 100% recall and rarely missed a letter. Sperling concluded that 100% of visual information is stored in iconic memory, but is only momentarily available for recall. So when participants are asked to report all nine letters, they cannot do it, because the letters fade from the sensory register before they have a chance to report them.

Studies show that our echoic memory also fades quickly but holds an incredible amount of information for a short period of time (Cowan, 1994; Lu, Williamson, & Kaufman, 1992). **Echoic memory** is what is stored in our auditory sensory register. Can you remember being in a conversation and having your attention drift? You then hear the voice of the person you have been talking to lift, and you realize that you have just been asked a question and you weren't listening. Your attention immediately comes back to the conversation and you ask, "What did you say?" Before the person has a chance to reply, you hear in your mind what was just asked and you are able to recover the question. This is because auditory echoes occur in the sensory register and last about three seconds before fading away. These experiments on iconic memory and echoic memory have helped us understand that the sensory register records almost 100% of the incoming information, but that it fades very quickly unless it is selectively attended to and passed on to short-term memory.

Short-Term Memory

When we perceive information by attending to it before it is lost from our sensory register, it is encoded in the **short-term memory (STM)**. In STM the information is further processed by using the working memory. **Working memory** is the part of STM that allows us to work on incoming information with strategies such as maintenance rehearsal and elaborative rehearsal (Brown, 1958; Peterson, 1959). Think of what happens when you've just gotten that telephone number from the operator. You use maintenance rehearsal when someone interrupts you to ask a question. When you go back to your phone number, what usually happens? If STM is full, then new incoming information pushes out old information that is forgotten—a process known as **displacement**. So unless information is repeated in STM, it will stay there for only a short period of time.

Miller's Magic Number

STM is limited not only in duration but also in its capacity. George Miller (1956) demonstrated in pioneering research that our working memory capacity is very limited. **Miller's Magic Number** is the term used to describe that STM has a capacity of about seven (plus or minus two) items, depending on the individual. Miller discovered this phenomenon by using a short-term digit test. He asked participants to remember lists of random numbers in sequence. He found that most people began to have difficulty somewhere between five and nine digits.

Our short-term recall seems to be a little better for numbers than it is for letters. Researchers speculate that this is because letters may have similar sounds that make the task slightly more confusing. Our STM recall is also slightly better for what we hear as opposed to what we see. We can process about as many words as we can speak in about two seconds (Cowan, 1994; Hulme & Tordoff, 1989). This means that at any given moment, we can process only a very limited amount of information.

Chunking

We should further elaborate on how information gets held in STM so that it can then move on to long-term memory storage. One's STM span is the maximum number of items that can be recalled without error after one presentation. For most people the number is six or seven items regardless of whether they are digits, letters, or words (Pollack, 1953).

This brings us to chunking. A chunk is one unit of information. **Chunking** is the process of combining several smaller units of information into one larger unit. This one unit can be individual numbers, letters, or words. The letters "b," "o," "y" when spoken separately are three separate units of information or chunks. If, however, we put these letters together to spell "boy," it becomes one chunk. We can build bigger and bigger chunks of information, which makes them easier to remember. For example, if we try to remember the words "smile," "the," "happy," "with," "boy," "the," we are likely to have difficulty because we are putting six chunks into our STM, about the maximum that can be maintained. On the other hand, if we put these separate words or chunks into a phrase that makes sense, such as, "The boy with the happy smile," we have reduced the load that the STM must handle to only one chunk, which then may be moved on to long-term memory.

FIGURE 8.11 *"The boy with the happy smile" is easier to memorize than all these words separately: "smile," "the," "happy," "with," "boy," "the."*

Long-Term Memory

Long-term memory (LTM) storage is where we hold information without having to rehearse it, and the information tends to stay for a long time. Our rehearsal of data in STM facilitates the transfer of that data into LTM. At times, even without rehearsal, information immediately accesses LTM, for example, September 11 or some other noteworthy event.

The capacity for LTM storage is large—probably unlimited (Matlin, 1998). Sometimes the hard drive of your computer, which might be considered the com-

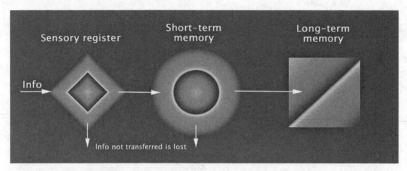

FIGURE 8.12 *The information processing model.*

puter's LTM, gets filled up and your computer slows down. It might even crash if you don't start deleting unwanted information or invest in an auxiliary hard drive. Since we've all experienced this problem, or at least heard about it, we know that the computer's hard drive does not have unlimited storage capacity. However, when was the last time you heard of someone who couldn't learn one more thing because all the space was used up in his or her long-term memory?

Some things seem to stay in our memory for a lifetime. For instance, one study found that people could recognize the faces of classmates they went to school with 25 years ago (Bruck, Cavanaugh, & Ceci, 1991). In another study, participants were able to remember their high school Spanish, French, or algebra 50 years after studying it (Bahrick & Hall, 1991).

Types of LTM

So far we have focused on episodic memory. **Episodic memory** refers to the episodes of your life, like your memory of going to a party last Friday night or your memory about the time you got the flu and couldn't go on the skiing trip with your friends. **Semantic memory** is memory for knowledge about the world. For example, it's your knowledge about what makes a verb different from a noun or your knowledge that the earth is round. When we recall an episodic memory, we often say, "I remember when . . . ," but when we retrieve a semantic memory, we tend to say, "I know that . . ." (Tulving, 1995). Episodic memory and semantic memory are also called declarative memory.

Procedural memory is your knowledge of how to perform certain tasks like riding a bike or driving a car. This type of memory is quite different from episodic and semantic memories. It is less connected to words and more connected to movement. Once you've become proficient at riding a bike, try explaining how to do it. You'll see it is difficult to put into words (to declare it). That's why procedural memory is also called nondeclarative memory.

Explicit and Implicit Memory

Explicit memory and implicit memory are two types of memory that have differing effects on behavior. **Explicit memory** occurs when you are trying to memorize something and you are consciously aware that you are trying to remember. For example, you use explicit memory when you study for a test.

An **implicit memory**, on the other hand, is formed when your previous experiences unconsciously influence your current memory (Schacter, 1996)—for example, when you are anxious and you bite your nails without thinking, because you usually bite your nails when you are anxious.

This implicit memory is due to priming. **Priming** is an unconscious mental process by which something registers in your memory without your being aware of it. Have you ever had the experience where you were in a group and you made a suggestion that your friend rejected? Maybe he or she even made fun of it. But then within a few weeks or months, he or she enthusiastically made exactly the same suggestion? What has happened? Is your friend trying to undermine you? Probably not. Your suggestion may have primed your friend's suggestion; that is, your suggestion was unconsciously processed in your friend's brain until it started to look good, and even started to look like his or her own.

Schacter (1996, p. 168) tells of a similar story about Sigmund Freud. Freud had a close friendship with the medical doctor Wilhem Fleiss, in which they shared many of their ideas. One day Freud told Fleiss his newest idea: All people are basically bisexual. Freud expected Fleiss to be astounded by this new idea, but that isn't what happened. Fleiss told Freud that he had told him exactly the same thing at an earlier time and Freud had rejected it. Once Fleiss reminded Freud of this, the memory came back to Freud. Thus, Freud was primed to come up with the same idea as Fleiss.

Retrieval

Retrieval is the process of getting information out of LTM storage into conscious awareness. Information is stored in memory in a network of associations, where each piece of information is interconnected with others. When you encode a piece of information into LTM you associate it with other items of information. This could be already-existing information or additional information that is occurring at the same time as the incoming information. For example, if you have been introduced to a new person and want to remember his name, "George," you may associate the name with the friend who introduced you, Joe. Joe's name is already stored in memory, so you just tag the new name as "George, Joe's friend." You could also tag George's name with other incoming information, "I met George at work, yesterday." The tags, hints, or identifying information attached to the new information are called retrieval cues and aid you in accessing the information later (Anderson et al., 1976).

Types of Retrieval

There are two types of retrieval: recall and recognition. In **recall**, a person retrieves information simply by searching memory. Trying to retrieve a name, a phone number, or Freud's theory is an example of a recall test. Generally in a recall test, you are not given any retrieval cues. An essay test is a good example of a partial recall test. You are given a few cues in the question, such as "Compare and contrast Freud's theory to Jung's theory." The words "Freud" and "Jung" serve as initial retrieval cues, but you will need to pull everything else out on your own. In a full recall test, you would not get any retrieval cues. The instructor might just say, "Write down everything you remember learning in the last two weeks," expecting that you will include Freud and Jung in your answer.

The second type of retrieval is recognition. **Recognition** requires you to match information presented to you to existing information in memory. When you are identifying a familiar face or name you are performing recognition retrieval. A multiple-choice exam is also a good example of a recognition task. You are given the question and the answer. All you have to do is recognize the correct answer. This differs from recall in that you do not have to supply the information, only recognize it. Recent brain-imaging studies show that the hippocampus seems to play an important role in recognition retrieval. When an individual is recognizing extremely familiar faces, there is brain activity in both hemispheres and the hippocampus and surrounding hippocampal region. When the faces are recently memorized, there is little activity in the hemispheres, and most of the brain activity is in the hippocampal regions (Henson, Shallice, Gorno-Tempini, & Dolan, 2002). Studies involving monkeys with hippocampal brain damage support this by demonstrating the monkeys' inability to do normal recognition tasks (Teng, Stefanacci, Squire, & Zola, 2000; Zola, Squire, Teng, Stefanacci, Buffalo, & Clark, 2000).

Reconstructive Memory

Originally it was thought that all experiences were permanently stored in the brain (Penfield, 1969). However, continuing research suggests that Sir Francis Bartlett, a pioneering memory researcher, was probably correct when he suggested that we store only part of the information we experience. Bartlett conducted a study in which he asked participants to listen to an Indian fable called **War of the Ghosts.** This is a story about an Indian who goes down the river with other Indians to battle another village of Indians. Contained in the story were several bits of information that really didn't make much sense. When participants were asked to recall the story, they omitted the facts that didn't make sense or changed them to make more sense in the story. Bartlett concluded that listeners had stored only the gist of the information from the story, and when they retrieved it, they filled in the gaps of missing information so that the story made sense. Bartlett concluded that our memory of events is a **reconstructive memory,** where we store only the highlights and piece together the event during retrieval using information that may or may not be accurate (Loftus & Loftus, 1980).

Context and Mood Effects on Retrieval

Findings from research suggest that memory retrieval is enhanced when the manner in which the material is originally encoded matches how it is later retrieved (Morris, Bransford, & Franks, 1977). For instance, in one study using college students, half the class were told they would be given a multiple-choice test, while the other half were told they would be taking an essay exam. When the actual tests were taken, however, only half the class got the type of test they expected.

The students taking the test they expected did better than those students who took the test in an unexpected format (d'Ydewalle & Rosselle, 1978). This indicates that the students, in preparing for the exam, used study techniques that were better suited to the type of test they thought they would be taking. Therefore, retrieving information for the unexpected format was more difficult. Thus, successful retrieval of memorized material depends on how well the original encoding strategy matches what will be later retrieved.

Tulving and Thompson (1973) conducted research that demonstrates that the physical environment is also important in the storing and retrieval of a memory. **Context-dependent memory** is the idea that information is easier to recall when a person is in the same physical environment that he or she was in when learning it. Research shows that students score better on tests if they take the test in the same physical environment in which they learned the information. In one study, members of a diving club were asked to memorize a list of words when they were underwater or on land. Later, they were asked to recall the list either underwater or on land. When the physical environment matched between memorizing and recall, the divers performed better (Godden & Baddeley, 1975).

Studies also show that people tend to recall information better if they are in the same emotional or psychological state as when the information was encoded. This is called the **state-dependent memory** effect (Bower, 1973). When people learn when they are drunk, they don't recall what they learned as well as if they had learned in a positive or sober state. However, they still recall better if they are drunk both when they attempt to learn the information and when they retrieve it. This has also been witnessed with marijuana usage. In numerous studies it has been found that if people smoke marijuana during the encoding phase of an experiment, they have difficulty remembering what they encoded. However, when they have a similar amount of marijuana in their systems during the retrieval phase of the experiment, they have no problem retrieving the encoded memory (Schacter, 1996).

Mood states also affect memory retrieval. There is a tendency to remember positive events from the past when you are in a positive mood, and sad events when you are sad (Ehrlickman & Halpern, 1988). The important point here is that if the learning mood state matches its retrieval state, then the retrieval is more accurate. Another interesting study that demonstrated this used spiders and snakes. Researchers exposed college students to spiders and/or snakes while they were learning a list of words. Students who were exposed to the snakes and spiders during recall remembered more words from the list than students who were not exposed to the snakes and spiders during recall (Lang, Craske, Brown, & Ghaneian, 2001).

Serial Position Effect

Although our long-term memories seem to have an unlimited capacity, certain things can affect how well our memories are retrieved. Many of you have played the name game, where everyone forms a circle and the first person says his name, perhaps with some adjective attached, such as "I'm Able Albert." The second in the circle says the first person's name (Able Albert) and then her own (Silly Susan). Then the third person says "Able Albert, Silly Susan," and adds her own name (Tiny Tameka), and so on. By the time it reaches the last person (Cool Carlos), naming all the names becomes quite a challenge. Often what happens is that everyone recalls the first two or three names with ease. This is also true for the last few names, but the names in the middle can be hit or miss. Why? This game demonstrates the serial position phenomenon. The **serial position phenomenon** demonstrates that we are more likely to remember the names (or words) that come first in a list as well as those that come last. Due to the **primacy effect,** we remember the first words in a list more easily than the later words because these words get the most rehearsal. This rehearsal moves them into LTM. Because of the **recency effect,** we recall the last words in a list because these are still in STM (Glanzer & Cunitz, 1966; Koppenaal & Glanzer, 1990).

The Biology of Memory

Explore
the hippocampus
in Chapter 3, p. 72

In the early 1950s, psychosurgery was used in an attempt to cure mental illness. **Psychosurgery** is a medical procedure that involves operating on part of the brain in an attempt to cure a mental illness. Patient H. M., as he is known in the scientific literature, suffered from severe epilepsy he developed when he was 16. His epilepsy may have been caused by a serious accident that occurred when he was seven. He was crossing the street and was hit by a boy on a bicycle. The blow to his head knocked him unconscious (Hilts, 1995). However, H. M.'s epileptic attacks did not begin for another nine years. His epilepsy became so disruptive that despite having an IQ of slightly above average, he could only work at the most menial jobs.

Dr. William Scoville, a graduate of Harvard Medical School, who was considered bold and wild by his friends, offered hope in a risky operation he said he could perform. His idea was that if he removed particular portions from the middle of H. M.'s brain, the epileptic seizures could be stopped. Dr. Scoville had never performed this operation before, *and* he did not know what those structures in the middle of the brain were for. Even his partner, Dr. Ben Whitcomb, advised against it. Yet on August 23, 1953, Dr. Scoville performed a **bilateral medial temporal lobe resection** on H. M., in which he inserted a silver straw into the middle of H. M.'s brain and sucked out much of his hippocampus on both sides of the brain along with other surrounding tissue.

When H. M. awoke from the operation, it was apparent that something had gone terribly wrong. He could not recognize his mother, and he had one of the worst seizures he had ever had in his life. The inability to retrieve old memories from LTM is called **retrograde amnesia.** In time, H. M. did begin to recognize his mother. His seizures decreased to the point where they could be controlled with medication. They went from occurring once a week to once every few months or less (Hilts, 1995). However, his memory was still disrupted in unusual ways. It is through H. M. that we have learned most of what we now know about how memories are formed within the brain.

H. M.'s Memory

Thanks to H. M., we now understand more about the functions of the parts of the brain that were removed. H. M. can still read and write; his slightly above average IQ is the same. Although H. M. has a good memory for things that he knew before the operation, he suffers from anterograde amnesia. **Anterograde amnesia** is the inability to store any new memories in LTM. Since H. M. cannot transfer new memories from his STM to his LTM, if you were introduced to him, he would remember your name and face for about 20 seconds. If you left the room for a short period and then came back, he would treat you as though he were meeting you for the first time. H. M. only has "immediate memory," which means he can hold onto new information for only about 20 seconds; as soon as he is distracted, the new information is gone. He does not remember any events that have happened to him or that have occurred in the world since his operation in 1953.

H. M. has maintained his original (presurgery) personality and his identity, since this is part of his intact LTM, but he has no idea what year it is, and he thinks he is as old as he was right before the surgery. However, his procedural memory (memory of how to perform tasks) is completely intact (Hilts, 1995). Researchers have demonstrated H. M.'s intact procedural memory by teaching him a star-tracing task. Each day, H. M. would come to the hospital and enter the testing room. The researchers would introduce themselves and give him instructions on how to trace the edges of a picture of a star, by looking at the star's reflection in the mirror (see Figure 8.13). Most people are not able to do this difficult task well the first time they try it (making many errors by tracing outside the lines), but with practice they improve. H. M. also did not do very well the first time he tried it, but each day when his examiners retaught him, he relearned it faster until he could finally do the task without making any errors. Each day, he could not remember ever having done the star-tracing task or remember the researchers he had met the previous day, because he could not store new memories in LTM. However, the fact that he relearned the task more easily each time indicated that he had not completely lost the previous day's procedural learning, despite having no recollection of ever being taught to do it (Schaffhausen, 2005). Researchers concluded that H. M.'s procedural memory influenced him unconsciously, causing him to perform the task better each time he traced the star.

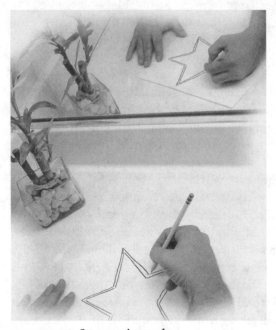

FIGURE 8.13 *Star-tracing task.*

Forgetting

Hermann Ebbinghaus (1850–1909) was the first psychologist to study memory and forgetting in a systematic way. He developed what he called the **method of savings** for measuring how much learning was "saved" from a previous learning attempt. If it took him 10 trials to learn nonsense syllables such as "pov," "tal," and "nel" and another 10 trials to relearn them, then no savings of the previous learning had taken place. If, however, it took him 10 trials to learn the nonsense syllables and only 5 trials to relearn them, there would be a savings of 50%.

One of Ebbinghaus's major contributions was the concept of the forgetting curve. The **forgetting curve** is the idea that most forgetting happens within the first nine hours of learning, with the first hour being the most vulnerable. After the first nine hours, there is a moderate decrease in forgetting over time (Slamecka & McElree, 1983). This is true whether you're memorizing nonsense syllables or verifiable facts. After the initial forgetting, it has been found that we can remember some things for a lifetime. Sometimes through lack of use we may need to brush up, but we will relearn the subject, whether it's typing or Spanish grammar, much faster than we did the first time. What are the implications of knowing this for your own study habits? Does this tell you anything about last-minute cramming for exams?

Why Do We Forget?

Various processes are involved in forgetting. For instance, **decay** is the process by which a mental representation of a stimulus is gradually lost. Think about that new phone number someone just gave you. If you don't do anything with the information (such as repeat it in your mind), it just fades away. Another process, **interference**, occurs when the storage or retrieval of information is affected by other information entering the memory system. Think of someone asking you a question while you are rehearsing that phone number—or even worse, the wise guy who starts reciting different numbers on purpose to make you forget. He is causing interference that is making it difficult for you to retain the phone number long enough in STM so that it might be stored in LTM.

There are two types of interference: retroactive and proactive. **Retroactive interference** occurs when the learning of new information interferes with recall of information you have already learned. You may have had this experience while trying to remember someone's name. Perhaps you just met someone named Scott (new information) and have been repeating his name in order to remember it. Then you bump into your good friend Shaun and can't seem to retrieve his name (old information), even though you have known him for years. The new name, Scott, may be interfering with your ability to retrieve the name Shaun. **Proactive interference** happens when information you already know interferes with learning or remembering new information. An example of this is if you have already learned Spanish (old information) in school and now you want to learn Italian (new information). You might find that your previous knowledge of Spanish interferes with your learning of Italian.

Forgetting and Normal Aging

As we get older, we unfortunately experience some changes in memory. Not being able to recall the name of a friend or a popular movie star, which we could do when we were younger, becomes more prevalent as we age. There have been decades of research comparing people over 70 with college-age students, and researchers have consistently found that on tests of explicit memory, older people do not do as well as college-age students on free-recall memory tests (like essay tests); however, these memory declines do not show up in *all* memory tasks. It has been found that on memory tests involving recognition tasks (like multiple-choice questions), older people do as well as younger people (Schacter, 1996).

Forgetting and Alzheimer's Disease

Severe memory impairment is one of the early signs of Alzheimer's disease (AD), but it is important to remember that AD is a disease and not an outgrowth of the normal aging process. It is a disease process brought about by a genetic predisposition and some unknown environmental factor or factors (Schacter, 1996).

Explore **Alzheimer's disease** in Chapter 3, p. 73

In AD, both episodic memory and semantic memory are progressively lost, making a person's ability to comprehend his or her world more and more difficult (Schacter, 1996). What is interesting is that, as with H. M., much of the Alzheimer's victim's implicit memory remains intact. It has been shown that recognition memory for pictures of familiar faces is impaired in AD patients (Diesfeldt, 1990), but Alzheimer's patients have the same preference for previously seen pictures as do healthy elderly participants. In other words, AD patients demonstrated a greater liking for previously viewed faces than for pictures of new faces. Since they cannot remember seeing these pictures before, their preference can only be due to intact implicit memory capacity (Winograd, Goldstein, Monarch, Peluso, & Goldman, 1999).

How Can You Improve Your Memory?

Knowing how your memory works can help you improve it. A good memory is very valuable for doing well in your courses. A good memory can also help you socially when you need to recall the name of the person to whom you were just introduced at a business meeting. But you need to use your memory in a way that makes it work most efficiently. Too often, students try to memorize information in a manner that actually makes it more difficult for them to remember. For instance, sometimes a student insists on rereading a whole chapter just before an exam. This is an inefficient use of time, and if this is all that the student does to prepare for the exam, he or she is not likely to do very well.

Listen Attentively

FIGURE 8.14 *Attending to information when it is first presented is important for later retrieval.*

Do you know why you forgot the name of the person to whom you were just introduced? One reason is that as soon as you met the individual, his or her name never made it past your sensory register. You didn't really hear it. Maybe the music was turned up too loud or you were thinking about something else. Did it ever occur to you that sometimes you can't remember information for a test because you never paid attention to the information initially? Try to improve your concentration in class by making eye contact with the professor when he or she is talking. If you find your mind wandering, then practice bringing your concentration back to the lecture. When studying or reading, taking frequent breaks will help you maintain a greater level of concentration during your study time.

Use Elaborative Rehearsal

Whenever you study for exams, you should be certain to use elaborative rehearsal. This means that you find connections between your new learning and what you already know. It is always easier to learn something if you can connect it with what you already have stored in memory. Simply rereading a chapter is too passive to enable your brain to encode the material.

Use Mnemonic Devices

Your ability to recall information is often associated with your ability to encode the material with adequate retrieval cues. One way to enhance your retrieval cue encoding is to learn various mnemonic devices. A **mnemonic device** is a way in which to organize or associate information you are learning in order to improve your capacity for recall (Bower, 1973; Higbee, 1977; Roediger, 1980). Learning to use mnemonic devices takes some practice, but the more you use them, the better your ability to recall information will become. Here are a few mnemonic devices to try:

1. Rhyming—making up rhymes is a common aid for remembering material. Perhaps as a child you learned the familiar rhyme "one is for fun, two is for shoes" in order to help you remember your numbers.

2. Method of loci—this technique is useful if you are trying to remember a list of items, such as a grocery list. Begin by selecting any familiar place, such as your home. Start placing the items on the list in locations in your house in an orderly fashion. That way you can visualize walking through your house and picking up all the items in each location in order to remember the items on the list.

3. First-letter technique—take the first letter of each item to be remembered and form a word, a phrase, or a sentence with those letters (Matlin, 1989). For example, if you want to remember these three mnemonics you could make a phrase with "R," "M," and "F," such as "Ray makes fire trucks." This would help you remember "rhyming, method of loci, and first-letter."

Activate Retrieval Cues

Try to find out what type of test you will be taking (multiple choice, essay, or short answer). Knowing the format of the test allows your encoding strategies to activate your retrieval strategies. For example, if you are learning terms and concepts, you can write a concept on one side of a flash card and the definition on the other. Isolating the information in this way prevents interference from similar concepts while you are retrieving the information. However, if you are studying for an essay exam, you will need to connect and integrate the information for an effective essay. Thus, flash cards will not be an effective way to study for an essay. Also, while taking a test, try to match mood states and the environmental states between learning and testing, in order to provide consistent retrieval states.

Use Primacy and Recency Effects to Your Advantage

FIGURE 8.15 *Do you know how to study for an exam?*

Since we tend to remember what we learned first (primacy) and what we learned last (recency), it's a good idea not to have study sessions that are too long. If you are using flash cards, go through the pack front side up and try to recall what is on the back. Then reverse the process. Then start at the middle of the pack and work forward or backward. Changing the order in which you learn items is important in order to take advantage of primacy and recency effects. It is also more efficient to actively study for a short time, take a break, and then have another short study session than it is to spend an hour cramming just before an exam. Distributed practice, on the whole, tends to be more effective than long study sessions for a number of reasons. It keeps you motivated, and you are less liable to become fatigued (Pauk, 1974). Also, by studying in short sessions, you minimize information "in the middle" of the session that might be more easily forgotten.

Minimize the Effects of Interference

Once you are able to recite some fact or principle three times, put that index card away for a while. Don't keep going over things you already know, since that will inhibit encoding of the material you haven't mastered yet. To further minimize interference, study or review before you go to sleep, so the day's events can't interfere with your processing of new memories.

Review Before the Exam

Do a final review of the information right before the exam, so that anything that has already happened that day will have less of a chance of interfering with the retrieval of the information during the test. If the test will be taken in a quiet classroom, try to review the material in a quiet place, such as at home or in the library. If the test will be taken in a somewhat noisy environment, such as a large lecture hall, try reviewing the material in a place with background noise, such as a busy cafeteria.

Overlearn the Material

Overlearning is practicing beyond the point of mastery. Most students will stop memorizing when they have learned most of the information. Studies show that even though you may get 90% correct when you test yourself, the stress during the exam can lower your retrieval to 75% (Krueger, 1929). To prevent this, you must overlearn the material. The best way to learn information beyond the point of mastery is to keep studying the material even after your self-testing shows that you remember 100% of the material.

Keep Your Mind and Body Sharp

Research studies show that the number-one thing you can do to improve your memory is to get enough sleep. Of course, this means that you must start studying soon enough so that you do not have to stay up all night. The other important element for memory is oxygen. When we get anxious, we don't breathe, and you can't get the oxygen necessary for memory retrieval to your brain. We can get more oxygen to our brain by breathing and drinking water. Make sure to drink plenty of water when you are studying and taking the test.

Chapter Summary

In this chapter we looked at the complexity of memory and saw that memory is not an exact videotape record of our lives. Recovered memory therapy attempts to uncover repressed memories, which may be interfering with current psychological functioning, through hypnosis, guided imagery, and journaling. Repressed memories refer to memories of which we are not consciously aware. However, there is little evidence to support the accuracy of these repressed memories.

In fact, most research results suggest that our memories of events are highly inaccurate. Research on eyewitness testimony has demonstrated that even a small piece of information can distort our memory of an event. This misinformation effect happens when a person is given new information after witnessing an event, thus changing what is remembered. Confabulation may also occur when a person unwittingly invents information to fill in the gaps in his or her memory and comes to believe the invention to be a fact. This may occur during hypnosis and is also probably present in reports of alien abductions.

We also explored how memory works. Three different levels of processing were discussed: encoding, storage, and retrieval. The three different memory stores were explored as outlined in the information processing model: sensory register (SR), short-term memory (STM), and long-term memory (LTM). The capacity and duration of the SR, STM, and LTM were examined in detail, expanding on the various research conducted that supports these theories.

Next, different types of LTM were discussed. Episodic memory is the storage of events in your life, and these events are marked with a time tag. Semantic memory is memory of your general knowledge about the world. Procedural memory is your knowledge of how to perform certain tasks, like riding a bike or driving a car. Explicit memory occurs when you are trying to memorize something and you are consciously aware that you are trying to remember. An implicit memory, on the other hand, is formed when your previous experiences unconsciously influence your current memory.

Retrieval is the process of getting information out of LTM storage into conscious awareness. We studied three types of retrieval: recall, recognition, and reconstructive memory. In recall, a person retrieves information simply by searching memory. Recognition requires you to match information presented to you to existing information in memory. With reconstructive memory, we store only the highlights and piece together the event during retrieval using information that may or may not be accurate. We also discussed the limitations that STM and LTM place on retrieval, and the effects of context on retrieval.

The biology of memory was explored by looking at different brain structures and their contributions to memory. H. M. demonstrated several memory deficiencies that caused researchers to conclude that the hippocampus is an important region for STM and for the ability to store and retrieve information from LTM.

Various aspects of forgetting were investigated next. Ebbinghaus's phenomenal discovery of the forgetting curve was explained. The forgetting curve is the idea that most forgetting happens within the first nine hours of learning, with the first hour being the most vulnerable. Other causes of forgetting discussed were decay and interference. Decay is the process by which a mental representation of a stimulus is gradually lost. Interference occurs when the storage or retrieval of information is affected by other information entering the memory system. There are two types of interference: retroactive and proactive. Retroactive interference occurs when the learning of new information interferes with recall of information already learned. Proactive interference happens when information you already know interferes with learning or remembering new information. Several aspects of how age-related diseases affect forgetting were also examined, such as Alzheimer's disease.

Finally, several techniques to improve memory were discussed. Practicing listening more attentively will ensure the information gets into STM, and learning various mnemonic devices will enhance your LTM encoding. Using elaborative rehearsal to find connections between your new learning and what you already know will improve memory storage and retrieval. Using mnemonic techniques will also help improve your memory. Also, it's a good idea to have short study sessions, to take advantage of the recency and primacy effects. Studying differently depending on the type of the exam, and reviewing right before the exam, will also help aid retrieval. Also, keeping the mood states and environmental states similar between learning and testing will enhance retrieval performance. Avoiding studying when other things might interfere is also recommended for better retrieval. In order to get 100% retrieval, you will need to overlearn the material. Lastly, make sure that you get enough sleep and enough oxygen to keep the mind and body primed for memory retrieval.

Knowledge Builder

RELATE TO YOURSELF

1. Alan Alda discussed a research study with Dr. Daniel Schacter in which the participants' brains were examined by a PET scan. In the future it may be possible to use PET scans to look into people's brains to see whether they are telling the truth. What do you think would be the disadvantage of this?

   _____

   _____

   _____

   _____

2. Discuss both sides of the memory debate. Take a side and defend your point of view with evidence from the research studies presented.

   _____

   _____

   _____

   _____

3. What did you think of eyewitness testimony before reading this chapter? Do you look at it differently now? Explain.

   _____

   _____

   _____

   _____

4. In 1961, as Betty and Barney Hill were driving home in the early hours of the morning, they were abducted by aliens. Can you give an alternative explanation for their abduction experience?

   _____

   _____

   _____

   _____

CHAPTER REVIEW QUESTIONS

1. Flashbulb memories are the only type of memories not subject to distortion. **T or F?**

2. If a person is very confident about his or her memory, this is a good sign that it is an accurate memory. **T or F?**

3. The cause of the majority of wrongful convictions is eyewitness misidentifications. **T or F?**

4. Memory for 9/11 was the only one of the flashbulb memories that did not exhibit any distortions. **T or F?**

5. Episodic memory is _____.

    (a) your memory for knowledge about the world

    (b) your memory for the things that have happened to you in your life

    (c) your memory for skilled movements

    (d) your unconscious memory

6. Which model of memory says that the information we remember best is the information that is most processed?

    (a) information processing   **(b)** parallel distributed processing

    (c) levels of processing   **(d)** transfer-appropriate processing

7. Which model of memory says that each new fact we learn becomes integrated with existing knowledge and influences the way we deal with the world?

    (a) information processing   **(b)** parallel distributed processing

    (c) levels of processing   **(d)** transfer-appropriate processing

8. The first words in a list are more easily remembered than the rest of the list because of _____.

    (a) the recency effect   **(b)** elaborative rehearsal

    (c) the primacy effect   **(d)** maintenance rehearsal

9. *Try this experiment:* Part I. Say the following letters to a friend: FB-IAO-LM-TVI-BMB-MW. As you say each letter group, pause a moment at the dash. Then have your friend repeat the letters from memory. How did your friend do?

_____

_____

_____

_____

Part II. Say the same letters, but this time say them like this: FBI-AOL-MTV-IBM-BMW. Did you note any difference in your friend's performance? Explain what happened by using your new knowledge from this chapter. Do the results of this experiment give you any ideas for changing the way you study for a test?

_____

_____

_____

_____

10. Dr. Scoville believed that if he removed the middle portions of H. M.'s brain (primarily the hippocampus), H. M.'s epileptic seizures would be cured. He had no research data to support his hypothesis. What do you think of this method of doing research?

_____

_____

_____

_____

11. *Activity:* Watch the movie *Memento* and compare it with what you have learned about H. M.

_____

_____

_____

_____

USEFUL WEB SITES

THE MEMORY EXHIBITION

http://www.exploratorium.edu/memory/

This Web site is like being at a live conference. It contains sheep dissections, exhibits, memory games, workshops, and articles on memory.

LIVE SCIENCE

http://www.livescience.com/memory/

This site has a lot of information on memory and brain fitness games to improve memory, attention, and processing speed.

MEMORY LOSS & THE BRAIN

http://www.memorylossonline.com/glossary/memory.html

This site has information on how memories are formed and an in-depth exploration of various forms of memory loss.

SHORT-TERM MEMORY TESTS

http://faculty.washington.edu/chudler/stm0.html &
http://faculty.washington.edu/chudler/puzmatch.html

Here are two Web sites where you can test your short-term memory.

MEMORY STORAGE SYSTEMS

http://www.nwlink.com/~donclark/hrd/learning/memory.html

This Web site contains a very thorough overview of the different memory storage systems.

SCIENCE MUSEUM

http://www.sciencemuseum.org.uk/on-line/brain/260.asp

This Web site is a virtual library of information about memory.

Chapter 9

Thinking, Language, Intelligence, and Creativity

by Deborah Yakel, PhD

The mind is everything. What you think you become.

—BUDDHA

One of Shakespeare's most memorable characters, Hamlet, proclaimed that humans were "noble in reason! . . . infinite in faculties! . . . in apprehension how like a god!" It is true that humans are capable of elaborative cognitive processes, but what causes some individuals to excel mentally above and beyond the average person? When we recall the most remarkable thinkers in history, many names come to mind—among them are Albert Einstein and Winston Churchill. Did you know that many of Churchill's teachers thought him mentally slow? Or that Einstein was labeled as a dunce in math as a child?

Einstein attended a university, but he often missed classes so that he could study physics at home. He annoyed so many of his teachers that he had difficulty finding a teaching position when he graduated, and he ended up working in a patent office. It was there that he figured out how to take abstract principles and apply them to devices. He noted that this inspired him to think long and hard about the fundamental properties of the universe. After years of hard work, Einstein published his *Special Theory of Relativity* (1905). His intellectual flexibility to break all the rules and view things differently marked him as one of the great thinkers of our time. However, Einstein proclaimed that his gift of fantasy should be credited more than any talent he might have had for absorbing knowledge. His methods of thinking resembled an artist's more than they did a scientist's, and yet he was able to discover some of the most profound scientific principles of our time (Clark, 1971).

FIGURE 9.1 *Albert Einstein. Courtesy of the Library of Congress.*

In this chapter we will explore thinking. How do people think? What mental processes are involved when you solve problems? How do we effectively measure how well people think? What constitutes intelligence? Are some people more intelligent than others; if so, why? Are creativity and intelligence related? Lastly, are there differences in the ways in which humans use language and thinking as compared to animals?

What Is Thinking?

Cognition refers to how we process, store, analyze, and use information mentally. The information we store in our mind constitutes our knowledge. **Thinking** involves using that knowledge to form concepts, inspire creativity, solve problems, and communicate with others. Thinking consists of several different modes of thought:

◆ **Imaginal thought** consists of images we perceive in our mind. We can imagine an elaborate beach scene or a simple apple. Either way, just by thinking we produce pictures in our mind.

◆ **Propositional thought** consists of the internal verbal language we perceive in our mind. As we think, we hear a steady, silent stream of sentences in our mind composed of the languages we know. Think of any object, for example, a cat. Are you able to think of this object visually without also mentally "hearing" its label? Can mental images exist without language?

◆ **Motoric thought** consists of mental representations of motor movements we perceive in our mind. For example, we can imagine ourselves riding a bike or cooking a meal.

Is Language Necessary for Thought to Occur?

Most linguists and psychologists today think that language does not determine how we think but that it does influence thought in various ways. It is possible that language affects how much detail we attend to and store with our experiences (Hunt & Agnoli, 1991). For instance, if you see a group of clouds and think they look like a horse, you are more likely to remember precisely how those clouds appeared than if you had no word to describe them other than "clouds" (Ellis, 1973). Language can also create and maintain stereotypical thinking. Briere and Lanktree (1983) demonstrated this by asking students to read one of two statements about psychology. The first statement implied that psychology is a male profession, whereas the second statement was written in gender-neutral language. Students who read the first statement rated psychology as a less attractive occupation for women than those who read the second statement.

Mental Representations and Thought

If language is not necessary for thought, then what is? Consider the case of Ildefonso, a man without language (Schaller, 1995). Ildefonso was born deaf and had no understanding of any spoken or signed language. He communicated by pantomime, unaware that words or gestures stood as symbols for things. He did not even know his own name. At age 27, he was living in Los Angeles, where he met Susan Schaller. Susan began teaching him sign language but soon learned he did not understand that objects had labels. Traditional methods of teaching sign language—by pointing to the object and then producing a sign—failed miserably. Eventually she was able to get him to understand by pantomiming a teacher teaching a student signs. When Ildefonso discovered that every object in the world had words to represent it, he wept at all the knowledge he did not know. Prior to his sign language training, it was impossible for Ildefonso to think in verbal form. His knowledge of the world was most likely represented in thought in the form of images.

Mental Images

FIGURE 9.2 *Synesthesia of a lemon.*

Mental images are representations that arise from stored information rather than from visual sensory input. They are not just visual representations. For example, your mental "picture" of a lemon may also include its pungent citrus odor and its sour taste (see Figure 9.2). Every sensory system can contribute to a mental image (Kosslyn & Shin, 1994; Paivio, 1971, 1975). In fact, some individuals have a rare form of imagery called **synesthesia**, in which mental images extend beyond normal sensory associations (Martino & Marks, 2001). For example, listening to music may cause a synesthetic person to also experience wild visual bursts of color.

Research has found that mental images have similar properties to actual perceptions of the same objects in the real world. For example, it takes less time to scan smaller objects than large objects mentally, just as it would if you were scanning with your eyes (Denis & Kosslyn, 1999). It also appears that images must fit into a mental space that has a limited size. Bigger objects must be imagined from farther away to fit into this mental space. This mimics actual visual perception, wherein we can see more of the visual scene the farther we are from it (Kosslyn, 1978). Similarly, the **mental rotation** of objects occurs in the same way that we are able to rotate the objects in the real world (Shepard & Cooper, 1982). It also appears that mental images activate the same brain areas as their corresponding sensory images (Farah, Weisberg, Monheit, & Peronnet, 1989; Kosslyn, Thompson, & Alpert, 1995; O'Craven & Karwisher, 2000)

We can also generate more images than we contain in our memory. A created image is constructed from combining existing memories into something novel, rather than simply remembering existing memories. Artists often mentally picture a new idea before beginning their project. Many of history's greatest intellects, such as Albert Einstein, Leonardo da Vinci, Galileo, and Thomas Edison (West, 1991), relied heavily on imagery. Current research shows that individuals with the ability to produce good mental images generally possess greater creativity than those who have poor mental imagery (Gonzalez, Campos, & Perez, 1997). Of course, not everyone can produce good images. According to McKellar (1965), about 2% of the population has poor visual imagery. Even for those with good mental imagery, it is important to remember that mental

Explore **reconstructive memory** in Chapter 8, p. 245

images are not snapshots but rather memories of the actual images. Our memories are reconstructed and highly subject to error (Reisberg & Chambers, 1991). We cannot store all the information that we encounter, so the mind has to decide which images will be useful. Even in combination with words, images are limited in the way that they can contribute to our thought processes.

Concepts and Categorization

A **concept** is a mental representation that consists of a grouping of objects or events. This could be a class or a group of objects, people, organizations, events, situations, or relations that share common characteristics or features. For example, "dog" is a concept that stands for a group of animals that share common features: fur, four legs, and a tail. Concepts are not images or word. They are expressed only by images and words (Kosslyn, 1980; Pinker, 1994). Grouping objects into concepts provides a way to store information. Concepts also help us organize our world and anticipate future events. They create **cognitive economy** by reducing the amount of cognitive effort required for thinking, understanding, and learning. Imagine what it would be like if you were unable to form concepts. Everything you encountered for the first time would be unfamiliar and would require a great deal of mental processing in order for you to understand it.

Three theories attempt to explain the nature of concepts. In the earliest theory, Aristotle proposed that concepts are defined by a set of features. For example, for the concept "bird," the features might be "feathers," "flies," "lays eggs," and "has a beak." In Aristotle's **classical theory**, all items in the concept share defining features (Medin, Proffit, & Schwartz, 2000). The second theory, **prototype theory**, states that a concept is formed on the basis of a mental example that embodies the most common and typical features of that set of objects (Rosch, 1978). For example, your prototype of a bird would probably be something like a robin or a sparrow since they typify an average bird (see Figure 9.3). Finally, the **exemplar theory** states that concepts can be represented by individual examples that are stored in memory from personal experiences (Estes, 1994). So, if you talk to your pet parrot every day, chances are your exemplar of a bird may be a parrot. Your exemplar of a parrot may override your prototype and become the most common representation of the concept "bird." However, most people do not encounter parrots every day. The birds they encounter frequently, such as robins and sparrows, are more likely to be their exemplars and their prototypes.

FIGURE 9.3 *House sparrow. Courtesy of the U.S. Department of the Interior, Fish and Wildlife Service.*

FIGURE 9.4 *Level of category. Courtesy of backgroundsarchive.com.*

Whether you store a concept by features, a prototype, or an exemplar, the concepts we form appear to be stored in hierarchies or nested categories. As individuals interact with new objects in their environment, they can easily place objects into categories because the brain is organized to store different concepts in different parts of the brain (Ilmberger, Rau, Noahchtar, Arnold, & Winkler, 2002). Psychologists have found that we tend to store concepts in a hierarchy at different levels of specificity (Rosch, Mervis, Gray, Johnson, & Boyes-Braem, 1976). The highest, most general level is called the **superordinate category**. The intermediate level of the hierarchy is called the **basic level category**. The most specific level of the hierarchy is called the **subordinate category**. For example, the item in Figure 9.4 would be represented as an animal at the superordinate level, as a dog at the basic level, and as a cocker spaniel at the subordinate level.

Courtesy of cepolina.com   Courtesy of backgroundsarchive.com

FIGURE 9.5 *Category level naming.*

Look at the items in Figure 9.5, and name them as quickly as you can.

Most likely you said a cat and a tree—both basic level labels. You could have given them labels of "an animal" and "a plant" from the superordinate level, but you didn't. You could have also named them at the subordinate level as a Persian cat and an oak tree. Rosch and her colleagues (1976) found that people tend to name objects at the basic level. Interestingly, it is also the first level of knowledge that children acquire, and it is a feat that is extremely difficult to replicate with computers (Rosch et al., 1976).

Some researchers theorize that concepts are not only organized by basic features into hierarchies but also organized by the brain into schemas (Rumelhart, 1975; Schank & Abelson, 1977). A **schema** is a mental framework for organizing concepts according to related themes or aspects of a particular situation. For example, a birthday schema would contain both cake and candles, even though these are not items that are normally stored together, because they do not share common features (Lin & Murphy, 2001). Piaget proposed that our mind is constantly trying to make sense of new, incoming information (Siegler & Ellis, 1996). We may organize concepts together because they frequently occur together in particular situations, as in the case of the concepts of cake and candles in the birthday schema. We may also organize new information with other concepts in the same category or with similar situations. For example, when a toddler sees a new four-legged animal (a "horsie"), he or she may **assimilate** that information into an already-existing schema of "doggies" because the new animal shares common features with dogs. Of course, this is inaccurate. The toddler will soon learn to adjust, or **accommodate**, his or her schemas to more accurately reflect the difference between a dog and a horse. He or she will refine the "doggie" schema so that its features are not so broad and the concept "horsie" can no longer fit into it. At this point he or she will construct a new schema, a "horsie" schema.

Problem Solving

Explore
trial-and-error learning
in Chapter 7, p. 212

Although the formulation of concepts is essential for thinking, it is not enough. Imagine that you have lost your car keys. You have a problem! Merely understanding the concepts involved will not help you solve your problem effectively. **Problem solving** is an attempt to overcome obstacles in order to reach a goal. We use a considerable array of strategies for solving the diverse range of predicaments we encounter. In some situations, we may arrive at solutions to problems by trial and error. **Trial-and-error learning** involves trying a variety of methods and eliminating those that don't work. This can be useful if you have a limited number of possible solutions. For example, Thorndike (1898) demonstrated that cats placed in puzzle boxes would escape by pushing on different parts of the cage until they stumbled onto the latch mechanism that released the door. If you were locked in a room, you might try the same trial-and-error approach. However, if you have a large number of possible solutions, this hit-or-miss approach is time consuming and not a very effective problem-solving strategy.

Sometimes a solution to a problem will suddenly appear with apparently little effort. Kohler (1924) referred to this as **insight**. This results from the mind restructuring the information when there is a new piece of the puzzle or when a new connection is made. Then all the elements of the problem suddenly fit together to form a solution. However, the greatest drawback to insight as a problem-solving strategy is that we generally don't have time to wait around for a sudden flash of insight to occur.

Problem-Solving Strategies

Many of our everyday problems are well-structured problems. Perhaps you are interested in calculating your grade in class or in setting up a study schedule. The information you need to accomplish your goal is likely to be close at hand. You are most likely to use either an algorithm or a heuristic to solve such a well-structured problem. An **algorithm** is a step-by-step set of rules that, if followed correctly, leads to a solution. Imagine that you find a wooden chest under your bed that you placed there when you were 10 years old. You remember that you placed several hundred dollars in it and locked it. You stare at the lock, realizing that you no longer remember the combination. You could use an algorithm to produce the combination by starting with 0-0-0 and then 0-0-1, until you had systematically worked your way through all 46,656 combinations. While this method is not very practical, it would guarantee a solution.

It might be more effective to use a heuristic to solve the problem. **Heuristics** are a mental shortcut that may or may not lead to a solution. They tend to simplify the problem by limiting the number of possible solutions. If you can remember numbers from past combinations, you might be able to use a shortcut to the above algorithm and use only a few numbers. Although this will not guarantee a solution, you may be able to arrive at a solution in less time.

The quickest strategy to get the money from the chest probably involves using a means-end analysis heuristic. In a **means-end analysis**, we identify differences between the present state and the goal state and make changes to reduce these differences (Newell & Simon, 1972). Most people would deduce that the one thing keeping them from getting the money was the lock, and they would just cut the lock off. Perhaps you would see the chest as the one thing keeping you from the money. Using an analogy from childhood—"breaking your piggybank open"—you might decide to take a hammer to the wooden chest and break it open. Although these are efficient solutions to this problem, other problems may require many changes to solve the problem. In addition, there may be restrictions on the changes that can be made. If we cannot break the lock or the chest because they are valuable, it is unlikely we would be able to use the means-end analysis heuristic or the analogy heuristic to solve our problem.

FIGURE 9.6 *Lily pond example. Courtesy of pdphoto.org.*

Another heuristic, **subgoal analysis**, involves breaking the problem into small intermediate steps that will lead toward a solution. Assume that you have a 14-page paper due in two weeks. It is unlikely that you will accomplish your goal by writing one page a day. Additionally, this will not result in a very coherent paper. Instead, you will probably break the project into a series of subgoals: doing the library research, making an outline, writing a draft, revising the final paper, and typing the references. By completing each subgoal, you move toward the ultimate goal of a quality paper in a more manageable way (Passer & Smith, 2004). Of course, for some problems, forming subgoals may become time consuming or cumbersome. Some problems cannot be subdivided, and others are so complex that it would take too much time to identify the subgoals (Hayes, 1966; Reed, 1996).

Working from the starting point toward your goal may not always be the most efficient way to solve a problem. Consider the following problem:

> Water lilies growing in a pond double in area every 24 hours (see Figure 9.6). On the first day of spring, only one lily pad is on the surface of the pond. Ninety days later, the pond is entirely covered. On what day is the pond half-covered? (Reisberg, 1997)

You could start at one lily pad and double it, continuing upward until you reach the number of days needed to cover the pond. However, it would be easy to make a mistake this way. In this case, it would be easier to use a **backward-working heuristic**. If we work backward from day 90, only one day, we arrive at the solution to our problem. The pond was half-covered on day 89 (Bourne, Dominowski, Loftus, & Healy, 1986; Hunt, 1994). Of course, most of us have been trained to solve problems in a forward linear fashion, so working backward may not readily occur to us.

Obstacles to Solving Problems

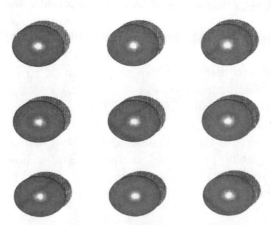

FIGURE 9.7 *Nine-dot problem.*

Many times when we are faced with a problem, familiar strategies often block our ability to readily perceive an answer. This is referred to as a **mental set**. A mental set is the tendency to use strategies that have worked in the past even though another strategy might work better (Luchins, 1946). The nine-dot problem is a good example of a mental set (see Figure 9.7). Attempt to connect all nine dots by drawing four straight lines without lifting your pencil from the paper or retracing any lines. The solution is found at the end of the chapter. If you had difficulty solving this problem, it is likely due to a mental set. You assumed that the straight lines should stay within the borders and that you couldn't join two dots with an angle.

Another obstacle to problem solving is functional fixedness. **Functional fixedness** refers to the inability to imagine objects being used in any

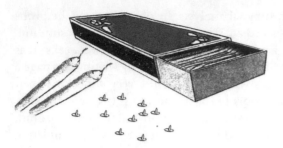

FIGURE 9.8 *Candle problem.*

way other than their familiar functions (Maier, 1931). Using only the material seen in Figure 9.8, devise a way to place the candle at eye level on a nearby door so that the wax will not drip on the floor as the candle burns. The solution is found at the end of the chapter. Most people cannot solve the problem when presented with the materials in the picture, because they cannot view the match box as anything other than its original function as a box that holds matches (adapted from Duncker, 1945). In order to solve the problem they must break out of this functional fixedness and perceive that the box can be used as a shelf to hold the candles. It is interesting that researchers have found that people who are more likely to experience a mental set are also likely to have problems with functional fixedness.

Language

Even though newborn infants cannot express themselves through the use of language, they can still communicate with us. **Communication** is an exchanging of information using sounds, smells, or gestures. So when an infant is screaming in the middle of the night, she is communicating to us that something is wrong. We try different things, such as changing her diaper, feeding her, or soothing her, until we figure out what she needs. By gurgling, cooing, and smiling, infants can communicate to us that they are happy. However, in order for infants to communicate with complicated or abstract ideas, they will need to acquire language. **Language** is a system of communication with a particular set of rules for combining symbols (sounds, written symbols, or hand signs), which can generate an infinite number of meaningful combinations.

The Acquisition of Language

Linguist Noam Chomsky (1975) has suggested that humans are born with a brain whose neural structure is ready to acquire language. This neural structure, the **language-acquisition device (LAD)**, allows us to recognize and produce the sounds and structure of language that we are exposed to in our environment. The LAD contains universal grammatical rules, which are common to all languages, including the various sign languages used across the world (Anderson & Lightfoot, 1999; Chomsky, 1987). It appears that we learn these grammatical structures without any formal instruction, just as we learn to sit, stand, and walk without any formal instruction (Pinker, 1994). This could account for children's ability to learn language in cultures where parents do not talk to infants less than 1 year of age (Locke, 1999). Children also have an amazing ability to learn language quickly. Studies show that the average 6-year-old child has already acquired a vocabulary of about 13,000 words (Carey, 1977; Pinker, 1994; Smith, 1926).

Explore **language development** in Chapter 12, p. 392

Learning theorist B. F. Skinner (1957) suggested that language is acquired by using basic learning principles. We initially learn by associating the sights of objects with the sounds of the words associated with those objects. This learning by association is simple **classical conditioning**. Then as we watch others produce the sounds of the words, we

FIGURE 9.9 *Burrhus Frederic Skinner (1904–1990). Courtesy of Carin Araujo/Wikipedia.*

imitate them. This process is called modeling, and it is a basic principle of **observational learning**. Finally, as we see the object and produce the correct sounds associated with it, others reinforce our success through smiles, hugs, and enthusiastic words of encouragement. The process of learning by reinforcement is called **operant conditioning**. Thus, Skinner argued that children learn to talk with the same process that he used to train pigeons to peck keys, and rats to press levers.

Elements of Language

Psycholinguistics is the study of how language is acquired, processed, understood, produced, and used. **Linguists** are professionals who study the nature of language. They believe that humans inherit a biological readiness to process language and have keen observation skills, which allow them to understand the basic elements of language. Linguists devote most of their study to the universal structures of language and the rules governing their use. These basic universal structures of language are phonemes, morphemes, graphemes, semantics, pragmatics, and syntax. Many linguists believe that the average person is a language expert (Chomsky, 1965; Pinker, 1994).

The basic elements of language that linguists have discovered are the same basic concepts each of us discovered as a child. Sounds that help distinguish meaning in a language are called **phonemes**. Each language has a set of phonemes, or speech sounds, specific to that language. For example, in English, when we say the word "rat," the "r" is much different than the trilled "r" in the word "arriba" in Spanish. Phonemes are the basic building blocks of a language. We can string these sounds together to form words—for example, "k" "a" "t" forms the word {cat}. As you can see, phonemes do not sound like the letters of the alphabet, but each letter has its own sound. The same sound may even be represented by different letters, such as the "a" in "stay" and the "ei" in "sleigh." And as you saw with "c," the same letter can represent different phonemes, as in {cat} and {cereal}. When children learn, they learn both the letters of the alphabet and their respective sounds. This process is called **phonetics**. It allows children to sound out words by reading their respective letters on a page. Phonemes are one of the first elements of language that children learn. They imitate speech sounds produced by adults in a process called babbling. About a hundred phonemes have been identified, but most languages consist of a much smaller set. English uses about 45 phonemes, but some languages have as few as 15 and others have as many as 85 (Solso, 1991).

FIGURE 9.10 *{cats}—not just two cats but also two morphemes. Courtesy of backgroundsarchive.com.*

When speech sounds are combined into the smallest units of meaning, called **morphemes**, a child has discovered words. Thus, {doggie}, {cookie}, and {dada} are all morphemes. Many words in English are single morphemes: dolphin, smile, tree, and house. Later, the child learns that prefixes and suffixes can also have meaning. When added to the end of a word, the suffix "-s" means "many" in English. Therefore, the word "cats" has two morphemes: {cat}, meaning a furry, four-legged creature, and {s}, meaning "many" (see Figure 9.10). The addition of the prefix "un-" reverses the meaning of the word it is placed in front of. So, the morpheme {un} in the word "unbelievable" indicates that something is not believable. Morphemes, either alone or in combination, form words and provide meaning in a language.

Linguists call the study of meaning **semantics**. This meaning can be derived from morphemes, words, or sentences. A word may have different meanings depending on the context in which it is used. This is called duality of structure. All human languages have duality of structure, wherein meaning is difficult to discern unless there is context. Noam Chomsky (1986, 1990) maintained that brain areas responsible for understanding meaning were different from brain areas that help us combine words into a sentence. So the actual words that compose a sentence are just the **surface structure**. The underlying meaning of the sentence is called the **deep structure**. This difference can be demonstrated by keeping the underlying meaning the same but changing the surface structure. For example, in the sentence "Suzie watched the dog," the surface structure and the deep structure are the same. However, we can change the surface structure by putting the sentence in passive voice: "The dog was watched by Suzie." The surface structure is changed, but the underlying meaning in the deep structure remains the same as in the first sentence.

There are additional characteristics of language that may aid us in communicating meaning. **Pragmatics** is the characteristics of spoken language that aid us in interpreting the social meaning of the communication. For example, the intonation used during speech signals meaning. We know that when someone's pitch rises at the end of a sentence, he or she is asking us a question. There are also nonverbal cues, such as gestures, that aid us in interpreting meaning. When someone says "Come here" and beckons with his or her hand, we know exactly where here is.

Ultimately, once a child begins to master words and their corresponding meaning, he or she begins to combine words into phrases. This will serve to communicate more complex meaning. However, it is not until the child learns the rules for combining words into sentences that he or she has mastered language. These grammatical rules are called **syntax**. Each language has a set of rules for combining words into sentences, but the rules may vary considerably between languages. Research shows that even sign languages, such as American Sign Language (ASL), have a rich and complex syntax.

Most languages also have a form of written expression, which is formally taught to children at school. Although this is not a necessary element of all communication languages, it is a component of most human languages. Some languages have symbols that stand for the sounds in their language. These could be alphabets, like in English, or syllabaries, like in Japanese. A syllabary has a single symbol that stands for a combination of sounds. In Japanese, there are individual symbols that represent "ko," "ka," "ke," and "ku." Other languages have symbols that stand for entire words. For example, Chinese has symbols called kanji. Each kanji is a pictorial symbol that represents an entire word. All written symbols used to express human languages are called **graphemes**.

Animal Communication vs. Language

Animals communicate in diverse ways. Many species of animals use sounds or gestures to warn about predators or to communicate basic needs for food and sex. Vervet monkeys make different calls or screams to warn other monkeys

FIGURE 9.11 *Honeybee dance. Courtesy of cepolina.com*

about dangers such as snakes, leopards, and eagles (Cheny & Seyfarth, 1990). Chimpanzees produce chutter and chirps to announce predators (Marler, 1967), and they also use physical gestures to communicate with other chimpanzees (Tomasello, Call, Nagell, Olguin, & Carpenter, 1994).

Communication is certainly not limited to primates. Penguins produce sounds to locate their mates when they are in a large group (Lengagne, Jouventin, & Aubin, 1999). Each species of songbird has its own song, just as humans have different dialects (Catchpole & Rowell, 1993). Even insects communicate (see Figure 9.11). When honeybees return to the hive, they do complex dances to signal to other bees the distance, location, and quality of the pollen they have just discovered (Esch, Zhang, Srinvasan, & Tautz, 2001; Gould & Gould, 1994). The female firefly imitates the flashing signals of other insects to lure them to her, and then she eats them (Hinojosa, Martin-Loeches, Munoz, Casado, & Pozo, 2004; Lachlan & Feldman, 2003).

Although it is clear that animals communicate, researchers remain unsure whether any animals produce language (Begley, 1998; Chomsky, 1965; Savage-Rumbaugh & Lewin, 1996). Language is a special form of communication that involves four components that other forms of communication do not appear to have:

1. *Abstract symbols*—humans use an arbitrary set of speech sounds, hand signs, and written symbols to represent their languages, and these symbols can have more than one meaning

2. *Abstract thoughts*—humans can use language to express thoughts or indicate objects, events, and ideas that are not physically present

3. *Syntax*—humans use complex rules of grammar to form words into meaningful phrases and sentences

4. *Infinite productivity*—humans can generate an unlimited amount of meaningful sentences using the rules of grammar and the abstract symbols used to express their language

Early Research on Animals' Use of Language

FIGURE 9.12 *Chimpanzee language studies. Courtesy of backgroundsarchive.com.*

Linguist Noam Chomsky (1965) suggested that animals do not have the ability to learn or express language, because their own communication lacks syntax, infinite productivity, and the ability for sounds to have more than one meaning. In an attempt to prove Chomsky's assumption incorrect, behaviorist Herbert Terrace (1979) taught sign language to a young chimpanzee he called **Nim Chimpsky** (see Figure 9.12). However, Nim's progress did not reach Terrace's expectations. Nim learned only about 125 signs and could string them together in only two- or three-word combinations. Nim would often run on with his hands, repeating words and stringing words together out of sequence. Terrace concluded that chimpanzees were not capable of grasping syntax or producing infinite combinations.

Not surprisingly, many ape-language researchers disagreed with Terrace. They felt his use of a sterile laboratory and constant training sessions in sign language produced an environment unlike that in which human children learn

(Fouts, 1994; Savage-Rumbaugh, 1987). Many researchers have argued that their animals have mastered at least a primitive grammar (Seyfarth & Cheny, 2003). For example, Gardner and Gardner (1969) taught sign language to a chimp named **Washoe**. Washoe learned about 160 signs for objects and actions, such as flower, give, come, open, and tickle. If Washoe wanted to be tickled, she would gesture, "You tickle Washoe." But if she wanted to tickle the researcher, she would sign, "Washoe tickle you." The ability to place the words in the correct order to vary the meaning of the sentence suggests a basic understanding of grammar (Gardner & Gardner, 1978).

Recent Research on Animals' Use of Language

In addition, Savage-Rumbaugh and her colleagues (1993) have observed several hundred instances in which the pygmy chimpanzee **Kanzi** has demonstrated an elementary understanding of syntax. For example, using a toy snake and a toy dog, he can respond appropriately to symbol commands of "Make the dog bite the snake" and "Make the snake bite the dog."

Originally, Sue Savage-Rumbaugh attempted to teach English to Kanzi's mother, Matata. Since chimpanzees do not have vocal cords that can produce human speech, Savage-Rumbaugh created a special computer keyboard with arbitrary symbols to represent English words. Matata did not do well. After two years of training, she learned only six of the pictures on the keyboard (Wise, 2000). However, her infant stepson, Kanzi, observed the training. Kanzi was not trained on how to use the keyboard, but he appeared to pick it up on his own (Savage-Rumbaugh, McDonald, Sevcik, Hopkins, & Rupert, 1986). When Matata's training ended, Kanzi spontaneously approached the keyboard and began to make requests. That first day he used the keyboard 120 times (Wise, 2000). Later, Kanzi's younger sister, Mulika, also demonstrated a grasp of syntax.

Explore **observational learning** in Chapter 7, p. 220

Kanzi quickly surpassed every other chimpanzee in his performance at the symbol board. By the time he was 6 years old, Kanzi could communicate with about 200 symbols and had been recorded using more than 13,000 utterances. He could also respond correctly to new sentence constructions. Furthermore, Kanzi also appeared to be capable of understanding some spoken language. One day he found a patch of wild strawberries growing outside the laboratory and began eating them. At the same time, he overheard the researchers talking about the strawberries. Later, whenever any of the researchers said "strawberries," Kanzi would head for the strawberry patch (Savage-Rumbaugh, 1987).

Of course, primates are not the only species that has demonstrated some language capability. Louis Herman and his colleagues have reported similar grammatical ability in bottle-nosed dolphins. Because dolphins have relatively large brains in relation to their bodies (Tyack, 2000), researchers are interested in their ability to produce language. Herman's research has shown that dolphins rarely confuse subject-verb-object word order requests that are signed to them (Herman, Richards, & Woltz, 1984). The bottle-nosed dolphins **Phoenix and Ake** can perform remarkably well when they are given hand signals or a series of whistles to perform behaviors in sequence. For example, if the researcher

FIGURE 9.13 *Dolphins and language. Courtesy of backgroundsarchive.com.*

signs to them to "put the Frisbee in the basket," they respond accordingly. If the researcher tells them to "put the basket in the Frisbee," they take the basket over to the Frisbee and try to put it in. They then go over to the "NO" button and press it to indicate that the behavior cannot be done (Herman, Kuczaj, & Holder, 1993; Herman & Uyeyma, 1993).

In addition, Phoenix and Ake can correctly respond to new sentences, which indicates an understanding of the basic rules of syntax (Herman, 1999). However, despite Herman's remarkable findings, some researchers still doubt that dolphins have the ability to use language (see Figure 9.13). They argue that dolphins might just be highly trained (Pinker, 1994). The dolphins in Herman's study can certainly perform complex behaviors in response to a researcher's commands. However, their current training does not include a way in which they can generate meaningful sentences using grammar to communicate with us. Thus, Louis Herman is working on a training method to teach the dolphins basic written symbols in an attempt to give them a tool to communicate with us in the future. Hopefully this will aid us in understanding the true nature of Phoenix and Ake's language abilities.

Defining Intelligence

Although language and problem solving seem to be key elements of intelligence, it is still unclear to researchers what to include in their definition of intelligence. The most widely accepted definition by psychologists is that **intelligence** is "the global capacity of the individual to act purposefully, to think rationally, and to deal effectively with the environment" (Wechsler, 1944, p. 3). However, most psychologists suggest that this is a very broad definition and should be refined to include problem-solving ability, capacity to acquire knowledge, abstract thinking or reasoning ability, memory, and adaptation to one's environment (Snyderman & Rothman, 1987). Beyond this, there is a great deal of disagreement among psychologists as to what constitutes intelligence.

The Origins of Intelligence

One of the current controversies concerning intelligence is whether it is due to genetic factors or environmental factors. Sir Francis Galton (1874) initiated the controversy by suggesting that intelligence is inherited. After observing several influential families in England, he concluded that intelligence was passed down through generations. He also attempted to understand ways in which the nervous system's efficiency might underlie mental abilities. However, the efficiency measures he proposed were not widely accepted, because they did not correlate well with mental activities. Still, most early theorists agreed with Galton in that intelligence is something we inherit.

There is also a lot of recent evidence to suggest that genes influence intelligence. Researchers have found evidence of genetic markers for intelligence on multiple genes (Fisher et al., 1999; Plomin, 1999; Plomin & Craig, 2001). It is expected that more genes contribute to intelligence and that they will be identified as research continues (Petrill, 2003). Researchers have long been aware that intelligence runs in families, but they are also aware that families share similar environments (Plomin & Petrill, 1997). Therefore, behavioral geneticists have had to find ways to divide the contribution of shared genes and shared environment in order to study heritability. Heritability is the degree to which a trait, such as intelligence, is influenced by genes (Merikangas & Risch, 2003).

Strong evidence for the role of heritability in intelligence comes from twin studies. Researchers at the Minnesota Center for Twin and Adoption Research tested 80 pairs of identical twins who were reared apart. The Minnesota Twin Study found that intelligence had a heritability of .60 to .70 (Bouchard, 1997b). McGue and colleagues (1993) also analyzed more than 100 studies containing over 100,000 pairs of relatives and found a heritability of .60 to .80 for intelligence. The data show that both genetics and environment played a role. The more closely two individuals were related, the higher the similarity in intelligence, suggesting a genetic component to intelligence. When identical twins were reared together, their intelligence scores were more similar than when they were raised apart. This suggests that environment is also a component in intelligence. In recent years, it has become fairly clear that both heredity and environment affect an individual's intellectual ability.

Many researchers do not agree with Bouchard's estimate of the role genetics plays in intelligence. Plomin and colleagues (1994) also analyzed a number of twin studies and found a heritability estimate of .52 for intelligence. This has led some psychologists to believe that some studies overestimate the contribution that genes make to an individual's intelligence. Although most researchers agree that both genetics and environment contribute to intelligence, they continue to fiercely debate over which plays the greater role in influencing intellectual ability.

Theories of Intelligence

Early in the twentieth century, Spearman (1927) discovered that scores on almost all cognitive ability tests were positively correlated. This led him to conclude that there was a general intelligence—which he called "g"—underlying all intelligent performance. He also noticed that individuals could vary on specific cognitive abilities. He proposed that these were specific intelligences, which he called "s." According to Spearman, when you perform a cognitive task, you are using both "g" and "s" intelligences.

Harvard psychologist Howard Gardner (Gardner & Hatch, 1989) rejects the notion of a general intelligence. Instead, his multiple intelligences theory suggests that there are eight different forms of intelligence: linguistic, logical-mathematical, spatial, bodily-kinesthetic, musical, interpersonal, intrapersonal, and naturalistic (Gardner, 1983).

♦ *Linguistic intelligence* is reflected in good reading comprehension and vocabulary. Writers, poets, and public speakers generally demonstrate good linguistic intelligence.

♦ *Logical-mathematical intelligence* consists of good math skills and reasoning. These attributes can be seen in scientists, philosophers, and mathematicians.

FIGURE 9.14 *Bodily-kinesthetic intelligence. Courtesy of wikipedia.org.*

♦ *Spatial intelligence* involves being able to mentally visualize objects and their relations—sculptors, painters, strategists, and architects are good examples.

♦ Dancers and athletes have good *bodily-kinesthetic intelligence* and are able to coordinate their bodily movements better than others (see Figure 9.14).

♦ Those with *musical intelligence*—musicians, composers, and singers—have abilities involving rhythm, tempo, and sound identification.

♦ People who are able to easily understand and interact with others have high *interpersonal intelligence.*

♦ Those who have a greater self-understanding have *intrapersonal intelligence.*

♦ Biologists, zoologists, and botanists all demonstrate a greater understanding of the patterns of nature and would be described as having a *naturalist intelligence.*

Gardner noted that cultures vary in how they value these intelligences, suggesting that Western societies value logical-mathematic and linguistic abilities, whereas non-Western societies value others.

Psychologist Robert Sternberg (1988b, 1995) disagrees with Gardner's theory of multiple intelligences. According to Sternberg, some of Gardner's intelligences are just specific abilities, whereas intelligence is a more general quality. Sternberg's **triarchic theory of intelligence** acknowledges both general intelligence and specific intelligences. Sternberg (1997) has proposed that successful intelligence consists of three types of intelligence. *Analytic intelligence* involves problem-solving abilities and is measured by traditional intelligence tests. *Creative intelligence* is the ability to come up with novel ideas using existing knowledge and skills. *Practical intelligence* is the ability to effectively adapt to the environment. Unlike other intelligence theories, Sternberg's theory examines how intelligence helps us adapt in everyday life. However, one of the major criticisms of his theory is that it is extremely difficult to test creative and practical intelligence (Gottfredson, 2003).

In his best-selling book, *Emotional Intelligence*, Daniel Goleman (1995) suggests that a theory of intelligence based solely on cognitive abilities is limited. He proposes that the ability to perceive, manage, and express emotions appropriately is a form of **emotional intelligence**. Emotional intelligence has four major components: the ability to perceive and respond to others' emotions effectively, the ability to understand and express your own emotions appropriately, the ability to control and regulate one's emotions, and the ability to use emotions to facilitate thinking and motivation (Mayer & Salovey, 1997). Researchers suggest that individuals with a high EQ (emotional quotient) tend to be better leaders and adapt better in the workplace than those with just a high IQ (Goleman, Boyatzis, & McKee, 2002; Yunker & Yunker, 2002). Goleman and colleagues have even developed a test to measure emotional intelligence, called the Emotional Competence Inventory (Boyatzis, Goleman, & Rhee, 2000).

Measuring Intelligence

Early researchers defined intelligence by specifying questions they thought would measure it. The area of psychology that studies the measurement of intelligence is called **psychometrics**. The intelligence tests widely used in our schools today are based on the first intelligence test, devised by Alfred Binet. In 1904, the French Ministry of Education commissioned Binet and his colleague Theodore Simon to devise methods that would identify children who required special help to get through school. Together, they devised a series of tests called the **Binet-Simon Intelligence Scale**, which measured children's memory, attention, and ability to understand similarities and differences. By 1908, Binet and Simon had assessed the age at which a child should be able to perform the tasks in these tests. To assess a child's intelligence, they asked the child to answer questions at the lowest age level first and allowed the child to continue until he or she could no longer perform the task. The age level at which the child could no longer answer the questions correctly was considered the child's mental age. A child's **mental age** was based on the number of items he or she got right as compared to the average number correct for children of various ages. If a child's accuracy score equaled the average accuracy score for 8-year-olds, then the child had a mental age of 8. Binet and Simon then calculated the child's intelligence by subtracting the child's mental age from his or her chronological age. If a child had a mental age of 8 but a chronological age of 6, then the child was considered bright. If a child had a mental age of 4 but was actually 8, then the child was considered retarded. However, this scoring system didn't always reflect the intelligence of the child accurately. It turned out that a 4-year-old with a mental age of 2 is more retarded than a 12-year-old with a mental age of 10. Researchers were thus left to find a way to represent a similar degree of retardation at different ages.

The Stanford-Binet Intelligence Scale

In 1912, William Stern refined Binet and Simon's scoring method. He developed the **intelligence quotient**, which consists of a child's mental age divided by chronological age and multiplied by 100. The Binet-Simon test has been revised numerous times in order to reflect our advancing understanding of the nature of intelligence. Lewis Terman of Stanford University was one of the first to revise the test, in 1916. Terman adapted items that enabled the test to measure adults' intelligence and applied Stern's concept of the intelligence quotient (Terman also introduced the abbreviation "IQ"). By 1920, over 4 million American children had taken the Stanford-Binet intelligence test, and Terman was able to establish new age-based averages from the data of large numbers of children. Administration of the Stanford-Binet became increasingly popular, and it was given to both children and adults.

Terman also revised the content of the original Simon-Binet test by analyzing an individual's response in four content areas: verbal reasoning, quantitative reasoning, abstract/visual reasoning, and short-term memory. One overall IQ score is calculated from the scores on the four subscales (Laurent, Swerdik, & Ryburn, 1992). However, it quickly became apparent that the **Stanford-Binet Intelligence Scale** was not very successful in measuring adult intelligence.

According to the original intelligence quotient, a 50-year-old adult with a mental age of 30 would be considered retarded. Obviously, the formula could not be applied to adults, because at a certain age, people achieve a certain level of mental maturity, and it doesn't continue to increase much over the remaining years. The Stanford-Binet Scale has been revised many times, and the current version, SB-V, is still commonly used to measure intelligence in individuals ages 2–23. However, intelligence tests devised by David Wechsler (1939) are the most widely used today.

The Wechsler Intelligence Scales

Wechsler felt that the Stanford-Binet test had many shortcomings, especially in measuring intelligence in adults. Wechsler argued that the concept of mental age could not be applied to adults, because an adult's intelligence is already fairly mature and does not change as much as a child's intelligence does. Therefore, Wechsler refined the scoring to reflect the amount that an individual's score deviates from the average score, rather than basing it on mental or chronological ages.

Wechsler also objected to the idea that one score could accurately represent something as complex as intelligence (Kaplan & Saccuzzo, 1989). His test, the **Wechsler Adult Intelligence Scale (WAIS)**, contains both verbal (VIQ) and nonverbal performance (PIQ) subtests, and produces an IQ score for each subtest and the overall test. Results have shown some discrepancies between VIQ and PIQ for certain ethnic populations. PIQ for some ethnic groups is as high as or higher than 100, whereas VIQ is below average for the same groups. This suggests that language may have a greater potential to bias the test in favor of some ethnic groups over others.

Wechsler also developed the **Wechsler Intelligence Scale for Children (WISC)** and, for children 4–6½ years of age, the **Wechsler Preschool and Primary Scale of Intelligence (WPPSI)**. The WISC is generally more accepted than the Stanford-Binet test because it has less of an emphasis on language, which some believe might provide a "fairer" measure of IQ in some ethnic groups. The WISC-IV consists of 15 separate subtests. Five of these tests measure verbal skills and make up the *verbal comprehension index*. The remaining 10 tests consist of nonverbal tests such as arranging pictures or repeating digits. The nonverbal tests are subdivided into the *perceptual reasoning index*, the *processing speed index*, and the *working memory index* (see Table 9.1). Each index generates its own IQ score, and these scores are combined into a comprehensive full-scale IQ score. The different kinds of IQ scores are helpful in aiding psychologists in understanding why a child might be exhibiting learning problems. The WAIS-IV, the WISC-IV, and the WPPSI-IV are the current versions of the Wechsler scales and are widely used today to test the IQs of adults and children.

IQ Categories

The Wechsler tests are devised so that an average person's score results in an IQ of 100. On the Wechsler intelligence scales, about 50% of the scores fall in

TABLE 9.1   Typical subtests on the Wechsler Intelligence Scale for Children (WISC-IV). Courtesy of Wood et al., *The World of Psychology*, 6th edition, 2008.

Verbal subtest	Sample item	Performance subtest	Sample item
Information	How many wings does a bird have?	Picture arrangement	Arrange a series of cartoon panels to make a meaningful story.
Digit span	Repeat from memory a series of digits, such as 3 1 0 6 7 4 2 5, after hearing it once.	Picture completion	What is missing from these pictures?
		Block design	Copy designs using blocks
General comprehension	What is the advantage of keeping money in a bank?		
Arithmetic	If 2 apples cost 15¢, what will be the cost of a dozen apples?		
Similarities	In what way are a lion and a tiger alike?		
Vocabulary	This test consists simply of asking, "What is a _____?" or "What does _____ mean?" The words cover a wide range of difficulty or familiarity.	Object assembly	Put together a jigsaw puzzle.
		Digit symbol	Fill in the missing symbols:

1	2	3	4
X	III	I	O

3	4	1	3	4	2	1	2

the average range, between 90 and 110 (see Figure 9.15). About 68% of the scores fall between 85 and 115. Scores falling between 85 and 90 are considered below average intelligence. Scores falling between 110 and 115 are considered above average intelligence. About 2% of the scores are below 70. Individuals with scores in this range are considered developmentally disabled (originally termed "mental retardation"). About 2% of the scores are above 130; those who score in this range are considered to have superior intelligence (originally termed "gifted").

Giftedness Range.   Lewis Terman (1925) conducted the earliest study on individuals scoring above 130 on IQ tests. Terman conducted a longitudinal study of 1,528 students with "genius" IQs. The participants' IQs were measured throughout their lifetime, and their scores ranged from 135 to 200. Terman concluded from these measurements that intelligence is basically innate and varies little across the life span (Cravens, 1992). In addition, Terman found that those who were intellectually superior were not necessarily physically inferior, contrary to the stereotype at the time. His participants excelled in almost all the areas he studied: intellectual, physical, emotional, moral, and social.

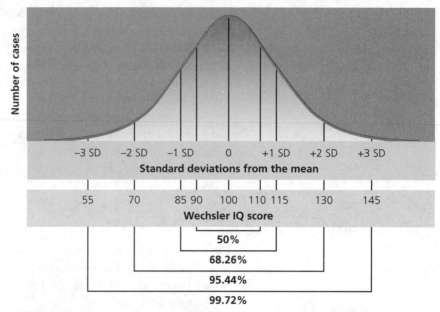

FIGURE 9.15 *The normal curve. Courtesy of Wood et al.,* The World of Psychology, *6th edition, 2008.*

He also debunked several other myths about "geniuses." It was often thought that there was a thin line between genius and madness. Terman's group actually enjoyed better mental health than the general population. It was also common for people to think that geniuses are "book smart" but generally do not have much common sense. Terman's participants were better adjusted both personally and socially than the general population (Terman & Oden, 1947).

Beginning in the 1920s, the term "gifted" was used to describe those with superior intelligence. However, the term is not widely used today to describe those who have IQ scores above 130. Today, the term **gifted** is used to describe individuals who have the following three qualities: exceptional ability, exceptional motivation, and exceptional creativity (Renzulli, 1986).

Developmentally Disabled Range.   Originally, individuals who scored below 70 on an IQ test were classified as mentally retarded. However, due to the negative stigma that has developed over time for the term "mental retardation," individuals with low IQ scores are no longer labeled as mentally retarded. Individuals with IQ scores below 70 are in the range of developmental disability. To be classified as being **developmentally disabled**, individuals must meet two criteria: (1) their IQ score is below 70, and (2) they have a severe deficiency in daily life functioning (Grossman, 1983). Causes of developmental disabilities include brain injuries, developmental deficiencies due to toxic exposure to chemicals or other hazards, and genetic abnormalities such as Down syndrome.

The degree to which individuals vary in developmental disability can range from mild to profound. Individuals with IQs ranging from 55 to 70 have a mild developmental disability. They are usually capable of grasping learning skills up to a sixth-grade level, and they may be able to have a job and live on their own. Those with an IQ from 40 to 55 have a moderate developmental disability. Most of these individuals are not able to grasp more than a second-grade academic level. They are able to lean some self-help skills and some social skills, but have difficulty working without a great deal of aid and generally need to live with others who can help them with their basic life skills. Severe developmental disability occurs with IQ scores between 25 and 40. These individuals can be trained in basic health habits through repetitive habit training, and they can learn to communicate verbally. Profound developmental disability occurs with IQ scores under 25. Profoundly developmentally disabled have rudimentary motor development and learn a very limited amount of self-help skills (Grossman, 1983).

Accuracy of Intelligence Testing

Intelligence tests can be administered either to an individual or to a group. The Stanford-Binet and the Wechsler scales are given to one person at a time, but it is often necessary due to budget limitations to administer intelligence tests to large groups. The California Test of Mental Maturity, the Cognitive Abilities Test, and the Otis-Lennon Mental Ability Test are widely used group intelligence tests.

All intelligence tests are judged for reliability and validity. **Reliability** means the test must consistently demonstrate the same score when the same person is tested and then retested on an alternative form of the test. The greater the similarity between the two scores, the more reliable the test. Even if a test is highly reliable, it is worthless if it is not valid. **Validity** is when a test accurately measures what it is intended to measure. There is quite a difference in opinion among psychologists over what actually constitutes intelligence, so the validity of IQ tests has been questioned. While the Wechsler Scales demonstrate high reliability, if you subscribe to a multiple intelligence theory such as Gardner's, you probably think that IQ tests are not a valid or accurate representation of an individual's intelligence.

Once a test has demonstrated reliability and validity, it must be standardized. **Standardization** means that there must be standard procedures for administering and scoring the test—the same instructions and the same amount of time must be given each time. In addition, **norms** by which all scores are interpreted must be established. This is accomplished by administering the test to large groups of people and then analyzing the mean and the standard deviation of the group tested.

Cultural Differences in Intelligence

Using intelligence testing, researchers have found disparities between intelligence scores of certain groups. For example, European Americans tend to score about 15 points higher on IQ tests than African Americans even when differences in income level are taken into account (Fagan & Holland, 2002). The average IQ of many minority groups in the United States is lower than that of European Americans (Loehlin, 2000; Perlman & Kaufman, 1990; Suzuki & Vraniak, 1994). However, some minority groups, such as Asian Americans, display higher average IQs than those of European Americans (see Figure 9.16).

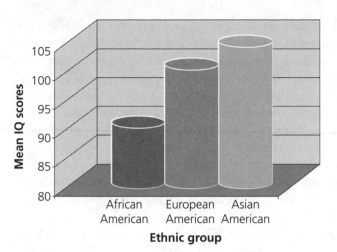

FIGURE 9.16 *Ethnic group differences in IQ score.*

What could cause this disparity? In 1969, Jensen fueled the flames of controversy over this subject by suggesting that cultural differences in IQ are due to heredity. He concluded this was the case because his analysis suggested that the heritability of intelligence is approximately .80. Years later, Herrnstein and Murray (1994) stoked the flames by implying in their widely discussed book, *The Bell Curve*, that ethnic disparities are at least partly genetic. Most psychologists argue that we must take into account the socially depressed environments where many minority children are raised.

Many individuals, not just ethnic minorities, live in environments where they are educationally disadvantaged. While the sheer numbers of European Americans living in poverty is greater than the number of ethnic minorities living in poverty, there is a disproportionate number of ethnic minorities living in poverty. Children raised in a low-income home often have fewer books and supplies, less privacy for study, and less parental assistance (Lott, 2002; McLoyd, 1998; Seifer, 2001). These environmental factors may account for some of the problems these children experience in achieving an IQ score comparable to children raised in middle- or high-income homes. Across all ethnicities, the average IQ scores are about 15 points lower among children from lower social classes (Seifer, 2001; Williams & Ceci, 1997). Thus it appears that socioeconomic status may play a more important role in lower IQ scores than belonging to a certain ethnic group.

Adoption studies support the influence of environment on intelligence scores. African American children from disadvantaged homes who were adopted into middle- and upper-class European American families showed an increase of about 10–15 points in their IQ scores. In addition, children raised in a home where the parents have a higher level of education also demonstrated higher IQ scores than children raised by parents with only a high school education (Scarr & Weinberg, 1976; Waldman, Weinberg, & Scarr, 1994). Finally, IQ scores have been rising for African Americans. Flynn (1999) suggests that perhaps this is due in part to increasing educational opportunities for African American children.

Some researchers suggest that the discrepancy in IQ scores between different ethnic groups may be caused by other cultural factors. For instance, the differences in IQ scores may reflect differences in the value each culture puts on educational achievement. Steinberg and colleagues (1992) studied 15,000 African American, Asian American, Hispanic American, and European American high school students and found that the importance they placed on academic achievement varied by ethnic group. In contrast, studies show that Asian Americans place little value on intellectual ability even though their IQ scores tend to be higher than other groups' (Li, 2003). Stevenson (1992) suggests that this is because they place a very high value on hard work and perseverance, to which their academic success can be attributed.

Another approach to examining the ethnic differences in IQ scores may be to take a closer look at the tests themselves. Many test items in IQ tests have been found to reflect the dominant European American middle-class culture in the United States. Those from other American cultures might be less familiar with these test items, and it might affect their IQ scores. Some ethnic groups may fail to understand instructions or test items due to language differences, or they may use different strategies for solving problems than those required by the tests (Miller-Jones, 1989). Researchers have been revising the original IQ tests for decades now, attempting to create a culture-fair intelligence test (Frey & Detterman, 2004). A **culture-fair intelligence test** uses culture-neutral questions and therefore does not penalize someone who is not from the dominant culture. However, it is now generally recognized that it is impossible to create a completely culture-free test. Any ability test will contain language that reflects the culture that is developing the test (Greenfield, 1997).

Gender Differences in Intelligence

Psychologists are also concerned with the differences found in IQ testing between men and women. Although the average overall intelligence test scores of men and women do not differ much, they do seem to vary on different aspects of intelligence (Brody, 2000a). Women tend to perform better on tests of perceptual speed, verbal fluency, mathematical calculation, and those requiring fine motor coordination. Men are better at throwing and catching objects and mathematical reasoning (Collins & Kimura, 1997). These differences appear to be present even in children. Girls on average have larger vocabularies than boys (Lutchmaya, Baron-Cohen, & Raggatt, 2002). Teenage girls perform better than teenage boys in reading and writing, but the boys do better in math and science (Hedges & Nowell, 1995). Although, these differences in abilities of men and women are quite small, they appear in most of the research (Halpern, 2000).

Researchers have suggested that these differences are due to both biological and environmental factors. Proponents of the biological approach suggest that hormones affect the developing brain differently and produce a variety of behavioral differences between men and women (Halpern & Tan, 2001; Nelson & Luciana, 2001). Environmental explanations suggest that behavior of boys and girls is shaped by gender roles. **Gender roles** are behaviors an individual exhibits because he or she thinks these are the expected behaviors of his or her gender. For example, many girls think that boys are supposed to be better at math, so the girls don't perform as well on math tests.

Steele (1997) coined the term **stereotype threat** to describe this phenomenon. A stereotype threat occurs when a member of a group fears that he or she will be evaluated based on a stereotype about his or her group. In one study, female and male students took a difficult math test. Prior to taking the test, the students were told that males typically score higher on the test. When the tests were scored, the female students scored significantly lower than their male counterparts. But when another group of male and female students who were not informed of any gender difference took the test, there was no difference in the performance between male and female students (Spencer, Steele, & Quinn, 1999). Simply reminding the female students of the stereotype that men are better at math than women lowered their scores.

Creativity

Creativity is the ability to think about something in original and useful ways. Researchers who develop traditional IQ tests suggest that any individual with an exceptionally high IQ is gifted. However, some psychologists argue that the concept of giftedness goes beyond intellectual factors and includes creativity. They suggest that gifted people have high levels of creativity and motivation, along with an ability to recognize the usefulness of their ideas and implement them (Renzulli, 1986). Child prodigy Alexandra Nechita is an excellent example of giftedness. When Alexandra was 2 years old, she colored for hours and was not interested in dolls or friends. Even today, at 23 years of age, she paints relentlessly and passionately on large canvases that sell for up to $80,000 apiece. Her high motivation, creativity, and her ability to productively use her talent are typical characteristics of gifted people (Wood, Wood, & Boyd, 2005).

Creativity and IQ

There is also evidence that creative people do not need to possess a high IQ. Arthur Fry, a chemist for the 3M company, was attempting to discover a very strong adhesive and failed. Instead, his research produced a weak adhesive that would allow paper to stick to things but could be easily removed. Fry initially could not think of any practical use for it. At the same time, Fry had a problem remembering where certain songs were in the church hymnal. He would leave slips of papers as bookmarks, but these were constantly falling out. Then it occurred to him that the weak adhesive he had discovered might hold the slips of paper in place, yet still allow him to remove them afterward. This sudden flash of insight led him to develop a modern marvel—the Post-it note.

Another creative mind stumbled upon information that led him to create another modern marvel. George de Mestral was walking his dog one day, and both of them returned with burrs stuck to their clothing. Curiosity led him to examine the burrs under a microscope to discover what made them so sticky. Upon examination, he discovered that the burrs were covered in tiny hooks. This knowledge, paired with his creativity, led him to develop Velcro. Both Fry and de Mestral were of average intelligence and yet displayed remarkable creativity.

In addition, it appears that individuals with low IQs can display some amazingly creative abilities. For example, Wendy Verougstraete is an extremely creative writer, and yet she cannot tie her shoes or cross the street by herself. Wendy has an IQ of 49, and yet she has a very rich vocabulary and enjoys telling stories. Wendy has Williams syndrome—a genetic birth disorder that includes a combination of extremely expressive verbal skills, extremely low IQ, and limited motor and spatial ability (Vicari, Bellucci, & Carlesimo, 2001). Children with Williams syndrome demonstrate an unusual liking for words. When asked to name an animal, they will list unusual animals such as an ibex or a newt (see Figure 9.17), whereas most children would say a dog or a cat (Bellugi, Korenberg, & Kilma, 2001). In addition, when they tell stories they express drama and emotions, varying the pitch of their voice and using attention-grabbing words. This suggests that intelligence and verbal skills may not be as related as researchers once thought.

FIGURE 9.17 *Newt. Courtesy of Christian Fischer.*

Autistic savants are individuals with autism who display amazing cognitive or artistic abilities. Autistics generally score quite low on IQ tests, presumably due to their communication skill deficits. About 10% of autistic individuals are savants. While some savants possess greater cognitive abilities in memory and mathematical calculating, others possess extremely creative abilities such as drawing, painting, or playing musical instruments without any training. For example, a 6-year-old girl named Nadia suffered from severe autism, yet she could draw gallery-quality pictures. Even though her IQ was between 60 and 70 and she could barely put two words together, she displayed remarkable creativity. Or consider Tom, a 13-year-old autistic boy who was blind and could not even tie his own shoes. He could play a difficult piano piece after hearing it just once, even though he had no musical training. In fact, he could even play one song with his left hand, another song with his right hand, and sing a third song—all at the same time (Ramachandran & Blakeslee, 1998; Sacks, 1985).

Creativity and Thought

It also appears that creative people tend to be divergent thinkers (Guilford, 1967). **Divergent thinking** is the generation of a number of useful and appropriate solutions to a problem in which there is no specific solution. Divergent thinking is original and involves the ability to associate ideas in an unusual way. It is also flexible, and divergent thinkers can switch quickly and smoothly from one set of ideas to another. It also requires the ability to formulate an abundance of ideas (Csikszentmihalyi, 1996). **Convergent thinking** is the narrowing down of alternatives to one solution by using knowledge and logic. Convergent thinking is typically the type of problem solving that is measured on IQ and achievement tests, where there is a known answer. Some researchers propose that divergent thinking is necessary in order to be creative, but convergent thinking is required to be able to tell the difference between good ideas and bad ideas (Csikszentmihalyi, 1996). Most experts agree that creative thinking does not occur quickly; rather, it is the product of intensive study, long reflection, motivation, and determination (Haberlandt, 1997; Snow, 1999). For instance, Mozart created 609 musical compositions before he died at the age of 35, and Einstein published 248 papers on his theory of relativity before it was finished.

Becoming More Creative

Robert Sternberg (1988b) suggested that creative people usually excel in five different components of creativity:

1. Imaginative thinking skills—creative individuals have the ability to see things in novel ways, to recognize patterns, and to make connections.

2. Expertise—creative people have a well-developed knowledge base, especially in their area of creativity. A well-developed knowledge base is essential because creativity involves taking these basic building blocks and combining them in novel ways.

3. A venturesome personality—creative individuals seek new experiences. They tolerate risk and persevere in the face of obstacles.

4. Intrinsic motivation—creative people are motivated primarily by interest, enjoyment, satisfaction, and the challenge of the work itself, rather than by external rewards.

5. A creative environment—creative people seek out environments that spark, support, and help them refine creative ideas. Most creative people have the emotional intelligence to socialize well with others, and they are mentored, supported, and challenged by their peers.

Many books offer techniques to help you improve your ability in all five of these areas. Even individuals who are not very creative can become more creative by learning strategies that enable them to look at things in novel ways.

Chapter Summary

We began by exploring thinking, which involves using knowledge to form concepts, inspire creativity, solve problems, and communicate with others. Thinking consists of three different modes: imaginal thought, which has to do with the images we perceive in our mind; propositional thought, which consists of the streams of sentences we hear in our mind; and motoric thought, which contains mental representations of motor movements we perceive in our mind.

Thought may include not only language but also mental images. Mental images are representations that arise from stored information rather than from visual sensory input. We appear to organize our mental representations into concepts and categories. A concept is a mental representation that consists of a grouping of objects or events. This could be a class or a set of objects, people, organizations, events, situations, or relations that share common characteristics or features. Classical theory, prototype theory, and exemplar theory are three theories on concepts. In classical theory, all items in the concept share defining features. Prototype theory states that a concept is formed based on a mental example that embodies the most common and typical features of that set of objects. Exemplar theory states that concepts can be represented by individual examples that are stored in memory from personal experiences.

People can easily place objects into categories because the brain is innately hardwired to store different concepts in different parts of the brain. Psychologists have found that we tend to store concepts in a hierarchy at different levels of specificity. The highest, most general level is the superordinate category. The intermediate level is the basic level category. The most specific level is the subordinate category. Some researchers theorize that concepts are not only organized by basic features into hierarchies but also organized by the brain into schemas. A schema is a mental framework for organizing concepts according to related themes or aspects of a particular situation.

In this chapter we also investigated different aspects of problem solving. Problem solving is an attempt to overcome obstacles in order to reach a goal. Individuals are most likely to use either an algorithm or a heuristic to solve a well-structured problem. An algorithm is a step-by-step set of rules that, if followed correctly, will lead to a solution. Heuristics are a mental shortcut that may or may not lead to a solution. Three problem-solving heuristics were discussed. A means-end analysis is a problem-solving strategy where we identify differences between the present state and the goal state and make changes to reduce that difference. Another heuristic, subgoal analysis, involves breaking the problem into small intermediate steps that will lead toward a solution. Finally, we learned that sometimes it is easier to use a backward-working heuristic than to attempt to solve problems in a forward linear fashion. Two obstacles to problem solving were discussed: a mental set and functional fixedness. A mental set is the tendency to use strategies that have worked in the past even if another strategy might work better. Functional fixedness refers to the inability to imagine objects being used in any way other than their familiar function.

The difference between communication and language was also explored in this chapter. Communication is an exchanging of information using sounds, smells, or gestures. Language is a system of communication with a particular set of rules for combining symbols, which can generate an infinite number of meaningful combinations. The way in which we acquire language was also examined. Some linguists believe that we have an inborn mechanism, called a language acquisition device, that enables us to learn the basic elements of language.

Linguists have studied the basic elements of language that are common to all human languages. The sounds that help distinguish meaning in a language are called phonemes. Each language has a set of phonemes, or speech sounds, specific to that language. When these speech sounds are combined into the smallest units of meaning, they are called morphemes. Linguists call this study of meaning "semantics." This meaning can be derived from morphemes, words, and sentences. Pragmatics is the characteristics of spoken language that aid us in interpreting the social meaning of the communication. Each language has a set of rules for combining words into sentences, but the rules may vary considerably between languages. These grammatical rules are called syntax. All written symbols used to express human language are called graphemes.

The debate over whether animals have language or whether they just communicate in less systematic ways was also discussed. The main reason that linguists and psychologists question this is that language is a special form of communication that involves four abilities not found in other forms of communication: use of abstract symbols, abstract thoughts, syntax, and infinite productivity.

Next we explored different theories of intelligence. Spearman's theory of intelligence suggests that there is a general intelligence and that there are specific intelligences. Gardner's multiple intelligences theory suggests that there are eight forms of intelligence: linguistic, logical-mathematical, spatial, bodily-kinesthetic, musical, interpersonal, intrapersonal, and naturalistic. Sternberg's triarchic theory of intelligence proposes that successful intelligence consists of three types of intelligence: analytic, creative, and practical. Goleman suggests that a theory of intelligence based solely on cognitive abilities is limited. He proposes that the ability to perceive, manage, and express emotions appropriately is a form of emotional intelligence.

This chapter also examined tests developed to measure intelligence. The Binet-Simon Intelligence Scale measures children's memory, attention, and ability to understand similarities and differences. However, there were limitations to the Binet test. It was not very accurate with adults, and psychologist David Wechsler believed that one score could not accurately represent something as complex as intelligence. Thus, he developed the Wechsler Adult Intelligence Scale (WAIS), the Wechsler Intelligence Scale for Children (WISC), and, for children 4–6½ years of age, the Wechsler Preschool and Primary Scale of Intelligence (WPPSI). IQ scores are separated into three categories: average intelligence (scores between 70 and 130), gifted (scores above 120), and developmentally disabled (scores below 70).

Of course, the reliability and validity of intelligence tests have been widely disputed. Cultural influences have been shown to affect the reliability of intelligence tests. Researchers have found disparities among intelligence scores of certain groups and have disagreed about whether they are largely due to cultural biases in the test or heritability. Gender differences in intelligence testing have also been observed. It is suspected that cultural gender roles are the cause. Gender roles are behaviors that an individual does because that is what he or she thinks is expected of his or her gender.

Finally, we examined the role of creativity in human behavior. Creativity is the ability to think about something in original and useful ways. Creative people tend to share five traits: imaginative thinking skills, expertise, a venturesome personality, intrinsic motivation, and creative environments. Creative people also tend to be divergent thinkers more often than convergent thinkers. Creativity does not require a high IQ, as there are savants who have low IQs and demonstrate high creativity. Also, a high IQ does not guarantee that someone will also have high creativity.

Knowledge Builder

RELATE TO YOURSELF

1. Think about the last time you did something creative. List all the things you did that you think contributed to your creative product. Compare them with the components of creativity listed in this chapter. Which creative components did you use?

_____

_____

_____

_____

2. Compare your own abilities to Gardner's eight intelligences. In which areas do you think you would score low, moderate, or high?

_____

_____

_____

_____

3. Quickly list below the first five objects that you think of. Now compare them to the hierarchical category levels on page 264. Did you find that you named objects with labels from the basic level category?

_____

_____

_____

_____

CHAPTER REVIEW QUESTIONS

1. Dolphins and primates do not demonstrate any ability to use or understand syntax. **T or F?**

2. Research suggests that creativity consists of more components than just a gifted level of intelligence. **T or F?**

3. Functional fixedness is the tendency to use strategies that have worked in the past even if another strategy might work better. **T or F?**

4. The word {cats} contains a single morpheme. **T or F?**

5. The internal language that we "hear" in our mind is called propositional thought. **T or F?**

6. The rules that we use for combining words into an infinite number of different sentences are called _____.

    (a) semantics   **(b)** morphemes

    (c) graphemes   **(d)** syntax

7. The process by which children apply words that they know to objects for which they do not yet have words is called _____.

    (a) babbling   **(b)** overgeneralization

    (c) overextension   **(d)** telegraphing

8. What do you call a step-by-step set of rules that, if followed correctly, will lead to a solution?

    (a) algorithm   **(b)** heuristics

    (c) mental set   **(d)** functional fixedness

9. The problem-solving strategy in which we identify differences between the present state and the goal state and make changes to reduce that difference is called _____.

    (a) backward-working heuristic   **(b)** means-end analysis

    (c) sub-goal analysis   **(d)** trial and error

10. *CRITICAL THINKING EXERCISE.* What are the similarities and differences among the classical theory, the prototype theory, and the exemplar theory of concept formation?

_____

_____

_____

_____

11. *CRITICAL THINKING EXERCISE.* Researchers continue to debate whether animals can produce language. List the four criteria for language that are used to examine this issue and give examples from animal research to support either side of the debate.

_____

_____

_____

_____

_____

_____

_____

12. *Consider the following scenario:* Joe lives in a poor area and his parents have a very limited income. Joe is good at finding ways to get the things he needs. What type of intelligence would you say that Joe exhibits? Why? Who developed the idea that this type of intelligence exists?

_____

_____

_____

_____

FIGURE 9.18 *Hobbit problem.*

13. *Consider the following scenario* (Matlin, 1998): Three hobbits and three orcs want to cross to the other side of a river. Unfortunately, they have only one boat, which will hold only two individuals at a time. There is no other way to cross the river. Also, orcs are always hungry! If more orcs than hobbits are left on either bank, the orcs will eat the hobbits. Devise a way to get the three hobbits and the three orcs to the other side of the river without harm. Now explain the problem-solving strategies you used to solve the problem.

_____

_____

_____

_____

USEFUL WEB SITES

PROBLEM-SOLVING STRATEGIES

http://www.une.edu.au/bcss/psychology/john-malouff/problem-solving.php

A comprehensive list of 50 problem-solving strategies and a thorough treatment of things you can do to increase your problem-solving abilities.

MACHIAVELLIAN MONKEYS & SHAKESPEAREAN APES: THE QUESTION OF PRIMATE LANGUAGE

http://nationalzoo.si.edu/Publications/ZooGoer/1995/6/machiavellianmonkeys.cfm

A great article from the National Zoo that discusses primates' and dolphins' communication abilities and intelligence.

TRANSLATE FAVORITE PHRASES INTO DIFFERENT LANGUAGES

http://world.altavista.com/

To unlock the confusion of Babel, use BABEL FISH, a unique program that can translate your phrases into several different languages.

TEST YOURSELF!

http://www.queendom.com/index.html

This site has many different tests—114 professionally developed and validated psychological tests, 111 just-for-fun tests, and 230 mind games and quizzes. Some are serious psychological tests, and some are just plain funny.

THE IQ TEST

http://www.iqtest.com/

Go here to take a free IQ test and to learn more about different types of IQ tests and their reliability.

THE CREATIVITY WEB

http://members.optusnet.com.au/~charles57/Creative/

The Creativity Web helps a person become more creative. It contains an exhaustive list of creativity techniques, books, software, and more.

SOLUTIONS TO PROBLEMS

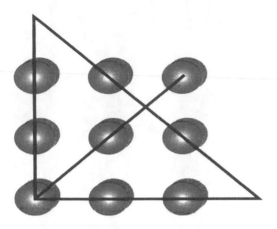

FIGURE 9.19 *The nine-dot problem.*

FIGURE 9.20 *The candle problem.*

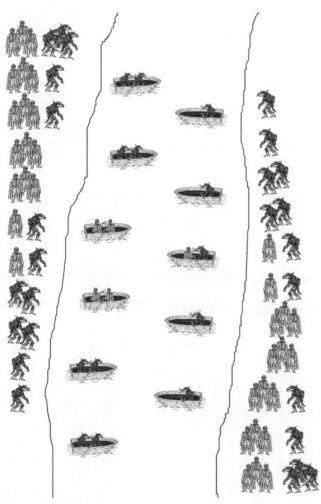

FIGURE 9.21 *The hobbit-orc problem.*

Chapter 10

Gender and Sexuality

by Amy Sweetman, MA, and Patricia Alexander, PhD

*Man is a creature who lives not upon bread alone,
but principally by catchwords; and the little rift
between the sexes is astonishingly widened by
simply teaching one set of catchwords to the girls
and another to the boys.*

—ROBERT LOUIS STEVENSON

How are men and women different? Are their differences inborn or a matter
of training? Why is someone gay? Just what is "normal" sex? In most cases,
gender-role and sexual behaviors exist on a continuum and cannot be neatly
categorized or simply explained. When trying to understand human sexuality, we need to recognize the complexity of human behavior and that it may
be difficult to draw firm conclusions about why people do what they do. A
famous sex researcher, Alfred Kinsey, stated, "Only the human mind invents
categories and tries to force facts into separate pigeonholes. The living world
is a continuum in each and every one of its aspects. The sooner we learn this
concerning sexual behavior, the sooner we shall reach a sound understanding
of the realities of sex" (Kinsey, Pomeroy, & Martin, 1948, p. 639). As human
beings, we like to organize things into categories in order to create satisfying
explanations for things. For example, society defines handedness according to
which hand we write with. However, most people have some behaviors in which
their right hand dominates and other behaviors in which their left dominates.
In other words, there seems to be different degrees of handedness in people.

Similarly, societies have tended to create a division of labor based on sex. Sex
refers to biological maleness or femaleness. Along with the various work tasks
deemed appropriate for men and women, there are typically behavioral or
gender role expectations that designate what are normal and appropriate
behaviors for men and women.

Handedness and sexuality issues are related in at least three ways. To start,
just as there are different degrees of handedness, there are different degrees

TABLE 10.1 Handedness continuum.						
Everything is done with the right hand	Most things are done with the right hand, but there are **some** things that have to be done with the left hand	Write with the right hand, but there are **lots** of things that are done with the left hand	Write and do most things **equally well** with the right and left hand	Write with the left hand, but there are **lots** of things that are done with the right hand	Most things are done with the left hand, but there are **some** things that have to be done with the right hand	**Everything** is done with the left hand

FIGURE 10.1 *In the past, left-handedness was thought to be the work of the devil.*

of sexual orientation and sexual identity. Also, the causes of left-handedness have not been clearly established, but it is theorized that biological factors that occur before birth have a major role in hand preference. Many aspects of sexual orientation and sexual identity are also thought to have a strong biological component that is subsequently influenced by social and other environmental forces. Finally, society tends to be unforgiving of behavior that strays from the norm. In earlier times left-handedness was thought to be the work of the devil or indicative of being cursed. These types of beliefs are no longer prevalent, thanks to a more scientific understanding of handedness. Scientific research has also helped us become more tolerant of differences in expressions of sexual orientation and sexual behavior over the past century. Later in this chapter we will find that there is another fascinating relationship between the phenomenon of handedness and issues of sexual orientation and sexuality identity.

Gender Differences

Take a look at the female brain and the male brain depicted in Figure 10.2. How do you feel about this picture? Do you think that male and female brains are very different from each other? This picture is a widely circulated joke

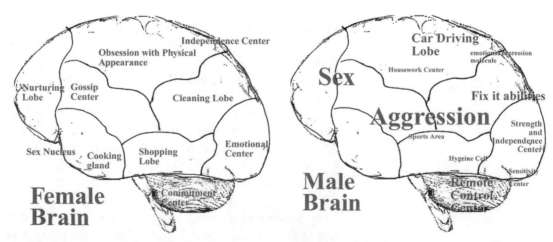

FIGURE 10.2 *It sometimes seems that there are more differences in the brains of men and women than is actually the case. Cartoon by Amy Sweetman. All rights reserved.*

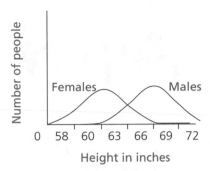

FIGURE 10.3 *Although the average male is taller than the average female, there is quite a bit of overlap.*

that plays on stereotypes of male and female behavior. **Stereotyping** is the tendency to make general conclusions about a large group of people. Common stereotypes for men are that they are independent, good at fixing things, concerned with obtaining status and power in the workplace, and aggressive. In their spare time they like to play sports, watch TV (with remote in hand), and play video games. Women, on the other hand, are commonly stereotyped as emotional, passive, nurturing, and good at cleaning, cooking, and caring for children. For their pastimes, they enjoy shopping and gossiping.

Figure 10.2 does *not* have scientific validity. There is no real shopping lobe or remote-control-addiction center in the human brain. Male and female brains are actually far more alike than they are different. However, improved research technology has revealed that subtle anatomical differences do occur in the lobes of male and female brains as well as in other subcortical structures (Cahill, 2005). Some of these differences are outlined in the sidebar. A note of caution is warranted here. These differences are averages. Just as the average female is shorter than the average male, we know that there are many instances where a particular man may be shorter than a particular woman. In other words, the broad generalizations, such as those pictured in the brain cartoon, should not be made for individuals.

Although differences in male and female brains have been found, it is not completely clear how these differences in brain structure developed. There is fairly strong evidence that points to a combination of genetic influences, hormones, and environmental factors (see, for example, Damaiso, 2002; Nopoulos, Flaum, O'Leary, & Andreasen, 2000). In terms of prenatal development, the body is organized by an interaction of genes and prenatal hormones. As part of the body, the brain would be expected to be likewise affected. The brain is an organ

Some of the Brain Differences Found in Men and Women

♦ The hypothalamus is widely cited as an area where men and women differ. Specifically, the preoptic and suprachiasmatic nucleus of the hypothalamus are larger in men than in women.

♦ The corpus callosum has been found to be larger in women than in men.

♦ The right and left amygdalae tend to process disturbing information differently in men and women.

♦ The hippocampus is larger in women than in men; it also seems to react to the environment and stress differently in men and women.

♦ Women have been found to have more language areas in their brain, and they recover their ability to produce language more readily than men after stroke damage.

♦ Processing differences between men and women have been found. For example, widely cited research indicates that women tend to use both hemispheres simultaneously when engaging in a cognitive task, whereas men tend to use one side or the other.

(Cahill, 2005)

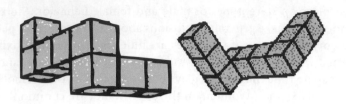

Look at these two pictures.
Determine if they are the same object.

How many synonyms can you think
of for this word within 30 seconds?

FIGURE 10.4 *Sex differences in performance levels on two cognitive tasks have been found. On average, women would excel in the task on the right, whereas men would dominate in the task on the left.*

Dominating at Both Ends of the Spectrum

Males who score over 700 on the SAT outnumber females who score over 700 by a ratio of 13:1.

Males with a learning disorder outnumber females with a learning disorder by a ratio of 6:1.

(Halpern, 2000)

FIGURE 10.5 *Gwen Stefani. Courtesy of Stephane Cardinale/People Avenue/Corbis.*

in constant flux; thus, any subtle biological differences between the brains of boys and the brains of girls that are present at birth are likely to be affected by experience and socialization practices, magnifying these initial differences to produce the distinctions found in more mature subjects (Rogers, 2001).

Given that there are several differences between male and female brains, do these anatomical differences correlate with intellect? Is one sex smarter than the other? As was discussed in Chapter 9, men and women have the same average intelligence, and there are very few areas where large differences have been found regarding mental abilities (Brody, 2000b). However, boys seem to be both blessed and cursed when it comes to school performance, which is likely to reflect intelligence. Boys seem to dominate in higher-level mathematics, but they are also more likely to have learning disorders such as dyslexia (a pattern-recognition disorder in which individuals have difficulty reading a large block of text or working with lots of numbers) and to suffer from attention deficit disorder. One area where boys have a definite advantage is in rapid mental spatial rotation, where subjects are asked to quickly rotate images in space. On average, girls talk earlier than boys and show more advanced language skills. Also, women are faster at finding words with similar meanings. Thus, it appears that there are slight differences between male and female abilities on very specific tasks. Environmental explanations have been offered for these sex differences, and most gender research on cognition and personality gives learning explanations equal billing with biological ones (A. Cohen, personal communication, February 1, 2008).

"I'm just a girl / Take a good look at me / Just your typical prototype": The pop star Gwen Stefani sings these lyrics, but what does it mean to be "just a girl"? Is there a typical prototype of a woman or man? Our entire society is divided according to this construct, as are other cultures. It is the first question asked about a child and one of the first questions listed on almost every form that we are required to fill out. Research continuously reflects the fact that gender expression is the complex interaction of biological, behavioral, social-cultural, and environmental forces. These forces seem to work in a reciprocal pattern in which each can influence the expression of the other.

Sexual Development

Genes are the hereditary material located within the chromosomes. Males and females have the same 22 pairs of chromosomes, but they differ on the 23rd pair. Women carry the X chromosome in their eggs. Some male sperm cells have an X chromosome, and others have a Y. If an X-carrying sperm fertilizes the egg (producing an XX cell), then female development is initiated. However, if a Y sperm fertilizes the egg, then the zygote (fertilized egg) will produce a male, or an XY chromosomal pattern. Genes located on the X and Y chromosomes affect the differentiation of the sex organ tissue. Both male and female sex organs develop out of the same tissue. The head of the penis is made from the same cells as the clitoris, and the outer lips of the vulva area are made from the same cells as the scrotum (the sac that holds the testicles) on a male. See Figure 10.6.

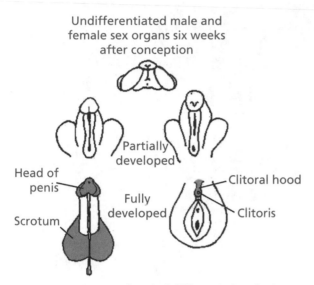

FIGURE 10.6 *Stages of genital differentiation during prenatal development. Image drawn by Steve Carballo, used with permission.*

Almost all embryos possess a set of precursors, or beginning forms of both male and female genitalia. In other words, for the first few weeks of development, all of us are capable of developing either male or female genitalia regardless of our chromosomal pattern. If testosterone is present in the womb at sufficient levels during weeks 7–11 of pregnancy, then the Wolffian duct system, the precursor of the male genitalia, develops. If testosterone is not present or not present in adequate levels, then our default setting is for the Mullerian ducts, the precursors of female genitalia, to mature. Several factors can interfere with this process of genital differentiation in the first trimester, such as genetic defects, insensitivity to hormones, or the ingestion of drugs. If there is a significant interference in the genital differentiation process, then the child may have the presence of ambiguous genitalia and secondary sex characteristics, or genitalia of the other sex.

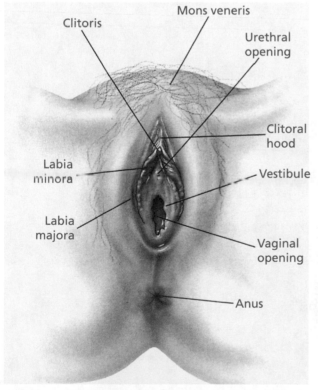

FIGURE 10.7 *The female genitalia (vulva), with the labia parted to show the vaginal and urethral openings. Courtesy of King,* Human Sexuality Today, *5th edition, 2005.*

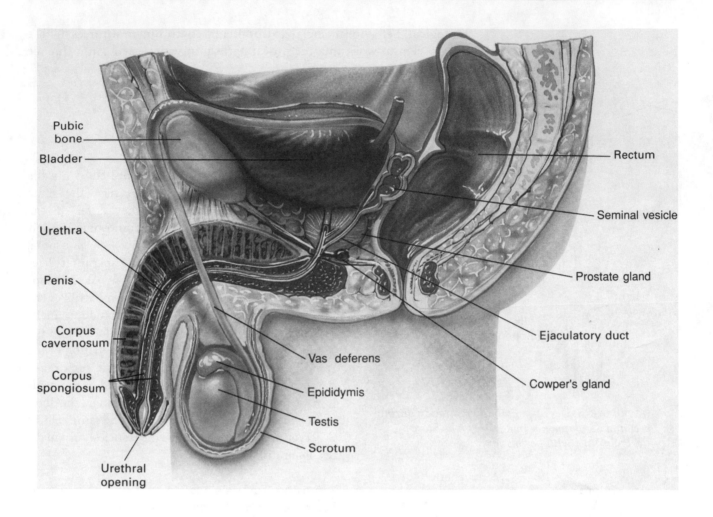

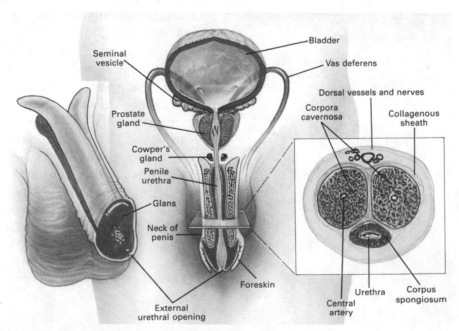

FIGURE 10.8 *The internal male reproductive system: (top) from a side view; (bottom) from a frontal view and section of the penis. Courtesy of King,* Human Sexuality Today, *5th edition, 2005.*

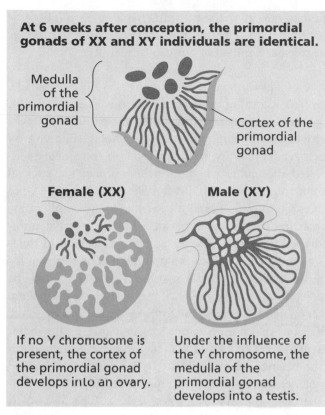

At 6 weeks after conception, the primordial gonads of XX and XY individuals are identical.

Medulla of the primordial gonad

Cortex of the primordial gonad

Female (XX)   **Male (XY)**

If no Y chromosome is present, the cortex of the primordial gonad develops into an ovary.

Under the influence of the Y chromosome, the medulla of the primordial gonad develops into a testis.

FIGURE 10.9 *The development of an ovary and a testis from the cortex and the medulla, respectively, of the primordial gonadal structure that is present six weeks after conception. Courtesy of Pinel,* Biopsychology, *7th edition, 2009.*

Atypical Gender Patterns

A condition of sexual ambiguity is called **hermaphroditism**. The term "hermaphrodite" comes from the union of Hermes and Aphrodite, Greek gods who formed a child with both sets of genitals. The term **intersex** is now commonly used to describe this condition. Researchers do not agree on the prevalence of this condition. Estimates range from less than 1% to 4% depending on how you define it (Fausto-Sterling, 2000; Sax, 2002). It should be noted that the term "intersex" encompasses many varieties of sexual ambiguity. For example, some intersex individuals have ambiguous genitalia at birth, while others show no signs of ambiguities until later in life when unexpected secondary sexual characteristics develop. **Secondary sex characteristics** are traits that distinguish us as being male or female but are not directly part of our reproductive system. Some examples of secondary sex characteristics are breasts, patterns of body and facial hair, waist-to-hip ratio, as well as muscle mass and fat development.

If a child is born with ambiguous genitalia, the parents of the child, along with medical experts, must decide on a course of action. It might seem that the answer to the sex determination would be to perform

Speaking of Hands

This chapter's introduction discussed handedness, which is hypothesized to be caused by prenatal hormone levels in the womb. Another aspect of our hands may also be determined by this variable. New research has revealed that our finger length on the right hand may be influenced by testosterone levels in the womb during prenatal development and is a sexually dimorphic trait—that is, it differs between males and females (Rahman & Wilson, 2003).

The ring fingers of males are generally longer than their index fingers, and the reverse is true for women. Research has examined how different

FIGURE 10.10 *The ring fingers of men are typically longer than their index fingers, whereas the reverse is true for women.*

finger-length patterns are related to male and female behaviors. Men with the more masculine pattern tend to have higher reproductive success over their lifetime, be more aggressive, and excel at sports. Women who display the more feminized pattern, with the two finger lengths reversed and with their ring and index fingers being similar in length, tend to have better reproductive success and a higher risk of breast cancer (Manning, 2002). Research suggests that the relative length of the second and fourth fingers is linked with sexual orientation (e.g., Putz, Galin, Sporter, & McBurney, 2004; Robinson, 2000). Homosexual women tend to display the more masculine pattern (Williams et al., 2000). Homosexual men and women show significantly lower 2:4 finger ratios in comparison to heterosexuals (Rahman & Wilson, 2003).

a chromosomal test and then raise the child accordingly. However, it is becoming clear that gender determination at birth is not an easy decision to make, as our genitalia are not the sole determinant of our gender identity.

Gender identity refers to our psychological feeling of being male or female. Just as genitals are organized according to prenatal hormone levels, the brain, which is also an organ of the body, may be influenced by these hormone levels. Although gender identity begins developing in early childhood, children may not be fully aware of their gender identity until puberty. Also, individuals' gender identity may be affected after puberty if abnormalities in secondary sexual characteristics become apparent. What would it feel like to be intersex? Since there are so many varieties, this question cannot be answered uniformly. Some intersexed individuals may feel completely unperturbed by their sexual ambiguity, while others report feeling intense shame, secrecy, and feelings of isolation. The Intersex Society of North America is a dominant activist group for the rights of intersex individuals. It advocates that the children's genitalia be left alone until they can determine for themselves if they would like to undergo surgery. This course of action may be very difficult for parents to embrace because of the strong gender divisions that dominate our society. However, the major problem with trying to assign sex to a child who has ambiguous genitalia is that the wrong sex may be assigned, which may lead to feelings of confusion and shame regarding their gender expression. These types of feelings are not limited to intersex individuals. Some people have these feelings even when their physical sexual differentiation shows no ambiguities.

The term transsexual is given to individuals who have the psychological experience that their gender identity is different from their biological sex. In some cases, the psychological term used to describe the distress over this condition is gender identity disorder. This disorder describes a child or an adult who has a strong cross-gender identification (not merely a desire for any perceived cultural advantages of being the other sex) and persistent discomfort with his or her sex or a sense of inappropriateness in the gender role of that sex (American Psychiatric Association, 2000a). It should be noted that this diagnosis is made only if the affected individual is significantly distressed by these feelings and if the quality of his or her life is impaired as a consequence. In addition, the diagnosis will not be made if the individual has a physical intersex condition such as that discussed in the preceding paragraph. Transsexuals usually report feeling this inconsistency between their biological sex and their gender identity early in life, but it may not appear until adolescence or later. Also, many report that the feeling increases over time. Some transsexuals choose to suppress their feelings regarding their gender in order to fit into society. However, as they age, it is common for many to decide it is more important to be true to their internal feelings than to be concerned with social constraints regarding their gender expression. There is a full range of behaviors that transsexuals engage in to reduce the inconsistencies they feel with regard to their gender identification and their body type. Some transsexuals seek plastic surgery, some seek hormone therapy, some dress as the opposite sex, and still others simply try to deal with it by seeking psychotherapy. In most cases, in order to get gender reassignment surgery (a sex-change operation), a person must go through psychological therapy and evaluation, hormonal therapy, and a *real-life test* that may last from one to two years in which they must live successfully as a person of the other sex.

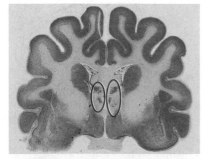

FIGURE 10.11 *Location of the BSTc in a cross-section of the brain.*

FIGURE 10.12 *Are gender differences the result of evolutionary history?*

The cognitive and anatomical brain differences found between men and women may help explain why some people feel as though they were born with the wrong genitalia. One widely cited research study found differences in an area in the bed nucleus of the stria terminalis (BSTc) in transsexual versus nontranssexual men (Zhou, Hofman, Gooren, & Swaab, 1995). This nucleus is located in the center of the brain and resides near parts of the basal ganglia and hypothalamus. Size differences in this nucleus have been found in men and women. Male-to-female transsexuals showed a BSTc area more similar to the female pattern of organization than to the male pattern.

The development of the area is not affected by adult level hormones, and it appears to be independent of sexual orientation. The exact function of this nucleus in behavior is not fully known, but these findings are suggestive.

Hormonal Theory of Sexual Differences

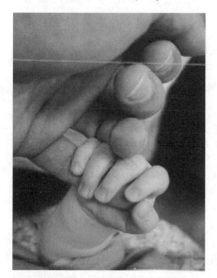

FIGURE 10.13 *Hormone levels may be influenced by a variety of factors such as holding a baby.*

Our circulating hormone levels affect our behavior. **Testosterone** is usually referred to as the male sex hormone, and **estrogen** is typically referred to as the female hormone. Both of these hormones are present in males and females, but in different proportions. Men tend to be more dominated by testosterone, and estrogen tends to dominate in women. The source of testosterone in women is the adrenal glands, and the source of estrogen in men is from a conversion process of testosterone made by the liver or fat cells. Testosterone is believed to be responsible for both aggression and the sex drive. A study of hormone levels in a large sample of men found that men with high testosterone levels were less likely to get married, and if they did get married, they were more prone to spousal abuse and infidelity (Booth & Dabbs, 1993).

As people age, their hormone levels change: estrogen levels fall in women, and testosterone lowers in men. This hormonal decrease unmasks the effect of the other sex hormones. It is common to see changes in men and women during the aging process. For example, women may become more assertive and career oriented, and men may become less work driven and more interested in family than they were during their youth. It is a common assumption that men reach their sexual peak in their late teens or early twenties, whereas women are frequently reported to reach their sexual prime in their late thirties. Although this statement is an overgeneralization, the observed trend may be due to the hormonal influence of testosterone, which exerts larger effects on younger males and older females.

The aging process is not the only thing that can affect hormone levels. Our behavior can influence our hormone levels as well. Testosterone levels in men fall as a result of marriage, for example, when an expectant father awaits the arrival of his newborn child, and even when he holds a baby (Fisher, 2004). On the other hand, testosterone can be increased in both males and females through exercising, thinking about sex, or winning a competition (Barash & Lipton, 1997).

Evolutionary Theory of Sexual Differences

Many differences between male and female brains have been confirmed, but why do these differences exist? The **evolutionary theory of sexual differences** seeks to explain behavioral and cognitive differences between males and females as being a result of their different survival tactics. The fundamental tenet of Charles Darwin's theory of evolution is *survival of the fittest*. He summed up his concept of natural selection with 10 words: "Multiply, vary, let the strongest live and the weakest die."

Early human beings are thought to have lived as hunters and gatherers for many centuries. Men, who were not weighed down by pregnancy or by the need to nurse a newborn, made better hunters. In order to hunt prey successfully, they had to rely on their visual and spatial abilities, which may explain why men tend to outperform women on visual-spatial tasks. In contrast, women, who were physically limited by their frequent pregnancies, were more suited for gathering edible plants and animals. They developed better spatial location memory than men in order to help them remember previously spotted food sources (Eagly & Wood, 2003). Also, since babies were breast-fed, it made sense that women would be the primary caregivers for young children. Women's best survival tactic was to rely on one another, which entailed using lots of communication when the men were off hunting. On the other hand, hunting can be more of a solitary activity and is best carried out with a minimum of verbal communication. The differences in survival behaviors may have resulted in more language areas in the female brain and an advantage in linguistic cognitive tasks.

> ### Men and Women Have Been Found to Differ in Their Answers to This Question
>
> What would upset or distress you more: imagining your mate having sexual intercourse with someone else, or imagining your mate forming a deep emotional attachment to someone else?

This theory has also been used to describe sexual behavior. A man's best tactic for increasing his gene pool is to reproduce with as many women as possible to increase his number of offspring. Men who did not desire multiple partners were less successful in passing on their genes and, therefore, became less numerous over time. On the other hand, women must devote a great deal of time and energy to pregnancy and child rearing, so their best survival tactic was to be very selective when choosing a mate. A woman's best choice would be someone who could provide the resources to help her successfully maintain her pregnancy and lactation in order to feed her child. If a woman had indiscriminate sex, doing so could create an unstable environment for raising children.

David Buss and his associates (1994) conducted a cross-cultural study of male and female sexual behaviors and preferences. In this study, he interviewed more than 10,000 men and women in 37 different cultures. He found a strong tendency for men to indicate a preference for multiple sex partners. However, he did not find this to be true of women. Additionally, he found gender differences regarding scenarios that would evoke the strongest forms of jealousy. Men reported being jealous over a partner's extramarital sexual intercourse more so than when seeing the partner talk to other men. This might be because men could not easily determine which children were their offspring without exerting sexual control over their women (Daly & Wilson, 1998). In contrast, women reported heightened jealousy in response to their mate forming an emotional bond with another as opposed to having a sexual relationship. Again, this can be explained

Why are you so messy in the bathroom?

It's part of my evolutionary past. I'm marking my territory.

FIGURE 10.14 *The evolutionary theory of sexual differences seeks to explain behavioral and cognitive differences in men and women as being a result of their distinct survival tactics. Courtesy of Amy Sweetman and Steve Carballo.*

due to the uncertainty men have over the paternity of their children. Every woman who gives birth can be 100% certain that the child carries her genes. For men, on the other hand, there is always a degree of doubt. In evolutionary terms, the consequence of a man raising a child who may not carry his genes but those of another man is the death of his line. Women feel more threatened by an emotional bond because it could lead to his leaving her and taking away his resources.

This theory has also been used to explain why men and women may place different emphasis on what they want in a mate. Buss reported that while men and women wanted the same top three things in a mate—intelligence, kindness, and love—some interesting sex differences did emerge. Women were more likely to look for financial status and height in a man. A survey of personal advertisements placed in newspapers and magazines also supported these findings. American women were twice as likely as men to list financial security as one of the main criteria for selecting a potential mate (Harrison & Saeed, 1977; South, 1991). In contrast, men placed more emphasis on physical beauty. Additionally, men tended to seek younger partners, whereas women across different cultures preferred partners who were three to four years older than themselves. Youth and physical attractiveness were indicative of health and the ability to bear children, whereas an older man would be more likely to have attained financial security and thus be a good provider.

Finally, this theory has been used to explain male and female stereotypical behaviors, such as the tendency for women to devote more time to shopping and self-care activities (to make themselves physically attractive), and for men to spend time on video games (to improve their target-directed motor skills and to engage in competitive activities). Shopping may also represent an evolutionary equivalent of gathering. Likewise, the male tendency to enjoy video games (Kubey & Larson, 1990) and sports could be reminiscent of those primordial days when men hunted and vied for status within the tribal hierarchy. This theory makes some interesting connections, but it is based on generalizations across groups of people that may be useful for explaining overall trends in behavior differences between men and women but does not address individual differences among men and among women.

Social Psychological Theories

There is another major factor that plays a crucial role in determining gender role behavior, and that is our experience. Gender role refers to behaviors that society expects from women and men. The environment undoubtedly influences our behavior. As with any other social role, gender role behavior is determined in part by cultural expectations. In any society, rules of conduct evolve that members of a society must adhere to in order to be considered "normal." These rules are based on the values held by the culture, and they define the boundaries of acceptable behavior within which there is generally some room for individual expression. Socially proscribed gender roles have a huge impact on us, as they influence the clothing we wear, the type of work we do, and, ultimately, the behaviors we are permitted to express. Social psychologists argue that traditionally stereotyped gender roles are grounded more in culture than in differing biological reproductive roles.

Society's division of labor between the sexes is the engine that drives self-differentiated behavior, because it outlines the social constraints under which men and women live their lives. Sex differences are viewed as accommodations to the differing restrictions and opportunities that a society maintains for its men and women, and sex-differentiated behavior is held to be dependent on a range of individual, situational, and cultural conditions (Deaux & LaFrance, 1998). Due to men and women occupying different social roles, they become psychologically different in ways that fit them to these roles. Since social organization continuously shifts in response to technological, ecological, and other historical changes, gender roles gradually evolve.

Despite this emphasis on the social environment, social structuralists typically acknowledge the importance of some genetically mediated sex differences. Physical differences between the sexes, particularly men's greater size and strength and women's childbearing and lactation, are important because they interact with shared cultural beliefs, social organization, and the demands of the economy to influence the sexual division of labor within a society and eventually produce psychological sex differences (Eagly, 1987). Thus, social structural theory views sex-differentiated tendencies as built in through accommodation to the existing sexual division of labor. In this approach, physical differences between the sexes are viewed as being one of several influences on role assignment according to gender.

Gender Role Behavior

Traditional gender role expectations for men are that they be independent, aggressive, fearless, work-oriented, powerful, and successful as well as in control of their emotions. These are typically referred to as *instrumental* or *agentic* traits. Traditional gender role expectations for women are that they be warm, helpful, supportive, family oriented, emotional, passive, and relationship oriented. Such qualities are summed up as *expressive* or *communal* traits. Early in life, children are made aware of gender role expectations through a number of avenues such as parental instructions, school experiences, and the media.

Our parents are the first to instill gender role expectations in us. From the moment of birth, boys and girls are treated differently. Infant girls are held gently, whereas infant boys are played with more roughly (Lips, 1995). Most toys and clothes are gender specific. Girls' rooms are more likely to be pink and contain dolls, whereas boys' rooms are more likely to be blue or red and have sports equipment and tools (Pomerleau, Boldue, Macuit, & Cosetts, 1990). Boys' toys tend to encourage spatial development, whereas girls' toys foster social skills. Parents talk to their girls more so than to their boys, and boys are encouraged to be more independent as well as careful about expressing their feelings.

The classroom is another prominent agent of socialization. From the beginning of preschool to graduation from high school, children who play according to traditional gender roles are more popular with their peers (Martin, 1989).

Disney's Female Gender Role Transition

***Snow White and the Seven Dwarfs* 1937**—Disney's first full-length film. Snow White is a helpless princess (who loves to clean) who is rescued. The stepmother is an evil witch who is consumed with beauty.

***Peter Pan* 1953**—Peter Pan says, "Girls talk too much," as he tells Wendy to hurry up and sew his shadow on. Tinkerbell is consumed with jealousy, as are the Mermaids and Wendy. Peter Pan must rescue almost all of the women in the movie.

***Sleeping Beauty* 1959**—A helpless princess is rescued by her handsome prince's true love kiss.

***Mary Poppins* 1964**—Mary Poppins is a nanny with magical powers who transforms a house into a neat and clean residence within minutes while simultaneously entertaining and educating the children.

***The Aristocats* 1970**—A high-class female cat who is the mother of three kittens gets displaced from her upper-class neighborhood and is rescued by a free-spirited alley cat.

***The Little Mermaid* 1989**—A mermaid falls in love with a human prince whom she rescues from a harsh storm. In the end, he rescues not only her but her entire family from an evil witch.

***Hercules* 1997**—When Hercules the hero tries to save the day, Meg the heroine tells him, "Back off! I can handle it." Later in the movie, she gives her own life to save his. The movie shows Hercules being emotionally wounded by rejection.

***Mulan* 1998**—A cross-dressing female joins the army and saves the entire country, along with the man she loves.

Research has found that girls and boys tend to participate equally in the classroom in the early grades, but by fifth grade, boys tend to dominate the majority of classroom discussions. They raise their hands more frequently and are called on more often. They seem more comfortable prevailing in classroom discussions and appear less self-conscious about making mistakes (Lips, 1995).

In addition to being shaped by the classroom environment, many children are influenced by the media. Our society has experienced a technological boom over the past generation, with the result that children are likely to spend many hours watching television and playing video or computer games. In fact, a nationwide survey conducted by the Kaiser Family Foundation in March 2005 estimated that the average child spends more than six and a half hours a day using some form of media, such as television, video games, computer games, or movies. According to this statistic, by the time the average child is 18 years old, he or she will spend more time watching television than being in the classroom.

Children may rely on characters in the media to help supply a definition of appropriate gender role behavior. The roles and actions of boys and girls have been changing for decades. For example, in Disney movies, girls have become more capable and less dependent. In other movies from the 1940s, typical female heroines were significantly shorter and lighter than their male counterparts. Today, movie couples are often approximately the same height, and the woman may, during the course of the film, demonstrate physical strength and cleverness. However, in children's cartoons, males still outnumber females by a ratio of 10:1 (Thompson & Zebrinos, 1997). Furthermore, an analysis of video games found that the vast majority of them reinforce traditional gender stereotypes. Even educational computer games tend to feature a male as the primary character. However, the good news is that our society is slowly transitioning away from promoting traditional gender roles. Both men and women have more freedom to explore a range of occupations and behaviors.

Rigid adherence to traditional gender roles is positively correlated with a variety of negative behaviors. For example, men who exhibit traditional male gender role behavior are more likely to engage in violence and rape and have higher rates of health problems (Murnen, Wright, & Kaluzny, 2002). Women who rigidly adhere to traditional gender roles are more likely to be depressed, suffer from anxiety disorders, and experience sexual dysfunction (Silverstein & Perlick, 1997).

> The truth is, a great mind must be androgynous, having the characteristics of both sexes.
>
> —Samuel Taylor Coleridge
> English poet, 1772–1834

These research findings suggest that more flexible gender role expectations may not only open up more opportunities for individuals, but may also lead to their having higher levels of self-esteem, as well as other signs of psychological and physical health.

An alternative to adherence to traditional gender roles is **psychological androgyny**. This term refers to an individual's integration of the expression of strong masculine and feminine traits within his or her personality. The word has Greek origins, with "andro" referring to male and "gyne" referring to female, and it means having both male and female parts. Psychologist Sandra Bem (1974) has written extensively on this concept and has developed a sex role inventory to measure levels of psychological androgyny in people, that is, the extent to which people attribute traditionally masculine and feminine characteristics to themselves. People who describe themselves as psychologically androgynous feel relatively free of gender role constraints and are thus more likely to express their unique personalities. Androgynous individuals are able to be flexible and to adjust their behavior to situational demands. This allows them to have a wider range of behaviors to call upon in diverse situations. For instance, a person may have the ability to be caring and concerned in an emotional situation as well as the ability to be a forceful and assertive leader when the occasion calls for it.

Psychological androgyny seems to be common among many of the new depictions of heroes in the media. Some of the new male and female superheroes are multidimensional, in that they express great strength along with emotional vulnerability. Spiderman is a heroic cartoon figure and a perpetual favorite among children. The Spiderman cartoons of the 1960s contained many sexist statements, such as, "The world should contain just men and children" and "Easy, Spiderman, she's just a woman." New versions of the cartoon occasionally show Spiderman being helped by a female superhero. Additionally, he regularly shows his sensitivity to the importance of being a partner in a relationship. In one episode, he states, "She is avoiding me, I know she is upset, I should be the first to go and make the apology." In two other cases, the Disney characters Mr. Incredible and Kim Possible are both shown to be strong when they need to be, but also sensitive and capable of being affected by a wide range of emotions.

Intimate Relationships

Most people rank having a healthy intimate relationship as a major component of happiness in life, and the research on happiness confirms that this is the case (e.g., Myers, 1991). Relationship issues are a key focal point in our society, as illustrated by their presence in our everyday conversations, our music lyrics and other forms of entertainment, as well as in our advertising. It is ironic that with all the emphasis on relationships, there is very little formal education provided to children and young adults on what constitutes a healthy relationship or how to have one. Unfortunately, this lack of education allows a variety of relationship myths to abound.

Myth 1: If you are in the right relationship, you will feel a constant peace and happiness within yourself.

One of the biggest relationship myths that the media tends to portray is the concept of "living happily ever after." Movies and television programs often portray relationships as being the cure-all for life's displeasure and promote the notion that if you find the right relationship, you will always be happy. This is not the case; instead, you are individually responsible for your own happiness. Relying on another person to bring you happiness will create resentment and frustration and will inevitably lead to disappointment. Research has found that happiness is largely determined by personality factors and by people engaging in thoughts and behaviors that require effort, such as setting goals and accomplishing them (Lyubomirsky, Baron-Cohen, & Raggatt, 2005). This is why self-esteem is thought to be crucial to having good relationships. Individuals with high levels of self-esteem are likely to engage in behaviors that bring personal satisfaction. Having self-esteem also fosters communication, since people with high self-esteem are usually comfortable with themselves and are able to express their feelings. They are less likely to expect their partners to be mind readers.

Finally, individuals with high self-esteem are more likely to be selective about the types of people they allow into their lives. Thus, it is not finding the right relationship that will bring personal happiness, but more likely that people who are good at being happy tend to choose and maintain relationships that foster happiness.

The Biological Connection

Biological research suggests that the release of two main chemicals, dopamine and cortisol, creates feelings of satisfaction. Dopamine is released as a result of being exposed to novel situations, and cortisol is released when the body is exposed to a physically, mentally, or psychologically stressful situation. By taking on new challenges that prompt both partners to grow, couples activate bodily processes that prompt the release of these two chemicals. Studies show that long-term couples who state that they are "still in love" report doing novel things together (Berns, 2005).

Myth 2: In order for a relationship to work, there needs to be lots of self-sacrifice by each partner.

In a healthy relationship, the partners assume responsibility for making themselves happy, so large amounts of self-sacrifice should not be required. It is important that compromise and cooperation take place, and sometimes people's individual wishes may have to be given up for the sake of the relationship. Even so, when individuals give up their own personal goals for the sake of the relationship, resentment and stagnation are likely to take over. Healthy relationships encourage the personal growth of the individuals in the relationship. The challenge of maintaining a relationship is to keep it viable, as the individuals within it continue to grow and change as a result of new experiences and greater maturity.

Explore
**the idea that
opposites attract**
in Chapter 11, p. 362

Myth 3: Opposites attract and have the most successful relationships.

Although we have heard that opposites attract, we are generally attracted to people of similar backgrounds, interests, attitudes, and beliefs. A healthy intimate relationship usually results from the combination of two individuals who have similar interests and values but individual goals. Research has found that we tend to be attracted to people who are similar to us in regard to age and physical characteristics such as height, weight, and race. It may be even more important for the longevity of a relationship to be attracted to someone who is similar to you in regard to values and personality traits. It is much easier to live with someone who has many of the same likes, dislikes, and habits that you do, and there tends to be less conflict in general when you agree on the basics of life (Antill, 1983; Carli, Ganley, & Pierce-Otay, 1991; Kim, Martin, & Martin, 1989).

If you are contemplating whether you are in a healthy relationship, you may want to ask yourself the following questions:

1. *Is my partner able to have healthy relationships with others?* If your partner is unable to have healthy friendships with others, the personality characteristics that contribute to this may also sabotage your attempts at having an intimate relationship with this person.

2. *Do I feel that my partner respects my personal goals?* Research supports the idea that individual happiness comes from setting personal goals and working toward their accomplishment (Alexander, 2007). If your intimate partner is unsupportive of your efforts to form and work toward goals, this interference may obstruct your ability to generate your own happiness.

3. *Do I feel that I am able to communicate my feelings regarding a wide range of subjects to my partner?* The feeling that you have to hide parts of yourself from your partner will create a large barrier to intimacy. A good relationship is one in which each partner can share whatever is on his or her mind.

Marriage Anyone?

After establishing a healthy relationship, it is natural to consider committing to each other through marriage. It is estimated that 90% of the population will get married at some point in their lives. Unfortunately, many marriages do not work out. Divorce rate statistics contain many ambiguities because of the techniques used to calculate them, but the general consensus is that a marriage today may have only a 50% chance of succeeding. Some key risk factors for getting a divorce are getting married before the age of 20, living together before marriage, and getting married because of an unplanned pregnancy.

People who marry during their teenage years are twice as likely to divorce as those who wait until they are in their twenties to get married (Norton & Moorman, 1987). In our society, our twenties is a time when we try out different roles and lifestyles to determine what suits us. Lots of self-discovery occurs at this time. Those who marry before the age of 20 may not have enough self-knowledge to make long-term decisions about a suitable partner, which could explain their high rates of divorce.

Many couples wrestle with the question of whether to live together before marriage. Common sense seems to indicate that if you can live together before getting married, the marriage is likely to be more stable because you have already determined that you are compatible. However, research has found that couples who cohabitate before marriage tend to have higher rates of divorce (Thompson

FIGURE 10.15 *In spite of the discouraging statistics about marriage success rates, about 90% of the population gets married at some point in their lives.*

Which of These Three Couples Will Make It?

♦ Christine and Landon have been married for five years. They report that they have never had a fight. They say they simply don't believe in wasting their time fighting.

♦ William and Sally have fights in which they yell at each other and slam doors. When they are not fighting, they are equally passionate in showing their love for each other.

♦ Maria and Sam talk things over when they disagree. They listen to each other and try to compromise.

Some Interesting Divorce Facts

♦ Couples who divorce tend to do so around their fourth year of marriage.

♦ Second marriages do not report higher levels of happiness than first marriages.

♦ Stepchildren increase the likelihood of divorce.

♦ The average time to remarry after a divorce is three years.

(Lamanna & Reidmann, 1997)

& Colella, 1992). It is unclear why, but one hypothesis is that couples who live together tend to be more liberal and are less opposed to exercising the option of divorce. Another explanation is that people who live together before marriage are less serious about the marital commitment and therefore more likely to end the relationship during times of trouble. If either of these explanations is correct, it does not suggest that living together before marriage *causes* the marriage not to work. Instead, these explanations suggest that the type of people who elect to live with their partner before marriage are also the sort of people who are not averse to dissolving the marriage if it does not appear to be working well.

A generation ago it was a common myth in U.S. culture that children serve to strengthen a marriage. Many times you would hear couples say that they were trying to have a child in order to "save the marriage." In actuality, marriages undergo great amounts of stress due to the birth of a child. For this reason, married couples tend to report a decrease in marital satisfaction after the birth of the first child (Somers, 1993). Overall, couples who do not have children report being about as happy as couples who have children (Myers, 1991). Furthermore, a strong relationship has been found between premarital pregnancy and marital unhappiness (Norton & Moorman, 1987), possibly because the partners felt pressured into the commitment.

John Gottman is one of the foremost leaders in marital research. He has spent 30 years conducting research on married couples. His research has focused on studying the quality of marital relationships by observing couples' physiological and emotional states. He monitors facial expressions, body movements, blood pressure, heart rate, and stress levels. Through his research he has identified factors that predict the success or failure of marriages. According to his findings, all three of the marriages of the three couples described in the sidebar should work out as long as there is a 5:1 ratio of positive to negative expressions. The couples' scenarios represent the three basic successful marital conflict styles. Christine and Landon have an avoidant conflict style marriage, William and Sally utilize the volatile conflict approach, and Maria and Sam have the validating conflict style. In the **avoidant conflict style**, couples avoid conflict and agree to disagree. In the **volatile conflict style**, couples have very passionate fights, which may include yelling, screaming, and even occasional name calling, but when they are not fighting, they tend to be equally adept at expressing their positive feelings. The **validating conflict style** is the type of relationship that psychologists have endorsed for years, where the couple engages in active listening and truly tries to understand each other's feelings in order to reach a compromise. Gottman (1994) states that although this third style is successful, it is not the only way to have a healthy marriage. All of the discussed marital conflict styles may be equally successful as long as negative emotions do not predominate. Personality factors and the degree of comfort with conflict also play a role in determining how a couple can resolve areas of difficulty.

One major problem that arises in heterosexual relationships stems from gender differences in response to conflict. Gottman found that during a conflict, men become more physiologically aroused than females. This "emotional flooding" causes men to shut down or **stonewall** in order to protect themselves from the intense feelings stirred up within them. Women, on the other hand, do not experience the high physiological arousal from the actual conflict, but their "emotional flooding" results from their husband's withdrawal from the conflict. This leads to a cyclical pattern where the man's attempt to reduce his intense emotions results in an increase in the woman's level of physiological arousal. Understanding of these gender differences in reaction to conflict can help couples develop a strategy of dealing with problems that will reduce the emotional intensity felt by both partners.

Even when partners are not in open conflict, they may convey frustration with each other through the expression of contempt. **Contempt** is defined as engaging in behavior that conveys a lack of respect for your partner. Gottman has found that this negative emotion can devastate a marriage. It usually manifests itself in body language, such as rolling the eyes, speaking with a condescending tone of voice, or intentionally saying things designed to psychologically wound your partner. Each marriage tends to have an emotional signature that is forged by the conflict style preferences of the partners. If the partners differ on their preferred mode of conflict, they tend to have more problems.

Sexual Expression

In the preceding section we discussed healthy intimate relationships and marriage. It is within these two arrangements that the majority of the population expresses its sexuality. Our sexual attitudes or beliefs are the major determinants of our sexual behavior. Many factors are involved in the development of our sexual attitudes, such as our personal life philosophy, moral teachings from parents, peer behavior, societal values, and media influences. These factors interact to determine your personal philosophy regarding what is right and wrong with regard to sexual expression. The decision to become sexually active in a relationship can have life-altering consequences. On one hand, it can serve to bring the relationship to a new level of intimacy and deepen the commitment and satisfaction of the relationship (Sprecher, 2002). On the other hand, it can bring forth negative consequences, such as feelings of guilt, shame, and disappointment if your experience does not conform to your own personal sexual attitudes and belief system. Additionally, it can have life-altering consequences such as an unwanted pregnancy, a sexually transmitted disease, or emotional trauma.

The following questions could be used as guidelines for acting on sexual feelings (Corey & Corey, 1993):

1. Will my actions hurt another person or myself?

2. Will my actions limit another person's freedom?

3. Will my actions violate another person's rights?

4. Are my actions consistent with my commitments?

Sexual Orientation

Sexual orientation is how we define who we are sexually attracted to. **Homosexuality** is defined as sexual attraction to individuals of the same sex, which is contrasted with **heterosexuality,** where the attraction is to individuals of the opposite sex. According to the National Health and Social Life Survey from 1992, 2% of men and 1% of women define themselves as being exclusively homosexual. About 4% of men and women have had at least one same-sex experience during adulthood, and about 4% of men and 2% of women have experienced same-sex attraction (Laumann, Gagnon, Michael, & Michaels, 1994). The 10% statistic that is often quoted as the estimated percentage of the population that is homosexual is from the 1940's national survey research of famous sex researcher Alfred Kinsey. It is believed that the reason why his statistic was higher than recent findings is because of population sample bias. However, sexual orientation is a difficult construct to define for a few reasons. First, behavior does not always reflect desire. For example, a person may engage in sexual intercourse with someone while not really being attracted to that person. Alternatively, individuals may refrain from engaging in sexual relations even though they experience desire. Finally, due to the social stigma that even today attaches to being homosexual, some people who have feelings of attraction toward members of their own sex may not acknowledge this even to themselves.

Kinsey organized a continuum of sexual orientation that outlines the variability of sexual behavior and attraction.

How would you classify the following individuals with regard to their sexual orientation?

1. Throughout her life, Ann has been involved with men, but she fell madly in love with Ellen for a couple years. Unfortunately, the relationship did not work out, and Ann resumed dating men. She is happily married to her husband and has two children. She states that she no longer finds herself attracted to women; her fling with Ellen was a one-time thing.

2. Lester enjoyed numerous sexual encounters with women prior to going to prison. In prison he engaged in sex acts with men on a regular basis, which he also enjoyed. Upon release from prison, he only dates women. He reports that his same-sex prison sexual experiences were caused by a lack of availability of females.

3. Susan was happily married to her husband for 25 years. When he died, she got a female roommate to help her share living expenses. Over their years as roommates, the two women formed a deep friendship that eventually evolved into a sexual relationship.

4. David has a very stressful job. He is married with three children and he enjoys sex with his wife. However, in order to relieve stress during his work day, he sometimes goes to a place where he pays a man to perform oral sex on him during his lunch break. He only does this when he feels large amounts of work-related pressure.

TABLE 10.2 **Sexual orientation continuum.**						
0	**1**	**2**	**3**	**4**	**5**	**6**
Exclusive heterosexual behavior with no homosexual expression	Predominant heterosexual behavior with incidental homosexual expression	Predominant heterosexual behavior but more than incidental homosexual expression	Equal homosexual and heterosexual behavior	Predominant homosexual behavior but more than incidental heterosexual expression	Predominant homosexual behavior with incidental heterosexual expression	Exclusive homosexual behavior with no heterosexual expression

Sexual orientation exists along a continuum that ranges from exclusive homosexuality to exclusive heterosexuality and includes various forms of bisexuality. **Bisexual** individuals experience sexual, emotional, and affectionate attraction to both their own sex and the opposite sex. People with a homosexual orientation are sometimes referred to as gay (both men and women) or as lesbian (women only).

Explore
Freudian psychoanalysis
in Chapter 13, p. 413

There are numerous theories about the origins of a person's sexual orientation. However, as noted by the continuum of sexual orientation expression, it is very difficult to define sexual orientation, let alone explain it. It is most likely that sexual orientation is similar to gender expression in that it is a result of a complex interaction of environmental, cognitive, behavioral, and biological factors.

In most people, sexual orientation is shaped at an early age. There is also considerable recent evidence to suggest that biology, including genetic or inborn hormonal factors, plays a significant role in a person's sexuality.

Sigmund Freud felt that sexual orientation developed during the phallic stage and that homosexuality resulted from difficulties in identifying with one's same-sex parent. He suggested that homosexual boys had an overbearing or overly close mother and a rejecting or distant father, while homosexual girls never resolved their penis envy. However, research has not found a particular family pattern that is indicative of the development of a homosexual sexual orientation. Homosexuals come from a variety of family structures. Evidence does not support the notion that single mothers are more likely to raise a homosexual child. Also, most children raised by homosexual parents grow up to be heterosexual.

Homosexuality is assuredly no advantage, but it is nothing to be ashamed of, no vice, no degradation, it cannot be classified as an illness; we consider it to be a variation of the sexual function produced by a certain arrest of sexual development.

—Quote taken from a letter written by Sigmund Freud, April 9, 1935

Learning theorists contend that early sexual experimentation and experiences may affect our sexual orientation development in that positive same-sex sexual experiences and negative opposite-sex sexual experiences could contribute to the development of a homosexual orientation. It is very difficult to examine this proposition, as childhood sexual experimentation is somewhat of a taboo subject in our culture and is thus difficult to document.

FIGURE 10.16 *Could these sheep be born gay?*

Some research suggests biological roots for sexual orientation. Simon LeVay (1991) reported structural differences in the brains of homosexual males. An area of the brain known as the third interstitial nucleus of the hypothalamus is twice as large in males as in females. LeVay found that this area in homosexual males was more similar to females than to heterosexual males. Other studies have found differences in both the preoptic nucleus, which is thought to regulate sexual behavior, and the suprachiasmatic nucleus (SCN), which regulates our daily rhythms (Swaab & Hofman, 1990). There are sex differences in the shape of the SCN and in the internal structural organization of these hypothalamic nuclei. In sheep, sex differences have been discovered in the medial preoptic area of the hypothalamus. Male sheep who display preferences of mating with other male sheep have a medial preoptic area that is similar to that of females. It should be noted that patterns of homosexual behavior have been found in more than 450 species of animals worldwide, including gorillas, bears, giraffes, dolphins, penguins, and flamingos (Bagemihl, 1999).

Twin studies also support the notion that homosexuality may have biological origins. If one identical twin is homosexual, the other twin has approximately a 50% chance of also being homosexual. If fraternal twins are studied, the likelihood drops to approximately 20% (Bailey & Pillard, 1991). If sexual orientation were completely biological, we would expect to see a 100% concordance rate among identical twin brothers. This finding again supports the notion that sexual orientation is an interaction of biological and social variables. Several studies have indicated a possible marker on the X chromosome (e.g., Hu, Pattatucci, Patterson, Li, Fulker, & Cherny, 1995). One study examined 40 pairs of gay non-twin brothers. In 33 of the pairs, the brothers had identical DNA markers on the end tip of the X chromosome. In addition, researchers found that gay males, in a sample of 114 gay men, were more likely than the general population to have gay male relatives on their mother's side of the family. However, they did not have a larger number of gay relatives on their father's side of the family (Hamer, Hu, Magnuson, Hu, & Pattatucci, 1993). A recent full genome-wide scan of sexual orientation in 156 men who came from 146 families with one or more gay brothers was recently conducted. The strongest markers for sexual orientation were found to come equally from maternal and paternal transmission (Mustanski et al., 2005). A reanalysis of one study revealed some evidence for maternal transmission, but the authors recommended that this study be replicated in order to confirm the findings (Mustanski et al., 2005).

A discussion on the causes of sexual orientation is important because, throughout history, human beings seem to be forgiving of nonnormative behaviors when biological causes are found. This chapter started with a discussion of handedness and how being left-handed was thought to be a curse. Children who displayed this hand preference were severely admonished. In many cases they were thought to have a mental disorder due to their hand preference.

If you are heterosexual, try answering some of these questions that are commonly asked of homosexuals?

1. When did you know you were heterosexual?

2. Do you think you could change your heterosexuality?

3. Are you sure you are heterosexual? Maybe all you need is to find the right same-sex partner.

4. What do you think caused your heterosexuality?

The same was true of sexual orientation. Prior to 1973, homosexuality was classified as a mental disorder. On the basis of evidence that homosexuals were no more likely than heterosexual individuals to be emotionally unstable or to have psychiatric disorders, homosexuality was removed as a diagnostic category in the *Diagnostic and Statistical Manual of Mental Disorders*. Mental health differences found among the general population were found to be much more related to social factors, such as being in a stable relationship and economic status, than to sexual orientation (Bailey, 1999). However, many homosexuals experience negative emotions due to society's lack of acceptance regarding their sexual orientation. When individuals "come out," or reveal their sexual orientation to others, they often face rejection and discrimination. Some people try to avoid the painful feelings that result from being socially ostracized by keeping their sexual orientation "in the closet," that is, by hiding their same-sex attractions. This course of action has been found to be psychologically stressful (Meyer, 2003). An even worse consequence is when they must face strong forms of homophobia. **Homophobia** is the irrational fear or strong negative feelings toward homosexual individuals. In extreme cases, homophobia may lead to verbal abuse or violence against homosexual individuals. A large percentage of homosexuals have been victims of some form of harassment due to their sexual orientation. All these factors may explain why homosexual adolescents have a much higher rate of attempted suicide than heterosexual adolescents. According to one survey, rates of attempted suicide for homosexual/bisexual males and females were 28.1% and 20.5%, respectively, versus 4.2% and 14.5% for their heterosexual counterparts (Remafedi, French, Story, Resnick, & Blum, 1998). It is hoped that these unfortunate statistics will be reduced as society continues to become more accepting of sexual orientation differences.

So What Happens During Sex?

William Masters and Virginia Johnson became famous for the research on sex that they conducted in the 1960s. One of their major accomplishments was developing a model of the **sexual response cycle**. They used various instruments to monitor bodily changes during sexual activity. From this research they developed a four-phase model of the human sexual response cycle, which are excitement, plateau, orgasm, and resolution. There are two basic physiological responses involved in each phase: vasocongestion and myotonia. **Vasocongestion** occurs when the tissues swell with blood, and **myotonia** refers to muscle tension. Vasocongestion occurs in parts of the body such as the penis, the testicles, the breasts, the vulva area (external female genitalia), and the vaginal wall. Myotonia is responsible for the muscle tensing that we experience in multiple parts of the body, such as the feet, the legs, the arms, and the face. In the first two phases, vasocongestion and myotonia are increasing, and in the third and fourth phases there is a reduction in these two processes. Following is a basic overview of the four phases.

Excitement

Myotonia and vasocongestion begin during excitement. In males, the penis becomes erect, and the testes swell and elevate. In females, the breasts and vulva swell, and the vagina becomes lubricated. The lubrication does not come from a particular gland but from the moisture released from the capillaries located in the vaginal wall, due to vasocongestion. Men may emit a few drops of fluid from the tip of their penis, which is released by the Cowper's gland. (Note: It is possible for this fluid to contain viable sperm.) However, not all men emit fluid, and some men may emit fluid during the plateau phase rather than the excitement phase. The exact function of the Cowper's gland is unknown, but a theory is that it may buffer the acidity of the urethra and facilitate the passage of sperm. Some people experience a form of sex flush, evidenced by a reddening of the face and chest area. This phase may last from minutes to hours.

Plateau

The plateau phase is a continuation of the excitement phase, but there is more intensity. Sexual tension continues to grow, and vasocongestion and myotonia increase. Near the end of the plateau phase, there are signs of impending orgasm. In men, the testicles become very swollen and completely elevate toward opposite sides of the penis. In females, the outer one-third of the vaginal canal becomes especially engorged with blood, creating a structure called the orgasmic platform, which can be experienced as a tightening effect of the initial entrance portion of the vagina. Also, the clitoris retracts or flattens out beneath the clitoral hood just prior to orgasm. This phase can be very brief, from a couple of seconds to a few minutes.

Orgasm

Orgasm is by far the most talked about stage of the sexual response cycle. It is also the shortest phase, typically lasting only seconds. In women, it consists of approximately 10–15 contractions of the muscles surrounding the vaginal and anal area. After reaching orgasm, a woman may return to the plateau phase, and with continued stimulation can again move to the orgasm phase (Masters & Johnson, 1966). In men, the orgasm stage has two phases. The first phase is called the emission stage, in which the seminal fluids are propelled into the urethra (a tube that runs through the penis and releases both semen and urine). This produces a feeling that orgasm is eminent. Then in the second phase, which is called expulsion, the semen is expelled out of the penis at the time of orgasm. Men also have contractions in the urethral and anal area.

In one research study, neuroscientist Gert Holstege and colleagues used a PET scan to examine brain activation during orgasm. He reported that during orgasm, areas of the cerebellum were activated and that there was a decrease in activity in the cortex and areas of the brain associated with fear and anxiety (Holstege, 2005). Oxytocin, a neurotransmitter that enhances social attachment, is also released during orgasm.

How Are Male and Female Orgasms Different?

Although male and female orgasms appear to be different—men experience two phases of orgasm in which semen is released—research has not found gender differences between subjective definitions of orgasm for males and females. More than 70 sex experts were given written descriptions of orgasm, and they were unable to determine whether the verbal description was that of a male or a female (Proctor, Wagner, & Butler, 1974).

Resolution

In this phase, the body returns to its original, nonexcited state. Some of the changes occur rapidly, whereas others take more time. The resolution phase begins immediately after orgasm if there is no additional stimulation. The refractory period is one of the significant differences in the sexual response cycles of men and women. It is a time when a man cannot return to the excitement, plateau, or orgasm phases through any kind of sexual stimulation. This period can last from a few minutes to days, depending on age and frequency of sexual activity, among other things. Women do not experience a refractory period, and they are capable of reaching orgasm again during the resolution stage. It is believed that most women have the potential for multiple orgasms (Masters & Johnson, 1966), but a woman may not want to have a second or third orgasm on a given day. In order to determine the woman's feelings on this matter, good communication between partners is extremely important.

The phases of human sexual response in men and women have similar patterns. The primary differences are in the time it takes for men and women to reach each phase, and in the ability of many women to achieve multiple orgasms.

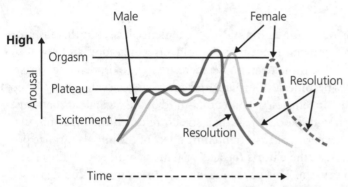

FIGURE 10.17 *Phases of human sexual response. Courtesy of Gerrig and Zimbardo,* Psychology and Life, *18th edition, 2008.*

How to Be a Better Lover

Although a basic understanding of the sexual anatomy of your partner and an appreciation of the differences between the male and female sexual response cycles will help you understand what happens during sex, the ultimate tool for increasing your effectiveness in your sexual encounters is the ability to talk to your partner about your sexual relationship. Sexual communication is one of the most difficult forms of communication due to a number of factors, such as the fact that our society does not readily encourage open discussions about sex, especially between men and women. Also, there is the fear that you may make your partner uncomfortable or that communication may lead to feelings of rejection. For example, a man may feel that if he asks his partner how to please her, she may interpret this as a sign of inexperience or incompetence. On the other hand, a woman may feel that if she tells her mate what she wants, she will be perceived as either easy or controlling. The best sex usually results from partners being spontaneous and in tune with each other's needs and desires. However, this is uncommon without open communication. To be a great lover, you need to be open to new experiences, have the desire to please your partner, and engage in communication about sex.

Here are some tips for good sexual communication:

1. Talk about sex outside of the bedroom, when you are not naked and the act has not just taken place. Our clothes give us protection and may take some of the awkwardness out of the exchange.

Sexual Dysfunctions

Hypoactive sexual desire disorder—person reports little to no sexual desire

Sexual aversion disorder—person reports extreme disgust/aversion to sexual encounters with a partner

Female sexual arousal disorder—woman reports inability to maintain adequate lubrication and swelling response of genitals

Male erectile disorder—man reports inability to maintain erection

Female orgasmic disorder—woman experiences an extended delay or inability to achieve orgasm

Male orgasmic disorder—man experiences an extended delay or inability to achieve orgasm

Premature ejaculation disorder—inability to control orgasm and ejaculation, which interferes with sexual relations

Vaginismus—recurrent or persistent involuntary spasm of the musculature of the outer third of the vagina, which interferes with sexual intercourse

Sexual pain disorder (dypaurenia)—unexplained genital pain occurring before, during, or after sexual intercourse

American Psychiatric Association (2000a)

2. Use humor and allow your partner to approach the sexual experience on his or her own terms. For example, make a suggestion such as, "Someday I would really like to 'rock your world' in the bedroom; let me know what I can do."

3. Talk about what you like in order to get your partner to tell you what he or she likes.

4. Body language is a great form of sexual communication. Pay close attention to what your partner is doing to you, and try doing it back to your lover. Also try to use body language to let your partner know what you like and don't like. In general, try to use as few words as possible when criticizing sexual behavior.

5. If you find that you must use criticism, use as many compliments as you can before saying something negative, and be specific about exactly what you want changed.

Sexual Dysfunction

Although sexual communication can go a long way toward improving a couple's sex life, some difficulties cannot be remedied through communication alone. For example, what if something goes wrong with sexual functioning? Laumann and colleagues (1999) estimated that about 40% of women and 30% of men experience sexual dysfunction at some point in their life. Sexual dysfunctions usually fall into four major categories: hypoactive sexual desire disorders, sexual pain disorders, sexual arousal disorders, and orgasmic disorders (see the sidebar for definitions of these disorders). However, most medical professionals agree that these conditions can only be diagnosed as sexual dysfunctions if the problem is ongoing for at least two months in a given year and is accompanied by personal distress. In other words, if a person occasionally experiences any one of these conditions, it may not be indicative of a sexual dysfunction. The causes of sexual dysfunction stem from a number of physical and psychological sources. It is best to be evaluated by a physician to rule out physical causes before assuming there are psychological reasons for sexual problems. Examples of physical causes are diabetes, excess weight, vascular conditions, cancer, medications, urinary tract infections, and hormonal changes due to pregnancy, breast-feeding, and menopause. Psychological factors associated with sexual dysfunction are guilt, relationship conflicts, depression, rape, and early childhood sexual abuse (Wilsnack, Vogeltanx, Klassen, & Harris, 1997). Also, life stressors such as a reduction in income or family-related stress may lead to an increase in sexual dysfunction risk (Laumann et al., 1999). Strong anxiety or stress in any form usually has a significant impact on the sexual response cycle.

Treatment of Sexual Dysfunctions

If a medical basis is determined, the physician will prescribe methods of treatment, ranging from medication to advice or education. If the cause is thought to be psychological, the person may seek help from a licensed psychologist or a licensed sex therapist (see the link at the end of the chapter for an online reference).

Psychotherapy strategies for sexual difficulties differ, depending on the nature of the dysfunction, but generally involve both education and prescribed activities for the individual or couple to practice. An example of a prescribed activity would be Kegel exercises for women to strengthen the pubococcygeus muscle, as women with weak pubococcygeus muscles generally have little or no vaginal sensation during intercourse (Kegel, 1952). Some positions for intercourse, such as the female-superior position (with the woman on top), help with premature ejaculation in the man and failure to achieve orgasm in the woman. Sensate focus exercises are intended to provide a couple with opportunities to enjoy each other without performance anxiety. The partners give each other sensual pleasure without thinking of what they are doing as foreplay to prepare for intercourse, because they have agreed ahead of time that there will be no intercourse. The stop-start technique is a method commonly employed to prevent premature ejaculation in men. The partners stop their sexual activity when the man approaches the point of orgasm and resume stimulation when his sensations subside. Repeated practice helps the man regulate ejaculation by familiarizing himself with the cues that precede the ejaculatory reflex. Therapists have reported success rates as high as 95% in treating premature ejaculation with this method (Segraves & Althof, 1998).

After reading about sexual dysfunction, you may have the following questions: What is normal? How often do others have sex? What do they do when they have sex? Are most people satisfied with their sex lives? These questions are difficult to answer because we typically have to rely on survey information. According to data from a respected national survey, here are some answers to the question "What is normal sex in America in the decade of 2000?"

The data are from the 2002 National Survey of Family Growth (NSFG) and are based on 12,571 in-person interviews with men and women 15–44 years of age.

- Among people 25–44 years of age, 97% have had sexual contact with an opposite-sex partner.

    - 97% have had vaginal intercourse.

    - 90% have had oral sex with a partner.

    - 40% have had anal sex with a partner.

- Males 30–44 years of age reported an average (median) of six to eight female sexual partners in their lifetimes.

- Among women 30–44 years of age, the median number of male sexual partners in their lifetimes was about four.

These statistics outline the current norms; however, survey data can be biased by a host of factors. Normal sexual behavior varies greatly. It is hoped that you will find a pattern of expression that meets your needs and those of your partner and that you will not be influenced by perceptions of what others are doing. However, there are some forms of sexual expression that are so different from the norm that they would be classified as abnormal behavior, which is our next topic of discussion.

The ABC News Primetime Live survey was conducted in 2004 by telephone with female interviewers only. A randomly selected national survey of 1,501 adults is reported to be a representative sample of adult Americans.

- 70% of men and 34% of women think about sex every day.

- 51% of all people said that they discussed fantasies with their partner. However, this is a more common behavior for younger people than for older people.

- 70% of all people reported that they were satisfied with their sex life.

- 35% of men versus 15% of women said that it was okay to have sex without an emotional commitment.

- 16% of adults said that they have cheated in a committed relationship; men were twice as likely to have cheated. Men were also likely to say that the reason for the infidelity was to fulfill a physical desire, whereas women were more likely to say it was to fulfill an emotional need.

Factors that relate to Americans' satisfaction with their sex lives were frequency of sex, how regularly they experienced orgasms, and whether they were married or in a committed relationship.

- 74% of men versus 30% of women said that they "always" experience orgasm. However, an additional 45% of women stated that they had an orgasm "most of the time."

- 80% of sexually active men and women reported that they have "the right amount" of sexual foreplay.

- 45 minutes is the average estimated amount of time for a sexual encounter, including foreplay.

- 85% of adults in committed relationships report having sex once a week.

- 41% report having sex several times a week.

- 8% report having sex daily.

Problematic Sexual Behaviors

FIGURE 10.18 *The dark side of sex.*

FIGURE 10.19 *Someone with the paraphilia of masochism may find this picture sexually arousing.*

Although sex can be a wonderful experience, there are aspects of sexuality that can have long-lasting negative physical and psychological consequences. Some people experience uncontrollable sexual desires that lead to sexual behaviors that hinder their own happiness and may even hurt others.

As is the case with other cultures, our society has boundaries for what it considers to be normal and abnormal sexual activities. There is a continuum regarding normal and abnormal behavior, just as there is with many other topics in this chapter. Atypical sexual behaviors are sexual activities that do not commonly occur in society. Paraphilia refers to a mental disorder characterized by sexual arousal in response to atypical stimuli. It can take the form of recurrent, obsessive sexual fantasies or behaviors that center on nonhuman objects. It may involve humiliation or experience of pain to gain sexual arousal, or incorporate children or other individuals who do not or cannot grant consent (Nevid, Rathus, & Greene, 2006). Paraphilias tend to cause problems in the individual's daily functioning. The diagnosis is dependent on a variety of factors, which are determined by societal expectations, the availability of a partner who is accepting of the unusual behavior, and the individual's personal feelings regarding the behavior.

The two main categories of paraphilias are noncoercive paraphilias and coercive paraphilias. With noncoercive paraphilias, the individuals seek partners who are willing participants. With coercive

Paraphilias

This list includes actually engaging in the behavior as well as having recurrent fantasies or urges.

Pedophilia—characterized by sexual activity with a child, usually age 13 or younger

Fetishism—sexual arousal from nonliving objects

Transvestic fetishism—sexual arousal from dressing in the clothes of the opposite sex (most transvestites are men)

Sexual sadism—sexual arousal from inflicting pain on another

Sexual masochism—sexual arousal from receiving pain, humiliation, or torture

Frotterism—sexual arousal from rubbing one's genitals on a nonconsenting individual

Voyeurism—sexual arousal from observing an unknowing and nonconsenting person usually unclothed and/or engaged in sexual activity

Exhibitionism—sexual arousal from exposing one's genitals to a stranger

paraphilias, individuals are sexually aroused by fantasies or urges to inflict either physical or emotional pain on unwilling victims. Coercive paraphilias are obviously dangerous and are illegal in most cases. Noncoercive paraphilias are harmful only when they motivate activities that are bothersome to the person's partner, serve as a substitute for human contact, or keep an individual from becoming aroused (or reaching orgasm) without performing the atypical sexual behavior (see the sidebar for examples of common paraphilias). It should be noted that paraphilias tend to be compulsive behaviors, which means that the individuals feel that they have no control over their behavior. Some people who suffer from a paraphilia never engage in the behavior, but they continually have uncomfortable fantasies and urges pertaining to them. Recent research suggests that individuals who suffer from paraphilias may engage in a variety of behaviors, and the tendency to engage in deviant sexual behavior may be due to a general lack of control (Abel & Osborn, 1992; Bradford, Boulet, & Pawlak, 1992). This theory is also supported by the observation that paraphilic behaviors tend to increase during times of stress.

Treatment of individuals with paraphilic behaviors is typically behavioral or cognitive psychotherapy. Another avenue is medication. One theory of paraphilias is that individuals have deficits in their serotonin activity levels. This has been supported by the fact that some individuals who engage in paraphilic behavior have been helped by antidepressant medication that boosts levels of serotonin (Balon, 1998).

Rape

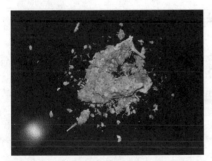

FIGURE 10.20 *Both GHB and Rohypnol can be in the form of a liquid or a powder that can easily be slipped into a drink.*

Rape is defined as a crime in which sexual activity is forced upon a nonconsenting partner. When most people think of rape, they think of a stranger coming out of the dark shadows and assaulting a victim. However, it is estimated that only 1% of all rapes are committed by strangers. The vast majority of rapes are committed by people the victims know. Thus, the most common form of rape is **acquaintance rape**, which is defined as forced intercourse by an individual with whom the victim has regular contact. Date rape is a subcategory of acquaintance rape and is a very common occurrence on college campuses. It is estimated that 5–15% of all female college students have been raped (Finkelson & Oswalt, 1995; Koss, 2000). Most date rapes occur under the influence of a mind-altering substance. It should be noted that the number one drug involved in date rape is alcohol. In fact, alcohol use is one of the four strongest predictors of date rape (Koss, 1989). When rapes occurred, half of the men perpetrators and women victims were either intoxicated or "mildly buzzed" at the time (Muehlenhard & Linton, 1987). Other commonly used date-rape drugs are **gamma-hydroxybutyric acid (GHB)** and **Rohypnol** (roofies). Both of these drugs are depressants, which produce extreme intoxication and amnesia. They come in the form of an odorless, tasteless liquid or a powder, and they are very dangerous when combined with alcohol, as they magnify its effects. Both GHB and Rohypnol circulate throughout the body system very quickly.

If the use of these drugs in the commission of a rape is suspected, testing should be done immediately, as the substances are undetectable after 12 to 48 hours.

If You or Someone You Know Has Been Raped

♦ If you have been raped, you should not change anything—do not change your clothes, take a shower, or brush your hair. Potential evidence will come from your keeping everything intact.

♦ Try to relax and re-create the scenario in which the rape took place, and make as many detailed notes as possible.

♦ Go to the police station or a rape trauma center as quickly as possible. Common date-rape drugs may pass through the body in as little as 12 hours. The longer you wait to go, the greater the chance that vital evidence will be lost and your memory will deteriorate.

It is estimated that only 1 in 10 rapes is reported to the police. Being raped can produce intense feelings of embarrassment, shame, anger, and guilt—which may be the reason for the lack of reporting. Another reason is the feeling that if the woman knows the perpetrator, she may be called into question when claiming to have been raped. Additionally, the woman may take responsibility for what has occurred. A research study found that only 27% of women whose assault met the legal definition of rape labeled their experiences as rape (Koss, 1989).

As with other topics covered in this chapter, sexual domination behaviors occur on a continuum. A large number of men report engaging in some form of sexually dominating behavior. For example, studies of the frequency of sexual assault among college students indicate that 25–60% of college men have engaged in some form of sexually coercive behavior (Berkowitz, 1992). **Sexual coercion** exists along a continuum, from forcible rape to nonphysical forms of pressure that compel girls and women to engage in sex against their will. The touchstone of coercion is that a woman lacks choice and faces severe physical or social consequences if she resists sexual advances. One study found that 30% of all male subjects said that they would commit a rape if they thought they could get away with it (Lonsway & Fitzgerald, 1994). Many men blame their women partners for date rape and state that it resulted from miscommunication.

FIGURE 10.21 *Alcohol consumption is involved in a majority of date-rape cases. Courtesy of yotophoto.com.*

Men and women differ in their definitions of rape. In one study, 88% of men whose behavior was reported as an assault that met legal definitions of rape indicated that their behavior was "definitely not rape" (Koss, 1989). Due to these factors, it is very difficult to create a profile of a typical rapist. It has been found that men who are extremely masculine in their gender role expression are more likely to engage in sexual aggression (Berkowitz, 1992; Muehlenhard & Falcon, 1990). Also, date rapes are more common in men who are in large masculine-oriented groups such as sports teams and fraternities (Gwartney-Gibbs & Stockard, 1989). This discussion has focused on males raping females, but it should be noted that there are rare cases of female rape and sexual coercion. Men are more commonly rape victims at the hands of other men.

In summary, to reduce your chances of being raped, be very specific in communicating your sexual boundaries and take care to limit your consumption of alcohol so that you have a better chance of exerting control over the situation. Also, take precautions to avoid potentially dangerous situations, such as being alone with a questionable individual or with a group of intoxicated people. Rape has many painful consequences, including depression, nightmares, anxiety, and sexual dysfunction. A rape could also result in the transmission of a sexually transmitted disease or an unwanted pregnancy.

Sexually Transmitted Diseases

Sexually transmitted diseases (STDs) are infections that are spread from person to person, primarily through sexual contact. The three main categories of infections are viral, bacterial, and fungal (see sidebar). Viral STDs, such as genital herpes (HSV) and human immunodeficiency virus (HIV), cannot be cured, but their symptoms can be managed with medication. Bacterial STDs, such as gonorrhea and chlamydia, can be cured with antibiotics. Fungal diseases, such as trichomoniasis and candidiasis, can be cured with antifungal agents. There are a wide range of symptoms that vary from no visible symptoms to extreme pain, illness, and in some cases, death. STDs occur most commonly in sexually active teenagers and young adults, especially those with multiple sex partners. According to the United States Department of Health and Human Services (2005), in the United States, approximately 19 million people are infected each year, and more than 65 million have an incurable STD. The overall incidence has increased dramatically in recent years.

Common Symptoms of STDs

♦ Any unusual discharge, especially with itching, burning, or odor

♦ Abdominal pain

♦ Genital sores or bumps

♦ Burning when urinating

♦ Itching around genitals

Since many STDs are **asymptomatic** (no symptoms are visibly present), people may be unaware of their infection status. If you have engaged in unprotected sexual relations, you should get tested for STDs to be certain of your condition. Although people may not show any signs of having an STD, they may still pass the infection on to others. The only sure way to avoid becoming infected with an STD is monogamy with an uninfected partner. Some complications of leaving STD infections untreated include pelvic inflammatory disease (PID), which is inflammation of the female reproductive organs, usually caused by germs or the growth of bacteria; inflammation of the cervix (cervicitis) in women; inflammation of the urethra (urethritis); inflammation of the prostate (prostatitis) in men; and fertility and reproductive system problems in both sexes. Also, a person infected with an STD is more likely to become infected with HIV, a very dangerous STD, due to having lesions in the genital area, which facilitates transmission of the virus.

FIGURE 10.22 *Some STDs are incurable and may even lead to death.*

The **human immunodeficiency virus (HIV)** attacks the immune system, which is the system of organs and glands that fight off infection. This virus is especially dangerous because it attacks the very part of our body that is responsible for maintaining our health. Currently HIV cannot be cured, but symptoms can be helped with medication. If the proper medication is not received, the immune system will be weakened to the point where it cannot effectively fight off illness, and the individual is likely to fall prey to an opportunistic infection. Opportunistic infections are infections that are common in our surroundings and that take advantage of the weakened immune system. When this happens, a new label is given to the set of symptoms, **acquired immunodeficiency syndrome (AIDS)**. HIV is the infection of a virus that attacks the immune system, whereas AIDS is the set of symptoms that HIV-positive people experience when their immune systems have been substantially compromised. The prognosis for a person with AIDS is poor, and serious intervention must occur, as there is a high probability of it being fatal.

People infected with HIV may spread the virus through sexual contact or by contact with an open wound of another person. When such contact occurs, the body fluids of the infected person have an opportunity to reach the bloodstream of the contacted person. The virus has also been spread through direct infusion of contaminated blood or blood products. Other sources of the viral spread are organ transplants or shared needles (Stine, 1995). A woman infected with HIV who becomes pregnant or breast-feeds can pass the virus on to her baby.

To stay safe from this dangerous virus, you merely need to control your own behavior. Talk to your partner or partners about past and present sexual prac-

Overview of Common Sexually Transmitted Diseases

Bacterial Infections

Chlamydia—the most common STD. Symptoms may be asymptomatic or a white, clear discharge and/or burning sensation in the genital area. It is treated with antibiotics.

Gonorrhea—may be asymptomatic or a white/yellow discharge from the genital or anal area. It is treated with antibiotics.

Syphilis—a disease that progresses over four different stages. The initial stage is characterized by a painless sore, which is then followed by a rash approximately 1–2 weeks later. It is treated with antibiotics in the early stages. If it is allowed to progress, however, it may be untreatable. The latent (hidden) stage of syphilis begins when the initial sore and subsequent rash disappear. This latent stage can last for years. The late stage develops in about 15% of people with untreatable syphilis. In the late stage, the disease may damage the internal organs and the brain seriously enough to cause death.

Viral Infections

Human papilloma virus—commonly called genital warts. Individuals may see small pink or gray wartlike marks on or around the genital area. However, sometimes the warts are so small, or located in obstructed places, that they are not visible. It is transmittable through sexual contact with the warts. This virus is not curable, but cryotherapy, a freezing procedure, may be used to remove the warts.

Herpes—Herpes simplex virus type one is generally called oral herpes. It causes cold sores or fever blisters on the mouth. It can be transferred to the genitals by oral genital contact. Herpes simplex type 2 produces painful, shallow sores on the genitals. The symptoms are painful reddish bumps or sores in the genital area that become visible approximately six to eight days after infection with genital herpes. It is not curable, but there are treatments that help reduce the symptoms. A person with this disease can experience outbreaks at any time. Drugs are available that can help ease the negative symptoms associated with the outbreaks.

Hepatitis B—this incurable virus causes inflammation of the liver, and it can be transmitted via sexual contact. Individuals exposed to this virus may be asymptomatic or may experience a variety of symptoms such as nausea, loss of appetite, or jaundice (yellow coloring of the skin).

Fungal Infections

Trichomonias—is caused by a parasite and may be transmitted through sexual intercourse. It may have symptoms of a foul-smelling discharge accompanied by burning and itching, but it may also be asymptomatic. A physician can prescribe a drug for treatment.

Candidiasis—is commonly called a yeast infection and is caused by an overgrowth of yeast fungus. These infections can be transmitted to and from males through sexual intercourse. The treatment is typically an over-the-counter cream or pill.

tices and drug use. Avoid sex with anyone who you know has had several sexual partners or whose sexual history you do not know. Whereas it is a good practice to ask potential partners about past sexual behavior, research suggests that you should not necessarily trust your potential mate's response, since 34% of the men and 10% of the women in the research samples said that they had lied about their behavior in order to have sex (Cochran & Mays, 1990). Thus, it is a good idea to require any potential sexual partner to have an HIV antibody test. Additionally, you should avoid being physically intimate with more than one partner. The more partners you have, the more you expose yourself to risk of infection. People with AIDS and those at risk for AIDS should not be considered safe sexual partners. Avoid anal sex, even with a condom. Although they are not 100% effective, you should use condoms and spermicidal barriers to reduce the possibility of transmitting the virus. The only truly safe sexual practice is electing not to be sexually active or limiting sex to one mutually faithful, uninfected partner, and not injecting drugs. If you use intravenous drugs, don't share needles (Corey & Corey, 1993).

Unplanned Pregnancy

Eighty-five percent of women engaging in fairly regular unprotected intercourse will become pregnant within one year. It is estimated that about 40% of pregnancies are unplanned. An unplanned pregnancy can be dealt with in many ways: altering your lifestyle to accept the role of becoming a parent, placing the child with an adoption agency, or obtaining an abortion. All these options

Some of the Available Birth Control Options

Hormonal forms—99% effectiveness with perfect usage. All methods work by preventing ovulation.

♦ **Pill**—there are different dosages of hormone pills.

♦ **Patch**—it looks similar to a Band-Aid; it secretes a constant flow of hormones into the skin. The patch must be changed weekly for three weeks and then not worn for one week.

♦ **Shot**—Depo-Provera is a hormone shot given once every three months.

♦ **Ring**—inserted into the vagina on a monthly basis, starting on the first day of the woman's menstrual period.

Barrier methods—act as a barrier against sperm getting to the egg. Effectiveness varies according to proper usage.

♦ **Condoms**—there are male and female varieties, but the most common is a rubber sheath inserted over the penis.

♦ **Diaphragm and cervical cap**—the device is inserted into the vagina prior to intercourse.

♦ **Spermicides**—a cream, foam, jelly, or film inserted into the vagina prior to intercourse.

♦ **Intrauterine device (IUD)**—prevents the embryo from attaching itself to the uterine wall.

Natural family planning methods—sex is avoided on days of ovulation. There are a variety of methods used to determine ovulation, such as counting the days of the menstrual cycle, taking the basal temperature, and examining cervical mucus.

carry emotional or financial burdens. Because an unplanned pregnancy has lasting consequences, it is best to take precautions so that you will not have to face this dilemma. A host of birth control options are available to you through your doctor or from nonprofit agencies such as Planned Parenthood. These agencies also have "morning after" or Plan B pills that can remedy "accidents" that may occur. The Plan B pills usually come in a package of two, with the first pill to be taken no later than 72 hours after the unprotected sexual intercourse, and the second pill to be taken approximately 12 hours after the first pill. It works by preventing ovulation or fertilization through an increased dosage of hormones. As much as 43% of the decline in abortions between 1994 and 2000 can be attributed to the use of emergency contraception (Henshaw, Singh, & Haas, 1999). Ultimately, awareness of the dangers of unanticipated pregnancy and STDs should prompt precautionary behavior that will serve as the best defense against any negative consequences of sexual expression.

Chapter Summary

Sexual behaviors are complex; thus any given person's sexual activities may defy categorization. There are subtle anatomical differences that are typical of male and female brains, particularly in the hypothalamus, the corpus callosum, the amygdala, and the hippocampus. Women tend to have more language areas in their brains than do men, and they tend to use both hemispheres simultaneously when engaging in cognitive tasks, unlike men. Men and women have the same average intelligence, although sexual differences in performance on certain cognitive tasks have been found.

Men typically possess one XY chromosomal pair, whereas women have an XX chromosomal pair. However, biological anomalies do occur, including hermaphroditism (an infant born with both male and female genitalia). Some human beings are born with the genitalia of one sex, but with a psychological sense of belonging to the other sex. This situation results in a gender identity disorder.

Behavioral and cognitive differences between men and women are explained in the evolutionary model as being the result of different survival tactics. Early human beings divided food-acquiring labors—men hunted game and women gathered plants. Men with good visual and spatial abilities were better hunters, and thus were more likely to survive and have offspring. Women, slowed down by pregnancy and childcare responsibilities, were more suited to gathering food that they could find, and thus they developed abilities suited to these tasks. Social constructionist theories attribute sex role differentiation to the social structure, suggesting that since men and women tend to occupy different social roles, they have become psychologically and behaviorally different in ways that fit them to these roles.

Psychologically androgynous individuals identify with both traditionally masculine and feminine attributes. Psychological androgyny is associated with greater adaptability and more satisfying intimate relationships.

Most people express the desire for an intimate relationship as one of their major goals in life. However, there are obstacles that can interfere with the achievement of intimacy. Three myths involving intimacy that can be problematic were described: in healthy relationships, our partner brings us happiness; relationships necessitate self-sacrifice; and opposites attract to form complementary relationships. Once a satisfactory intimate relationship has been established, the couple may naturally wish to marry. Yet divorce statistics, showing that half of all marriages end in divorce, can be discouraging. Marital researcher John Gottman discovered that successful marriages have a substantially higher proportion of positive exchanges than negative ones. Both the presence of "stonewalling" and the expression of contempt predict a poor relationship outcome, as does the presence of a great deal of criticism.

Much attention has been devoted to understanding homosexual behavior. It is by now clear that homosexual and heterosexual preferences exist on a continuum; thus it is simplistic to categorize people as being strictly heterosexual or homosexual. Homosexuality affects only a small proportion of the population. At present, it is thought to come about as a result of an interplay among biological, social, behavioral, and environmental factors.

Masters and Johnson's research on the human sexual response cycle shows that there are four phases of the cycle: excitement, plateau, orgasm, and resolution. During the resolution phase, men experience a refractory period during which they cannot return to the excitement phase, no matter how much stimulation they receive. Women, however, are capable of having several orgasms in quick succession.

Sexual dysfunctions fall into four categories: sexual desire disorders (the person reports little or no sexual desire), sexual pain disorders (pain is experienced during intercourse), sexual arousal disorders (men who experience impotence or women who don't become lubricated), and orgasmic disorders (men or women experience an extended delay or inability to achieve orgasm). Sexual dysfunctions are treated first with a medical exam to determine whether the dysfunction is the result of a physical or a psychological problem. Medical problems are often treated with medication. Psychological issues are generally treated with education and behavioral exercises, typically practiced with a partner.

Negative aspects of sexual expression are those that incorporate an unwilling victim into the sex act. Noncoercive paraphilias do not harm others and include desires such as men feeling compelled to dress in women's clothing (transvestitism) or focusing on a particular type of object as a source of sexual excitement (fetishism). Coercive paraphilias, such as frotterism (e.g., rubbing up against a nonconsenting person in public), sexual sadism (which may include inflicting pain on a consenting partner but may also entail victimizing unwilling participants), or exhibitionism (e.g., males displaying their genitals to unsuspecting bystanders), are harmful to others. Rape is another example of sexual activity forced onto a nonconsenting person, with destructive emotional consequences. STDs, the most serious of which is HIV/AIDS, range from being nuisances to having fatal consequences. Finally, an unplanned premarital pregnancy can limit the potential development of a young parent, as well as limit the opportunities of any child that might come from the pregnancy.

Knowledge Builder

RELATE TO YOURSELF

1. What aspects of your own behavior do you feel are the product of societal gender role expectations?

   _____

   _____

   _____

   _____

2. This chapter discussed the topic of psychological androgyny. Do you think that you are androgynous? What qualities, if any, that are traditionally assigned to the other sex do you see yourself as possessing?

   _____

   _____

   _____

   _____

3. After reading the section on relationships, do you feel that you express the behaviors required to maintain a healthy intimate relationship? If so, what are those behaviors?

   _____

   _____

   _____

   _____

4. Three marital conflict styles—avoidant, volatile, and validating—were discussed in this chapter. Which style do you feel you currently use in your relationship, and which would you be most comfortable with in a long-term relationship? Which style, if any, have you witnessed in your parents?

   _____

   _____

   _____

   _____

CHAPTER REVIEW QUESTIONS

1. Male and female embryos have the ability to develop either male or female sex organs. **T or F?**

2. Physical differences have been found in male and female brains. **T or F?**

3. The basic idea of the evolutionary theory of sexual differences is that male and female brains are different due to their environmental survival requirements. **T or F?**

4. Male and female hormone levels change as a result of age. **T or F?**

5. If you are in the right relationship, you will have everlasting happiness. **T or F?**

6. You are more likely to be raped by a stranger than by someone you know. **T or F?**

7. Most pregnancies that occur are unplanned. **T or F?**

8. Which style of marital conflict is most likely to lead to a successful marriage?

    (a) avoidant   **(b)** volatile

    (c) validating   **(d)** all of the above

    (e) none of the above

9. _____ is a term in psychology that refers to a mental disorder characterized by obsessive sexual fantasies or behaviors that cause problems in the individual's daily functioning.

    (a) Sexual dysfunction   **(b)** Paraphilia

    (c) Frotterism   **(d)** Sexual orientation

10. What is the most common date-rape drug?

    (a) GHB   **(b)** Rohypnol

    (c) caffeine   **(d)** alcohol

11. Which of the following sexually transmitted diseases is curable?

    (a) chlamydia   **(b)** genital warts

    (c) HIV   **(d)** herpes

12. Differentiate among the following terms: intersexual, transsexual, and homosexual.

_____

_____

_____

_____

13. Why is it difficult to define abnormal sexual behavior?

_____

_____

_____

_____

14. List some of the negative consequences associated with engaging in sexual activity and how you can avoid them.

_____

_____

_____

_____

_____

_____

_____

15. This chapter focused on the theme of continuums. List and describe the different behaviors that were illustrated as expressing themselves on a continuum.

_____

_____

_____

_____

USEFUL WEB SITES

INTERSEX SOCIETY OF NORTH AMERICA

http://www.isna.org/

Discusses different issues related to intersexualism.

AMERICAN PSYCHOLOGICAL ASSOCIATION

http://www.apa.org/pubinfo/answers.html

Answers your questions about sexual orientation and homosexuality.

AMERICAN ASSOCIATION OF SEX EDUCATORS, COUNSELORS AND THERAPISTS

http://www.aasect.org/

Can help you locate a sex therapist and answer many questions about sexuality.

BBC SEX ID TEST

http://www.bbc.co.uk/science/humanbody/sex/add_user.shtml

An online test that examines a host of gender-related constructs and provides you with a fascinating analysis of your personal performance.

PLANNED PARENTHOOD

http://www.plannedparenthood.org

Can answer all your questions regarding birth control.

RAPE, ABUSE & INCEST NATIONAL NETWORK

http://www.rainn.org/

Provides information on rape issues.

CENTERS FOR DISEASE CONTROL AND PREVENTION

http://www.cdc.gov/nchstp/dstd/disease_info.htm

Provides general information about STDs.

11

Social Psychology

by Christopher Hayashi, MA

Man is a social animal.

—BENEDICT SPINOZA, *ETHICS*

On August 27, 2005, Hurricane Katrina brought about unprecedented devastation to the southern states of Louisiana and Mississippi. The city of New Orleans was the most heavily hit. Winds of 165 mph pelted the city for more than 26 hours. Huge waves from the gulf caused a major levy to break, leaving much of the city literally underwater. The entire city's population had to be evacuated, as food and clean drinking water became increasingly unavailable. Homes and businesses were destroyed, and many lives were lost.

During the days and weeks that followed, the government and many U.S. citizens joined together in an attempt to deal with the aftermath of Hurricane Katrina. Americans opened their hearts and their wallets, donating millions to aid those who had lost everything they owned. The residents of nearby Houston and other cities throughout the nation opened their doors to the now-homeless people. Volunteers paid their own way and traveled to the devastated city to help in the rescue effort. Foreign countries sent money and supplies, and people around the world did what they could to relieve the suffering of those who had lost so much. Senator Bill Frist, who visited the devastated region to personally lend a helping hand, called the horrible situation "America's Challenge" and bolstered the hopes of the citizens of New Orleans by promising that we would soon see "America at its very best." And indeed, we did.

FIGURE 11.1 *Hurricane Katrina brought out the very best and the worst in people.*

But Hurricane Katrina also brought out a darker side of human nature, one that many of us would rather pretend does not exist. Along with the uplifting stories of people giving of themselves to help those in need, news coverage also showed people at their very worst. People were shown looting the now-abandoned stores and homes. Violence and gunfire erupted in some parts of the city amid the chaos. Disturbing video footage of police officers

FIGURE 11.2 *The destruction left many in need of a helping hand. Others took advantage of the chaos. Courtesy of yotophoto.com.*

savagely beating a 64-year-old man was shown on the news; many claimed the assault stemmed from the accumulated frustration resulting from the horrific situation.

Many Americans were also outraged at the perceived lack of urgency and subsequent delayed response by the federal government. Many were appalled that it took nearly four days after the hurricane had struck to organize a rescue effort. Meanwhile, thousands of people were left stranded on their rooftops for days as the floodwaters refused to subside. Fingers were pointed, as many felt that the disaster should have been foreseen and steps should have been taken to evacuate the city and avoid the subsequent loss of life that ultimately ensued.

Finally, because the population of New Orleans was predominantly poor and African American, many Americans felt that race and class discrimination played a role in the lack of urgency in the federal government's response. Many believed that the response would have been much different had the disaster taken place in a more affluent area of the country. President Bush himself took partial responsibility for the situation and admitted that the devastation caused by Hurricane Katrina shed light on an even larger problem—a social and political system that was inadequate in many ways.

Defining Social Psychology

What can we learn from the events that preceded and followed Hurricane Katrina? Perhaps the field of social psychology can help us understand how this horrible situation brought out both the best and the worst in human nature. **Social psychology** is the branch of psychology that attempts to understand how individual behavior is affected by the social environment and the presence of other people.

I'm sure you have noticed the many ways that your own thoughts and behaviors are influenced by the people around you and by the social situations in which

FIGURE 11.3 *To what extent is behavior a function of the situations in which we find ourselves? Photograph by Debbie Whittaker.*

you find yourself. In some situations, it may seem as if we are entirely different people altogether. For example, think of the way you might act at a crowded music concert performed by your favorite band. Is it the same way you would act at Sunday brunch? Are you the same person when you are with your close friends as opposed to a group of strangers? Do you act the same when you are at home with your family as opposed to when you are at school or work?

As human beings, we spend much of our time interacting with others. We go to school and we go to work. We spend time with our family and hang out with our friends. Even the mundane task of making a quick run to the grocery store involves a multitude of social interactions. For instance, we might interact with other customers as we walk down the aisles. We chat with the cashier as we are checking out. We even communicate with other drivers as we navigate our way to the store and back home. We spend much of our waking hours in the presence of other people, whether they are friends, family, fellow students, coworkers, or complete strangers. Because we spend so much of our time interacting with others, social psychologists are interested in how our behavior is affected and influenced by the presence of these people and the various social environments in which we might find ourselves throughout our lives. Social psychology suggests that the social situation is often quite powerful in shaping and influencing many aspects of our behavior.

Social Psychology vs. Sociology: Focusing on the Individual

Because many fields attempt to understand how the social environment influences behavior, the field of social psychology has considerable overlap with many other disciplines. Answers to the question of how behavior is affected by the environment can be derived from the fields of anthropology, philosophy, and sociology. Sociology is perhaps social psychology's closest related discipline. In fact, a social psychology class at your school might be dually listed as both a psychology course and a sociology course.

So what is the difference between the field of social psychology and the field of sociology? Whereas sociology attempts to answer how *groups* of people (gender groups, ethnic groups, social classes, etc.) are affected by various social factors, the focus of social psychology is the individual. Of course, psychology studies how people behave in groups, but social psychology specifically attempts to address how the *individual* is influenced by the presence of others and the social situation. Social psychology assumes that we are all affected by our surroundings, and the particulars of each situation influence our behavior in distinct and often predictable ways.

Key Issue: Nature vs. Nurture

By now you have probably spent time studying how various biological factors shape and mold your behavior. No doubt you have already studied the role of genetics in explaining many of your behaviors. You have seen how genes shape us in our parents' image, whether we like to admit it or not. You have studied how various parts of the brain control specific aspects of our behavior, and how subtle fluctuations in our hormone or neurotransmitter levels can have a rather profound effect on how we think, feel, and act. You might be asking yourself, "Do social psychologists suggest that our physiology has no influence on how we behave?"

Contemporary thought within the field of social psychology acknowledges that biology plays an important role in shaping human behavior. Yet at the same time, our individual experiences, our personal histories, and, most importantly, the situations in which we find ourselves can and often do exert just as strong of an influence in shaping how we think, feel, and act. Social psychology rests on the foundation that all people—regardless of differences in biological predisposition, personality, or personal history—are influenced by specific social situations. Therefore, the goal of social psychology is to understand the general ways in which we are *all* influenced by the things going on around us.

This chapter will allow you to understand how common behaviors that you see all around you are influenced by specific social circumstances. For example, we will discuss exactly what specific social situations make it more likely that two people will form a friendship. We will also see what social factors make it likely that two people will fall in love. We will identify what social situations increase the likelihood of people receiving help when they are in need (prosocial behavior), along with the social situations that increase the likelihood that people engage in behaviors that cause harm to others (aggression). We will see why so many of us, regardless of our individual differences, are likely to be motivated by the same kinds of leaders, find the same kinds of people attractive, and also be guilty of holding stereotypes and prejudices.

I welcome you to the fascinating world of social psychology!

Why Is Social Psychology Important?

Explore
**behavior as a
reflection of personality**
in Chapter 13, p. 428

Social psychologists suggest that when observing the behavior of others, we have the tendency to automatically assume that their behavior is a direct reflection of their personality. In other words, we assume that people's behavior matches who they are inside. When you go out to eat at a restaurant and see someone fail to leave a tip, do you automatically assume that the person is cheap? Wouldn't you assume that if you were to see this person at another restaurant or in any other situation, he or she would do the same thing? You may be correct, but you might have also just made what social psychologists refer to as the "fundamental attribution error."

The **fundamental attribution error** is the tendency to underestimate the influence of social and situational factors when judging why others behave the way they do (Ross, 1977). Perhaps the person you saw in the restaurant was in a huge hurry and simply forgot to leave a tip. Perhaps there were a multitude of other reasons why the person didn't leave a tip. The point is that most of us don't take the time to consider situational explanations for others' behavior. We are quick to assume that people's behavior reflects their personality. In other words, we are quicker to make a *dispositional attribution* than a *situational attribution*. A **dispositional attribution** is when we attribute the behavior of others to their personality traits. A **situational attribution** is when we attribute the behavior of others to the specific social circumstances. Generally, we tend to focus more on situational factors when we explain our own behavior. This greater attention paid to the situation when explaining our own behavior while instead focusing on dispositional factors when explaining the behavior of others is known as the **actor/observer difference** (Jones & Nesbitt, 1972).

But why do we make the type of attributions that we do? Part of the reason why we are quicker to make dispositional attributions and overlook situational factors when judging the behavior of others is that it is simply easier to do (Gilbert & Malone, 1995). Because we see so many events occur throughout the day, it is necessary to make quick interpretations of events and get on with our lives. In contrast, if we are to make a situational attribution, we must take the extra time to critically evaluate the particulars of the situation. When others' behavior has relatively little effect on us, what is the point of taking this extra time and devoting this extra energy?

In summary, I hope you have come to understand that social psychologist are interested in the ways we are all affected by the people and the events going on around us. Perhaps it is not necessarily the events themselves but rather our individual perception of those events that ultimately influences how the social environment affects us. Let us now take a critical look at how we actually perceive the world around us.

How We Form Our Views of the Social World

Social Cognition and Social Perception

> Nothing is or isn't, only thinking makes it so.
>
> —Anais Nin

See if you can answer the following riddle: A father and his son are involved in a terrible automobile accident. The father is killed, but the son survives. An ambulance arrives on the scene and rushes the son to the emergency room. Critically injured, the son requires emergency surgery. A surgeon is called and the son is quickly prepped. The surgeon steps into the operating room, takes a look at the patient, and immediately says, "I cannot operate on him. He is my son!"

Before you read on, stop for a moment and ask yourself how this is possible. Didn't the father die in the car accident? How did he all of a sudden appear in the operating room?

The answer to this riddle is in fact quite simple—the doctor is his mother!

Although in retrospect the answer is quite obvious, why are so many of us stumped? If you had difficulty answering this riddle, you probably made the quick assumption that the doctor was a man. If so, your social cognition and social perception have hindered you from looking at this situation in an unbiased way. More specifically, previous knowledge acquired through your past experiences, the way that you have organized this information in your mind, and the way that you have used this information to interpret this new situation have led you astray. In other words, your past experiences have created a habitual pattern of interpreting events that makes it difficult to view the world in an unbiased way.

FIGURE 11.4 *Does this person match your "schema" for a doctor?*

What can we learn from this example? We have already established that social psychologists are interested in how the social environment and the presence of other people influence the behavior of the individual. But we must also realize that not all of us

FIGURE 11.5 *When you think of a chair, is this the first thing that comes to mind?*

perceive the world in exactly the same fashion. A person's individual perception of a social situation is a key component of how the social environment ultimately shapes behavior. The way in which we individually view the social environment is what is called **social perception**.

Prior experiences and previous knowledge shape our beliefs about and perceptions of how the world works. We all have similar prior experiences in this world that lead us to view it in a similar fashion most of the time, but because we also have significant differences in our past personal experiences, the way we view the world may significantly differ from others' views. The accumulation of knowledge gained through our unique personal experiences can lead us to view our world in unique and individual ways. Whether a situation brings out the best or worst in us is truly tied to our perceptions of it.

Whereas social perception refers to the way we view the world, **social cognition** refers to the way we mentally *organize* information and think about the world. The way that information is stored in the mind can also have a profound effect on how we view the world, thus altering our social perception. Social psychologists suggest that humans have a cognitive tendency to mentally organize the world by creating schemas. **Schemas** are organized bodies of general information and knowledge regarding persons, places, and things (Bartlett, 1932; Taylor & Crocker, 1981). For example, consider your schema for "chair." You've probably included the fact that it is an object with four legs and a seat, and it is something upon which you sit. You have a mental picture of what a chair looks like, and it is against this prototype that you compare all other chairs you might encounter.

So what are we getting at here? Let's reexamine the riddle from the beginning of this section. Can you see how your schema of a doctor might have hindered you from immediately knowing the answer to the riddle? Your schema of a doctor probably included the fact that doctors are often male. Of course, there are plenty of female doctors, and when we encounter one we are not at all surprised; our schemas are modifiable to meet the demands of the situation. But oftentimes, the fact that our social perception and social cognition rely so heavily on the use of schemas keeps us from viewing the world in a completely unbiased manner.

FIGURE 11.6 *Much of how the social environment affects us is tied to how we view it.*

We use schemas to help us make sense of a world filled with an abundance of information. Schemas help us interpret and adapt to new situations that we encounter each day, and they help us efficiently navigate our daily lives. Can you imagine entering every situation in your daily life without previous information or knowledge about how the world works? You would be completely lost! Social psychologists suggest that most of our social perception is spent in this "automatic processing mode," which allows us to be more efficient in making sense of what is going on around us. At times, this efficiency is at the cost of accuracy, as evidenced by our difficulty with the father/son riddle. But now that we appreciate how our social perception and cognition influence our behavior, we can tackle our first topic—prejudice.

Prejudice

In 2006, the movie *Crash* won an Oscar for best picture. In the story, the lives of eight seemingly ordinary characters living in Los Angeles dramatically intersect. Of particular interest is the *reason* that their lives become irrevocably intertwined. The connections that are formed among the characters are invariably a result of each of their individually held prejudices toward one another. The movie takes place over a span of 36 hours and sheds light on a behavior that has interested social psychologists for decades. In the movie, prejudice is portrayed as a behavior in which we all engage, no matter how good our intentions might be. The movie brings to our awareness those beliefs that we often unconsciously hold but that shape our interactions with the social world. The characters find that acting on individually held prejudices results in dire consequences, just as it often does in the real world.

Attitudes and Attitude Formation

Prejudice is a type of attitude. To truly understand prejudice, it is first important to more generally understand how our attitudes are formed and exactly what they are. An **attitude** is defined as an enduring system of beliefs, feelings, and behavioral tendencies concerning people, objects, or ideas. One way of understanding an attitude is to break it down into these various components. Social psychologists suggest that attitudes have three distinct components: the affective component, the behavioral component, and the cognitive component.

The ABC's of Attitudes

The **affective component of an attitude** refers to the *emotional response* associated with a person, place, or idea. For example, when you think of the New York Yankees, how do you feel? When you think of the war in Iraq, does it stir positive or negative emotions? Rarely do we feel completely neutral about anything in this world. It is certainly true that our attitudes vary in the strength of the emotional response they trigger in us. But if we have any previous knowledge about a particular subject, we are subsequently prone to feel either positively or negatively.

FIGURE 11.7 *You were not born preferring Pepsi to Coke. Your preference for certain brands is an attitude shaped by experience.*

The **behavioral component of an attitude** refers to how our preexisting and preestablished ideas guide our *actions*. For example, if your favorite color is blue, you probably wouldn't buy a yellow car. If your political values are conservative and you identify with the Republican Party, you probably wouldn't vote for a democratic candidate in the next election. If your favorite type of cuisine is Thai food, you probably wouldn't spend as much time at the local Mexican restaurant as you would the local Thai restaurant if given a choice. In other words, our beliefs, likes, and dislikes influence what we choose to do and not to do in our daily lives.

Finally, the **cognitive component of an attitude** refers to the *logic* and rationale behind our attitudes. Our attitudes toward ideas, people, and things in this world are often based on facts and information that we believe to be true. For example, your political affiliation and your voting patterns are probably highly influenced by what you perceive to be "right" in this world.

Attitude Formation

Social psychologists are also interested in how our attitudes are formed, for two reasons: (1) because we are not born with our attitudes, our attitudes must be a product of the social environment, and (2) because our attitudes guide and influence our behavior. Let's take a deeper look at each of these ideas.

No one was born preferring Pepsi to Coke. Not a single person came into this world with a preference for a type of music, a clothing style, a favorite color, a favorite sports team, a political ideology, or even an inherent core sense of morals and values. Although some of these things might be essential aspects of who we are as individuals, it is important to realize that our attitudes are primarily products of the social environment and the social worlds in which we were raised and continue to live. Our attitudes are derived and shaped by the accumulation of the individual experiences we have throughout our lives, influencing what we like and do not like in this world.

Explore **observational learning** in Chapter 7, p. 220

In Chapter 7, "Learning," you investigated the various ways in which your behavior was changed by the experiences you have had. You read about various types of learning such as observational learning, classical conditioning, and operant conditioning. Just to remind you, classically conditioned behaviors refer to learned involuntary responses to stimuli. Operant conditioning refers to voluntary behavioral changes that occur as a function of reinforcement or punishment (Skinner, 1948). Observational learning refers to learning that occurs as a result of watching others. These types of learning can be applied to understanding how our attitudes are created, strengthened, and even changed.

For example, let's say that you are in an adventurous mood and decide to dine at a restaurant that serves a type of food you have never tried before. After eating at this restaurant, you develop the worst case of food poisoning ever. Following this horrible experience, you probably wouldn't return to that restaurant any time soon, nor would you be too excited about joining your friends if they decided to go out for that same type of food, even if they went to a different restaurant. From that day forward, the mere mention of that type of food would probably bring a look of disgust to your face and a sense of queasiness to your stomach. Your attitude toward the restaurant, that type of food, and anything related has been classically conditioned.

Conversely, what if you had an entirely different experience at that same restaurant? This time, not only did you enjoy the food, but you also had a fabulous evening listening to music, dancing, *and,* as it just so happened, meeting the love of your life. Remember that operant conditioning states that our behavior is shaped through reinforcement and punishment. How do you think you'd feel about the culture from which that food came now? If you had such a great experience, it might even help you decide where to take your next vacation.

FIGURE 11.8 *Would Nike be as popular as it is if it was not endorsed by popular athletes? Courtesy of David Young-Wolff/PhotoEdit, Inc.*

To see another great example of these principles at work, look no further than the closest TV or magazine. Why do you think companies hire likable celebrities to endorse their products? Do you think Nike would be as popular as it is if it didn't have Michael Jordan, one of the greatest basketball players ever, as its spokesman? How about Catherine Zeta-Jones and T-Mobile?

Companies often pair their products with beautiful models, catchy tunes, humorous scenarios, or other things that evoke positive feelings in us. Their hope is that repeated exposure to a commercial will affect your attitude toward the product. They are relying on the principles of classical and operant conditioning to shape your attitudes toward their products. They also hope that we will imitate the behaviors of these famous people, whom we can only hope to be like. On a similar note, politicians point out all the good things that will come if we vote for them, and emphasize all the bad things that will happen if we vote for the other candidate. Our attitudes are constantly being shaped by the things we see and hear each day.

Understanding Prejudice

Now that you have an idea of how attitudes are formed, let us return to the specific topic introduced at the beginning of the chapter. **Prejudice** is a negative attitude harbored by an individual toward a person based on the person's membership in a group. Have you ever had somebody approach you and you felt as if you knew something about this individual simply by his or her physical appearance? Have you ever seen someone with a particular color of skin and assumed that you could guess the individual's favorite type of music and favorite foods? Have you ever judged someone by the clothes he or she was wearing? Were you stumped by the riddle at the beginning of the chapter? Most people would probably answer yes to at least one of these questions.

Social psychologists suggest that we all harbor prejudices, no matter how good our intentions may be. We all are raised interacting with others, and it is inevitable that we form attitudes toward them. Thus, it is also inevitable that we will form prejudices.

Prejudice and the ABCs of Attitudes

As discussed earlier, all attitudes have affective, behavioral, and cognitive components. Since prejudice is a type of attitude, perhaps the best way to understand its nature is to consider it in terms of these components.

The affective component of an attitude refers to the feeling or emotional response toward the person, place, or thing. Rarely do we feel completely neutral about anything; almost everything evokes some form of emotional response within us. Although it is possible to have a positive prejudice, research investigating the nature of prejudice has often focused on the *negative* feelings toward individuals based on their group membership.

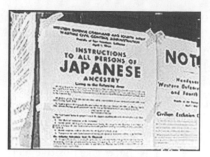

FIGURE 11.9 *In 1942, all U.S. citizens of Japanese ancestry were forced to leave their homes and possessions and were placed in relocation camps throughout the United States for more than two years. Many lost everything they owned. Courtesy of yotophoto.com.*

The behavioral component of an attitude refers to how these preexisting ideas guide our actions. The behavioral manifestation of prejudice is known as discrimination. **Discrimination** refers to the unfair treatment of people based on their group membership. Two forms of discrimination you are probably familiar with are racism and sexism. Whereas **racism** usually refers to the unfair treatment of someone based on his or her membership in a racial group, **sexism** refers to the unfair or unethical treatment of someone because of his or her sex.

Finally, the cognitive component refers to the logic, thoughts, or rationale associated with our attitude. With prejudice, the cognitive component is what we refer to as a stereotype. A **stereotype** is a generalization about someone based on his or her group membership. We automatically assume that people have certain attributes simply because they are members of a particular group.

Prejudice in the World Today

When people think of the topic of prejudice, they are quick to think of racial prejudice. However, social psychologists do not limit their study of prejudice simply to the topics of race or sex. Anything can serve as the basis of prejudice—religion, political affiliation, age, and even hair color. But social psychologists are particularly interested in racial prejudice and sexual prejudice because they are often so blatant and cause so much harm within our society.

Social psychologists suggest that although outright acts of prejudice and discrimination have generally decreased in society, prejudice and discrimination still continue to widely exist. Some psychologists even suggest that general levels of prejudice associated with race and sex have remained relatively unchanged. However, they have become more covert and hidden. People often hide their prejudices in social situations to avoid being called a racist or a sexist, but their prejudices are readily revealed when social identification is no longer a threat (Dovidio & Gaertner, 1996). Social psychologists refer to covert prejudice tied to one's race and sex as **modern racism** and **modern sexism**.

Changing Our Attitudes and Reducing Prejudice

FIGURE 11.10 *Some people will assume many things about this woman on the basis of her clothing alone. Do you? Courtesy of yotophoto.com.*

As discussed previously, social psychologists suggest that attitudes can be broken into their components. Since prejudice is an attitude, each component represents a path for changing our attitude and managing our prejudices.

Since attitudes are shaped by our experiences, they can also be changed by new experiences. For example, what if we generally feel negatively toward going to school, but one semester have a great time in a particular class? Our attitude will probably be changed via the emotional or affective route. What if we talk to a counselor on campus and she makes us realize that those who earn a college degree make 25% more money each year than those who do not have a degree? Our attitude might be changed via the cognitive route; the purpose of school now makes sense. Of course, the stronger our attitudes are, the stronger the experiences will need to be to change them.

Cognitive Dissonance Theory

We have looked at how our attitudes can be changed through both the cognitive route and the emotional route, but how can attitudes be shaped via the behavioral route? Although common sense suggests that behavior is a product of attitude, social psychologist Leon Festinger proposed the opposite. Festinger proposed that attitude can be a product of one's behavior. In other words, the behaviors in which we engage can shape and mold our attitudes.

Festinger (1957) proposed that one's actions must be consistent with one's attitudes. More specifically, if we engage in behaviors that are opposite of what we believe, Festinger suggested that a sense of psychological discomfort arises, which he called cognitive dissonance. The **cognitive dissonance theory** states that this feeling of psychological discomfort motivates us to take some form of action to reduce the state of discomfort (Aronson, 1998). How is this done? If we cannot change our actions, the only alternative is to change our attitude.

According to Festinger, attitude change can occur when people engage in behaviors that are opposite their current attitudes and beliefs. This might seem a bit backward, but according to this theory, our attitudes are often a result of behavior, and not the other way around. For example, imagine that you have always wanted a fancy BMW, but instead you bought a more economical Toyota. The feeling of psychological tension that might result because you did something opposite your previous beliefs might motivate you to focus more readily on all the positive characteristics that your new Toyota has over a BMW. Over time you would most likely develop a much more favorable impression of Toyotas than you ever had before.

On a similar note, according to this theory, if you want to have a positive attitude toward school, make sure you attend every class. If you want to change your feelings of lost love for an ex-boyfriend or ex-girlfriend, stop doing the little things that you currently do for him or her. According to this theory, this "love" that we might still feel for an ex might not stem so much from what he or she does for us, but rather what we do for him or her.

Reducing Our Prejudices

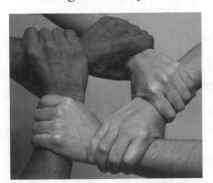

FIGURE 11.11 *Does the simple act of having contact with individuals from different groups reduce prejudice?*

Since prejudice is an attitude, the same paths to change attitudes can be used to reduce prejudice as well. If you want to change your own prejudices, take the opportunity to hang out with people toward whom you are prejudiced and be sure to look for information that disconfirms your stereotypes. The **contact hypothesis** proposes that levels of prejudice are reduced as people from different groups interact with one another. Contact with others gives us the opportunity and the knowledge to challenge the logic and accuracy of our preexisting ideas. It also allows new, positive emotional experiences to arise and replace past, negative experiences that contribute to our prejudices.

Other research has shown that certain conditions must exist in order for our prejudices to be reduced. These conditions include equal status among individuals, multiple contacts, intimate contact, and working toward a common goal (Allport, 1954; Amir, 1969, 1976; Sherif, 1966; Wilder, 1984). If these conditions are not present, contact among individuals from different groups can actually lead to the strengthening of a prejudice. How could lack of these conditions increase prejudice? Remember, our social cognitions and perceptions are not always perfect. We often tend to see the world as we want to see it or are conditioned to see it. We like to believe that we are correct in our assumptions about the world and often choose to focus on certain aspects of a person or situation that confirm our already-existing beliefs. The tendency to ignore information that disconfirms our existing belief and focus on information that supports our existing beliefs is known as the **confirmation bias** (Jones, Schultz-Hardt, Frey, & Thelan, 2001).

Now that we have considered how our thoughts are shaped by the social environment, let us now turn to a few topics and areas of research within social psychology that address very specific and direct ways in which our behavior is influenced by those around us.

How the Presence of Others Affects Specific Aspects of Our Behavior

FIGURE 11.12 *Can social factors help explain the abuse that occurred at Abu Ghraib prison?*

In April 2004, images of American soldiers abusing Iraqi prisoners in the Abu Ghraib prison plastered our television sets, our newspapers, and our magazines. No doubt the images were disturbing. Iraqi war prisoners were photographed naked while they were being humiliated and physically abused. In a 53-page report obtained by the *New Yorker*, Major General Antonio M. Taguba described some of the horrific events that had occurred, which included breaking chemical lights and pouring the phosphoric liquid on detainees, beating detainees with a broom handle, threatening male detainees with rape, sodomizing a detainee with a chemical light and a broom stick, using military working dogs to frighten and intimidate detainees, and allowing a guard dog to bite a detainee. The situation was particularly disturbing for Americans who perceived the U.S. military as representing morality and righteousness. Many were baffled and asked how such a horrible thing could have happened.

We must remember that social psychology suggests that the social situation can and often does have a very powerful effect on the behavior of individuals. Not only is it able to bring out the very best in human nature, but it also has the power to bring out the very worst. Social psychologists interested in the power of social influence have spent much time studying the particular behaviors of obedience, compliance, and conformity. The research on these behaviors demonstrates three ways in which our behavior is directly changed by the presence of others around us. It might also help explain how this horrible event could have occurred.

Obedience

In the 1960s, researcher Stanley Milgram conducted a now-famous experiment investigating the power of social influence. He placed an ad in a local newspaper in an attempt to recruit people for what was supposed to be a psychological test on memory. However, the true topic of the experiment was

FIGURE 11.13 *Stanley Milgram's shock generator.*

obedience—a change in behavior by an individual that stems from receiving a direct command from a person in a position of authority. Milgram was interested to see what social factors influence the extent to which people will obey such commands. More specifically, he was interested in the social factors that would lead others to carry out a behavior that would directly harm another person.

The volunteer subjects entered a small room and were seated at a desk. On the desk was a small machine that they were told was an electrical shock generator. The subjects were then told by the researcher in a white lab coat that they were part of a memory experiment. They were informed that it was their job to serve as the "teacher" and to read part of a list of words over a microphone to a person serving as a subject in the next room. The subject was to indicate which word came next in the sequence by pressing a particular button. Each time the person answered incorrectly, the teacher was required to administer an electrical shock to the subject. With each successive wrong answer, the intensity of the shock was to be increased.

In reality, there was no one in the other room actually receiving electrical shocks. Instead, a confederate of the experiment sat in the next room and played tapes of a man screaming in pain as if he were actually receiving electrical shocks. Yet the subject serving as the teacher was led to believe that there was indeed someone in the next room receiving the shocks that he was delivering.

Milgram wanted to see how far the subjects who were acting as teachers would progress in the level of shock they would administer if an authority figure told them to do so. What surprised him and others in the field of psychology was that an astonishing 65% of the participants delivered a potentially lethal shock to the person they believed was in the next room (Milgram, 1963). This classic experiment illustrated how easily good people could be influenced by the social situation to do truly horrible things. Milgram identified the following as some of the factors affecting levels of obedience:

♦ Proximity of the experimenter—participants displayed higher levels of obedience if the experimenter in charge of the study was in the same room and physically close.

♦ Legitimacy of the authority figure—participants displayed higher levels of obedience when they perceived the authority figure as legitimate.

♦ Proximity of the victim—participants displayed higher levels of obedience if the victim was physically or emotionally distant from them.

♦ Assumption of responsibility—participants were much more obedient when they felt that somebody else would assume responsibility for their actions. (Milgram, 1974)

It is important to keep in mind that the people who signed up for the experiment were not that different from you or me. You probably believe that you would be one of the strong-willed people who would simply walk out of the experiment. This further demonstrates the fundamental-attribution error discussed previously. But the results certainly suggest otherwise. The key idea is that various situational factors can combine to bring out the very worst in basically good people.

Explore
the use of deception in research
in Chapter 2, p. 52

No doubt, the information that Milgram's experiment revealed about the nature of obedience was abundant and contributed much to the field of social psychology. However, the ethical nature of this experiment has been called into question because of the use of deception and the extreme distress caused to the participants of the study.

Perhaps Milgram's experiment can help us better understand some of the most atrocious acts of inhumanity that have been witnessed throughout history. Perhaps his classic experiment can help us understand what happened in the Abu Ghraib prison as well. Well-known Stanford psychologist Philip Zimbardo (2007) recently published a book called *The Lucifer Effect*, which discusses how these principles can be readily applied to the situation at Abu Ghraib and more generally how some situations bring out the worst in all of us.

Compliance

Whereas obedience involves changing our behavior because of an authority figure's command, **compliance** refers to a change in our behavior because someone makes a *request* of us. Someone is simply asking us to do something, but the person isn't necessarily in a position of authority.

Just as there are specific social factors that increase levels of obedience, levels of compliance can also be increased by manipulating the social situation. The next time you visit a car dealership, see if you can spot some of these practices in action.

When individuals have previously yielded to a small request, they are significantly more likely to yield to a larger subsequent request. This is known as the **foot-in-the-door approach**. For example, if I was selling magazine subscriptions, I would be more likely to be able to sell you 10 subscriptions if I had convinced you to buy even a single subscription earlier in the year. On the other hand, when we are approached with a large request that we decline, we are subsequently more likely to yield to a smaller request. Using the same example, if I was to ask you to buy 10 magazine subscriptions and you turned me down, I would be much more likely to get you to buy just 1 than if I had made an initial request for you to buy just 1. We often feel guilty and concede to the small request, which might have been the person's goal from the very beginning (Freedman & Fraser, 1966). This is known as the **door-in-the-face approach**. Both of these techniques are frequently used to increase the likelihood that people will oblige a request. So the next time somebody calls you and tries to get you to subscribe to the daily newspaper, watch out, because the individual's next question after you turn him or her down might be, "Well, how about just the Sunday edition?"

Conformity

> The reward of conformity is that everyone likes you except yourself.
>
> —Rita Mae Brown

At times we modify how we act, what we do, or how we look simply because of the way the people around us are behaving. Even when no one is commanding us to do something and no requests are being made of us, there are times when we change our behavior out of a desire to fit in with the group. This change of behavior is known as **conformity**—a change in behavior simply designed to match the behavior of others around us.

Researcher Soloman Asch was one of the first to experimentally attempt to answer the question as to why people conform. In his now-famous "line study," subjects were shown a line and asked to pick from a group of three lines which line most closely matched the length of the line that they were shown. The experiment was conducted in a group setting, with other confederates of the experiment present. Asch was interested to see how often an individual would go along with the group and report an obviously incorrect answer, simply to match the responses of the other members of the group. Although 100% of the subjects chose the correct line when they were in the room alone, an overwhelming 75% of the respondents conformed to the group's response at least once out of 12 trials when they were in the presence of others. Only 25% of the respondents remained steadfast and reported their own correct response throughout each trial, ignoring the responses of the other group members. The results indicated that people conformed to the group about one-third of the time when an obviously incorrect response was given (Asch, 1951). The subjects would rather be wrong than go against the group.

Why would the subjects go along with the group's obviously wrong answer? Social psychologists suggest that one of the main reasons people often go along with the group and push aside their own ideas is simply due to the desire to fit in. **Normative conformity** is a change in our behavior that is caused by the desire to belong to and to meet the standards of a group. When we feel pressured to buy a certain kind of jeans or dress in such a way as to fit in with our peers, we are engaging in normative conformity. For example, your teacher might pose a question to the class of which you know the answer. However, you choose not to offer your answer because no other students are raising their hands. When you question the accuracy of your answer and it subsequently influences your behavior, you are engaging in normative conformity. Normative conformity is especially prevalent in highly cohesive groups, where group unanimity is critical. Often the motivating factor for why we engage in normative conformity is to avoid the sense of social rejection that comes from standing out from the group (Deutsch & Gerard, 1955).

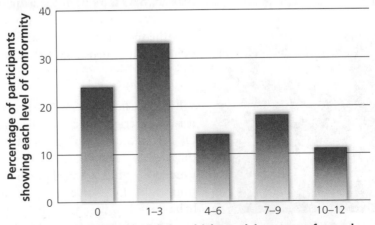

FIGURE 11.14 *Results of the Asch line judgment study.*

FIGURE 11.15 *Fashionable back tattoos . . . normative conformity?*

Normative conformity is the result of the social norms established within a particular group. **Social norms** are appropriate behaviors agreed upon within a group. There are many subtle examples of social norms all around us. Have you ever noticed how people act when they walk into a crowded elevator? They quietly press the button, face the door, and refrain from looking or speaking. They are abiding by social norms. Have you ever looked at pictures of your parents when they were your age and laughed at the clothes they were wearing? You can see how social norms can and do change over time.

If you have ever traveled or spent time in another country, you no doubt have seen how social norms can dramatically differ as a function of culture. One great example of how cultures differ is with regard to interpersonal distance or personal space. At what distance do you begin to feel uncomfortable when someone is standing next to you or talking to you? On a recent flight I took while in the country of Turkey, I had the pleasure of sitting between two men engaged in a lengthy conversation. They leaned over to talk to each other as if I wasn't sitting in the seat between them. Because my idea of personal space was much different, I felt quite awkward the whole time, while they probably thought nothing of the situation.

There are also circumstances when we go along with the behavior of others not because of our desire to gain the group's acceptance, but because we aren't quite sure how to act or respond in a particular situation. In this case, we are likely to act in accordance with the group due to **informational social influence**—going along with the group because we assume that the group has knowledge that we personally lack. When we encounter an ambiguous situation in which we are not quite sure of the right decision, we look to others as a source of information and mimic their behavior. In other words, we assume that two heads are better than one and automatically believe that the group must know more than we do. This is further facilitated when the person trusts the group's judgment and/or lacks confidence in his or her own judgments.

Prosocial Behavior

FIGURE 11.16 *Helping those in need. Why do we do it?*

Although we have been focusing on some of the negative aspects of how our behavior is shaped by those around us, social psychology is also interested in how the social environment influences human behaviors that are positive and benefit others. **Prosocial behavior** is any behavior intended to help or benefit another.

Why do we help others? Is it because we are inherently good people? Perhaps it is to experience the good feeling that lending a helping hand brings to us. Or is it because helping others when they need it increases the likelihood that we can cash in the favor when we need help from that same person sometime in the future? Social psychologists have been trying to answer the question as to why people sacrifice their time, money, and energy to engage in behaviors that often have little or no immediate benefit to themselves. Social psychologists are interested in the social factors that lead to people helping others in need.

Factors Influencing Prosocial Behavior

Imagine that you arrive home, your house is burning down, and there are people trapped inside. Who are you more likely to run into the house to save? Would it matter if the individual was a friend versus a stranger, young versus elderly? Would it matter if the individual was a millionaire, and by saving his or her life, you would be offered a huge reward? In short, there are a variety of reasons and social factors that influence who and why we help.

Sociobiologists who emphasize evolutionary factors that contribute to the development of social behaviors take the stance that prosocial behavior can be explained by the benefits we perceive we will receive when we help others. According to the **social norm of reciprocity**, helping others in a time of need increases the likelihood that they will help us in the future when we are in need. We increase our chances of survival by being able to "cash in" these favors in the future. Furthermore, the **theory of kin selection** suggests that we are more likely to help blood relatives because helping them increases the likelihood that our own genes will make it to the next generation (Burnstein, Crandall, & Kitayama, 1994).

Social psychologists suggest that there are other reasons why people help. More specifically, there are particular social situations that increase the likelihood of our lending a helping hand. In terms of predicting helping behavior, personality tells only part of the story. As with the behaviors we have already studied in this chapter, the particularities of the social situation can be used to predict the likelihood of helping. Two major theories have been used to explain the phenomenon of prosocial behavior.

The first of these theories is the **exchange model** of prosocial behavior, which suggests that the likelihood of helping others is a function of the costs of helping. In short, helping others is motivated by maximizing benefits and minimizing costs. If the cost of offering assistance is large, people are less likely to engage in prosocial behavior. However, if costs are small and the potential benefits are large, then there is an increased likelihood that people will help.

Anytime we offer a helping hand, there is an inherent cost we must pay. The cost might be money or some other material possession or it may simply be our time, energy, and effort. But we always receive something when we help others. Sometimes in helping others we are truly helping ourselves. Sometimes helping others simply makes us feel good about ourselves, giving us a "helper's high."

The exchange model tells only part of the story as well. People often engage in prosocial behavior when there is little to be personally gained. Helping behavior that is not motivated by self-interest and that often incurs significant costs to the helper is what social psychologists refer to as **altruism**. The empathy-altruism theory has been widely used to explain this apparent phenomenon (Batson, 1991). The **empathy-altruism theory** suggests that our ability to experience the emotions and feelings of another is the vital ingredient for predicting the likelihood of people offering assistance when the situation is highly demanding of time, energy, or other resources. When we feel

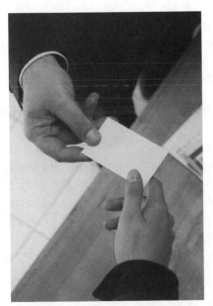

FIGURE 11.17 *Sometimes we help others because we expect them to help us when we are in need.*

empathy for someone, we are more likely to help, regardless of the cost. If we can relate to the other person's pain and distress, we will offer assistance. Perhaps the motivation is to reduce our own personal distress.

Why People Don't Help

To fully understand the nature of prosocial behavior, it is also important for us to understand the reasons why people *do not* help. We have already seen that people are less likely to help when the costs of helping outweigh the rewards, especially if there is no feeling of empathy. But social psychologists have also identified other social circumstances that decrease the likelihood that individuals will receive a helping hand when they are in need.

In one of the most famous case studies in all of social psychology that occurred in the 1960s, a woman by the name of Kitty Genovese was walking home one night after work in New York City. As the story goes, she was attacked and dragged into an alley between two apartment buildings. She screamed for help as she attempted to fight off the assailant, but to no avail. Kitty Genovese was brutally murdered.

The interesting part of the story is what happened when the police found her body. As they went around to the various apartments on each side of the alley and asked if anyone had heard her cries for help, no fewer than 38 people said they had heard her screaming. What was fascinating (as well as quite disturbing) was that not one single person went to her aid. Only one person even made the effort to pick up the telephone and call the police.

Now it would be easy to dismiss the actions (or lack thereof) of all 38 people who heard her cries for help as being the result of selfish people with a severe lack of any basic sense of humanity, but what are the odds that all 38 people who heard her cry for help fit into this category? If we made this assumption, we might be guilty of making the fundamental attribution error, as discussed earlier in this chapter. Perhaps social psychology can provide some alternative explanations of this terrible occurrence. Can you guess what the most frequent response from the 38 witnesses was when the police asked why they didn't help the victim? As you might have guessed, most people responded that they thought someone else would do it!

This common misconception is what social psychologists call the **diffusion of responsibility theory**. This theory states that the likelihood that any one individual will step forward to offer assistance decreases as the number of people present becomes greater in a situation in which help is required. The main reason is that the responsibility to help becomes spread out, or "diffused," among all those present as everyone assumes that someone else will step up to offer the needed assistance. Whereas common sense suggests that we would be better off being in a crowded room if an emergency arose, the evidence collected that supports the diffusion of responsibility theory suggests we would be much better off if there was only one other person in the room.

FIGURE 11.18 *Kitty Genovese, a victim of the diffusion of responsibility?*

Other research has shown that people do not help because they do not know the proper from of assistance, they don't notice the event, or they don't perceive

FIGURE 11.19 *The scene of the Kitty Genovese murder.*

the event as an emergency (Latane & Darley, 1968). In an ambiguous situation, we often look to others as a source of information. The **bystander effect** states that in an emergency situation, if no one else around us perceives the event as an emergency, then we, too, are likely to perceive the event in the same manner and ultimately not offer assistance to the person in need. This is yet another way in which the social situation can influence our behavior and cause us to act in a particular way that is inconsistent with whom we may think we are.

Recent research has suggested that some of the facts of the Kitty Genovese story have been exaggerated or distorted. The journal *American Psychologist* recently published an analysis of this case and showed that it was more likely closer to a dozen people who heard her cry for help but did nothing (Manning, Levine, & Collins, 2007). Nonetheless, this incident spurred a plethora of research into understanding social situations that decrease the likelihood that people will fail to help those around them who are in need.

Aggression

Let us now turn our attention to human behavior at its very worst. Psychologists define **aggression** as any behavior intended to cause either physical or emotional harm to another individual. Of course, aggression can take many forms—hostile words, a punch thrown, or intentionally cutting someone off on the freeway. But what is the difference? Aggression can be usefully separated into two subtypes: instrumental and hostile (Berkowitz, 1993).

Types of Aggression

Although we typically think of aggression as associated with the emotion of anger, there are behaviors that social psychologists consider acts of aggression that do not involve anger. Can you think of a behavior intended to hurt someone but in which there are no negative feelings directed toward the target? What about a football player tackling someone on the opposite team? How about a soldier firing upon an unknown enemy on the battlefield? These qualify as acts of aggression in that they are intentional acts designed to cause harm. The intent to cause physical harm (if not death) is certainly present in these situations. However, it is possible that in each situation, the emotions of hatred or anger are not present. These acts can be classified as **instrumental aggression**, in which there is an intention to cause harm to another person as a means of achieving a goal or to obtain something of value.

FIGURE 11.20 *Aggression—wanting to hurt someone else. Courtesy of Bill Aron/PhotoEdit, Inc.*

At other times, people desire to cause emotional or physical pain to another person and the action does involve anger or hostility. Aggressive acts associated with feelings of anger are often referred to as **hostile aggression** or **emotional aggression**. Has someone ever provoked you in such a way that it resulted in a fistfight? Have you ever spread a nasty rumor about someone you didn't like? Have you ever gotten very angry at someone while driving and told the other driver that he or she was "number one" with a certain finger in the air? If so, your intent was most likely to get the fleeting satisfaction of causing someone else pain or discomfort. Terrible isn't it?

Almost all species of animals exhibit some form of aggressive behavior. Aggressive behavior serves an important evolutionary function. In animals, the most physically dominant male of the group is usually the most aggressive and has an increased likelihood of passing on his genes by scaring off other potential suitors and mating with available females. The most aggressive male may also have the most access to food and other resources through his ability to intimidate others in the group.

Research has identified a variety of biological factors related to aggression. Some research has suggested a positive correlation between blood levels of testosterone and acts of physical aggression (Boyd, 2000). Males of most species are more affected by levels of testosterone, and in almost all cultures in the world, a majority of the acts of physical violence are committed by males. Low levels of the neurotransmitters serotonin and GABA have also been linked to aggression (Bernhardt, 1997).

Although our aggressive tendencies may have their roots in our primitive past, social psychologists are interested in identifying situational and social factors that increase the likelihood of bringing out the "inner beast" inside all of us. It is easy to understand why individuals might intentionally hurt someone else if they personally have something large to gain, but social psychologists are particularly interested in the situational factors that lead people to "lose their cool" and lash out in anger. Let's take a look at some of these social factors.

Social Learning Theory

FIGURE 11.21 *Modeling an aggressive behavior?*

Social learning theory suggests that aggression is a learned product of our environment. More specifically, our behavior is shaped by reinforcement and punishment, as well as by observing the behavior of others. **Modeling** involves the imitation of the behavior of others. When children observe someone they admire acting aggressively, they are more likely to imitate the aggressive behavior than if there is a model portraying a nonaggressive behavior. When children are reinforced or rewarded for engaging in aggressive behavior, the likelihood that they will repeat the behavior in the future increases.

In the famous Bobo doll experiment, conducted by Bandura, Ross, and Ross (1961), children either watched an adult play aggressively with a blow-up Bobo doll (kicking and hitting it with a hammer) and other toys or watched an adult play nonaggressively with the Bobo doll and other toys. Afterward, children were placed in a room with similar toys, and the researchers observed how they played. As you might expect, children who saw the adult play roughly with the Bobo doll were significantly more likely to imitate those behaviors and kick and punch the doll than those who witnessed an adult play nicely with the doll. Maybe the reason that the apple doesn't fall far from the tree is due to more than just our genes. Recent research suggests that the television programs we watch, the movies we see, and the video games that our children play can and do increase the likelihood of aggressive behavior (Anderson & Bushman, 2001; Johnson, Cohen, Smailes, Kasen, & Brooks, 2002).

Discomfort

FIGURE 11.22 *Pain or discomfort increases the likelihood of aggression.*

Social psychologists have shown that any form of physical or emotional discomfort increases the likelihood that we might act aggressively. Have you ever noticed how nasty you can be toward others when you are in a bad mood? Ever stubbed your toe and when someone asks if you are all right, you bark back at him or her with a nasty reaction? Ever notice how irritable you can be after a long day of work, when you are tired and exhausted?

Even something as simple as a change in the weather can create a situation in which we are more likely to aggress. Longitudinal studies of crime records have shown that a positive correlation exists between the amount of violent crime (assault, murders, etc.) and an increase in temperature and humidity (Anderson, Bushman, & Groom, 1997). Generally speaking, the more unpleasant the situation in which we find ourselves, the more prone we are to engage in behaviors intended to hurt others.

Alcohol

The presence and consumption of alcohol have been shown to be positively correlated with the increased occurrence of aggression (Bachman & Peralta, 2002; Leonard & Quigley, 1999). Numerous studies have shown that those under the influence of alcohol are significantly more likely to engage in acts involving physical aggression such as assault, rape, and homicide (Desmond, 1987; White, 1997). Alcohol serves as a disinhibitor and physiologically decreases our ability to pull the "emergency brake" when we are angry or upset.

Interpersonal Attraction: Why Do We Like the People We Do?

Life without love is like a tree without blossoms or fruit.

—Kahlil Gibran

John Dunn said that no man is an island. It is also said that our friends are the family that we choose for ourselves. Without friends and family, our lives might be meaningless and no doubt very lonely. We rely on the people in our lives for love, support, and companionship. They are the people upon whom we lean when times are difficult. They are also the people to whom who we disclose our most cherished secrets and with whom we rejoice when we accomplish great things.

Why is it that we have the friends we do? Why is it that we seem to like some people more than others? Why is it that we are attracted to and want to date certain types, but prefer to remain simply friends with others?

FIGURE 11.23 *Friends are the family we choose for ourselves.*

Research on this topic has focused on the determinants of interpersonal attraction. Social psychologists have identified a couple of key factors that lead to both the positive feeling we have for others and the likelihood that a relationship will subsequently develop. These determinants include proximity, familiarity, similarity, reciprocal liking, and physical attractiveness.

Proximity and Familiarity

Research investigating **proximity** suggests that we are most likely to develop positive feelings toward people we see the most and with whom we interact the most. For example, our friends are most likely the people with whom we work, people we meet at school, or often mutual friends (Berscheid & Reiss, 1998). If we do not have the opportunity to interact with someone, it is nearly impossible for any type of relationship to develop.

But why is it that the people with whom we coincidentally interact the most are the ones who later become the people with whom we voluntarily and freely choose to spend our time? According to the **mere exposure effect**, repeated exposure to a stimulus increases our attraction and positive feelings toward that stimulus (Zajonc, 1968). In other words, proximity breeds **familiarity**, or a sense that one knows someone else. Perhaps simply being in the presence of someone affords us the opportunity to see all of his or her positive qualities.

For a quick example of how familiarity breeds liking, think of the people you like the most in your psychology class. I would venture to guess that it is the people who sit close to you and with whom you have a chance to interact. So in your next class, be sure to pick the seat next to someone you'd really like to get to know. I bet before reading this chapter you didn't think that social psychology could improve your dating life.

Similarity

FIGURE 11.24 *Similarity is one factor that leads people to have positive feelings toward each other. Courtesy of Bill Aron/PhotoEdit, Inc.*

We are also more likely to develop positive feelings for people who are similar to us. People who share our values, attitudes, and beliefs seem to be more attractive to us. Past research has indicated that we like to establish relationships and spend time with people who enjoy doing the same things that we do and who hold the same priorities and beliefs (Chen & Kenrick, 2002). Perhaps they provide a sense of personal validation.

If you believe that being physically fit is important, it is likely that you like to spend time with people who are health conscious as well. If you are an avid reader, you probably like people with whom you can discuss the latest best seller. If you are a big sports fan, you probably enjoy spending time with others who are knowledgeable about the local baseball team and with whom you can talk sports.

On the opposite side of the coin, people who are passionate about things that we could care less about are not the people we enjoy being around. Ever notice how difficult it is to hold a conversation with someone with whom you share no common interests? There's simply nothing to talk about.

But what about the old adage "opposites attract"? Isn't there any truth to support the idea that people who are different from us are the people we find attractive? Most research supports the idea that it is similarity that is most influential in determining whether two people will feel positively toward each other. Some past research suggests that opposites can attract and that **complementarity** can have an effect. More specifically, we like people who are different from us if they possess qualities that we personally lack but admire. We are also attracted to people who serve to complete what we perceive as missing in ourselves. Nonetheless, most research strongly suggests that what we have in common is much more powerful than what is different between two people.

Reciprocal Liking

In Dale Carnegie's best-selling book *How to Win Friends and Influence People*, one of his recommendations in making a positive impression on people is to "lavish praise and compliments" (1936). In other words, if you want people to like you, make sure that you like other people, and certainly don't forget to tell them how great they are. We feel positively toward people who pay us compliments and say nice things about us. In short, we like people who like us (Berscheid & Reis, 1998). The idea that we are more likely to have positive feelings for those that we know have positive feelings for us is known as **reciprocal liking**.

Let's look at an example. Imagine that you are at a party and you meet an individual named Bob. Over the course of the evening, you and Bob discuss a mutual friend named Sue. At the end of the evening, you shake Bob's hand, tell him it was nice to meet him, and wish him a good evening. When you arrive at work on Monday, you run into Sue in the hall, and she says to you, "Hey, I heard you met Bob this weekend. He said he had a great time talking with you, enjoyed your company, and mentioned that he hopes he gets the chance to enjoy your company some time in the future." Now the next time you run into Bob, how do you think you'll feel about Bob? Why, you'll like Bob, of course. Why do you like him? Well, Bob likes you. In short, we seem to feel positively about people who make us feel good about ourselves. Almost all of us enjoy a compliment and having people notice our positive qualities.

Physical Attractiveness

Of all the determinants that predict the likelihood of having positive feelings for someone, the most influential by far is the person's physical appearance. As shallow as it may seem, we are more likely to have positive feelings for someone whom we perceive as being good-looking. Some research has indicated that physical attractiveness is somewhat more important for men, but other studies have shown that there seems to be little gender difference between women and men with regard to the importance of this factor, especially during the initial stages of liking (Regan & Berscheid, 1999; Zebrowitz, Hall, Murphy, & Rhodes, 2002).

We often perceive that physically attractive people also have a number of other positive characteristics. This tendency to believe that a person must have other positive characteristics when we perceive they have a certain positive trait is known as the **halo effect**. In this case, we have a tendency to associate good looks with high social skills, health, independence, and even intelligence (Dion, Berscheid, & Walster, 1972; Feingold, 1992). Perhaps all the money that people spend on makeup, gym memberships, fashionable clothes, and plastic surgery is for a valid reason.

FIGURE 11.25 *Which of the determinants of interpersonal attraction draw these two famous people together? Physical attractiveness.*

Research has also attempted to answer the question of whether there are universal, cross-cultural standards of beauty. Others suggest that one's perception of beauty is more consistent with the old adage "beauty is in the eye of the beholder." In other words, there are differences in what individuals perceive as being physically attractive. It seems that there is evidence on both sides.

A number of characteristics are universally recognized as being associated with physical attractiveness. These include a youthful appearance, a smile, and symmetry of the face (Chen, Shaffer, & Wu, 1997). For men, attractive facial features include large eyes, prominent cheekbones, and a large chin. For women, a small nose, large eyes, narrow cheeks, and high eyebrows seem to be universally attractive (Cunningham, Barbee, & Pike, 1990). Research suggests that all these characteristics might be associated with reproductive health and therefore serve as an explanation as to why they are important to us, especially in romantic relationships.

However, you can probably give a number of examples of physical attractiveness being shaped by unique, individual perceptions. Would you be attracted to your girlfriend if she had elongated earlobes? Would your boyfriend seem as attractive to you if he wore a skirt? Would members of other cultures think it odd for women to walk around on elevated platforms called "high heels"? In short, a plethora of cultural differences regarding physical attractiveness exist around the world and are a testament to the fact that we certainly don't all perceive what is beautiful as being exactly the same thing.

Some researchers are concerned that in cultures such as the United Sates the media are promoting a standard of beauty that is dangerous, unhealthy, and simply unattainable for most. Take, for instance, the ideal form of the female body, which is often portrayed as excessively thin. Whereas at one point in recent history the ideal form for the female body was curvaceous and robust, today the ideal female form as promoted by magazine advertisements and other forms of media is one that borders on levels of self-starvation. There are concerns that such ideals promote unsafe eating practices and behaviors (anorexia and bulimia) for women in their attempt to attain this ideal body type.

Theories of Love

How about the especially strong feeling we develop for those select few people throughout our lives? What factors contribute to feelings of love? Perhaps it is best if we begin by defining what we mean by that word.

In the English language, the word "love" is used quite liberally. But when we say, "I love you, Mom," we mean something entirely different than when we say we are "in love" with someone. We even use the word to describe how we feel about our favorite food: "I love a good steak every once in awhile." Although the word is identical, the meaning, feeling, and implications are entirely different.

All of the relationships that we have in our life do not fit into the same category. We have different types of feelings and attraction toward our family than we do toward our friends. Our feelings toward people in whom we are romantically interested fit into a different category altogether. There are a variety of ways we can classify the types of love that we have for the people in our lives.

Passionate Love vs. Companionate Love

FIGURE 11.26 *Passionate love is much different from companionate love.*

Passionate love is defined as an intense feeling for another that has a sexual or erotic content. It is accompanied by hope and expectation for the future and involves the idealization of the object of one's affection. Have you ever noticed how, at the beginning of a romantic relationship, the other person seems like the greatest person you have ever met? Perhaps this is because we are only focusing on the individual's most positive qualities. Also, we have the tendency to put our best foot forward at the beginning of a relationship in an attempt to present ourselves in the most favorable light.

Research indicates that passionate love exists in nearly every culture in the world (Jankowiak, 1997). Most likely it is something with which we can all identify. It is the type of love often portrayed in Hollywood movies and in trashy romance novels. The problem is that much research indicates that romantic love tends to diminish over time. Soon enough the awestruck "he can finish my sentences" adorations turn into annoyed "why does he keep interrupting me?" gripes. At times such love is not reciprocated by the target of our affection, making us feel empty, sad, and upset. It is a volatile love to say the least, but perhaps it lays the path and groundwork for development of another type of love that keeps couples together indefinitely.

FIGURE 11.27 *Companionate love is the type of love we feel for a friend.*

Companionate love is a positive feeling and attraction to someone that is characterized by feelings of trust, concern, warmth, and friendship. Most of our relationships fit into this category. Whereas romantic love seems prone to diminish over the course of time, companionate love seems more steadfast and enduring. And whereas romantic love is often a roller coaster ride with the corresponding highs, lows, and gut-wrenching turns, most cases of companionate love follow a steadily increasing trend. Companionate love has its basis in feelings of admiration and respect. Research indicates that relationships based on companionate love are the ones from which people derive the most satisfaction (Kiraly, 2000).

Sternberg's Triangular Theory of Love

Robert Sternberg (1988a) proposed yet another theory of love—the triangular theory of love. Sternberg believes that there are not just two kinds of love, but rather seven. Sternberg's **triangular theory of love** suggests that seven kinds of love can be derived from the varying combination of three main ingredients: passion, intimacy, and commitment. **Passion** involves sexual desire and physiological arousal. **Intimacy** involves feelings of closeness. **Commitment** involves investments in the future of the relationship. The combination of these main ingredients yields seven types of love:

♦ Intimacy: simply liking someone but with no passion or sense of commitment for the future (e.g., a simple friendship)

♦ Fatuous love: feeling passion toward someone and being committed to that person but lacking intimacy

♦ Infatuation: associated with strong feelings of passion for someone but with no intimacy or commitment

♦ Empty love: simply being committed to someone but without any feeling of passion or intimacy (e.g., an empty and unfulfilling marriage)

♦ Romantic love: feeling strong passion for someone and feeling close to him or her (intimacy) but with no commitment for the future

♦ Companionate love: the feeling and experience of intimacy and commitment toward the relationship but lacking a sense of passion

♦ Consummate love: love that contains passion, intimacy, and commitment (e.g., the perfect, ideal, and all-encompassing love, or perhaps the love we have for the person we want to marry)

Group Processes

Group behavior includes the many ways our behavior is influenced when individuals are members of a specified group. A **group** is defined as two or more people who interact and are interdependent upon one another. **Interdependence** means that the behaviors of each group member influence and affect the others in a tangible way.

Just being at the same place at the same time as others does not qualify as a group. Let us now look at some of the ways our behavior is changed when we are a member of an identifiable group.

Group Decisions

When you have an important decision to make, don't you often go to other people for advice? Isn't your decision ultimately shaped by their input and insight? In most societies, it is rare that important decisions are made by an individual. Instead, critical decisions are usually made by a panel of individuals or a defined group. For example, the Supreme Court of the United States comprises nine judges. Their job is to make some of the most important decisions within our society. Large companies often have a board of corporate executives in charge of making important decisions. In fact, the important decisions made at your college are most likely made by committees composed of individuals you see every day.

Regardless of the environment or the particular situation, decision making is a dynamic process. Let us look at some of the particular social environments that lead to both good and bad decision making in a group setting.

Group decisions are usually superior to decisions made by individuals for a variety of reasons. When making an important decision, the group benefits from the accumulated knowledge of each group member. Ideally, each member of the group contributes unique information that is relevant to the problem, ultimately resulting in a superior decision. Furthermore, groups typically

FIGURE 11.28 *A group decision . . . for better or for worse?*

make better decisions, especially when unique information is shared and the most competent members within the group exert the greatest influence (Schafer & Crichlow, 1996).

However, groups do not always make decisions that are superior to those made by individuals. Group decisions are not impervious to error, and certain situations exist where the specific interactions of the group members lead to poor decisions being made. Any aspect of group interaction that leads to poor decision making is referred to as **process loss** (Steiner, 1972). One type of process loss is groupthink (Janis, 1982). **Groupthink** occurs when members of the group are overly concerned with maintaining group cohesiveness. The emphasis on maintaining good relations and cordiality among members interferes with the group's ability to critically examine the problem. In this situation, critical information is often overlooked, since dissenting opinions that might affect the morale of the group are withheld. The ultimate result is that a less-than-optimal decision is made, often with dire consequences.

They say that hindsight is 20/20, but let's take a look at some important decisions of the recent past and see if some of these factors can be applied. Recall the effects of Hurricane Katrina described at the outset of this chapter. The Federal Emergency Management Association (FEMA), the organization responsible for preparing for national hazards and organizing a response, came under attack for its lack of foresight and action in the days before Hurricane Katrina struck the southern states of Louisiana and Mississippi. Michael D. Brown, the director of FEMA (who ultimately resigned a short time after the disaster), claimed that the destruction that the hurricane brought was "unforeseeable." However, it was later noted that the problems associated with the levy that eventually broke were well documented, but policymakers chose to ignore them.

FIGURE 11.29 *Was the lack of urgency during Hurricane Katrina brought about by similar factors that contribute to groupthink?*

But what was it exactly that made the organization believe that the category five hurricane would not wreak as much havoc and bring about the amount of devastation that it did? Why did the members fail to consider the fact that the levy that broke was designed to withstand a category four hurricane but not a category five? Was Brown, who was reported to be judging horse shows prior to his position in the organization, too unqualified yet too influential in the decision-making process? Some suggested that the lack of organized response by FEMA was due to the nature of a bureaucracy, whereas others contended that important individuals within the organization simply failed to realize the urgency of the situation. Regardless of the reason, a majority of Americans and much of the world felt that the response could have been much, much better.

Were any of the following antecedents or symptoms of groupthink present in FEMA's response to Hurricane Katrina?

♦ A highly cohesive group

♦ Insulation of group members from outside sources

♦ A highly directive leader who makes his wishes known

♦ Lack of a systematic procedure to evaluate both the pros and the cons of the decision

♦ An illusion of invulnerability (Janis, 1982)

Only time will tell if the tremendous loss of life could have been avoided. We are not here to point fingers but to learn from our mistakes so that we do not repeat them in the future. It does seem likely that better decisions could have been made along the way that would have decreased the level of devastation brought about by Hurricane Katrina.

Our Performance on Tasks

A recent survey stated that the average person's greatest fear is having to give a speech in public. Somehow this ranked even higher than death which was third on the list. So, you're telling me that at a funeral, most people would rather be the guy in the coffin than have to stand up and give a eulogy.

—Jerry Seinfeld

To understand how our performance on tasks is affected by the presence of others, consider the case of the moderately famous basketball player Robert Horry. Unless you are a basketball fan, you probably aren't too familiar with the name. But if you are a fan of the NBA team the Sacramento Kings, you no doubt know the name all too well.

In the 2002 playoffs, Horry was playing for the Los Angeles Lakers. During game four of the western conference finals, Horry became a legend for Lakers fans everywhere. With the Kings narrowly winning the game and the final seconds ticking away, Horry scooped up a loose ball that had miraculously bounced his way, calmly set his feet, and shot a three-point basket. The ball went through the hoop as the buzzer sounded, with the Lakers successfully defeating the Sacramento Kings and derailing their chances of winning a world championship. For many players, this would be the shining moment of their careers. For Horry, it was just one of many similar moments throughout his career.

What is of particular interest is that Robert Horry is not one of the greatest basketball players in the league. But his knack for being in the right place at the right time and being cool under pressure earned him the nickname "big shot Rob." He had made many just as important shots throughout his career and would even do so again in the future. Robert seems to thrive in situations where other players get nervous and choke.

FIGURE 11.30 *In 2002, Robert Horry hit a game-winning shot to beat the Sacramento Kings. Social facilitation theory at work?*

On a similar note, have you ever had to give a speech in front of your class or a group of people? Many people admit that public speaking is one of their biggest fears. Why is it that some people are able to be as "cool as a cucumber" the second they step in front of a group of people, whereas for the rest of us, our hands shake, our voice trembles, and we feel as if we might just lose our lunch right then and there. For better or for worse, our behavior is no doubt affected when we know that others are watching us.

Social psychologists have attempted to understand the reasons people seem to have a change in their performance when they are in the presence of other people. Robert Zajonc (1968) proposed that the presence of others results in a state of physiological arousal when we know that we are being watched. For simple, well-learned tasks, our performance is enhanced. This is what Zajonc called the **social-facilitation theory**. Simple things that we already do well, we do even better while in this state of arousal. The presence of others gives us an extra little push.

FIGURE 11.31 *Our performance on tasks changes when we know others are watching us.*

However, for complex tasks that require concentration and skill, our performance is often compromised. We perform things poorly in the presence of other people if we do not know how to do them extremely well. Researchers have proposed reasons as to why the presence of others decreases our performance on some tasks. Two of the explanations include the following:

♦ The **distraction-conflict theory** states that the presence of others diverts our attention from the task at hand and ultimately results in an impaired performance (Baron, 1986).

♦ The **evaluation apprehension theory** states that it isn't so much the mere presence of other people that affects our performance, but the knowledge that we are being watched (Aiello & Douthitt, 2001).

But what happens when the presence of others results in a state of arousal and at the same time makes us less noticeable? What happens when we can blend in with the crowd so that our individual behavior is less observable than normal? This is what is called **deindividuation**. When group members gain this feeling of anonymity, oftentimes a decreased sense of inhibition arises and people engage in behaviors in which they wouldn't normally engage (Zimbardo, 1970). Under these circumstances, people are more likely to engage in acts of antisocial behavior. Mobs and riots are good examples of some of the negative effects of deindividuation.

Oftentimes our behavior is influenced by the social roles in which we are placed. **Social roles** are defined as shared expectations regarding how people behave when they are placed in certain positions. In a classic study known as the Stanford Prison experiment, individuals were randomly assigned to the role of either a prison guard or a prisoner in a simulated prison built on the Stanford University campus. Although the subjects were not in a real prison, they began to lose their personal identity and adopt the corresponding attitudes and behaviors of either prisoners or prison guards.

FIGURE 11.32 *Being part of a crowd can increase the likelihood that we will do things we would not ordinarily do.*

Could the actions of the prison guards at Abu Ghraib discussed earlier in this chapter be explained by some of these factors? Many suggest that the deindividuation the soldiers felt by wearing the same uniform, masks, and being part of a group contributed to their increased acts of aggression. Some of the guards who abused the prisoners even wore makeup on their faces that made them even more indistinguishable. Or perhaps they were simply obeying the commands of authority figures and felt little sense of responsibility for their actions. Do you remember the Stanley Milgram experiments discussed earlier in the chapter? The social situation has the power to bring out both the very best and the very worst in all of us.

Chapter Summary

It is a common misconception that our behavior is primarily a function of who we are as individuals. But as we have seen in this chapter, many of our behaviors are strongly influenced by the social environment and specific situations. In fact, one could argue that to a certain extent, all human behaviors are influenced by what is going on in the environment. This chapter provided an overview of how we form our ideas about the world in which we live and how those ideas shape our interaction with the world, how we act, and how we behave. We established how the field of social psychology distinguishes itself from sociology and other fields that study human behavior in a social context.

We discussed the way our views of the social world are shaped (attitudes), and how our cognitive habits such as the fundamental attribution error and prejudice often lead to perceptions of the world that are not precisely accurate. We also identified specific social situations that increase the likelihood of obedience, conformity, or compliance occurring. We examined the topics of prosocial behavior and aggression and demonstrated that there are certain social conditions under which we are all more likely to act kindly or behave in a hostile nature. We saw that certain social conditions exist that increase the likelihood that people will have positive feelings toward each other and thus relationships will be likely to develop. We also saw that certain conditions may exist where our performance on tasks may be either enhanced or impaired while we are in the presence of others. Finally, we saw that circumstances can exist that lead groups to make either superior or inferior decisions compared to decisions made by a single individual. For better or for worse, almost all of our behaviors are influenced by the world around us.

Knowledge Builder

RELATE TO YOURSELF

1. Describe how social psychology's contribution to the understanding of human behavior could help you in a specific aspect of your life.

2. You secretly have a crush on someone you have just met. How could you apply your knowledge of the determinants of interpersonal attraction described in this chapter to get this individual to like you?

3. Differentiate between times when you have engaged in instrumental and hostile aggression. Provide an example of each.

4. Describe a time when you engaged in normative conformity. Describe a time when your behavior was shaped by informational social influence.

5. On your drive home, you see someone on the side of the road with a flat tire. Discuss how the empathy-altruism theory of helping would influence the likelihood that you would pull over and lend a hand.

_____

_____

_____

_____

6. Pick a relationship that you have in your life. Describe which of Sternberg's types of love best describes this relationship. Why?

_____

_____

_____

_____

CHAPTER REVIEW QUESTIONS

1. Research into the determinants of interpersonal attraction has demonstrated that there are some facial characteristics and physical traits that are perceived as being more attractive in almost all parts of the world. **T or F?**

2. Social psychology places an emphasis on how the social environment and situational factors influence behavior. **T or F?**

3. Social psychologists believe that few people truly engage in prejudice. **T or F?**

4. Cognitive dissonance refers to a state of discomfort that occurs when our actions directly correspond with our beliefs about ourselves. **T or F?**

5. According to the foot-in-the-door theory of compliance, if you agree to a small request initially, it is much easier to deny a larger request at a later time. **T or F?**

6. Stanley Milgram was investigating _____ in his classic teacher-learner shock study.

    (a) the effects of punishment on learning

    (b) the effects of reinforcement on learning

    (c) factors associated with obedience to authority

    (d) prosocial behavior

7. We misjudge the causes of another person's behavior because we overestimate internal, personal factors and underestimate external, situational influences. This is called _____.

    (a) delusional thinking   **(b)** prejudice

    (c) the fundamental attribution error   **(d)** the self-serving bias

8. _____ is a generally negative attitude directed toward people simply because of their membership in a specific group.

    (a) Prejudice   **(b)** Stereotyping

    (c) Cognitive biasing   **(d)** Empathy

9. When you change your behavior as a result of the real or imagined group pressure to do so, you are engaged in a process called _____.

    (a) norm compliance   **(b)** obedience

    (c) conformity   **(d)** mob rule

10. The student council has an important decision to make regarding the homecoming dance. Although the president's choice of a "somewhere over the rainbow" theme may be more expensive, the student council members all go along with it because they want to avoid an argument. The group may have just engaged in which of the following?

     (a) aggression   (b) similarity
     (c) social facilitation theory   (d) groupthink

USEFUL WEB SITES

PBS WEB SITE: A CLASS DIVIDED

http://www.pbs.org/wgbh/pages/frontline/shows/divided/etc/view.html

UNDERSTANDING PREJUDICE.ORG WEB SITE

http://www.understandingprejudice.org/

SOCIETY FOR PERSONALITY AND SOCIAL PSYCHOLOGY

http://www.spsp.org/

SOCIETY FOR THE PSYCHOLOGICAL STUDY OF SOCIAL ISSUES

http://www.spssi.org/

SOCIETY FOR EXPERIMENTAL SOCIAL PSYCHOLOGY

http://www.sesp.org/

THE STANFORD PRISON EXPERIMENT WEB SITE

http://www.prisonexp.org/

INFLUENCE AT WORK: THE PSYCHOLOGY OF PERSUASION

http://www.influenceatwork.com/

A LIST OF DOCTORAL PROGRAMS IN SOCIAL PSYCHOLOGY

http://www.socialpsychology.org/socprogs.htm

LOOKING TO GET INVOLVED IN PROSOCIAL BEHAVIOR?

http://www.volunteermatch.org/

Chapter 12

Developmental Psychology

by Elizabeth Shobe, PhD

Constant development is the law of life, and a man who always tries to maintain his dogmas in order to appear consistent drives himself into a false position.

—MAHATMA GANDHI

What Is Developmental Psychology?

Mahatma Gandhi thought that continuous change in an individual's beliefs was natural, and, indeed, change is apparent in every aspect of life. In this chapter on developmental psychology, you will see that development is continuous throughout our lifetime. It redefines our capabilities, who we are, and what we do. But what does development mean? Simply put, **development** means changes that occur over time. Developmental psychologists study changes in human behaviors, skills, and abilities, from conception to death. They may study changes in specific behaviors across several years of life, or they may concentrate their efforts on a particular age level. The information gathered by developmental psychologists provides a broad understanding of how behaviors and abilities develop. Developmental psychology is a uniquely integrative field, drawing from and informing many other areas of psychology, including neuroscience and physiology, learning, cognition, social psychology, personality, educational psychology, and psychopathology. Developmental psychology overlaps with many fields because it is the study of how a wide spectrum of behavior develops.

Physical Development

Arnold Gesell (1880–1961)

Arnold Gesell (pronounced "geh-ZEL") profoundly impacted the field of developmental psychology, as well as the manner in which countless teachers, physicians, and parents approach the developing child. Although he died more than

40 years ago, his work still impacts the daily lives of children. Gesell's ideas are firmly rooted in an evolutionary and biological approach. He advocated the idea that children develop along a biologically determined sequence that is unaffected by the environment (Gesell, 2007). His most notable contributions include the principles of development, the principle of individuating maturation, and the importance of individual difference for maturational readiness.

Gesell was very much influenced by **recapitulation theory** (Hall, 1904), which is the assertion that ontogeny recapitulates phylogeny. **Ontogeny** refers to the development of an animal from conception to death, and **phylogeny** refers to the evolutionary development of a species. "Ontogeny recapitulates phylogeny" means that the developmental stages of the individual reflect the developmental stages of the species. Consider that at conception, a human is a single cell that divides into two cells, then four cells, and so forth. This recapitulates that all life started with one-celled animals that divided, and so on. A more frequently used example of recapitulation is the development of the brain. In an individual, prenatal (before birth) brain development basically begins with the pons and the medulla (breathing, heart rate), the thalamus (senses), and the hypothalamus (feeding, fleeing, fighting, and mating), followed by the cortex. In evolutionary history, consider that reptiles have a hindbrain, thalamus, and hypothalamus (they have basic bodily functions, senses, and survival instincts). Lower mammals (e.g., rats) have a cortex, but it is smooth, and primates have pretty well-developed cortexes, with the latest in this lineage, humans, having the most well-developed cortex. The development of an individual human brain recapitulates the evolutionary development of the brain.

Explore **the medulla** in Chapter 2, p. 75

Gesell's emphasis on evolution and biology is also evident in his principle of **individuating maturation**. Individuating maturation refers to the idea that development proceeds in a genetically preprogrammed sequence. Therefore, the experiences in a child's life should exert relatively minor influence over the course of his or her development but they cannot play a causal role. While Gesell was a dedicated researcher who spent countless hours documenting and describing normal development, he is also well known for his work promoting individual differences. While behaviors develop along a predetermined sequence, people vary from one another in the expression of various traits, and these traits are highly stable within the individual as he or she matures. One example is the stability of intelligence, where children who tend to perform in the top percentiles on intelligence assessments continue to perform at the top in subsequent measurements throughout their lives. Similarly, those who perform in the bottom ranges tend to stay at the bottom throughout their development. Later in the chapter, we will question the stability of intelligence. In the normal population, under normal circumstances, performance on intelligence tests is quite stable across the life span. Similarly, easygoing babies turn into easygoing toddlers. Normal development, therefore, means that a child should achieve certain tasks in an order that is consistent with the species. However, the manner in which a child expresses that achievement is determined by genetically programmed individual differences.

Gesell's emphasis on the importance of individual differences also includes the notion of maturational readiness. **Maturational readiness** is the assertion that individuals vary in the rate at which they develop motor behaviors, adaptive behaviors (e.g., alertness, intelligence), language, and social behaviors. Normal children will reach milestones in a predictable sequence, and new behaviors or achievements are possible only after the child has physically or psychologically matured to a certain level—a readiness level. You simply cannot teach a child to read before he or she is ready, nor can you teach a child to talk, jump, walk, or do algebra before he or she has the physical and psychological structures in place to accept the teachings. So, playing Mozart to a baby or placing a violin in a child's hands will not increase his or her likelihood of being a musical prodigy at age 3. Further, you will become quite frustrated trying to teach any 6-year-old quantum physics. This may seem rather obvious to you. Indeed, the notion of maturational readiness has become common knowledge, demonstrating the far-reaching and long-lasting impact of Arnold Gesell.

Development in the Womb

For centuries, scientists believed in preformation, which is the belief that all of our body parts are preformed in the embryo, and that these parts simply become bigger as we grow. This idea was abandoned when scientists were able to look through high-powered microscopes and failed to find tiny beings inside embryos. Today, we understand that characteristics emerge and prenatal development tends to follow three **laws of developmental direction**: (1) the **cephalo-caudal law** states that development begins at the head (cephalo) and proceeds to the tail (caudal); (2) the **proximo-distal law** states that development begins in the center of the body and then proceeds to the extremities; and (3) the **gross-fine law** states that general, rudimentary parts become specific, finely detailed parts. As you continue to read about the development of the fetus, you will readily see how these laws apply.

The **prenatal period** runs from conception to birth and is divided into three periods: germinal, embryo, and fetus. During the **germinal period** (approximately the first two weeks after conception), the fertilized egg (**zygote**) moves through the fallopian tube and begins to divide (**mitosis**), first into 2 cells (30 hours after fertilization), then 4, then 8, then 16, then 32, and so on. These cells are all undifferentiated, meaning that they perform no specialized functions and they share the exact same genetic material. As the cells divide they form a sphere, and if the sphere divides during mitosis and each sphere continues to develop, **identical twins** will be born. Within three to four days of moving through the fallopian tube, the cells form into a hollow ball called a **blastocyst**, part of which becomes the placenta, the umbilical cord, and other supporting structures. This is known as the **trophoblast**. The other part of the blastocyst, the **embryoblast**, becomes the embryo, or child. At approximately one week postconception, the blastocyst (about 100–150 cells) enters the uterus. If after a few days it comes into contact with the uterine wall, it will send tendrils into the lining of the wall. This inhibits the menstrual flow, and the lining of the uterus will not be sloughed off as part of the regular menstrual cycle. **Implantation** of the blastocyst into the uterine wall is the end of this period, which lasts approximately two weeks. The potential baby is officially attached to the mother.

At the start of the **embryonic period**, tiny blood vessels from the trophoblast establish a connection with the mother's blood system through the wall of the uterus. These tiny blood vessels become the **placental barrier**, which allows nutrients from the mother's blood to pass through to the child and for waste to leave. The embryonic period lasts until approximately the eighth week, during which time the **embryo** (formerly the embryoblast) becomes three layers. The **endoderm** layer is the innermost, and it develops into the inner organs such as the digestive tract, the respiratory system, the pancreas, and the circulatory system. The middle layer, or **mesoderm**, becomes muscles, bones, the circulatory system, and the excretory system. The outer layer, or **ectoderm**, becomes the skin, the hair, the nails, and the brain and spinal cord. All organs are formed during the embryonic period and are somewhat rudimentary.

The **fetal period** lasts from the ninth week up until birth. During this time all the organs present during the embryonic period are refined and developed, and the fetus dramatically increases its weight and height. At approximately 26 weeks the fetus is able to live outside the womb, but several organs, including the lungs, may be dangerously underdeveloped.

Growth during the prenatal period is extremely rapid and occurs in every aspect of the body. Interference with this growth at any point during this critical time has the potential to affect the formation of several of the body's organs and systems. The result can be physical and mental abnormalities called **birth defects**. Growth of the baby can be affected by exposure to disease, chemicals, and/or radiation, all of which are collectively termed **teratogens**. The effects of different teratogens can range from low birth weight (from cigarette smoke) to mental retardation (e.g., from heavy alcohol consumption), depending on when they are introduced. Teratogens present during the germinal period can prevent the blastocyst from ever implanting (no child can develop), can wreak havoc on major organs and organ systems (such as the brain and spinal cord) during the embryonic stage, and can halt the refinement of organs and body parts that characterize the fetal period.

Various teratogens have different effects at different times during pregnancy. Drinking alcohol during the first three months of pregnancy can result in facial and skull abnormalities, whereas drinking alcohol later in the pregnancy can affect the baby's growth both pre- and postnatally. Alcohol consumption can also result in **fetal alcohol syndrome (FAS)**, which is characterized by poor motor coordination and development, head and facial abnormalities (such as flattened nose, eyes set widely apart, thin upper lip), heart defects, slower development, and/or obvious learning and cognitive disabilities including mental retardation. Increases in the amount of alcohol consumed by the mother tend to increase the number of these characteristics that are likely to be present in the newborn. As little as one drink per day can slow fetal growth and increase the likelihood of a miscarriage, and only 1.5 ounces per day can affect intelligence and psychomotor skills (Larroque, Kaminski, & Dehaene, 1995; O'Connor, Sigman, & Casari, 1993). Even one episode of binge drinking can adversely affect the development of the fetus by raising its blood alcohol level beyond a manageable level.

Similarly, increased amounts of cocaine ingestion by the mother may result in increases in the number and severity of observed problems in the newborn, and these problems can continue throughout the child's life. Cocaine is perhaps the most harmful drug to a fetus. Problems include irritability; feeding difficulties (poor sucking, vomiting, weight loss); extreme sensitivity to light, sounds, and movement; inability to console oneself; brain abnormalities; malformation of circulatory and digestive systems; poor reflexes; emotional unresponsiveness; and emotional, cognitive, and physical delays throughout childhood. Infants may go through cocaine withdrawal, characterized by fever and inability to regulate temperature. Sadly, these already-troubled infants are also much more likely to endure poverty, abuse, and neglect due to being raised in an environment of drug-addicted parent(s). Interestingly, early intervention through prenatal care, counseling of parents and caregivers, and instruction on how to care for these special babies can significantly improve the lives of these children, so that they have a much higher likelihood of reaching the same levels of development as their peers, starting as early as three months (Griffith, 1992; Kaplan, 2000).

Brain Development

The brain undergoes changes throughout life, with the most dramatic changes occurring prenatally, in the early years, and in adolescence (Spear, 2000). The brain begins as a neural tube. By four weeks' gestation, two distinct parts have emerged: one that will lead to the thalamus, the hypothalamus, and cortex structures, and one that will lead to the development of all brain stem structures. By 12 weeks' gestation, the four lobes of the cortex begin to emerge, and growth for the remainder of gestation is concentrated on the cortex. Incidentally, this concentration of cortical growth is a distinctly mammalian trait. At approximately six months, the folds of the cortex begin to develop and continue until birth, at which time the neocortex, the cerebellum, and the end of the brain stem are the only visible parts, as the neocortex has covered every other structure.

At birth, the brain weighs approximately 25% of the weight of the average adult's brain. At six months, it weighs approximately 50% of the average adult's brain, and by age 2 it is 75% of the weight of an adult's brain (Cowan, 1979; Restak, 1984). Most of the neurons you will ever have (about 100 billion) were present before you were born—by about the seventh month of gestation (Rakic, 1995; Shatz, 1992). This means that neurons were being generated at about 250,000 per minute, a process referred to as **neuron proliferation**. During gestation, neurons move to different locations in the brain in a process known as **neuronal migration**. The early development of the brain actually produces more neurons than you need in the first few years of life, so the brain starts **thinning** out excess neurons (some die) and synapses (connections between neurons are removed). The process of thinning does not necessarily mean that we are born with more neurons than we will ever have. Rather, recent discoveries have indicated that several brain regions exhibit **postnatal neurogenesis**, which is the formation of new brain and nerve cells, and most likely this occurs throughout our lifetime (Nelson, 2004).

Two possible reasons for the overproduction and subsequent thinning of neurons are (1) to allow experience to determine which neurons are vital and which can be discarded, and (2) to ensure plasticity. **Plasticity** means that new, unspecialized neurons can be flexible in their functioning, which is useful if brain injury or nerve damage occurs. Plasticity also refers to the formation of new synaptic connections.

Neurons become specialized through a process known as **differentiation**, where they are enlarged and form synapses with other neurons. Neuronal differentiation occurs mostly after birth, and in some regions may continue into adulthood. Many neurons require stimulation through experience to become differentiated, without which the corresponding behavior can be markedly impaired. One classic study illustrating the interplay between neuronal differentiation and experience was done by Hubel and Weisel (1979) on newborn kittens. They found that newborn kittens that were placed in an environment without vertical edges and lines failed to develop the cells in the cortex necessary for seeing these lines and could not help but bump into objects bearing only vertical lines. As little as 20 minutes' exposure to vertical lines was sufficient to encourage the differentiation of these cortical cells, even in animals subsequently placed in the vertically impoverished environments.

If you've ever been around a newborn, you have no doubt observed signs that the brain stem and midbrain—responsible for the most basic reflexes (swallowing), sensations (pain), and functions (breathing, digestion, elimination)—are well developed at birth. As you might also expect, areas of the cortex responsible for thinking, planning, movement, problem solving, and memory are much less differentiated at birth. Further, the areas of the cortex responsible for sensation and motor function mature much earlier than the frontal cortex, which is responsible for thinking, problem solving, and language. In general, by six months many reflexive behaviors disappear and are replaced by more voluntary behavior, reflecting development of the cortex.

Explore **synapses** in Chapter 3, p. 76

As the child grows through toddlerhood, thinning of excess synapses along with simultaneous increases in myelination result in enhanced language skills (frontal cortex, left temporal lobe), problem solving (frontal and prefrontal cortex), and imagination (visual cortex). A major burst in language skills occurs between the ages of 3 and 6, which coincides with heightened activity in Broca's and Wernicke's area (Fischer & Rose, 1996), as well as a growth spurt in the left cerebral hemisphere (Reeve, 1998). The developing cerebellum enables noticeable increases in motor coordination.

Between ages 7 and 16, there is another dramatic *decrease* in synapses (Huttenlocher, 1979, 1984). This substantial thinning most likely occurs for synapses that are not used and for a large-scale restructuring of neural connections to enable mature processing and functions. Abnormally high numbers of synapses are associated with mental retardation. Thus the **synaptic pruning** process appears to make the adolescent brain more efficient and less energy-consuming than it would otherwise be (Rakic, Bourgeois, & Goldman-Rakic, 1994).

Although neurons and synapses are thinned, during adolescence the brain increases myelination, which speeds the transmission of action potentials along axons. Maturation of myelin during adolescence occurs in prefrontal, frontal, parietal, and temporal areas and may contribute to the integration of these areas (Luna & Sweeney, 2004). The increases in myelination in the prefrontal and frontal areas coincide with dramatic increases in cognitive processing abilities at

Explore
myelin sheath
in Chapter 3, p. 76

this age. Not surprisingly, the area of the brain responsible for impulse control, the **dorsal lateral prefrontal cortex**, remains immature in adolescence, not reaching full maturity until the individual is in his or her early twenties. Adolescence is also marked by increases in gray matter in the hippocampus and amygdala (Geidd, Castellanos, Rajapakse, Vaituzis, & Rapoport, 1997). The end of adolescence sees marked improvement in response inhibition, planning, and organizational skills (Fuster, 1989). The basic observation here is that major changes in brain development coincide with pronounced pruning and myelination. As you will see in subsequent discussions throughout this chapter, hallmarks of psychological development reflect these brain changes toward more mature processing of and thinking about information, as well as an increase in processing speed.

Sensory Development

Newborns differ from adults in their ability to see fine details (acuity) and color. At birth, newborns' acuity is about 20/660 (Courage & Adams, 1990), making their vision quite blurry, with high-contrast areas being most visible. To give you an idea of what this vision is like, imagine viewing an object from 660 feet away. The appearance to you of the details of an object 660 feet away is how an infant sees details that are only 20 feet away—totally blurry. Newborns' inability to see details may be the reason why they seem most interested in high-contrast areas, such as black-and-white alternating lines (Cohen, Deloache, & Strauss, 1979). The distance at which babies seem to prefer viewing an object is approximately 10 inches, which coincides with the distance between the mother's breast and her face. Their acuity improves to adult levels by six months.

Infants' color vision is comparable to adults also by six months. In one study on infant color vision, 4- and 5-month-old infants were presented with circles colored blue, red, green, and yellow, and boundary colors such as yellow-green and blue-red (Bornstein, 1992a). The circles were presented in pairs and the amount of time the infants spent looking at each color was measured (termed "looking time"). The researchers found that infants much preferred (looked at longer) the blue and red circles, whereas green, yellow, and green-yellow were the least preferred. It also appears as though infants have some color vision at birth, with infants as young as 1 day old being able to discriminate between colored and white stimuli.

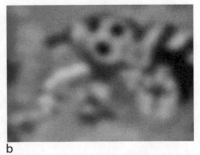

a   b

FIGURE 12.1 *(a) Normal vision (b) Infant vision.*

In contrast to vision, hearing is well developed at birth, but it is slightly less sensitive (20–30 decibels less) than the hearing level of adults. In fact, shortly after birth, newborns prefer their mother's voice to a stranger's, indicating familiarity with the sound through exposure in the womb. Newborns discriminate among different pitches, being most responsive to those found in the range of the human voice. At birth, newborns will orient toward sounds, demonstrating sound-localization abilities. They also prefer music and rhythmic sounds (Rock, Trainer, & Addison, 1999; Walk, 1981) and can be startled and distressed by loud or sudden sounds.

Smell also appears to develop much sooner than vision. Breast-fed newborns prefer cotton pads that have been worn inside their mother's bra to pads of other nursing mothers (Schaal, 1986). Interestingly, even bottle-fed infants prefer the scent of the pad worn by a nursing mother in contrast to one worn by a non-nursing mother (Makin & Porter, 1989). While there may be implications that humans are naturally drawn toward human milk, more relevant here is that infants can discriminate smells as early as two days. As might be expected, taste is also well developed in newborns, and research has demonstrated that newborns as young as 2 hours old can discriminate among salty, sweet, bitter, and sour. They seem to prefer sweet, as indicated by the accompanying facial expression (which appears to be happiness) and an increased heart rate. Perhaps because of their poor vision, newborns must be especially adept at utilizing smell and taste for survival.

Also important for survival, the somatosenses (pain, touch, temperature) are well developed at birth. Newborns respond positively to touch and strongly to pain, and they cry when cold or wet. Within the first two weeks of life, swaddling a baby (wrapping the baby burrito-style in a blanket) will soothe and comfort him or her because of the warmth and the slight pressure, both of which enable the baby to feel secure (Shelov, 1998). Additionally, several reflexes present at birth are elicited in response to touch. For example, when a baby's cheek is touched, the baby reflexively turns his or her head to face the object. This is called the **rooting reflex**. They also jerk their foot back and cry in response to a needle prick to the heel (necessary for a blood test). These reflexes make it easier for babies to find food and avoid injury.

Motor Skill Development

The laws of developmental direction apply not only to anatomical development but also to motor skill development. For example, consistent with the cephalo-caudal law (head to tail), infants develop control over their eye movements earlier than their neck movement, which is still earlier than arm and leg movement. Consistent with the proximo-distal law, infants are able to sit up before they are able to coordinate their two hands. And, consistent with the gross-fine law, infants learn large movements before finer ones, such as raking an object toward them before mastering the pincer grasp (index finger to thumb).

Infants are born with no fewer than 25 reflexes, most of which disappear by six months. Beyond reflexes, we can distinguish between gross motor behavior and fine motor behavior, although these are not the only methods of classifying behaviors. Gross motor behaviors enable postural control and locomotion, and fine motor movements include smaller movements for object manipulation (e.g.,

FIGURE 12.2 *Childhood play serves a key function in development of coordinated movement.*

reaching, grasping, and pulling). See Table 12.1 for the developmental sequence of motor behaviors.

Skills in locomotion (running, jumping, climbing, and hopping), manipulation (throwing and catching), and postural movements (balancing and rolling) continue to increase into early childhood. Motor skills that appear to be well developed are still those that mostly involve large muscles (gross motor), but the child makes advances in fine motor skills, too. These skills are just not as smoothly executed as the gross motor skills. However, by 4 years old, children can hold a pen using their fingers and have begun to control the movements of the pen with their finger muscles. Examination of the writing of preschoolers (ages 3–5) reveals shaky lines drawn with jerky or scribbling movements, and this may require considerable effort for the younger preschoolers, whereas older children are able to write discernable letters and/or numbers.

During the elementary school years, motor skills continue to be refined with increases in running speed, distance jumping, balance, and both throwing distance and accuracy. Significant gender differences in running ability appear at about age 11, with boys tending to outperform girls, and superior skill at throwing

TABLE 12.1 Development of motor behavior (adapted from Bukatko & Daehler, 2004).

Age	Skill
8 weeks	Holds head upright
2 months	Rolls from back to side
3 months	Reaches for objects
4 months	Turns from stomach to back
5–7 months	Sits without support
8–9 months	Sits without help, crawls
9–14 months	Stands without support, cruises (walks while holding furniture), uses pincer grasp
8–12 months	Walks with support
12–14 months	Drinks from cup, walks alone, scribbles
18 months	Runs
20 months	Kicks ball, throws ball
2–3 years	Jumps, balances on one foot, catches ball with outstretched arms
3–4 years	Walks up stairs alternating feet, performs standing long jump (1 ft.), catches ball by pulling arms toward chest, uses scissors, hops
4–5 years	Gallops, catches with one hand, dresses without help
5–6 years	Walks on balance beam, performs standing long jump (3 ft.), catches and throws similar to an adult, writes letters and numbers

appears slightly earlier (Gallahue, 1989). However, it is important to note that motor skill development does require practice, and boys may simply get more practice than girls during the preceding elementary school years.

Cognitive Development

Jean Piaget (1896–1980)

Jean Piaget (pronounced "pee-ah-ZHAY") profoundly influenced our knowledge of how children think and how thought processes develop. Piaget suggested that thinking and intellect develop over four successive stages, each of which is characterized by new skills as well as new ways of interpreting and organizing information and experiences. In Piaget's theory, progressing from one stage to the next entails broadening applications of existing knowledge and adding new kinds of knowledge. Knowledge is seen as consisting of schemata. A schema (singular form of schemata) is a body of knowledge pertaining to a particular idea or concept. For example, in infants, a schema is formed of things that are "suckable." Infants tend to respond to the environment as though most objects are suckable, but eventually their schema gets modified to include only a few categories of things that should go into the mouth. Piaget argued that cognitive development reflects the processes of assimilating new information into existing schemas and then, if necessary, accommodating new information by modifying existing schemas or creating new ones. These processes result in four general shifts or stages in cognition: sensorimotor, preoperational, concrete operational, and formal operational.

During the sensorimotor stage (birth–2 years), behavior consists primarily of simple motor responses to sensory stimuli (such as reflexes). The child's schemas consist mostly of sensory and motor knowledge. The sense of self emerges at this time, which means that the toddler becomes aware of his or her own body belonging to him or her. A major milestone that occurs during this period (between seven and nine months) is the concept of object permanence. Object permanence is the knowledge that something or someone continues to exist, even if the child cannot see, hear, touch, smell, or taste it. Before object permanence develops, it is rather easy to remove an object of intense fascination (such as a piece of paper) by obstructing it from view without incurring a protest from the child. After object permanence, however, obstructing the object may incur great distress because the baby knows it is still there—and still wants it. As any caregiver can tell you, the phrase "easy as taking candy from a baby" only applies to infants lacking object permanence (but don't give babies candy). Incidentally, sometimes removal of an object is not so easy in babies supposedly lacking object permanence, and this has raised some question about the validity of object permanence as a cognitive marker of this stage.

Children in the preoperational stage (ages 2–7) have significant language increases and can represent things using symbols (e.g., pretend play emerges), which is referred to as representational thought. Cognitive markers at this stage include egocentricity and animistic thought. Egocentric thought refers to the inability of children to think from another's point of view. This is not selfishness, as in the sense of greed or not wanting others to have things. Rather, the egocentric child thinks that others' perspectives match his or her own. A child exhibiting egocentric behavior may smile to, shrug, or nod into the phone when responding to questions posed by his grandma at the other end of the receiver. **Animistic thought** is the belief that all objects possess qualities of living things. A child may say that flowers get really happy when it rains or that her teddy bear was hurt when sat on.

The cognitive milestone in the **concrete operational stage** (ages 7–12) is the ability to think about the operation of concrete objects (objects that physically exist and are subject to the laws of physics). This means that children know and can think about the capabilities, movements, and qualities of concrete objects. This is perhaps best illustrated in their understanding of the concept of conservation. **Conservation** is the knowledge that an object retains all of its properties, even when placed in different contexts that may alter its appearance. The classic test of this is to sit a child in front of two empty glasses, one short and one tall. Then show the child a quantity of water in a third glass, and pour the entire quantity into the short glass. Refill the third glass to the same level, show the child, and then pour it into the tall glass. Because of the size differences, the water in each glass will look different. Simply ask the child which glass has more water. A child with the concept of conservation will know that they both contain the same amount, but a child in the preoperational stage will choose one because of its appearance and his or her inability to think about the liquid's properties and how it should perform (operate). Incidentally, if a preoperational child is guided, he or she will arrive at the correct answer. For example, if presented with two rows of 10 pennies each, with one row spaced farther apart, a preoperational child may say the longer row has more pennies. However, if the child is encouraged to look more closely and counts the pennies, he or she will realize that both rows are the same, exhibiting conservation. This is the concrete operational stage because the child cannot do the same with abstract things and has difficulty thinking hypothetically ("what if . . .").

In the **formal operational stage** (age 12–adulthood), the ability to think about and perform operations with abstract concepts emerges, as does hypothetical thinking. The adolescent in this stage can imagine long chains of behaviors and consequences, and can also reason about objects and events that are impossible in the real world. Interestingly, adolescents also show egocentrism in this stage in the form of personal fable and imaginary audience. **Personal fable** is the belief that the adolescent's thoughts are completely unique, and that no other has experienced the same thoughts or can understand (Elkind, 2001). **Imaginary audience** is the belief that the adolescent's behaviors are the focus of everyone else's thoughts, and we see this manifest in adolescents as self-consciousness.

FIGURE 12.3 *The task of conservation—both glasses have the same amount of liquid.*

Perceptual Development

Do babies understand what they are sensing? This is a difficult question to assess in very young infants, and the procedure is mainly to observe what they look at and for how long. If an infant turns to look at an object, the object has grabbed his or her attention. If the infant fixates on that object, then he or she is processing the object in a more meaningful way (Cohen, 1972). This requires perception. Salapatek (1968, 1975) showed infants up to the age of 2 months a picture of a circle inside a triangle. Those younger than 2 months looked mainly at the edges of the triangle, whereas the 2-month-olds looked separately at the features of the triangle and the features of the circle. This suggests that by 2 months of age, infants at least perceive two objects. Also, young infants seem to have a definite preference for faces, suggesting that at least they perceive these stimuli to be different from all others. Infants who are 3 to 5 weeks old stare at the outer edges of the face, but by 7 weeks old they prefer the eyes. In one study, even infants with a mean age of 53 minutes preferred facelike stimuli (an oval shape with two dots for eyes and a dot for a nose vs. the inverse of one dot above two dots).

Color perception appears to be similar to that of adults by 4 months of age. Adults perceive color categories, depending on the wavelength of light. Wavelengths between 450 and 489 nm are perceived as blue, 510–540 nm as green, 570–590 nm as yellow, and 615–650 nm as red. Most colors are seen by adults as categorically being one color or another. Sky blue, navy blue, cornflower blue, and royal blue are all "blue" and are different from violet, purple, and lavender, which belong to the category "purple." In one study, 4-month-olds were repeatedly presented with a single color until they lost interest (habituated). Then the infants were presented with one of two other colors, and their looking time was measured. One of the colors was in the same color category as the original, habituated stimulus, and the other was in a different color category. The infants were more interested in (looked at longer) the color that adults perceive to be in a different category than the color that would be classified as belonging to the same category. This suggests that infants as young as 4 months have category perception for colors. They understand them as more than just sensations of wavelength.

Walk and Gibson (1961; Gibson & Walk, 1960) studied depth perception by developing an apparatus known as the visual cliff. The **visual cliff** is a large glass table upon which a crawling baby is placed. Just under the glass on one end (shallow end) is a solid surface with a checkerboard pattern. The same surface is placed a few feet below the glass at the other end (deep end) of the table, giving the appearance that there is a drop. Seven-month-old infants will not crawl over the deep end, even when they are enticed to do so by their mothers. Additionally, the heart rates of these infants increase when placed over the visual cliff, which presumably reflects a fear response. Although only crawling infants can use the visual cliff, a decrease in heart rate has been observed in much younger infants who are lowered over the deep side. It is probable that the decrease in heart rate is not a reflection of fear, and the change in heart rate indicates that these babies in fact perceive a difference in depth.

FIGURE 12.4 *Children usually perceive a visual cliff and hesitate to crawl forward. Courtesy of Mark Richards/PhotoEdit, Inc.*

Memory Development

Are we born with memory? One well-known study by DeCasper and Spence (1986) suggests that memory begins to develop prenatally. In their study, they asked pregnant mothers to repeatedly read aloud a Dr. Seuss book (*The Cat in the Hat*) during their last six weeks of pregnancy. Infants only a few days old were tested using a modified pacifier that measured the rate of sucking, higher rates indicating preference. The intensity of pacifier sucking was measured under two conditions: listening to the mother read the Dr. Seuss book and listening to the mother read a different book. The findings were that the newborns had a higher sucking rate while listening to Dr. Seuss—a finding that suggests the newborns were already familiar with this story or pattern of sounds, indicating that some memory is developed and functioning prior to birth. Indeed, while playing a recording of their mother reading a poem and a female stranger reading the same poem, Kisilevsky, Hains, and Lee (2003) found differences in heart rates two weeks *before* birth.

While we may be born with memory capabilities, they do not seem to be very good. Recall that Piaget argued that object permanence does not develop until after nine months, and once the object disappears, it is forgotten. Diamond (1985) found evidence suggesting that babies remember the object exists, but do not remember where it has gone. In her study, 7½-month-old infants were presented with an object, which was then hidden. Infants who were permitted to immediately search for the object found it. However, when there was a delay of just two seconds between hiding the toy and allowing the infants to search for it, the infants searched the wrong place. Thus, the infants remembered the toy existed, but in just two seconds forgot where it was.

Carolyn Rovee-Collier and her colleagues (1980) have extensively studied the development of memory in children 2–18 months old. They tested whether and for how long infants (ages 2–6 months) remembered that kicking would cause a mobile to move. In the study, infants were placed in their cribs with a ribbon tied around their ankle. The ribbon was attached to a string that pulled on a mobile overhead, moving it. The infants kicked vigorously, making the mobile move; they then lay still until the mobile died down, and then they kicked again. It was during this time that the infants learned that kicking made the mobile move. The researchers tested the infants' memory for the mobile between 1 and 42 days. The infants had the ribbon tied to their ankle again, and if the infant remembered the mobile, they kicked more. Two-month-olds remembered the mobile for less than a week, 3-month-olds remembered for about a week, and 6-month-olds for about two weeks.

In another study, Rovee-Collier and Hayne (1987) measured the memories of children 6–18 months old for pressing a lever to make a train move around a track. Again, the 6-month-olds remembered for about two weeks that the lever would make the train go; 9-month-olds remembered for about six weeks, 12-month-olds for about eight weeks, 15-month-olds for 10 weeks, and 18-month-olds for about 13 weeks.

By age 2, memory capabilities have improved substantially, and toddlers are able to report on events that happened months prior. However, if you've ever known a 3- or 4-year-old, you may suspect that some of the things he or she remembers may not have actually happened. For example, my son and his friend Nicholas are absolutely positive that they have been to Hawaii, when, in fact, not only have they never been, but also there are no pending plans to go. Apparently, over the course of several days and several incidences of engaging in play in which a volcano in Hawaii erupted, they became downright convinced that we were leaving for Hawaii "tomorrow." After another couple of weeks of this sort of play, both of the boys became absolutely convinced they had been to Hawaii and had seen lava erupting from a volcano. The upshot is that now they don't constantly request to go to Hawaii because, apparently, we've already been. More relevant here, however, is how could such a false memory (and ludicrous scenario, at that) have developed?

One explanation may be that children have trouble with source monitoring. **Source monitoring** is the process of determining whether the source of a memory is real or imagined. Foley and Ratner (1998) asked one group of 6-year-olds to physically act out the activity of flying like an airplane, another group was asked to imagine what it would feel like to fly like an airplane, and the third group was asked to imagine what they would look like if they were flying like an airplane. The children were later asked if they'd actually flown around the room. Those who imagined what it would feel like to fly like an airplane made the most source errors, believing they had actually flown around the room like an airplane. False memories are normally distinguished from real memories by their lack of detail and personal experience. However, when we have a very detailed account or a personal experience (even if imagined), we may have trouble with source monitoring and come to believe that we experienced something we did not. This happens to adults, too, and sometimes we wonder if a very realistic and detailed dream actually happened (and we may ask someone else for confirmation).

A second explanation for the false memories may be due to the biasing effects of suggestion, to which children appear especially susceptible. In one study (Leichtman & Ceci, 1995), a man visited a classroom of children aged 3, 4, 5, and 6 years old and walked around for two minutes. The children were assigned to one of four conditions: (1) they were told in advance about a very clumsy man coming to visit, (2) they were told in advance about the clumsy man, and it was suggested in a post-visit interview that he tore a book and spilled chocolate, (3) they were told nothing in advance, but it was suggested in a post-visit interview that he tore a book and spilled chocolate, (4) they were told nothing before or after the visit (control condition). Ten weeks later the children were asked if they saw the man tear a book or spill chocolate (neither of which he did). For those told in advance (condition 1), the 3- and 4-year-olds reported witnessing the events about 20% of the time, and the 5- and 6-year-olds reported witnessing the events about 10% of the time. The 3- and 4-year-olds who were told in advance and exposed to the post-interview suggestions (condition 2) said that they witnessed these things over 40% of the time, whereas only about 10% of the 5- and 6-year-olds reported the same. The 3- and 4-year-olds who heard just the post-visit suggestion (condition 3) reported witnessing the acts just under 40% of the time, and the 5- and 6-year-olds reported witnessing the acts less than 10% of the time. Interestingly, none of the 5- and 6-year-olds in the control condition said they witnessed the events, and 5% of the 3- and 4-year-olds said they did. At the least, the control condition illustrates that children's memories can be highly accurate. However, the reports from the children in the other conditions show that children's memories can be easily biased.

Elizabeth Loftus (2004, 2005; Loftus & Davis, 2006) has consistently reported that adults are also somewhat susceptible to suggestion, but the prevalence of this susceptibility appears to be greater in children than in adults.

Language Development

As you learned in Chapter 9, children acquire language along a predictable continuum that begins with crying (from birth), to cooing (1–2 months), to consonant sounds (3 months), to babbling (by 6 months), and finally to patterned speech (about 12 months). However, they appear to recognize and prefer the sounds in their native language as early as two days, suggesting that they were learning about their language while listening inside the womb. The most frequent sounds in infant babbling are "b," "d," "m," "n," and "p." These sounds are also found in the first words uttered by infants, which tend to be the labels for mother and father in a variety of dissimilar languages (e.g., mama and dada in English, eema and aba in Hebrew, mama and papa in Russian, and umma and babba in Chinese). Deaf babies follow a similar progression, and if they are exposed to sign language, they do **manual babbling**, which is rhythmic and repeated hand movements (Petitto & Marentette, 1991). Deaf children cease their vocal babbling by 10 months. Additionally, the ability to produce sounds in one's own language requires repeated practice during which the child attempts to match his or her own sounds with those of his or her native language. Deaf people sound the way they do when they try to speak because they cannot receive feedback about their own speech; hearing children who are able to make sounds after being prevented from doing so during these early, critical months (due to medical conditions) sound the same way deaf children do, from which they rapidly recover. Thus, practice listening to one's own speech appears to be crucial.

While many infants produce their first word (**patterned speech**) between the ages of 10 and 13 months, they understand the meanings of words much earlier. For example, by approximately six months, infants will look longer at a picture of their mother if they have heard the word "mommy" and longer at a picture of their father if they have heard the word "daddy," but they showed no difference in looking time at strangers' pictures after hearing these words (Tincoff & Jusczyk, 1999). By nine months, this looking time extends to objects that have been named.

Explore
language
in Chapter 9, p. 262

In most cultures the first 50 words of a child's vocabulary refer to people, food, animals, clothes, toys, vehicles, furniture and household items, personal items (e.g., book, watch, key), outdoor objects (e.g., snow), and places (e.g., pool) (Caselli, Bates, & Casadio, 1995; Nelson, 1973). Children's speech typically consists of one-word utterances up until about 18 months, and their vocabulary at that time is limited to 100 words or less. However, much of their speech at this time is in **holophrases**, which are single words used to represent an entire phrase. A 15-month-old may just say "juice," rather than "I want juice."

Up until children are about 2 years old, their meanings for words may be different from those of adults, these errors reflecting overextensions, underextensions, and overlaps. An **overextension** is to generalize the meaning of a word beyond its true meaning—using the word "car" to refer to cars, buses, vans, trucks, and trains. An **underextension** is the opposite; it limits the use of a particular word, such as using "truck" to refer to the child's father's pickup truck but not other trucks. An **overlap** is overextending the use of a word to refer to different objects, but also underextending to refer to only some of the same objects.

TABLE 12.2 The course of language development.

Age	Language ability	Reference
Newborn	Prefers baby talk, a.k.a. "motherese."	(Fernald & Kuhl, 1987)
1–2 months	Perceives speech sounds, produces cooing.	(Eimas, Siqueland, Jusczyk, & Vigorito, 1971)
4.5 months	Recognizes the sound of his or her name.	(Mandel, Jusczyk, & Pisoni, 1995)
6 months	Duplicated babbling (repeating a consonant-vowel sound such as "babababa"). Understands some words, such as "mommy" and "daddy."	(Oller, 1980; Tincoff & Jusczyk, 1999)
9 months	Distinguishes common or likely speech sounds in native language from those of foreign languages.	(Jusczyk, Luce, & Charles-Luce, 1994)
10–13 months	Speaks first words.	
1 year old	Uses idiomorphs—words invented by the child to represent an object, such as saying "foof" to refer to cereal.	(Hakuta, 1986)
18 months	Begins vocabulary spurt, speaks fewer than 50 words.	
2 years old	Has a vocabulary of 50+ words, naming explosion. Simple multiword combinations. Distinguishes between grammatically correct and incorrect sentences.	(Gleitman, Gleitman, & Shipley, 1972; Goldfield & Resnick, 1990)
24–36 months	Develops conversational skills.	(Bloom, Rocissano, & Hood, 1976)
3 years old	Has a vocabulary of 1,000 words.	
4 years old	Writes letters, own name.	
5–6 years old	Connects the visual image of letters and words to sounds, a necessary precursor for reading.	(Cunningham, Perry, & Stanovich, 2001)
6 years old	Has a vocabulary of 10,000 words. Narrative discourse or ability to tell a good story.	(McCabe & Peterson, 1991)
6–7 years old	Understands conversational differences between describing facts and telling a good story.	(Hicks, 1991)

Between the ages of 18 months and 21 months, there is a vocabulary spurt in which children double their vocabulary and do so again between 21 and 24 months. Vocabulary acquisition continues to increase rapidly, and by first grade, children understand approximately 10,000 words; by age 10, they understand 40,000 words. How this rapid acquisition of matching word to meanings (after a single exposure as 2–3-year-olds) is accomplished is termed the **riddle of induction**. Markman (1989, 1992) suggests that when interpreting a sentence such as "This is a [insert new vocabulary word here]," children restrict their conclusions about the unknown word's meaning to (1) the whole object, not just part of it, (2) the shape of similar objects having the same name instead of objects with the same colors or of the same sizes having the same names, (3) new words refer to objects other than those they already know, and (4) new words refer to other objects in the same category.

Intellectual Development

Earlier in our discussion of Arnold Gesell, we alluded to the idea that intelligence is a stable characteristic, partially genetically determined. Sometimes, however, unique circumstances enable researchers to approach a problem differently, and reach a very different conclusion. This is precisely what occurred for Skeels and Dye (1939) in their studies of children from an orphanage. During their initial assessments of intelligence, they found two girls (ages 13 and 16 months) to be severely retarded (functioning at 7- and 8-month levels), and they were subsequently sent to an institution for the retarded. Six months later, Skeels visited the institution and observed the two little girls functioning at appropriate levels for their age. A follow-up several months later revealed the same: the girls were perfectly normal and not at all retarded. What happened? As it turned out, there was no children's ward when the girls were placed in the institution, so they were necessarily placed with adult retarded women. These women constantly played with the children, cared for them, and showered them with affection. The girls also received special treatment from the nurses. It appeared as though the enrichment from the environment in which they were placed played a strong role in developing their intelligence.

In a more formal test of the hypothesis, the researchers placed one group of below-average-intelligence orphans with the retarded women and left another normal-intelligence group in the orphanage. Tests of the children's performance after two and a half years revealed that the children who were placed with the retarded women had shown and maintained the same gains as the first two girls, and some of the children who remained in the orphanage had actually decreased in intelligence. A follow-up of these children 30 years later (Skeels, 1966) revealed that the children who were placed with the retarded women grew to be normal, productive citizens, whereas the children who remained in the orphanage were mostly institutionalized their whole lives or were employed in menial jobs (Salkind, 2004). On the basis of the research of Skeels and Dye, intelligence may not be so stable after all.

Similarly, there is much evidence suggesting that animals placed in an enriched environment (i.e., with toys, minimal stressors) perform better and have more synaptic connections in their brains than animals placed in impoverished environments. It is important to note, however, that an environment such as an orphanage or one that is impoverished is *not* normal. When individuals are placed in an environment that is not normal, we might expect their behaviors to also be "not normal." Thus, we may expect that characteristics such as intelligence ought to be stable over time if the developmental context is normal. But we must also acknowledge that in an abnormal environment, the display of an individual's characteristics may be askew, and when placed in a normal environment, those characteristics either "get back on track" or "get on the right track."

Social and Emotional Development

Erik Erikson (1902–1994)

Erik Erikson emphasized the importance of social and cultural factors in the course of development throughout the life span (birth to death). Erikson recognized that development is achieved by the interplay among biological processes, cognitive processes (thinking, reasoning), and social processes (becoming part of society). Erikson believed that social and emotional development proceeded through a series of eight stages determined by age. Each stage is characterized by a conflict that must be resolved. Successful development depends on the degree to which the conflicts are successfully resolved, with previous resolutions affecting future ones. These stages are briefly described in the following paragraphs.

Stage 1: Basic trust vs. mistrust (infancy: birth to 1 year). At this age, infants are confronted with a conflict between developing trust in their world or developing mistrust. Trust is developed when the infant's needs are met and the infant learns that his or her world or environment is a safe place to be. These infants learn to trust others and eventually themselves. Mistrust is developed when the infant's experiences lead the infant to believe that his or her world is an unsafe and/or unpredictable, uncomfortable place. These infants mistrust others and may even mistrust their own sense of reality.

Stage 2: Autonomy vs. doubt (toddlerhood: 1–3 years). At this age, children either develop autonomy, the belief that they can control their own body, or develop self-doubt. This is the age of toilet training. Children resolve this conflict positively if caregivers encourage them to explore within a safe environment and if their independence is supported. The resolution will be negative if they are shamed by mistakes, overprotected, or pushed into doing things they either do not want to do or are not yet able to do. Children who are forced into toilet training or reprimanded for a lack thereof may learn self-doubt.

Stage 3: Initiative vs. guilt (early childhood: 3–6 years). This conflict characterizes children's willingness to become more independent of their caregivers, to try new things, and to test limits. Children will develop initiative if they are provided opportunities to try new behaviors independently of their caregivers and are encouraged to discover their environment for themselves. Children will feel guilt over their independent efforts if they are surrounded by negative attitudes and a lack of opportunities.

Stage 4: Industry vs. inferiority (middle childhood: 6 years to adolescence). Children at this age continually face new social and academic challenges. If they believe they can acquire skills that enable them to confront and overcome these challenges to become effective problem solvers, they will resolve this conflict with a sense of industry. This requires adequate training, good role models, and adequate education. If the training is lacking and they have no role models for skill building, they will fail to meet these challenges and be unprepared for meeting them in the future, resulting in feelings of inferiority.

Stage 5: Identity vs. role confusion (adolescence: 12 to 20 years). This stage reflects the struggle of adolescents to develop a self-identity and a clear picture of their beliefs, attitudes, and feelings. To arrive at a self-identity, adolescents must have opportunities to explore different pathways and receive positive feedback about their beliefs, attitudes, and feelings. Adolescents whose identities are unduly influenced by their parents may resolve this conflict with confusion, not arriving at a self-identity.

Stage 6: Intimacy vs. isolation (young adulthood: 20 to 40 years). Young adulthood is characterized by creating and maintaining intimate relationships with others. Lonely or ostracized individuals are less likely to be successful at intimacy, which can lead to a sense of isolation from social networks. Resolution of earlier conflicts may also be necessary for the success of intimate relationships during this age.

Stage 7: Generativity vs. stagnation (middle adulthood: 40 to 60 years). This conflict is about creating something that will be valuable to future generations (e.g., family, business, ideas). Having a sense of purpose and productivity during these years will enable positive resolution of this conflict. People who lack enrichment, people who believe they have no meaningful accomplishments, or people who are stagnated (e.g., someone in a dead-end job or who loses a job) have resolved this conflict negatively.

Stage 8: Integrity vs. despair (old age: 60+ years). In this last conflict, individuals reflect on their accomplishments and the events in their lives. They determine whether they have found contentment in various aspects of their life. If they have, then they resolve this conflict with integrity. If they believe their lives to have been mostly unsatisfactory, they may resolve this conflict with despair. Resolution of this final conflict is highly dependent on how previous conflicts have been resolved.

Temperament

The consistent individual difference in the type and intensity of emotional reaction to events is referred to as **temperament**, the scientific study of which was initiated by Arnold Gesell. Some believe that an individual's temperament is unchanging, is their core personality, and is central to the full development of personality, while others are less convinced of the relationship between temperament and personality. Generally, temperament encompasses such characteristics as activity level, emotional disposition/mood, adaptability, reactivity, and persistence. From a longitudinal study of 133 children from birth to young adulthood, Thomas and Chess (1986) proposed the classification of infants/children as having easy, difficult, or slow-to-warm temperaments based on an assessment along nine dimensions. Children with easy temperaments are happy; have predictable or regular routines for eating, sleeping, and so forth (rhythmicity); and are adaptable or flexible (can readily change behavior to accommodate a new situation). Those with difficult temperaments frequently fuss and cry, have irregular sleeping and eating routines, and are upset by sudden changes or newness. Slow-to-warm temperaments are a combination of easy and difficult, being upset by new experiences but gradually adapting to them or responding less intensely, and having a low activity level.

Temperament is believed to be inherent in the individual (biologically or genetically based) and stable across time. Happy, adaptable infants become toddlers willing to try new experiences, whereas infants who are upset by new experiences may resist major transitional periods, such as adjusting to school. Difficult children have a greater risk of having attention problems, being aggressive, and developing psychological and adjustment problems as they mature (Rothbart, Ellis, & Posner, 2004). Some have suggested that the experiences of an individual can render some temperament characteristics as more pronounced or less pronounced. **Goodness of fit**, the fit between the child's temperament and the parents' expectations and behavior toward the child, may affect the modification of temperament. For example, caregivers of a difficult baby who react negatively by intolerance, by withdrawing, or by being unresponsive have little chance of altering their baby's temperament as compared to caregivers who reinforce good behaviors and respond positively with structured experiences. However, the ability of experience to affect temperament has received inconsistent support, further illustrating its strong biological foundation.

There is evidence suggesting that the temperament of an infant affects **parenting style** and behaviors (e.g., Bates, 1987; Neiderhiser, Reiss, Hetherington, & Plomin, 1999). Children who are slow-to-warm benefit from parents who prepare the child for change and allow them ample time to adjust. Children whose temperaments lead them to be impulsive and uninhibited are more likely to receive severe and aggressive punishments from parents (Bates, Bayles, Bennett, Ridge, & Brown, 1991), and as a result of being reacted to aggressively, they become aggressive. Perhaps the immediate environment has less of an impact on temperament than it does on parenting style, and parenting style (and later behaviors of teachers and other adult influences) can affect the expression of temperament by teaching the child how to behave and react to different situations. Temperament is an additional example of how an individual's behavior is a product of his or her nature inextricably intertwined with his or her environment.

Attachment

Attachment is an emotional bond (i.e., love or affection) between an infant (animal or human) and another individual, such as a parent or a caregiver. Development of attachment proceeds through three phases (Ainsworth, Blehar, Waters, & Wall, 1978). The initial preattachment phase lasts for the first three months, and the infant shows no preference among caregivers. The attachment-in-the-making phase, between 2 and 7 months, is when infants prefer familiar people to provide care. Lastly, at 6 or 7 months to 24 months, the clear-cut-attachment phase emerges, and the infant very clearly prefers his or her primary caregiver. It is during this stage that **separation anxiety** (distress over leaving the primary caregiver) and **stranger anxiety** (fear of strangers) are seen. Often we see that the primary caregiver is the mother, and in a stressful situation the infant will likely reach for the mother over the father. However, in the natural home setting, infants seem to equally prefer the father and the mother. This is perhaps because, in this setting, fathers soothe the

FIGURE 12.5 *Infants become attached to their primary caregivers.*

infants as often as their mothers, and fathers engage in significant interaction with them that may or may not be of a different kind from the mother (Lamb, Sternberg, & Podromidis, 1992).

Ainsworth and her colleagues (Ainsworth, 1973; Ainsworth et al., 1978) also identified several kinds of attachment by using the strange situation method to observe infants' behaviors. The **strange situation method** consists of exposing the infant to a series of situations with and without the presence of the mother. It begins with the mother and the infant in a room, with the infant on the floor with toys and the mother in a chair (mother, baby); followed by the entrance of a stranger, who gives the infant a toy (mother, baby, stranger); followed by the mother leaving (stranger, baby); the mother then returns and the stranger leaves (mother, baby); then she leaves again (baby); the stranger comes into the room (stranger, baby); and lastly, the mother returns again (mother, baby). Each situation lasts for three minutes. Of interest is how the baby reacts when the mother leaves the room and when she returns. Does the baby miss her, and is the baby glad she has returned?

Infants who are **securely attached** show mild distress when the mother leaves, eagerly go to her when she returns, and are readily soothed by her, but then return to their playing. Securely attached infants identify the mother (or caregiver) as a source of comfort and enjoyment, perhaps trusting her or him to be there when needed. Indeed, parents of securely attached infants are more sensitive and responsive to the baby's needs, are cooperative and predictable, and engage in more physical contact. Securely attached infants tend to be happier, more cooperative, and better adjusted in school and with peers. When they reach toddlerhood, they are less aggressive, better at problem solving, and better liked by others than are insecure toddlers. Secure attachments are the most common.

Insecure infants can be categorized as either avoidant or ambivalent/resistant (these are not the only categories, just the ones more commonly agreed upon). Infants with **avoidant attachment** do not fuss when the mother leaves or during her absence, and generally ignore her when she returns. They clearly avoid being close to and interacting with her. These infants are more likely to have caregivers who are less likely to meet their emotional needs, such as comforting, and expect caregivers to be unresponsive. Infants with **ambivalent/resistant attachment** are overly clingy and anxious at the start of the strange situation method. They become severely distressed (screaming, tantrums) by her leaving and alternate between pushing her away and clinging to her upon her return. These infants appear to be unable to cope in her absence, but they do not seem glad or relaxed when she returns, or at any time in her presence. These two kinds of insecurely attached infants are more likely to have parents who are abusive, mentally ill, neglectful, or slow to meet their children's needs. They show little affection and are rejecting or unpredictable. Insecure infants are also more likely to have psychological disorders later in life. **Nonattachment** occurs when children have no opportunity to form an emotional bond with a caregiver, as may be the case in some orphanages or institutions or when children are placed in constantly shifting foster care. These children may have trouble developing emotional bonds with others.

Why is attachment so important for psychological well-being? According to Bowlby (1980), attachment to a caregiver is critical for survival. Spitz (1965) observed that institutionalized infants whose basic survival needs were taken care of but who were rarely, if ever, held or provided contact with a caregiver were more likely to develop depression, show decreased activity, become sick, and even die. Some clues about why this happens may come from the work of Harry Harlow (1958). In Harlow's studies, infant monkeys were removed from their mother's care at birth and placed with two surrogate mothers: one wire mesh "surrogate mother" that supplied the food, and one cloth "surrogate mother." Under conditions of stress (a mechanical spider introduced), the monkeys ran to the cloth surrogate, and under normal conditions, the monkeys spent most of their time cuddling with the cloth monkey. Harlow concluded that the physical contact (termed **contact comfort**) of the cloth monkey was more important in fostering attachment than the nourishment provided by the wire monkey. It may be that a lack of contact is so severely stressful for some infants in institutions that the expected pattern of physiological reactivity to stress occurs, namely, sickness and death.

Early attachments form the framework of love and affection for the future. If these attachments are maladaptive or nonexistent, an adult may lack empathy and may not be able to care about others or form normal social bonds with them. Further, securely attached individuals learn that they can trust their caregivers, respond to needs, show more sympathy in childhood, be more socially active, and exhibit leadership qualities (Weinfield, Ogawa, & Stroufe, 1997). Fortunately, most infants are securely attached, and the less-than-ideal styles of attachment can be reversed if the caretaking situation changes for the better.

Social Interactions

FIGURE 12.6 *The infant's smile provides a strong social signal to caregivers.*

Within 6 weeks of age, the newborn smiles for the first time, quickly bringing enthusiastic responses and sparking the beginnings of his or her social life. Babies are also keenly interested in human faces, and when presented with a human face, babies may smile and seem to expect some form of interaction in return. If the infant smile is ignored or unreciprocated, the baby will look away and may become visibly distressed. This is known as the **still face effect**. The still face effect illustrates that social interaction is highly valued at a very early age. As children grow, their social interaction increases in complexity, and they develop different kinds of social relationships with parents, siblings, and peers.

Parents and parenting styles (how parents interact with their children) play an important role in the child's social development. Researchers have identified four parenting styles (e.g., Baumrind, 1966, 1989, 1991a, 1991b). **Authoritarian** parents use threats and physical punishment to achieve strict obedience to their authority. These parents rarely explain or use reasoning to influence children's behaviors, and they are less nurturing. **Permissive** parents set few limits, and the children are permitted to dictate their own schedules for their daily rituals of play, meals, and bed. These parents are also less nurturing than the other types of parents, or they are uninvolved. Children of authoritarian or permissive parents exhibit more deviant behavior, poor peer relations, and less social responsibility. **Authoritative** parents use more rewards, reasoning, and explanation to influence behavior. They are clear in their communications and encourage communication with their children. They are highly nurturing and supportive.

FIGURE 12.7 *Siblings significantly influence each other's social development.*

Children of authoritative parents exhibit a characteristic called instrumental competence. **Instrumental competence** is competence in sociability, such as friendliness, cooperation, independence, and achievement oriented. **Uninvolved** parents (or the rejecting-neglecting type) are emotionally detached, being more interested in their own activities than in their child's. They rarely interact with the child and are uninvolved with events in the child's life, such as school functions, sports, friends, and interests. Children of uninvolved parents are more likely to exhibit social problems such as higher incidence of aggression and alcohol use during adolescence, and lower self-esteem.

While less is known about the effects of sibling relationships on social development, these relationships are unique and significant. The average American has only one sibling. Before the arrival of a sibling, the firstborn child receives all available parental attention and nurturing, but this decreases significantly (particularly, maternal attention) upon the arrival of a sibling. This can markedly affect the behavior of the firstborn child, who may become demanding, clingy, angry, or depressed or may exhibit general "brattiness." From this, the sibling relationship may become either friendly or hostile. The relationship between the siblings may depend on how well the firstborn was prepared for the newborn, and if the firstborn is allowed involvement in the care of the newborn. Hostile or negative relationships may be seen if there was a drastic decrease in interaction between the mother and the firstborn when the newborn arrived. In addition to the new sibling being viewed as competition for parents' affection, the firstborn may believe that the parents are treating him or her differently, which can build resentment (Dunn, 1988). As siblings grow, they engage in more conflict with each other than with their friends, but if parents intervene with a more authoritative style and a less authoritarian style, the frequency of conflict tends to diminish. Siblings also provide an important source of emotional support in times of family problems or crisis.

As children grow, their social interactions expand to include people outside their family. By two months, infants take an interest in other infants, indicated by looking time, and the complexity of interactions with other infants increases to smiling, vocalization, reaching, and crawling to the other by nine months. By one year, babies show social interaction by responding to peers with complementary emotional expressions. Between the ages of 1 and 2, social interactions incorporate language and become more complex, and prosocial behaviors such as empathy and turn-taking emerge. Children at this age engage in **parallel play**, where they play next to each other but do not interact. By age 3, they engage primarily in **cooperative play**, which is interaction with others, including games, role playing, and construction. Helping and sharing behaviors emerge during this time. By age 4, children engage more frequently in **associative play**, which is when they work using the same materials or on the same project but do not incorporate others in their task. Conflict in social relationships also emerges at around ages 3 or 4, with higher conflicts among the more sociable children.

FIGURE 12.8 *Children engaged in associative play.*

When the child is 6, his or her peer group increases in size as does the amount of time the child spends with peers (presumably due to the academic setting and involvement in extracurricular and community activities). Friendships at this age are often defined by shared interests and successful play, and for children between the ages of 7 and 9, friendships are aimed toward gaining peer acceptance. For children between 6 and 12 years of age, physical aggression greatly diminishes and is replaced by prominent verbal aggression (name calling, teasing); play consists of games and rules.

During adolescence, the number of friends tends to decrease, but these friendships become more significant and are based on intimacy and self-disclosure. Their social identities form around **cliques** (close-knit, typically same sex, group of friends who share common interests) and crowds. **Crowds** are a larger group of similarly stereotyped individuals who are defined by the actions, beliefs, and attitudes of the members, such as geeks, goths, stoners, preps, or jocks. Cliques enable intimacy and self-disclosure, whereas crowds are a source for additional activities and meeting nonclique people, particularly those of the opposite sex.

Moral Development

A woman is near death from a special kind of cancer. There is a drug that is likely to save her, but it costs $2,000 per dosage. The sick woman's husband, Heinz, has gone to everyone he knows to borrow the money, and he has tried every legal means, but he could only collect about $1,000. He asked the doctor/scientist who discovered the drug for a discount or to let him pay later, but the doctor/scientist refused. Should Heinz break into the laboratory and steal the drug for his wife? Why or why not?

This is a classic problem of moral reasoning presented to students, and it is one of the original dilemmas Lawrence Kohlberg used in his pioneering research on the development of moral reasoning. We each have our opinion of what Heinz should do, or what we would do if faced with the same dilemma, but a yes or no answer may not be nearly as telling as the reason for why we would do it. It is this justification that indicates the sophistication of an individual's moral reasoning. Morality can be conceptualized as doing the right thing for the right reason, and, drawing from the work of Piaget, Kohlberg argued that moral reasoning develops over a series of stages as the individual matures. He suggested six stages grouped into three levels. These stages are described in the following paragraphs, and each includes a stage-appropriate answer to Heinz's dilemma.

Preconventional Level

At the **preconventional level**, stage 1 and stage 2 morality is determined by the consequences of the behavior. Children under 9 years old typically use this rationale.

Stage 1 (**obedience**). A behavior is wrong if the consequence is punishment, and it is right if the consequence is reinforcement. Heinz's decision to steal: No, because he will go to prison; yes, or his wife will yell at him.

Stage 2 (**self-interest**, also known as instrumental relativist). A behavior is right if it furthers the individual's own interests, and there is little regard for how another might benefit. This stage is commonly represented by the "I'll scratch your back if you scratch mine" mentality. Heinz's decision to steal: Yes, because if his wife lives, she will take care of him, or he loves her and wants her near.

Conventional Level

At the **conventional level**, stage 3 and stage 4 morality is determined by social rules, and it is commonly seen in children ages 9 to 19 years.

Stage 3 (**conformity**, a.k.a. interpersonal concordance). Having learned social expectations of "good boys and girls," children believe a behavior is right if others will judge them as good if they engage in the behavior. Heinz's decision to steal: Yes, because his friends and family expect him to do what it takes to save his wife, and he does not want to appear callous; no, because he would be branded a thief and ostracized by others in the community.

Stage 4 (**law and order**). Having learned societal rules, children believe behaviors must conform to laws dictated by society. At this stage, the individual provides an answer that is based on the belief that a working society requires that its individual members follow a strict adherence to the law. Heinz's decision to steal: No, the law prohibits stealing, and if everyone broke the law, there would be chaos.

Postconventional Level

At the **postconventional level**, stage 5 and stage 6 morality is determined by internalized principles, and it may develop over the remainder of a lifetime.

Stage 5 (**human rights** or **social contract**). By this stage, individuals adhere to an internalized set of ethics that reflects commonly agreed upon principles of social justice and human rights. If a behavior violates these ethical principles, then it is wrong, regardless of the law. If the ethical principles are in conflict with the law, then the law should be changed, illustrating a respect for the law but not absolute obedience. Heinz's decision to steal: Yes, because life is more important than money and the price of the drug is in conflict with social welfare; no, because there is a social contract that we pay for goods received.

Stage 6 (**universal ethics**). In this stage, decisions about behavior are made through abstract reasoning and an understanding of universal ethical principles such as a right to life, justice, or honesty. This level of moral reasoning requires the individual to fairly assess other people's points of view, and the law is not a consideration. Heinz's decision to steal: Yes, because life is of higher value than objects, no, because it is dishonest and violates the druggist's autonomy.

Presented here are possible justifications for yes or no answers to Heinz's dilemma, and Kohlberg argued that these explanations indicate one's level of moral reasoning. Kohlberg also suggested that advances in moral reasoning occur when individuals are dissatisfied with their reasoning about a current moral dilemma, and roughly coincide with advances in Piaget's stages of cognitive development. Progression through the stages proceeds in an orderly fashion in that stages are not skipped, but an individual may occasionally revert back to an earlier stage to resolve a particular dilemma. However, in Kohlberg's research and that of others, individuals with stage 6 reasoning are rare, and some have even questioned the inclusion of stage 6 at all. In modern times, people who are likely to have reached stage 6 include Mahatma Gandhi and Martin Luther King, Jr., who both argued that laws without a foundation of justice are moot.

Kohlberg's stages of moral development have been criticized on the grounds that his research is based on a sample of men and thus excludes women's moral reasoning and the concept of caring. However, negligent or inconsistent differences have been observed between men and women in their reasoning using Kohlberg's stages. It is plausible that Kohlberg's stages do not capture all of the reasoning an individual may use when making decisions about moral dilemmas.

Chapter Summary

In this chapter you learned about the kinds of issues that developmental psychologists study and that development refers to changes that occur throughout the life span. Several aspects of physical development were discussed, including stages and processes of prenatal development, brain development, sensory development, and motor behavior. You learned about cognitive development, including perception, memory, language, and intelligence. Social and emotional development were presented, including temperament, attachment, and social interaction. You should by now realize that almost everything that makes you human has gone through a developmental process, physically, mentally, or socially. Further, development continues across the life span, although our focus in this chapter was largely from conception through young adulthood. You learned about three pioneers in the field—Arnold Gesell, Jean Piaget, and Erik Erikson. Although these pioneers were introduced in separate sections, if you look closely at their ideas, and specifically compare the children's ages discussed by Erikson and Piaget, you will see that their theories are complementary. This reinforces the point that development occurs in the whole individual; the types of social conflicts that arise coincide with the types of cognitive thinking that are predominant at the time. The individual differences discussed by Gesell fit nicely into this framework.

You should also realize that the so-called nature-nurture debate is practically moot. You have grown, and continue to grow, into the person you are because of the interaction of your nature and your environment, and the two cannot be teased apart. You may also realize at this point that development occurs on a smooth continuum and also as stages where large gains are observed. Lastly, while your genes enable you to make developmental strides, your experiences affect the expression of those genes and the paths that lead to the changes that create the whole, integrated, and unique *you*.

Knowledge Builder

RELATE TO YOURSELF

1. If you saw a pregnant friend drinking alcohol, what reasons could you give her to convince her not to drink while pregnant?

_____

_____

_____

_____

2. How do you think your parenting style would be affected by a baby who has an easy versus difficult temperament? How could you avoid negative responses to a difficult baby?

_____

_____

_____

_____

3. What kinds of questions would you pose to a child to ascertain if he or she was in the concrete or formal operational stage?

_____

_____

_____

_____

4. In what stage of moral development are you, and what is one example of your behavior that supports your opinion?

_____

_____

_____

_____

CHAPTER REVIEW QUESTIONS

1. The preoperational stage is characterized by simple motor responses to sensory stimuli. **T or F?**

2. The stage of moral development is determined by the rationale for solving moral dilemmas. **T or F?**

3. Development progresses according to three laws of developmental direction. **T or F?**

4. Periods of increased myelination and pruning coincide with major physical, cognitive, and social changes. **T or F?**

5. Infants cannot see colors until about 6 months of age. **T or F?**

6. Toddlers are less susceptible to problems with source monitoring than are adults. **T or F?**

7. Both deaf infants and hearing infants babble. **T or F?**

8. Adolescents who are free to explore their identity develop identity confusion. **T or F?**

9. In a strange situation study, a child who seems anxious from the start and throws tantrums when the mother leaves the room is exhibiting which style of attachment?

   (a) secure   (b) ambivalent

   (c) avoidant   (d) nonattachment

10. The process in which children acquire words as rapidly as they do has been termed _____.

    (a) the riddle of induction   (b) epigenesis

    (c) assimilation   (d) source monitoring

11. In which stage is geocentricism prominent?

    (a) sensorimotor and formal operational

    (b) sensorimotor and concrete operational

    (c) concrete and formal operational

    (d) preoperational and formal operational

12. In which of the following styles of attachment does the child rarely appear to be relaxed around the mother?

    (a) secure   (b) ambivalent/resistant

    (c) avoidant   (d) anxious

13. *Consider the following scenario:* What kinds of elements would you include if you were to design an environment for infants and toddlers (such as a day care or a playroom) and wanted to maximally stimulate their senses, exercise their motor skills, and encourage their memory and language skills?

14. *Consider the following scenario:* As a counselor, you are confronted with a parent who has a baby born with a cocaine addiction. What kinds of problems should the caretaker look for as the baby develops?

15. Compare the development of the five senses.

16. What commonalities do you see among Gesell, Piaget, Erikson, and/or Kohlberg in this chapter? Do you see any conflicting ideas?

USEFUL WEB SITES

WEB SITES WITH LINKS TO VARIOUS TOPICS

www.psy.pdx.edu/PsiCafe/Areas/Developmental/

www.socialpsychology.org/develop.htm

http://www.devpsy.org/links/index.html

http://classweb.gmu.edu/awinsler/ordp/topic.html

http://www.mhhe.com/socscience/devel/

www.vanguard.edu/faculty/ddegelman/amoebaweb/

http://www.psychology.org/

PICTURES OF BRAIN DEVELOPMENT

http://www.med.harvard.edu/AANLIB/home.html

PIAGET REVIEW AND CRITIQUE

http://hubcap.clemson.edu/~campber/piaget.html

ATTACHMENT

http://www.psychology.sunysb.edu/attachment/

PARENTING

http://parenthood.library.wisc.edu/Topics.html

CONVERSATIONS WITH CHILDREN

http://childes.psy.cmu.edu/

MORAL REASONING

http://tigger.uic.edu/~lnucci/MoralEd/index.html

DEVELOPMENTAL PSYCHOLOGY DIVISION OF THE AMERICAN
PSYCHOLOGICAL ASSOCIATION

http://classweb.gmu.edu/awinsler/div7/homepage.shtml

GOVERNMENT STATISTICS

http://childstats.gov/

JOURNAL OF APPLIED DEVELOPMENTAL PSYCHOLOGY

www.sciencedirect.com/science/journal/01933973

DEVELOPMENTAL PSYCHOLOGY JOURNAL

www.sciencedirect.com/science/journal/00121649

13

Personality

by William July, PhD, and Patricia Alexander, PhD

Personality can open doors, but only character can keep them open.

—ELMER G. LETTERMAN

What Is Personality?

FIGURE 13.1 *Your personality can be thought of as a mask.*

When you say someone has a great personality, what do you mean? Often we mean the person is likable, easy to get along with, or even interesting. In one sense this is a description of personality. However, there is much more to personality than what we see on the surface. Personality is one of those words with a dual meaning. It means one thing in common everyday English and means something more specific in the science of psychology. In psychology, **personality** can be defined as a relatively consistent set of thoughts, emotions, and behaviors. The term "personality" originates from the Latin word *persona,* meaning "mask." Ancient actors wore detailed masks displaying thoughts, emotions and behaviors. That is why the concept of a mask is connected to what is meant by personality (Schultz & Schultz, 2005).

Personality is a well-studied concept in psychology, yet psychologists still have many unanswered questions. In this chapter we will delve into some of those questions and examine a few of the theories that have attempted to shed light on this fascinating topic. Additionally, we will investigate the extent to which scientific research supports various aspects of personality theory.

How Is Personality Assessed?

FIGURE 13.2 *There are a number of techniques used to assess personality. Courtesy of Michael Newman/PhotoEdit, Inc.*

For psychologists, assessing personality is similar to the way an artist sketches a portrait. The artist begins with some basic tools, sketching skills, and a subject. Likewise, psychologists use a number of techniques as well as their knowledge and experience to assess personality. These techniques can be broadly grouped into four distinct categories on the basis of the method used: interviews, objective tests, projective tests, and behavioral observation.

When psychologists develop assessment instruments, they need to determine whether the new instruments measure what they are supposed to measure. If they do, the instruments are said to have validity (Groth-Marnat, 1990). Another test that a new instrument needs to pass in order to be considered viable is that it must be reliable. In general, a test has reliability when it is consistent, although there are several types of consistency that are considered when determining the reliability of a personality test. The most common type is test-retest reliability, which means that when a group of people takes the assessment instrument at one point and then takes the instrument again, say, a month later, the scores should be consistent. That is, people in the group who scored high in Time 1 should also score high in Time 2, and those who scored low in Time 1 should also score low in Time 2. This type of consistency implies that the assessment tool is measuring a trait that is stable over time. Since personality is expected to be stable over time, a personality assessment tool should reflect that stability.

Interviews

Much like a job interview, personality assessment through an interview process involves asking questions to seek information. A psychologist may use a structured format, an unstructured format, or a combination of the two. Structured interviews feature direct questions put to the interviewee. If the assessment is being done as part of a research project, there is an advantage to asking everyone the same questions in the same order, as this provides a standard basis for evaluation. If the assessment is being done in a therapy context, a structured interview ensures that necessary questions are asked in order to determine how to best help the client.

FIGURE 13.3 *The interview process is one way in which psychologists assess personality. Courtesy of Phototake/Alamy.*

Structured interviews have been developed that can be conducted via computer, and, interestingly, it turns out that most people are more open with information about themselves when answering questions on a computer than when responding in a face-to-face interview. It may be that interviewees don't worry about being "judged" by a machine.

Unstructured interviews have a less formal approach, which allows for the exploration of personality through longer answers to questions from the interviewer. For example, if the interviewee is seeking therapy, the interviewer may simply begin with the question, "What brings you here today?" Unstructured interviews also allow the interviewer the opportunity to improvise relevant and probing questions during the interview.

Interviews are quick ways to gain information about the interviewee. After all, who knows you better than you? However, they do have limitations. The interviewee may lack insight into his or her motives and wishes, or may be reluctant to divulge information that will cast him or her in an unfavorable light.

Objective Tests

Have You Ever Had a Personality Assessment?

Here are some typical situations in which you might be asked to take a personality assessment:

♦ Applying for a new job

♦ Being promoted to a new or different type of position

♦ Seeking information on the best career for you

♦ Receiving couples' counseling

♦ Being assessed for mental disorders

♦ Seeking education-related assessments

Personality inventories are also known as **objective tests**. These assessments are considered objective because they do not involve the subjective judgments of an interviewing or observing psychologist, as in direct interviews and behavioral observation. These assessments are usually designed as multiple-choice or true-false format questionnaires. Individuals' test results are compared with standardized data to assess personality. Well-known personality inventories include the **Minnesota Multiphasic Personality Inventory (MMPI-2)** and the Myers-Briggs Type Indicator (MBTI).

Research shows high validity for the MMPI-2, which means that it can accurately assess personality traits associated with particular mental disorders (Garb, 2003; Kubisyzn et al., 2000). The inventory is composed of more than 500 items in the form of true/false statements such as, "People constantly conspire against me," "I like fire," and "Someone is always watching me." Although these are not actual items from the MMPI-2, they give you an idea of the inventory. The MMPI-2 has 10 scales, which form a profile of the person's personality. These 10 scales are hypochondriasis, depression, hysteria, psychopathic deviate, masculinity/femininity, paranoia, psychasthenia, schizophrenia, mania, and social introversion. Other aspects of personality the MMPI evaluates are alienation from self, alienation from others, ego inflation, shyness, addiction potential, responsibility, level of motivation, self-doubt, family discord, fears, cynicism, and inability to disclose (Schultz & Schultz, 2005).

Whereas the MMPI-2 is an instrument that is designed to assess pathology, the **Myers-Briggs Type Indicator (MBTI)** is often used with normal populations, such as college students, to help them choose majors and develop career goals. The MBTI has four personality dimensions, which combine to create 16 personality types. The four dimensions are introversion-extroversion, intuitive-sensing, judging-perceiving, and thinking-feeling.

Projective Tests

Projective tests allow the test taker to assign meaning to pictures such as ambiguous scenes or inkblots. After viewing the stimulus, the test taker assigns or "projects" meaning onto the image. The idea behind the projective test is that the meaning projected onto the object yields insight into the personality traits and possible psychopathology of the test taker. This assumption is known as the projective hypothesis. From the psychodynamic perspective, these instruments are thought to reveal unconscious conflicts or wishes of the examinee that are not accessible through direct questioning or any other personality assessment instrument.

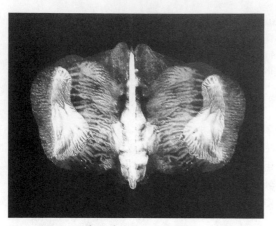

FIGURE 13.4 *What do you see in this picture?*

The Rorschach Inkblot Test is perhaps the most widely known personality test. Though most people would not know it by its formal name, they would likely recognize it as the "inkblot" test upon seeing one of its abstract images. Created in 1921 by Swiss psychiatrist Hermann Rorschach, this test asks a person to view an inkblot image and tell the examiner what it might be. Where one person sees a cat in the inkblot, another person may see a pregnant cow, for example.

Research of the Rorschach test offers mixed results—some studies show that the test can assess personality, whereas other studies indicate that the test has low validity and that it doesn't assess personality so much as a person's temporary mental processes. For example, you see an inkblot and it appears to you as a mother abandoning her child. Does this tell anything about you or about your temporary memory of a news segment you saw on TV last night? For these reasons, the Rorschach is considered a controversial test of personality (Schultz & Schultz, 2005).

Psychologist Henry Murray created the Thematic Apperception Test (TAT) in 1938. The TAT employs black-and-white pictures that are intentionally unclear in meaning. The test taker is asked to create a story with a beginning, a middle, and an end to explain the picture. Typically the subject is shown a series of pictures in an order in which the psychologist can look for a similar theme that runs through the stories told by the subject. Common themes that examinees might project into the ambiguous scenes are the need for achievement or a need for affiliation, or their stories may suggest interpersonal difficulties.

As with the research on the Rorschach test, research on the TAT offers mixed results as well. Some studies show that the test can assess personality, whereas other studies show that the test has low validity. Most psychologists consider this test to be controversial (Schultz & Schultz, 2005).

Behavioral Observation

Similar to interviews, behavioral observation allows the psychologist to gather direct information on the person being assessed. The psychologist doing the assessment is trained in a variety of techniques that allow the interpretation of meaning from observed behaviors. One example of behavioral observation can be found in marriage and family therapy. Therapists can gain valuable insight into a couple's dynamics from watching their interactions, body language, and even tonal inflections during discussions, role playing, and other exercises.

Which Method Is Best?

Each approach has clear advantages and disadvantages. For example, a skilled psychologist may use direct observation to detect nuances not indicated on a personality inventory. On the other hand, a personality inventory may detect possible psychopathologies that a psychologist using a projective technique or making behavioral observations might overlook. Since each approach has inherent strengths and weaknesses, the best method is a combination or battery of tests. In a test battery, the results from each test yield different and valuable information. When an experienced psychologist reviews the data from a test battery, he or she can make a more accurate evaluation.

Psychoanalytic Theory

Sigmund Freud is perhaps the most widely known person in psychology. This is because he pioneered the first form of talk therapy, known as psychoanalysis. Although Freud's theory of personality formation was wildly popular for about 60 years, most psychologists today do not embrace it in its original form. In fact, an early basis for the growth of his personality theory came from three directions: (1) those agreeing with Freud, (2) those agreeing with Freud in general, but adding their own approach, and (3) those who had theories very different from Freud's. In this section we will examine Freud's personality theory as well as similar theories developed by neo-Freudian theorists such as Carl Jung, Alfred Adler, Karen Horney, and Erik Erikson. Today there are psychotherapists who embrace theoretical perspectives that agree with Freudian theory to varying degrees. The school of thought that embraces Freud and all the theorists who modified Freud's original theory is known as the psychodynamic school. The psychodynamic model is based on the idea that there are powerful mental processes that remain hidden from conscious awareness, which nevertheless influence a person's behavior (Sulloway, 1983).

Freud's Levels of Consciousness

Freud posited that the human consciousness is divided into three levels: the conscious, the preconscious, and the unconscious. The **conscious** level consists of thoughts a person is easily aware of recalling. The **preconscious** level contains thoughts not immediately within the conscious mind but easily accessible. For example, a friend or relative may tell a funny story that involves you but you may not remember the incident. After you are given a few clues, however, you think hard and you recall the incident. The **unconscious** level consists of your deepest thoughts, feelings, and motivations, which are not accessible during normal awareness. Freud (1900/1953) believed this third level possessed many of the keys to personality and behavior.

Freud's levels of consciousness can be pictured as an iceberg, with the conscious level being the tip rising just out of the water, the preconscious being at water level, and the unconscious being the larger part concealed below the water.

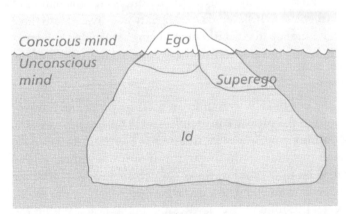

FIGURE 13.5 *Freud theorized that consciousness is similar to an iceberg, as most of it is hidden.*

Common Uses and Misuses of Freudian Terms

Death wish is often misunderstood as the desire to take extreme chances with one's life. Actually, Freud's reference to a death wish means the desire for a person to be in a state of ultimate peace and balance. Freud believed this could only be achieved in death.

Egotistical is often used to describe a person who has an inflated sense of self-worth. Actually, ego refers to Freud's definition of that part of the self that is operating at the conscious level. So, to have a strong ego means that one is rational.

Freudian slips are seemingly meaningless slips of the tongue interpreted as having a deeper meaning representing a person's innermost thoughts.

Libido in popular culture is used to refer to the sex drive. While this is partly correct, Freud's definition of libido actually refers to the overall energy or drive of a person.

Oedipus complex is an allusion to the Greek character Oedipus, who kills his father and marries his mother. Freud believed young boys secretly harbor unconscious sexual desires for their mothers and are jealous of their fathers.

Pleasure principle, as it is used in popular culture, refers to having a good time without worrying about the consequences. Similarly in Freudian theory, this refers to the id's desire to seek pleasure and avoid pain as a primary motivation, without taking reality into account.

Referring to someone as "anal" in ordinary conversation refers to an overly detail-oriented, anxious type of person. The term comes from Freud's anal-retentive-type personality, which represents a fixation during the second stage of psychosexual development.

Referring to something as "Freudian" in lay terms generally means it is sexually suggestive, possessing a hidden sexual meaning, or symbolic of sex in some manner.

Freud's Structure of the Personality

Another component of Freud's psychoanalytic theory offers an explanation of the structure of personality. Freud believed the personality was divided into three parts: the id, the ego, and the superego. Rather than being actual physical structures in the brain, these components refer to the theoretical mechanics of the brain's operation.

The **id** is the part of the personality operating on basic instincts and motivations. The id operates from the **pleasure principle**, seeking pleasurable experiences and avoiding painful experiences in an attempt to relieve the tension brought on by pressures that life puts on the psyche. It operates without regard to consequences, and, if left unchecked by the other personality structures, the id would lead us to make dangerous and rash decisions that jeopardize our health and safety. The id creates our uninhibited daydreams and fantasies. Within the id are instincts that are part of our common human nature, such as the sexual instinct, an aggressive instinct, and the survival instinct.

An Argument Between the Id, the Ego, and the Superego

This example illustrates how Freud's structures of personality interact. This dynamic interaction is implied in the term "psychodynamic." Imagine a person walking by a bakery and looking in the window to see a fresh tray of chocolate chip cookies. The smell is wafting out the door of the bakery and it's almost lunchtime.

Id: Hey, let's get some cookies.

Ego: Well, I'd like to honor that request, but we've picked up some weight over the winter and we've got to shape up for the summer. Before you know it we'll be heading for the beach in a swimsuit.

Id: Whatever! Let's get some cookies. It won't hurt.

Ego: No. Just one of those cookies has almost an entire day's fat grams.

Id: So what? I want some cookies!

Superego: Id, don't be greedy. You can't have everything you want all the time. We're moving along now because it's best for us to skip the cookies and focus on eating healthy food. Let's go.

Ego: Yeah, we don't need to be late for work. I don't know. Maybe we can get just one on the way home.

Id: I want a dozen, now!

Ego: Be quiet, Id. We're not getting any now.

Superego: We should feel good. We did the right thing.

In Freud's theoretical framework, the **ego** serves as the "executive" of the personality in that it manages the pressures from the id, the superego, and reality. The ego emerges when the child is introduced to the rules and norms for behavior in society and thus begins to realize the constraints created by reality, particularly in the form of parental directives. The ego prevents the id's impulsiveness from causing harm—for example, by ignoring parental rules. This is why the ego is said to operate on the **reality principle** as opposed to the id's pleasure principle. However, as Freud noted, the id is not always simply under the control of the ego and has ways of influencing the ego. The ego must also take into account the demands of the superego.

The **superego** works on the **morality principle**, providing overall moral guidance to the personality. The conscience emerges as a means by which the individual gauges whether a behavior is morally appropriate, that is, a list of things that one should not do. The **ego ideal** consists of things that we know will make us feel good about ourselves when we do them. It is the aspect of the superego that encompasses those actions for which the child has been consistently rewarded. When a person does not do what the superego values as right, the result is guilt, whereas when we follow the dictates of the ego ideal, we tend to feel proud of ourselves (Hall & Lindzey, 1970).

Defense Mechanisms

One can see that the interaction of the id, the ego, and the superego are not easily aligned. In Freud's theory, these personality structures compete for dominance. The result is strain on the psyche that causes the individual to **repress** desires or thoughts that are unacceptable to the ego, pushing them into the unconscious region of the psyche. An individual may resort to other ego **defense mechanisms** as well. Freud believed that the psyche creates defense mechanisms to keep from being overwhelmed by anxiety due to these competing structures of personality. Defense mechanisms allow us to create reasons to make our actions feel understandable and acceptable even when they are not. They are not inherently bad or wrong, because they enable us to cope, but they can also be dangerous since they deny or distort reality. Finally defense mechanisms operate on an unconscious level, so the person is not aware of employing them.

As an example in which defense mechanisms might be helpful, police officers, firefighters, and paramedics use them in performing their daily duties. These professionals often witness gory scenes, heartbreaking tragedy, and extreme violence as part of their jobs. In the face of such things, these individuals might intellectualize rather than respond emotionally. Intellectualizing allows them to unconsciously manage the anxiety they are experiencing. This is a useful mechanism, within limits. For example, a paramedic responding to the scene of a terrible auto accident might get on the radio and tell the dispatcher, "We have a major auto and pedestrian accident here. The pedestrian has suffered a severe head injury with multiple lacerations. He also has serious trauma to his chest and abdomen. One of the witnesses is not physically injured but highly distressed and will also need medical attention." The paramedic is intellectualizing, or translating the highly emotional content into a less distressing form. In this way, the paramedic is shielded from the panic and dread normally aroused by such a scene and is able to treat those who are injured. Most psychologists would agree that defense mechanisms operate in a protective manner and are not problematic unless they seriously distort reality (Newman, Duff, & Baumeister, 1997; Taylor & Armor, 1996).

Psychosexual Stages of Development

Perhaps one of Freud's most controversial beliefs was the psychosexual stages of development. Freud theorized that all children develop through **psychosexual stages**, which occur during approximately the first 12 years of life. These

TABLE 13.1 Defense mechanisms.

Defense mechanism	Summary	Example
Denial	Refusing to accept unpleasant realities	Refusing to admit a drug addiction
Displacement	Using a less threatening object for the original object of impulse	Yelling at a younger sibling because your mother yelled at you
Intellectualization	Ignoring emotions by focusing on words or ideas	Focusing on funeral costs instead of the pain of losing a loved one
Projection	Transferring unacceptable thoughts to others	Accusing your mate of being attracted to other people because you are
Rationalization	Using socially acceptable excuses for unacceptable behavior	Saying you are going to exceed the speed limit because everyone else speeds
Reaction formation	Suppressing unacceptable urges by exaggerating the opposite	Being vehemently against pornography because you are secretly enchanted by it
Regression	Responding to a threat in a manner characteristic of an earlier stage of development	Curling into the fetal position when facing danger
Repression	Preventing traumatic thoughts from being remembered easily	Forgetting the details of a terrible auto accident
Compensation	Overcoming a personal defect or perceived weakness by excelling in the same or another area	Working out with determination to overcome physical frailty
Sublimation	Substituting constructive activities for unacceptable impulses	Venting anger by taking karate lessons

stages correspond to erogenous zones from which the child receives pleasure at each respective stage. Freud believed each stage presented a developmental conflict between the child's healthy and unhealthy approach to life. If the child did not successfully move through a stage, he or she would be said to have developed a **fixation**, that is, the child would get stuck on that particular stage of development.

The Oral Stage

The **oral stage** takes place from birth to 18 months. The infant receives gratification through using the mouth for sucking, eating, and biting. Parents play a critical role in the formation of the child's personality, since they can overindulge the child through the gratification of pleasures obtainable through the mouth. If the child's mouth gets stimulated whenever he or she wants something, the child can get stuck or orally fixated—he or she will always crave for this oral overindulgence. This fixation can lead to the development of an oral personality—adults who are overly dependent on others to provide and care for them. This is exhibited by being passive, gullible, overly optimistic, impatient, and restless (Schultz & Schultz, 2005).

Conversely, a fixation can also occur due to undergratification during the oral stage. Parents can frustrate children by not letting them have sufficient amounts of oral gratification. In this scenario, children can also get fixated on needing this oral stimulation. Children raised under these conditions might develop the form of oral personality characterized by pessimism about the world, mistrust toward others, aggression, and social withdrawal. Freud believed that parents need to find a way to provide the child with ample oral stimulation to support the development of a healthy personality. Freud believed orally fixated children would exhibit behaviors indicative of this fixation throughout life—for example, excessive drinking or chain smoking (Schultz & Schultz, 2005).

The Anal Stage

FIGURE 13.6 *Toilet training is part of the anal stage. Courtesy of Debbie Whitaker.*

In the **anal stage** (18 months to 3 years), children receive satisfaction through the anus by either having or retaining bowel movements. Freud theorized that parental efforts at toilet training cause conflict between children and their parents. Toilet training is a frustrating experience for children, and they can rebel against their parents either by defecating (expulsion of feces) whenever or wherever they want or by retaining feces in spite of parents' urging them to defecate. Rebellion against parents and stimulation of anal muscles give children pleasure. If they get stuck on the pleasures of anal-retentive behavior, they might develop an anal-retentive personality characterized by extreme neatness, stubbornness, and stinginess. If, however, they get stuck on anal-expulsive behavior, they might develop an anal-expulsive personality characterized by messiness, defiance, recklessness, and extreme disorganization in life (Schultz & Schultz, 2005).

The Phallic Stage

During the **phallic stage** (between 3 and 6 years), children find pleasure in their genitals. For example, children begin to masturbate alone and with other children. At this stage, Freud's controversial Oedipus complex begins—the boy develops a sexual attraction to his mother (Oedipus is a character from Greek mythology who kills his father and marries his mother). The Oedipal complex manifests itself in the boy's need to displace his competitor—his father. This lust for mother and wish to kill father causes castration anxiety in the boy. In other words, he fears that his father knows of his desires and will punish him by cutting off his penis. In Freud's theory, the boy can become stuck on this complex and develop a phallic personality characterized by narcissism (excessive self-love due to castration anxiety) and/or homosexuality (his mother will be his only romantic choice, so no other woman will have a significant romantic role in his life). The boy can resolve his Oedipal complex by repressing his sexual attraction to his mother and his wish to kill his father, and by identifying with his father. Through identification, the boy vicariously (through his father) can have his mother (Monte, 1999).

For a girl, the Oedipus complex is initiated by the castration complex that precipitates a weakening of her *cathexis* (the process of investment of mental or emotional energy in a person, object, or idea) for the mother and an instituting of a cathexis for the father (Hall & Lindzey, 1970). The Oedipus complex affects girls of the same age (3–6) as it does the boy. When a young girl realizes that she does not have a penis, she feels that she has already been castrated. She blames her mother for allowing this to happen. When she looks at her mother, she realizes that her mother is also missing this organ, which is the symbol of power. The girl is drawn toward her father because he possesses a penis, his power or status symbol. She hopes that through association with him, she will gain the symbolic power represented by the penis, which is something she lacks and wants. Freud referred to this as penis envy. In this complex, the girl experiences sexual attraction toward her father and wants to displace her competitor—her mother.

The girl can resolve her complex by repressing her lustful and aggressive urges, and through identifying with her mother. However, in theory, if this is unsuccessful and the girl gets stuck in the Oedipal complex, she can develop phallic personality characterized by homosexuality and/or insecurity. She will always romantically want her father, and no other male will be able to spark her romantic interest.

Another controversial notion of Freud's was his view of how girls experienced the phallic stage. Freud believed girls in the phallic stage experienced **penis envy** due to their lack of a penis. Penis envy results in the girl always being mildly insecure throughout her life even if she does resolve her Oedipal complex. However, if her Oedipal complex is not resolved, a very high level of insecurity will plague the girl throughout her life. Freud believed girls did not ever fully overcome penis envy, and for that reason, in Freud's view, women are inherently more insecure than men (Schultz & Schultz, 2005).

The Latency Period

The **latency period** occurs from age 6 to puberty. In this stage, children develop socially and also repress sexual urges while engaging in socially acceptable activities. The dormant sexual impulses are redirected into nonsexual outlets, such as learning how to do things that will be useful in adulthood (Monte, 1999).

TABLE 13.2	Freud's psychosexual stages of development.			
Stage	**Age**	**Erogenous zone**	**Conflict**	**How fixation affects the adult personality**
Oral	0–18 months	Mouth	Weaning	Deriving excessive pleasure from oral tasks such as eating, drinking, or other activities
Anal	18 months–3 years	Anus	Toilet training	Anal retentive: overly concerned about neatness and stubborn behavior
				Anal expulsive: Rebellious and destructive behavior
Phallic	3–6 years	Genitals	Overcoming Oedipal complex	Males: Castration anxiety and problems with authority figures, overly concerned about getting a mate
				Females: Penis envy, flirtatiousness, overly concerned about getting a mate
Latency	6–puberty	None	Interacting with same-sex peers	Asexuality
Genital	Puberty to adult	Genitals	Having intimate relationships with the opposite sex	Isolation and withdrawal from others

The Genital Stage

The last stage is the **genital stage**, which begins at the onset of adolescence. This stage is based on creating relationships with the opposite sex in which sexual desires can be resolved. Success at this stage largely depends on the resolution of conflicts in previous stages. If a person was unable to resolve the conflicts from previous stages, at this stage the person may be more prone to promiscuity than is typical for teenagers at this age.

Objections to Freud's Theory

Despite being a tremendous influence on modern psychology, Freud's theory of personality draws fire from critics on several significant issues:

♦ Freud's theories have not been tested with a diversity of cultures. Freud used his own case studies for his evidence rather than having a variety of cases from which to test his theories; thus, he based his views on Viennese women who were 18–25 years old. It is questionable whether these women were representative of the entire human population.

♦ The unconscious mind is too abstract to test. Therefore, proof of psychoanalytic theories is difficult to establish.

♦ Freud focused too much on biological instincts such as the sex drive and self-preservation drives such as hunger and thirst.

♦ Freud's psychoanalytic theory is sexist. For example, the assertion that women experience penis envy assumes that the male gender is inherently superior.

Certain aspects of Freud's theory, though, seem to be supported by research evidence. For example, defense mechanisms seem to exist; boys 3–6 years of age are more affectionate with their mothers than with their fathers. Boys are also more aggressive toward their fathers than toward their mothers. Girls 3–6 years of age are more affectionate with their fathers than with their mothers, and girls are more aggressive toward their mothers than toward their fathers (Schultz & Schultz, 2005).

Neo-Freudians

As previously discussed, not all early theorists agreed with Freud. Indeed, one of Freud's largest contributions to psychology may have been the chain reaction that he caused from those who disagreed with him. It was from this foundation that many new theories were postulated by other psychologists. Three influential neo-Freudians were Carl Jung, Alfred Adler, and Karen Horney.

Carl Jung (1875–1961)

Perhaps the best-known neo-Freudian among the public is Carl Jung. Jung disagreed with Freud's idea of human behavior being motivated merely by primal needs within the unconscious. Jung believed the unconscious mind also had spiritual motivations in addition to the sexual and aggressive instincts emphasized by Freud.

Jung's theory divides the psyche into three parts. The first is the ego, which Jung identified with the conscious mind. He concluded that the unconscious mind consisted of the **personal unconscious** and the **collective unconscious**. The personal unconscious includes anything that is not presently conscious but that can be easily recalled. It is the result of an individual's own life experiences. It contains "complexes," which are organized constellations of feelings, thoughts, perceptions, and memories that exist within the personal unconscious and act as a kind of magnet attracting to it various experiences (Jung, 1934/1960). For example, the mother complex consists of experiences with mothers in general and from the child's experiences with his or her own mother. Ideas, feelings, and memories relating to the mother form a complex and may behave like an autonomous unconscious personality, which has energy and a mental life of its own. It may seize control of the personality in order to carry out its own ends (Monte, 1999).

The personal unconscious is like most people's understanding of the unconscious in that it includes both memories that are easily brought to mind and memories that have been suppressed for some reason. But it does not include the instincts that Freud envisioned as a central aspect of the unconscious mind.

The collective unconscious contains universal memories shared among all human beings, as well as **archetypes**, which are universal ideas present in all people. Jung believed that evidence for the existence of a collective unconscious was found in the similarities across cultures in art, mythology, and religion, which tend to be reflected in common images consistent in meaning throughout the entire human race, as well as common patterns of thinking, feeling, and behaving. Jung believed that the collective unconscious and the archetypes within it are not learned, but instead are inherited genetically from our ancestors. In other words, we are born with a collective unconscious.

Like Freud, Jung believed the unconscious mind was always at work. However, Jung's concept of the collective unconscious was very different from Freud's concept of the unconscious mind. Jung suggested that our collective unconscious already had knowledge of certain concepts and images. Therefore, when a person had an experience linking the conscious contemporary world with the collective unconscious knowledge, the collective unconscious served as a resource that offered great insight. Freud believed such insights could only result from years of psychoanalysis, whereas Jung concluded that they were inherently a part of the human mind in a spiritual sense.

As evidence to support Jung's theory, Jungian scholars point out that people from many different cultures, regardless of their religious convictions, describe near-death experiences in similar ways. Common details of this experience include feeling as though you are floating or hovering, having an out-of-body feeling, encountering friends and relatives who are dead, and experiencing warmth, divine love, peace, and a bright light. Jung suggested that this sort of experience—consisting of a pattern of thoughts, feelings and behaviors—is evidence of the collective unconscious in action, of a near-death archetype. Other evidence put forward to support the idea of universal archetypes includes the existence of common symbols in art and the common human experience of reverence for nature.

The Collective Unconscious.

To better understand Jung's conception of the unconscious mind, we have to delve into archetypes. They are often embedded in images from which all human beings can derive a common meaning. Let's discuss some common archetypal images prominent in literature, art, and even in movies. For example, the movie *Star Wars* contains many archetypal images, such as the wise old man, the animal, and the shadow (Darth Vader). Another movie with similar archetypal images is *The Matrix*, with Neo as the archetypal hero and Morpheus as the archetypal image of a wise old man. One reason for the success of these films is their ability to convey a message through the use of archetypal imagery to which people can relate. The number of archetypes is unlimited, but the following paragraphs discuss a few that illustrate how archetypes operate.

FIGURE 13.7 *The wicked witch from* The Wizard of Oz *is an example of the villain archetype. Courtesy of PhotoFest.*

The **mother archetype** is easy to understand when you consider what a mother represents to most people. A woman's tendency to be caring, nurturing, and selfless with her offspring forms the core of the mother archetype. The archetypal image of a mother can be seen in the famous sculpture *Pietà* by Michelangelo, in which mother Mary holds her dead son, Christ. The **father archetype** represents authority, and the **family archetype** represents connection and belonging.

Two important archetypes are the **anima** and the **animus**, which represent, respectively, the feminine aspects in men and the masculine aspects in women. Jung considered the expression of both the masculine and feminine sides in an individual as necessary for full personality development. Furthermore, the existence of anima in males and animus in females enables us to relate to members of the opposite sex. A man who hates women would be considered to be

Archetypes in Art, Literature, Theater, and Film

The *hero* often represents sacrifice and victory of goodness over evil. Examples of archetypal heroes are Luke Skywalker in *Star Wars*, Harry Potter in the *Harry Potter* series, and all the comic book superheroes. The collective unconscious is represented by a figure having knowledge, such as the *wise old man*—for example, Gandalf in *The Lord of the Rings* and Merlin in *King Arthur*. The villain—for example, Darth Vader—represents the *shadow*.

? Can you identify archetypes in a book, a play, or a movie you're familiar with?

at war with his own anima. A woman may project her ideal image of manliness (her animus) onto a potential mate and then be disappointed if that man does not live up to the standards she carries internally.

The **persona** goes with the **shadow archetype** to form a pair. The persona is that part of ourselves of which we are conscious and which we see when we look in a mirror. However, it is only the outer self; there is more that lies within us. Most of us cannot see beneath the masks we wear, and sometimes we are not aware that our public personalities are masks that disguise other aspects of ourselves that are less acceptable to us.

There is something behind our mask, and that is our shadow. If the persona is everything we like about ourselves, then the shadow is everything we dislike about ourselves, the darker side that we deny. The shadow archetype represents things we fear about ourselves or don't want to think about due to their negative nature. Like our real shadow, our psychic shadow clings to us even when we turn our backs on it. We project our shadows onto others in a scapegoat fashion, rejecting in them what we don't wish to acknowledge about ourselves.

The **self archetype** is the most important archetype. It represents an integration of and a balance between the conscious and the unconscious, the anima and the animus, our thinking and feeling aspects, our sensing and intuiting sides, the persona and the ego, as well as our tendencies toward introversion or extroversion.

Jung viewed human nature as consisting of polarities: A male also has female aspects, and the reverse is true as well. We may be extroverted, but we have an introverted side. We may be essentially thinking beings, but we have reservoirs of feelings. We may be conscious beings, but within us there are cauldrons of unconscious raw material seeking outward expression. We live on a physical plane, but we also have a spiritual self. Jung represented the self archetype with mandalas, which are circular structures that are symmetrical from right to left and from top to bottom, representing that balance of opposites within each of us.

FIGURE 13.8 *Aragorn from* The Lord of the Rings *is an example of the hero archetype. Courtesy of New Line/Everett Collection.*

Jung's Eight Personality Types.
Jung's most accepted contribution to personality theory was his discovery of the extroversion/introversion dimension. Extroverted individuals incorporate the following mental processes: thinking, feeling, sensing, and intuiting. Sensation tells us through our senses that a thing exists. Sensation is concerned with orientation to reality (Jung, 1968). Intuition is the ability to predict and know, but not on the basis of evidence—as in when you are driving on the highway and you get a strong gut feeling that something bad will happen behind you. You are extra attentive, and in a few minutes you are able to react in time to the huge truck almost hitting you from behind. Jung thought that one of these processes tends to dominate an individual, whereas the other end of the continuum tends to be less pronounced. Thus, he believed that there are four extroverted types

FIGURE 13.9 *Despite looking the same, the members of this marching band have different personality types.*

of personality: extroverted thinking, extroverted feeling, extroverted sensing, and extroverted intuiting. There are also four introverted types: introverted thinking, introverted feeling, introverted sensing, and introverted intuiting (Schultz & Schultz, 2005). The MBTI, discussed in the assessment section, is based on Jung's personality types.

Objections to Jung's Theory. Research evidence supports the notion that people can be extroverted or introverted. Even though some studies show that eight personality types exist, other research studies show that there might be more than eight personality types. Jung's concepts of the collective unconscious and the existence of archetypes are controversial, and the vast majority of contemporary psychologists do not accept them. The concept of the collective unconscious is difficult to test using scientific methods. The existence of archetypes is currently under investigation, as well as the notion that these archetypes are genetically transmitted to us from our ancestors (Schultz & Schultz, 2005). As intriguing as Jung's ideas are, there is a lack of scientific evidence to support them, except for the extroversion/introversion personality dimension.

Alfred Adler (1870–1937)

Alfred Adler was a follower of Freud's, but he disagreed with Freud over the importance of internal dynamics such as sexual drives. Adler viewed social interaction as a critical factor in shaping personality. He theorized that individuals are motivated by their individual goals as well as their central purpose in life, which is a **striving for superiority**. In Adler's view, all human beings initially form feelings of inferiority as a result of feeling helpless and incompetent as infants and small children. This natural feeling of inferiority leads to a striving for superiority, which usually leads to the development of sense of competence or mastery. This, in turn, allows the person to experience self-acceptance. The positive results of the natural feelings of inferiority from childhood are a social consciousness and an interest in the welfare of other people. The negative side of struggling with these feelings can be the development of an **inferiority complex**, which can trigger aggressive behavior or excessive jealousy. Adler accepted Freud's concept of an inborn aggressive drive, which tends toward cruelty, but proposed that the drive becomes converted through the demands of cultural and parental censure into altruism, charity, and sympathy. Adler considered this transformation to be the hallmark of healthy development. He believed that friendship, love, and work are the central concerns of adult life.

Adler was convinced that personality is affected by birth order (see sidebar for details as to the expected effects). During the past half century, there has been significant research interest in the effects of birth order in an attempt to verify Adler's theory (e.g., Salmon & Daly, 1998; Sulloway, 1995). Researchers have attempted to find links between personality traits and birth order, but the connection has not been strongly substantiated. This may be due to the complexity of family configuration, in which any effects of birth order are significantly modified by the details of each family situation, such as the sex of the children, how close they are in age, and whether the family has been dissolved by parental divorce and reconstituted by remarriage.

Does Birth Order Affect Personality?

Firstborn

Positives: independent and authoritative
Negatives: insecure and defensive

The oldest child has to endure being dethroned by the next child. He or she then has to learn to share. Parental expectations are usually very high. This child is often given responsibility and is expected to set an example for younger siblings. This child may become authoritarian or strict or feel that power is his or her right. If encouraged, he or she can become helpful. The firstborn may turn to the father after the birth of the next child.

Second Born

Positives: competitive and achievement oriented
Negatives: domineering

The second child always has someone ahead to set the pace for development. Second-born children are more competitive, wanting to overtake the older child. This child may become a rebel or try to outdo everyone. Competition can deteriorate into rivalry.

Middle Child

Positives: balanced temperament and fairness oriented
Negatives: feelings of neglect

The middle child is "sandwiched" between siblings and thus may feel squeezed out of a position of privilege and significance. This child may be even-tempered and have a "take it or leave it" attitude. He or she may have trouble finding a place or may become a fighter of injustice.

Youngest Child

Positives: ambitious
Negatives: dependent and seeks pampering

The youngest child may have many "mothers" and "fathers" and tends to be educated by older siblings. This child is never dethroned and wants to be bigger than the others. He or she may have huge plans that never work out. The youngest is frequently spoiled and can stay the "baby."

Only Child

Positives: independent and achievement orientated
Negatives: shy and passive

With an only child, the parents have no previous experience in parenting. The child receives 100% of the attention from both parents. This child may become a rival of one parent and can also be overprotected and spoiled. As a result, an only child likes being the center of adult attention, often has difficulty sharing with peers, prefers adult company, and uses adult language.

(Adler, 1930; Sulloway, 1995)

Karen Horney (1885–1952)

Karen Horney's theory focuses on **basic anxiety**. Horney was the foremost psychoanalytic theorist in the area of **neurosis**, and her ideas helped transform the view of neurosis. She did not see anxious thinking as unique to the neurotic individual; rather, she posited that all individuals experience the same dynamics as those considered neurotic, but those who successfully cope with their basic feelings of anxiety develop healthy personalities. Neurotic individuals may attempt to cope with intense levels of anxiety in one of three ways: (1) by becoming aggressive, assuming that the best defense is a good offense; (2) by withdrawing, with the idea that minimizing contact with others minimizes the opportunity to be hurt; and (3) by becoming dependent, assuming that safety can be found in the protection offered by a stronger, more competent person.

Womb Envy?

Karen Horney responded to Freud's suggestion that women have penis envy with her own theory. Horney suggested that men might experience womb envy as a result of their inability to bear children. As evidence, she offered examples of male attempts to continue to "live on" by assigning their names to children and attempting to make a permanent impact on society.

? How do you feel about penis envy and womb envy?

Horney also posited that we all have the need for affection and approval. When an intimate relationship or marriage breaks up, the need for affection and approval is in jeopardy of not being met. For most individuals, this crisis can be managed, and they will maintain a relatively normal state of psychological functioning. However, the needs of the neurotic are much more intense, and the neurotic individual experiences a crisis of coping with an extreme level of anxiety as a result.

Erik Erikson (1902–1994): The Life-Span Approach

Erik Erikson's **life-span development** theory does not emphasize the unconscious forces influencing the development of personality as do Jung's and Freud's. Instead, he believed that our conscious experience of our environment and our ability to make conscious choices are the most important factors in personality development. He emphasized the influence of social relationships on shaping personality. There are eight stages of development, according to Erikson, and each stage influences some important personality aspects. Freud believed that our experiences from the initial five years of our childhood are the most critical for personality development, whereas Jung emphasized the midlife period (ages 35–45) as probably the most important phase of personality development. For Erikson, adolescence is the most significant stage.

Explore
Erikson's theory
in Chapter 12, p. 394

Research seems to support Erikson's view of the stages of personality development as well as the idea that the extent to which the crisis associated with each stage is resolved and has positive and negative effects on subsequent development (e.g., Domino & Affonso, 1990; McAdams, de St. Aubin, & Logan, 1993; Ochse & Plug, 1986). However, research evidence does not support Erikson's conclusion that a sense of identity forms by age 18 in most people. Today, at least, identity formation seems to be a longer process, so that by the age of 25, a majority of people have formed the sense of who they are and what they want to do with their lives. These people may continue to change, but less drastically, throughout their lives. Some studies show that identity formation occurs in many people throughout their lifetime rather than being solidified by age 25. Erikson is also criticized for not talking sufficiently about the effect of specific cultures on the development of personality even though he properly acknowledged the effects of the environment on personality development (Schultz & Schultz, 2005).

Humanistic Theories

Humanistic personality theories value the individual's perception of reality and do not attribute personality to genes, human nature, or unconscious influences. Humanists believe that people have free will, which means that their behavior is directed by their own choices, regardless of external influences. They contend that behavior is primarily organized around the positive motive for self-fulfillment (Alexander, 2007). The humanistic theory places emphasis on understanding the perception of the world held by the individual person. Humanistic theorists support the idea that people are naturally good, and, if allowed to develop normally, they will move in a positive manner toward self-fulfillment.

Abraham Maslow/Self-Actualization

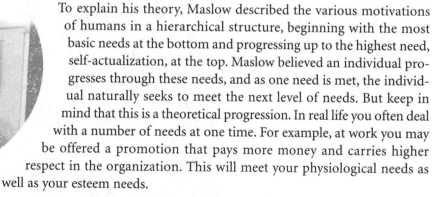

Explore
Maslow's hierarchy
in Chapter 6, p. 169

Abraham Maslow was a notable humanistic theorist. Maslow's work has been used in a number of practical applications, such as business, motivation training, and education. Maslow theorized that individuals have the desire to reach their highest potential. He termed this self-actualization. To explain his theory, Maslow described the various motivations of humans in a hierarchical structure, beginning with the most basic needs at the bottom and progressing up to the highest need, self-actualization, at the top. Maslow believed an individual progresses through these needs, and as one need is met, the individual naturally seeks to meet the next level of needs. But keep in mind that this is a theoretical progression. In real life you often deal with a number of needs at one time. For example, at work you may be offered a promotion that pays more money and carries higher respect in the organization. This will meet your physiological needs as well as your esteem needs.

To describe these motivations, Maslow created a hierarchy of needs. At the most basic level are *physiological* needs: the need for food, clothing, and shelter. We need to eat, we need to have oxygen to breathe, and we need to be sheltered from a rain or snow storm. *Safety and security* needs are the next level—for example, the need to live in a safe neighborhood or the desire to work at a job without the fear of being fired or laid off. Needs for *love and belonging* make up the next level. This includes the need for friends, relationships, or memberships in organizations—for example, the need to have friends to hang out with on the weekend or the need to have a boyfriend or girlfriend. *Esteem needs* are divided into two levels. Maslow believed individuals have a need for esteem from those in their environment, such as recognition and notoriety—for instance, receiving an award for being the most outstanding salesperson. A need for self-esteem

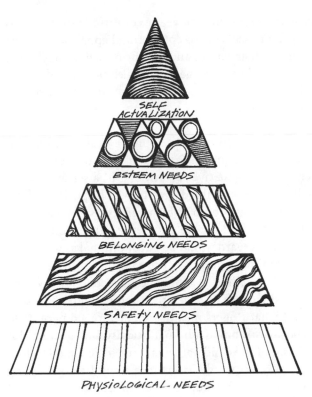

FIGURE 13.10 *Maslow's hierarchy of needs.*

also takes the form of a desire for confidence and independence. An example would be believing that you are a good salesperson regardless of whether you win an award or are recognized for your skills by someone else. The highest level of need is *self-actualization*, which refers to fulfillment of one's full potential. Although Maslow posited that self-actualization is a key motivation for all people, he felt that only a few people ever actually achieved it. Much of the world's population struggles with attempting to meet their most basic needs. Examples of those whom Maslow considered self-actualized were the 30 "good specimens of humanity" he studied in order to discover the qualities they had in common. These individuals include Eleanor Roosevelt, Albert Einstein, Abraham Lincoln, Thomas Jefferson, Jane Adams, Ludwig von Beethoven, Walt Whitman, and Henry David Thoreau. Of course, one need not be famous or a world leader to achieve self-actualization.

Carl Rogers

The self-concept theory of Carl Rogers proposes that the most critical element in the determination of personality is an individual's perception of the self, or **self-concept**. A related concept, **self-esteem**, refers to how you feel about yourself, that is, your evaluation of your worth given your self-concept or image of yourself.

Rogers noticed that a central goal of his therapy clients seemed to be to become their "real self." Rogers eventually concluded that the formation of a healthy personality was the result of **congruence** (Hall & Lindzey, 1970). Specifically, he suggested that a well-adjusted personality stems from an overlapping of an individual's self-concept with the experiences that the individual has with others and the rest of the environment, which reflects the **true self**. In other words, when your subjective reality matches external reality (the world as it is), you have congruence. For example, if you consider yourself a kindhearted person, and your friends, coworkers, and family also describe you that way, then you have a high degree of congruency. Another aspect of congruence is agreement between the **ideal self**, the person you would ideally like to be, and the self-concept, the person you see yourself as being. On the other hand, a poorly adjusted personality results from **incongruence**, that is, when there exists a large discrepancy among the self-concept, the ideal self, and the experiences that give the person a sense of his or her true self.

As a humanistic psychologist, Rogers had a positive belief about humanity. He contended that all individuals are born with the natural tendency to grow to their highest level of self-expression. At this level, the individual would achieve happiness and also benefit society and the world. A natural question to ask is that if an individual has an inherent tendency to grow to be the best person he or she can be, then why doesn't everyone reach this goal? Rogers believed the answer to this question was based on the love an individual received as a child. Rogers examined whether the love a child received from parents was conditional.

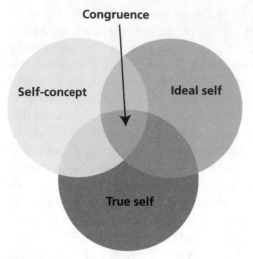

FIGURE 13.11 *Congruence.*

Children experiencing conditional love, or **conditions of worth** as Rogers termed it, grew to see love, acceptance, and appreciation from others as dependent on their actions and specific behaviors. Such children learn to avoid expressing their true thoughts, emotions, and behaviors. Rogers believed that the result was that this blocked the development of the true self.

Rogers suggested that the answer to developing a healthy child with a strong sense of self-esteem and self-acceptance was to provide him or her with **unconditional positive regard**, that is, a sense of being valued for oneself regardless of the degree to which specific behaviors are approved of or disapproved of by parents or significant others (Alexander, 2007). If a child were to experience only unconditional positive regard, then self-regard would be unconditional as well (Hall & Lindzey, 1970). Often the concept of unconditional positive regard is misunderstood to mean children should be allowed to do anything and everything they want in the name of developing individuality and self-esteem. However, that is not what Rogers meant. He encouraged parents to discourage inappropriate behaviors, but as a humanistic psychologist, he also believed in separating criticism of the child's actions from criticizing the child as a person. In other words, Rogers would assert that a child who is acting poorly toward classmates is not a bad child, but is an inherently good child doing bad things. That is, the child has intrinsic merit regardless of his or her behavior at that particular moment in time. This is the essence of positive regard.

Objections to Humanistic Theory

Rogers developed client-centered therapy, which represented one of the first alternatives to psychodynamic therapy. The most significant contribution of humanistic theory has been its positive view of human nature and the encouragement it gives for seeking self-awareness and personal growth. However, research has not consistently shown client-centered therapy to be effective (Greenberg, Watson, & Lietaer, 1998; Patterson, 2000). Whereas some studies show client improvement compared to control subjects, others do not. Even so, Rogers had a positive influence on the practice of psychotherapy in that his techniques of conducting therapy, such as reflective listening, have been incorporated into therapeutic practice even outside the humanistic school.

Behavioral Theories

The **behaviorist** school, founded by John B. Watson, focused on overt behavior and gave up attempts to determine what was going on inside the human mind. Watson's purpose in limiting his focus to the study of behavior was to allow psychology to develop as a true science, sticking to observable, measurable phenomena. Behaviorists don't deny the influence of genetics, nor do they deny that people have thoughts and feelings (internal states), but they believe that these mental states are subject to the same learning principles as are overt behaviors. In his research, Watson focused on how reflective, involuntary behavior could be conditioned. Later, B. F. Skinner expanded the purview of behaviorism by studying voluntary behavior rather than reflexive behavior. He concluded that when such behaviors were followed by consequences that the person or animal found pleasing, then the voluntary behavior tended to be repeated. If a person engaging in a behavior found that the environmental consequences were unpleasant, then the behavior was less likely to be repeated in the future. Eventually, each person develops a set of behavior patterns or habits, which are the closest thing to having a "personality" that these early behaviorists would consider. Since the explanation as to why each of us has formed the behavioral habits we have lies outside us—in the environmental consequences that have followed those behaviors in the past—then there is little need to have a theory of personality. From the behaviorist perspective, people don't do things because they have certain personality traits; they do them because they have found these behaviors to be reinforcing in the past. Thus, Lamont doesn't study for his exams because he is conscientious; he studies because he has found that doing so has enabled him to get good grades.

Explore
operant conditioning
in Chapter 7, p. 211

Around 50 years ago, psychologists within the behaviorist school began to reincorporate subjective experiences in their explanations as to why people develop certain behavior patterns. They began to doubt that learning principles were sufficient to explain people's behaviors and personalities. A branch of behaviorism, social-cognitive learning theory, emerged, which incorporates roles for both situational and cognitive variables in determining behavior (Nevid, Rathus, & Greene, 2006). Social-cognitive learning theory goes beyond the approach developed by early behaviorists by taking into account mental processes such as people's expectations of success or failure (self-efficacy) and their beliefs about their ability to control their fate (locus of control).

Social-Cognitive Learning Theory

Bandura's Self-Efficacy

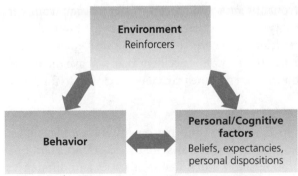

FIGURE 13.12 *Bandura's reciprocal determinism. Courtesy of Wood et al.,* The World of Psychology, *6th edition, 2008.*

Albert Bandura believed that the way people think significantly affects their personality and behavior. Bandura is credited with adding the theory of reciprocal determinism to the understanding of personality. Rather than viewing personality as simply a function of the individual's response to the environment, Bandura postulated that the individual is part of creating the environment as well. The person's actions create circumstances that elicit specific responses from others, which in turn impact how the person views himself or herself. Bandura saw personality as shaped by the environment, the person's own behavior, and the psychological processes of the individual.

One psychological process important to Bandura was the extent to which a person has a sense of **self-efficacy**. Self-efficacy refers to our beliefs that we can perform adequately in a given situation (Bandura, 1977). We need to have skills to successfully perform tasks with competence, but we also need to have the conviction that we know how to implement the skills in an effective manner. The strength of our convictions regarding our effectiveness determines whether we even try to cope with difficult situations (Alexander, 2007). We tend to avoid situations when we believe ourselves unable to handle them, as we experience them as threatening. Yet we tackle situations that we judge ourselves to be capable of successfully managing. Bandura theorized that individuals gain a sense of high or low self-efficacy on the basis of their successes and failures in dealing with the environment. Our degree of self-efficacy regarding our performance also influences our sense of locus of control.

Rotter's Locus of Control

Julian Rotter contended that personality and behavior are the direct result of an individual's expectations combined with specific outcomes within his or her environment. In other words, what you feel should happen is either reinforced or denied by your environment. For example, when you try a new task, you don't know if you will be good at it. But if you try and succeed, you gain confidence. That confidence leads to **cognitive expectancies** of doing well. Cognitive expectancies refer to the person's expectations of future success on the basis of past experiences. This confidence could also transfer to other challenges.

When a person believes that he or she can exert control over and master new challenges presented by the external environment, he or she is said to have an **internal locus of control**. Individuals who feel that the external environment controls them and that they have little effect on events around them are said to have an **external locus of control**. Rotter was convinced that people could learn to have more of an internal locus of control and develop self-confidence by setting realistic goals and achieving them.

Trait Theories

Trait theory states that personality traits and characteristics make up your personality. As a result, personality traits and characteristics have a powerful influence on those you choose as friends, the type of work you find enjoyable, and whom you select as a mate. It's usually not by accident that we have the friends we have or marry the person we marry. Some traits tend to cluster to form **personality types**.

As you may have already realized, understanding personality is a complex undertaking. A central question to settle is which **traits** are the most important ones to measure when trying to understand individual similarities and differences. Early theorists attempted to solve this puzzle by employing a number of approaches. Gordon Allport identified approximately 4,500 English words that could possibly refer to personality traits (Allport & Odbert, 1936). However, this

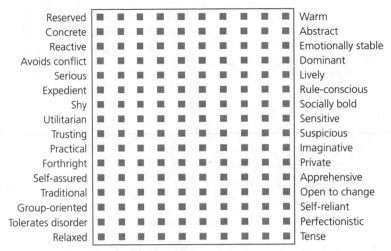

FIGURE 13.13 *The 16PF Personality Profile. Courtesy of Wood et al.,* The World of Psychology, *6th edition, 2008.*

number was clearly unmanageable in any study of personality dimensions. Later, Allport (1937) grouped the vast array of descriptive words into a hierarchy, with the most central ones at the top.

The unwieldy number of traits continued to be a difficult issue in personality theorists until new researchers took on the enormous task of further distilling the personality traits. One researcher, Raymond Cattell (1950, 1965, 1990), identified similarities among a number of personality characteristics. He was then able to reduce the number of characteristics into distinct categories using a statistical technique known as **factor analysis**. Cattell's work led him to create a number of personality tests. He is perhaps best known for his Sixteen Personality Factors (16PF) Test, which is still used today to assess personality for a variety of reasons such as vocational counseling, couples counseling, and treatment planning (Pearson Assessments, 2005).

Hans Eysenck (1967, 1982, 1990) narrowed the list of personality traits further to only three key factors: extraversion–introversion (E), neuroticism (N), and psychoticism (P). Extraversion refers to the characteristic of being outgoing, whereas introversion is characterized by having reserve; a tendency to keep to oneself. Introverts are shy and not eager to engage others socially, as they are easily overstimulated. Neuroticism implies a temperamentally anxious person who is moody, touchy, and chronically tense. Psychoticism suggests poor impulse control, a tendency toward sensation-seeking, and an unsociable nature, all of which make the individual prone to delinquency. While the psychoticism dimension did not turn out to be useful, the other two dimensions have been shown to be of great utility in explaining individual similarities and differences.

The "Big Five" Model

The most popular trait theory used today is the **Big Five model**, also called the five-factor model (FFM) (McCrae & Costa, 1990, 1997, 1999; McCrae et al., 2000). This model has become popular because it utilized factor analysis to bring together the myriad personality traits from the various theories. This approach allows a much more manageable view of personality traits. Incidentally, the five factors combine to spell OCEAN, providing an easy way to remember them.

O—Openness: People scoring high in this factor are creative, curious, and open to new experiences and ideas. Those scoring low in this factor tend to be highly conventional and less interested in new ideas and experiences.

C—Conscientiousness: Those scoring high in this factor are self-disciplined and responsible. Low scorers tend to be undependable, careless, and unorganized.

E—Extroversion: People with a high extroversion score enjoy meeting new people, being involved in conversations and social gatherings, and showing affection. Low scorers tend to be introverted and withdrawn.

A—Agreeableness: People scoring high in this factor are warm, cooperative, and trusting. Individuals scoring low in this factor tend to be more prone to argument, irritability, and being uncooperative.

N—Neuroticism: This factor refers to emotional stability. Individuals scoring high on this factor are unstable, anxious, and moody. Those scoring low on this factor tend to be calm and emotionally balanced.

FIGURE 13.14 *Thinking of the OCEAN is an easy way to remember the Big Five model.*

Are Trait Theories Universal?

There is evidence that personality traits may be universal. Cross-cultural studies indicate that characteristics of the Big Five model are not limited to one culture but appear to be present in multiple cultures (McCrae et al., 2000; Paunonen & Ashton, 1998; Salgado, 1997). Furthermore, Buss (1991, 1999) found a strong substantiation for evolutionary advantages of individuals who were more open, conscientious, extroverted, agreeable, and low on neuroticism. Interestingly, research has provided evidence that even animals such as nonhuman primates have personality characteristics that can be understood using the Big Five model (Fouts & Mills, 1997).

Although trait theories may seem to be a logical approach to understanding personality, there are well-substantiated arguments against these theories. The first argument is that trait theory fails to explain human behavior. Trait theories are said to effectively describe personality, but they do not explain much about behavior (Digman, 1997). A second argument states that trait theory does not offer data indicating which personality traits are stable, which change, and why traits may not remain stable over a lifetime. The third major argument is that trait theory doesn't sufficiently enable us to predict behavior; that is, behavior may actually change depending on the situation faced by an individual, so situational factors may be more important to consider than personality traits (Mischel & Shoda, 1999).

Personality and Culture

FIGURE 13.15 *Culture plays a big role in your personality.*

Culture has a large influence on personality theory and the understanding of human behavior. We all view the world through a cultural lens comprised of the values and norms we learn from our society. We learned these values and norms as children, and they created our sense of what is right, wrong, normal, and abnormal.

The theories presented in this chapter were derived exclusively from theorists in Western cultures. They do not necessarily reflect the personality theories and behaviors of other cultures. For example, Western countries such as the United States are **individualistic**, meaning that most Americans are taught to place a high value on individual freedom and self-expression. However, in more **collectivist** cultures, such as China, the notion of being an individual separate from one's family, tribe, or village is not considered a desirable behavior or personality trait. Thus, one culture's desirable trait can be another culture's inappropriate behavior.

Biological Theories

Has anyone ever told you that you act just like your mother or father? That statement may have a lot of truth to it in terms of personality characteristics being transmitted genetically. In this section we will examine some of the current theories reflecting the effect of genes and brain chemistry on behavior.

Brain and Neurochemical Influences on Personality

Explore **brain imaging techniques** in Chapter 2, p. 44

Although many brain structures may perform similar functions, a few structures have unique functions. Much has been made of the specialized tasks associated with the right and left hemispheres of the brain. It is inaccurate to assume, however, that the right side of the brain exclusively handles artistic tasks and that the left is dedicated to language abilities. In fact, both hemispheres are involved in language and art, and the hemispheres work together through communication of information across the bundle of axons that make up the corpus callosum. Even so, the right hemisphere dominates in processing the creative thinking involved in artistic expression, and the left dominates in the logical thinking required for tasks such as language processing. Brain research has been greatly advanced with the introduction of technologies such as MRI, fMRI, and PET scans. For example, Tellegen (1985) found that introversion and extroversion are associated with specific areas of the brain. An area in the prefrontal cortex appears to be active in people experiencing positive mood states and underactive in people experiencing depression.

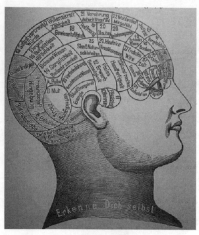

FIGURE 13.16 *Phrenology map demonstrating the different areas associated with certain personality traits.*

The role of brain regions in shaping personality was recognized in the nineteenth century by the German physician Franz Gall, who created a once-popular view called **phrenology**. Gall theorized that skull shape corresponded to the over- or underdevelopment of parts of the brain that were thought to correspond to specific personality characteristics. Therefore, bumps on the skull were presumed to indicate personality traits. For example, a bump in the area thought to control aggression would mean that the person tends to be very aggressive. If there was an indentation in the region for aggression, that person would be expected to be minimally aggressive. A major embarrassment for Gall occurred when a skull was placed in front of him for evaluation of its owner's personality. Gall proclaimed the person to be highly moral and deeply religious. Actually, the skull belonged to the Marquis de Sade, a notoriously sadistic individual who intentionally hurt others to gain sexual pleasure. Furthermore, the Marquis de Sade openly hated any form of religion. This and many other examples of erroneous phrenological assessment demonstrated that phrenology was not a viable method for personality assessment.

FIGURE 13.17 *Phineas Gage. Courtesy of Warren Anatomical Museum, Francis A. Countway Library of Medicine.*

Although phrenology has been completely discredited, Gall appears to have been right about brain regions influencing personality characteristics. Modern research supports the notion that aspects of personality may be controlled by certain brain regions. Aggression can be influenced by changes in the brain, such as damage to the frontal lobes or to the amygdala. The case study of Phineas Gage provided the earliest evidence of this. Gage sustained damage to his frontal lobes when a mining accident caused a pipe to enter his face below his cheekbone and exit through the top of his head, taking a section of his frontal lobes with it. Although Phineas lived, his personality changed from that of a congenial fellow who was popular with the men he supervised at the mine, to an aggressive person who had difficulty getting along with others. There are other cases of people suffering from brain tumors that put pressure on the amygdala. This stimulation of the amygdala often leads to uncontrollable aggressive outbursts. When the tumor is removed, these people become less aggressive, showing a link between changes in the brain and aspects of personality. Lesions (damaged areas) in the amygdala can have the same effect.

Genetics and Personality

Behavioral genetics is the study of the impact of genes on human behavior, or the **heritability** of human characteristics. Heredity has already been demonstrated to have a strong influence on personality, so that it is now clear that just as you have inherited genes that help determine your height and body size, you have also inherited genes that shape your personality.

To study the influence of genes on personality, researchers rely on twin studies. Twin studies provide an opportunity to compare the similarities among identical twins as compared with fraternal twins. Identical (monozygotic) twins are formed from a single egg and have the same genes. Therefore, they look the same and often behave similarly. In contrast, fraternal (dizygotic) twins are born at

Explore
**the effects of
neurotransmitters**
in Chapter 3, p. 80

the same time but develop from different eggs. They share about 50% of the same genes, just as ordinary siblings and parents and their children do. Twin studies suggest that as much as half of personality may be genetically determined (Bouchard, 1997a; Rowe, 1997).

Other types of kinship studies are also conducted to examine the genetic similarity of parents and their biological and/or adopted children. Research in this area has shown moderate correlations between parents and biological children and very low correlations between the personalities of parents and their adopted children (Bouchard, 1997a; Bouchard & Loehlin, 2001; Loehlin, McCrae, Costa, & John, 1998). Although the study of genetic influences on personality is promising, it is no more conclusive than other theories of personality (Macoby, 2000).

Neurochemical processes are another potential determinant of personality. Certain behaviors have been found to be associated with the concentrations of neurotransmitters and other chemicals in the brain. For example, risk-taking behavior has been associated with low levels of the enzyme monoamine oxidase (MAO) (Zuckerman, 1994). MAO affects the neurotransmitter dopamine by suppressing its release, which affects the ability of a person to experience a relaxed and calm state. Therefore, when MAO inhibits dopamine, it increases the need for activity and sensation seeking (Depue & Collins, 1999).

Interactionist Theory

In reality, no personality theory explains everything we want to know about personality development and change. To understand personality, most psychologists use the **interactionist approach** and draw on a combination of the factors presented in this chapter, weighing each to a greater or lesser extent. An interactionist approach divides the construction of personality into four parts (Bouchard, 1997a; Plomin, 1997; Talbot, Duberstein, King, Cox, & Giles, 2000; Wright, 1998):

♦ 40–50% genetic: inherited genetic traits

♦ 27% nonshared environmental factors: the manner in which an individual's genes adapt to a particular environment

♦ 7% shared environmental factors: traits developed from parent, family of origin, and immediate environment, such as the community in which a person lives

♦ 16–26% unknown factors: unknown factors and testing errors

This theory holds that personality can only be understood by considering the genetic heritage of the individual, the person's child-rearing experiences, the era in which the person grew up, the stage of life the individual is currently in, the significant relationships in the person's life, and other influential environmental factors.

TABLE 13.3 Summary of personality theories.		
Theory	**Theorist(s)**	**View of personality**
Trait & Five-factor model	Allport, Cattell, Eysenck	Personality is the result of inherited traits and the environment of an individual
Psychoanalytic/ Psychodynamic	Freud, Adler, Jung, Horney	Operations within the unconscious determine personality
Humanistic	Rogers, Maslow	Your individual experience of reality determines your personality
Social/Cognitive	Bandura, Rotter	The way you think and the experiences you have shape your personality
Biological		Personality is the result of genetics and neurochemical functioning of the nervous system
Interactionist		A perspective suggesting personality is a combination of all the above theories

Chapter Summary

In psychology, personality can be defined as a generally consistent set of thoughts, emotions, and behaviors. Psychologists use a variety of techniques to assess personality, such as interviews, objective tests, projective tests, and behavioral observations. Psychologists must check assessment tools for reliability and validity. Reliability refers to the assessment tool's consistency; validity has to do with the tool's accuracy, in other words, whether the tool measures what it is supposed to measure.

Interviews are a method of gaining information about a person by asking the person direct questions, and the interview format may be structured or unstructured. Personality inventories such as the MMPI-2 are another type of self-report strategy, in which people answer questions about themselves in a paper-and-pencil or computer format. Unlike the interview and personality inventory strategies, behavioral observation does not involve self-report, which relies on people to honestly and accurately report on their thoughts, feelings, and behaviors. Instead, people's behaviors are carefully watched, and their personality traits are inferred from their actions.

Projective tests such as the Rorschach inkblot and the Thematic Apperception Test (TAT) are based on the projective hypothesis—that when people are presented with an ambiguous stimulus, they will project their unconscious wishes and conflicts onto the stimulus and reveal unconscious material that can help resolve their psychological problems.

Several theories have been developed to explain personality structure and development. The perspectives discussed in this chapter were the psychoanalytic/psychodynamic orientation, humanistic theory, behavioral and social-cognitive learning theories, biological theories, and the interactionist theory.

Freudian psychoanalysis introduced a theory of personality development that involves the progression of children through five psychosexual stages of development: the oral, anal, phallic, latency, and genital stages. At each stage, a crisis must be mastered for healthy development. Failure to do so results in fixation and might result in a psychological disorder.

Neo-Freudians began to modify Freudian theory in light of their own experiences with patients. Collectively, these subsequent theories and the original psychoanalytic theory make up the psychodynamic school. Carl Jung, one of the early neo-Freudians, contributed to personality theory by discovering the extroversion/introversion dimension. This dimension, combined with three others, produced eight personality types in a personality type system devised by Jung. He expanded Freud's concept of the unconscious to include the collective unconscious, which he described as a repository of the experiences of our ancestors that have been passed on genetically. The collective unconscious contains archetypes, which are universal representations or prototypes of human beings, such as the mother, the hero, and the guru (wise old man).

Alfred Adler believed that birth order shapes personality. Firstborns tend to be more achievement oriented and domineering than later-born children. This neo-Freudian also proposed the idea that all children begin life in a state of incompetence and thus develop a "striving for superiority" (or mastery) in order to attain self-acceptance and acceptance by society. Those who do not gain mastery develop an inferiority complex and, as adults, may attempt to gain the approval of others in a childish fashion.

Karen Horney proposed that the central concern of childhood is to feel secure. Children who did not manage to feel secure developed basic anxiety and subsequently behaved in nonfunctional ways intended to reduce anxiety. Erik Erikson modified Freud's initial five stages of development by adding three adult stages of development. Erikson also changed the focus on personality development from Freud's internal, unconscious dynamics toward social relationships as primary shapers of personality.

The humanist perspective maintains that people are motivated to fulfill their potential. Ideally, individuals can become self-actualized, but only after other more pressing needs are met. According to Carl Rogers, to develop fully, people need unconditional positive regard from a significant person, usually their mothers. Another sign of a fully functioning person is congruence, or agreement among the three aspects of self: self-concept, the ideal self, and the true self.

The behaviorist position on personality states that your past experiences prompt you to form habits, which are then expressions of your personality. The social-cognitive learning model incorporates cognitive factors, such as taking into account how your past experience shapes your expectations about future events, and your expectations influence your behavior patterns.

Trait theories explore which sets of personality dimensions best predict future behavior. The Big Five model suggests that five traits are particularly good ways to understand individual similarities and differences in personality. The five traits are extroversion, conscientiousness, agreeableness, neuroticism, and openness to experience.

Biological theories suggest that brain chemistry and function affect personality. Some support for biological influences on personality come from kinship studies and case studies of personality change as a result of brain damage. Brain research has been aided by the introduction of brain-imaging technologies such as MRI, fMRE, and PET scans that allow researchers to examine living brains in action.

Finally, the interactionist approach holds that the various theories of personality are most useful if integrated to explain the complexities of human personality.

Knowledge Builder

RELATE TO YOURSELF

1. How has your family impacted the development of your personality?

   _____

   _____

   _____

   _____

2. What would cause your personality traits to change over time?

   _____

   _____

   _____

   _____

3. Can a projective personality test determine your personality accurately?

   _____

   _____

   _____

   _____

4. Which theories of personality do you think best represent your way of thinking about the similarities and differences among people? Explain why you think the way you do. In other words, what evidence do you have to support your ideas?

   _____

   _____

   _____

   _____

CHAPTER REVIEW QUESTIONS

1. Personality inventories are more accurate than projective tests. **T or F?**

2. Freud's theory of the personality is currently the most popular one among clinical psychologists. **T or F?**

3. Unconditional positive regard means to never blame anyone for anything. **T or F?**

4. Genes play a small role in behavior; the environment is more important. **T or F?**

5. Personality is influenced by social relationships, particularly in early childhood. **T or F?**

6. The sexual drive, the aggressive instinct, and the instinct for self-preservation are all important factors in _____.

   (a) social-cognitive theories   (b) biological theory

   (c) psychoanalytic theory   (d) humanistic theory

   (e) all personality theories

7. The _____ is only motivated by gaining pleasure and avoiding pain.

   (a) superego   (b) ego

   (c) id   (d) collective unconscious

8. The _____ stores thoughts and ideas universal to humanity.

   (a) preconscious   (b) reality principle

   (c) subconscious   (d) collective unconscious

9. The Big Five personality traits include all of the following EXCEPT _____.

   (a) conscientiousness   (b) affability

   (c) openness   (d) extroversion

10. The personality theorist who coined the term "inferiority complex" was _____.

   (a) Sigmund Freud   (b) Carl Jung

   (c) Carl Rogers   (d) Alfred Adler

11. Erikson's theory departed from the Freudian model by _____.

   (a) disputing the idea of penis envy

   (b) placing more emphasis on conscious experience than on unconscious processes

   (c) introducing a "striving for superiority" as the essential goal of childhood

   (d) proposing the idea of a collective unconscious in addition to the personal unconscious

12. According to Rogers, providing positive regard to children fosters _____.

   (a) hardworking adults   (b) an integrated self-archetype

   (c) self-acceptance and self-esteem   (d) a striving for superiority

13. Which of the following is not a step in Abraham Maslow's hierarchy of needs?

   (a) love and belongingness   (b) happiness

   (c) safety and security   (d) self-esteem

   (e) self-actualization

14. *Consider the following scenario:* Adam was known to be quiet and reserved in high school. After graduating he went to a local community college and earned a degree while taking acting lessons to learn to be more outgoing. In college he participated in a couple of plays as a minor character. Eventually he moved to Los Angeles when relocated by his company. There, his love for theater was reborn, and he auditioned for a few plays. A talent agent spotted him in a show and asked him to audition for a television comedy. The show became a hit and eventually he had his own spin-off show. Adam was no longer quiet and introverted. He began throwing lavish parties and was known as Hollywood's most notorious bachelor. How can we explain the discrepancy between Adam's personality in high school and his present behavior?

   _____

   _____

   _____

   _____

15. *Consider the following scenario:* A student goes to the vocational counseling center on campus seeking career advice. The student is interested in a career in marketing and asks the counselor for leads on a summer internship. The vocational counselor asks the student to take a battery of personality assessments and vocational assessments. The tests reveal the student has a strong desire to serve people and would be well suited for a career in social services. How should the student weigh the results of the tests with her present plans for a career in business?

_____

_____

_____

_____

16. Describe how Bandura's theory of self-efficacy could be used to help an individual learn to be successful.

_____

_____

_____

_____

17. What is the relationship between culture and personality development?

_____

_____

_____

_____

USEFUL WEB SITES

ALFRED ADLER INSTITUTES

http://ourworld.compuserve.com/homepages/hstein/birthord.htm

Informative charting of Adler's birth-order-related views on personality.

ALLPSYCH ONLINE: THE VIRTUAL PSYCHOLOGY CLASSROOM

http://allpsych.com/personalitysynopsis/contents.html

Comprehensive and concise review of major personality theories. This site is an excellent general psychology resource and well worth a bookmark on your browser.

PERSONALITY TYPOLOGIES

http://www.myersbriggs.org/

The official Web site of the Myers-Briggs Type Indicator explains how the typology works and how you can take it to find out your personality type.

LIFE COLORS PERSONALITY INVENTORY

http://203.210.106.133/lifecolorslite.html

Free online personality inventory correlating your personality type with a color and specific characteristics.

HOLLAND'S CAREER PERSONALITY TYPES

http://facweb.bhc.edu/Advising/Counseling/Services/Develop/Interests.htm

Explore John Holland's theory on how certain personalities fit best in specific types of work by taking this free online inventory.

A note to the reader: Online personality inventories and tests are not comprehensive and should not be relied on. For actual testing, consult a licensed psychologist.

PERSONALITY THEORIES

http://www.ship.edu/~cgboeree/perscontents.html

A comprehensive listing of personality theories including biographical information on the theorists.

UNIVERSITY OF TEXAS ANIMAL PERSONALITY RESEARCH

http://www.utexas.edu/opa/news/03newsreleases/nr_200312/nr_psychology031203.html

This link connects to the review of a study suggesting that personality exists in dogs.

THE PERSONALITY PROJECT: RESEARCH PROJECT

http://test.personality-project.org/

By clicking this link, you can participate in a current personality research project on the Big Five traits.

PERSONALITY AND CONSCIOUSNESS

http://pandc.ca/

Comprehensive resource of personality theorists featuring links to related sites and relevant books.

BORDERLINE PERSONALITY DISORDER

http://www.nimh.nih.gov/publicat/bpd.cfm

An overview of this well-known but highly misunderstood personality disorder.

MENTAL HEALTH

http://www.webmd.com/content/article/60/67116.htm

This Web site features in-depth discussions of several mental disorders. It also provides information for those who may need help with mental disorders.

MINNESOTA TWIN FAMILY STUDY

http://www.psych.umn.edu/psylabs/mtfs/

A leading longitudinal study of twins offers insights into the debate on the effect of genes on personality and behavior.

GENES & BIOLOGY IN PERSONALITY

http://allpsych.com/personalitysynopsis/biologicaltrends.html

A quick reference discussing relevant factors in the discussion of the role of genetics in biology in personality development and behavior.

BEHAVIORAL GENETICS

http://www.ornl.gov/sci/techresources/Human_Genome/elsi/behavior.shtml

A comprehensive discussion on the influence of genetics on human behavior.

Chapter 14

Psychological Disorders

by Patricia Alexander, PhD

Nothing is at last sacred but the integrity of your own mind.

—RALPH W. EMERSON

What Is Abnormal?

When would you say that a person's behavior goes beyond the point of being unusual and becomes abnormal? Where would you draw the line between ordinary sadness and depression? How can a distinction be made between behavior that is creative or eccentric (interesting) and actions that are bizarre (sick)? These are difficult questions to answer.

One critical component of normal functioning is the ability to adapt to a changing environment. We human beings (and other living things) face continuous challenges to our survival, and we must respond flexibly in order to thrive. Those of us who cannot function effectively by adjusting to diverse situations are at risk of perishing.

Psychopathology is a term used to suggest that a person has a significant enough impairment in functioning to be considered outside the normal realm. Psychopathology interferes with a person's ability to face the daily pressures that are a normal part of the struggle to exist; in other words, psychopathology hinders his or her ability to adapt. Some central factors used in identifying **abnormal behavior** are how unusual it is in terms of its statistical frequency, whether it violates social norms, involves a faulty perception of reality, produces excessive personal distress, or leads to self-defeating or dangerous behavior.

Statistical Infrequency/The Behavior Is Unusual

Explore
the normal curve
in Chapter 2, p. 48

A reasonable criterion for defining what is abnormal can be to think of it in a literal sense of the person's behavior being substantially different from that of most other people in a given culture. Statistical abnormality simply means that the behavior is infrequent. Abnormal behavior may merely differ from normal behavior in terms of quantity rather than quality. That is, many mentally ill people have problems that are exaggerations of the thoughts and behaviors we all have. Using a statistical criterion, whatever two-thirds of people do is normal, as it is within one standard deviation from the mean in either direction, showing either slightly more or slightly less of the characteristic. On the other hand, if we behave differently from 95% of the population (departing more than two standard deviations from the mean), this is one standard for considering a characteristic or behavior to be unusual enough to be considered abnormal. If our behavior is in the range between average (what two-thirds of the population is like) and the 95% cutoff point designating statistical abnormality, then we have departed somewhat from the average and would be considered to be in the low average or high average range.

This definition of abnormality isn't entirely satisfactory, since there are rare positive characteristics that are also "abnormal" using a statistical criterion. Having an IQ over 130 meets the criterion for statistical abnormality, but it is not considered abnormal in the usual sense of being a problem. Having no stage fright or no test anxiety would be statistically unusual, since it is common for people to suffer from these problems. The performance of Olympic gold medalists is certainly statistically abnormal. As you can see, generally only behavior that is unusual in a negative direction—in other words, actions or subjective experiences that are also disturbing—would be considered abnormal.

FIGURE 14.1 *Having no test anxiety is unusual but not necessarily abnormal.*

Another limitation of this definition of abnormality is that some negative characteristics are not statistically abnormal but are still undesirable. For instance, being overweight to the point of obesity is fairly common in the United States, but it is nevertheless a pathological condition. According to the National Center for Health Statistics, one-third of Americans are overweight. The general population suffers from a great deal of depression and anxiety, and yet both disorders substantially lower the quality of life, so we do not consider these common ailments acceptable. Nicotine dependence is listed as a disorder, although it isn't particularly rare. To determine the prevalence of various psychological disorders, the U.S. National Institute of Mental Health (NIMH) took a census of psychological disorders during the 1980s. Drawing from this study, Narrow, Rae, Robins, and Regier (2002) estimated that one in six Americans suffers clinically significant mental disorders in a year.

The Behavior Violates Social Norms

What is customary for most people to do in normal life varies from culture to culture. Social **norms** refer to how people with similar backgrounds are expected to behave in a given social situation. An action is socially unacceptable if it violates a particular culture's norms. Since behavior deemed normal in one culture may be viewed as abnormal in another, abnormal behavior is determined in part by the *context* in which it occurs. For example, consider a man in white robes who sits down on a street corner and begins chanting, holding his arms out in front of him. Is he mentally ill? In the United States he would probably be looked at suspiciously, yet in India he might be revered as a holy man. A woman who sits in front of her home cutting intricate patterns into her flesh with a knife and rubbing mud and ashes into the open and bleeding wounds might be hospitalized for her own protection in the United States, whereas if the woman is a member of the Korongo tribe in Africa, she would be considered to be doing something ordinary, merely making scars on her skin to enhance her beauty.

FIGURE 14.2 *Scarification in some African cultures is a social norm, not a sign of abnormality.*

Social nonconformity may also be a basis for judgments of normality. Abnormal behavior can sometimes be viewed as a failure in socialization. The person in question has not adopted the usual rules for social conduct. This negative nonconformity must be distinguished from the departures from normal behavior found in creative people and others with a high level of functioning. Nonconformity does not automatically indicate psychopathology, nor does adherence to social norms guarantee "mental health," since people who rigidly conform to rules or standards without making reasonable exceptions may also be showing a symptom of a mental disorder, such as obsessive-compulsive personality disorder.

One of the functions of social norms is to allow us to predict what others around us are likely to do. This enables us to feel less anxious than we otherwise would feel when we are out in public. An expectation we have of other human beings is that they will converse with us. All known cultures classify people as abnormal if they either fail to communicate with others or are consistently unpredictable in their actions. Keep in mind that although we have been discussing abnormal behavior as being tied to what is acceptable practice in a given culture, some behaviors, such as depression and schizophrenia, are found in virtually all cultures, which suggests that not all mental disorders are defined by social norms found within a given culture (Castillo, 1997; Draguns, 1990a, 1990b).

The Behavior Is Maladaptive or Self-Defeating

An unusual and disturbing behavior is more likely to be considered abnormal if it is destructive, that is, harmful to the person or to others. A behavior is considered maladaptive if it interferes with our ability to survive and accomplish our goals in life. Actions that lead to unhappiness or that keep us from fulfilling our social roles are also considered maladaptive. An example of this would be substance abuse that is extensive enough to cause a person to lose his or her job and become estranged from his or her family. A smoker's habit damages not only the smoker but also those exposed to the secondhand smoke. This view of abnormality focuses more on behavior than on what the person is experiencing internally. However, sometimes recurrent troublesome thoughts and negative emotions can be considered covert behaviors. **Covert behaviors** are responses that are internal, such as frequent self-deprecatory thoughts that have a depressing effect on a person's mood.

The Perception of Reality Is Faulty

FIGURE 14.3 *Famous painter van Gogh lost touch with reality—he cut off his ear, wrapped it in a newspaper, and gave it to a prostitute as a gift. Courtesy of Francis G. Mayer/Corbis.*

FIGURE 14.4 *Wearing "rose-colored glasses" can stave off depression. How?*

A cardinal principle of mental health is that the person has an accurate perception of reality. To be **psychotic** is to be seriously deficient in possessing an understanding of reality that concurs with the perception that others have of what is going on. If the person's interpretation of reality is seriously flawed—for example, by suffering hallucinations (perceptions in the absence of stimuli) or delusions (false beliefs about reality)—then the person is considered to be psychotic.

There are tests to measure psychosis, known as **mental status exams**. In their simplest form they look at whether the person is oriented in terms of knowing who he or she is (not another Santa Claus, please!), where he or she is at the present moment, and what is the approximate date (you're not living as an American colonist in the 1700s are you?).

For many years, psychologists placed no qualification on the necessity of a clear perception of reality as being a criterion for mental health. However, a large body of research on the explanatory styles that distinguish depressed people from happy people has demonstrated that there are limits to the rule that an accurate perception of reality is vital to mental health (Sweeney, Anderson, & Bailey, 1986). Depressed people tend to view setbacks in their lives in a systematically different way than do people who are not depressed. When something bad happens, depressed individuals tend to see the incident as global (it affects the rest of their lives), as permanent (it's always going to be this way), and as a personal failing (it's my fault). People who aren't depressed see things in a different light. They view setbacks as temporary (it won't last), limited (not infecting other areas of their lives), and not as their fault (it doesn't reflect on me). This latter quality could be construed as a projection of blame onto others, which could be a mild sign of mental illness, as it represents a distortion of reality. However, this mental habit seems to work well for people in that it serves to protect against depression. Depressed people have often been shown to have a more accurate perception of reality than do people who are not depressed, a phenomenon known as **depressive realism**. Thus, it seems that although being overly optimistic distorts reality slightly, it works well for people by staving off depression. So, an accurate perception of reality does not guarantee mental health. Optimism prompts an overly rosy perception of reality, which in turn boosts the person's sense of self-efficacy and self-esteem, which then elevates mood and increases the sense of optimism, so that a cycle is formed.

Subjective Discomfort (Personal Distress)

A person may have the sense that he or she should be happier or less depressed. Such an individual may seek therapy because he or she feels abnormal or different from other people in a negative way. Another person may feel extremely fearful and notice that others do not seem to suffer the same degree of anxiety.

FIGURE 14.5 *Euphoria sometimes manifests itself as a feeling that one can fly, and although the feeling is great, it is obviously not a sign of mental health.*

This criterion for assessing abnormality also has limitations. It assumes that depressed people are aware of their situation in comparison to others. Believe it or not, people may not know that they are depressed. For one thing, if the state of depression has lasted a long time, such is the case with dysthymic disorder, being depressed could feel normal in the sense that it is the way the person typically feels.

Another problem with subjective discomfort as a criterion for abnormality is that some people with maladaptive behavior have no experience of misery as a result of their actions. In some instances of mental illness, such as a manic episode, individuals say they feel "great"—even euphoric. When working with those who have personality disorders, therapists find that these individuals usually cause discomfort in others more so than within themselves. They experience their problematic behaviors as a core aspect of their way of being in the world, and they blame other people for any relationship problems that crop up.

Finally, many people experience negative emotions that are normal reactions to unpleasant life events. Distressing levels of anxiety, sadness, and/or anger are only considered a disorder if they are lasting and disrupt your ability to function well enough to accomplish your goals in life.

The Behavior Is Dangerous

Actions that present a danger to oneself or others may be considered abnormal and can be the basis for involuntarily hospitalizing a person, at least temporarily. A person in the throes of a manic episode is likely to act on impulse, without exercising enough caution to protect himself or herself or others. Those suffering from schizophrenia or other psychotic disorders may be unaware of their actual surroundings as they attend to their private thoughts or feelings and thus may not realize they are standing in the street or in the rain. As with the other definitions of abnormality, determining whether a behavior is dangerous has loopholes. Killing during wartime is almost universally acceptable across cultures, as is killing in self-defense in a nonwartime context. Bungee jumping, rock climbing, and race-car driving are dangerous activities, although, for some reason, people who engage in them aren't considered abnormal. On the other hand, many mental disorders lower the quality of a person's life without actually endangering it.

The Medical Model

The medical model treats mental illness as similar to physical illness, in that both are viewed as stemming from physiological problems. Abnormal behavior is seen as "diseaselike" and capable of being diagnosed and treated, largely with medication. The causes of abnormal behavior are thought to be internal rather than a function of the interaction between the person and the environment. One piece of evidence supporting the medical model is that many disorders, when treated with medication, show dramatic symptom relief.

Whereas those adhering to the medical model consider mental disorders to be the result of a disease, many psychologists believe that disorders result from an interaction of physiological, mental, environmental, and behavioral influences. They contend that all behavior is best understood as a result of the interaction of genetic and other biological factors, the individual's inner psychological dynamics, and his or her life experiences. The complex interaction among the potential causes of psychopathology calls for a blended bio-psycho-social perspective.

Insanity

Insanity is a legal term applied to those who have committed criminal acts but are judged to have been in a mental state at the time of the crime that prevented them from understanding their responsibilities to other members of society. If judged mentally incompetent, people are not held legally responsible for their behavior in the same way that normal people are held accountable. For instance, Ted Kaczynski mailed bombs to unsuspecting victims at universities and airlines, many of whom were killed or maimed. He distrusted technology and believed he was saving humanity from it by killing people he considered to be technologically proficient. During his trial, he was diagnosed by mental health professionals as suffering from paranoid schizophrenia. Even though his primary hope for avoiding a death sentence rested on an insanity plea, Kaczynski resisted taking this route during his trial, as he saw himself as more of a man delivering society from evil than as a person suffering from a mental disorder.

FIGURE 14.6 *Many people were killed or maimed when opening mail containing bombs sent to them from Ted Kaczynski, the notorious Unabomber. Kaczynski was once an untenured professor at UC Berkeley. Courtesy of AP/Wide World Photos.*

So Which Method for Identifying Abnormality Is Correct?

In practice, we typically identify abnormal behavior by using several criteria rather than a single criterion. This is largely because each criterion, as we have seen, is flawed or incomplete. Subjective discomfort accounts for most instances in which a person voluntarily seeks professional help. The judgment by others that a person needs help usually occurs when the person *does something* such as hit a person, have a hallucination, or be difficult to get along with. If this behavior *gains the attention* of or *annoys* a person in a position of power, such as an employer, a teacher, a parent, or a spouse, then that person *does something* about it. The diagnosis of a psychological or **mental disorder** is made when there is a significant impairment in functioning. Generally speaking, the problem must persist over a period of time in order for a diagnosis to be deemed appropriate.

Diagnosing Abnormality: The *Diagnostic and Statistical Manual of Mental Disorders*

Psychological disorders are grouped into categories according to common features or symptoms. Over a period of decades, the diagnostic categories have been refined and validated using research evidence. The current edition of the diagnostic manual used in the United States and Canada, the *Diagnostic and Statistical*

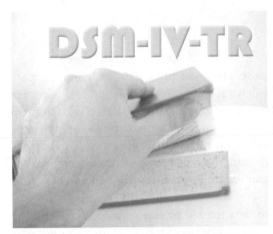

FIGURE 14.7 *Professionals use the* DSM-IV-TR *to diagnose mental disorders.*

Manual of Mental Disorders (4th ed. [DSM-IV-TR]), contains more than 300 recognized mental disorders.

The *DSM-IV-TR* ("TR" stands for "text revision," which was published in 2000) is organized along five axes. *Axis I,* Clinical Syndromes, includes a classification of syndromes as well as conditions that may be the focus of clinical attention. "Clinical disorders" are the patterns of abnormal behavior that impair functioning and cause the individual distress. "Other conditions" include academic, vocational, or social problems that may be the focus of diagnosis or treatment but do not constitute mental disorders. *Axis II,* Personality Disorders and Mental Retardation, discusses chronic disorders that typically are present throughout the individual's life. Personality disorders are enduring patterns of maladaptive behavior that impair interpersonal relationships, and mental retardation is an impairment in normal cognitive functioning. *Axis III,* General Medical Conditions, covers conditions that are the direct cause of a mental disorder. For example, hypothyroidism may cause depression, and hyperthyroidism can cause anxiety symptoms. Medical conditions that affect the understanding or treatment of a mental disorder but are not direct causes of the disorder are also listed in *Axis III. Axis IV,* Psychosocial and Environmental Problems, covers problems that are believed to affect the diagnosis, treatment, or outcome of a disorder. These can include such issues as losing one's job, getting a divorce, being homeless and lacking social support, having a close friend or relative die, and being exposed to war or a natural disaster. Positive life events, such as a job promotion, may also be listed but only when they create problems for the client, such as difficulty in adapting to the changed nature of work relationships. *Axis V,* Global Assessment of Functioning, refers to the client's overall psychological, social, and occupational functioning. The clinician rates the highest level of performance achieved for at least a few months during the preceding year, and this is an indication of what is possible for the person. The current level of functioning is also judged by the clinician.

Evaluating the *DSM-IV-TR*

Explore
treatment of disorders
in Chapter 15, p. 488

The current diagnostic manual is helpful in standardizing diagnosis and treatment, facilitating communication among professionals as well as among those in the helping professions and their patients. It does have limitations, however. Whereas the manual completely describes symptoms, it doesn't explain their causes nor does it suggest a form of treatment.

Studies have found that use of the *DSM-IV-TR* leads to reliable diagnoses. For example, one study found 83% agreement among clinicians diagnosing psychiatric patients (Riskind, Beck, Berchick, Brown, & Steer, 1987). In any event, use of the diagnostic manual is financially necessary since most North American health insurance companies require a *DSM-IV-TR* diagnosis (Myers, 2004).

Personality Disorders

General Characteristics

Individuals with personality disorders have deeply ingrained, enduring patterns of thinking, perceiving, and behaving that generally cause problems in their relationships. Personality disorders are inflexible patterns of behavior that are mostly troublesome to others. Unlike some of the disorders covered in this chapter, symptoms of personality disorders do not occur in episodes, with periods of normal behavior in between. Instead, these disorders are an integral part of the individual's core personality that continuously affect the person's behavior.

Explore
personality traits
in Chapter 13, p. 430

The symptoms of personality disorders tend to be **ego syntonic**, which means that the person's behavior is experienced as consistent with his or her self-image. "It's just the way I am," the individual might say. The troublesome behaviors feel natural or normal to the person. When things go wrong interpersonally, these individuals tend to project blame onto others. This is why they are likely to have problematic relationships. Furthermore, when they have problems, they don't engage in any soul-searching or try to mend their ways. Due to their tendency to project blame, they do not learn from their bad experiences. They believe that it is not their problem; rather, others are at fault.

Personality disorders are exaggerations of normally occurring personality traits; thus there are no clear boundaries to indicate pathology. When a person meets enough of the criteria in the *DSM-IV* for a personality disorder, the diagnosis is made. Interestingly, research indicates that people who qualify for one personality disorder are likely to meet the criteria for several (Dahl, 1986; Timmerman & Emmelkamp, 2001; Widiger, Frances, Warner, & Bluhm, 1986).

Types of Personality Disorders

Paranoid personality disorder has suspiciousness as a defining trait—the tendency to interpret other people's actions as deliberately threatening or demeaning. Paranoid people ascribe evil motives to others, and they blame others for their own mistakes and failures. They tend to be overly sensitive to criticism, whether real or imagined, and to hold grudges against others when they think they have been mistreated. They question the sincerity and trustworthiness of friends and associates, and they seldom confide in others. Feeling that they need to be on guard against harm, they tend to remain hypervigilant. Other people perceive them as cold, scheming, devious, and humorless.

People with **schizoid personality disorder** tend to be loners. They are withdrawn, usually having no close friends. Typically wrapped up in abstract ideas rather than thoughts about people, they pursue solitary interests. Their isolation from others is ego syntonic, which means that the disorder doesn't concern them. They are inclined to be aloof and without warm, tender feelings for other people, as well as indifferent to praise, criticism, and the sentiments of others. Their faces don't show emotion, and they rarely exchange social smiles or nods.

FIGURE 14.8 *Foretelling the future by someone with schizotypal personality disorder.*

Those with **schizotypal personality disorder** dress and behave in ways that are odd, eccentric, or peculiar, but they are not disturbed enough to warrant a diagnosis of schizophrenia. People with this disorder may experience unusual perceptions, such as feeling the presence of a deceased family member in the room. They may engage in magical thinking, such as entertaining the idea that others can sense their feelings or that they can foretell the future. People suffering from schizotypal personality disorder are likely to be anxious in social situations, even when interacting with people they know, and they are especially anxious around strangers. Their anxieties seem to be associated with paranoid thinking, such as the fear that others mean them harm.

Antisocial personality disorder gets more research attention than other personality disorders because people with this disorder cause problems for other people. Individuals with **antisocial personality disorder** have little regard for others and tend to violate their rights. They are irresponsible, egocentric, cynical, unsympathetic, ungrateful, and exploitive in their dealings with others. They tend to engage in deceitfulness, such as repeated lying, use of aliases, or conning others for personal profit or pleasure. The diagnostic manual lists several other characteristics of individuals with antisocial personality disorder, including failure to conform to social norms with respect to lawful behaviors, as indicated by repeatedly performing acts that are grounds for arrest. Studies show that more than 65% of all people with antisocial personalities have been arrested, usually for crimes such as robbery, vandalism, rape, or even murder. In addition, people with this disorder show symptoms indicative of problems in frontal lobe functioning, such as impulsivity (failure to plan ahead); irritability; low frustration tolerance; aggressiveness, as shown by repeated physical fights or assaults; reckless disregard for safety of self or others; and consistent irresponsibility, as demonstrated by repeated failure to sustain consistent work behavior or to honor financial obligations. Furthermore, people with an antisocial personality disorder show inadequate conscience development, as demonstrated by a lack of remorse over having hurt, mistreated, or stolen from another person (American Psychiatric Association, 2000).

Other features of antisocial personality disorder are a lack of anxiety even when performing risky and illegal activities, and an inability to profit from negative experiences. This may be in part because they blame others for their own mistakes and socially deviant behavior. They cause others harm but aren't a problem for themselves (as far as they can see). Eventually, as they reach middle age, many people with this personality disorder begin to grasp the consequences of their remorseless dealings with others and may desist from some of their objectionable behaviors.

The individual must be at least 18 years old to meet the criteria for this diagnosis, and there must have been evidence of conduct disorder before the age of 15. A child who is diagnosed with conduct disorder has demonstrated a pattern of truancy, lying, physical cruelty or aggression toward people or animals, vandalism, stealing, and/or other behaviors that have gotten him or her into trouble with the authorities.

Borderline personality disorder gets its name from the idea that the person is on the edge of reality, suffering identity problems or fluctuations in self-image.

FIGURE 14.9 *Self-destructive behavior, such as overdosing on pills, is common in borderline personality disorder.*

The person's sense of self is unstable. There is often a high degree of aggression associated with this disorder—such as self-destructive behavior (recurrent suicidal gestures or self-mutilation), inappropriate, intense anger, and recurrent fights—resulting in unstable and intense interpersonal relationships.

A hallmark of the borderline personality disorder is difficulty being alone, which sometimes leads to frantic efforts to avoid abandonment. This is accompanied by, and perhaps prompted by, chronic feelings of emptiness. In addition, the person tends to be manipulative, unpredictable, moody, easily frustrated, and impulsive, as demonstrated by excessive spending, eating, or engaging in promiscuous sexual activity.

People with **narcissistic personality disorder** are likely to have a grandiose, exaggerated sense of self-importance. They tend to be preoccupied with receiving attention and need to be loved and admired by others. They tend to be self-absorbed to the extent that they disregard the rights and feelings of others. Some narcissists are preoccupied with fantasies of success, and they tend to be interpersonally exploitive in serving their own goals. Erich Fromm (1973) has described this disorder as follows:

> Narcissism can be described as a state of experience in which only the person himself, *his* body, *his* needs, *his* feelings, *his* thoughts, *his* property, everything and everybody that pertain to *him* are experienced as fully real, while everybody and everything that does not form part of the person or is not an object of his needs is not interesting, is not fully real, is perceived only by intellectual recognition, while *affectively* without weight and color. (p. 201)

This passage illustrates how a person with a narcissistic personality lacks empathy for the feelings or plight of others, disregarding the other person's rights and feelings. They can be superficially charming and friendly, but they see people as pawns who can serve their interests. They seek and surround themselves with sycophants who lavish them with unconditional praise and will agree with their viewpoint. Their fragile self-esteem is revealed by their preoccupation with how others regard them. Their extreme vulnerability to being wounded by criticism from others may cause their friends, coworkers, and family members to feel as though they are walking on eggshells around the narcissistic person.

FIGURE 14.10 *Being inappropriately seductive during an interview for a cashier at a grocery store might point to histrionic personality disorder.*

Histrionic personality disorder describes a person, usually a female, who engages in attention-seeking behavior and displays excessive emotionality. Individuals with this disorder are uncomfortable in situations in which they are not the center of attention and thus may be theatrical or sexually seductive in appearance and behavior to draw attention to themselves. They constantly seek reassurance, approval, or praise and are overly concerned with physical attractiveness. They may display rapidly shifting and shallow expressions of emotion. Those with histrionic personality disorder are self-centered; their actions are directed toward obtaining immediate satisfaction; and they have no tolerance for the frustration of delayed gratification (American Psychiatric Association, 2000).

FIGURE 14.11 *Hypersensitivity to negative evaluation is typical in avoidant personality disorder.*

With **avoidant personality disorder**, individuals exhibit the same social withdrawal as do schizoids, but the motivation is different. Avoidant people withdraw to avoid rejection, shame, or humiliation. They are hypersensitive to negative evaluation, showing an apprehensive alertness to any sign of social denigration. They may see ridicule or disparagement where none was intended. These individuals are too fearful of criticism to seek out other people, yet they desire affection and are often lonely and bored. Their fears prompt them to avoid work or school activities that involve significant interpersonal contact. This is the only personality disorder that is **ego dystonic** (also called **ego alien**), meaning the person wishes to be rid of the disorder. While those with avoidant personality disorder do suffer and want to be rid of the disorder, it feels to the person like his or her normal state of being.

People with an **obsessive-compulsive personality disorder** tend to be perfectionists: overly conscientious, rigid, and excessively concerned with rules, order, efficiency, and work. They are controlling, and they may insist that everyone do things their way. They have difficulty relaxing, doing anything just for fun, and expressing warm feelings. This personality disorder is differentiated from a similarly named type of anxiety disorder, obsessive-compulsive disorder, in that the former is ego syntonic and the latter is ego alien (American Psychiatric Association, 2000). This disorder fits Freud's formulation of the anal retentive personality.

Explore
the functions of the frontal lobes
in Chapter 3, p. 70

Those who suffer from **dependent personality disorder** give up the responsibility for important aspects of their lives to others, by allowing them to make most of the dependent person's important decisions, such as where to live, what job to take, and whom to date. Due to a lack of self-confidence, people with a dependent personality disorder believe themselves to be incompetent or stupid and are thus reluctant to initiate projects or do things on their own. They display an unwillingness to mature or take responsibility for themselves. In order to get other people to like them, they may volunteer to do things that are unpleasant or demeaning. They are frequently preoccupied with fears of being abandoned and may feel devastated when close relationships end. When this happens, another relationship is urgently sought as a source of care and support.

Causes of Personality Disorders

Biological research on antisocial and borderline personality disorders has focused on the frontal lobes of the cerebral cortex, an area of the brain that helps inhibit impulsive, aggressive behavior. Since there is extensive evidence that genes play a role in shaping personality, it is likely that personality disorders are at least in part hereditary. In particular, schizotypal, antisocial, borderline, and narcissistic personalities tend to run in families. Many theorists are convinced that problematic family relationships are at the root of personality disorder formation. Various family dynamics have been linked to personality disorders. For example, researchers have found associations between sexual abuse or neglect and antisocial and borderline personality disorders (Golier et al., 2003; Luntz & Widom, 1994;

McLean & Gallop, 2003), between parental overprotection/ authoritarianism and the development of dependent personality disorder (Bornstein, 1992b), and between moralistic and rigid parents and obsessive-compulsive personality disorder (Oldham, 1994).

Anxiety Disorders

General Characteristics

It is normal, even adaptive, to be somewhat anxious about our health, social relationships, exams, careers, world hunger, terrorism, and other things. Anxiety also prompts us to get regular medical checkups, study for exams, and take other appropriate action in response to potential threats. Although anxiety is a natural human experience, those with anxiety disorders suffer from a level of unease that is extreme in relation to any existing threat. When anxiety is intense, prolonged, and out of proportion to any actual danger, it may meet the criteria for an anxiety disorder.

Types of Anxiety Disorders

Generalized anxiety disorder is characterized by a relatively constant state of tension, excessive worry, and diffuse uneasiness. The person may also be restless, easily tired, or irritable. These symptoms may disturb the person's sleep or make concentration difficult. The person may also be hypersensitive to sudden or unexpected stimuli, which may cause him or her to overreact. The anxiety does not have a distinct source, such as a particular object or situation—an aspect of the disorder that Freud termed "free-floating" anxiety. Whereas the symptoms of this disorder are pretty ordinary, their persistence is unusual, lasting for at least six months. Additionally, they are very typically an ongoing aspect of the way the person experiences the world throughout his or her lifetime. The extent of the worry or dread is beyond being a realistic reaction to any real threat and interferes with the person's normal functioning.

Panic disorder is characterized by sudden, unpredictable, intense, and recurrent short-term episodes of severe anxiety or dread. The person may experience shortness of breath, choking sensations, trembling, dizziness, and heart palpitations. Although the individual may feel as though he or she is having a heart attack and likely to die, the attacks aren't generally life-threatening. They happen fast and make the person feel out of control, as well as distressed to the point of sheer terror. What makes panic attacks turn into a panic disorder is fear of having an attack at a time when doing so would either put the person in physical danger, such as while driving an automobile, or at risk of social embarrassment (American Psychiatric Association, 2000). Two to three percent of the population is likely to be diagnosed with panic disorder sometime during their lifetimes (Barlow, 2002).

Phobias are unrealistic fears of specific objects, activities, or situations. A person's ordinary life may be disrupted by avoidance of the dreaded object or situation. Phobias fall into three main categories: specific phobias, social phobia, and agoraphobia.

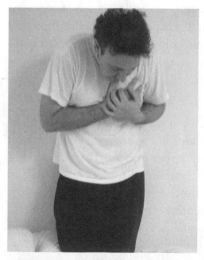

FIGURE 14.12 *Individuals suffering a panic attack may feel as though they are having a heart attack.*

TABLE 14.1 **Specific phobias.**	
Specific phobia	**What the person fears**
Acrophobia	High places
Nyctyophobia	The dark
Pathophobia	Disease
Claustrophobia	Enclosed places
Hematophobia	Blood
Mysophobia	Germs
Arachnophobia	Spiders
Ophidiophobia	Snakes
Astrophobia	Lightning
Zoophobia	Animals

Specific phobias may be attached to virtually any object or situation. Fear of objects most frequently involves animals such as snakes, spiders, sharks, and bees. Fear of the dark or a fear of heights suggests roots in an evolutionary process that serves the purpose of keeping people safe.

Almost everyone has a few mild phobias. In fact, phobias are the most common form of mental disorder (Nevid, Rathus, & Greene, 2006). About 10% of the general population will experience a specific phobia at some point in their lives (Kessler et al., 1994). Typical phobias are a fear of heights, enclosed spaces, the dark, and bugs. A phobia that is strong enough to be incapacitating produces overwhelming anxiety that may cause vomiting, wild climbing and running, or fainting.

We are all appraised and evaluated by other people all the time. People experiencing **social phobia** avoid certain social situations—such as eating or speaking in public, dating, talking with authority figures, or meeting new people—where they might encounter the scrutiny of others (Raulin, 2003). They worry that, when with others, they will be observed, evaluated unfavorably, and humiliated.

FIGURE 14.13 *Many agoraphobics avoid leaving the safety of their homes.*

Agoraphobia is the most disruptive type of phobia. It refers to fear of having a panic attack and losing control in public places or unfamiliar situations. People with agoraphobia wish to avoid any situations that might set off panic attacks, situations in which escape would be difficult or help might not be forthcoming. Sufferers tend to fear leaving the house or other familiar surroundings, or even being away from a safe person. Agoraphobia is often diagnosed in conjunction with panic disorder.

Obsessive-compulsive disorder (OCD) is diagnosed when a person is troubled by repetitive thoughts and related actions, which are ego alien. It is classified as an anxiety disorder because patients suffer tension if they try to resist their obsessions and compulsions. In its mildest form, obsessive-compulsive disorder is like an annoying habit that the person just can't seem to break, such as the persistent reoccurrence of a song in the person's head or the urge to engage in fingernail biting (American Psychiatric Association, 2000). In its most severe form, it involves a thought (rumination) or activity (ritual) that literally controls every aspect of a person's life to the exclusion of everything else.

Obsessions are thoughts or images that intrude into consciousness against a person's will. The ideas are inappropriate and distressing. Obsessions usually give rise to **compulsions**, as the person attempts to neutralize the bothersome thought with another thought or an action. Compulsions are irrational behaviors that a person feels driven to repeat. The acts are performed in a ritualistic pattern, often

FIGURE 14.14 *Hand washing is dangerous when it becomes a compulsion. Skin on the hands can become cracked and bleed, leaving the person open to infection.*

at a very high frequency. For example, a person may engage in hand washing, manipulate objects such as keys or worry beads, or turn a faucet or light switch on and off. The behavior is not an end in itself but is designed to produce or prevent some future event or situation. However, either the activity is not connected in a realistic way with what it is designed to produce or prevent, or it is clearly excessive.

Acute stress disorder (ASD) occurs within one month after exposure to an extremely traumatic event and lasts no longer than a month. ASD and post-traumatic stress disorder share many common features. Both disorders involve reexperiencing the traumatic event in flashbacks, as though the experience were happening again. They also prompt avoidance of stimuli associated with the event as well as give way to a heightened state of bodily arousal, emotional distress, impairment of functioning, nightmares, hypervigilance, insomnia, an exaggerated startle response, and irritability. Other than time of onset and duration, the major feature that differentiates post-traumatic stress disorder from ASD is dissociation. People with ASD report dissociative symptoms such as emotional numbing or feelings of detachment from themselves or their environment.

Post-traumatic stress disorder (PTSD) is a prolonged maladaptive reaction to a traumatic experience that is life-threatening in nature. The reaction may last many months, years, or even decades. Situations such as car accidents, military combat, a natural disaster, or violent physical assault may precipitate intense fear and feelings of helplessness that cause the victim to persistently reexperience the terrifying event. The disorder may not appear until many months or years after the event. About 72% of people in the United States have experienced a traumatic event at some time in their lives, with about 8% experiencing PTSD. Thus, not all people who experience traumatic events are doomed to develop this disorder.

Causes of Anxiety Disorders

Some aspects of anxiety can be explained from a biological perspective. There is good evidence pointing to innate differences in the ease with which individuals become physiologically aroused in response to internal and external stimuli (Raine, 1999). This could reflect an inherited predisposition toward autonomic nervous system arousal that renders such individuals vulnerable to developing anxiety disorders.

It is also the case that human beings seem to be biologically prepared to fear certain objects and situations but not others (Seligman, 1971). Fear of heights, fear of lightning, and fear of dangerous animals such as snakes, spiders, bees, and sharks seem to be obviously adaptive mechanisms (Cook, Hodes, & Lang, 1986). In the past, those who were not afraid of such things might not have survived long enough to produce offspring.

From a learning theory perspective, anxiety may develop through classical conditioning of fear (Schwartz, 1984), through stimulus generalization, through reinforcement, or through observational learning. The originally conditioned fear may also generalize to encompass fears of other situations that have never actually been experienced. Once a fear has been conditioned, avoidance of stimuli that elicit the fear is maintained by the reduction in anxiety that results from avoidance maneuvers. For instance, having been bitten by a dog, a person may feel anxious when around any dog, and experience a flood of relief after moving away from a dog that has been spotted. Finally, we learn to fear certain objects and situations through vicarious conditioning, after observing others react with fear.

Explore
**learning theory—
classical conditioning**
in Chapter 7, p. 200

Cognitive approaches focus on the distorted thinking that prompts those suffering from anxiety disorders to overestimate the threat posed by situations they encounter. For example, a woman suffering from social phobia may perceive criticism where none exists. If she learns to remind herself that most people are preoccupied with their own tasks, rather than dwelling on what she is doing wrong, she may experience some relief.

Somatoform Disorders

General Characteristics

In the case of somatoform disorders, psychological problems are converted to physical complaints. The presence of physical symptoms suggests a medical condition, but the symptoms are not fully explained by any medical condition, by substance abuse, or by any other mental disorder (American Psychiatric Association, 2000). People with somatoform disorders are distressed by their condition and are not faking it. In order for a diagnosis to be appropriate, the symptoms must cause significant impairment in social, occupational, or other areas of functioning.

Types of Somatoform Disorders

Conversion disorders result when anxiety is converted into physical symptoms. There may be a loss of motor or sensory function, which becomes a prolonged disability. For instance, the patient may be unable to hear, to speak, or to feel

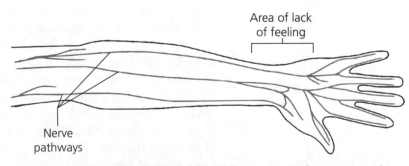

Area of lack
of feeling

Nerve
pathways

FIGURE 14.15 *Glove anesthesia doesn't make anatomical sense, since the nerves that serve each of the fingers run down the entire length of the arm.*

anything from the wrist to the fingertips, a condition known as "glove anesthesia." This condition doesn't make anatomical sense, since no combination of nerves serves this area alone, so the loss of feeling has to have a psychological rather than a medical cause.

Hypochondriasis is characterized by a person's unrealistic interpretation of relatively common physical sensations and bodily symptoms. It typically involves the development of an irrational preoccupation with or fear of having a major or even terminal disease. For example, a middle-aged man may notice swollen lymph nodes in his neck that are due to a common type of infection and jump to the conclusion that he has a cancerous tumor.

Somatization disorder is similar to hypochondriasis except that symptoms appear before the age of 30, typically in adolescence. Pain or a feeling of "sickliness" may be felt for a large part of the person's life. The individual experiences a number of symptoms characterized by pain, gastrointestinal distress, sexual problems, and pseudoneurological symptoms. They may include double vision, muscle weakness, stomachache, diarrhea, painful menstruation, or sexual indifference (American Psychiatric Association, 2000).

With **pain disorder**, the person experiences either pain in the absence of physical cause or much more pain than is warranted by the physical cause. The pain must be of sufficient severity to cause significant distress or impairment in important areas of daily life, such as in the person's work or social obligations.

Body dysmorphic disorder refers to a preoccupation with a real or imagined defect in appearance. If a slight physical anomaly happens to be present, the person's concern is noticeably excessive. The preoccupation causes clinically significant distress or impairment in social, occupational, or other important areas of functioning. A young woman may have slightly more body hair than usual for women and be convinced that everyone is looking at it and thinking of nothing else.

Causes of Somatoform Disorders

Psychoanalytic theorists suggest that an underlying unconscious conflict may be displaced onto a body part to produce body dysmorphic disorder or channeled into physical symptoms, which results in conversion disorder (Merskey, 1995). From a behavioral perspective, the "sick role" can be reinforcing because others respond to the person with sympathy and the sufferer may be relieved of his or her normal responsibilities or may escape anxiety-evoking situations (Miller, 1987). Cognitive theorists suggest that hypochondriasis and panic disorder may share a common cause, which is a distorted way of thinking that leads the person to misinterpret minor changes in bodily sensations as signs of a life-threatening illness (Salkovskis & Clark, 1993). Hypochondriasis may also serve as a self-handicapping strategy in that poor performance can be blamed on failing health. Finally, somatoform disorders may provide a means of diverting attention to physical complaints in order to avoid thinking about other life problems.

Dissociative Disorders

General Characteristics

FIGURE 14.16 *Wartime horrors, such as this building that was destroyed after a bombing, are fruitful grounds for spawning a dissociative disorder.*

Dissociative disorders are characterized by a splitting apart of significant aspects of experience from memory or consciousness. It is normal to experience one's physical and psychological self as consistent over time and in different situations. In dissociative states, people experience a disruption in the usually integrated functions of consciousness, memory, identity, or perception of reality (American Psychiatric Association, 2000). As with anxiety disorders, dissociative disorders represent ways of dealing with overwhelming anxiety levels.

Types of Dissociative Disorders

Dissociative amnesia is characterized by an inability to remember significant personal information and is usually of a traumatic or stressful nature that is too far-reaching to be explained by ordinary forgetfulness (American Psychiatric Association, 2000). It may include an inability to remember one's name, address, or details about one's past. More commonly, it involves a failure to recall events pertaining to an occurrence perceived as personally disastrous. The memory loss is reversible.

Dissociative fugue involves a sudden inability to recall one's past as well as confusion about one's personal identity or the assumption of a new identity, combined with unexpected and purposeful travel away from home or one's customary place of work. For example, a solider may witness his buddy being killed by a mortar shell and block out the horror with a dissociative episode, at the same time fleeing the battle scene without conscious awareness of being a soldier in the act of desertion.

Formerly known as multiple personality disorder, **dissociative identity disorder (DID)** is characterized by the presence of two or more distinct identities or personality states within the same person that recurrently take control of that individual's behavior. The disorder is accompanied by an inability to recall important personal information that is too extensive to be explained by ordinary forgetfulness. Each personality state has a characteristic way of perceiving, thinking, and behaving. Only one of the personality states predominates at any given time.

This disorder is rare and controversial, and some psychologists question whether the phenomenon of multiple personalities actually exists. They suggest instead that it is a form of role playing acquired by observational learning and reinforcement (Reisner, 1994; Spanos, 1994; Spanos, Weekes, & Bertrand, 1985). Others propose that patients sometimes fake the disorder or come up with "alters" in an unconscious effort to please a therapist who inadvertently encourages multiple personalities to emerge. However, the majority of psychologists believe that DID is a genuine, although rare, disorder.

FIGURE 14.17 *An aspect of depersonalization is a feeling that one is living in a dream; the external world seems unreal.*

Depersonalization disorder is characterized by a persistent or recurrent episode of feeling detached from one's mental processes or body that is accompanied by intact reality testing. The person's grasp on reality remains unaffected, so the person is able to respond to questions and interact normally with the environment during an episode. This feeling of estrangement from oneself is ego alien. The individual may feel mechanical or robotic, may experience sensory amnesia, or may have a sense of unreality about the external world. In a traumatic situation, this kind of psychological separation may help keep a person from being overwhelmed by anxiety. From time to time, many people experience a sense of detachment from their bodies. Since depersonalization is a common experience, a diagnosis would be made only if the symptoms are prolonged and severe, distressing, or they impair functioning.

Causes of Dissociative Disorders

Dissociations are often precipitated by traumatic events such as natural disasters, wartime horrors, or marital strife. A psychodynamic explanation of dissociative disorders is that they provide an escape from intolerable psychological conflicts by giving up the continuity of the self, by disowning a part of themselves. Painful memories, thoughts, and feelings are repressed, causing a "splitting off" (separation) of unacceptable impulses and troubling recollections from conscious awareness.

Cognitive theorists suggest that avoidance of guilt and shame is accomplished through not thinking about disturbing acts. Genetic and environmental factors may explain dissociation well, as those who develop dissociative disorders tend to have certain personality traits in common and also have typically suffered child abuse or other forms of childhood trauma. Certain personality traits, such as poor self-awareness, a tendency to fantasize, a high degree of suggestibility, openness to altered states of consciousness, and a high degree of dependency on others, may predispose people to develop dissociative experiences in the face of extreme stress.

Mood Disorders

General Characteristics

Mood disorders involve an extreme level of mood that is inappropriate to the situation. The two main types of mood disorders are bipolar disorder (mania and depression) and unipolar disorder (depression only). Depression is far more common than bipolar disorder. About 16% of the population experiences significant depression at some time in their lives (Nevid et al., 2006), whereas less than 2% of the population is affected by bipolar disorder (Raulin, 2003).

Types of Mood Disorders

The main feature of **bipolar disorder** is alternating manic and depressive moods. When in a manic state, the person experiences a natural high and is euphoric, cheerful, and elated. The thought process is expansive, prompting the individ-

FIGURE 14.18 *Bipolar disorder consists of alternating depressed and manic moods.*

ual to feel that anything is possible. The person has a positive self-image and unrealistic expectations of success. Since these individuals often have delusions of grandeur, believing that they have special powers or talents, clearly their judgment is impaired. They are also likely to experience rapid shifts of thought and may be irritable, particularly when their wishes are frustrated (American Psychiatric Association, 2000). This elevated mood may last for a few days or as long as a few months.

On a behavioral level, the person displays a whirlwind of activity and appears "super charged." He or she may go on buying sprees, take on new work duties, or make plans on a grand scale. In a manic state, people may talk constantly and be inappropriately loud, or their speech may become incoherent if it comes out too rapidly. They may be extremely distractible and restless. Hypersexuality along with abandonment of moral restraint may also be evident.

Physical signs of mania involve deep-seated changes in bodily function. The person often sleeps only a few hours per night. Since this mode of existence cannot continue indefinitely, it's understandable that few individuals who experience mania seem to avoid depression. For this reason, people who have had a few manic episodes are diagnosed as having a bipolar disorder.

A major depressive episode is signaled by two or more weeks of depressed mood or the loss of pleasure in activities that the person normally finds enjoyable. This is accompanied by other symptoms that might include changes in appetite, changes in sleep, decreased energy, difficulty concentrating, suicidal ideation, and feelings of worthlessness or guilt.

On a behavioral level, depressed people are likely to be inactive and lethargic. Withdrawal from others is common. However, there is such a thing as agitated depression, characterized by jerky and rapid behaviors such as pacing and hand-wringing.

Depression has physical consequences, known as the vegetative signs of depression. The depressed person may experience a loss of appetite and a consequent weight loss, or he or she may gain weight, as some people eat in an attempt to feel better. Sleep disturbances such as trouble falling asleep, waking up in the night, or not feeling rested after a night's sleep are likely to occur. Women's menstrual cycles may cease temporarily. A depressed person is likely to experience decreased sexual desire (and decreased desire or motivation of any kind).

FIGURE 14.19 *Pacing behavior is often seen in depression.*

Depression takes more than one form. A person can suffer from **major depressive disorder**, which involves episodes of depression followed by a lessening of the symptoms, or from **dysthymic disorder**, which is a less intense but relatively constant state of depression for at least two years. A person could also have dysthymic disorder and suffer major depression as well, a condition known as double depression.

Causes of Mood Disorders

The causes of bipolar disorder are not clear. The disorder does tend to run in families. There is some indication that the brains of people with bipolar disorder use more glucose (the brain's "fuel," or, in other words, its energy source) than the brains of normal subjects.

Biological theories of depression focus on neural, biochemical, and physiological mechanisms underlying the development of depression. Three neurotransmitters that have been associated with depression are serotonin, norepinephrine, and dopamine. The levels of serotonin and norepinephrine are often lower in depressed people than in nondepressed people, and drugs that increase the levels of these neurotransmitters in the brain tend to alleviate depression. Low levels of dopamine may be the cause of some forms of depression, but not others (Depue, Arbisi, Spoont, Leon, & Ainswoth, 1989).

There is ample evidence of genetic factors in both major depression and bipolar disorder (e.g., Mendlewicz & Rainer, 1977; Wender et al., 1986). The concordance rates for major depression in monozygote (identical) twins is more than twice as high as for dizygote (fraternal) twins (Bertelsen, Harvald, & Hauge, 1977). For bipolar disorder, the concordance rates are three times higher in monozygotic twins than in dizygotic twins (Bertelsen et al., 1977; Mendlewicz, 1985). A **concordance rate** indicates in pairs of twins the rate at which both twins have the same disorder.

Psychodynamic theory suggests that anger may become directed against the self, resulting in depression. The early loss of a mother or the failure of parents to satisfy an infant's need for a loving attachment (i.e., rejecting parents) could render the child vulnerable to depression.

A behavioral view of depression suggests that depressed people withdraw from social situations because they lack the energy to engage in social interaction and because such activities no longer bring them pleasure. This withdrawal makes it difficult for depressed people to have enjoyable experiences, so their depression is maintained by lack of positive reinforcement from the environment. Another behavioral theory of depression employs the **learned helplessness** model, which proposes that people become depressed because they learn to view themselves as helpless to control the reinforcements in their environment. At some time in the past, they found themselves in a predicament and were helpless to improve their situation; thus, they came to regard their efforts as fruitless. After once seeing their efforts as pointless, they no longer strive to help themselves, even in situations where their efforts would pay off.

A cognitive perspective focuses on a sense of having lost something, whether it is a loved one, a job, or self-esteem, as a cause of depression. Furthermore, Aaron Beck identified specific patterns of thinking that are associated with depression. For example, depressed people may engage in **selective perception**, which means that they only notice the negative events in their lives and overlook the positive ones. A cognitive triad of negative perceptions, consisting of a negative attitude about oneself, about the environment, and about the future, is typical of people who are depressed (Beck, Freeman, & Associates, 1990; Clark & Beck, 1999).

FIGURE 14.20 *Perceiving this glass as half empty means focusing on the negative. It can be viewed as half full, too. Depressed people often have a negative perception.*

Explore
humanistic theory
in Chapter 13, p. 426

For humanists, depression can be a consequence of failure to find meaning in one's life. People are not satisfied merely to have enough to eat and to feel safe when they lie in bed at night. They tend to long for a sense of purpose in their lives, to give their existence meaning. In addition, human beings have a natural drive to explore, which in the past gave them an evolutionary advantage in that they were more likely to find food sources if they searched for them. However, moving forward in life involves doing new things, which can be anxiety provoking. Those who shrink back from striving due to the anxiety it entails may feel guilty when they face not having lived up to their potential. From a humanist perspective, the realization that they are settling, coasting through life, and playing it safe instead of going for the gold can result in depression.

Schizophrenia

General Characteristics

People suffering from **schizophrenia** tend to have major disturbances in perception, language, thought, emotion, and behavior, with signs that such disturbances of this nature have occurred for at least six months. The individual must display a number of characteristic symptoms, but the common misconception that schizophrenics have a split personality is not one of them. The term "schizophrenia" does indeed imply that there is a split, but it is more of a break with reality that is meant, as the schizophrenic person responds to an inner world of accusatory voices or paranoid ideas.

Symptoms of Schizophrenia

People with schizophrenia show a variety of symptoms, although a person diagnosed with this disorder rarely displays all of its signs. Symptoms vary in intensity from person to person, but the core ones include incoherent speech and/or irrationality (Brislin, 1993; Draguns, 1990b). In general, the symptoms are grouped into two categories: **positive symptoms** or **negative symptoms**. To describe a symptom as positive doesn't mean that it is good, but instead denotes that the person with schizophrenia has experiences that others do not. On the other hand, negative symptoms are things lacking in a person suffering from schizophrenia that are typically found in a nonschizophrenic person.

Thought disorders are among the positive symptoms. They represent a collection of problems that involve difficulty in thinking clearly or in expressing a coherent train of thought. The most common form of thought disorder is a **loosening of associations** (also called derailment). It involves jumping from one topic to another, making the schizophrenic person's conversation difficult or impossible to follow (Raulin, 2003). The listener is left with the impression that what is being said would make sense if only he or she could listen just a little more closely. A word salad—random words put into sentences that are gramatically correct yet convey no meaning—produces a similar experience in the listener. For example, a schizophrenic might declare, "I am elected

FIGURE 14.21 *A "word salad" refers to words formed into a sentence that conveys no meaning.*

by god almighty and never again until life do us part" or "I have saw many lots from my or now pot."

Neologisms refer to the making up of words. For instance, one schizophrenic patient referred to people she thought were plotting against her as "clandestites," a term that is apparently based on the word "clandestine" but has no meaning except to this patient (Raulin, 2003). Finally, some schizophrenics string words together on the basis of their sound, or the "clangs" they make. **Clang associations** involve the repetitious use of similar-sounding words. An example is, "She loved to sing, zing, ping, and bing, but nowhere to fling, bing, ming."

Delusions are a second category of positive symptoms, and they are defined as false beliefs about reality that the person clings to and resists considering evidence that disputes them. All of us have mistaken ideas at times. Students sometimes come to class not knowing a quiz or exam has been scheduled. Whereas a student's false belief about an exam date is easily corrected, the delusions of a psychotic person are not so easily shaken by evidence to the contrary. Instead, the person who produces evidence against a strongly held delusion may be viewed by a schizophrenic person as attempting to deceive. In addition, a schizophrenic's delusions tend to be bizarre in that they are implausible and not related to ordinary life experiences (American Psychiatric Association, 2000).

There are several types of delusions. **Delusions of influence** are the false beliefs that one's thoughts, feelings, or actions are being controlled by external agents; that one's private thoughts are being broadcast indiscriminately to others; that thoughts are being inserted involuntarily by alien forces; or that some mysterious agency has robbed one of one's thoughts. **Delusions of grandeur** are unfounded beliefs that one has some great, unrecognized talent, knowledge, or insight; that one has a special relationship with an important person or with God; or that one is a prominent person (Raulin, 2003). **Delusions of persecution** are mistaken beliefs that one is being cheated, spied on, followed, poisoned, harassed, or plotted against. **Delusions of reference** occur when events unrelated to the schizophrenic person are given personal significance. For example, a person suffering from schizophrenia may assume that a newspaper article or a television program is sending a special personal message to him or her. Finally, **somatic delusions** are false beliefs about one's body.

FIGURE 14.22 *A delusion of persecution may involve the conviction that one is being followed.*

Hallucinations are another type of positive symptom. They are perceptual experiences that are not based on external reality, but instead are fabrications created by the psychotic person's brain. Auditory hallucinations, or hearing voices, are the most common type, followed by visual hallucinations. A hallucination involving sight may consist of formed images, such as of people, or of unformed images, such as flashes of light. Tactile hallucinations involve feeling things in the absence of external stimuli. People may even have taste or smell hallucinations.

A final positive symptom, **grossly disorganized behavior**, may take a variety of forms. A catatonic schizophrenic may hold a rigid and often bizarre posture for hours. The person may display rigidity with a resistance to being moved or demonstrate "waxy flexibility" by being flexible enough to be bent and reshaped by another person as though made of wax. A person suffering from disorganized schizophrenia may display a childlike silliness, with giggling or cackling laughter that is unconnected with what is happening around the person. Other behavioral manifestations of schizophrenia include echolalia (repeating what others say) and echopraxia (which refers to imitating the gestures of others many times over).

Negative symptoms of schizophrenia include **affective flattening**, **alogia**, **avolition**, and **asociality**. Affective flattening refers to the external expression of emotion. A schizophrenic is likely to show some form of reduced emotionality, such as anhedonia, the inability to experience pleasure; blunted affect, a reduced level of emotionality; or flat affect, no emotionality and/or the inability to express emotions.

Alogia refers to a poverty of speech or a poverty of content in the speech. People with alogia rarely talk, and when they do, their speech is often noticeably sparse. Avolition represents apathy or an energy deficit. People with this symptom don't care about basic behaviors such as self-grooming, so they remain disheveled and dirty. They may spend day after day doing nothing. Asociality is a lack of interest in social relations. People displaying asociality have no friends and apparently have no desire to make friends. Their detachment from others is usually accompanied by the elaboration of an inner world in which the person develops illogical and fantastic ideas that have little or no relationship to reality.

Types of Schizophrenia

FIGURE 14.23 *Catatonic stare.*

There are three main subtypes of schizophrenia: paranoid, catatonic, and disorganized. The most common subtype is **paranoid schizophrenia**. This person has better personality integration than do either of the other two subtypes and typically suffers from grandiose and persecutory delusions.

Catatonic schizophrenia is exemplified by catatonic stupors, in which the patient becomes immobile for hours, days, or even years. While in a catatonic state, the person is mute and unresponsive to the environment. The stupor may sometimes alternate with motor agitation.

In **disorganized schizophrenia**, the patient's speech may become incoherent and may include baby talk, childish giggling, clang associations, and loose associations that may give a punlike quality to his or her speech. The individual may wear a silly smile and engage in inappropriate, shallow laughter with little or no provocation. He or she may also have bizarre mannerisms, display obscene behavior, and lack any signs of modesty. Delusions of disorganized schizophrenics are usually of a sexual, religious, hypochondriac, or possibly persecutory nature.

When a person who is clearly schizophrenic does not meet the criteria for one of the subtypes, that person is diagnosed with undifferentiated schizophrenia.

Undifferentiated schizophrenia is a classification reserved for those who meet the criteria for schizophrenia but don't fall neatly into one of the three classifications.

Causes of Schizophrenia

It is highly unlikely that a single factor is responsible for schizophrenia or any other form of psychopathology. The possible causal links that have been uncovered are numerous and can generally be categorized as biological, psychological, social, and environmental in nature.

A major finding that supports a genetic basis to schizophrenia comes from twin studies. There is nearly a 50% likelihood of a second identical twin becoming schizophrenic, given that one twin has already been diagnosed with the disorder. People who have a biological relative with schizophrenia have about 10 times the risk of developing schizophrenia as do members of the general population. Among adopted children, schizophrenia occurs more frequently among those from biological parents with schizophrenia than among children of normal biological parents. Conversely, children born to normal parents but raised by schizophrenic adoptive parents are at the same risk of developing schizophrenia as are children raised by normal parents.

The Genain identical quadruplets (born 1930)—Nora, Iris, Myra, and Hester, all of whom developed some manifestation of schizophrenic disorder—are a classic example of genetic influence. The odds of any four randomly chosen people all being diagnosed as having schizophrenia are 1 in 100 million. The sisters' problems began in high school. Since that time, they have been in and out of hospitals. However, if genes were the sole contributor to schizophrenia, then every identical twin of a person with schizophrenia would develop the disorder. Instead, only half do, which suggests there are other causes of the disorder.

Explore **dopamine** in Chapter 15, p. 485

Neurotransmitters may also play a role in schizophrenia. The "dopamine hypothesis" suggests that schizophrenia involves either an excess of the neurotransmitter dopamine or an overreactivity of dopamine receptors in the brains of people with schizophrenia. The major source of evidence for the dopamine model is found in the effects of antipsychotic drugs called major tranquilizers or neuroleptics, which often reduce the symptoms of schizophrenia. Neuroleptic drugs block dopamine receptors, thereby reducing the level of dopamine activity. As a consequence, neuroleptics inhibit excessive transmission of neural impulses that may give rise to schizophrenic behavior patterns. Another source of evidence for the dopamine hypothesis is the effect of high doses of amphetamines, which (1) produce symptoms remarkably similar to paranoid schizophrenia in people who do not have schizophrenia, and (2) exacerbate psychotic symptoms in many but not all people with the disorder.

Cerebral atrophy has also been observed in the brains of some schizophrenic patients. The brains of schizophrenics are about 5% smaller, on average, in total volume than those of normal individuals, with the greatest volume reductions being in the cerebral cortex. CT (computed tomography) scans and MRIs (magnetic resonance imaging) have shown that three out of four people with schizophrenia show enlarged lateral ventricles, and many have a reduced volume in the limbic system, particularly in the hippocampus. Enlarged ventricles are a sign of loss of brain tissue, or cell loss.

Environmental factors include family dynamics and sociocultural factors. Family characteristics—such as the tendency of family members to express hostile and critical comments toward the schizophrenic relative, to be overly involved in the schizophrenic person's life, and to habitually communicate in a manner that lacks clarity—have been linked with schizophrenia (Nevid et al., 2006). Sociocultural factors include the evidence that the majority of people with schizophrenia come from the lower socioeconomic classes. Lower socioeconomic class is defined as having a high school education or less and an occupation that requires few skills and little training. Research evidence generally supports the **downward drift hypothesis** as an explanation of this link, which is the proposal that schizophrenia makes it hard for people to achieve educationally and occupationally and that they therefore drift into lower social classes (Goldberg & Morrison, 1963; Lystad, 1957; Turner & Wagonfeld, 1967). However, the fact that schizophrenia is found throughout the world with roughly the same frequency suggests that sociocultural factors do not make a substantial contribution to the risk of developing schizophrenia. The variability in sociocultural experiences among people throughout the world is substantial, yet the proportion developing schizophrenia remains constant at 1% of the population (Gottesman, 1991).

Delusional Disorders

General Characteristics

A **delusional disorder** is characterized by one or more nonbizarre delusions that last for at least one month. Whereas a patient with schizophrenia has delusions that tend to be bizarre, that is, not derived from ordinary life experiences, delusions that are nonbizarre involve situations that could conceivably occur in real life. Other than suffering from the impact of his or her delusions, the delusional person does not exhibit markedly impaired functioning or bizarre behavior. The individual does not suffer from disorganized speech, affective flattening, or the bizarre behaviors characteristic of schizophrenics. However, hallucinations that are related to the delusional system may be present (American Psychiatric Association, 2000).

Types of Delusional Disorders

An **erotomanic type** delusion is a false belief that another person, usually of higher status, is in love with the delusional person. Once in awhile, movie stars are the focus of attention from such individuals. **Jealous type** delusions center on the conviction that the individual's sexual partner is unfaithful. **Somatic type** delusions are characterized by the belief that the person has some physical defect or general medical condition. You may recall from an earlier section that **grandiose type** delusions are characterized by an inflated sense of worth, power, knowledge, identity, or special relationship to a deity or famous person and that **persecutory type** delusions involve the person's conviction that he or she (or someone to whom the person is close) is being malevolently treated in some way (American Psychiatric Association, 2000).

Mental Illness vs. Mental Health

In this chapter we have considered some serious mental disorders that people face. We have discussed criteria for determining whether behavior is abnormal. One of those criteria was "subjective discomfort," or, in other words, the experience of the individual that his or her life should be better and that there should be less anxiety, anger, or sadness in it.

For the span of its 125 plus years of existence, the field of psychology has been largely occupied with alleviating human misery. Within the past few years, Martin Seligman and other psychologists have expressed concern that we are living in an age of epidemic levels of depression. Anxiety disorders are also extremely common, as was noted earlier. It is clear that much still needs to be done to develop preventive and curative strategies to help people lead more fulfilling lives.

Within the past several decades, many psychologists have turned to the study of exceptionally healthy individuals in hopes of obtaining some signposts that might serve to guide people toward optimal living. An early example of this was Maslow's study of 30 "good specimens" of humanity and their common characteristics, which enabled him to describe the self-actualized person. More recently, psychologists have engaged in the scientific study of happiness (Diener, 1984; Kahneman, Diener, & Schwarz, 1999; Myers, 1991). It turns out that the majority of people consider themselves to be at least fairly happy, and that a person's general level of happiness seems to function as an ongoing trait. Happy people like themselves, are optimistic and outgoing, and believe that they control their own destinies. They tend to experience "flow," which means that they have good skills and opportunities to engage in challenging and rewarding activities that employ their skills. This research is part of a new area of study called positive psychology. **Positive psychology** provides an inspiring perspective on how psychologists hope to enable people to function in an optimal fashion. Rather than merely eliminating misery and distressing levels of dysfunction, psychologists are exploring what it takes to live life to the fullest and how to remove obstacles to the ongoing experience of well-being.

Chapter Summary

"Psychopathology" is a term used to suggest that a person has a significant-enough impairment in functioning to be considered outside the normal realm. Some central factors used in identifying abnormal behavior are how unusual the behavior is in terms of its statistical frequency, whether it violates social norms, and whether it is maladaptive, involves a faulty perception of reality, produces excessive personal distress, or leads to either self-defeating or dangerous behavior.

Statistical frequency defines abnormality in terms of how unusual the behavior is, whereas the violation of social norms compares a person's behavior with what is acceptable behavior in a given culture. Maladaptive behavior is any action that interferes with our ability to accomplish our goals in life. Mental health is associated with an accurate perception of reality, and mental disorder is sometimes defined as loss of touch with reality. The medical model treats mental illness as a disease of the body.

Personality disorders are enduring maladaptive patterns of behavior that cause people to have problematic relationships. There are 10 types of personality disorders, the most studied of which is antisocial personality disorder, since it represents a threat to society. The nine other types are paranoid, schizoid, schizotypal, borderline, narcissistic, histrionic, obsessive-compulsive, avoidant, and dependent personality disorders.

Anxiety disorders involve levels of anxiety that are intense enough to be extremely painful and to interfere with the sufferer's ability to accomplish his or her goals in life. Generalized anxiety disorder refers to a level of anxiety that is not particularly intense but is constantly evident. In contrast, panic disorder involves episodes of intense anxiety that afflict a person out of the blue and then subside. Those suffering from a phobia have an irrational fear of an object or situation. The cardinal signs of obsessive-compulsive disorder are the presence of thoughts that intrude into conscious awareness and prompt the person to engage in compulsive behaviors to avoid intolerable levels of anxiety. Acute stress disorder and post-traumatic stress disorder involve an abnormally strong response to a life-threatening situation in which the person is not sure of survival.

Somatoform disorders and dissociative disorders are anxiety based. Somatoform disorders are those in which psychological distress is converted into physical symptoms. Types of somatoform disorders are conversion disorder, hypochondriasis, somatization disorder, pain disorder, and body dysmorphic disorder. With dissociative disorders, psychological distress causes psychological impairment, such as memory loss or a splitting off of parts of the self. The types of dissociative disorders are dissociative amnesia, dissociative fugue, dissociative identity disorder, and depersonalization.

Mood disorders involve extreme and inappropriate levels of mood that interfere with the person's ability to function. The two types of mood disorders are depression and bipolar disorder. Whereas depression is among the most common mental disorders, bipolar disorder affects less than 2% of the population.

Schizophrenia is defined by positive symptoms, such as thought disorders, and the presence of delusions and/or hallucinations. Negative symptoms are often present as well, such as asociality (a withdrawal from contact with others), affective flattening (a lessened level of emotionality), avolition (a lack of motivation), and alogia (a poverty of speech or a poverty of the content in the speech). There are three types of schizophrenia: paranoid, catatonic, and disorganized. There is also a designation of undifferentiated schizophrenia for people whose symptoms don't fit any of the three main categories.

Delusional disorders belong to the schizophrenic spectrum disorders and involve nonbizarre delusions, which are less severe than the delusions found in schizophrenic patients. The types of delusional disorders are erotomanic, jealous, somatic, grandiose, and persecutory.

The causes of many mental disorders are as yet unknown. Various explanations include genetic and other biological factors, social and psychological factors, and other environmental factors. Many disorders seem to involve an inherited vulnerability that is likely to be activated by environmental stresses.

During the past several decades, psychologists have become interested not only in alleviating human misery but also in studying human potential for happiness and for living life to the fullest. This new line of research has led to the development of a new subfield in psychology known as positive psychology.

Knowledge Builder

RELATE TO YOURSELF

1. Think of a time when you observed a stranger and decided that this person was suffering from a mental disorder. Which of the criteria discussed in the chapter did you use? Did you use more than one criterion?

_____

_____

_____

_____

2. There are probably times when you were adept at adapting to your environment and other times when you didn't seem to be as effective at doing so. What factors seemed to contribute to your fluctuating ability to cope with the situations in which you found yourself?

_____

_____

_____

_____

3. Depersonalization is supposed to be a common disorder. It can involve feeling robotlike, as if you were mechanically going through the motions in a detached manner. Have you ever had an experience such as this, perhaps after pulling an all-nighter while studying for exams? If so, what was it like?

_____

_____

_____

_____

4. Anxiety disorders are quite common. All of us can relate to being stressed at times. Can you think of a period in your life when your anxiety level reached a point where it interfered with your ability to function? If so, how did you cope?

_____

_____

_____

_____

CHAPTER REVIEW QUESTIONS

1. Schizophrenia is the same as "split personality." **T or F?**

2. There is one widely accepted standard for determining when behavior should be considered abnormal. **T or F?**

3. Dissociative identity disorder (formerly called multiple personality disorder) is a common form of mental illness. **T or F?**

4. Mental disorders tend to occur in consistent proportions across cultures, so it is meaningful to talk in terms of a worldwide prevalence of any given disorder. **T or F?**

5. A person who experiences depression is more likely to seek therapy than a person who has an antisocial personality disorder. **T or F?**

6. Which of the following is NOT a criterion for determining that behavior is abnormal?

    (a) it is dangerous

    (b) it doesn't conform with social norms

    (c) it is not ethical

    (d) it causes personal distress in the form of depression, rage, or anxiety

7. All official mental disorders are listed in the _____.

    (a) MMPI-2   (b) DSM-IV-TR

    (c) Stanford-Binet   (d) WAIS-III

8. The personality disorder that gets a lot of research attention because it poses a threat to society is _____.

    (a) antisocial   (b) borderline

    (c) schizoid   (d) avoidant

9. An antisocial personality would rarely be identified on the basis of _____.

    (a) resistance to authority   (b) subjective discomfort

    (c) impulsive, selfish behavior   (d) absence of guilt or remorse

    (e) a tendency to manipulate others

10. Individuals who are excessively narcissistic, dependent, or antisocial are characterized as having _____.

    (a) panic disorders   (b) generalized anxiety

    (c) conversion reactions   (d) psychosis

    (e) personality disorders

11. The anxiety disorder commonly associated with panic disorder is _____.

    (a) generalized anxiety disorder   (b) post-traumatic stress disorder

    (c) agoraphobia   (d) social phobia

12. Obsessive-compulsive disorder is to _____ as obsessive-compulsive personality disorder is to _____.

    (a) ego alien; ego syntonic   (b) ego alien; ego dystonic

    (c) ego syntonic; ego alien   (d) ego syntonic; ego antisyntonic

13. Of the following mental disorders, which is the rarest type?

    (a) major depression   (b) panic disorder

    (c) dissociative identity disorder   (d) depersonalization

14. Obsessions, compulsions, panic, and phobias are formally classified as _____ disorders.

    (a) affective   (b) neurotic

    (c) anxiety   (d) psychotic

    (e) dissociative

15. The somatoform disorder that is described as an irrational fear of having a terminal disease or condition is _____.

    (a) hypochondria   (b) somatotization disorder

    (c) body dysmorphic disorder   (d) conversion disorder

16. The new name for multiple personality disorder is _____.

    (a) schizophrenia   (b) dissociative amnesia

    (c) depersonalization   (d) body dysmorphic disorder

    (e) dissociative identity disorder

17. _____ is a much more common disorder than is _____.

    (a) Depression; bipolar disorder

    (b) Dissociative identity disorder; depersonalization

    (c) Schizophrenia; bipolar disorder

    (d) Schizophrenia; depression

18. Your conviction, not based on any evidence, that a famous person is in love with you could be a sign of a(n) _____ disorder.

    (a) schizophrenic   **(b)** erotomaic form of delusional

    (c) dissociative   **(d)** grandiose type of delusional

19. The subfield of psychology that studies optimal living rather than psychological disorder is known as _____.

    (a) self-actualization   **(b)** humanistic psychology

    (c) nirvana psychology   **(d)** positive psychology

20. *Consider the following scenario:* Jeremy had gone for treatment because he had been rejected by the army for psychiatric reasons and "wanted to do whatever was necessary to get into the army and go to Iraq." Over the course of several weeks of therapy, little happened. Jeremy remained guarded and maintained that there really wasn't anything wrong. He showed almost no affective responses and claimed that his ideal was Grissom, the intellectual, unemotional, and central character of *CSI: Crime Scene Investigation.* One week, as he was leaving his therapy session, he announced that he had "figured out what was going on and knew what to do." Three days later he was hospitalized. He had threatened to blow up an army recruiting post, claiming that aliens from another planet had taken over. He believed that he was one of the last "true" earth men and that the aliens had already infiltrated the bodies of most human beings. What is your diagnosis of Jeremy?

_____

_____

_____

_____

21. *Consider the following scenario:* Due to his unreasonable fear of germs, Howard Hughes made people who worked with him wear white gloves, sometimes several pairs, when handling documents that he would later touch. When newspapers were brought to him, they had to be in stacks of three so he could slide the middle one out by grasping it with a tissue. To escape contamination by dust, he ordered that masking tape be put around the doors and windows of his cars and houses (Fowler, 1986). How would you diagnose Hughes' condition?

_____

_____

_____

_____

22. *CRITICAL THINKING EXERCISE.* What are the similarities and differences between the social phobia disorder and the avoidant personality disorder?

_____

_____

_____

_____

23. *CRITICAL THINKING EXERCISE.* How is the concept of mental health different from the idea of being normal?

_____

_____

_____

_____

USEFUL WEB SITES

ENCYCLOPEDIA OF MENTAL DISORDERS

http://www.minddisorders.com/

MENTAL HEALTH MATTERS: LIST OF PSYCHOLOGICAL DISORDERS

http://www.mental-health-matters.com/disorders/list_alpha.php

This site provides a complete list and explanation of the DSM-IV psychological disorders.

INTERNET MENTAL HEALTH

http://www.mentalhealth.com/p20-grp.html

This site provides information on disorder symptoms and treatments.

PSYCH CENTRAL *DSM-IV* MENTAL DISORDERS INDEX

http://psychcentral.com/disorders

Index of symptoms and treatments of mental disorders.

PSYCHOLOGICAL DISORDERS

http://psychology.suite101.com/article.cfm/
psychological_disorders

This site has symptoms, treatments, and statistics relating to psychological disorders.

WORLD HEALTH ORGANIZATION

http://www.google.com/search?hl=en&q=mental+disorders&
btnG=Google+Search

Complete list of psychiatric disorders and adult symptoms of mental health disorders.

15

Therapies

by Binh Nguyen, MA

> *It may be necessary to encounter defeats, so you can know who you are, what you can rise from, and how you can come out of it.*
>
> —MAYA ANGELOU

Therapy: History and Origins

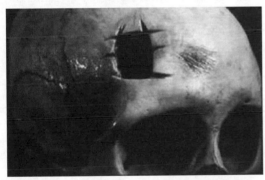

FIGURE 15.1 *Evidence of trephination, a hole drilled in the skull to allow evil spirits to escape, is seen here.*

During the Stone Age, psychological disorders were not well understood, and treatment modalities left much to be desired. Prehistoric societies believed that evil spirits and demonic possessions caused abnormal behaviors, and drastic measures needed to be employed to remove the unwelcome supernaturals. One such measure was discovered by an archaeological finding of skulls in Europe and South America. The discoveries revealed evidence of a "curative" practice called **trephination**, a technique consisting of drilling an opening through the skull of a person to allow the evil spirits to escape, thereby eradicating the abnormal behavior (Selling, 1940). Unfortunately, many "patients" did not survive this procedure and died without justification.

Amid the darkness rose a speck of light, a visionary who deviated from using demonology as an explanation for abnormal behavior. The visionary was Hippocrates (ca. 460–377 BCE), an outstanding physician sometimes referred to as the "father of medicine." Hippocrates believed that imbalances of vital fluids, or humors, in the body and mind can create deterioration in health and give rise to abnormal behaviors. For instance, an excessive amount of one of the humors, such as phlegm, was thought to cause a person to be lethargic; too much black bile could produce depression; extra blood could create a sanguine disposition; and an overabundance of yellow bile could make a person quick-tempered. Although Hippocrates' theory of ill humors is not considered credible today, it is believed that his theory notably paved the way for the medical explanation of abnormal behavior, a view that states that psychological disorders may be caused by biological mechanisms.

Around the fifteenth to the seventeenth centuries, witchcraft became a popular explanation for abnormal behavior. Witch-hunting, with the help of a manual called the Malleus Malleficarum (The Witches' Hammer), rounded up and killed more than 100,000 accused witches. Although some of the accused showed signs of atypical behavior, most did not display any signs of abnormality or maladaptiveness. Nonetheless, these innocent victims were still captured, labeled as witches, and subjected to abominable no-win tests. One such test was the water-float test, in which the hands and feet of the accused were bound and the body was dipped into water. If the accused floated, impurity was declared, and the person would be burned at the stake. If the suspect drowned, then innocence was proved. Either way, once suspected of witchcraft, the person would most likely end up dead. Over time, it appears that accusations of witchcraft were just a convenient method of seizing property and disposing of social aggravations and political adversaries (Spanos, 1978).

The late fifteenth and early sixteenth centuries gave rise to a large number of asylums in Europe that were converted from hospitals and monasteries to house and care for mental patients as well as beggars and homeless people. As the asylums became overcrowded, many patients were left in deplorable conditions. Individuals were chained to their beds without medical treatment, left to wander about unassisted, or whipped in order to prevent violent outbursts (Asimov, 1997). One famous asylum in London, St. Mary's of Bethlehem Hospital, even allowed the public to buy tickets to come and taunt its patients.

It was not until 1793 that the mentally ill were treated humanely. Philippe Pinel (1745–1826), chief physician at LeBicetre in Paris, argued that patients are sick people whose illnesses should be treated with kindness and sympathy rather than with chains and beatings. Pinel moved patients from darkened dungeons to well-ventilated rooms and conversed with them in the hope that showing caring and understanding would restore them back to normal functioning. Many patients did improve greatly over a brief period of time and were released from the hospital.

Pinel's efforts led to **moral treatment**, an approach that emphasized moral guidance and respectful procedures, and quickly became popular throughout Europe and the United States. While Pinel's work was quite influential, it was the work of Dorothea Dix (1802–1887), a politically active Bostonian schoolteacher, that gave rise to many of the state hospitals in the United States and Europe. She fought heartily for new laws and greater government funding to improve the treatment of people with mental disorders (Bickman & Dokecki, 1989).

In the following sections, we will examine several forms of therapy for abnormal behavior and mental processes. These include drug therapies, psychosurgery, psychotherapies, alternative therapies, and cross-cultural counseling.

Biological Treatments

Most of the biological treatments for psychological disorders and abnormal behaviors center around drug therapies (e.g., antipsychotics, antidepressants, antianxiety drugs, and mood stabilizers). The drugs are thought to stabilize the unbalanced neurotransmitters in the brain. Drugs may be beneficial for correcting some forms of behavior, but they are not without limitations, such as having debilitating and sometimes dangerous side effects. Other types of biological treatments, such as psychosurgery, electroconvulsive therapy, and transcranial magnetic stimulation, are also used as alternatives to or in combination with drug therapies to treat people with psychological problems.

Antipsychotic Drugs

Developed in the 1950s, **antipsychotic drugs**, such as Haldol, Thorazine, Clozaril, and Risperdal, are primarily used in treating people with severe psychotic disorders (those that involve a loss of touch with reality), such as schizophrenia. Antipsychotic drugs work by blocking or reducing the receptor sites that respond to the neurotransmitter dopamine, thereby decreasing agitation, confusion, hallucinations, and delusions in at least 65% of the patients who take them (Breier, 2001).

One of the major potential side effects of the "older" antipsychotic drugs, **tardive dyskinesia**, a condition that creates involuntary control of the lip and tongue and facial tics (Albers, Hahn, & Reist, 2004), occurs in about 20% of the people who take them. This condition is less likely to occur among people who take Clozaril, a "newer" antipsychotic drug, although about 1–2% of those treated with Clozaril will develop some medical complications (Hector, 1998). One such complication is agranulocytosis, a condition in which the bone marrow stops producing white blood cells, thereby increasing the patient's chances of infection.

Antidepressant Drugs

The 1950s marked an earnest beginning for **antidepressant drugs** as a treatment tool for major depression and, later, other mood and anxiety disorders. It has been estimated that antidepressants generate improvement in 65–75% of patients and complete recovery in 40–50% of depressed patients who sustained the use of their medication (Frazer, 1997; Hammen, 2003).

The first generation of antidepressants, known as **tricyclics**, work by blocking the reuptake of serotonin and norepinephrine at the neuron's axon terminal, thus allowing these neurotransmitters to linger longer at the synapse to enhance their actions. Though tricyclics, such as Elavil and Tofranil, can reduce symptoms of depression in more than 50% of the cases, they usually require two–four weeks to take effect and can sometimes have unpleasant side effects, such as dry mouth, dizziness, forgetfulness, and weight gain (Frazer, 1997).

Since the late 1980s, a second category of antidepressants has become popular for the treatment of depression. These drugs are collectively known as **selective serotonin reuptake inhibitors (SSRIs)**, and they work by blocking the reabsorption/reuptake of serotonin at the neuronal synapse (Anderson, 2000).

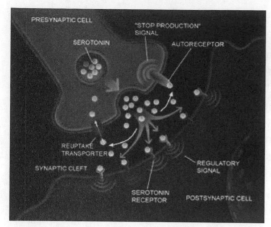

FIGURE 15.2 *Some antidepressants work by blocking neurotransmitter reuptake, which promotes more neurotransmitters in the synapse. To better understand this reuptake process, see Chapter 3, "Biopsychology."*

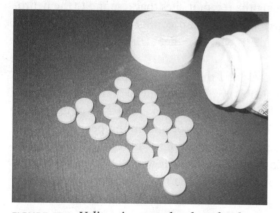

FIGURE 15.3 *Valium is a popular drug for the treatment of anxiety disorders.*

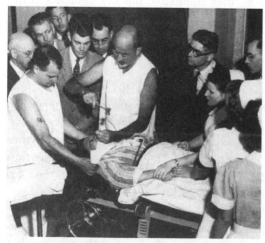

FIGURE 15.4 *Many patients who underwent prefrontal lobotomies suffered serious consequences.*

The three most widely prescribed SSRIs are Prozac (fluoxetine), Paxil (paroxetine), and Zoloft (sertraline). Though SSRIs may be safer than tricyclics and have fewer side effects, those who take SSRIs are still prone to headaches, insomnia, diarrhea, and sexual dysfunction (Masand & Gupta, 2002; Sadock & Sadock, 2003).

Another category of antidepressants is **monoamine oxidase inhibitors (MAOIs)**, prescribed mostly for people who do not respond to tricyclics or SSRIs. MAOIs work by blocking the body's enzymes that destroy the norepinephrine and serotonin in the synapse, thus increasing the availability of these neurotransmitters at the receptor sites (Thase, Frank, Mallinger, Hammer, & Kupfer, 1992). MAOIs produce similar side effects to those of tricyclics. People taking MAOIs must avoid certain foods and beverages containing tyramine, or they run the risk of a stroke or heart attack.

Antianxiety Drugs

Antianxiety drugs, more commonly known as minor tranquilizers, are typically prescribed for people who have abnormal levels of anxiety. Tranquilizers come from a class of drugs called **benzodiazepines** and include well-known drugs such as Valium, Librium, and Xanax. Benzodiazepines work by increasing the activity of the inhibitory neurotransmitter GABA, thus producing a calmer and less excitable effect in the user. Though antianxiety drugs may be fast-acting and effective as a treatment remedy, they are not without side effects, which can range from dizziness and impaired motor coordination to psychological and physiological dependence (Rivas-Vazquez, 2003). For this reason, clinicians prescribe antianxiety drugs as a short-term remedy for a highly stressful situation rather than as a long-term cure.

Mood Stabilizers

For bipolar disorder, **lithium carbonate**, a naturally occurring salt, is effective for controlling both manic and depressive episodes. This mood stabilizer can create improvement in 60–80% of bipolar patients (Walden, Normann, Langosch, Berger, & Grunze, 1998) and can quiet the manic state in approximately 5–10 days. Despite lithium's therapeutic promise, its dosage needs to be monitored closely, because high levels can create kidney, thyroid, and nervous system complications (Schou, 1997). For this reason, anticonvulsant drugs, such as Depakote or Tegretol, may be suggested as alternatives to lithium, with similar effectiveness but with fewer side effects (Bowden et al., 2000).

Psychosurgery

Psychosurgery is a type of biological treatment for people with severe or obstinate psychological disorders. It is designed to remove parts of the brain and create a permanent change in mood and behavior. Antonio Egas Moniz (1874–1955), a Portuguese neurologist, invented

TABLE 15.1 **Drugs and their labels.**			
Category of psychotropic drugs	**Chemical class**	**Generic name**	**Trade name**
Antianxiety	Benzodiazepines	Diazepam Cholordiazepoxide Alprazolam	Valium Librium Xanax
	Nonbenzodiazepine	Buspirone	Buspar
Antidepressants	Tricyclics (TCAs)	Amitriptyline Imipramine Doxepine	Elavil Tofranil Sinequan
	Monoamine oxidase inhibitors (MAOIs)	Phenelzine Tranylcypromine	Nardil Parnate
	Selective serotonin reuptake inhibitors (SSRIs)	Fluoxetine Paroxetine Scrtraline	Prozac Paxil Zoloft
	Other antidepressants	Bupropion Venlafaxine	Wellbutrin Effexor
Mood stabilizers/ Antimanic		Lithium carbonate Carbamazepine Divalproex	Eskalith Tegretol Depakote
Antipsychotics	Phenothiazines	Chlorpromazine Trifluoperazine Thiordazine	Thorazine Stelazine Mellaril
	Butyrophenones	Haloperidol	Haldol
	Atypical antipsychotics	Clozapine Risperdal	Clozaril Risperidone

an operation called *prefrontal lobotomy* in the 1930s to help alleviate symptoms of severe mental disorders. Moniz's technique consisted of inserting a sharp device into the forebrain to sever nerve tissues connecting the prefrontal lobes to other areas of the brain. Although Moniz was awarded a Nobel Prize for his work, his procedure was never scientifically validated, and many patients who underwent prefrontal lobotomies were left emotionally withdrawn, paralyzed, or dead. The practice of prefrontal lobotomies has been discontinued.

Electroconvulsive Therapy (ECT) was first popularly used in the 1930s and 1940s to decrease symptoms of schizophrenia. Currently it is more commonly used to treat suicidally depressed patients. Since some patients do not respond to antidepressants and others do not get relief from their depressive symptoms for two to six weeks after taking antidepressants, ECT can serve as an effective

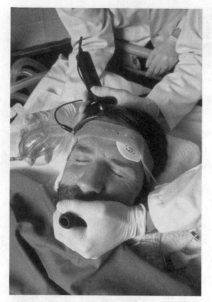

FIGURE 15.5 *ECT treatment relies on proper positioning of an electrode that stimulates one's temple with electrical current. Courtesy of Photo Researchers, Inc.*

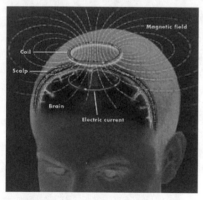

FIGURE 15.6 *rTMS utilizes a coil-emitting magnetic field. This treatment is effective for depression and is easier to administer than ECT.*

immediate treatment, albeit the possibility of side effects such as memory loss exists. Although the exact mechanism explaining why ECT is effective in the treatment of depression is unclear, it does not stop as many as 100,000 people a year from engaging in this practice (Mayo Foundation, 2006). The procedure usually requires electrodes to be hooked up to either one side (unilateral ECT) or both sides (bilateral ECT) of the patient's brain while a small voltage of electric current is passed through to the brain, causing seizures that last approximately one minute. After 6–12 sessions of this process, usually done twice a week for several weeks, around 60–70% of once-depressed patients report improvement as symptoms of depression disappear. Possible side effects may include temporary memory lapse for some individuals and permanent brain damage for others. Advocates of ECT have stated that, when used properly, ECT is safe and effective, with no risk of detectable brain damage, long-term cognitive impairment, or significant memory loss (Abrams, 1992). ECT can produce rapid improvement in a person's mood, and when compared with other treatment modalities, it is as effective as cognitive or drug therapy (Goforth & Holsinger, 2007).

Toward the end of the twentieth century, researchers began experimenting with a milder alternative to ECT as a treatment option. This alternative is **repetitive transcranial magnetic stimulation (rTMS)**, a procedure in which an electromagnetic coil is pressed against the scalp of an awake and unsedated patient. The coil transmits high-intensity magnetism to the brain. As with ECT, researchers have not determined how rTMS brings relief to patients with major depression, but certain research has shown rTMS's effectiveness in reducing depressive symptoms among patients who have not responded to medication (Fitzgerald et al., 2003). The advantages of using rTMS to ECT include easier administration and no memory loss.

Psychotherapies

Psychotherapies are treatment strategies used by trained professionals to help clients deal with their emotional distress or with mental disorders through various psychological techniques and procedures designed to increase communication, self-disclosure, and self-awareness. Clients are encouraged to explore conflicts and gain insight into personal problems, change harmful thought processes and self-defeating behaviors, and improve social and occupational functioning.

Psychoanalysis

Psychoanalysis, developed by Sigmund Freud, attempts to help anxiety-ridden patients uncover unconscious and unresolved motivations, desires, and conflicts via an intensive and lengthy process. The goal is to balance the demands of the impulsive id and the highly critical superego to form a balanced ego. To obtain the goal of uncovering materials from the unconscious, patients are told to engage in **free association**, revealing whatever feelings, thoughts, or experiences come to mind, for an elaborate interpretation, or deciphering of motivations, by the psychotherapist. **Dream analysis**, a technique used to interpret and apply meaning to the content of a person's dream, is also used to help unlock the deep secrets in the deeper layers of the person's mind (Wolitzky, 1995).

During therapy, the client is encouraged to express strong feelings to bring about an emotional release, or a **catharsis**. **Transference**, a client's responses to the therapist that treat the therapist as if he or she is reacting to another influential person in his or her life, is also utilized to help resolve the client's hidden problems. Sometimes **resistance**, the client's unconscious unwillingness to bring distressing material into the open due to the emotional pain it invokes, will occur. It is then up to the psychotherapist to break through the resistance to help with the healing process (May, 1996).

Traditional psychodynamic therapy can involve more than 900 sessions and take at least four years to complete. Some clients never complete this long and enduring process. Thus today, many therapists employ a shorter version, usually lasting from 12 to 20 sessions, called brief psychodynamic therapy. Here, the goals are set by the client and the therapist at the beginning of therapy, and the focus is on bringing forth unconscious conflicts and feelings in a more direct fashion. Recent research has shown brief psychodynamic therapy to be an effective form of psychotherapy for the treatment of anxiety disorders (Hager, Leichsenring, & Schiffler, 2000).

Humanistic Therapy

In contrast to psychodynamic therapy, humanistic therapy does not put any emphasis on the resolution of unconscious conflicts and desires. Instead, the focus of humanistic psychologists is on helping clients gain insight into their self-worth and discover their own unique potential as growing human beings. Humanistic therapists believe in the ability of clients to understand their problems, dismantle their distress, and take responsibility for their future by changing and promoting growth and fulfillment (Bohart, 1995).

Developed by Carl Rogers (1902–1987), **client-centered therapy**, also known as person-centered therapy, is one of the most frequently used humanistic approaches to treatment. Client-centered therapists believe that most of the client's problems are derived from a discrepancy between the *ideal* self (what one wants to be, based on parental, societal, or one's own expectations) and the *true* self (the reality of oneself, based on one's past and present experiences) leading to feelings of incongruence and disconnectedness within oneself. The goal of client-centered therapy, then, is to guide the client through self-reflection toward self-acceptance and a more realistic connection and congruence of the selves (Hill, 2000).

FIGURE 15.7 *Client-centered therapy relies on the therapist's positive regard, empathy, and genuineness. Courtesy of David Buffington/Getty Images.*

To help the client reach congruency and reach his or her maximum potential, or the fully functioning person, Rogers (1951) stated that it is essential that the client-centered therapist display the following characteristics in therapy:

♦ **Unconditional positive regard:** The therapist will not place any conditions of worth on the client and will be completely accepting and respectful of the client even if the client's thoughts and behaviors seem improper or illogical.

♦ **Genuineness:** The therapist needs to be completely honest with the client and with himself or herself regarding his or her own feelings about the process; this will allow for more open and honest communication within the therapeutic setting.

♦ **Empathy:** The therapist should be able to actively listen, reflect on, and truly understand the client's feelings and position; the therapist should also be able to see events from the client's perspective and provide neutral responses to encourage movement in a favorable direction.

With the therapist's consistent use of unconditional positive regard, genuineness, and empathy, the client will eventually adopt similar ideas to evaluate himself or herself and thus may adjust his or her ideal self to match that of his or her own standards rather than only the standards of his or her parents or those of society.

Behavioral Therapy

Borrowing from the concepts of operant and classical conditioning, **behavior therapy** offers action-oriented strategies to help people reduce or eliminate maladaptive behavior (Kazdin, 2002). Behavior therapists believe the cause of behavior is neither innate nor unconscious, but instead is derived from observational learning, negative associations, and/or reinforcement and punishment. Behavior therapy utilizes short-term therapy that generally involves three procedures: (1) identifying the problematic behavior and how often it occurs; (2) changing the behavior by utilizing strategies that best fit the client (counter-conditioning procedures, social skills training, re-education, etc.); and (3) continually assessing change and monitoring progress. Treatment is considered effective when the client shows evidence of constructive new behavior in place of previously existing maladaptive behavior.

Systematic Desensitization

Psychiatrist Joseph Wolpe (1958) was one of the pioneers of a classical conditioning therapeutic technique called systematic desensitization, a multistage course of action in which clients are trained in deep muscle relaxation and taught to relax when confronting an anxiety-provoking stimulus or situation. Systematic desensitization is a gradual procedure that involves the following key steps:

1. The client is asked to create an *anxiety-provoking stimulus*, starting with the image or situation that creates the least amount of anxiety and progressing to that which creates the most.

2. Then the client is asked to gradually *imagine* these vivid scenarios one at a time while being guided through deep relaxation procedures. This continues until the client is able to imagine the most anxiety-provoking scenario without feeling anxious.

3. Eventually, the client is asked to confront the stimulus or situation in real life. This can take the form of the following:

    ♦ **Gradual in-vivo exposure,** where the client exposes himself or herself slowly and gradually to the anxiety-provoking stimulus or situation.

FIGURE 15.8 *Gradual in-vivo exposure can help decrease phobias (in this case, fear of dogs).*

♦ **Flooding**, where the client is exposed to the fear all at once for an extended period until the anxiety decreases; the sessions usually last no longer than two hours and should not end until the client shows a discernible decrease in anxiety compared with the beginning of the session.

♦ **Virtual reality exposure**, where clients are exposed to the fear stimulus via a computer-generated, three-dimensional visage that appears in head-mounted video display; this type of therapy has been used and found to be successful for claustrophobia, arachnophobia, acrophobia, and social phobia (Emmelkamp, Bruynzeel, Drost, & van der Mast, 2001; Lee, Ku, Jang, & Kim, 2002; Rothbaum, Hodges, Smith, Lee, & Price, 2001; Wald & Taylor, 2002).

Aversion Therapy

FIGURE 15.9 *Disulfiram (Antabuse) can cause aversive reactions when mixed with alcohol.*

Another treatment that employs classical conditioning concepts is **aversive conditioning**. This kind of treatment consists of repeatedly pairing an aversive stimulus with an undesirable habit, such as smoking, drinking, or nail biting, so that a negative association will form and such habits will be eradicated. Some examples of aversive stimuli that have been used are electric shocks, unpleasant visual images, and nausea-inducing substances. For instance, a therapist may have the client take disulfiram (Antabuse), a substance that causes extreme nausea when combined with alcohol, to create an unpleasant sensation whenever the client imbibes alcohol. Over time, an association between alcohol and nausea forms, and the client will experience extreme discomfort at the idea of ingesting alcohol.

Behavior Modification

Utilizing operant conditioning concepts, **behavior modification** seeks to change behavior by using reinforcement to increase a desirable behavior and punishment or extinction to decrease an undesirable behavior. Behavior modification techniques are effective for changing people's behavior in various settings such as mental hospitals, schools, or even at home.

A behavior modification procedure that is both popular and widely used is the **token economy**, a system of compensation in which appropriate behaviors are rewarded with symbolic tokens in the forms of stars, poker chips, or play money that can later be exchanged for items and/or privileges such as food, clothing, games, more time with an activity, or trips to various places (Kazdin, 1994). For decades, token economies have been successfully used in mental institutions to help people with chronic schizophrenia improve their social interactions and self-help skills (Allyon & Azrin, 1965). In addition, token economies have also helped young people who are mentally retarded, autistic, and delinquent to ratify and improve their behaviors.

Social Skills Training

Many problems can arise for people with mental disorders who are socially inadequate or unassertive (Bower & Bower, 1976/1991). **Social skills training** attempts to resolve deficits in social skills and shapes suitable interactions through modeling and reinforcement. When approaching or interacting with others, clients use the skills they have been taught in order to formulate *what* to say to obtain a preferred response, *how* to go about the task, and *when* the appropriate timing would be to accomplish such a goal. The training usually commences with a discussion of appropriate responses in a social situation followed by a demonstration in video format. Thereafter, the client is asked to role-play the situation and then receives constructive feedback and/or reinforcement from the therapist. Outside the therapeutic setting, the client is instructed and encouraged to apply the newly acquired skills to novel situations.

FIGURE 15.10 *Effective social skills training can increase self-confidence and enhance interpersonal relationships.*

Research on the improvement of social interactions among people with autism spectrum disorders (ASD) has provided a myriad of appropriate and successful social skills intervention techniques to help them make and keep friends. One such technique is the use of peer mediated interface, whereby trained peers contribute to the intervention by initiating social exchanges or responding swiftly and adequately to the initiation of the person with ASD (McEvoy, Odom, & McConnell, 1993). The use of peers allows teachers and therapists to be facilitators instead of active participants and, through time, will facilitate a generalization of the skills achieved with peers in the natural environment.

Cognitive Therapy

Similar to behaviorists, **cognitive therapists** have long discarded the view that abnormal psychological functioning was the result of medical illness. Instead, they assume that maladaptive behaviors stem from irrational thoughts, beliefs, and ideas, which therapy will attempt to change. With **cognitive restructuring**, cognitive therapists guide their clients through the identification of irrational and self-defeating thoughts and then alter the thoughts to eradicate the maladaptive feelings and behaviors.

FIGURE 15.11 *Irrational beliefs and negative thought patterns can increase stress and lower self-esteem.*

In the 1950s, Albert Ellis, a clinical psychologist, developed **rational-emotive therapy (RET)** as a treatment strategy for those whose maladaptive behaviors and distressed feelings were derived from illogical and destructive beliefs (Kottler & Brown, 1999). Later it was revised to rational-emotive behavior therapy (REBT) to include both the cognitive and behavior aspects of the person. Ellis suggested that people generally attain a unique set of assumptions about the world and themselves that assists them in reacting and dealing with the situations that occur around them. These assumptions can sometimes take the form of negative reflection in what Ellis calls *basic irrational assumptions* (Ellis, 1979, 1987). People often unconditionally possess these irrational assumptions, which can veer individuals away from their competent judgment in everyday situations and jeopardize their chances of success and happiness. According to Ellis, the following assumptions commonly arise:

♦ The idea that you should be thoroughly competent at everything

♦ The idea that you do not have control over your happiness

♦ The idea that you need someone stronger than yourself to be dependent on

♦ The idea that your past history greatly influences your present life

♦ The idea that there is a perfect solution to human problems

Thus, one goal of RET/REBT is to infiltrate these negative assumptions and replace them with rational and healthier ones so that the emotions and behaviors of the client become less distressing and more constructive.

Albert Ellis's explanation of irrational assumptions goes along with Aaron Beck's idea of *automatic thoughts* in his theory of **cognitive therapy**, developed with the goal of helping clients stop their negative thoughts and replace them with more objective ones (Beck, 1991). Beck identified a variety of illogical thought processes and distorted thinking patterns (see Table 15.2) that clients engage in, which is similar to Ellis's list of irrational assumptions.

TABLE 15.2 **Thinking distortions.**

Name	Description
Selective attention	Seeing only the negative features of an event
Magnification	Exaggerating the importance of undesirable events
Overgeneralization	Drawing broad negative conclusions on the basis of a single insignificant event
All-or-nothing thinking	Seeing things in black-and-white categories
Mental filter	Picking out a single negative detail and dwelling exclusively on it
Disqualifying the positive	Rejecting positive experiences by insisting they "don't count"
Jumping to a conclusion	Making negative interpretations although there are no definite facts
Emotional reasoning	Assuming that your negative emotions reflect the way things really are
"Should" statements	Thinking that you "must" or "ought to" do something
Labeling and mislabeling	Attaching a negative to yourself or others for a behavior error
Personalization	Seeing yourself as a cause of some negative external and uncontrollable event

These patterns of illogical thoughts unfortunately contribute to the development of depression and anxiety in people. Thus, in order to improve the conditions of their clients, cognitive therapists must have their clients recognize and comprehend the effects that negative cognitions have on their feelings and behaviors. The cognitive approach gives alternative ways for clients to transform their negativity into more productive thoughts, which can benefit them in their perception of everyday activities. Depressed people who are treated with Beck's approach improve significantly more than those who receive no treatment and about the same as those who receive biological treatments (Hollon & Beck, 1994). Beck's cognitive therapy has also been successfully applied to panic disorders and other anxiety disorders (Beck, 1993).

Cognitive Behavior Therapy

Cognitive behavior therapy (CBT) focuses on changing irrational beliefs and modifying maladaptive behaviors by integrating the cognitive restructuring techniques of cognitive therapy and the behavioral modification techniques of behavior therapy (Watson & Tharp, 2007). With Albert Ellis's (1973) *rational emotive behavior therapy* and Meichenbaum's (1975) *self-instructional methods*, clients are encouraged to challenge core beliefs that are causing distress, change them with constructive statements, and adjust their behaviors. Generally, CBT is recommended for those suffering from mood disorders, social phobia, agoraphobia, post-traumatic stress disorder (PTSD), obsessive-compulsive disorder, and attention deficit/hyperactivity disorder.

CBT employs the following techniques and homework assignments to help clients modify negative thoughts and change inappropriate behaviors:

♦ Cognitive rehearsal: Patients are asked to practice positive self-statements in the face of difficult situations

♦ Behavioral modeling: Patients are encouraged to try out responses to situations discussed and modeled in therapy sessions

♦ Journals: Patients are asked to record thoughts, emotions, and behaviors to show potential negative thoughts that could lead to damaging actions

Generally, short-term success rates for CBT range from 50 to 65%. The American Psychiatric Association (2000b) reported that among psychotherapeutic approaches, CBT has one of the best-documented efficacies for treatment of major depressive disorder.

Group Therapy

People with a dire need to share their tribulations with others and to seek support from others typically find themselves in a **group therapy** setting with a therapist and about 7 to 11 additional clients sharing similar issues. Depending on the nature of the group (victims of sexual abuse, spouses/children of alcoholics, sufferers of divorce, etc.) and the therapeutic orientation of the lead therapist (CBT, behavioral, client-centered, etc.), the members will meet about once a week to express their thoughts and feelings in a contained nonthreatening envi-

FIGURE 15.12 *Group therapy can decrease feelings of isolation and provide support for individuals dealing with problems that they think are unique to themselves.*

FIGURE 15.13 *Family therapy can strengthen communication and create structural change in the family dynamics.*

ronment, to appropriately learn and share their problems with others, and to observe and practice ways of relating interpersonally. Actively engaging in a group therapy setting can provide clients with insight into their own problems, decrease the sense of shame and isolation experienced by clients who feel they are alone, and allow clients to try out effective problem-solving techniques.

Family Therapy

Family therapy is a special type of group therapy in which parents and children enter treatment as a unit in order to improve communication patterns and resolve interpersonal conflicts. Instead of treating the individual, the family therapist attempts to change the dynamics of the family as a whole, or a *system* of relationship. The premise behind the systems approach is that no individual is solely responsible for the problems that occur within the family; instead, the problems arise from a myriad of interactions among family members. Thus, to create change within the family, all the components of the system must change.

Family therapy utilizes an eclectic approach to treatment, ultimately attempting to reduce tension and improve functioning of the members by helping them recognize the positive as well as the negative aspects of their relationship. The most widely used family therapy techniques may include validation, reframing, detriangulation, and structural change. In **validation**, the therapists convey their acceptance and understanding of the clients' feelings and wishes. They also offer clients new ways of reconceptualizing, or **reframing**, their problems. For example, clients may need to see that the problem is not that the child is depressed; rather, the problem is within the marriage and family unit as a whole. In a family system, **triangulation** may occur solely among the family members or among the family members and an "outsider." Triangulation is when a third person (child, therapist, etc.) is unsuspectingly solicited in a conflict-ridden dyadic relationship, which results in his or her inadvertently "covering up" or "defusing" the problem of the actual people in conflict. In this situation, the therapists try to promote an environment of detriangulation, a process in which the attention is shifted away from the identifying patient, or "scapegoat," and focused on the family members actually in conflict. Further, a *structural change*, or restructuring of the family alliance (e.g., a mother-son unit), is encouraged in order to bring collaboration and balance to the family system (Minuchin & Fishman, 1981).

Self-Help Groups

Sometimes referred to as *support groups*, **self-help groups** are voluntary organizations created to help people with similar problems meet and support one another in overcoming a behavioral or mental problem. These group meetings are generally free and are not directed by any licensed health-care professional, although the group leader may have had some prior training in facilitation techniques. Each year, as many as 10 million U.S. adults attend a myriad of self-help

FIGURE 15.14 *Alcoholics Anonymous is a support group that helps people overcome their alcohol-related problems.*

groups, including support groups for alcohol/substance abuse, survivors of child abuse, single-parent child rearing, gay/lesbian relationships, weight reduction, and a vast number of medical diseases (cancer and AIDS among others). Though hundreds of self-help groups have blossomed in the past half century, the very first support group to pave the way was pioneered in 1935 by Alcoholics Anonymous, which still exists today across the United States.

What properties of self-help groups make them most effective as healing devices? Researchers have found that sharing among members of support groups provides attendees with valuable information regarding disorders and treatment, an outlet for cathartic release of the pain and suffering commonly shared by all members, and/or a place where a sense of hope and control can be restored to the sufferer (Schiff & Bargal, 2000). Regardless of the reasons for seeking and joining support groups, the attendees must be strongly affiliated with and be robustly satisfied with the group in order to effectively gain and maintain prolific change (Morgenstern, Labouvie, McCrady, Kahler, & Frey, 1997).

Cybertherapy

With advances in cutting-edge technology, psychotherapy does not necessarily need to occur in a traditional office setting. **Cybertherapy**, a style of treatment in which clients receive therapy from a licensed professional over the Internet, is one alternative to a face-to-face interaction between client and therapist. Much debate has ensued over the merits and shortcomings of cybertherapy. On the one hand, cybertherapy is flexible in the service of its delivery and the population served. It allows for treatment to occur in places where physically reaching a therapist might be a hardship, either due to weather/road conditions or due to a physical handicap. Additionally, for individuals who are more comfortable with writing versus speaking, cybertherapy allows them the freedom to reveal their thoughts and feelings in a way that is more effective for their healing process.

Explore **psychological disorders** in Chapter 14, p. 452

FIGURE 15.15 *Cybertherapy is a way to gain and maintain access to mental health professionals.*

On the other hand, many therapists consider cybertherapy less than an optimal form of treatment. First, there is no way to guarantee anonymity and confidentiality for the client on the Internet, so the information provided may potentially be compromised. Second, without face-to-face contact, the therapeutic alliance between the client and the therapist may suffer, as bonding may not occur due to a lack of "personal" interactions. Third, cybertherapy creates a loss of metacommunication, such that certain significant verbal and bodily cues that the client presents in face-to-face interactions will go unnoticed when communicating via computer. At present, though cybertherapy may be more effective than no treatment at all (Lange, van de Ven, Schrieken, & Emmelkamp, 2001), there is little research on whether cybertherapy may be as effective as face-to-face therapy.

Eye Movement Desensitization and Reprocessing (EMDR)

FIGURE 15.16 *EMDR at work.*

In the late 1980s, Dr. Francine Shapiro, a senior research fellow at the Mental Research Institute in Palo Alto, California, developed **eye movement desensitization and reprocessing (EMDR)** as a therapeutic treatment for people suffering from anxiety disorders, especially PTSD. In EMDR, the client is asked to picture an image that is associated with a traumatic event while the therapist moves a finger back and forth in front of the client's eyes for 20 to 30 seconds or more. Next, the client reports to the therapist any thoughts, feelings, or bodily sensations experienced during the process. The steps are then repeated multiple times until the client is emotionally desensitized to the original effects of the traumatic event.

Research evidence from many carefully controlled studies sustained the beneficial effects of EMDR in the treatment of PTSD (Power et al., 2002; Rothbaum, 1997; Taylor et al., 2003; Wilson, Becker, & Tinker, 1995, 1997). The American Psychiatric Association gave EMDR the same status as CBT in its effectiveness for PTSD treatment, and the Department of Veterans Affairs and the Department of Defense stated EMDR was one of four therapies given the highest level of evidence and recommendation for treatment of PTSD. At present, it is uncertain how EMDR actually works, although some therapists attempt to make a connection between EMDR and systematic desensitization (a behavioral approach), stating that it is not the eye movements per se that create the improvements but the mere exposure of the traumatic mental imagery that produces the positive change (Taylor et al., 2003).

Cross-Cultural Counseling

Explore
**cross-cultural effects
on personality**
in Chapter 13, p. 433

As diversity in the United States increases, it becomes progressively important for therapists to become more culturally aware of the different types of people who visit their offices. Therapists need to be sensitive to the personal backgrounds (collectivistic values, norms, and cultural practices) and individual experiences of their clients in order to provide competent and appropriate therapeutic services (La Roche & Maxie, 2003; Wong, Kim, Zane, Kim, & Huang, 2003). In addition, therapists need to be cognizant of their own biases and avoid ethnic stereotyping (Lee & Richardson, 1991). Ultimately, it is necessary for therapists to remember that just because a particular type of therapy works for one group of people, it does not necessarily mean it will work for another group (Sue, 2003). We will now discuss important therapeutic issues of Native Americans, Asian Americans, African Americans, and Latino/a Americans.

Native Americans

Although Native Americans make up less than 1% of the U.S. population, their health problems exceed those of other Americans in a disproportionate fashion. Their age-adjusted mortality rate when compared with the rates of other Americans was 465% greater for alcoholism, 184% greater for accidents, 46% greater for suicide, and 39% greater for homicide (USDHHS, 1996). Given the statistics, Native Americans may be in dire need of effective mental health. In spite of this, Native Americans continue to be underserved in the psychotherapy arena because of their resistance to professional counseling and the cultural gap that exists between them and the Westernized psychotherapists.

When treating Native Americans—aside from being aware of the message behind various nonverbal communication cues such as eye contact, hand and body gestures, and facial expressions that carry subtle but important meaning—therapists should be ready to handle the heavy cultural baggage that their client has experienced for many years (Rabasca, 2000a; Renfrey, 1992). Therapists should be able to provide emotional support and understanding of the oppression and loss of land and identity that the Native American client has experienced that has contributed to the detriment of their mental health.

Occasionally, therapy with Native American clients should incorporate certain components of their culture to make the process more sensitive and effective. For instance, indigenous ceremonies such as sweat lodges, where purification and cleansing rituals are emphasized, are therapeutic for Native American clients who feel their problems are caused by unplacated malicious evil spirits. They believe their mind, body, and spirit will heal after the ceremonious rituals (Lefley, 1990).

Asian Americans

In 2000, the U.S. Census reported close to 12 million Asian Americans residing in the United States. Yet it seems that study after study has found that mental health services are underutilized by the Asian American population, although Asian Americans exhibit more severe mental instability than non Asian Americans (Sue, 1998). The underutilization of both outpatient and inpatient services may be due to the Asian belief that the mind and body coexist as one, and treatment should not be separated. Under many circumstances, the Asian American client's negative mental health will manifest itself into physical symptoms, and the medical physician's expertise will be sought instead of the expertise of the mental health professional. In addition, there is a stigma in sharing personal problems outside the family, thus bringing shame and loss of face to the family.

Asian American clients use much restraint when talking about themselves and their feelings; thus, the therapist working with Asian American clients should not expect immediate self-disclosure (Sue & Sue, 1990). Instead, therapists should exercise patience, allowing the clients' problems and emotions to unveil themselves slowly as the clients become more comfortable and less conflicted about revealing personal information.

Intervention during the therapeutic process should emphasize structure and action, with specific plans for change outlined and directed (Lin & Cheung, 1999; Root, 1993). Cognitive therapy and behavioral therapy with detailed techniques in systematic desensitization, relaxation, and meditation exercises are effective for reducing stress and rechanneling thoughts toward a positive direction. To keep attrition of Asian American clients at a low rate, cross-cultural researchers suggest the following: avoid excessive formality with the client; be aware of the shame and humiliation that encompasses attending therapy; understand the dynamics between parents and children; and avoid talks of hospitalization for somatic complaints without first considering less intrusive measures (Paniagua, 1994).

FIGURE 15.17 *Building positive rapport can create a comfortable sharing environment for the Asian American client.*

African Americans

Although African Americans make up 13% of the U.S. population, their psychological disorders have been underdiagnosed, their use of mental health services is low, and their dropout rate for psychotherapy is high (Sanchez-Hucles, 2000). Unless a strong alliance is developed between client and therapist and a sense of trust occurs, it is unlikely that the African American client will return after the first session. Historically, African Americans have been mistreated and oppressed, and they still face inequities in a multitude of areas, including employment, education, health care, and housing. Those who had sought treatment were exposed to insensitive therapists, pathologized, and overmedicated (Sanchez-Hucles, 2000). It is therefore important to note that the African American client may be suspicious toward the therapist's intentions and may be reserved toward self-disclosure, especially in the early stages of therapy (Greene, 1985).

When working with the African American population, it is crucial for therapists to explore issues of racial identity and racial prejudice and discrimination, and assess how these factors influence psychological functioning and mental health utilization. In addition, therapists must recognize their own ethnic and racial attitudes and how their thoughts and feelings affect the way they conduct therapy (Nickerson, Helms, & Terrell, 1994). Giving the African American client an overview of therapy and inviting active participation in setting goals for improvement may be a good start to building trust and confidence in the therapeutic setting.

Effective multicultural counseling considers African American clients in their sociocultural context, including their family dynamics, community support, and religious spirituality. The African American family extends beyond the nuclear family into the realms of nonblood relations, and they give and receive social support from various community networks such as grandparents, neighbors, church members, and preachers. Thus, therapists should have their African American clients define their concept of family and identify their social support groups when considering using "kin" as a social support tool (Brooks, Haskins, & Kehe, 2004).

Religious spirituality has long been used by the African American community to direct their lives and provide guidance for their emotional distress and psychological problems (Helms & Cook, 1999). It is in their church that they can escape rejection imposed by society and find solace and validation in their racial identity (Cook & Wiley, 2000). Consequently, many African Americans find their identification with and participation in church activities as more beneficial and more effective than psychotherapy in the promotion of their mental health (Grier & Cobbs, 1968). Thus, it is perhaps advantageous for mental health professionals to recognize the church as a resource for successful psychotherapy.

Latino/a Americans

According to the 2000 U.S. Census, Latinos/as accounts for 12.5% of the U.S. population, and they are one of the fastest-growing populations, with an increase of 57% from 1990 to 2000 (Guzman, 2001). They are, however, slow to seek treatment, and when they do, more than 50% drop out after one treatment (Thurman, Swaim, & Plested, 1995). Multiple factors, such as language, economics, and sociocultural values, account for underutilization rates and early termination.

Many Latinos/as are referred to the mental health community by the medical system. This is largely due to their belief that strong emotions cause deterioration in physical health, and, thus, medical advice must be received. When counseling Latino/a clients, it is important to understand that their identity is determined by their roles within the family (De La Cancela & Guzman, 1991). *Familismo* is a strong sense of commitment, loyalty, reciprocity, and solidarity as well as interdependence and cooperation to the family (Falicov, 1998). The roles of the *macho* and the *marianismo* are also important to consider when providing intervention; the male (*macho*) is given the responsibility of being the head of the household, the provider, and the protector of the family, while the female (*marianismo*) is dictated to care for the family and children.

Many Latinos/as place great value on *personalismo*—dignity and self-worth, respect for others, and reciprocity (Ho, 1987), with higher regard given to those who support and provide for the family than those who have social standing and material goods (Comas-Diaz, 1997). Another value of the Latino/a culture is *simpatia*, or a personality characteristic that promotes and maintains harmonious and pleasant interpersonal relationships by avoiding conflicts and de-escalating negative behaviors (Triandis, Marin, Lisansky, & Betancourt, 1984; Yep, 1995).

Within the therapeutic setting, it is essential that therapists recognize the conflict between the Latino/a value of interdependence and the American value of independence and self-reliance. Respecting the differences in values and responding appropriately instead of imposing the majority culture's values will build *confianza*, or trust, and enhance the effectiveness of psychotherapy (Gloria, Ruiz, & Castillo, 2004). Therapists should remember that although there is holistic information in understanding the cultural background and values of the Latino/a clients, each person should be considered individually in treatment. His or her personal life experiences, age, level of acculturation, and religious ideals should be assessed in order to provide a valuable and successful individualized treatment plan.

Evaluating Psychotherapy

Effectiveness of Psychotherapy

More than four decades ago, British psychologist Hans Eysenck (1952) created uproar among the mental health community when he shockingly declared that psychotherapy was ineffective as a treatment method for psychological disorders. Eysenck's declaration was met with a bout of researchers developing more accurate methodologies to evaluate the effectiveness of psychotherapy.

Ultimately, a **meta-analysis**, a statistical method in which the results of many studies are combined and analyzed, was devised and used to help researchers draw conclusions about psychotherapy's effectiveness. One meta-analysis conducted by Smith, Glass, and Miller (1980) examined the results of 475 studies that compared a group of people who were given various types of psychotherapy with a control group who did not receive any treatment at all. The results of this meta-analysis proved Eysenck's original claim about psychotherapy's ineffectiveness to be wrong. In fact, it showed that people who received psychotherapy improved more than about 80% over those who did not receive treatment, although it did not find that one type of psychotherapy was more effective than another.

Other meta-analyses have also been conducted with results similar to those of Smith and colleagues. They show that psychotherapy works and that its positive effects are long-lasting (Lambert, 2001; Lambert & Bergin, 1994; Lipsey & Wilson, 1993). Some research even investigated clients' attitudes toward psychotherapy. For example, *Consumer Reports*, with the assistance of Martin Seligman (1995), sent out a large number of surveys to its readers and received 22,000 responses. The following is a summary of the results:

♦ In general, clients who received psychotherapy showed substantial improvement in subjective ratings of mental health.

♦ Clients who received drug therapy coupled with CBT showed a slightly higher rate of improvement than those who received psychotherapy alone.

♦ Clients who received long-term therapy, especially for more than six months, showed more improvement than those who received short-term therapy.

Choosing a Therapist

Locating and choosing a therapist can be an arduous and overwhelming experience for those already under an immense psychological strain. The following are suggestions for when, where, and who to search for professional help.

When

There are no set rules for when you should seek professional help for your problems, but if you experience one or more of the following, you should consider talking to a qualified psychotherapist about your concerns:

♦ An extreme change in sleep, appetite, energy level, or social activities

♦ Feeling sad and crying frequently

♦ Hearing voices that tell you what you should do, or you have a sense that someone is out to get you

♦ Feeling anxious and having physical reactions to everyday events

♦ Being frightened by animals or things you know should not be fear-provoking

♦ Being hypervigilant and having frequent nightmares about events that occurred in the past

Where

Psychotherapists are located in a number of places. You can find listings of psychologists, psychiatrists, marriage and family therapists, and social workers on Internet search engines (e.g., *www.google.com* or *www.yahoo.com*), in the Yellow Pages, at community mental health centers, in newspaper advertisements, at college and university student health facilities, and through crisis hotlines.

Who

Making a decision to see either a psychologist or a psychiatrist is arbitrary, as both are equally effective in providing successful psychotherapy. However, if you are concerned about the credentials of the therapist and want to confirm his or her authenticity, you can just simply ask the therapist about his or her qualifications and licenses. Most legitimate therapists have copies of their licenses on-site, either posted on the wall or in an easily accessible location. Table 15.3 shows a list of types of therapists, their credentials, and their specialties.

Generally, if you would like to uncover problems, conflicts, or desires through a lengthy period of time, you will fare best with a psychodynamic therapist. If you would like to change specific behaviors (cure phobic reactions, enhance social skills, change negative habits, etc.) in a short number of sessions, then it would be best to seek the advice of a behavior therapist. If low self-esteem and negative, hopeless, or irrational thinking patterns are your underlying characteristics (such as in people with mood disorders or anxiety disorders), requesting the help of a cognitive therapist would yield the most beneficial results. More likely than not, you will probably end up seeing a psychotherapist who is *eclectic* in his or her approach. That is, the individual's approach to psychotherapy is not limited to one school of treatment but combines a wide variety of schools of therapy.

In order for therapy to be successful, it mostly depends on the relationship between the therapist and the client, and depends little on the type of degree that the therapist possesses or the type of therapy he or she practices (Hubble, Duncan, & Miller, 1999). A positive rapport and a sense of comfort and trust

TABLE 15.3 **Types of therapists, their degrees, and their specialties.**		
Discipline	**Degree/Training**	**Specialties**
Psychologist	PhD (doctor of philosophy) or PsyD (doctor of psychology) 5–8 years beyond a BA/BS	Diagnosis, testing and treatment using various modalities
Psychiatrist	MD (medical doctor) 8 years beyond a BA/BS	Biological treatment, psychopharmacology, and some psychotherapeutic modalities and orientations
Social worker	MSW (master of social work) 2 years beyond a BA/BS	Family therapy or behavior therapy, oftentimes in community-based settings
Master's level therapists	MA (master of arts) or MS (master of science) or MEd (master of education) or licensed MFT (marriage and family therapy) 2 years beyond BA/BS	Family therapy, vocational readjustment, alcoholism and drug abuse counseling
Psychiatric nurse specialist	BSN (bachelor of science in nursing) or MSN (master of science in nursing) 0–2 years beyond a BA/BS	Inpatient psychiatric care, supportive therapy using various modalities

will lay the foundation for a constructive therapeutic alliance. Therapy should be about the client, not about the therapist. It is essential to have warmth, integrity, sincerity, sympathy, and mutual respect between the client and the therapist. Goals should be set and discussed in the first session, and a possible end date should be conferred. Don't expect miracles, but don't give up too easily. Give the therapist a fair chance, and if therapy is not proceeding in a direction you're comfortable with, you should not hesitate to terminate therapy or change therapists.

Chapter Summary

Therapy: History and Origins

Beliefs on the causes of abnormal behaviors have changed across time and place. Demonology and spirit possession were popular beliefs during the Stone Age. During the Middle Ages, Hippocrates employed the medical model to explain that abnormal behaviors were caused by imbalances of humors in the mind and body. Beliefs about witchcraft were popular from the fifteenth to the seventeenth centuries. Asylums arose during the fifteenth century, but it was not until the late eighteenth and nineteenth centuries that conditions improved in the hospitals and patients were treated humanely.

Biomedical Therapy

Antipsychotic drugs, antidepressant drugs, antianxiety drugs, and mood stabilizers such as lithium carbonate are types of psychotherapeutic medications used to treat psychological disorders. Generally, antipsychotic drugs are used to treat people with schizophrenia and other psychotic disorders, antidepressant drugs treat people with depression, antianxiety drugs treat people with anxiety disorders, and mood stabilizers help people with bipolar disorder. Drugs may be effective in treating psychological disorders, but some come with severe side effects, such as depression and tardive dyskinesia.

In addition to drug therapy, psychosurgery techniques such as electroconvulsive therapy (ECT) and repetitive transcranial magnetic stimulation (rTMS) are used to treat people with severe psychological disorders. Psychosurgery procedures, such as lobotomies, were utilized in the 1930s but are no longer performed.

Psychotherapies

Psychoanalysis helps clients uncover unconscious conflicts and desires by the use of free association, dream interpretation, and transference. Humanistic therapy capitalizes on unconditional positive regard, genuineness, and empathy to help clients self-reflect and reach self-actualization. Behavioral therapy attempts to change behavior by making use of systematic desensitization techniques, aversion therapy, token economies, and social skills training. Cognitive therapy attempts to change irrational thoughts by employing cognitive restructuring techniques. Cognitive behavior therapy (CBT) employs rational-emotional behavioral therapy and self-instructional techniques to change irrational beliefs and maladaptive behaviors. Group therapy allows several clients to work together in one setting and helps them feel less isolated. Family therapy provides an environment for family members to detriangulate and produce change within the family structure. Cybertherapy is therapy without face-to-face contact for clients who are more comfortable revealing their thoughts via writing anonymously through a computer instead of verbal communication. EMDR assists clients to become emotionally desensitized to traumatic events by creating an environment where images are repeated multiple times.

Cross-Cultural Counseling

It is important for therapists to become more aware of the diversity in the United States and to provide more culturally sensitive approaches to therapy. Therapy with Native Americans should incorporate components of the culture, such as indigenous ceremonies, to make the process more effective. Asian American clients will fare better when there is emphasis on structure and action, with specific directions for change. Success with African American clients usually requires community, family, and spiritual support. It is useful to recognize values such as *familismo, simpatia,* and *confianza* to effectually deal with Latino/a clients.

Evaluating Psychotherapy

With the use of meta-analysis, researchers have shown the positive and long-term effects of psychotherapy. When choosing a therapist, it is important to recognize when you need help, where to locate a therapist, and who you will be most successful receiving treatment from.

Knowledge Builder

RELATE TO YOURSELF

1. What would your life be like if you were considered "crazy" back in the sixteenth century?

_____

_____

_____

_____

2. If your behavior was explosive, aggressive, and out of control, would you allow Dr. Freeman to perform a prefrontal lobotomy on you? Why or why not?

_____

_____

_____

_____

3. Under what personal conditions would you consider using cybertherapy as a mode for therapy?

_____

_____

_____

_____

4. You're taking antipsychotics to help decrease the psychotic symptoms of schizophrenia. What side effects might you be experiencing?

_____

_____

_____

_____

CHAPTER REVIEW QUESTIONS

1. Antidepressants are effective as a treatment for depression because they increase levels of serotonin and norepinephrine in the brain. **T or F?**

2. The Malleus Malleficarum was a liquid concoction used to treat people with psychological disorders in the nineteenth century. **T or F?**

3. Behavior therapy is a nondirective psychotherapy developed by Carl Rogers. **T or F?**

4. Psychoanalysis attempts to uncover people's psychological problems by using techniques of free association and dream interpretation. **T or F?**

5. When utilizing community mental health services, primary interventions are efforts made to reduce the number of new cases of mental disorders in the community. **T or F?**

6. _____ is a side effect of antipsychotic medications that causes uncontrollable tremors and lip smacking.

   (a) Narcolepsy   **(b)** Tardive dyskinesia

   (c) Agranulocytosis   **(d)** Seasonal affective dysfunction

7. Mentally exposing clients to an anxiety-provoking stimulus slowly while teaching them relaxation exercises is a behavioral technique called _____.

   (a) aversion therapy   **(b)** flooding

   (c) cybertherapy   **(d)** systematic desensitization

8. Ellis's REBT deals with changing client's irrational _____.

   (a) unconscious desires   **(b)** behaviors

   (c) beliefs   **(d)** consumption

9. Family therapy employs all of the following therapeutic techniques *except* _____.

   (a) gradual exposure   **(b)** detriangulation

   (c) validation   **(d)** reframing

10. Rogers's client-centered therapy utilizes all of the following concepts in therapy *except* _____.

    (a) genuineness   **(b)** cognitive restructuring

    (c) empathy   **(d)** unconditional positive regard

11. When dealing with arachnophobia, _____ might not be an effective behavioral treatment to use since it requires the full exposure to the spider at once and may lead to more emotional distress.

    (a) flooding
    (b) systematic desensitization
    (c) gradual in-vivo exposure
    (d) aversion therapy

12. Cognitive behavior therapy has been shown to be effective in the treatment of which disorder(s)?

    (a) major depressive disorder

    (b) attention deficit/hyperactivity disorder

    (c) post-traumatic stress disorder

    (d) all of the above

13. You should seek a therapist when _____.

    (a) you feel sad and cry frequently

    (b) you feel anxious and have strong negative reactions to everyday events

    (c) you are hypervigilant and have frequent nightmares

    (d) all of the above

14. *Consider the following scenario:* You have an intense fear of heights, although your profession as a pilot requires you to fly an airplane almost every day. What kind of therapy would you seek, and what techniques are most effective for you to overcome your fear of heights?

    _____

    _____

    _____

    _____

15. *Consider the following scenario:* You just went through a horrid and emotionally draining divorce and are currently feeling depressed and lonely. You're wondering if you're alone in your feelings and if there are people out there who have undergone such an experience and can offer helpful advice. Which type of treatment would you seek?

    _____

    _____

    _____

    _____

16. *Consider the following scenario:* You have just gone through a psychological assessment and have been diagnosed as having major depression with suicidal tendencies. What combination of therapeutic modalities should be employed under this situation to help you through this rough time?

_____

_____

_____

_____

17. *CRITICAL THINKING EXERCISE.* Most psychologists would not recommend using psychoanalysis for the treatment of marital problems. Why do you think this might be?

_____

_____

_____

_____

USEFUL WEB SITES

AMERICAN PSYCHIATRIC ASSOCIATION

http://www.psych.org/

This Web site provides information on available and accessible quality psychiatric diagnosis and treatment. It features more than 35,000 U.S. and international member physicians working together to ensure humane care and effective treatment for all persons with mental disorders, including mental retardation and substance-related disorders.

NATIONAL PSYCHOLOGICAL ASSOCIATION FOR PSYCHOANALYSIS

http://www.npap.org

This Web site provides an abundance of psychotherapy in general and psychoanalysis in particular. It also features a month-by-month calendar of upcoming professional workshops, seminars, and conferences as well as the online version of the Psychoanalytic Review.

ALBERT ELLIS INSTITUTE

http://www.albertellisinstitute.org/aei/index.html

This Web site posts information on Albert Ellis's approach to cognitive therapy and features a response from Dr. Ellis himself to a question posed by the general public.

METANOIA

http://www.metanoia.org

This Web site is the best place to start when looking for an e-therapist (cybertherapy). It lists therapists whose credentials have been referenced by Mental Health Net.

EMDR (EYE MOVEMENT DESENSITIZATION AND REPROCESSING) INSTITUTE, INC.

http://www.emdr.com/

This Web site provides detailed information on the history and theory of EMDR as a treatment technique for decreasing symptoms of PTSD. This site also contains links to a list of evidence for EMDR's efficacy, EMDR clinicians, and training faculty.

CALIFORNIA BOARD OF BEHAVIORAL SCIENCES (BBS)

http://www.bbs.ca.gov/

This Web site contains information about licensing procedures, continuing education, and laws for people who are interested in becoming a marriage and family therapist (MFT), a licensed clinical social worker (LCSW), or a licensed educational psychologist (LEP) or who already have a license in these fields.

16

Health and Stress

by Robert Flome, MA, MFT, DAPA

Fasten your seat belts. It's going to be a bumpy night.

—BETTE DAVIS

Stress will always be a part of your daily life. You will be challenged to cope with it throughout your life. Numerous studies have shown a strong connection between stress and disease. Major causes of death, such as cancer, cardiovascular disease, infection, and stroke, are all closely associated with stress. In order to cope with stress, you must be able to manage its psychological and physical impact on you. By having a healthy lifestyle that includes positive thinking, regular exercise, good nutrition, sleep, relaxation, and avoidance of harmful substances, you can decrease your likelihood of suffering from the illnesses and diseases that come from stress.

Defining Health and Stress

Health is a state of physical, mental, and social well-being. A healthy person has energy, vitality, fitness, a sense of purpose, and an optimistic perception of life. The greatest benefit of good health is the absence of disease. For health is a wonderful state of a balance between the body and the mind. It is this healthy balance that promotes cell development and growth, both of which are needed in order to support life.

The six subcategories of optimal health include physical, emotional, social, intellectual, occupational, and spiritual health (Hettler, 1980). **Physical health** is made up of good nutrition, physical fitness, medical self-care, and control of substance abuse. **Emotional health** includes stress management, effective coping skills, and optimistic appraisals of the environment. **Social health** is when you have a social network of family, friends, and community, while **intellectual health** focuses on education, achievement, and career development. **Occupational health** is the ability to gain personal satisfaction and enrichment from one's work, school,

FIGURE 16.1 *When stressors are greater than coping skills.*

hobbies, or volunteer activities. Finally, there is the **spiritual health** of love, hope, peacefulness, and charity. You experience optimal health when all six subcategories of health are in balance.

Stress is the internal and external behavioral reaction to physical, chemical, environmental, and emotional factors that may strain your tolerance level and eventually destroy your ability to cope. This is followed by physiological and emotional changes that cause decreased immunity, which can eventually lead to disease and even death. According to Lazarus and Folkman (1984), stress is the result of an individual's perception of a potentially difficult situation in which his or her cognitive evaluation determines whether the stressful situation is a challenge or a threat. A **stressor** is the situation, experience, or event that causes physiological and emotional arousal. The body weakens when stressors become greater than your coping skills. Without effective intervention, the strain and tension from stressors can deplete the body's resources and make it more susceptible to injury and disease.

Stress can be seen as the internal, psychological, and physical responses to external factors coming from sensory stimuli or situations in the environment. It begins when you appraise that the stressor exceeds your ability to cope. Emotions of fear, worry, and anxiety start to appear, which then trigger physiological changes in the body. Stressors become overwhelming when you appraise them as a threat. As the stressors become chronic, cognitive and physiological changes begin to lower the body's immunity. Without an immunological defense, the stage is set for disease to invade the body.

Types of Stressors

Travel down the road of life can be a bumpy ride. Stressors are the potholes in the road that cause the ride to be rocky if you have poor coping skills. There are six types of stressors: frustration, hassles, pressures, life change units, conflict, and life-threatening traumatic events. A stressor can be the daily obstacles, called frustration, or the small and irritating inconvenient hassles of everyday life. Stressors are also the pressures in life that cause you to change. Life-adjustment events are another example of a stressor that results in having problems adjusting to changes. These life events can be either positive situations, such as winning $10 million, or negative situations, such as being diagnosed with diabetes. Another type of stressor is an intra-psychic conflict, which produces tension and anxiety because of the difficulty in making a choice. The last type of stressor is a life-threatening traumatic event. This stressor causes extreme anxiety symptoms such as fear, flashbacks, avoidance, hypervigilance, and nightmares.

Stressors can be physical, such as in starvation, an earthquake, or in loud industrial noises. They can also be emotional, as seen with the loss of a parent, divorce, or a difficult day at work. You can experience a single stressor or deal with multiple ones at the same time. The greater the stressor's intensity, amount, dura-

FIGURE 16.2 *She left me for my brother!*

tion, and irreversibility, the more severe the stress becomes if you lack effective coping tools.

The following example illustrates the major impact and effects that multiple stressors have on the body and the mind. Brad had been fired from his job. Two days later he found his wife in bed with his brother. Three days later while his house was burning down, Brad was in his doctor's office receiving news that he has diabetes. A couple of days later, Brad was notified by the IRS that he owes $22,000 in back taxes. Shortly thereafter, he became depressed and couldn't function at work. Brad felt guilty and saw no hope for the present or the future. He began to isolate himself from his friends and had thoughts about suicide. Brad's self-isolation and suicidal ideation were the result of a failure to successfully cope with stressors.

Let's explore the types of stressors that you face in life. Although these stressors may not look dangerous, they can all be deadly, for they all have the ability to destroy your physical and psychological well-being.

Frustration

Frustration occurs when an obstacle causes resistance that blocks you from reaching a goal. The following two examples show how frustration arises when interacting with the environment. Debbie, a senior in high school, needs a 4.0 grade point average (GPA) in order to be accepted to UCLA. Since seventh grade she has always maintained a 4.0 GPA, but in her last semester of high school she received a "B" in physics. Steve, a 16-year-old high school student, is very attracted to his classmate Heidi. Steve would like to take her out on a date but can't because he doesn't have enough money. Both of these examples demonstrate frustration when obstacles block a person from achieving a goal.

As frustration becomes chronic, resilience in coping with the stressor tends to weaken, which then allows the intensity of the stressor to increase. At this point, the sympathetic branch of the autonomic nervous system is activated, triggering the fight-or-flight response. Physiological arousal begins with an increase of norepinephrine and epinephrine. As chronic frustration persists, a physical and emotional exhaustion called **burnout** may emerge and begin to wear down the body's immunological system in people with poor coping skills. This is followed by a decrease in the body's antibodies that are needed to fight infection. The stage is now set for acquiring diseases such as muscle pain, chronic fatigue, and even cancer or heart failure.

FIGURE 16.3 *The feeling of frustration.*

Along with causing physical deterioration, burnout will have a detrimental impact on your cognitive and emotional state by possibly causing a negative attitude, a lack of motivation, depression, and anxiety. As you can see, frustration is harmful to your health. Effective treatments for frustration include aerobic exercise, relaxation techniques, meditation, yoga, good nutrition, and biofeedback, as well as being resilient and resourceful in figuring out new routes to the goal.

Hassles

Hassles are the annoying inconveniences in life that result from troublesome situations or events that you interpret as stressful. Common reactions to hassles include irritation and anger. Hassles can be caused by the little stressors at home, at school, or at your job. Hassles can also be seen on vacations when you have to wait for hours at the airport in order to get security screening or when arrangements you have made in advance don't work out as planned.

Psychosomatic disorders are medical conditions caused at least in part by psychological factors. The more daily hassles in life, the higher the probability of your being in a bad mood and coming down with a psychosomatic disorder. DeLongis, Folkman, and Lazarus (1988) studied the effects of daily hassles on men and women and found an association between hassles and physical ailments such as headaches, sore throats, backaches, and the flu.

There are, however, ways to buffer the harmful effects of daily hassles. One way is through the positive experiences in life called **uplifts**. Uplifts help decrease the physiological and emotional reactions to stress. By destroying the harmful effects of a hassle, uplifts help buffer the body against stressors. Examples of uplifts include falling in love, receiving a job promotion, winning the lottery, and having a good time at a concert. **Reframing** is another way to eliminate the negative emotional effects of hassles. This is done by turning an annoying situation into a funny joke or finding a positive meaning from the hassle. Essentially, the individual creates uplifts out of whatever life events have transpired.

Pressures

Pressures are the distress that come from feeling threatened by a negative situation. Pressure can also arise when trying to defend against a perceived threat by attempting to avoid the negative experience. The following examples illustrate how pressure causes avoidant behaviors. Michael feels pressure at his job because he has to work long hours or face the punishment of being fired. He begins to frequently call in sick. Susie avoids having sexual intercourse with her husband because he refuses to take a bath. Susie feels pressure and distress each time she uses an excuse in order to avoid making love with her husband.

Life Change Units

FIGURE 16.4 *A life-changing moment. (Honey, are you sure this is our hotel room?)*

Transitioning to a new environment involves adjusting to unfamiliar people, tasks, or situations (Sykes & Eden, 1985). Personal networks help with transitions by building social relationships, forming groups, communicating, and collaborating. When an existing personal network is no longer useful in smoothing the transition to the new situation, your physical and mental health becomes affected (Takai, 1989). Examples of **life change units** (LCUs) include a new marriage, the birth of a firstborn child, a job promotion, being diagnosed with a disease, and retirement. When a combination of these LCUs happen at the same time, your level of stress increases. The elevated stress level begins to affect the body's immunological system by interfering with antibody production. It is these antibodies that are needed in the fight against infection. Without sufficient amounts of antibodies, disease, and possibly even death, can result.

FIGURE 16.5 *Marriage is worth 50 LCUs.*

The relationship between stress and physical illness was explored by Holmes and Rahe (1967). They examined major changes that one could possibly experience during the life span. Each one of these events was then allotted an LCU value. From their research they found that people who experienced a large amount of life adjustments during the last 12 months had a higher probability of developing illness.

The **Social Readjustment Rating Scale (SRRS)**, shown in Table 16.1, is an evaluation tool used to assess an individual's total LCUs. In order to evaluate the number of LCUs recently experienced, an individual would mark off the life events he or she has experienced in the last 12 months. The marked LCU values are then added up, and the total number of LCUs is used to predict the probability of the individual acquiring an illness within the next two years.

Just for fun, take a few moments to fill out the SRRS. Check off all the events that you have experienced in the last year. When finished, add up your individual LCUs. A score of 300 or more indicates a greater than 80% chance that you will come down with an illness within the next two years. A score between 200 and 299 translates into a 50% chance. A score of 150–199 indicates a 33% chance of acquiring a disease. Scores less than 150 indicate that you are unlikely to get any illnesses.

Research has shown that the SRRS has limitations. Gender differences can affect the type of answers given on the SRRS due to the way men and women employ different coping mechanism when confronted with stress. Gist and Lubin (1999) reported that men have a structured, outward focus and take a systematic approach when dealing with stress, whereas women tend to seek emotional and social resources. Liebert (1999) stated that testosterone helps keep men from breaking down in the face of stress and danger, whereas women tend to be depressed and anxious when affected by interpersonal and family stressors. A serious weakness of the SRRS is low correlation found between the LCU scores and illness (Dohrenwend & Dohrenwend, 1981). A possible explanation for this might be that there are reasons other than experiencing life changes that cause people to become sick. A third limitation is that the SRRS does not consider the meaning of an event for each individual taking the test. For example, the number of LCUs for the death of a spouse might depend on how the surviving spouse perceived whether he or she had derived satisfaction or dissatisfaction from the marriage. A fourth limitation is that the SRRS does not consider the individual's coping resources. Those who have excellent coping skills are able to handle many stressors without succumbing to illness.

Even so, if you found that your LCU count was high, you might consider taking steps to prevent the potentially harmful effects due to your need to cope with so many life events in one time period. You may be able to put some stressors on hold while you deal with others. Consider getting better organized by making a prioritized daily to-do list. You may also want to postpone a move or hold off on making a job change or going on a diet.

Conflict

A **conflict** is the feeling you have when two or more motives clash with each other, resulting in the inability to make a decision. As an example, Tommy wants to join the armed forces. After visiting various recruiters from the different

TABLE 16.1 Social readjustment rating scale.

Rank	Life event	Life change unit value	Your points
1	Death of spouse	100	
2	Divorce	73	
3	Marital separation	65	
4	Jail term	63	
5	Death of close family member	63	
6	Personal injury or illness	53	
7	Marriage	50	
8	Getting fired at work	47	
9	Marital reconciliation	45	
10	Retirement	45	
11	Change in health of family member	44	
12	Pregnancy	40	
13	Sex difficulties	39	
14	Gain of a new family member	39	
15	Business readjustment	39	
16	Change in financial state	38	
17	Death of a close friend	37	
18	Change to different line of work	36	
19	Change in number of arguments with spouse	35	
20	Taking out loan for major purchase (e.g., home)	31	
21	Foreclosure of mortgage or loan	30	
22	Change in responsibilities at work	29	
23	Son or daughter leaving home	29	
24	Trouble with in-laws	29	
25	Outstanding achievement	28	
26	Spouse beginning or stopping work	26	
27	Beginning or ending school	26	
28	Change in living conditions	25	
29	Revision of personal habits	24	
30	Trouble with the boss	23	
31	Change in work hours or conditions	20	
32	Change in residence	20	
33	Change in school	20	
34	Change in recreation	19	
35	Change in church activities	19	
36	Change in social activities	18	
37	Taking out a loan for a lesser purchase (e.g., car or TV)	17	
38	Change in sleeping habits	16	
39	Change in number of family get-togethers	15	
40	Change in eating habits	15	
41	Vacation	13	
42	Christmas	12	
43	Minor violation of the law	11	
		Total	

Mark all the events that you have experienced in the last 12 months. Next, add up the points to determine your life stress score. Then use the scale to assess your probability of developing a major health problem within the next two years.

Life Change Unit Scale

> 300:	80% chance in the next two years
200–299:	50% chance in the next two years
150–199:	33% chance in the next two years
< 150:	unlikely chance in the next two years

FIGURE 16.6 *Conflicts are one big headache.*

branches, Tommy discovers that he likes both the Marines and the Navy. He's having trouble deciding which branch to join. Tommy has a conflict.

What do you experience when you're involved in a conflict? It feels like being in the middle with both arms pulled in opposite directions. There are four types of conflict that can affect you: approach-approach, avoidance-avoidance, approach-avoidance, and double-approach-avoidance.

1. **Approach-approach conflicts** are when you need to pick between two pleasurable goals that are equal in value. Michael is graduating from high school and has been accepted to both Harvard and Princeton. Both schools are excellent, yet he can't decide which to choose. The stressors of this conflict cause him to experience headaches and insomnia. This type of conflict is the easiest to resolve. What do you think Michael should do?

2. **Avoidance-avoidance conflicts** arise when you have two or more unpleasurable options that can result in displeasing consequences, and you must choose one of the options. Julia has a painful toothache that needs treatment. However, she fears all dental work because of an incident that happened five years ago when a dentist pulled out the wrong tooth. This caused her to experience pain and resulted in an infection that lasted for five months. Should Julia tolerate the pain from her tooth, or should she go to the dentist? Either choice will be unpleasant for her.

3. **Approach-avoidance conflicts** are when you reach a positive goal that has an unpleasurable outcome. Lena is a rising actress who is becoming popular with her American audience. She has just been asked to sign a contract to appear in a movie that can make her a superstar. Lena will be in Paris for nine months during the filming of the movie. The producers will not allow family members to go. Lena is very much in love with her husband, Bob, and they are always together. Lena begins to worry as she feels the stress from the conflict of finding fame at the expense of not being with her husband. What do you think she should do?

4. **Double approach-avoidance conflict** is when you find it difficult to decide between options that have both pleasurable and unpleasurable outcomes. Carla is in a position where she must choose between two jobs. The first job is prestigious and pays well, but the boss is always angry. The other job, with a smaller company, pays less, but the boss has a well-known reputation for caring about her employees. What would you do in Carla's position? Any decision you make will most likely have pleasant and unpleasant consequences.

Avoidance, compromise, aggression, and accommodation are inappropriate ways to deal with conflict. Actions like these can result in anxiety, anger, manipulation, and worry. These types of behaviors will not resolve a conflict; they can only make it worse.

One way to deal with conflict is to measure the benefits of each decision. By doing this, you are able to make a reasoned decision. Begin by listing all the positive benefits of each decision. Then, using the measurement scale of 1 = small, 2 = medium, 3 = maximum, write the appropriate score for each benefit. Total the score for each decision and determine which one has the most points. The highest score helps in determining the best option to take in order to resolve the conflict. This technique can help you feel comfortable making a decision.

Conflicts can also arise in relationships with two or more people. This is seen when people have opposite interests in mind. Inappropriate ways to deal with this type of conflict include launching personal attacks, withdrawing into silence, or being compliant by giving in. Any one of these negative ways of coping can put stress on the relationship and leave the conflict unresolved.

There is a positive way to deal with this type of conflict. By using **conflict resolution**, all parties involved are motivated to come to an agreement in order to work out a settlement. The results are a win-win situation for both parties. The **integration approach** to conflict resolution maximizes the gains by using creative procedures. Conflict resolution is most effective when all parties are empathetic to one another's needs and behave in a manner demonstrating mutual cooperation.

FIGURE 16.7 *Jack and Jill enjoying conflict resolution, and each other.*

The following example illustrates how much fun conflict resolution can be. Jill calls her husband, Jack, at work and tells him that he's getting lazy in his romantic behaviors. She says to him, "Tonight I would like you to take me to a fancy restaurant for a romantic evening." Jack tells Jill, "We don't have enough money to go to a restaurant, and by the way we need to do the taxes tonight." Both partners acknowledge Jack's objections. Through conflict resolution, Jack and Jill decide that the best solution is to first go to the supermarket and buy gourmet food. They then head home and prepare a romantic candlelight dinner. After dinner, Jack and Jill head upstairs to enjoy some satisfying lovemaking. Then they walk hand-in-hand downstairs, ready to take on the challenge of doing the taxes.

Can this type of resolution for a conflict help a marriage? Heavey, Layne, & Christensen (1993) found that conflict resolution promoted satisfaction in romantic relationships, while Fileinger and Thomas (1988) reported that conflict resolution helps maintain the stability of the relationship.

Traumatic Events

It is extremely frightening when you experience a traumatic event that is life threatening. Victims of traumatic events can develop symptoms of **post-traumatic stress disorder (PTSD)**. The *Diagnostic and Statistical Manual of Mental Disorders* (American Psychiatric Association, 2000a) states that the essential feature of PTSD is the development of characteristic symptoms following exposure to an extreme traumatic stressor that involves direct personal experience of an event that causes actual or threatened death, or threats to one's physical integrity. It also includes witnessing an event that involves death. Other stressors that may cause PTSD include injury or threat to the physical

FIGURE 16.8 *PTSD can cause emotional numbness.*

integrity of another person, learning about an unexpected or violent death or serious harm, and threat of death or injury experienced by a family member or a close associate. Traumatic events can be seen in automobile accidents, combat, rape, a kidnapping, being a hostage, terrorist attacks, and natural disasters. Symptoms from the trauma arise a month or more following the event. Trauma can affect more than one person at the same time. In the 9/11 terrorist attacks and with Hurricane Katrina's disastrous effects on the Gulf Coast, the world witnessed how millions of people can be traumatized by a single event.

PTSD symptoms have a negative effect on daily life. Expressing emotions about the trauma decreases negative symptoms and increases the cognitive evaluation of the experience (Pennebaker, 1990). Seligman (1975) reports that combining the psychotherapy techniques of prolonged exposure and stress inoculation in the treatment of PTSD resulted in a high cure rate. Eye movement desensitization reprocessing (EMDR) is another psychotherapy intervention that has been used in the treatment of this type of stressor. How EMDR works is still not known, and currently there is research that supports and does not support this therapeutic intervention.

The Body's Physiological Response to Stress

Fight-or-Flight Response

When confronted with a threat, you either hold your ground and meet the threat head on (fight) or escape from it (flight) in order to prevent harm. Both fight and flight require a large amount of energy and cardiopulmonary capacity. The fight-or-flight response is activated by physical stimuli or situations in which a threat is appraised by the brain. This is followed by a state of physiological arousal as the body prepares to deal with the stressor. The unfolding of the body's physiological, psychological, and biochemical response to stress can best be described in the following sequence of events:

♦ At first the stimuli are appraised as a threat.

♦ The amygdala then activates the hypothalamus, which stimulates the pituitary gland's release of adrenocorticotropic hormone (ACTH).

♦ ACTH activates the adrenal cortex to make corticoids for the purpose of increasing the glucose that is needed for energy.

♦ At the same time, the hypothalamus arouses the sympathetic nervous system, which in turn stimulates adrenal gland production of epinephrine (adrenaline) and norepinephrine. These arousal hormones excite the body by increasing respiratory rate, blood glucose, blood pressure, heart rate, and blood flow to the muscles and brain. They also activate the release of glycogen from the liver for the purpose of providing the body with continuous energy.

General Adaptation Syndrome

When sensing a threat, the body reacts by gathering together its physiological defenses for the purpose of combating infection, trauma, and emotional stress. The work of Hans Selye (1976) provided the classical model for how organisms adapt to stress. Selye found that an organism responds to stress with a predictable pattern in an attempt to restore internal homeostasis. Prolonged stress forces you to adapt to it in order to maintain a balance in the face of the stressor, but the organism eventually reaches a point where sustained resistance to the stressor is no longer possible. What follows is a decline in function and performance as well as damage to the body. Selye's General Adaptation Syndrome (GAS) is a predictable sequence of physiological and psychological events that organisms exhibit in reaction to stressors.

The three sequential stages of the GAS (Table 16.2) are as follows:

1. **Alarm stage**—Appraising the situation as threatening, the body responds to stress by stimulating the sympathetic nervous system into action in order to get it ready to confront the threat. Heart rate, blood pressure, and respiratory rate increase. Blood circulating through the digestive tract is redirected to the skeletal muscles for strength. At the same time, the immunological system is increasing antibodies and T-killer cells. Glucose pumps into the bloodstream in order to supply the extra energy that will be needed during this state of excitation.

2. **Resistance stage**—The body's resources are now at maximum levels as the organism continues to be exposed to the stress. As the body adapts to the stress, its vital resources become depleted and drained, while at the same time, the fight-or-flight response begins to damage organs in the body. To prevent further organ injury, the body retreats by deactivating the sympathetic nervous system. The body changes from an offensive mode to a defensive one as it continues to fight off stress. Psychosomatic

TABLE 16.2 Selye's stages of the GAS.

Alarm stage	Resistance stage	Exhaustion stage
▲ Heart rate	Cortisol damages organs	Allergies
▲ Blood pressure	Electrolyte imbalance	▼ Adrenal gland activity
▲ Respiratory rate	▼ Sympathetic nervous system	Fatigue
▲ Blood flow to skeletal muscle	▼ Immune system	Depression
▲ Antibodies	▼ Physical activity	Suicide
▲ T-killer cells	▼ Nutrient absorption	Scar tissue formation
▲ Blood glucose	Tissue damage	Infection
▲ Epinephrine	Physical fatigue	Stroke
▲ Cortisol	Mental fatigue	Heart attack
▲ Inflammation	Hypertension	Cancer
Perspiration	Headache	Multiorgan failure
Excitation	Stomach pain	Death

symptoms such as stomach pain, skin rash, eating disorders, weak immune system, high blood pressure, physical and mental fatigue, muscle pain, and headaches can appear during this stage.

3. **Exhaustion stage**—As the chronic stress continues, the body's organs and immunological system weaken more and become damaged. The psychosomatic symptoms worsen and can lead to the development of diseases such as cancer, hypertension, stroke, and myocardial infarction. Multiorgan failure may follow.

The GAS is an evolutionary survival mechanism that helps you respond to environmental threats. Activation of the GAS protects the body during an emergency. In this respect, acute activation of the GAS is helpful. Unfortunately, with prolonged stress, long-term activation of the GAS becomes harmful to the body as the chances of acquiring psychosomatic symptoms and succumbing to disease increase.

The Effects of Stress on the Immune System

The function of the white blood cells in the immune system is to fight off all types of infection for the purpose of maintaining health. The two major groups of white blood cells are lymphocytes and phagocytes. Lymphocytes comprise the B-cells, which respond to infection by producing antibodies. Phagocytes and macrophages also defend against disease by engulfing infection through the process of phagocytosis. Two other types of lymphocytes are T-cells, which search for and destroy infection, and the natural killer cells, which detect tumor cells early and prevent them from growing.

Part of the body's response to stress is to release neurotransmitters such as norepinephrine, epinephrine, corticosteroids, and endorphins. Unfortunately, these neurotransmitters have a negative effect on the body's immunological system by impairing function and decreasing its efficiency. The neurotransmitters of the corticosteroids and catecholamine have an immunosuppressive effect, while the **endorphins** lower the effectiveness of natural killer T-cells. This sets the stage for the invasion of microorganisms that cause infection.

With chronic stress comes the increased probability of acquiring a disease. Every system in the body has the potential to be damaged by stress. Numerous studies have shown a link between stress and physical health problems (Cohen, Tyrrell, & Smith, 1993; Cohen & Williamson, 1988). Examples of stress-triggered illnesses include colds, flu, diabetes, asthma, bronchitis, osteoporosis, impotency in males, amenorrhea in woman, cancer, and cardiovascular disease.

It is possible for our immune system to be weakened by disease, such as in the case of **acquired immune deficiency syndrome (AIDS)**. This immune deficiency disease is caused by the human immunodeficiency virus (HIV), which infects the body by attaching to the CD4 receptor on the T-cell lymphocytes. The infected T-cells are gradually destroyed over a period of years. With insufficient T-cells in the body, the B-cells antibody production is hampered. As the body's immune system functioning declines, opportunistic pathogenic microorganisms multiply rapidly and produce destructive diseases such as pneumocystis carinii pneumonia, tuberculosis, and Kaposi's sarcoma. When this happens, the HIV-infected individual is said to have AIDS.

HIV is transmitted through sexual intercourse, where there is contact with blood, secretions of the vagina, or semen from the man. It can also be transmitted through direct inoculation, as in the sharing of contaminated needles by IV drug users. A third way that you can contact HIV is through blood transfusions.

At this time there is no cure for HIV. Millions of people around the world are infected. Stephenson (2005) reported that HIV/AIDS infection continues to expand globally, with more than 40 million people now estimated to be infected with the virus. Serious HIV/AIDS epidemics are in sub-Sahara Africa, where 30% of the pregnant women are infected, while Eastern Europe, central Asia, and east Asia are growing at rapid epidemic rates due to IV drug use and commercial sex (Mayer & Pizer, 2005). Since first being diagnosed in the early 1980s, HIV continues to have a high infection rate in the United States, with homosexual men and IV drug users making up the largest population. The Centers for Disease Control (2004) estimates that among the diagnosed HIV infections in the United States in 2003, 63% were among men who had sexual contact with other men, 50% were among African Americans, 32% were among Caucasians, and 16% among Hispanics. HIV infection appears to be growing rapidly among minority populations. Ways to prevent the transmission of HIV/AIDS include education, elimination of contaminated needles by IV drug users, testing of blood products, and using condoms for sexual intercourse.

The study of **psychoneuroimmunology** focuses on how the mind and body interact with each other. This science was formed in 1964, when George Solomon and his colleague inferred that stress could affect the immune system by decreasing a person's lymphocytes. Following Solomon and Moos's study, Ader and Cohen (1975) conditioned the suppression of the immune response. Psychoneuroimmunology has helped researchers find out how the central nervous system, the endocrine system, and psychosocial factors affect the immunological system. Due to stress, your negative sensory input, thinking, behavior, feelings, and perception can have pathological consequences on the central nervous system, which then affect the endocrine and immunological systems. Stressful situations such as bereavement, divorce, lack of social support, unemployment, and taking final exams can result in a decrease in your lymphocytic response. On the bright side, research has demonstrated that positive psychological events can benefit health by strengthening the immune response. Phillips and Smith (1990) studied the effects of symbolically meaningful events on terminally ill patients and found that anticipating celebrations such as Passover for Jewish men and the Chinese Harvest Moon Festival for Chinese women often prolonged the lives of those suffering from cancer or cardiovascular disease.

Psychological Correlates of Stress

Personality Factors

Factors within your own personality can affect how you perceive the intensity of a stressor. One personality factor that determines your effectiveness in coping with a stressor is called your locus of control. Your view of how much control you have over a stressor helps determine whether you will be harmed by it.

FIGURE 16.9 *I believe in the internal locus of control.*

An **external locus of control** is the feeling of having no power in controlling what happens in your life. You believe that it is fate, luck, or chance that determines how the world will treat you. This type of person appraises stressful situations as being threatening and harmful, resulting in negative emotions such as anger. An **internal locus of control** is when you feel in control of your behavior and consequences. With the internal locus of control, stressors are seen not as threats but as challenges.

This positive appraisal produces a happy mood, motivation, energy, and excitement. Those with an internal locus of control have more fulfillment and happiness in their life. They are also better problem solvers and decision makers.

Can some people handle a stressful situation better than others? This question can be answered by looking at another personality factor, **hardiness**. Being in control, following through on commitments, and looking forward to the challenge of life are what hardiness is all about. Hardy people have an internal locus of control and **self-efficacy**. Having the personality factor of self-efficacy gives you the confidence of knowing that you're capable of handling most situations. According to Bandura (1995), self-efficacy is the belief in one's capabilities to organize and execute a course of action required to manage a prospective situation. Self-efficacy helps hardy people believe in their ability to perform optimally in challenging situations. With a sense of self-efficacy, you have the confidence to make the appropriate choices in difficult situations.

Another factor that affects how one copes with stress is determined by whether the glass is seen as half full (optimism) or as half empty (pessimism). Those who believe that good things will happen to them are optimists. The positive appraisal of an optimist allows you to focus on the positive side of life.

Positive psychology, which is a new branch of psychology, believes that by becoming an optimist, you can utilize the tools necessary to be happy and to successfully get through the difficult times in life. According to Seligman (2002), positive psychology focuses on three overlapping areas. The first is the pleasant life. It includes embracing positive feelings and emotions, which in turn helps enhance healthy relationships and interest in life. The second is the good life, which is the feeling of being in control and looking forward to engaging in life activities. With the good life comes the belief in being able to face all your tasks in life. The third area is called the meaningful life. This is a positive feeling of well-being brought on by having a meaningful purpose in life and by belonging to and contributing to your environment. By focusing on your ability for love and work, compassion, self-knowledge, self-control, curiosity and integrity, you may be able to tolerate and overcome harmful stressors.

Pessimists expect negative things to always happen to them. A pessimist usually feels negative emotions such as anger, rage, hostility, fear, and anxiety. The pessimist's attitude and beliefs make him or her highly susceptible not only to stress but also to its harmful effects on health. How you successfully overcome and handle stress will depend on whether you perceive the stressor as a satisfying challenge that is beneficial and rewarding or as a threat.

FIGURE 16.10 *I hope he can take it.*

Can a stressful situation that you perceive as uncontrollable affect the way you interpret and deal with future stressors? According to Seligman (1975), the cognitive learning theory of **learned helplessness** is when you experience negative situations that you're unable to control that can then result in the expectation of being helpless. This results in giving up when experiencing future stressors because you believe that your actions are useless. By giving up, you make no effort to behave and think in ways that can make things better for you. Not feeling in control of negative situations can result in passivity, which may then be followed by depression. With low expectations of personal control, the motivation to take on the challenges of future stressors is gone. This results in the individual continuing to be depressed and also being susceptible to the harmful effects of stress.

Another personality factor that influences how you deal with stress is whether you are a Type A personality. In Type A personality, there are characteristic patterns of behavior that produce emotional stress. Studies have shown an association between Type A personality and cardiovascular disease. Type A personalities produce constant emotional stress, which activates the sympathetic nervous system to release norepinephrine. This neurotransmitter stimulates the heart to work harder. At the same time, the stress triggers an increased amount of cholesterol from the liver to the bloodstream, where it is then deposited in the coronary arteries by low density lipoproteins. Blood flow eventually becomes obstructed. Hypertension develops, as the heart must work harder to pump blood through the constricted arteries. The decrease in blood flow causes a lack of oxygen to the heart muscle, which can result in a myocardial infarction and possibly death. Characteristics of a Type A personality include hard-driving, competitive, ambitious, multitask oriented, demanding, fast eater, loud speaker, and aggressive in a hostile manner. It is believed that the increased blood testosterone levels of Type As cause them to have aggressive behaviors. Although Type As have a high rate of success and achievement, they also experience a higher incidence of cardiovascular disease than Type B personalities. Seligman (1994) reported that Type As have more heart attacks than Type Bs. It appears that Type Bs do not exhibit aggression or hostility. In fact, time constraints are not an issue for them. Even though Type Bs are just as ambitious as Type As, they give themselves permission to play and relax without feeling guilty.

Social Factors

FIGURE 16.11 *A social support system of friends helps reduce stress.*

A good social support system made up of family and friends can protect you from the harmful effects of stress. Those who have at least one person in whom they can confide are less vulnerable to the impact of stress (Cohen & Wills, 1985). Being able to talk to an empathetic, understanding, and validating person about how you feel is therapeutic. Most people usually feel better after venting their negative feelings. Having trust in another makes you comfortable with sharing your deepest feelings and fears.

Having social support during times of stress also helps the decision-making process. By first evaluating the opinions of others, you are more equipped to make a decision. In regard to social support and stress, Cohen and Wills (1985) reported appraisal support as the best buffer against stress. Having other people available to help appraise the stressful situation contributes to better physical and psychological health among individuals who are experiencing stress. By having a good social support network, you seldom develop psychosomatic symptoms and usually do not become anxious or depressed. In contrast, people living alone without any social support are highly susceptible to stress's harmful health effects on the body.

Ineffective Coping Styles

Many people cope with stress in inefficient ways, such as through aggression, withdrawal, overly used defense mechanisms, and psychoactive drug abuse. Although these inappropriate ways of dealing with stress can provide temporary relief from tension, they do not eliminate or solve the problems caused by the stressor. In fact, these poor coping styles only make matters worse.

Aggression

Aggression is the acting-out of emotions through destructive behaviors. Aggression arises from your reaction to the frustration of not being able to achieve a goal. As an example, 6-year-old Brad is told by his mother that he can't go outside and play. Brad reacts aggressively by throwing toys at his mother with the intention of hurting her.

Aggression doesn't have to be an active behavior. **Passive-aggressiveness** is when you are too scared to assert your feelings in an appropriate manner. So, through passive and covert behaviors, you oppose the other person's request. Behaviors observed with this style of coping include procrastinating, stonewalling, being stubborn and inefficient, and not remembering.

The following example illustrates how passive-aggressiveness operates. Steve and Maria are at home discussing their financial problems. Steve tells Maria that she needs to get a job. Maria becomes angry and tells Steve that he's a lazy bum and has to make more money by working harder at his job. Steve is furious with Maria's remark but is too scared to assert his true feelings because of her hot temper. That night, as Steve lays awake in bed, he hears Maria singing their wedding song in the shower. Steve knows that this is the signal that Maria wants to make love. As Maria climbs into bed, Steve turns away from her and pretends that he's asleep.

Withdrawing

Sometimes you try to deal with stress by withdrawing from it. Withdrawing results in avoidance of dealing with a situation that doesn't go away—a young adult moves out of state in order to get away from his overly protective, domineering parents; a woman who feels the tension from a bad marriage may withdraw from the relationship by getting involved in an affair with a coworker. By withdrawing, you neither solve the problem, nor do you get rid of the stress.

Avoidance does have its advantages when dealing with stress. You can deal with a stressor by avoiding the negative situation until you find the skills that are

Id → Ego ← Superego

↓
↓
↓   **Escape from anxiety**
↓
↓
↓

Defense mechanism

FIGURE 16.12 *Etiology of defense mechanisms.*

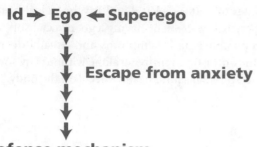

Explore
defense mechanisms
in Chapter 13, p. 415

needed to cope with the stressor. Removing yourself from the situation allows time to regroup in order to obtain the resources to deal with the issue.

Defense Mechanisms

Defense mechanisms are irrational and unconscious ways of the ego to defend against anxiety. According to Freud's psychoanalytic theory (1915/1957), personality is determined by the dynamic relationship among the id, the ego, and the superego. The primitive id operates under the pleasure principle of seeking satisfaction while avoiding pain. The id desires food, sex, protection, and aggression. It has no sense of reality, nor does it tolerate tension. The ego guides the id through the reality of the external world. Under the reality principle, the ego senses, tests, and adapts to the external world. The ego also takes on the role of showing the id realistic and safe ways to achieve satisfaction and pleasure. The superego represents the morality and conscience of society and opposes the actions of the id.

The superego restricts the ego from helping the id. This puts the ego in a conflict. By fulfilling the desires of the id, the ego feels the guilt that arises from the superego. If the ego decides to ignore the id and follow the moral boundaries of the superego, it then feels the frustration and tension from the id. Unable to satisfy the id and the superego at the same time, the ego becomes filled with anxiety. In order to avoid feeling anxious or tense, the ego escapes from the conflict through defense mechanisms (Figure 16.12) that decrease the ego's tension. This protects the ego from feeling anxious and/or guilty and keeps our self-esteem high. Different types of defense mechanisms become problematic when overused to the extent that the individual doesn't deal with the conflict.

Psychoactive Drug Use

Explore
psychoactive drugs
in Chapter 5, p. 149

The use of addictive substances is another example of inappropriately coping with stress. On the surface, the use of psychoactive drugs for dealing with or escaping from stress gives an initial feeling of pleasure, satisfaction, and happiness, as the drug alters mood, perception, consciousness, and behavior. But in reality, the continual use and abuse of a drug creates more stress, which worsens the intensity of the tension. This can result in psychological mental disorders such as psychosis, depression, anxiety, and medical problems like cirrhosis of the liver, lung cancer, and HIV.

The association between psychoactive drugs and the relief of stress can be seen by the brain's neurotransmitters' effect on mood. The brain produces four monoamine neurochemical transmitters that control your mood, energy level, happiness, and tolerance of pain. **Dopamine** is a catecholamine neurotransmitter substance that influences motivation, concentration, learning abilities, and motor movement. The second monoamine neurotransmitter, **serotonin**, regulates mood, appetite, aggressiveness, and impulse control. **Norepinephrine**, the third monoamine, keeps you alert and awake. **Epinephrine**, the fourth neurotransmitter, triggers the release of stored glucose from muscle tissue for the purpose of providing energy for the body. It should be noted that a fifth neurotransmitter, beta endorphins, decreases pain and gives the individual a feeling of euphoria. Beta endorphins are from the catecholamine family and are opiates.

As you perceive a stressor as a threat, your body goes into action. Upon the initial onset of stress, the first stage of the **General Adaptation Syndrome (GAS)** begins, resulting in the release of these neurotransmitters into the bloodstream. As the body enters the second stage of the GAS, the neurotransmitters begin to be depleted. Through the process of reuptake, they are conserved by crossing back over the synapse and returning to the sending neuron. The decrease in these neurotransmitters in the blood causes depression, insomnia, lack of energy, poor concentration, and increased sensitivity to pain.

Now here's where initial pleasure is derived from the use of psychoactive drugs. Abused substances such as cocaine and amphetamines block the reuptake of the neurotransmitters from the blood back to the neuron. This creates a state of happiness, alertness, and energy. Other psychoactive drugs such as nicotine and caffeine stimulate the reward/pleasure center in the nucleus accumbens and ventral segmental area of the brain. These drugs activate the reward/pleasure center, resulting in an increase in dopamine. The pleasurable feeling that one gets from dopamine becomes the reinforcing factor for the continual use and abuse of these psychoactive drugs.

Alcohol is a psychoactive depressant. Coping with stress by using alcohol can result in abuse and dependency. With alcohol dependency comes the craving for the drug and the inability to stop drinking. Alcohol dependency becomes evident with the development of withdrawal symptoms such as anxiety, sweating, nausea, and tremors. Alcohol can only make stress worse, not better. In the short run it clearly reduces stress, but the long run is a different story. The negative consequences of alcoholism include depression, anxiety, relationship problems, loss of job, legal problems, suicide, accidents, injury, cirrhosis, insomnia, irritability, aggression, malnutrition, and brain damage.

You would think that the adverse effects of alcohol would stop a person from wanting to drink, but that's not the case. In the United States alone, 110 million Americans drink alcohol, and 14 million of them suffer from the destructive effects of alcoholism. One reason for the popularity of alcohol is its effects on the GABA neural receptors. Alcohol binding at the GABA receptor sites results in decreased anxiety and inhibition. Alcohol abuse is associated with a negative mood. Merikangas and Gelerntor (1990) reported a strong positive relationship among depression, alcohol abuse, and dependence. People use alcohol to self-medicate when they are depressed.

FIGURE 16.13 *Why aren't things getting better?*

Nicotine is a widely used addictive stimulant drug that activates the dopamine reward/pleasure center and triggers the release of

FIGURE 16.14 *Dying for a smoke!*

norepinephrine, epinephrine, and beta endorphins. Nicotine's effect on the ventral tegmental area of the dopaminergic system quickly makes you dependent on smoking. The World Resource Institute (1998–1999) reported that the current death toll attributed to tobacco in developing countries is one in eight, while in developed countries it's one in four. Causes of death from smoking cigarettes include chronic bronchitis, emphysema, bronchogenic cancer, and myocardial infarctions.

Stress appears to be a powerful motivator for smoking. According to Perkins and Grobe (1992), as stress increases in intensity, the craving for cigarettes also increases. Kaplan and Sadock (1998) reported that the pleasurable feeling derived from cigarettes becomes a reinforcer for addiction along with psychological factors such as social gatherings, drinking alcohol, and eating. When you're physiologically addicted, cessation of smoking can result in the development of withdrawal symptoms in the first couple of hours. These symptoms, which can continue for months, include increased appetite, weight gain, irritability, headaches, concentration problems, and feeling sleepy.

FIGURE 16.15 *Caffeine can make stress worse.*

Another widely used psychoactive stimulant is caffeine. Individuals use caffeine to combat some of the effects of stress, which include being sleepy, fatigued, or otherwise not alert. The stimulation from caffeine is caused by the blocking of the adenosine receptors in the brain. This results in a mild physical and psychological stimulation. The average dosage of caffeine in one cup of coffee is 90–100 mg. When caffeine levels go above 150 mg, you can experience nervous system toxicity. Sue, Sue, and Sue (1994) reported that two cups of coffee can produce symptoms such as irritability, headaches, fatigue, and a craving for caffeine. Dosages greater than 300 mg can cause depression and anxiety symptoms. Caffeine increases the intensity of stress and causes restlessness, nervousness, excitement, insomnia, a flushed face, rambling speech, and cardiac arrhythmias. Caffeine is another example of how using a psychoactive drug to cope with stress only increases it.

Stress Management

Coping Styles

To prevent and fight back against the harmful effects of stress, you need to incorporate stress management into your everyday life. A stress management program is the best way to protect against the dangers of stress. Stress management is utilized in three areas: changing thoughts, physiology, and behavior. Stress has a great effect on your thoughts. Decreasing intrusive and anxiety-provoking thoughts that are a typical response to stressors can be done through a variety of cognitive behavior therapy techniques. **Cancellation** is an excellent intervention that allows you to get rid of continuously intrusive and distressing thoughts. Cancellation works by blocking the process of storing a memory. The **stage theory of memory** states that there are three stages of memory. Each stage allows you to hold information for a set amount of time. The first stage is the sensory register, which holds the sensory experience for a quarter of a second.

Explore **memory** in Chapter 8, p. 235

The second stage consists of the information held in short-term memory. The stimuli are held in short-term memory for 30 seconds. By rehearsing stimuli in short-term memory, they become permanently stored in the third stage, long-term memory, where they may become constant intrusive negative thoughts that cause distress, anxiety, and depression.

The cancellation technique creates interference and forgetting of negative intrusive thoughts. While the information is stored in the short-term memory, the intervention distracts your attention from the intrusive thought. This results in the thought being forgotten, as it falls out of the short-term memory. The cancellation technique should be started immediately at the first sign of an intrusive negative thought. It works like this: Immediately close your eyes and say the word "blue" for 10 seconds. Then take a deep breath and say "blue" for another 10 seconds. Repeat this procedure three more times. By blocking the negative stimuli from being transferred to the long-term memory, you are able to decrease the frequency and intensity of distressing negative thoughts.

Thought stopping is another method that helps decrease the frequency and intensity of stress-producing, obsessive negative thoughts. This technique is simple to learn. When an obsessive negative thought enters your mind, close your eyes and clap your hands for 30 seconds while repeatedly yelling "stop!" To avoid embarrassment in front of people, a mental scream can be used. The command "stop" becomes a distracter, which is incompatible with the obsessive thought. Thought stopping should then be followed by **thought substitution,** where you think about positive, reassuring, self-accepting affirmations. Your stress level can be greatly decreased by controlling your thoughts.

Another way to control stress is by **scheduling worries**. By using this technique, you allow yourself to focus on worrying for 30 minutes a day at a specific time. It is only at this specified time that worrying should occur. If any negative obsessive thoughts arise outside the scheduled worry time, you should tell the thought that it "needs to wait until its scheduled time to worry." Because the scheduling of worries is inconvenient and time consuming, you realize that it is not worth spending time worrying about negative thoughts. Scheduling of worries helps you control negative thoughts produced by stress.

Using stress management can also allow you to change your body's physiological responses to stress by reversing sympathetic nervous system excitability, which can prevent injury to the body's organs. Techniques used in changing the body's physiology include biofeedback, exercise, progressive muscle relaxation, breathing control, meditation, and yoga.

Biofeedback is a therapeutic technique in which you learn to voluntarily change and control various automatic physiological functions such as heart rate, blood pressure, temperature, muscle tone,

FIGURE 16.16 *Sit back, relax, and imagine that you're in Malibu.*

and blood flow. With biofeedback, electronic instruments receive the stress-related physiological signals from the body. This information is fed back to the person either visually or auditorily. Through biofeedback training, operant conditioning allows you to learn how to change stress's harmful physiological responses to healthy ones. In biofeedback, a computer records the various changes in physiology caused by the stress reaction. The physiological feedback that is recorded includes cortical brain waves, cortical blood flow, muscle tension, peripheral temperature and blood flow, heart rate, and breathing frequency. You then learn techniques to change and regulate these various physiological responses. Shahidi and Salmon (1992) found that biofeedback was useful in decreasing blood pressure and heart rate, while Gamble and Elder (1993) reported that biofeedback was successful in decreasing muscle tension.

The following example illustrates how biofeedback works. Paul suffers from hypertension. His doctor told him that his high blood pressure is due to stress and recommends that he try biofeedback. While hooked up to the biofeedback machine, Paul watches his blood pressure rise to 140/95. Following this, he begins to utilize learned relaxation techniques, such as progressive muscle relaxation. This results in the lowering of his blood pressure to 120/80 on the monitor. He continues this procedure for a set amount of time. After a while, Paul is able to lower his blood pressure without using any of the biofeedback equipment. Biofeedback is used in the treatment of asthma, grand mal epilepsy, migraine and tension headaches, cardiac arrhythmias, hypertension, headaches, anxiety, and stress.

Jacobson's progressive relaxation technique is another physiological approach to managing stress by creating relaxation through the release of muscle tension. Jacobson (1974) reported that the body reacts to stress-provoking thoughts and situations with muscle tension. This physical tension then triggers anxiety. Muscle relaxation decreases the physiological tension and the anxiety that results from it.

This technique is easy to learn. Just sit back comfortably in a chair. Tense the muscles of the arms, hands, and fingers for 5 seconds and then relax them for 30 seconds. Repeat this procedure one more time. Then follow the same procedure for the head, face, neck, and shoulders. Next, move on to the chest, stomach, and lower back. Finish with the thighs, buttocks, calves, and feet. Tensing and relaxing many muscles at one time can achieve relaxation. Mastering this technique enables you to counteract the muscle tension that typically occurs in response to stress.

Another technique used in stress management to change your tension level and brain chemistry is **breathing control**. This simple procedure begins with inhaling slowly through the nose and into the lungs, where the breath is held for five seconds before exhaling. During inhalation, count to five, followed by holding your breath while counting to five again. Then exhale for another count of five. This procedure is repeated five times. Breathing control stimulates the release of endorphins, which gives you a feeling of peacefulness, relaxation, and an increased tolerance to pain.

FIGURE 16.17 *Yoga.*

Yoga is a Hindu technique that achieves relaxation and peace of mind through concentration, deep meditation, controlled breathing, and various body posture positions. Yoga allows for the healthy balance and connection between body and mind. As discussed throughout the chapter, the body's response to stress results in the stimulation of the fight-or-flight response of the sympathetic nervous system, causing blood flow to be redirected to the muscles in the body. This results in the increase of muscle tension.

Practicing yoga activates the parasympathetic nervous system to decrease heart rate, blood pressure, and respiratory rate. Another benefit of yoga is reduced blood flow to the muscles, which results in relaxation. Blood flow is redirected to the gastrointestinal and immune systems, resulting in better digestion of foods and increased immunity. Benefits of yoga include stronger muscles, better digestion, relaxation, energy, improved posture and balance, as well as flexibility and vitality. In a study on the effects of yoga on mood, Harvey (1983) reported that yoga breathing exercises increased vigor and decreased tension, depression, and fatigue.

FIGURE 16.18 *Practicing TM.*

Transcendental meditation (TM) allows you to achieve relaxation by blocking out the negative thoughts and feelings that cause stress. This results in the mind changing to a passive state of relaxation. TM is simple to do, and you begin by closing your eyes and repeating a mantra either silently or out loud. The mantra can be any calming word or sound—for example, "one" or "blue." With TM, stressful thoughts are changed to peaceful ones. Relaxation is achieved as the parasympathetic nervous system takes over control of the body's various functions. According to Bensen (1975), TM creates an altered state of consciousness that decreases cardiovascular activity and increases relaxation. In order for TM to be effective, you need to be in a quiet environment while maintaining passive thinking in a comfortable position. This is followed by chanting the mantra while focusing on an object.

FIGURE 16.19 *Aerobic exercise.*

Exercise is another physiological way to reduce stress. According to Davis, Robbins-Eshelman, and Mckay (1996), exercise is an excellent outlet for the body during the fight-or-flight arousal state. Exercise allows for the release of the natural chemicals that have been building up during the stress response. The release of these chemicals results in the body returning to a normal homeostasis. Crews and Lander (1987) reported that exercise can reduce the harmful cardiovascular effects of stress. The United States Surgeon General (1996) stated that regular exercise helps prevent heart disease, diabetes, and a host of other diseases. Aerobic exercise also causes the release of catecholamine endorphins throughout the body, which results in a feeling of well-being and a reduction in anxiety. Psychologically, exercise can increase self-esteem while decreasing muscle tension. Another benefit of exercise is that it is one of the best ways to lose weight.

Examples of various aerobic exercises include jogging, walking, bicycle riding, and using a stair stepper. For aerobic exercise to be effective, you need to increase your heart rate to 60–80% of the maximum heart rate. To find your maximum heart rate, subtract your current age from 220. Next, figure out your target heart rate by multiplying your maximum heart rate by .7 (70% of your maximum heart rate). If your heart rate is below 60%, pick up the pace. If it's above 80%, then slow down. Exercising 30 minutes a day, four to seven times a week will not only reduce stress but also improve cardiovascular function and the body's immunological response to stress-related disorders.

Behavioral changes are a third way you can buffer the harmful effects of stress. The following examples demonstrate how positive behaviors can help in the management of stress.

Nutrition is a behavioral change used to decrease stress. When the body is under stress, the digestive system doesn't function properly. This results in food not being properly digested and nutrients not being absorbed into the stomach. Stress also causes deficiencies in protein, magnesium, calcium, and vitamins B, C, and D. Balanced nutrition is essential in the fight against stress. Lacking appropriate nutrients decreases the body's ability to fight stress. Ness and Powles (1997) reported that diets low in fruits and vegetables and high in saturated fats were associated with cardiovascular heart disease, diabetes, and some cancers.

A healthy diet includes daily servings of whole grains, fresh vegetables, fresh fruit, low-fat dietary products, and protein from lean meat, dairy, and beans. A healthy diet should also include essential vitamins and minerals, fatty acids, and carbohydrates. Chocolate, used wisely and in moderation, can help with stress by activating the body's release of mood-enhancing opiates, which causes you to experience a pleasant mood. Stress can also make you turn to dangerous comfort foods that are starchy and salty and can thus result in weight gain. Snacking on low-calorie, low-fat foods such as fresh fruits, pretzels, and unbuttered popcorn can help keep weight down. Stress also increases cravings for snacks that are high in sugar and fat. The increased energy from sugars is only short term and results in decreased blood sugar later and a loss of energy.

Problem-focused coping is another behavioral technique used to decrease stress. Developed by Lazarus (1966), this method allows you to develop strategies for removing the stressor. The procedure in utilizing this technique is achieved by educating a person about the problem, changing behaviors, and taking action. Through the process of planning, you are able to take time in forming an action plan that will either overturn the threatening circumstances or at least decrease its harmful effects. Problem-focused coping can be seen in the following example, where Tim is experiencing stress at work because his boss is a demanding Type A personality. Every day, Tim hears his coworkers speak angrily about work. Tim is aware of the harmful effects of stress and chooses to deal with the problem in a proactive manner. His high level of motivation to change has encouraged him to give up cigarettes and coffee, eat healthful foods, enroll in a yoga class, exercise five times a week, go to a weekly support group for employees who work in a negative environment, and vent his feelings about his boss to friends who are empathetic. By using problem-focused coping, Tim is able to be happy and productive at work. According to Meichenbaum (1974), you should perceive a threat or a provocation as a problem that needs to be solved, and identify and evaluate what aspects of the situation have potential for changing. Lazarus and Folkman (1984) view problem-focused coping as a process that focuses on

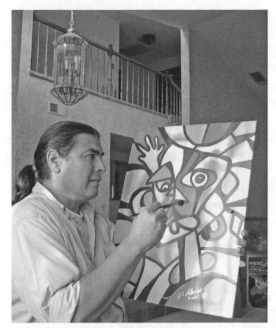

problem-solving strategies that include generating solutions, weighing alternatives, and learning new skills and behaviors in order to overcome the stressor.

Creative arts such as art, music, dance, and writing are healthy behaviors that enable you to gain self-awareness and cope with the symptoms of stress. Creative arts help a person who is experiencing stressors to express hidden emotions. This aids in the reduction of stress, fear, and anxiety.

Through art you are able to express and even project thoughts and feelings about stress, anxiety, and fears. Wolberg (1995) stated that individuals may project their conflicts into a physical form through art and thus express their feelings. Art can be helpful when you're experiencing stress and at the same time having trouble verbalizing feelings. Engaging in artwork triggers internal body activity that contributes to relaxation by decreasing a person's heart rate and blood pressure.

FIGURE 16.20 *The great artist J. S. Valencia relaxes with art.*

Music is another way to relieve stress. Coordinated musical resonance may evoke pleasure, while rhythmic cadence stimulates motor activity and relieves stress (Wolberg, 1995). By singing, you can express emotions that concern inner feelings of fear and frustration. Fultz (1966) reported that music may serve to promote self-confidence and control hyperactivity. Dance and movement help you communicate feelings and conflicts. Dance allows for emotional release and helps relieve anxiety. A solo dance performance, improvisations, folk dancing, and ballroom dancing help externalize feelings (Rosen, 1957). Writing is another excellent way to express feelings when you are having trouble verbalizing emotions. Writing promotes the connection between the conscious and the unconscious. This connection increases the self-understanding needed in order to cope with stress.

Chapter Summary

Health is a state of physical, mental, and social well-being. The six subcategories of optimal health include physical, emotional, social, intellectual, occupational, and spiritual health. Physical and emotional reactions to stress can strain your body's reserves and eventually cause damage. There is ample evidence of a strong association between stress and disease. What is also clear is that you have the opportunity to avoid the harmful and deadly effects of stress.

Types of stressors include frustration, daily hassles, pressures, conflicts, and traumatic events. Holmes and Rahe attempted to quantify the impact of stressors by using life change units (LCUs) to predict the likelihood of succumbing to illness. Although this strategy was ambitious, it failed to take into account several important factors in determining whether any given person is likely to be made ill by having to cope with a large number of stressful life experiences.

When you appraise an event as threatening, your sympathetic nervous system is aroused and mobilizes the body to defend against the perceived threat. The physiological activation of the fight-or-flight mechanism can be helpful in dealing with a momentarily stressful situation. If the experience of stress becomes chronic and overwhelming, there can be possible destruction to the body's immunological system. Hans Selye discovered this process and termed it the General Adaptation Syndrome (GAS). The GAS begins with the alarm stage, is followed by the resistance stage, and ends with the exhaustion stage. This last stage can result in disease, and possibly even death.

Personality factors also contribute to your ability to cope with stress. Positive personality factors such as having an internal locus of control, hardiness, self-efficacy, optimism, and Type B personality help you cope. Hardy people perceive stressors as challenges they can overcome. Negative personality factors that include an external locus of control, pessimism, learned helplessness, and Type A personality can cause you to appraise stressors as threatening. This can result in an experience of stress that is physiologically and emotionally overwhelming to the body. Social factors also play an important role in helping people manage stress. Having social support during times of stress makes us much less vulnerable to being harmed by it.

People may deal with stress in ineffective ways, such as by becoming aggressive, withdrawing from the situation, employing defense mechanisms, or using psychoactive drugs. On the other hand, successful management of stress is the key to a happy and healthy life. This is accomplished by changing your thoughts, physiology, and behaviors. Life's stressors can often be reframed as challenges rather than threats. Incorporating a consistent stress management program of exercise, nutrition, relaxation, cognitive restructuring, creativity, and optimistic thinking will benefit a person's mental health and physical well-being, and at the same time neutralize the negative effects of stress.

Knowledge Builder

RELATE TO YOURSELF

1. List all the stressors that you are currently experiencing. What type of stress management program could you following in order to buffer your stress?

   _____

   _____

   _____

2. Do you have a stress management program? If so, what stress management techniques are you currently practicing? If not, what type of stress management techniques would you like to begin using?

   _____

   _____

   _____

3. Going back to the last three generations in your family, write down the health issues of each family member. Who in your family may have had a stress-related illness?

   _____

   _____

   _____

4. Are you a Type A or Type B personality? How has your type of personality helped you achieve your goals? How has it prevented you from not getting what you want in life?

   _____

   _____

   _____

   _____

CHAPTER REVIEW QUESTIONS

1. The parasympathetic nervous system triggers the fight-or-flight response. **T or F?**

2. Research has shown a connection between stress and illness. **T or F?**

3. Projection is an example of a defense mechanism. **T or F?**

4. It's been proved that chronic use of alcohol greatly decreases the intensity of stress. **T or F?**

5. Chronic stimulation of the sympathetic nervous system lowers antibodies. **T or F?**

6. Depletion of serotonin in the blood during stress can result in depression. **T or F?**

7. The relaxation that one feels after drinking alcohol is due to the stimulation of the _____ receptors.

    (a) ABBA   (b) REM

    (c) GABA   (d) PABA

8. _____ is the study of the effects of psychological factors on the immune system.

    (a) Biophysics   (b) Psychoneuroimmunology

    (c) Physiology   (d) Psychology

9. The _____ produce(s) epinephrine and norepinephrine.

    (a) lymphocytes   (b) parasympathetic nervous system

    (c) heart   (d) sympathetic nervous system

10. Positive experiences in life that cancel out the harmful effects of hassles are called _____ .

    (a) uplifts   (b) stressors

    (c) downlifts   (d) psychoactive drugs

11. *Consider the following scenario:* Your best friend, Brenda, has had a three-year stormy relationship with her boyfriend, Ted. Today, Brenda got into an argument with him. Following the argument, she visits you at your home. Even though you're friendly toward her, Brenda is verbally abusive to you. Suddenly, she begins to cry and says, "I don't know why I act this way toward you." What can you tell Brenda to help her understand why she is behaving this way?

_____

_____

_____

_____

12. *Consider the following scenario:* New Orleans has been your home for the last 10 years. You love the city's history, music, food, and lifestyle. Suddenly, you're warned that Hurricane Katrina will be hitting New Orleans in less than a day. You decide to stay at a shelter during the hurricane. You survive the disaster, but the following day you see dead bodies floating in the water. The next day you feel emotionally numb, hypervigilant, and distressed whenever you're reminded of the hurricane. You then begin to have flashbacks, insomnia, and a sense of a foreshortened future. How do you explain your condition?

_____

_____

_____

_____

13. *CRITICAL THINKING EXERCISE.* What are the similarities and differences between frustration and hassles?

_____

_____

_____

_____

14. *CRITICAL THINKING EXERCISE.* What is the relationship between serotonin and depression?

_____

_____

_____

_____

USEFUL WEB SITES

THE STRESS MANAGEMENT SOCIETY

http//www.stress.org.uk

This site has a free stress guide and also a Web shop for purchasing stress management products.

STRESS EDUCATION CENTER

http://www.distress.com

This site has a certified stress management program for those interested in helping others who are experiencing stress.

STRESS FREE NET

http://www.stressfree.com

This is a good site for those interested in assessing and measuring their stress level. You can even speak to a psychologist about your stress.

NATIONAL CENTER FOR PTSD

http://www.ncptsd.org

This site was created within the Department of Veterans Affairs to address the science of PTSD. It has valuable information on the psychological effects of Hurricane Katrina and the war in Iraq.

AMERICAN INSTITUTE OF STRESS

http://stress.org

A nonprofit organization dedicated to understanding the effects of stress on health, the mind-body relationship, and self-healing.

TOWNSEND INTERNATIONAL PTY LTD

http://www.stresstips.com

This Web site offers a free weekly stress management journal. It also contains stress management tips, relaxation CDs, and lots of practical resources for people who are stressed.

STRESS MANAGEMENT RESOURCE CENTRE

http://www.davidposen.com/pages/resmain.html

This Web site provides straightforward advice on how to manage stress and take control of your life. It contains good tips on coping with stress on the job and also during the holidays.

References

Abduction of Barney and Betty Hill. (n.d.). Retrieved on July 29, 2005, from http://www.subversiveelement.com/alienAbductionHills~ns4.html

Abel, G. G., & Osborn, C. (1992). The paraphilias. The extent and nature of sexually deviant and criminal behavior. *Psychiatric Clinics of North America, 15*(3), 675–687.

Abrams, R. (1992). *Electroconvulsive therapy.* New York: Oxford University Press.

Adami, P., Konig, P., Vetter, Z., Hausmann, A., & Conca, A. (2006). Post-traumatic stress disorder and amygdala-hippocampectomy. *Acta Psychiatrica Scandinavica, 113*(4), 360–364.

Addolorato, G., Leggio, L., Abenavoli, L., & Gasbarrini, G. (2005). Neurobiochemical and clinical aspects of craving in alcohol addiction: A review. *Addictive Behaviors, 30*(6), 1209–1224.

Ader, R., & Cohen, N. (1975). Behaviorally conditioned immunosuppression. *Psychosomatic Medicine, 37*(4), 333–340.

Adler, A. (1930). *The education of children.* Chicago: Henry Regnery.

Aiello, J. R., & Douthitt, E. A. (2001). Social facilitation from Triplett to electronic performance monitoring. *Group Dynamics: Theory, Research, and Practice, 5,* 163–180.

Ainsworth, M. (1973). The development of infant-mother attachment. In B. Caldwell & H. Ricciuti (Eds.), *Review of child development research* (pp. 49–68). Chicago: University of Chicago Press.

Ainsworth, M., Blehar, M. C., Waters, E., & Wall, S. (1978). *Patterns of attachment: A psychological study of the strange situation.* Hillsdale, NJ: Lawrence Erlbaum.

Albers, L. J., Hahn, R. K., & Reist, C. (2004). *Handbook of psychiatric drugs.* Laguna Hills, CA: Current Clinical Strategies Publishing.

Alexander, T. (2007). *Personal development and human relations: A lamp along the way.* Boston: Pearson Custom Publishing.

Allport, G. W. (1937). *Personality: A psychological interpretation.* New York: Holt, Rinehart and Winston.

Allport, G. W. (1954). *The nature of prejudice.* Reading, MA: Addison-Wesley.

Allport, G. W., & Odbert, H. S. (1936). Trait-names: A psycho-lexical study. *Psychological Monographs: General and Applied, 47,* 1–21.

Allyon, T., & Azrin, N. H. (1965). The measurement and reinforcement of behavior of psychotics. *Journal of the Experimental Analysis of Behavior, 8,* 557–583.

Alzheimer's Association. (2003). *New Alzheimer projections add urgency to search for prevention, cure.* Retrieved October 28, 2005, from http://www.gswi.org/current_issues/AD_projections.htm

American Psychiatric Association. (2000a). *The diagnostic and statistical manual of mental disorders* (4th ed.). Washington, DC: Author.

American Psychiatric Association. (2000b). *Practice guidelines for the treatment of patients with major depressive disorder* (2nd ed.). Washington, DC: Author.

American Psychological Association. (2003). *Careers for the twenty-first century.* Washington, DC: Author.

American Psychological Association. (2006). *2003 Doctorate employment survey.* Washington, DC: APA Research Office.

Amir, Y. (1969). Contact hypothesis in ethnic relations. *Psychological Bulletin, 71*(5), 319–342.

Amir, Y. (1976). The role of intergroup contact in change of prejudice and ethnic relations. In P. A. Katz (Ed.), *Toward the elimination of racism* (pp. 73–123). New York: Plenum Press.

Anand, B. K., & Brobeck, J. R. (1951). Hypothalamic control of food intake in rats and cats. *Yale Journal of Biological Medicine, 24,* 123–140.

Anderson, C. A., & Bushman, B. J. (2001). Effects of violent video games on aggressive behavior, aggressive cognition, aggressive affect, physiological arousal, and prosocial behavior: A meta-analytic review of the scientific literature. *Psychological Science, 12*(5), 353–359.

Anderson, C. A., Bushman, B. J., & Groom, R. W. (1997). Hot years and seriously deadly assault: Empirical test of the heat hypothesis. *Journal of Personality and Social Psychology, 73,* 1213–1223.

Anderson, D. J. (2007, December). Genes and circuits for emotional behavior in mice and flies. Lecture at Cal Tech, Pasadena, CA.

Anderson, I. (2000). Selective serotonin reuptake inhibitors versus tricyclic antidepressants: A meta-analysis of efficacy and tolerability. *Journal of Affective Disorders, 58*(1), 19–36.

Anderson, R. C., Pihert, J. W., Goetz, E. T., Schallert, D. L., Stevens, K. V., & Trollip, S. R. (1976). Instantiation of general terms. *Journal of Verbal Learning and Verbal Behavior, 15,* 667–679.

Anderson, S. R., & Lightfoot, D. W. (1999). The human language faculty as an organ. *Annual Review of Physiology, 62,* 697–722.

Antill, J. K. (1983). Sex role complementarity versus similarity in married couples. *Journal of Personality and Social Psychology, 45,* 145–155.

Aronson, E. (1998). Dissonance, hypocrisy, and the self-concept. In E. Harmon-Jones & J. S. Mills (Eds.), *Cognitive dissonance theory: Revival with revisions and controversies* (pp. 21–36). Washington, DC: American Psychological Association.

Arwas, S., Rolnick, A., & Lubow, R. E. (1989). Conditioned taste aversion in humans using motion-induced sickness as the US. *Behavioral Research and Therapy, 27*(3), 295–301.

Asch, S. E. (1951). Effects of group pressure on the modification and distortion of judgments. In H. Guetzkow (Ed.), *Group, leadership, and men* (pp. 177–190). Pittsburgh: Carnegie University Press.

Asimov, I. (1997). *Isaac Asimov's book of facts.* New York: Random House (Wings Books).

Aston-Jones, G., & Cohen, J. D. (2005). An integrative theory of locus coeruleus-norepinephrine function: Adaptive gain and optimal performance. *Annual Review of Neuroscience, 28,* 403–450.

Atkinson, R. C., & Shiffrin, R. M. (1968). Human memory: A control system and its control processes. In K. W. Spence (Ed.), *The psychology of learning and motivation* (pp. 90–195). New York: Academic Press.

Axtell, R. E. (1993). *Do's and taboos around the world* (3rd ed.). New York: John Wiley.

B

Bachman, R., & Peralta, R. (2002). The relationship between drinking and violence in an adolescent population: Does gender matter? *Deviant Behavior: An Interdisciplinary Journal, 23,* 1–19.

Bagemihl, B. (1999). *Biological exuberance: Animal homosexuality and natural diversity.* New York: St. Martin's Press.

Bahrick, H. P., & Hall, L. K. (1991). Lifetime maintenance of high school mathematics content. *Journal of Experimental Psychology: General, 120,* 54–75.

Bailey, J. M. (1999). A family history study of male sexual orientation using three independent samples. *Behavior Genetics, 29*(2), 79–86.

Bailey, J. M., & Pillard, R. C. (1991). A genetic study of male sexual orientation. *Archives of General Psychiatry, 48,* 1089–1096.

Baker, R. A. (1998, February). A view of hypnosis. *Harvard Mental Health Letter, 14*(8), 5.

Baker-Ward, L., Gordon, B., Ornstein, P. A., Larus, D., & Chubb, P. (1993). Young children's long-term retention of a pediatric examination. *Child Development, 64,* 1519–1533.

Balon, R. (1998). Pharmacological treatment of paraphilias with a focus on antidepressants. *Journal of Sex and Marital Therapy, 24*(4), 241–254.

Bandura, A. (1977). Self-efficacy: Toward a unifying theory of behavioral change. *Psychological Review, 84,* 191–215.

Bandura, A. (1995). *Self-efficacy in changing societies.* Cambridge: Cambridge University Press.

Bandura, A., Ross, D., & Ross, S. A. (1961). Transmission of aggression through imitation of aggressive models. *Journal of Abnormal and Social Psychology, 63,* 575–582.

Barash, D. P., & Lipton, J. E. (1997). *Making sense of sex: How genes and gender influence our relationships.* Washington, DC: Island Press.

Bard, P. (1934). On emotional expression after decortication with some remarks on certain theoretical views: Part I. *Psychological Review, 41,* 309–329.

Barlow, D. H. (2002). *Anxiety and its disorders: The nature and treatment of anxiety and panic* (2nd ed.). New York: Guilford.

Baron, R. S. (1986). Distraction/conflict theory: Progress and problems. In L. Berkowitz (Ed.), *Advances in experimental social psychology* (Vol. 19, pp. 1–40). Orlando, FL: Academic Press.

Bartlett, F. C. (1932). *Remembering.* Cambridge, England: Cambridge University Press.

Bates, J. E. (1987). Temperament in infancy. In J. Osofsky (Ed.), *Handbook of infant development* (2nd ed., pp. 1101–1149). Oxford, England: John Wiley & Sons.

Bates, J. E., Bayles, K., Bennett, D. S., Ridge, B., & Brown, M. M. (1991). Origins of externalizing behavior problems at eight years of age. In D. J. Pepler & K. H. Rubin (Eds.), *The development and treatment of childhood aggression* (pp. 93–120). Hillsdale, NJ: Erlbaum Associates.

Batson, C. D. (1991). *The altruism question: Toward a social-psychological answer.* Hillsdale, NJ: Erlbaum.

Baumrind, D. (1966). Effects of authoritative parental control on child behavior. *Child Development, 37,* 887–907.

Baumrind, D. (1989). Rearing competent children. In W. Damon (Ed.), *Child development today and tomorrow* (pp. 349–378). San Francisco: Jossey-Bass.

Baumrind, D. (1991a). The influence of parenting style on adolescent competence and substance use. *Journal of Early Adolescence, 11,* 56–95.

Baumrind, D. (1991b). Parenting styles and adolescent development. In J. Brooks-Gunn, R. Lerner, & A. C. Peterson (Eds.), *Encyclopedia of adolescence* (pp. 746–758). New York: Garland.

Beck, A. T. (1991). Cognitive therapy: A 30-year retrospective. *American Psychologist, 46,* 368–375.

Beck, A. T. (1993). Cognitive therapy: Past, present, and future. *Journal of Consulting and Clinical Psychology, 63,* 919–927.

Beck, A. T., Freeman, A., & Associates. (1990). *Cognitive therapy of personal disorders.* New York: Guilford.

Begley, S. (1998, January 19). Aping language. *Newsweek, 131,* 56–58.

Bellisle, F. (1999). Glutamate and the UMAMI taste: Sensory, metabolic, nutritional and behavioural considerations. A review of the literature published in the last 10 years. *Neuroscience & Biobehavioral Reviews, 23*(3), 423–438.

Bellugi, U., Korenberg, J. R., & Kilma, E. S. (2001). Williams's syndrome: An exploration of neurocognitive and genetic features. *Journal of Clinical Neurosciences Research, 1*[Special issue] 217–229.

Bem, S. L. (1974). The measurement of psychological androgyny. *Journal of Consulting and Clinical Psychology, 42,* 151–165.

Bensen, H. (1975). *The relaxation response.* New York: William Morris.

Berger, R. J., & Oswald, I. (1962). Effects of sleep deprivation on behaviour, subsequent sleep, and dreaming. *Journal of Mental Science, 108,* 457–465.

Berkowitz, L. (1992). College men as perpetrators of acquaintance rape and sexual assault: A review of recent research. *Journal of American College Health, 40,* 175–181.

Berkowitz, L. (1993). *Aggression: Its causes, consequences and control.* New York: McGraw-Hill.

Bernhardt, P. C. (1997). Influence of serotonin and testosterone in aggression and dominance: Convergence with social psychology. *Current Directions in Psychological Science, 6,* 44–48.

Berns, G. (2005). *Satisfaction: The science of finding true fulfillment.* New York: Henry Holt.

Bernstein, D., Penner, L., Clarke-Stewart, A., & Roy, E. (2006). *Psychology* (7th ed.). Boston: Houghton Mifflin.

Bernstein, D. A., Penner, L. A., Clarke-Stewart, A., & Roy, E. J. (2008). *Psychology* (8th ed.). Boston: Houghton Mifflin.

Berscheid, E., & Reis, H. T. (1998). Attraction and close relationships. In D. T. Gilbert, S. T. Fiske, & G. Lindzey (Eds.), *The handbook of social psychology* (4th ed., Vol. 2, pp. 193–281). New York: McGraw-Hill.

Bertelsen, B., Harvald, B., & Hauge, M. (1977). A Danish twin study of manic-depressive disorders. *British Journal of Psychiatry, 130,* 330–351.

Betty and Barney Hill Abduction. (n.d.). Retrieved July 20, 2005, from http://www.ufocasebook.com/Hill.htm

Bickman, L., & Dokecki, P. (1989). Public and private responsibility for mental health services. *American Psychologist, 44*(8), 1133–1137.

Biederman, I. (1993). Visual object recognition. In A. I. Goldman (Ed.), *Readings in philosophy and cognitive science.* Cambridge, MA: MIT Press.

Biederman, I., Rabinowitz, J., Glass, A., & Stacy, E. (1974). On the information extracted from a glance at a scene. *Journal of Experimental Psychology, 103,* 597–600.

Biello, S., & Dafters, R. (2001). MDMA and fenfluramine alter the response of the circadian clock to a serotonin agonist in vitro. *Brain Research, 920,* 202–209.

Bloom, L., Rocissano, L., & Hood, L. (1976). Adult-child discourse: Developmental interaction between information processing and linguistic knowledge. *Cognitive Psychology, 8,* 521–552.

Bohart, A. C. (1995). The person-centered therapies. In A. S. Gurman & S. B. Messer (Eds.), *Essential psychotherapies* (pp. 107–148). New York: Guilford.

Bolles, R. C., Collier, A. C., Bouton, M. E., & Marlin, N. A. (1978). Some tricks for ameliorating the trace-conditioning deficit. *Bulletin of the Psychonomic Society, 11*(6), 403–406.

Booth, A., & Dabbs, J. M. (1993). Testosterone and men's marriages. *Social Forces, 72,* 463–477.

Bornstein, M. H. (1992a). Perception across the life cycle. In M. H. Bornstein & M. E. Lamb (Eds.), *Developmental psychology: An advanced textbook.* Hillsdale, NJ: Lawrence Erlbaum Associates.

Bornstein, R. F. (1992b). The dependent personality: Developmental, social, and clinical perspectives. *Psychological Bulletin, 112,* 3–23.

Bouchard, T. J., Jr. (1997a). The genetics of personality. In K. Blum & E. P. Noble (Eds.), *Handbook of psychiatric genetics* (pp. 273–296). Boca Raton, FL: CRC Press.

Bouchard, T. J., Jr., (1997b). IQ similarity in twins reared apart: Findings and response to critics. In R. J. Sternberg & E. Grigorenko (Eds.), *Intelligence, heredity, and environment* (pp. 479–502). New York: Cambridge University Press.

Bouchard, T. J., Jr., & Loehlin, J. C. (2001). Genes, evolution, and personality. *Behavior Genetics, 31*(3), 243–273.

Bourne, L. E., Dominowski, R. L., Loftus, E. F., & Healy, A. F. (1986). *Cognitive processes* (2nd ed.). Englewood Cliffs, NJ: Prentice Hall.

Bouton, M. E., & Bolles, R. C. (1979). Contextual control of the extinction of conditioned fear. *Learning and Motivation, 10*(4), 445–466.

Bowden, C., Lecrubier, Y., Bauer, K., Goodwin, G., Greil, W., Sachs, G., et al. (2000). Maintenance therapies for classic and other forms of bipolar disorder. *Journal of Affective Disorders, 59*(1), S57–S67.

Bower, G. H. (1973, October). How to ... uh ... remember! *Psychology Today,* 63–70.

Bower, S. A., & Bower, G. H. (1991). *Asserting yourself: A practical guide for positive change.* Reading, MA: Addison-Wesley. (Original work published 1976)

Bowlby, J. (1980). *Attachment and loss: Loss.* London: Hogarth.

Boyatzis, R. E., Goleman, D., & Rhee, K. S. (2000). Clustering competence in emotional intelligence: Insights from the emotional competence inventory. In R. Baron & J. D. A. Parker (Eds.), *Handbook of emotional intelligence: Theory, development, assessment, and application at home, school, and in the workplace.* San Francisco, CA: Jossey-Bass.

Boyd, N. (2000). *The beast within: Why men are violent.* London: Greystone Books.

Bradford, J. M. W., Boulet, J., & Pawlak, A. (1992). A multiplicity of deviant behaviors. *Canadian Journal of Psychiatry, 37*(2), 104–108.

Breedlove, M. S., Rosenzweig, M. R., & Watson, N. V. (2007). *Biological psychology: An introduction to behavioral, cognitive and clinical neuroscience* (5th ed.). Sunderland, MA: Sinauer Associates.

Brehm, S., Kassin, S., & Fein, S. (2005). *Social Psychology* (6th ed.). Boston: Houghton Mifflin.

Breier, A. (2001). A new era in the pharmacotherapy of psychotic disorders. *Journal of Clinical Psychiatry, 62*(Suppl. 2), 3–5.

Briere, J., & Lanktree, C. (1983). Sex role-related effects of sex bias in language. *Sex Roles, 9,* 625–632.

Brislin, R. W. (1993). *Understanding culture's influence on behavior.* Fort Worth, TX: Harcourt Brace.

Brody, J. E. (2000a, April 25). Memories of things that never were. *New York Times,* D8.

Brody, L. R. (2000b). The socialization of gender differences in emotional expression: Display rules, infant temperament, and differentiation. In A. H. Fischer (Ed.), *Gender and emotion: Social psychological perspectives* (pp. 24–47). New York: Cambridge University Press.

Brooks, L. J., Haskins, D. G., & Kehe, J. V. (2004). Counseling and psychotherapy with African American clients. In T. B. Smith (Ed.), *Practicing multiculturalism: Affirming diversity in counseling and psychology* (pp. 145–166). San Francisco: Pearson.

Brown, D. P., Scheflin, A. W., & Hammond, D. C. (1998). *Memory, trauma treatment, and the law.* New York: W. W. Norton.

Brown, J. (1958). Some tests of the decay theory of immediate memory. *Quarterly Journal of Experimental Psychology, 10,* 12–21.

Brown, R., & Kulik, J. (1977). Flashbulb memories. *Cognition, 5,* 73–99.

Bruck, M., Cavanaugh, P., & Ceci, S. (1991). Forty something: Recognizing faces at one's 25th reunion. *Memory and Cognition, 19*(3), 221–228.

Bruck, M., Hembroke, H., & Ceci, S. J. (1997). Children's reports of pleasant and unpleasant events. In J. D. Read & D. S. Lindsay (Eds.), *Recollections* of trauma: Scientific evidence and clinical practice (pp. 45–51). New York: Plenum Press.

Brummet, P., Edgar, R., Hackett, N., Jewsbury, G., Taylor, A., Bailkey, N., et al. (2003). *Civilization past and present* (10th ed.). Boston: Allyn & Bacon.

Buchanan, T. W. (2007). Retrieval of emotional memories. *Psychological Bulletin, 133*(5), 761–779.

Buck, R. (1985). Prime theory: An integrated view of motivation and emotion. *Psychological Review, 92,* 389–413.

Bukatko, D., & Daehler, M. W. (2004). *Child development: A thematic approach* (5th ed.). Boston: Houghton Mifflin.

Burnham, M., Gaylor, E., & Anders, T. (2006). Sleep disorders. In J. Luby (Ed.), *Handbook of preschool mental health* (pp. 186–207). New York: Guilford Press.

Burnstein, E., Crandall, C. S., & Kitayama, S. (1994). Some neo-Darwin decision rules for altruism: Weighing clues for inclusive fitness as a function of the biological importance of the decision. *Journal of Personality and Social Psychology, 67,* 773–789.

Buss, D. M. (1991). Evolutionary personality psychology. *Annual Review of Psychology, 42,* 459–491.

Buss, D. (1994). *The evolution of desire: Strategies of human mating.* New York: Basic Books.

Buss, D. M. (1999). *Evolutionary psychology: The new science of the mind.* Boston: Allyn & Bacon.

Buss, D. M., Larsen, R. J., Westen, D., & Semmelroth, J. (1992). Sex differences in jealousy: Evolution, physiology, and psychology. *Psychological Science, 3*(4), 251–255.

C

Cahill, L. (2005, May). His brain, her brain. *Scientific American, 292,* 40–47.

Cain, W. S. (1973). Spatial discrimination of cutaneous warm. *American Journal of Psychology, 86,* 169–181.

Cannon, W. B. (1927). The James-Lange theory of emotions: A critical examination and an alternative theory. *American Journal of Psychology, 39,* 106–124.

Cannon, W. B., & Washburn, A. L. (1912). An explanation of hunger. *American Journal of Physiology, 29,* 441–454.

Carey, F. (1977). The child as a word learner. In M. Halle, J. Bresnan, & G. Miller (Eds.), *Linguistic theory and psychological reality* (pp. 264–293). Cambridge, MA: MIT Press.

Carli, L. L., Ganley, R., & Pierce-Otay, A. (1991). Similarity and satisfaction in roommate relationships. *Personality and Social Psychology Bulletin, 17*(4), 104–113.

Carnegie, D. (1936). *How to win friends and influence people.* New York: Simon & Schuster.

Carpenter, S. (2000). Psychologists tackle neuroimaging at APA-sponsored Advanced Training Institute. *Monitor on Psychology, 31,* 42–43.

Cartford, M. C., Gould, T., & Bickford, P. C. (2004). A central role for norepinephrine in the modulation of cerebellar learning tasks. *Behavioral & Cognitive Neuroscience Reviews, 3*(2), 131–138.

Caselli, M. C., Bates, E., & Casadio, P. (1995). A cross-linguistic study of early lexical development. *Cognitive Development, 10,* 159–199.

Castillo, R. J. (1997). *Culture and mental illness: A client-centered approach.* Pacific Grove, CA: Brooks/Cole.

Catchpole, C. K., & Rowell, A. (1993). Song sharing and local dialects in a population of the European wren Troglodytes troglodytes. *Behaviour, 125,* 67–78.

Cattell, R. B. (1950). *Personality: A systematic, theoretical, and factual study.* New York: McGraw-Hill.

Cattell, R. B. (1965). *The scientific analysis of personality.* Baltimore: Penguin.

Cattell, R. B. (1990). Advances in Cattellian personality theory. In L. A. Pervin (Ed.), *Handbook of personality: Theory and research* (pp. 101–110). New York: Guilford Press.

Centers for Disease Control. (2005). HIV prevalence, unrecognized infection and HIV testing among men who have sex with men—five US cities—June 2004–April 2005. *Journal of American Medical Association, 294,* 674–676.

Chamberlain, S. R., del Campo, N., Dowson, J., Muller, U., Clark, L., Robbins, T. W., et al. (2007). Atomoxetine improved response inhibition in adults with attention deficit/hyperactivity disorder. *Biological Psychiatry, 62*(9), 977–984.

Chen, F., & Kenrick, D. T. (2002). Repulsion or attraction?: Group membership and assumed attitude similarity. *Journal of Personality and Social Psychology, 83*(1), 111–125.

Chen, N. Y., Shaffer, D. R., & Wu, C. H. (1997). On physical attractiveness stereotyping in Taiwan: A revised sociocultural perspective. *Journal of Social Psychology, 137,* 117–124.

Cheny, D. L., & Seyfarth, R. M. (1990). *How monkeys see the world.* Chicago: University of Chicago Press.

Chomsky, N. (1965). *Aspects of the theory of syntax.* Cambridge, MA: MIT Press.

Chomsky, N. (1975). *Reflections on language.* New York: Praeger.

Chomsky, N. (1986). *Knowledge of language: Its nature, origin, and its use.* New York: Praeger.

Chomsky, N. (1987). Language in a psychological setting. *Sophia Linguistica Working Papers in Linguistics, No. 22,* 567–574 (Sophia University, Tokyo).

Chomsky, N. (1990). *On the nature, use, and acquisition of language.* In W. G. Lycan (Ed.), *Mind and cognition* (pp. 627–646). Oxford, England: Blackwell.

Clark, D. A., & Beck, A. T. (1999). *Scientific foundations of cognitive theory and therapy for depression.* New York: Wiley.

Clark, R. W. (1971). *Einstein: The life and times.* New York: World Publishing.

Cochran, S. D., & Mays, V. M. (1990). Sex, lies, and HIV. *New England Journal of Medicine, 322,* 774–775.

Cohen, L. B. (1972). Attention-getting and attention-holding processes of infant visual preference. *Child Development, 43,* 869–879.

Cohen, L. B., Deloache, J. S., & Strauss, M. S. (1979). Infant visual perception. In J. Osofsky (Ed.), *Handbook of infant development.* New York: Wiley.

Cohen, S., Tyrrell, D. A. J., & Smith, A. (1993). Negative life events, perceived stress, negative affect, and susceptibility to the common cold. *Journal of Personality and Social Psychology, 64,* 131–140.

Cohen, S., & Williamson, G. (1988). Perceived stress in a probability sample in the United States. In S. Spacapan & S. Oskamp (Eds.), *The social psychology of health* (pp. 31–67). Newberry Park, CA: Sage.

Cohen, S., & Wills, T. A. (1985). Stress, social support and the buffering hypothesis. *Psychological Bulletin, 98,* 310–357.

Colburn, S. H., Shinn-Cunningham, B., Kidd, Jr., G., & Durlach, N. (2006). The perceptual consequences of binaural hearing. *International Journal of Audiology, 45*(Suppl. 1), S34–S44.

Cole, R. P., & Miller, R. R. (1999). Conditioned excitation and conditioned inhibition acquired through backward conditioning. *Learning & Motivation, 30*(2), 129–156.

Coleman, D. I. (1979). Obesity genes: Beneficial effects in heterozygous mice. *Science, 203,* 663–665.

Collins, D. W., & Kimura, D. (1997). A large sex difference on a two-dimensional mental rotation task. *Behavioral Neuroscience, 111,* 845–849.

Comas-Diaz, L. (1997). Mental health needs of Latinos with professional status. In J. G. Garcia & M. C. Zea (Eds.), *Psychological intervention and research with Latino populations* (pp. 142–165). Boston: Allyn & Bacon.

Compton, W. (2005). *Introduction to positive psychology.* Belmont, CA: Thomson Wadsworth.

Constantini, M., & Haggard, P. (2007). The rubber hand illusion: Sensitivity and reference frame for body ownership. *Consciousness and Cognition: An International Journal, 16*(2), 229–240.

Cook, D. A., & Wiley, C. Y. (2000). Psychotherapy with members of African American churches and spiritual traditions. In P. S. Richards & A. E. Bergin (Eds.), *Handbook of psychotherapy and religious diversity* (pp. 369–396). Washington, DC: American Psychological Association.

Cook, E. W., III, Hodes, R. L., & Lang, P. J. (1986). Preparedness and phobia: Effects of stimulus content on human visceral conditioning. *Journal of Abnormal Psychology, 95,* 195–207.

Coren, S., Ward, L. M., & Enns, J. T. (1999). *Sensation and perception* (5th ed.). Orlando, FL: Harcourt Brace College Publishers.

Corey, G., & Corey, M. S. (1993). *I never knew I had a choice.* Belmont, CA: Brooks/Cole.

Cory-Slechta, D. A., O'Mara, D. J., & Brockel, B. J. (1999). Learning versus performance impairments following regional administration of MK-801 into nucleus accumbens and dorsomedial striatum. *Behavioral Brain Research, 102*(1–2), 181–194.

Courage, M. L., & Adams, R. J. (1990). Visual acuity assessment from birth to three years using the acuity card procedures. *Optometry and Vision Science, 67,* 713–718.

Cowan, N. (1994). Mechanisms of verbal short-term memory. *Current Directions in Psychological Science, 3,* 185–189.

Cowan, W. M. (1979). The development of the brain. In *The brain: A scientific American book* (pp. 56–67). New York: W. H. Freeman.

Craik, F. I. M., & Lockhart, R. S. (1972). Levels of processing: A framework for memory research. *Journal of Verbal Learning & Verbal Behavior, 11,* 671–684.

Craik, F. I. M., & Tulving, E. (1975). Depth of processing and the retention of words in episodic memory. *Journal of Experimental Psychology, 104,* 268–294.

Cravens, H. (1992). A scientific project locked in time: The Terman genetic studies of genius, 1920s–1950s. *American Psychologist, 47,* 183–189.

Crews, D. J., & Lander, D. M. (1987). A meta-analytic review of aerobic fitness and reactivity to psychosocial stressors. *Medical Science Sport Exercise, 19,* S114–S120.

Crews, F. (1995). *The memory wars: Freud's legacy in dispute.* London: Granta.

Crowder, R. G. (1992). Sensory memory. In L. R. Squire (Ed.), *Encyclopedia of learning and memory* (pp. 607–609). New York: Macmillan.

Crowne, P. D. (2007). *Personality theory.* New York: Oxford University Press.

Csikszentmihalyi, M. (1996, July/August). The creative personality. *Psychology Today, 29,* 36–40.

Cunningham, A. E., Perry, K. E., & Stanovich, K. E. (2001). Converging evidence for the concept of orthographic processing. *Reading and Writing, 14*(5–6), 549–568.

Cunningham, A. J., Barbee, A. P., & Pike, C. L. (1990). What do women want? Facialmetric assessment of multiple motives in the perception of male physical attractiveness. *Journal of Personality and Social Psychology, 59,* 61–72.

D　Dahl, A. (1986). Some aspects of the DSM-III personality disorders illustrated by a consecutive sample of hospitalized patients. *Acta Psychiatrica Scandinavica, 73,* 61–66.

Dalgleish, T., Rosen, K., & Marks, M. (1996). Rhythm and blues: The theory and treatment of seasonal affective disorder. *British Journal of Clinical Psychology, 35*(2), 163–182.

Dalí, S. (2007). *Diary of a genius.* New York: Solar Books.

Daly, M., & Wilson, M. (1998). The evolutionary social psychology of family violence. In C. Crawford & D. Krebs (Eds.), *Handbook of evolutionary psychology: Ideas, issues and applications* (pp. 431–456). Mahwah, NJ: Erlbaum.

Damaiso, A. R. (2002, August). How the brain creates the mind [Electronic version]. *Scientific American,* 4–9.

Damasio, A. R. (2005). *Descartes' error: Emotion, reason, and the human brain* (paperback ed.). New York: Penguin Books.

Damasio, A. R., Damasio, H., & Van Hoesen, G. W. (1982). Prosopagnosia: Anatomical basis and behavioral mechanisms. *Neurology, 32,* 331–341.

Damasio, H., Grabowski, T. J., Tranel, D., Hichwa, R. D., & Damasio, A. R. (1996). A neural basis for lexical retrieval. *Nature, 380,* 499–505.

Darwin, C. (1874). *The descent of man, and selection in relation to sex* (2nd ed.). New York: A. L. Burt.

Darwin, C. (1979). *The expression of emotions in man and animals.* London: Julian Friedmann Publishers. (Original work published 1872)

Davis, M. (1974). Sensitization of the rat startle response by noise. *Journal of Comparative and Physiological Psychology, 87*(3), 571–581.

Davis, M., Robbins-Eshelman, E., & Mckay, M. (1996). *The relaxation & stress reduction book* (4th ed.). Oakland, CA: New Harbinger Publications.

Deaux, K., & LaFrance, M. (1998). Gender. In D. Gilbert, S. T. Fiske, & G. Lindzey (Eds.), *Handbook of social psychology* (4th ed., pp. 788–827). New York: Random House.

DeCasper, A. J., & Spence, M. J. (1986). Prenatal maternal speech influences newborns' perception of speech sounds. *Infant Behavior and Development, 9*, 133–150.

Deckers, L. (2001). *Motivation: Biological, psychological, and environmental.* Boston: Allyn & Bacon.

De La Cancela, V., & Guzman, L. P. (1991). Latino mental health service needs: Implications for training psychologists. In H. F. Meyers et al. (Eds.), *Ethnic minority perspectives on clinical training and services in psychology* (pp. 59–64). Washington, DC: American Psychological Association.

DeLongis, J. R., Folkman, S., & Lazarus, R. S. (1988). The impact of daily stress on health and mood: Psychological and social resources as mediators. *Journal of Personality and Social Psychology, 54*, 486–495.

Denis, M., & Kosslyn, S. M. (1999). Scanning visual images: A window on the mind. *Current Psychology of Cognition, 18*, 409–465.

Depue, R. A., Arbisi, P., Spoont, M. R., Leon, A., & Ainswoth, B. (1989). Dopamine functioning in the behavioral facilitation system and seasonal variation in behavior: Normal population and clinical studies. In N. E. Rosenthal & M. C. Blehar (Eds.), *Seasonal affective disorders and phototherapy* (pp. 230–259). New York: Guilford.

Depue, R. A., & Collins, P. F. (1999). Neurobiology of the structure of personality: Dopamine, facilitation of incentive motivation, and extraversion. *Behavioral and Brain Sciences, 22*, 491–517.

Desmond, E. W. (1987, November 30). Out in the open. *Time, 130*, 80–90.

Deutsch, M., & Gerard, H. G. (1955). A study of normative and informational social influence upon individual judgment. *Journal of Abnormal and Social Psychology, 51*, 629–636.

Diamond, A. (1985). The development of the ability to use recall to guide action as indicated by infants' performance on A-B. *Child Development, 56*, 868–883.

Diefendorff, J. M., & Richard, E. M. (2003). Antecedents and consequences of emotional display rule perceptions. *Journal of Applied Psychology, 88*, 284–294.

Diener, E. (1984). Subjective well-being. *Psychological Bulletin, 93*, 542–575.

Diesfeldt, H. (1990, December). Recognition memory for words and faces in primary degenerative dementia of the Alzheimer type and normal old age. *Journal of Clinical Experimental Neuropsychology, 12*(6), 931–945.

Digman, J. M. (1997). Higher-order factors of the Big Five. *Journal of Personality and Social Psychology, 73*(6), 1246–1256.

Dion, K., Berscheid, E., & Walster, E. (1972). What is beautiful is good. *Journal of Personality and Social Psychology, 24*, 285–290.

Dohrenwend, B. S., & Dohrenwend, B. P. (1981). Life stress and illness: Formulation of the issues. In B. S. Dohrenwend & B. P. Dohrenwend (Eds.), *Stressful life events and their contents* (pp. 1–27). New York: Prodist.

Domino, G., & Affonso, D. D. (1990). A personality measure of Erikson's life stages: The inventory of social balance. *Journal of Personality Assessment, 54,* 576–588.

Domjan, M. (2003). *The principles of learning and behavior* (5th ed.). Belmont, CA: Thomson/Wadsworth.

Domjan, M. (2006). *The principles of learning and behavior* (5th ed., active learning ed.). Belmont, CA: Thomson/Wadsworth.

Domjan, M., & Purdy, J. E. (1995). Animal research in psychology: More than meets the eye of the general psychology student. *American Psychologist, 50,* 496–503.

Doty, R. L. (2001). Olfaction. *Annual Review of Psychology, 52,* 423–452.

Dovidio, J. F., & Gaertner, S. L. (1996). Affirmative action, unintentional racial biases, and intergroup relations. *Journal of Social Issues, 52,* 51–57.

Draguns, J. G. (1990a). Applications of cross-cultural psychology in the field of mental health. In R. W. Brislin (Ed.), *Applied cross-cultural psychology* (pp. 302–324). Newbury Park, CA: Sage.

Draguns, J. G. (1990b). Normal and abnormal behavior in cross-cultural perspective: Specifying the nature of the relationship. *Nebraska Symposium on Motivation 1989, 37,* 235–277.

Duffy, F. H. (1994). The role of quantified electroencephalography in psychological research. In G. Dawson & K. W. Fischer (Eds.), *Human behavior and the developing brain* (pp. 125–143). New York: Wiley.

Duggan, J. P., & Booth, D. A. (1986). Obesity, overeating, and rapid gastric emptying in rats with ventromedial hypothalamic lesions. *Science, 231,* 609–611.

Duncker, K. (1945). On problem solving. *Psychological Monographs, 58*(5, Whole No. 270).

Dunn, J. (1988). Connections between relationships: Implications of research on mothers and siblings. In R. Hinde & J. Stevenson-Hinde (Eds.), *Relationships within families: Mutual influences.* Oxford: Clarendon Press.

Durgin, F. H., Evans, L., Dunphy, N., Klostermann, S., & Simmons, K. (2007). Rubber hands feel the touch of light. *Psychological Science, 18*(2), 152–157.

Dutton, D. G., & Aron, A. P. (1974). Some evidence for heightened sexual attraction under conditions of high anxiety. *Journal of Personality and Social Psychology, 30,* 510–517.

d'Ydewalle, G., & Rosselle, H. (1978). Text expectations in text learning. In M. M. Gruneberg, P. E. Morris, & R. N. Sykes (Eds.), *Practical aspects of memory* (pp. 609–617). Orlando, FL: Academic Press.

E Eagly, A. H. (1987). *Sex differences in social behaviour: A social-role interpretation.* Hillsdale, NJ: Erlbaum.

Eagly, A. H., & Wood, W. (2003). The origins of sex differences in human behavior: Evolved dispositions versus social roles. In C. B. Travis (Ed.), *Evolution, gender, and rape* (pp. 265–304). Boston: MIT Press.

Ehrlickman, H., & Halpern, I. N. (1988). Affect and memory: Effects of pleasant and unpleasant odors on retrieval of happy and unhappy memories. *Journal of Personality and Social Psychology, 55,* 769–779.

Eibl-Eibesfeldt, I. (1971). *Love and hate: The natural history of behavior patterns*. New York: Holt, Rinehart & Winston.

Eimas, P., Siqueland, E., Jusczyk, P., & Vigorito, J. (1971). Speech perception in infants. *Science, 171*, 303–306.

Ekman, P. (1993). Facial expression and emotion. *American Psychologist, 48*, 384–392.

Ekman, P. (1994). Strong evidence for universals in facial expressions: A reply to Russell's mistaken critique. *Psychological Bulletin, 115*, 268–287.

Ekman, P., & Friesen, W. V. (1975). *Unmasking the face*. Englewood Cliffs, NJ: Prentice-Hall.

Ekman, P., Friesen, W. V., O'Sullivan, M., Chan, A., Diacoyannia-Tarlatzis, I., Heider, K., et al. (1987). Universals and cultural differences in the judgments of facial expressions of emotion. *Journal of Personality and Social Psychology, 53*, 712–717.

Ekman, P., & Rosenberg, E. L. (Eds.). (2005). *What the face reveals: Basic and applied studies of spontaneous expression using the facial action coding system (FACS)*. New York: Oxford University Press.

Elkind, D. (2001). Much too early. *Education Matters, 1*, 9–15.

Ellis, A. (1973). *Humanistic psychotherapy: The rational-emotive approach*. New York: Julian Press.

Ellis, A. (1979). The practice of rational-emotive therapy. In A. Ellis & J. Whiteley (Eds.), *Theoretical and empirical foundations of rational-emotive therapy*. Monterey, CA: Brooks/Cole.

Ellis, A. (1987). A sadly neglected cognitive component in depression. *Cognitive Therapy & Research, 11*(1), 121–145.

Ellis, H. C. (1973). Stimulus encoding processes in human learning and memory. In G. H. Bower (Ed.), *The psychology of learning and motivation* (Vol. 7, pp. 124–182). New York: Academic Press.

Emmelkamp, P. M. G., Bruynzeel, M., Drost, L., & van der Mast, C. A. P. G. (2001). Virtual reality treatment in acrophobia: A comparison with exposure in vivo. *CyberPsychology & Behavior, 4*, 335–339.

Esch, H. E., Zhang, S., Srinvasan, M. V., & Tautz, J. (2001). Honey-bee dances communicate distances measured by optic flow. *Nature, 411*, 581–583.

Estes, W. K. (1994). *Classification and cognition*. New York: Oxford University Press.

Eysenck, H. J. (1952). The effects of psychotherapy: An evaluation. *Journal of Consulting Psychology, 16*, 319–324.

Eysenck, H. J. (1967). *The biological basis of personality*. Springfield, IL: Charles C. Thomas.

Eysenck, H. J. (1982). *Personality, genetics, and behavior: Selected papers*. New York: Praeger.

Eysenck, H. J. (1990). Biological dimensions of personality. In L. A. Pervin (Ed.), *Handbook of personality: Theory and research* (pp. 244–276). New York: Guilford Press.

F Fagan, J. F., & Holland, C. R. (2002). Equal opportunity and racial differences in IQ. *Intelligence, 30*, 361–387.

Falicov, C. J. (1998). *Latino families in therapy: A guide to multicultural practice.* New York: Guilford Press.

Fancher, R. E. (1979). *Pioneers of psychology.* New York: Norton.

Farah, M. J., Weisberg, L. L., Monheit, M. A., & Peronnet, F. (1989). Brain activity underlying mental imagery. *Journal of Cognitive Neuroscience, 1*(4), 303–316.

Fausto-Sterling, A. (2000). *Sexing the body: Gender politics and the construction of sexuality.* New York: Basic Books.

Feingold, A. (1992). Good-looking people are not what we think. *Psychological Bulletin, 111,* 304–341.

Fernald, A., & Kuhl, P. (1987). Acoustic determinants of infant preference for motherese speech. *Infant Behavior and Development, 10,* 279–293.

Ferster, C. B., & Skinner, B. F. (1957). *Schedules of reinforcement.* New York: Appleton-Century-Crofts.

Festinger, L. (1957). *A theory of cognitive dissonance.* Stanford, CA: Stanford University Press.

Fileinger, E. E., & Thomas, S. J. (1988). Behavioral antecedents of relationship satisfaction and adjustment. A five-year longitudinal study. *Journal of Marriage and the Family, 50,* 785–795.

Filley, C. M., Rollins, Y. D., Anderson, C. A., Arciniegas, D. B., Howard, K. L., Murrell, J. R., et al. (2007). The genetics of very early onset Alzheimer disease. *Cognitive and Behavioral Neurology, 20*(3), 149–156.

Finkelson, L., & Oswalt, R. (1995). College date rape: Incidence and reporting. *Psychological Reports, 77*(2), 526.

Fischer, K. W., & Rose, S. P. (1996). Dynamic growth cycles of brain and cognitive development. In R. W. Thatcher & G. R. Lyon (Eds.), *Developmental neuroimaging: Mapping the development of brain and behavior* (pp. 467–561). San Diego: Academic Press.

Fisher, H. (2004). *Why we love: The nature and chemistry of romantic love.* New York: Henry Holt.

Fisher, P. J., Turic, D., Williams, N. M., McGuffin, P., Asherson, P., Ball, D., et al. (1999). DNA pooling identifies QTLs on chromosome 4 for general cognitive ability in children. *Human Molecular Genetics, 8,* 915–922.

Fiske, S. T. (2004). *Social beings: A core motives approach to social psychology.* New York: Wiley.

Fitzgerald, P. B., Brown, T. L., Marston, N. A. U., Daskalakis, J., de Castella, A., & Kulkarni, J. (2003). Transcranial magnetic stimulation in the treatment of depression: A double-blind, placebo-controlled trial. *Archives of General Psychiatry, 60,* 1002–1008.

Flemons, D. (2005). Hypnosis and relaxation scripting. In G. P. Koocher, J. C. Norcross, & S. S. Hill (Eds.), *Psychologists desk reference* (pp. 332–337). New York: Oxford University Press.

Flint, R. W., Jr. (2006). Biopsychology. In B. Vukok (Ed.), *Psychology: Exploring our universe within* (pp. 67–99). Boston: Pearson Custom Publishing.

Flynn, J. R. (1999). Searching for justice: The discovery of IQ gains over time. *American Psychologist, 54,* 5–20.

Foley, M. A., & Ratner, H. H. (1998). Distinguishing between memories for thoughts and deeds: The role of prospective processing in children's source monitoring. *British Journal of Developmental Psychology, 16*, 465–484.

Fouts, D. H. (1994). The use of remote video recordings to study the use of American Sign Language by chimpanzees when no human is present. In R. A. Gardner, B. T. Gardner, A. B. Chiarelli, & F. X. Plooij (Eds.), *The ethological roots of culture* (pp. 271–284). Dordrecht, Netherlands: Kluwer.

Fouts, R., & Mills, S. T. (1997). *Next of kin: What chimpanzees have taught me about who we are.* New York: Morrow.

Fowler, R. D. (1986, May). Howard Hughes: A psychological autopsy. *Psychology Today, 20*(5), 22–33.

Franklin, J. (1987). *Molecules of the mind: The brave new science of molecular psychology.* New York: Atheneum Publishers.

Franz, K., & Koob, G. (2005). The neurobiology of addiction. In R. Coombs (Ed.), *Addiction counseling review* (pp. 33–58). Mahwah, NJ: Lawrence Erlbaum Publishers.

Frazer, A. (1997). Antidepressants. *Journal of Clinical Psychiatry, 58*(6, Suppl.), 9–25.

Fredrickson, B. L. (2001). The role of positive emotions in positive psychology: The broaden-and-build theory of positive emotions. *American Psychologist, 56*, 218–226.

Fredrickson, B. L., & Levenson, R. W. (1998). Positive emotions speed recovery from the cardiovascular sequelae of negative emotions. *Cognition and Emotion, 12*, 191–220.

Freedman, J. L., & Fraser, S. C. (1966). Compliance without pressure: The foot-in-the-door technique. *Journal of Personality and Social Psychology, 4*, 195–203.

Freud, S. (1913). *The interpretation of dreams* (A. A. Brill, Trans.). New York: Macmillan. (Original work published 1900)

Freud, S. (1953). The interpretation of dreams. In *Standard edition. Vols. 4 and 5.* London: Hogarth Press. (Original work published 1900)

Freud, S. (1957). Instincts and other vicissitudes. In J. Rickman (Ed.), *A general selection from the works of Sigmund Freud* (pp. 70–86). New York: Anchor Books. (Original work published 1915)

Frey, C. F., & Detterman, D. K. (2004). Scholastic assessment or *g? Psychological Science, 15*, 373–378.

Fromm, E. (1973). *The anatomy of human destructiveness.* New York: Holt.

Fultz, A. F. (1966). Music therapy. *Psychiatry Op, 3*, 32–35.

Funder, D. C. (2004). *The personality puzzle* (3rd ed.). New York: W. W. Norton.

Fuster, J. M. (1989). *The prefrontal cortex: Anatomy, physiology, and neuropsychology of the frontal lobe.* New York: Raven Press.

G Gabrieli, J. D. E. (1998). Cognitive neuroscience of human memory. *Annual Review of Psychology, 49*, 87–115.

Gaffan, D. (2001). What is a memory system? Horel's critique revisited. *Behavioural Brain Research, 127*(1–2), 5–11.

Galati, D., Scherer, K. R., & Ricci-Bitti, P. E. (1997). Voluntary facial expression of emotion: Comparing congenitally blind with normally sighted encoders. *Journal of Personality and Social Psychology, 73,* 1363–1379.

Galef, B. (1998). Edward Thorndike: Revolutionary psychologist, ambiguous biologist. *American Psychologist, 53,* 1128–1134.

Gallahue, D. L. (1989). *Understanding motor development.* Carmel, IN: Benchmark.

Galton, F. (1874). *English men of science: Their nature and nurture.* London: Macmillan.

Gamble, E., & Elder, S. (1983). Multimodal biofeedback in the treatment of migraine. *Biofeedback and Self-Regulation, 8,* 383–392.

Garb, H. N. (2003). Incremental validity and the assessment of psychopathology in adults. *Psychological Assessment, 15,* 508–520.

Garcia, J., & Koelling, R. A. (1966). Relation of cue to consequence in avoidance learning. *Psychonomic Science, 4,* 123–124.

Gardner, H. (1983). *Frames of mind.* New York: Basic Books.

Gardner, H., & Hatch, T. (1989). Multiple intelligences go to school: Educational implications of the theory of multiple intelligences. *Educational Research, 18,* 4–10.

Gardner, R. A., & Gardner, B. T. (1969). Teaching sign language to a chimpanzee. *Science, 165,* 664–672.

Gardner, R. A., & Gardner, B. T. (1978). Comparative psychology and language acquisition. *Annals of the New York Academy of Sciences, 309,* 37–76.

Geidd, J. N., Castellanos, F. X., Rajapakse, J. C., Vaituzis, A. C., & Rapoport, J. L. (1997). Sexual dimorphism of the developing human brain. *Progress in Neuropsychopharmacology and Biological Psychiatry, 21,* 1185–1201.

Gesell, A. (2007). Developmental diagnosis: Normal and abnormal child development—Clinical methods and pediatric applications. New York: Harper.

Geyer, L. H., & Dewald, C. G. (1973). Feature lists and confusion matrices. *Perception and Psychophysics, 14,* 479–482.

Gibson, E. (1969). *Principles of perceptual learning and development.* Englewood Cliffs, NJ: Prentice-Hall.

Gibson, E. J., & Walk, R. D. (1960). The visual cliff. *Scientific American, 202,* 64–71.

Gilbert, D. T., & Malone, P. S. (1995). The correspondence bias. *Psychological Bulletin, 117,* 21–38.

Giles, J. (2004). Neuroscience: Change of mind [Electronic version]. *Nature, 430,* 14.

Gist, R., & Lubin, B. (Eds.). (1999). *Response to disaster, psychosocial community, and ecological approaches.* Ann Arbor, MI: Taylor and Francis.

Glanzer, M., & Cunitz, A. (1966). Two storage mechanisms in free recall. *Journal of Verbal Learning and Verbal Behavior, 5,* 351–360.

Gleitman, L. R., Gleitman, H., & Shipley, E. F. (1972). The emergence of the child as grammarian. *Cognition, 1,* 137–164.

Gloria, A. M., Ruiz, E. L., & Castillo, E. M. (2004). Counseling and psychotherapy with Latino and Latina clients. In T. B. Smith (Ed.), *Practicing multiculturalism: Affirming diversity in counseling and psychology* (pp. 167–189). San Francisco: Pearson.

Godden, D. R., & Baddeley, A. D. (1975). Context-dependent memory in two natural environments: On land and underwater. *British Journal of Psychology, 66,* 325–331.

Goforth, H. W., & Holsinger, T. (2007). Rapid relief of severe major depressive disorder by use of preoperative ketamine and electroconvulsive therapy. *Journal of ECT, 23,* 23–25.

Goldberg, E. M., & Morrison, S. L. (1963). Schizophrenia and social class. *British Journal of Psychiatry, 109,* 785–802.

Goldfield, B. A., & Resnick, J. S. (1990). Early lexical acquisition: Rate, content and the vocabulary spurt. *Journal of Child Language, 17,* 171–183.

Goldstein, E. B. (2002). *Sensation & Perception* (6th ed.). Belmont, CA: Thomson/Wadsworth.

Goleman, D. (1995). *Emotional intelligence.* New York: Bantam.

Goleman, D., Boyatzis, R. E., & McKee, A. (2002). *Primal leadership: Realizing the power of emotional intelligence.* Boston: Harvard Business School Press.

Golier, J. A., Yehuda, R., Bierer, L. M., Mitropoulou, V., New, A. S., Schmeidler, J., et al. (2003). The relationship of borderline personality disorder to posttraumatic stress disorder and traumatic event. *American Journal of Psychiatry, 160,* 2018–2024.

Gondola, J. C., & Tuckman, B. W. (1982). Psychological mood state in "average" marathon runners. *Perceptual and Motor Skills, 55*(3, pt 2), 1295–1300.

Gonzalez, M. A., Campos, A., & Perez, M. J. (1997). Mental imagery and creative thinking. *Journal of Psychology, 131*(4), 353–364.

Gosserand, R. H., & Diefendorff, J. M. (2005). Emotional display rules and emotional labor: The moderating role of commitment. *Journal of Applied Psychology, 90,* 1256–1264.

Gottesman, I. I. (1991). *Schizophrenia genesis: The origins of madness.* New York: W. H. Friedman.

Gottfredson, L. S. (2003). Dissecting practical intelligence theory: Its claims and evidence. *Intelligence, 31,* 343–397.

Gottman, J. M. (1994). *Why marriages succeed and fail.* New York: Simon & Schuster.

Gould, J., & Gould, C. G. (1994). *The animal mind.* New York: Freeman.

Greenberg, L. S., Watson, J. C., & Lietaer, G. (Eds.). (1998). *Handbook of experiential psychotherapy.* New York: Guilford Press.

Greene, B. A. (1985). Considerations in the treatment of Black patients by White therapists. *Psychotherapy, 22,* 389–393.

Greenfield, P. (1997). You can't take it with you: Why ability assessments don't cross cultures. *American Psychologist, 52,* 1115–1124.

Grier, W. H., & Cobbs, P. M. (1968). *Black rage.* New York: Basic Books.

Griffith, D. R. (1992, September). Prenatal exposure to cocaine and other drugs. *Phi Delta Kappan,* 30–34.

Grilly, M. D. (2002). *Drugs and human behavior* (4th ed.). Boston: Allyn & Bacon.

Grossman, H. J. (Ed.). (1983). *Manual on terminology and classification in mental retardation.* Washington, DC: American Association on Mental Deficiency.

Groth-Marnat, G. (1990). *Handbook of psychological assessment* (2nd ed.). New York: Wiley.

Guilford, J. P. (1967). *The nature of human intelligence.* New York: McGraw Hill.

Guzman, B. (2001). *The Hispanic population* (Current Population Reports, C2KBR/01-3). Washington, DC: U.S. Census Bureau.

Gwartney-Gibbs, P., & Stockard, J. (1989). Courtship aggression and mixed-sex peer groups. In M. A. Pirog-Good & J. E. Stets (Eds.), *Violence in dating relationships: Emerging social issues* (pp. 185–204). New York: Praeger.

H

Haberlandt, D. (1997). *Cognitive psychology* (2nd ed.) Boston: Allyn & Bacon.

Hager, W., Leichsenring, F., & Schiffler, A. (2000). When does a study of different therapies allow comparisons of their relative efficacy? *Psychother. Psychsom. Med. Psychol., 50,* 251–262.

Hakuta, K. (1986). *Mirror of language: The debate on bilingualism.* New York: Basic Books.

Hale, R. J., Zeillinga, B., Chanton, P. J., & Spiller, A. H. (2003, August). Questioning the Delphic oracle. *Scientific American, 289,* 66–73

Hall, C. S., & Lindzey, G. (1970). *Theories of personality* (2nd ed.). New York: Wiley.

Hall, G. S. (1904). *Adolescence: Its psychology and its relations to physiology, anthropology, sociology, sex, crime, religion, and education* (2 vols.). New York: Appleton.

Hall, J. (2002). Culture-Africa: Attempts made to outlaw dangerous superstitions. *Inter Press Service.* Retrieved on May 29, 2008, from http://www.aegis.com/news/ips/2002/Ip020412.html

Halpern, D. F. (2000). *Sex differences in cognitive abilities* (3rd ed.). Mahwah, NJ: Erlbaum.

Halpern, D. F., & Tan, U. (2001). Stereotypes and steroids: Using a psychobiosocial model to understand cognitive sex differences. *Brain and Cognition, 45,* 392–414.

Hamer, D. H., Hu, S., Magnuson, V. L., Hu, N., & Pattatucci, A. M. (1993, July 16). A linkage between DNA markers on the X chromosome and male sexual orientation. *Science, 261,* 321–327.

Hammen, C. (2003). Mood disorders. In G. Stricker & T. A. Widiger (Eds.), *Handbook of psychology: Clinical psychology* (Vol. 8, pp. 93–118). New York: Wiley.

Handel, S. (1995). Timbre perception and auditory object identification. In B. C. J. Moore (Ed.), *Hearing* (pp. 425–461). San Diego, CA: Academic Press.

Hardy, J. D., & Oppel, T. W. (1937). Studies in temperature sensation III. The sensitivity of the body to heat and the spatial summation of the end organ responses. *Journal of Clinical Investigation, 16,* 533–540.

Harlow, H. F. (1958). The nature of love. *American Psychologist, 13,* 673–685.

Harrison, A. A., & Saeed, L. (1977). Let's make a deal: An analysis of revelations and stipulations in lonely hearts advertisements. *Journal of Personality and Social Psychology, 35,* 257–264.

Harvey, J. R. (1983). The effects of yogic breathing exercises on mood. *Journal of the American Society of Psychosomatic Dentistry and Medicine, 30* (2), 39.

Hayes, J. R. (1966). Memory, goals, and problem solving. In B. Kleinmuntz (Ed.), *Problem solving: Research, method, and theory* (pp. 243–246). New York: Wiley.

Heavey, C. L., Layne, C., & Christensen, A. (1993). Gender and conflict structure in marital satisfaction. A replication and extension. *Journal of Consulting and Clinical Psychology, 61,* 16–27.

Hector, R. I. (1998). The use of clozapine in the treatment of aggressive schizophrenia. *Canadian Journal of Psychiatry, 43,* 466–472.

Hedges, L. V., & Nowell, A. (1995). Sex differences in mental test scores, variability, and numbers of high-scoring individuals. *Science, 269,* 41–45.

Helms, J. E., & Cook, D. A. (1999). *Using race and culture in counseling and psychotherapy: Theory and process.* Boston: Allyn & Bacon.

Hensel, H., & Witt, I. (1959). Spatial temperature gradient and thermoreceptor stimulation *Journal of Physiology, 148,* 180–187.

Henshaw, S. K., Singh, S., & Haas, T. (1999). The incidence of abortion worldwide. *International Family Planning Perspectives, 25*(Suppl. January), S30–S38.

Henson, R., Shallice, T., Gorno-Tempini, M., & Dolan, R. (2002). Face repetition effects in implicit and explicit memory as measured by fMRI. *Cerebral Cortex, 12,* 178–186.

Hergenhahn, B. (2001). *An introduction to the history of psychology.* Belmont, CA: Wadsworth Publishers.

Herman, L. M. (1999). Cited in J. Maestro, Dialogue with a dolphin. *San Diego Union-Tribune,* E1.

Herman, L. M., Kuczaj, S. A., & Holder, M. D. (1993). Responses to anomalous gestural sequences by a language-trained dolphin: Evidence for processing of semantic relations and syntactic information. *Journal of Experimental Psychology: General, 122,* 184–194.

Herman, L. M., Richards, D. G., & Woltz, J. P. (1984). Comprehension of sentences by bottlenosed dolphins. *Cognition, 16,* 129–219.

Herman, L. M., & Uyeyma, R. J. (1993). The dolphin's grammatical competency: Comments on Kako. *Animal Learning & Behavior, 27,* 18–23.

Hernandez, L., & Hoebel, B. G. (1989). Food intake and lateral hypothalamic self-stimulation covary after medial hypothalamic lesions or ventral midbrain 6-hydroxydopamine injections that cause obesity *Behavioral Neuroscience, 103,* 412–422.

Herrmann, N., Lanctot, K. L., & Khan, L. R. (2004). The role of norepinephrine in the behavioral and psychological symptoms of dementia. *Journal of Neuropsychiatry & Clinical Neuroscience, 16*(3), 261–276.

Herrnstein, R. J., & Murray, D. (1994). *The bell curve.* New York: Free Press.

Herz, R. S., & Cupchik, G. C. (1995). The emotional distinctiveness of odor-evoked memories. *Chemical Senses, 20*(5), 517–528.

Herz, R. S., McCall, C., & Cahill, L. (1999). Hemispheric lateralization in the processing of odor pleasantness versus odor names. *Chemical Senses, 24*(6), 691–695.

Hetherington, A. W., & Ranson, S. W. (1940). Hypothalamic lesions and adiposity in the rat. *Anatomical Record, 78,* 149–172.

Hettler, B. (1980). Wellness promotion on a university campus. *Family Community Health, 3*(1), 77–95.

Heymsfield, S. N., Greenberg, A. S., Fujioka, K., Dizon, R. M., Kushner, R., Hunt, T., et al. (1999). Recombinant leptin for weight loss in obese and lean adults. *Journal of American Medical Association, 282,* 1568–1575.

Hicks, D. (1991). Kinds of narrative: Genre skills among first graders from two communities. In A. McCabe & C. Peterson (Eds.), *Developing narrative structure* (pp. 55–88). Hillsdale, NJ: Erlbaum.

Higbee, K. L. (1977). *Your memory: How it works and how to improve it.* Englewood Cliffs, NJ: Prentice Hall.

Hill, C. E. (2000). Client-centered therapy. In A. Kazdin (Ed.), *Encyclopedia of psychology* (Vol. 2, pp. 106–108). Washington, DC & New York: American Psychological Association and Oxford University Press.

Hill, W. F., & Wallace, W. P. (1967). Reward magnitude and number of training trials as joint factors in extinction. *Psychonomic Science, 7,* 267–268.

Hilts, P. J. (1995). *Memory's ghost: The nature of memory and the strange tale of Mr. M.* New York: Simon & Schuster.

Hinojosa, J. A., Martin-Loeches, M., Munoz, F., Casado, P., & Pozo, M. A. (2004). Electrophysiological evidence of automatic early semantic processing. *Brain and Language, 88,* 39–46.

Ho, M. K. (1987). *Family therapy with ethnic minorities.* Beverly Hills, CA: Sage.

Hockenbury, D., & Hockenbury, S. (2006). *Psychology* (4th ed.). New York: Worth Publishers.

Holland, P. C., & Rescorla, R. A. (1975). Second-order conditioning with food unconditioned stimulus. *Journal of Comparative and Physiological Psychology, 88*(1), 459–467.

Hollander, E. (2005). Obsessive-compulsive disorder and spectrum across the life span. *International Journal of Psychiatry in Clinical Practice, 9*(2), 79–86.

Hollon, S. D., & Beck, A. T. (1994). Cognitive and cognitive-behavioral therapies. In A. E. Bergin & S. L. Garfield (Eds.), *Handbook of psychotherapy and behavior change* (4th ed., pp. 428–466). New York: John Wiley & Sons.

Holmes, T. H., & Rahe, R. H. (1967). The social readjustment rating scale. *Journal of Psychosomatic Research, 11,* 213–218.

Holstege, G. (2005). Central nervous system control of ejaculation. *World Journal of Urology, 23*(2), 109–114.

Hu, S., Pattatucci, A. M. L., Patterson, C., Li, L., Fulker, D. W., Cherny, S. S., et al. (1995). Linkage between sexual orientation and chromosome Xq28 in males but not in females. *Nature Genetics, 11,* 248–256.

Hubble, D. H., Duncan, B. L., & Miller, S. D. (Eds.). (1999). *The heart and soul of change: What works in therapy.* Washington, DC: American Psychological Association.

Hubel, D. H., & Wiesel, T. N. (1962). Receptive fields, binocular interaction, and functional architecture in the cat's visual cortex. *Journal of Physiology, 160,* 106–154.

Hubel, D. H., & Wiesel, T. N. (1963). Receptive fields of cells in the striate cortex of very young visually inexperienced kittens. *Journal of Neurophysiology, 26,* 994–1002.

Hubel, D. H., & Wiesel, T. N. (1979). Brain mechanisms of vision. *Scientific American, 241,* 150–162.

Hulihan, J. (1997). Ice cream headache. *British Medical Journal, 314,* 1364.

Hulme, C., & Tordoff, V. (1989). Working memory development: The effects of speech rate, word length, and acoustic similarity on serial recall. *Journal of Experimental Child Psychology, 47,* 72–87.

Humphreys, G. W. (1998). The neural representation of objects in space: A dual coding account. *Philosophical Transactions of the Royal Society, 353,* 1341–1352.

Hunt, E. (1994). Problem solving. In R. J. Sternberg (Ed.), *Thinking and problem solving: Handbook of perception and cognition* (2nd ed., pp. 263–288). San Diego, CA: Academic Press.

Hunt, E., & Agnoli, F. (1991). The Whorfian hypothesis: A cognitive psychology perspective. *Psychological Review, 98,* 377–389.

Huttenlocher, P. R. (1979). Synaptic density of human frontal cortex-developmental changes and effects of aging. *Brain Research, 163,* 195–205.

Huttenlocher, P. R. (1984). Synapse elimination and plasticity in developing human cerebral cortex. *American Journal of Mental Deficiency, 88,* 488–496.

Hyman, I. E., Jr. (2000). The memory wars. In U. Neisser & I. E. Hyman, Jr. (Eds.), *Memory observed: Remembering in natural contexts* (pp. 375–379). New York: Worth.

Hyman, I. E., Husband, T. H. R., & Billings, F. J. (1995). False memories of childhood experiences. *Applied Cognitive Psychology, 9,* 181–197.

Ilmberger, J., Rau, S., Noahchtar, S., Arnold, S., & Winkler, P. (2002). Naming tools and animals: Asymmetries observed during direct electrical cortical stimulation. *Neuropsychologia, 40,* 695–700.

Ingram, R. E., & Siegle, G. J. (2001). Cognition and clinical science: From revolution to evolution. In K. S. Dobson (Ed.), *Handbook of cognitive-behavioral therapies* (2nd ed., pp. 111–137). New York: Guilford Press.

Ivey, J. (2000). *Boys Town: The constant spirit.* Chicago: Arcadia Publishing.

Izard, C. E. (1977). *Human emotions.* New York: Plenum Press.

Izard, C. E. (1994). Innate and universal facial expressions: Evidence from developmental and cross-cultural research. *Psychological Bulletin, 114,* 288–299.

Izawa, C. (1999). *On human memory: Evolution, progress & reflecting on the 30th anniversary of the Atkinson Model.* Mahwah, NJ: Erlbaum Associates.

Jacobs, G. (1999). *Say goodnight to insomnia.* New York: Holt Books.

Jacobson, E. (1974). *Progressive relaxation.* Chicago: University of Chicago Press, Midway Reprint.

Jahnke, J. C., & Nowaczyk, R. H. (1998). *Cognition.* Upper Saddle River, NJ: Prentice Hall.

James, W. (1884). What is an emotion? *Mind, 9,* 188–205.

James, W. (1890). *The principles of psychology.* New York: Henry Holt and Company.

Janis, I. L. (1982). *Groupthink: Psychological studies of policy decision and fiascoes* (2nd ed.). Boston: Houghton Mifflin.

Jankowiak, W. (1997). *Romantic passion: A universal experience.* New York: Columbia University Press.

Jensen, A. R. (1969). How much can we boost IQ and scholastic achievement? *Harvard Educational Review, 39,* 1–123.

Johnson, J. G., Cohen, P., Smailes, E. M., Kasen, S., & Brooks, J. (2002). Television viewing and aggressive behavior during adolescence and adulthood. *Science, 295,* 2468–2471.

Jones, E., Schultz-Hardt, S., Frey, D., & Thelan, N. (2001). Confirmation bias in sequential information search after preliminary decision: An expansion of dissonance theoretical research on selective exposure to information. *Journal of Personality and Social Psychology, 80,* 557–571.

Jones, E. E., & Nesbitt, R. E. (1972). The actor and the observer: Divergent perceptions of the causes of behavior. In E. E. Jones, D. E. Kanouse, H. H. Kelley, R. E. Nesbitt, S. Valins, and B. Weiner (Eds.), *Attribution: Perceiving the causes of behavior* (pp. 79–94). Morristown, NJ: General Learning Press.

Jones, H. M., & Pilowsky, L. S. (2002). Dopamine and antipsychotic drug action revisited. *British Journal of Psychiatry, 181*(4), 271–275.

Joseph, R. (1992). The limbic system: Emotion, laterality, and unconscious mind. *Psychoanalytic Review, 79*(3), 405–456.

Julien, R. M. (2003). *A primer of drug action* (9th ed.). New York: Worth Publishers.

Jung, C. G. (1960). A review of the complex theory. In *Collected works. Vol. 8* (pp. 201–204). Princeton, NJ: Princeton University Press. (Original work published 1934)

Jung, C. G. (1968). *Analytical psychology: Its theory and practice* (The Tavistock Lectures). New York: Pantheon.

Jusczyk, P. W., Luce, P. A., & Charles-Luce, J. (1994). Infants' sensitivity to phonotactic patterns in the native language. *Journal of Memory and Language, 33,* 630–645.

K

Kahneman, D., Diener, E., & Schwarz, N. (1999). *Well-being: The foundations of hedonic psychology.* New York: Russell Sage Foundation.

Kalat, W. J. (2003). *Biological psychology* (8th ed.). Belmont, CA: Wadsworth/Thomson Learning.

Kandel, E. R., Schwartz, J. H., & Jessell, T. M. (1991). *Principles of neural science* (3rd ed.). East Norwalk, CT: Appleton & Lange.

Kaplan, H. I., & Sadock, B. J. (1998). *Synopsis of psychiatry* (7th ed.). Baltimore: Williams and Wilkins.

Kaplan, P. (2000). *A child's odyssey* (3rd ed.). Belmont, CA: Wadsworth.

Kaplan, R. M., & Saccuzzo, D. P. (1989). *Psychological testing: Principles, applications, and issues.* Pacific Grove, CA: Brooks/Cole.

Kazdin, A. E. (1994). Methodology, design, and evaluation in psychotherapy research. In A. E. Bergin & S. L. Garfield (Eds.), *Handbook of psychotherapy and behavior change* (4th ed., pp. 19–71). New York: John Wiley & Sons.

Kazdin, A. E. (2002). Applied behavior analysis. In M. Hersen & W. H. Sledge (Eds.), *Encyclopedia of psychotherapy* (Vol. 2, pp. 1–6). San Diego: Academic Press.

Kegel, A. (1952). Sexual functions of the pubococcygeus muscle. *Western Journal of Surgery, Obstetrics, and Gynecology, 60,* 521–524.

Kellaway, P. (1945). Pathways of transmission to the cochlea. *American Journal of Psychology, 58,* 25–42.

Kessler, R. C., McGonagle, K. A., Zhao, S., Nelson, C. B., Hughes, M., Eshleman, S., et al. (1994). Lifetime and 12-month prevalence rates of DSM-III-R psychiatric disorders in the United States: Results from the national comorbidity survey. *Archives of General Psychiatry, 51,* 8–19.

Kew, J.N.C., & Kemp, J. A. (2005). Ionotropic and metabotropic glutamate receptor structure and pharmacology. *Psychopharmacology, 179*(1), 4–29.

Kihlstrom, J. F. (2003). Hypnosis and memory. In J. H. Byrne (Ed.), *Learning and memory* (2nd ed., pp. 240–242). Farmington Hill, MI: Macmillan Reference.

Kim, A., Martin, D., & Martin, M. (1989). Effects of personality on marital satisfaction. *Family Therapy, 16*(3), 243–248.

Kinsey, A. C., Pomeroy, W. B., & Martin, C. E. (1948). *Sexual behavior in the human male.* Philadelphia: W. B. Saunders.

Kiraly, Z. (2000). The relationship between emotional self-disclosure of male and female adolescents' friendships (gender differences, ninth grade). *Dissertation Abstract International: Section B: The Sciences & Engineering, 60*(7-B), 3619.

Kirsch, I. (1996). Hypnotic enhancement of cognitive behavioral weight loss treatments: Another meta-reanalysis. *Journal of Consulting and Clinical Psychology, 64,* 517–519.

Kirsch, I., & Lynn, S. (1998). Dissociation theories of hypnosis. *Psychological Bulletin, 123,* 100–115.

Kisilevsky, B. S., Hains, S., & Lee, K. (2003). Effects of experience on fetal voice recognition. *Psychological Science, 14,* 220–224.

Klatsky, R. L. (1980). *Human memory: Structures and processes* (2nd ed.). New York: W. H. Freeman.

Kobayashi, H., Sawamura, Y., & Ikeda, J. (2005). A tumor in the medulla oblongata producing beta-HCG and AFP. *Journal of Clinical Neuroscience, 12*(6), 709–711.

Kohler, W. (1924). *The mentality of apes.* New York: Harcourt Brace.

Kohler, W. (1927). *The mentality of apes.* London: Methuen.

Kolb, B., & Whishaw, I. Q. (2003). *Fundamentals of human neuropsychology* (5th ed.). New York: Worth Publishers.

Kolb, B., & Whishaw, I. Q. (2006). *Introduction to psychology* (2nd ed.). New York: Worth Publishers.

Koppenaal, L., & Glanzer, M. (1990). An examination of the continuous distractor task and the "long term recency effect." *Memory and Cognition, 18,* 183–195.

Koss, M. P. (1989). Hidden rape: Sexual aggression and victimization in a national sample of students in higher education. In M. Pirog-Good & J. Stets (Eds.), *Violence in dating relationships.* New York: Praeger.

Koss, M. P. (2000). Blame, shame, and community: Justice responses to violence against women. *American Psychologist, 55,* 1332–1343.

Kosslyn, S. M. (1978). Measuring the visual angle of the mind's eye. *Cognitive Psychology, 10,* 356–389.

Kosslyn, S. M. (1980). *Image and mind.* Cambridge, MA: Harvard University Press.

Kosslyn, S. M., & Shin, L. M. (1994). Visual mental images in the brain: Current Issues. In M. J. Farah & G. Ratcliff (Eds.), *The neuropsychology of high-level vision: Collected tutorial essays. Carnegie Mellon symposia on cognition.* Hillsdale, NJ: Erlbaum.

Kosslyn, S. M., Thompson, W. I., & Alpert, N. N. (1995). Topographical representation of mental images in primary visual cortex. *Nature, 378,* 496.

Kottler, J. A., & Brown, R. W. (1999). *Introduction to therapeutic counseling.* Monterey, CA: Brooks/Cole.

Krueger, W. C. F. (1929). The effect of overlearning on retention. *Journal of Experimental Psychology, 12,* 71–78.

Kubey, R. W., & Larson, R. (1990). The use and experience of the new video media among children and young adolescents. *Communication Research, 17,* 107–130.

Kubisyzn, T. W., Finn, S. E., Eyde, L. D., Kay, G. G., Meyer, G. J., Moreland, K. L. et al. (2000). Empirical support of psychological assessment in clinical health care settings. *Professional Psychology: Research and Practice, 31,* 119–130.

L

La Roche, M. J., & Maxie, A. (2003). Ten considerations in addressing cultural differences in psychotherapy. *Professional Psychology: Research and Practice, 34,* 180–186.

Lachlan, R. F., & Feldman, M. W. (2003). Evolution of cultural communication systems. *Journal of Evolutionary Biology, 16,* 1084–1095.

Lamanna, M. A., & Reidmann, A. (1997). *Marriages and families* (6th ed.). Belmont, CA: Wadsworth.

Lamb, M. E., Sternberg, K. J., & Podromidis, M. (1992). Nonmaternal care and the security of infant-mother attachment: A re-analysis of the data. *Infant Behavior and Development, 15,* 71–83.

Lambert, M. J. (2001). The effectiveness of psychotherapy: What a century of research tells us about the effects of treatment. *Psychotherapeutically speaking— Updates from the Division of Psychotherapy* (29). Washington, DC: American Psychological Association.

Lambert, M. J., & Bergin, A. E. (1994). The effectiveness of psychotherapy. In A. E. Bergin & S. L. Garfield (Eds.), *Handbook of psychotherapy and behavior change* (4th ed., pp. 143–189). New York: Wiley.

LaMotte, R. H., & Mountcastle, V. B. (1975). Capacities of humans and monkeys to discriminate vibratory stimuli of different frequency and amplitude: A correlation between neural events and psychological measurements. *Journal of Neurophysiology, 38,* 539–559.

Lang, A., Craske, M., Brown, M., & Ghaneian, A. (2001). Fear-related state dependent memory. *Cognition and Emotion, 15,* 695–703.

Lang, P. J. (1994). The varieties of emotional experience: A meditation on James-Lange theory. *Psychological Review, 101,* 211–221.

Lang, P. J. (1995). The emotion probe: Studies of motivation and attention. *American Psychologist, 50,* 372–385.

Lange, A., van de Ven, J., Schrieken, B., & Emmelkamp, P. M. G. (2001). Interapy, treatment of posttraumatic stress through the Internet: A controlled trial. *Journal of Behavior Therapy & Experimental Psychiatry, 32*(2), 73–90.

Larroque, B., Kaminski, M., & Dehaene, P. (1995). Moderate prenatal alcohol exposure and psychomotor development at preschool age. *American Journal of Public Health, 85,* 1654–1661.

Larsen, R., & Buss, D. (2005). *Personality psychology: Domains of knowledge about human nature.* Boston: McGraw Hill.

Latane, B., & Darley, J. M. (1968). Group inhibition of bystander intervention. *Journal of Personality and Social Psychology, 10,* 215–221.

Laumann, E. O., Gagnon, J. H., Michael, R. T., & Michaels, S. (1994). *The social organization of sexuality: Sexual practices in the United States.* Chicago: University of Chicago Press.

Laumann, E. O., Paik, A., & Rosen, R. C. (1999). Sexual dysfunction in the United States: Prevalence and predictors. *Journal of the American Medical Association, 281*(6), 537–544.

Laurent, J., Swerdik, M., & Ryburn, M. (1992). Review of validity research on the Stanford-Binet Intelligence Scale: Fourth Edition. *Psychological Assessment, 4,* 102–112.

Laver, A. B. (1972). Precursors of psychology in ancient Egypt. *Journal of the History for the Behavioral Sciences, 8,* 181–195.

Lazarus, R. S. (1966). *Psychological stress and the coping process.* New York: McGraw Hill.

Lazarus, R. S. (1991). Cognition and motivation in emotion. *American Psychologist, 46,* 352–367.

Lazarus, R. S., & Folkman, S. (1984). *Stress, appraisal and coping.* New York: Springer.

Leahey, H. (2004). *A history of psychology: Main currents in psychological thought* (6th ed.). Upper Saddle River, NJ: Pearson Education.

Lee, C. C., & Richardson, B. L. (1991). *Multicultural issues in counseling: New approaches to diversity.* Alexandria, VA: AACD.

Lee, J. M., Ku, J. H., Jang, D. P., Kim, D. H., Choi, Y. H., Kim, I. Y., et al. (2002). Virtual reality system for treatment of the fear of public speaking using image-based rendering and moving pictures. *Cyberpsychology & Behavior, 5*(3), 191–195.

Lefley, H. P. (1990). Culture and chronic mental illness. *Hospital and Community Psychiatry, 41,* 277–286.

Leichtman, M. D., & Ceci, S. J. (1995). The effects of stereotypes and suggestions on pre-schoolers' reports. *Developmental Psychology, 31,* 568–578.

Lemonick, M. D. (2002, June 3). Lean and hungrier. *Time, 159,* 54.

Lengagne, T., Jouventin, P., & Aubin, T. (1999). Finding one's mate in a king penguin colony: Efficiency of acoustic communication. *Behavior, 136,* 833–846.

Leonard, K. E., & Quigley, B. M. (1999). Drinking and marital aggression in newlyweds: An event-based analysis of drinking and the occurrence of husband and marital aggression. *Journal of Studies on Alcohol, 60,* 537–545.

Lerner, R. M. (2001). *Concepts and theories of human development* (3rd ed.). Mahwah, NJ: Erlbaum.

LeVay, S. (1991). A difference in hypothalamic structure between heterosexual and homosexual men. *Science, 258,* 1034–1037.

Levin, R. J. (2004). Smells and tastes—Their putative influence on sexual activity in humans. *Sexual and Relationship Therapy, 19*(4), 451–462.

Li, S. C. (2003). Biocultural orchestration of development plasticity across levels: The interplay of biology and culture in shaping the mind and behavior across the life span. *Psychological Bulletin, 129,* 171–194.

Liebert, M. A. (1999). Toward optimal health: The experts response to stress. *Journal of Women's Health and Gender-Based Medicine, 8,* 10.

Lin, E. L., & Murphy, G. L. (2001). Thematic relations in adults' concepts. *Journal of Experimental Psychology: General, 130,* 3–28.

Lin, K., & Cheung, F. (1999). Mental health issues for Asian Americans. *Psychiatric Services, 50*(6), 774–780.

Lindsay, S. D., Hagen, L., Read, D. J., Wade, K. A., & Garry, M. (2004). True photographs and false memories. *Psychological Science, 15,* 149–154.

Lindsay, S. D., & Read, D. J. (Eds.). (1997). *Recollections of trauma: Scientific evidence and clinical practice.* New York: Plenum Press.

Lips, H. M. (1995). Gender-role socialization: Lessons in femininity. In J. Freeman (Ed.), *Women: A feminist perspective* (5th ed., pp. 128–148). Mountain View, CA: Mayfield.

Lipsey, M., & Wilson, D. (1993). The efficacy of psychological, educational, and behavioral treatment: Confirmation from meta-analysis. *American Psychologist, 48,* 1181–1209.

Locke, J. L. (1999). Towards a biological science of language development. In M. Barrett (Ed.), *The development of language* (pp. 373–395). Philadelphia: Psychology Press.

Loehlin, J. C. (2000). Group differences in intelligence. In R. J. Sternberg (Ed.), *Handbook of intelligence* (pp. 176–193). New York: Cambridge University Press.

Loehlin, J. C., McCrae, R. R., Costa, P. T., Jr., & John, O. P. (1998). Heritabilities of common and measure-specific components of the common and measure-specific components of the Big Five personality factors. *Journal of Research in Personality, 32*(4), 431–453.

Loftus, E. F. (1975). Leading questions and the eyewitness report. *Cognitive Psychology, 7,* 550–572.

Loftus, E. F. (1978). Reconstructive memory processes in eyewitness testimony. In B. D. Sales (Ed.), *Perspectives in law and psychology* (pp. 115–144). New York: Plenum.

Loftus, E. F. (1993). The reality of repressed memories. *American Psychologist, 48,* 518–537.

Loftus, E. F. (2002, Summer). Memory faults and fixes. *Issues in Science and Technology, 18,* 41–59.

Loftus, E. F. (2003, March). Perspectives. *Neuroscience, 4,* 231–234.

Loftus, E. F. (2004). Memories of things unseen. *Current Directions in Psychological Science, 13,* 145–147.

Loftus, E. F. (2005). Memory for a past that never was. In D. L. Hamilton (Ed.), *Social cognition: Key readings.* New York: Psychology Press.

Loftus, E. F., & Burns, T. E. (1982). Mental shock can produce retrograde amnesia. *Trends in Cognitive Science, 6,* 299–305.

Loftus, E. F., & Davis, D. (2006). Recovered memories. *Annual Review of Clinical Psychology, 2,* 469–498.

Loftus, E. F., & Ketcham, K. (1994). *The myth of repressed memory.* New York: St. Martin's Press.

Loftus, E. F., & Loftus, G. R. (1980). On the permanence of stored information in the human brain. *American Psychologist, 35,* 409–420.

Loftus, E. F., & Pickerell, J. E. (1995). The formation of false memories. *Psychiatric Annals, 25,* 720–725.

Loftus, E., & Zanni, G. (1975). Eyewitness testimony: The influence of wording of a question. *Bulletin of the Psychometric Society, 5,* 86–88.

Longer, E. (1989). *Mindfulness.* Reading, MA: Addison Wesley.

Lonsway, K. A., & Fitzgerald, L. F. (1994). Rape myths: In review. *Psychology of Women Quarterly, 18,* 133–164.

Lott, B. (2002). Cognitive and behavioral distancing from the poor. *American Psychologist, 57,* 100–110.

Lu, Z. L., Williamson, S. J., & Kaufman, L. (1992). Behavioral lifetime of human auditory sensory memory predicted by physiological measures. *Science, 258,* 1668–1670.

Luchins, A. S. (1946). Classroom experiments on mental set. *American Journal of Psychology, 59,* 295–298.

Luna, B., & Sweeney, J. A. (2004). fMRI studies of the development of response inhibition. *Annals of the New York Academy of Sciences, 1021,* 296–301.

Luntz, B. K., & Widom, C. S. (1994). Antisocial personality disorder in abused and neglected children grown up. *American Journal of Psychiatry, 151,* 670–674.

Lutchmaya, S., Baron-Cohen, S., & Raggatt, P. (2002). Fetal testosterone and vocabulary size in 18- and 24-month-old infants. *Infant Behavior and Development, 24,* 418–424.

Lutz, J. (2000). *An introduction to learning and memory.* Long Grove, IL: Waveland Press.

Lystad, M. M. (1957). Social mobility among selected groups of schizophrenics. *American Sociological Reviews, 22,* 288–292.

Lyubomirsky, S., Baron-Cohen, S., & Raggatt, P. (2005). Pursuing happiness: The architecture of sustainable change. *Review of General Psychology, 9,* 111–131.

M Mackintosh, N. J. (1974). Classical conditioning: Basic operations. In *The Psychology of Animal Learning* (pp. 8–40). London: Academic Press.

Macoby, E. E. (2000). Parenting and its effects on children: On reading and misreading behavior genetics. *Annual Review of Psychology, 51,* 1–27.

Madigan, S., & O'Hara, R. (1992). Short-term memory at the turn of the century: Mary Whiton Calkins's memory research. *American Psychologist, 47,* 170–174.

Magner, L. N. (1992). *A history of medicine.* New York: Marcel Dekker.

Mahowald, M., & Ettinger, M. (1990). Things that go bump in the night: The parsomnias revisited. *Journal of Clinical Neurophysiology, 7,* 119–143.

Maier, N. R. F. (1931). Reasoning in humans: II. The solutions of a problem and its appearance in consciousness. *Journal of Comparative Psychology, 12,* 181–194.

Makin, J. W., & Porter, R. H. (1989). Attractiveness of lactating females' breast odors to neonates. *Child Development, 60,* 803–811.

Mandel, D. R., Jusczyk, P. W., & Pisoni, D. B. (1995). Infants' recognition of sound patterns of their own names. *Psychological Science, 6*(5), 314–317.

Manning, J. T. (2002). *Digit ratio: A pointer to fertility behavior and health.* New Brunswick, NJ: Rutgers University Press.

Manning, R., Levine, M., & Collins, A. (2007). The Kitty Genovese murder and the social psychology of helping: The parable of the 38 witnesses. *American Psychologist, 62,* 555–562.

Markman, E. (1989). *Categorization and naming in children.* Cambridge, MA: MIT Press.

Markman, E. (1992). Constraints on word learning: Speculations about their nature, origins, and domain specificity. In M. R. Gunnar & M. P. Maratsos (Eds.), *Minnesota symposium on child psychology* (pp. 59–97). Hillsdale, NJ: Erlbaum.

Marler, P. (1967). Animal communication symbols. *Science, 35,* 63–78.

Martin, C. L. (1989). Children's use of gender-related information in making social judgments. *Developmental Psychology, 25,* 80–88.

Martin, J. B., & Riskind, P. N. (1992). Neurologic manifestations of hypothalamic disease. *Progress in Brain Research, 93,* 31–40.

Martini, H. F., Ober, W. C., Garrison, C. W., Welch, K., Hutchings, R. T., & Ireland, K. (2004). *Fundamentals of anatomy & physiology* (6th ed.). Upper Saddle River, NJ: Prentice Hall.

Martino, G., & Marks, L. E. (2001). Synesthesia: Strong and weak. *Current Directions in Psychological Science, 10,* 61–65.

Masand, P. S., & Gupta, S. (2002). Long-term side effects of newer-generation antidepressants: SSRIs, venlafaxine, nefazodone, bupropion, and mirtazapine. *Annals of Clinical Psychiatry, 14,* 175–182.

Maslow, A. H. (1970). *Motivation and personality* (2nd ed.). New York: Harper & Row.

Masters, W. H., & Johnson, V. E. (1966). *Human sexual response.* Boston: Little Brown.

Matlin, M. W. (1989). *Cognition* (2nd ed.). New York: Holt, Rinehart & Winston.

Matlin, M. W. (1998). *Cognition* (4th ed.). Fort Worth, TX: Harcourt Brace College Publishers.

May, C., & Hasher, L. (1998). Synchrony effects in inhibitory control over thought and action. *Journal of Experimental Psychology: Human Perception and Performance, 24,* 326–330.

May, M. (1996). Resistance: Friend or foe? *American Journal of Psychotherapy, 50*(1), 32–44.

Mayer, J. D. (2005). A tale of two visions: Can a new view of personality help integrate psychology? *American Psychologist, 60,* 294–307.

Mayer, J. D., & Salovey, P. (1997). What is emotional intelligence? In P. Salovey & D. J. Sluyter (Eds.), *Emotional development and emotional intelligence: Educational implications* (pp. 3–31). New York: Basic Books.

Mayer, K., & Pizer, H. F. (2005). AIDS pandemic: Impact on society and science. *Journal of American Medical Association, 294,* 849.

Mayeux, R. (2003). Epidemiology of neurodegeneration. *Annual Review of Neuroscience, 26,* 81–104.

Mayo Foundation. (2006). *Electroconvulsive therapy (ECT): Treating severe depression and mental illness.* Rochester, MN: Author. http://www.mayoclinic.com/health/electroconvulsive-therapy/MH00022

Mazur, J. E. (2002). *Learning and behavior.* Upper Saddle River, NJ: Prentice Hall.

McAdams, D. P., de St. Augin, E., & Logan, R. L. (1993). Generativity among young, midlife, and older adults. *Psychology and Aging, 8,* 221–230.

McCabe, A., & Peterson, C. (1991). *Developing narrative structure.* Hillsdale, NJ: Lawrence Erlbaum.

McCrae, R. R., & Costa, P. T. (1990). *Personality in adulthood.* New York: Guilford.

McCrae, R. R., & Costa, P. T. (1997). Personality trait structure as a human universal. *American Psychologist, 52*(5), 509–516.

McCrae, R. R., & Costa, P. T. (1999). A five-factor theory of personality. In L. A. Pervin, & O. P. John (Eds.), *Handbook of personality: Theory and research* (pp. 139–153). New York: Guilford.

McCrae, R. R., Costa, P. T., Jr., Ostendorf, F., Angleitner, A., Hrebickova, M., Avia, M. D. et al. (2000). Nature over nurture: Temperament, personality, and life span development. *Journal of Personality & Social Psychology, 78*(1), 173–186.

McEvoy, M. A., Odom, S. L., & McConnell, S. R. (1993). Peer social competence intervention for young children with disabilities. In S. L. Odom, S. R. McConnell, & M. A. McEvoy (Eds.), *Social competence of young children with disabilities* (pp. 113–133). Baltimore: Paul H. Brookes.

McGue, M., Bouchard, T. J., Jr., Iacono, W. G., & Lykken, D. T. (1993). Behavioral genetics of cognitive ability: A life-span perspective. In R. Plomin & G. E. McClearn (Eds.), *Nature, nurture, and psychology* (pp. 59–76). Washington, DC: American Psychological Association.

McKellar, P. (1965). The investigation of mental images. In S. A. Bartnet & A. McLaren (Eds.), *Penguin science survey B (biological sciences)* (pp. 79–94). New York: Penguin Books.

McLean, L. M., & Gallop, R. (2003). Implications of childhood sexual abuse for adult borderline personality disorder and complex posttraumatic stress disorder. *American Journal of Psychiatry, 160,* 369–371.

McLoyd, V. (1998). Socioeconomic disadvantage and child development. *American Psychologist, 53*(2), 185–204.

McNally, R. J. (2006). Cognitive abnormalities in post-traumatic stress disorder. *Trends in Cognitive Sciences, 10*(6), 271–277.

McNally, R. J., Lasko, N. B., Clancy, S. A., Macklin, M. L., Pitman, R. K., & Orr, S. P. (2004). Psychophysiological responding during script-driven imagery in people reporting abduction by space aliens. *Psychological Science, 15*(7), 493–497.

Medin, D. L., Proffit, J. B., & Schwartz, H. C. (2000). Concepts: Structure. In A. Kazdin (Ed.), *Encyclopedia of psychology* (pp. 162–169). Washington, DC & New York: American Psychological Association and Oxford University Press.

Meichenbaum, D. H. (1974). The clinical potential of modifying what clients say to themselves. In M. J. Mahoney & C. E. Thoresen (Eds.), *Self-control: Power to the person* (pp. 103–117). Monterey, CA: Brooks/Cole.

Meichenbaum, D. H. (1975). Self instructional methods. In F. H. Kanfer & A. P. Goldstein (Eds.), *Helping people change: A textbook of methods* (pp. 357–391). New York: Pergamon.

Melzack, R., & Wall, P. D. (1965). Pain mechanisms: A new theory. *Science, 150,* 971–979.

Mendlewicz, J. (1985). Genetic research in depressive disorders. In E. E. Beckham & W. R. Leber (Eds.), *Handbook of depression: Treatment, assessment, and research* (pp. 795–815). Homewood, Il: Dorsey Press.

Mendlewicz, J., & Rainer, J. D. (1977). Adoption study supporting genetic transmission in the manic depressive illness. *Nature, 268,* 327–329.

Merikangas, K. R., & Gelerntor, C. S. (1990). Comorbidity for alcohol and depression. *Psychiatric Clinic of North America, 13,* 613–632.

Merikangas, K. R., & Risch, N. (2003). Will the genomics revolution revolutionize psychiatry? *American Journal of Psychiatry, 160,* 625–635.

Merskey, H. (1995). *The analysis of hysteria: Understanding conversion and dissociation* (2nd ed.). London: Gaskel/Royal College of Psychiatrists.

Meyer, I. H. (2003). Prejudice, social stress, and mental health in lesbian, gay, and bisexual populations: Conceptual issues and research evidence. *Psychological Bulletin, 129,* 674–697.

Milgram, S. (1963). Behavioral study of obedience. *Journal of Abnormal and Social Psychology, 67,* 371–378.

Milgram, S. (1974). *Obedience to authority: An experimental view.* New York: Harper & Row.

Miller, E. (1987). Hysteria: Its nature and explanation. *British Journal of Clinical Psychology, 26,* 163–173.

Miller, G. A. (1956). The magical number seven, plus or minus two: Some limits on our capacity for processing information. *Psychological Review, 63,* 81–97.

Miller, N. E. (1985). The value of behavioral research on animals. *American Psychologist, 40,* 423–440.

Miller-Jones, D. (1989). Culture and testing. *American Psychologist, 44,* 360–366.

Minuchin, S., & Fishman, H. C. (1981). *Family therapy techniques.* Cambridge, MA: Harvard University Press.

Mischel, W., & Shoda, Y. (1999). Integrating disposition and processing dynamics within a unified theory of personality: The cognitive-affective personality system. In L. A. Pervin & O. P. John (Eds.), *Handbook of personality: Theory and research* (pp. 531–545). New York: Guilford Press.

Miyata, M. (2007). Distinct properties of corticothalamic and primary sensory synapses to thalamic neurons. *Neuroscience Research, 59*(4), 377–382.

Mombaerts, P. (1999). Molecular biology of odorant receptors in vertebrates. *Annual Review of Neuroscience, 22,* 487–509.

Monte, C. F. (1999). *Beneath the mask.* Fort Worth, TX: Harcourt Brace.

Moore, R. Y. (1997). Circadian rhythms: Basic neurobiology and clinical applications. *Annual Review of Medicine, 48,* 253–266.

Morgane, P. J., & Mokler, D. J. (2006). The limbic brain: Continuing resolution. *Neuroscience & Biobehavioral Review, 30*(2), 119–125.

Morgenstern, J., Labouvie, E., McCrady, B. S., Kahler, C. W., & Frey, R. M. (1997). Affiliation with Alcoholics Anonymous after treatment: A study of its therapeutic effects and mechanisms of action. *Journal of Consulting and Clinical Psychology, 65,* 768–777.

Morris, C. D., Bransford, J. D., & Franks, J. J. (1977). Levels of processing versus transfer-appropriate processing. *Journal of Verbal Learning and Verbal Behavior, 16,* 519–533.

Muehlenhard, C. L., & Falcon, P. L. (1990). Men's heterosocial skill and attitudes towards women as predictors of verbal sexual coercion and forcible rape. *Sex Roles, 23*(5), 241–259.

Muehlenhard, C. L., & Linton, M. A. (1987). Date rape and sexual aggression in dating situations: Incidence and risk factors. *Journal of Counseling Psychology, 34*(2), 186–196.

Murnen, S. K., Wright, C., & Kaluzny, G. (2002). If "boys will be boys" then girls will be victims? A meta-analytic review of the research that relates masculine ideology to sexual aggression. *Sex Roles, 46,* 359–375.

Murray, E. A. (2007). The amygdala, reward and emotion. *Trends in Cognitive Sciences, 11*(11), 489–497.

Mustanski, B. S., DuPree, M. G., Nievergelt, C. M., Bocklandt, S., Schork, N. J., & Hamer, D. H. (2005). A genomewide scan of male sexual orientation. *Human Genetics, 116*(4), 272–278.

Myers, D. G. (1991). *The pursuit of happiness: Who is happy—and why.* New York: Morrow.

Myers, D. G. (2004). *Exploring psychology* (6th ed.). New York: Worth.

N

Narrow, W. E., Rae, D. S., Robins, L. N., & Regier, D. A. (2002). Revised prevalence estimates of mental disorders in the United States. *Archives of General Psychiatry, 59,* 115–123.

Nash, M. R. (2001, July). The truth and the hype of hypnosis. *Scientific American, 285*(1), 46–55.

Nathan, D., & Snedeker, M. (2001). *Satan's silence.* Lincoln, NE: Authors Choice Press.

Neiderhiser, J. M., Reiss, D., Hetherington, E. M., & Plomin, R. (1999). Relationship between parenting and adolescent adjustment over time: Genetic and environmental contributions. *Developmental Psychology, 35,* 680–692.

Neisser, U. (1967). *Cognitive psychology.* New York: Appleton-Century-Crofts.

Nelson, C. A. (2004). Brain development during puberty and adolescence. *Annals of the New York Academy of Sciences, 1021,* 105–109.

Nelson, C. A., & Luciana, M. (2001). *Handbook of developmental cognitive neuroscience.* Cambridge, MA: MIT Press.

Nelson, K. (1973). Structure and strategy in learning to talk. *Monographs of the Society for Research on Child Development, 38*(1–2, Serial No. 149).

Ness, A. R., & Powles, J. W. (1997). Fruits, vegetables and cardiovascular disease: A review. *International Journal of Epidemiology, 26,* 1–13.

Nesse, R. M. (1990). Evolutionary expression of emotions. *Human Nature, 1,* 261–289.

Neves, G., Cooke, S. F., & Bliss, T. V. P. (2008). Synaptic plasticity, memory and the hippocampus: A neural network approach to causality. *Nature Review Neuroscience, 9*(1), 65–75.

Nevid, J. S., Rathus, S. A., & Greene, B. (2006). *Abnormal psychology in a changing world* (6th ed.). Upper Saddle River, NJ: Prentice Hall.

Newell, A., & Simon, H. (1972). *Human problem solving.* Englewood Cliffs, NJ: Prentice Hall.

Newman, L. S., Duff, K., & Baumeister, R. (1997). A new look at defensive projection: Thought suppression, accessibility, and biased person perception. *Journal of Personality and Social Psychology, 72,* 980–1001.

Nickerson, K. J., Helms, J. E., & Terrell, F. (1994). Cultural mistrust, opinions about mental illness, and Black students' attitudes toward seeking psychological help from White counselors. *Journal of Counseling Psychology, 41,* 378–385.

Nopoulos, P., Flaum, M., O'Leary, D., & Andreasen, N. C. (2000). Sexual dimorphism in the human brain: Evaluation of tissue volume, tissue composition and surface anatomy using magnetic resonance imaging. *Psychiatry Research: Neuroimaging, 98*(1), 1–13.

Norton, A. J., & Moorman, J. E. (1987). Current trends in marriage and divorce among American women. *Journal of Marriage and the Family, 49,* 3–14.

O

Ochse, R., & Plug, C. (1986). Cross-cultural investigation of the validity of Erikson's theory of personality development. *Journal of Personality and Social Psychology, 50,* 1240–1252.

O'Connor, M. J., Sigman, M., & Kasari, C. (1993). Interaction model for the association among maternal alcohol use, mother-infant interaction, and infant cognitive development. *Infant Behavior and Development, 16,* 177–192.

O'Craven, K. M., & Karwisher, N. (2000). Mental imagery of faces and places activates corresponding stimulus-specific brain regions. *Journal of Cognitive Neuroscience, 12*(6), 1013–1023.

O'Hara, S. (2005). *What can you do with a major in psychology? Real people, real jobs, real rewards.* Hoboken, NJ: John Wiley & Sons.

Oldham, J. M. (1994). Personality disorders: Current perspectives. *Journal of the American Medical Association, 272,* 213–220.

Oller, D. K. (1980). The emergence of the sounds of speech in infancy. In G. Yeni-Komshian, J. F. Kavanagh, & C. A. Ferguson (Eds.), *Child phonology: Vol. 1 production* (pp. 93–112). New York: Academic Press.

O'Neil, H. F., & Drillings, M. (1994). *Motivation: Theory and research.* Hillsdale, NJ: Lawrence Erlbaum.

Oren, D., & Terman, M. (1998). Tweaking the human circadian clock with light. *Science, 279,* 333–334.

Ost, J. (2003). Seeking the middle ground in the "memory wars": Essay book review. *British Journal of Psychology, 94,* 125–139.

Ost, J., Vrij, A., Costall, A., & Ball, R. (2002). Crashing memories and reality monitoring: Distinguishing between perceptions, imaginations and "false memories." *Applied Cognitive Psychology, 16,* 125–134.

P

Padilla, M. A. (1988). Early psychological assessments of Mexican-American children. *Journal of the History of the Behavioral Sciences, 24,* 111–117.

Paivio, A. (1971). *Imagery and verbal processes.* New York: Holt, Rinehart & Winston.

Paivio, A. (1975). Perceptual comparison through the mind's eye. *Memory and Cognition, 3,* 635–647.

Paniagua, F. (1994). *Assessing and treating culturally diverse clients: A practical guide.* Thousand Oaks, CA: Sage.

Parkinson, W. L., & Weingarten, H. P. (1990). Dissociative analysis of ventromedial hypothalamic obesity syndrome. *American Journal of Physiology, 259,* 829–835.

Partala, T., Jokiniemi, M., & Surakka, V. (2000, November). *Pupillary responses to emotionally provocative stimuli.* Poster session presented at the Eye Tracking Research & Application Symposium, Palm Beach, FL.

Passer, M. W., & Smith, E. S. (2004). Language, thinking, and intelligent behavior. In T. Dorwick (Ed.), *Psychology: The science of mind and behavior.* New York: McGraw Hill.

Pastorino, E., & Doyle-Portillo, E. (2006). *What is psychology?* Belmont, CA: Wadsworth/Thomson Learning.

Patterson, C. H. (2000). *Person-centered approach and client-centered therapy: Essential readers.* Ross-on-Wye, England: PCCS Books.

Pauk, W. (1974). *How to study in college.* Boston: Houghton Mifflin.

Paunonen, S. V., & Ashton, M. C. (1998). The structured assessment of personality across cultures. *Journal of Cross-Cultural Psychology, 29,* 150–170.

Pavlov, I. P. (1927). *Conditioned reflexes.* London: Oxford University Press.

Pearce, J. M., Redhead, E. S., & Aydin, A. (1997). Partial reinforcement in appetitive Pavlovian conditioning with rats. *Quarterly Journal of Experimental Psychology B: Comparative and Physiological Psychology, 50*(4), 273–294.

Pearson Assessments. (2005). Retrieved June 8, 2008, from http://www.pearsonassessments.com

Pendergast, M. (1996). *Victims of memory: Sex abuse accusations and shattered lives* (2nd ed.). Hinesburg, VT: Upper Access.

Penfield, W. (1969). Consciousness, memory, and man's conditioned reflexes. In K. Pribam (Ed.), *On the biology of learning* (pp. 129–168). New York: Harcourt Brace Jovanovich.

Pennebaker, J. (1990). *Opening up.* New York: William Morrow.

Perennou, D. A., & Bronstein, A. M. (2005). Balance disorders and vertigo after stroke: Assessment and rehabilitation. In M. Barnes, B. Bobkin, & J. Bogoussalavsky (Eds.), *Recovery after stroke* (pp. 320–396). New York: Cambridge University Press.

Perkins, J. E., & Grobe, J. E. (1992). Increased desire to smoke during stress. *British Journal of Addiction, 87,* 1037–1040.

Perlman, M. D., & Kaufman, A. S. (1990). Assessment of child intelligence. In G. Goldstein & M. Hersen (Eds.), *Handbook of psychological assessment* (pp. 127–129). New York: Pergamon Press.

Perry, C. (n.d.). *Key concepts in hypnosis.* Retrieved August 29, 2005, from http://davidhutchinson.net/projects/fmsf/hypnosis.htm

Peterson, C. (2006). *A primer in positive psychology.* New York: Oxford University Press.

Peterson, J. R., & Peterson, M. J. (1959). Short term retention of individual verbal items. *Journal of Psychology, 66,* 421–435.

Petitto, L. A., & Marentette, P. F. (1991). Babbling in the manual mode: Evidence for the ontogeny of language. *Science, 251,* 1493–1496.

Petrill, S. A. (2003). The development of intelligence: Behavioral genetics approaches. In R. J. Sternberg, J. Lautrey, & T. I. Lubart (Eds.), *Models of intelligence* (pp. 17–34). Washington, DC: American Psychological Association.

Pezdek, K. (2003). Event memory and autobiographical memory for the events of September 11, 2001. *Applied Cognitive Psychology, 17,* 1033–1045.

Phelps, E. A. (2006). Emotion and cognition: Insights from studies of the human amygdala. *Annual Review of Psychology, 57,* 27–53.

Phillips, D. P., & Smith, D. G. (1990). Postponement of death until symbolically meaningful occasions. *Journal of the American Medical Association, 263,* 1947.

Pierce, W. D., & Epling, W. F. (1995). *Behavior analysis and learning.* Englewood Cliffs, NJ: Prentice Hall.

Pinel, J. P. J. (2006). *Biopsychology* (6th ed.). Boston: Pearson Education.

Pinker, S. (1994). *The language instinct.* New York: William Morrow.

Plomin, R. (1997, May). Cited in B. Azar, Nature, nurture: Not mutually exclusive. *APA Monitor,* p. 32.

Plomin, R. (1999). Genetics and general cognitive ability. *Nature, 402,* C25–C29.

Plomin, R., & Craig, I. (2001). Genetics, environment, and cognitive abilities: Review and work in progress toward a genome scan for quantitative trait locus associations using DNA pooling. *British Journal of Psychiatry, 40,* 41–48.

Plomin, R., Owen, M. J., & NcGuffin, P. (1994). The genetic basis of complex human behaviors. *Science, 264,* 1733–1739.

Plomin, R., & Petrill, S. A. (1997). Genetics and intelligence: What's new? *Intelligence, 24,* 53–77.

Plotnik, R. (1998). *Introduction to psychology.* Pacific Grove, CA: Brooks/Cole.

Plotnik, R. (2002). *Introduction to psychology* (6th ed.). Pacific Grove, CA: Wadsworth-Thomson Learning.

Plotnik, R. (2005). *Introduction to psychology* (8th ed.). Belmont, CA: Thomson Wadsworth.

Plutchik, R. (1980). A general psychoevolutionary theory of emotion. In R. Plutchik & H. Kellerman (Eds.), *Emotion: Theory, research, and experience: Vol. 1. Theories of emotion* (pp. 3–33). New York: Academic.

Pollack, I. (1953). The assimilation of sequentially coded information. *American Journal of Psychology, 66,* 421–435.

Pomerleau, A., Boldue, D., Macuit, G., & Cosetts, L. (1990). Pink or blue: Environmental stereotypes in the first two years of life. *Sex Roles, 22,* 359–367.

Power, K. G., McGoldrick, T., Brown, K., Buchanan, R., Sharp, D., Swanson, V., et al. (2002). A controlled comparison of eye movement desensitization and reprocessing versus exposure plus cognitive restructuring, versus waiting list in the treatment of post-traumatic stress disorder. *Journal of Clinical Psychology and Psychotherapy, 9,* 299–318.

Preston, J. D., O'Neal, J. H., & Talaga, M. C. (2005). *Handbook of clinical psychopharmacology for therapists* (4th ed.). Oakland, CA: New Harbinger Publications.

Proctor, F., Wagner, N., & Butler, J. (1974). The differentiation of male and female orgasm: An experimental study. In Rathus et al. (Eds.), *Human sexuality in a world of diversity.* Upper Saddle River, NJ: Pearson Education.

Pruessner, J. C., Dedovic, K., Khalili-Mahani, N., Engert, V., Pruessner, M., Buss, C., et al. (2008). Deactivation of the limbic system during acute psychosocial stress: Evidence from positron emission tomography and functional magnetic resonance imaging studies. *Biological Psychiatry, 63*(2), 234–240.

Pynes, M. (2005, September 19). Brain scans that spy on the senses. *Seeing, hearing, and smelling the world: A report from the Howard Hughes Medical Institute.* Retrieved October 25, 2005, from http://www.hhmi.org/senses/e110.html

R

Rabasca, L. (2000a, March). Listening instead of preaching. *Monitor on Psychology, 31,* 50–51.

Rahman, Q., & Wilson, G. D. (2003). Sexual orientation and the 2nd and 4th finger length ratio: Evidence for organising effects of sex hormones or developmental instability? *Psychoneuroendocrinology, 28*(3), 288–303.

Raine, A. (1999). Murderous minds: Can we see the mark of Cain? *Cerebrum, 1,* 15–30.

Rakic, P. (1995). Corticogenesis in human and nonhuman primates. In M. S. Gazzaniga (Ed.), *The cognitive neurosciences* (pp. 127–145). Cambridge, MA: MIT Press.

Rakic, P., Bourgeois, J. P., & Goldman Rakic, P. S. (1994). Synaptic development of the cerebral cortex: Implications for learning, memory, & mental illness. In J. van Pelt, M. A. Corner, H. B. M. Uylings, & F. H. Lopes da Silva (Eds.), *Progress in brain research: Vol. 102. The self-organizing brain: From growth cones to functional networks* (pp. 227–243). Amsterdam: Elsevier.

Ramachandran, V. S., & Blakeslee, S. (1998). *Phantoms in the brain: Probing the mysteries of the human mind.* New York: Morrow.

Ratsma, J. E., Van Der Stelt, O., & Gunning, W. B. (2002). Neurochemical markers of alcoholism vulnerability in humans. *Alcohol & Alcoholism, 37*(6), 522–533.

Raulin, M. L. (2003). *Abnormal psychology.* Boston: Allyn & Bacon.

Read, J. D., & Lindsay, D. S. (1997). *Recollections of trauma: Scientific evidence and clinical practice.* New York: Plenum Press.

Recanzone, G. H., & Sutter, M. L. (2008). The biological basis of audition. *Annual Review of Psychology, 59,* 119–142.

Reed, S. K. (1996). *Cognition: Theory and applications* (4th ed.). Pacific Grove, CA: Brooks/Cole.

Reeve, A. (1998). Cerebral lateralization. *Journal of Psychosomatic Research, 44,* 641–642.

Reeve, J. (1997). *Understanding motivation and emotion* (2nd ed.). Fort Worth, TX: Harcourt Brace.

Regan, P. C., & Berscheid, E. (1999). *Lust: What we know about sexual desire.* Thousand Oaks, CA: Sage.

Reisberg, D. (1997). *Cognition: Exploring the science of the mind.* New York: W. W. Norton.

Reisberg, D., & Chambers, D. (1991). Neither pictures nor propositions: What can we learn from a mental image? *Canadian Journal of Psychology, 45,* 336–348.

Reisner, A. D. (1994). Multiple personality disorder diagnosis: A house of cards? *American Journal of Psychiatry, 151,* 629.

Remafedi, G., French, S., Story, M., Resnick, M. D., & Blum, R. (1998). The relationship between suicide risk and sexual orientation: Results of a population-based study. *American Journal of Public Health, 88*(1), 57–60.

Renfrey, G. S. (1992). Cognitive-behavior therapy and the Native American client. *Behavior Therapy, 23,* 321–340.

Renzulli, J. S. (1986). The three-ring conception of giftedness: A developmental model for creative productivity. In R. J. Sternberg & J. E. Davidson (Eds.), *Conceptions of giftedness* (pp. 51–92). New York: Cambridge University Press.

Repressed-memory case won't be retried. (1996, July 3). *New York Times.* Retrieved September 20, 2005, from http://query.nytimes.com/gst/fullpage.html?res=9D0CE5DF1039F930A35754COA960958

Rescorla, R. A., & Wagner, A. R. (1972). A theory of Pavlovian conditioning: Variations in the effectiveness of reinforcement and nonreinforcement. In *Classical Conditioning II: Current Research and Theory* (pp. 64–99). New York: Appleton-Century-Crofts.

Restak, R. M. (1984). *The brain.* New York: Bantam.

Revensuo, A. (2000). The reinterpretation of dreams: An evolutionary hypothesis of the function of dreaming. *Behavioral & Brain Science, 23,* 877–903.

Richardson, J. T. E., & Zucco, G. M. (1989). Cognition and olfaction: A review. *Psychological Bulletin, 105*(3), 352–360.

Riskind, J. H., Beck, A. T., Berchick, R. J., Brown, G., & Steer, R. A. (1987). Reliability of DSM-III diagnoses for major depression and generalized anxiety disorder using the structured clinical interview for DSM-III. *Archives of General Psychiatry, 44,* 817–820.

Rivas-Vazquez, R. A. (2003). Benzodiazepines in contemporary clinical practice. *Professional Psychology: Research and Practice, 34,* 424–428.

Robertson, G. L. (1983). Thirst and vasopressin function in normal and disordered states of water balance. *Journal of Laboratory and Clinical Medicine, 101,* 351–371.

Robinson, S. (2000). The ratio of 2nd to 4th digit length and male homosexuality. *Evolution and Human Behavior, 21*(5), 333–345.

Rock, A. M. L., Trainer, L. J., & Addison, T. L. (1999). Distinctive messages in infant-directed lullabies and play songs. *Developmental Psychology, 35,* 527–534.

Roediger, H. L. (1980). The effectiveness of four mnemonics in ordering recall. *Journal of Experimental Psychology: Human Learning and Memory, 6,* 558–567.

Roediger, H. L. (1990). Implicit memory: Retention without remembering. *American Psychologist, 45*(9), 1043–1056.

Rogers, C. (1951). *Client-centered therapy: Its current practice, implications and theory.* London: Constable.

Rogers, C. R. (1961). *On becoming a person.* Boston: Houghton Mifflin.

Rogers, L. (2001). *Sexing the brain.* New York: Columbia University Press.

Rollman, G. B. (1991). Pain responsiveness. In M. A. Heller & W. Schiff (Eds.), *The psychology of touch* (pp. 91–114). Hillsdale, NJ: Lawrence Erlbaum Associates.

Root, M. P. (1993). Guidelines for facilitating therapy with Asian American clients. In D. R. Atkinson, G. Morten, & D. W. Sue (Eds.), *Counselling American minorities: A cross-cultural perspective* (pp. 211–224). Madison, WI: Brown & Benchmark.

Rosch, E. H. (1978). Principles of categorization. In E. H. Rosch & B. B. Lloyd (Eds.), *Cognition and categorization* (pp. 27–48). Hillsdale, NJ: Erlbaum.

Rosch, E., Mervis, C. B., Gray, W. D., Johnson, D. M., & Boyes-Braem, P. (1976). Basic objects in natural categories. *Cognitive Psychology, 8,* 382–439.

Rosen, E. (1957). *Dance in psychotherapy.* New York: New York Bureau of Publications; Teachers College, Columbia University Press.

Rosenzweig, M. R., Breedlove, S. M., & Watson, N. V. (2005). *Biological psychology, An introduction to behavioral and cognitive neuroscience* (5th ed.). Sunderland, MA: Sinauer Associates.

Ross, L. (1977). The intuitive psychologist and his shortcomings: Distortions in the attribution process. In L. Berkowitz (Ed.), *Advances in experimental social psychology* (Vol. 10, pp. 173–220). Orlando, FL: Academic Press.

Roth, T. (2004). Characteristics and determinants of normal sleep. *Journal of Clinical Psychiatry, 65* (Suppl. 16), 8–11.

Rothbart, M. K., Ellis, L. K., & Posner, M. I. (2004). Temperament and self-regulation. In R. F. Baumeister & K. D. Vohs (Eds.), *Handbook of self regulation: Research, theory, and applications* (pp. 357–370). New York: Guilford Press.

Rothbaum, B. (1997). A controlled study of eye movement desensitization and reprocessing in the treatment of post-traumatic stress disordered sexual assault victims. *Bulletin of the Menninger Clinic, 61,* 317–334.

Rothbaum, B. O., Hodges, L., Anderson, P. L., Price, L., & Smith, S. (2002). Twelve-month follow-up of virtual reality and standard exposure therapies for the fear of flying. *Journal of Consulting and Clinical Psychology, 70,* 428–432.

Rothbaum, B. O., Hodges, L., Smith, S., Lee, J. H., & Price, L. (2001). A controlled study of virtual reality exposure therapy for fear of flying. *Journal of Consulting & Clinical Psychology, 68,* 1020–1026.

Rovee-Collier, C. K., & Hayne, H. (1987). Reactivation of infant memory: Implications for cognitive development. In H. W. Reese (Ed.), *Advances in child development and behavior* (Vol. 20, pp. 185–238). New York: Academic Press.

Rovee-Collier, C. K., Sullivan, M. W., Enright, M., Lucas, D., & Fagen, J. W. (1980). Reactivation of infant memory. *Science, 208*(4448), 1159–1161.

Rowe, D. C. (1997). Genetics, temperament, and personality. In R. Hogan, J. Johnson, & S. Briggs (Eds.), *Handbook of personality psychology* (pp. 105–176). New York: Academic Press.

Rudski, J. M. (2000). Effects of delay of reinforcement on superstitious inferences. *Perceptual and Motor Skills, 90*(3), 1047–1058.

Rumelhart, D. E. (1975). Notes on schema for stories. In D. G. Bobrow & A. M. Collins (Eds.), *Representations and understanding: Studies in cognitive science* (pp. 211–236). New York: Academic Press.

S   Sacks, O. (1985). *The man who mistook his wife for a hat.* New York: Summit Books.

Sacks, O. (1996). *An anthropologist on Mars: Seven paradoxical tales.* Essex, UK: Vintage.

Sadock, B. J., & Sadock, V. A. (Eds.). (2003). *Synopsis of psychiatry: Behavioral sciences/clinical psychiatry.* Philadelphia: Lippincott Williams & Wilkins.

Sahakian, W. S. (Ed.). (1968). *History of psychology: A source book in systematic psychology.* Itasca, IL: F. E. Peacock Publishers.

Sajith, S. G., & Clarke, D. (2007). Melatonin and sleep disorders associated with intellectual disability: A clinical review. *Journal of Intellectual Disability Research, 51*(1), 2–13.

Salapatek, P. (1968). Visual scanning of geometric figures by the human newborn. *Journal of Comparative and Physiological Psychology, 66,* 247–258.

Salapatek, P. (1975). Pattern perception in early infancy. In L. Cohen & P. Salapatek (Eds.), *Infant perception: From sensation to cognition* (pp. 133–248). New York: Academic Press.

Salgado, J. F. (1997). The five factor model of personality and job performance in the European community. *Journal of Applied Psychology, 82,* 30–43.

Salkind, N. J. (2004). *An introduction to theories of human development.* Thousand Oaks, CA: Sage Publications.

Salkovskis, P. M., & Clark, D. M. (1993). Panic disorder and hypochondriasis. Special issue: Panic, cognitions and sensations. *Advances in Behaviour Research and Therapy, 15,* 23–48.

Salmon, C. A., & Daly, M. (1998). Birth order and familial sentiment? Middleborns are different. *Evolution and Human Behavior, 19*(5), 299–312.

Sanchez-Hucles, J. (2000). *The first session with African Americans: A step-by-step guide.* San Francisco: Jossey Bass.

Sandman, C. A., & Hetrick, W. P. (1995). Opiate mechanisms in self-injury. *Mental Retardation & Developmental Disabilities Research Reviews, 1*(2), 130–136.

Sarafino, E. P. (2001). *Behavior modification: Principles of behavior change.* Long Grove, IL: Waveland Press.

Savage-Rumbaugh, E. S., McDonald, K., Sevcik, R. A., Hopkins, W. D., & Rupert, E. (1986). Spontaneous symbol acquisition and communicative use by pygmy chimpanzees *(Pan paniscus). Journal of Experimental Psychology: General, 115,* 211–235.

Savage-Rumbaugh, E. S., Murphy, J., Sevcik, R. A., Williams, S., Brakke, K., and Rumbaugh, D. M. (1993). Language comprehension in ape and child. *Monographs of the Society for Research in Child Development, 58*(3, 4), 1–256.

Savage-Rumbaugh, S. (1987). Communication, symbolic communication and language: Reply to Seidenberg and Petitto. *Journal of Experimental Psychology: General, 116,* 288–292.

Savage-Rumbaugh, S., & Lewin, R. (1996). *Kanzi.* New York: Wiley.

Sax, L. (2002). How common is intersex? A response to Anne Fausto-Sterling. *Journal of Sex Research, 39,* 174–179.

Scarborough, E., & Furumoto, L. (1987). *Untold lives: The first generation of American women psychologists.* New York: Columbia University Press.

Scarr, S., & Weinberg, R. A. (1976). I.Q. test performance of black children adopted by white families. *American Psychologist, 31,* 726–739.

Schaal, B. (1986). Presumed olfactory exchanges between mother and neonate in humans. In J. LeCamus & J. Cosnier (Eds.), *Ethologie et Psychologie de l'Enfant* (pp. 101–110). Toulouse, France: Private IEC.

Schacter, D. L. (1996). *Searching for memory: The brain, mind and the past.* New York: Basic Books.

Schacter, D. L., Gilbert, D. T., & Wegner, D. M. (2007). *Psychology.* New York: Worth Publishers.

Schacter, S., & Singer, J. (1962). Cognitive, social, and physiological determinants of emotional state. *Psychological Review, 69,* 379–399.

Schafer, M., & Crichlow, S. (1996). Antecedents of groupthink: A quantitative study. *Journal of Conflict Resolution, 40,* 415–435.

Schaffhausen, J. (2005, July). The day his world stood still. *Brain connection.* Retrieved August 30, 2005, from www.brainconnection.com/topics/?main=fa/hm-memory

Schaie, K. W. (1965). A general model for the study of developmental problems. *Psychological Bulletin, 64,* 92–101.

Schaller, S. (1995). *A man without words.* Berkeley, CA: University of California Press.

Schank, R., & Abelson, R. (1977). *Scripts, plans, goals, and understanding.* Mahwah, NJ: Erlbaum.

Schiff, M., & Bargal, D. (2000). Helping characteristics of self-help and support groups: Their contribution to participants' subjective well-being. *Small Group Research, 31,* 275–304.

Schloss, P., & Williams, D. C. (1998). The serotonin transporter: A primary target for antidepressant drugs. *Journal of Psychopharmacology, 12*(2), 115–121.

Schmolk, H., Buffalo, E. A., & Squire, L. R. (2000). Memory distortion over time: Recollections of the O. J. Simpson trial verdict after 15 months and 32 months. *Psychological Science, 11,* 39–47.

Schou, M. (1997). Forty years of lithium treatment. *Archives of General Psychiatry, 54,* 9–13.

Schultz, D., & Schultz, S. (2005). *Theories of personality* (8th ed.). Belmont, CA: Thomson Wadsworth.

Schwartz, B. (1984). *Psychology of learning and behavior* (2nd ed.). New York: Norton.

Schwartz, B. (1989). *Psychology of learning and behavior* (3rd ed.). New York: Norton.

Scientific American Frontiers. (n.d.). *Introductory psychology: True or false* (video). New York: Worth Publishers.

Sedlaczek, O., Grips, E., Bazner, H., Claus, A., Wohrle, J., & Hennerici, M. (2005). Infarction of the central cerebellar arbor vitae and transient loss of spatial orientation. *Neurology, 65*(1), 168.

Segraves, R. T., & Althof, S. (1998). Psychotherapy and pharmacotherapy of sexual dysfunctions. In P. E. Nathan & J. M. Gorman (Eds.), *A guide to treatments that work* (pp. 447–471). New York: Oxford University Press.

Seifer, R. (2001). Socioeconomic status, multiple risks, and development of intelligence. In R. J. Sternberg & E. L. Grigorenko (Eds.), *Environmental effects on cognitive abilities* (pp. 59–82). Mahwah, NJ: Erlbaum.

Seligman, M. E. P. (1971). Phobias and preparedness. *Behavior Therapy, 2*, 307–320.

Seligman, M. E. P. (1975). *Helplessness: On depression, development, and death.* San Francisco: Freeman.

Seligman, M. E. P. (1994). *What you can change and what you can't.* New York: Alfred A. Knopf.

Seligman, M. E. P. (1995). The effectiveness of psychotherapy: The *Consumer Reports* study. *American Psychologist, 50*, 965–974.

Seligman, M. E. P. (2002). *Authentic happiness: Using the new positive psychology to realize your potential for lasting fulfillment.* New York: Free Press.

Seligman, M. E. P., Rashid, T., & Parks, A. C. (2006). Positive psychotherapy. *American Psychologist, 61*(8), 774–788.

Selling, L. S. (1940). *Men against madness.* New York: Greenberg.

Selye, H. A. (1976). *The stress of life.* New York: McGraw-Hill.

Sergent, J., & Signoret, J. L. (1992). Varieties of functional deficits in prosopagnosia. *Cerebral Cortex, 2*, 375–388.

Seyfarth, R. M., & Cheny, D. L. (2003). Signalers and receivers in animal communication. *Annual Review of Psychology, 54*, 145–173.

Shahidi, S., & Salmon, P. (1992). Contingent and noncontingent biofeedback training for type A and B health adults: Can type As relax by competing? *Journal of Psychosomatic Research, 36*, 477–483.

Shatz, C. J. (1992). The developing brain. *Scientific American, 267*(3), 60–67.

Shelov, S. P. (1998). *Caring for your baby and young child.* New York: Bantam Books.

Shepard, R. N., & Cooper, L. A. (1982). *Mental images and their transformations.* Cambridge, MA: MIT Press/Bradford Books.

Shepherd, G. M. (1994). *Neurobiology.* New York: Oxford University Press.

Sherif, M. (1966). *In common predicament: Social psychology of intergroup conflict and cooperation.* Boston: Houghton Mifflin.

Sherwood, L. (2004). *Human physiology: From cells to systems.* Belmont, CA: Brooks/Cole—Thomson Learning.

Shuman, D. W. (1997). Framing the questions of the admissibility of expert testimony about recollections of trauma in the United States. In J. D. Read

& D. S. Lindsay (Eds.), *Recollections of trauma: Scientific evidence and clinical practice* (pp. 495–500). New York: Plenum Press.

Shweder, R. A., & Sullivan, M. A. (1993). Cultural psychology: Who needs it? *Annual Review of Psychlogy, 44*, 497–523.

Siebert, M., Markowitsch, H. J., & Bartel, P. (2003). Amygdala, affect and cognition: Evidence from 10 patients with Urbach-Weithe disease. *Brain, 126*(12), 2627–2637.

Siegel, J. M. (1999). The evolution of REM sleep. In R. Lydic & H. A. Baghdoyan (Eds.), *Handbook of behavioral state control* (pp. 87–100). Boca Raton, FL: CRC Press.

Siegle, G., Granholm, E., Ingram, R., & Matt, G. (2001). Pupillary and reaction time measures of sustained processing of negative information in depression. *Biological Psychiatry, 49*, 624–636.

Siegler, R. S., & Elllis, S. (1996). Piaget XE "Piaget, J." on childhood. *Psychological Science, 7*, 211–215.

Silberstein, R. B., Farrow, M. M., Levy, F., Pipingas, A., Hay, D. A., & Jarman, F. C. (1998). Functional brain electrical activity mapping in boys with attention-deficit/hyperactivity disorder. *Archives of General Psychiatry, 55*, 1105–1112.

Silverstein, B., & Perlick, E. (1997). Depression mixed with anxiety, somatization, and disorder eating: Relationship with gender-role-related limitations experienced by females. *Sex Roles, 36*(11–12), 709–724.

Skeels, H. M. (1966). Adult status of children with contrasting early life experiences: A follow-up study. *Monographs of the Society for Research on Child Development, 31*(Serial No. 105).

Skeels, H. M., & Dye, H. (1939). A study of the effects of differential stimulation on mentally retarded children. *Proceedings of the American Association on Mental Deficiency, 44*, 114–136.

Skinner, B. F. (1938). *The behavior of organisms: An experimental analysis.* New York: Appleton-Century-Crofts.

Skinner, B. F. (1948). Superstition in the pigeon. *Journal of Experimental Psychology, 38*, 168–172.

Skinner, B. F. (1957). *Verbal behavior.* Englewood Cliffs, NJ: Prentice Hall.

Skinner, B. F. (1966). Operant behavior. In W. K. Honig (Ed.), *Operant behavior: Areas of research and application* (pp. 12–32). New York: Appleton-Century-Crofts.

Skinner, B. F. (1981). Selection by consequences. *Science, 213*, 501–504.

Slamecka, N. J., & McElree, B. (1983). Normal forgetting of verbal lists as a function of their degree of learning. *Journal of Experimental Psychology: Learning, Memory and Cognition, 9*, 384–397.

Sleepwalking. (n.d.). Retrieved March 17, 2008, from http://www.emedicinehealth.com/sleepwalking/article_em.htm

Smith, M. E. (1926). An investigation of the development of the sentence and the extent of vocabulary in children. *University of Iowa Studies in Child Welfare, 3*(5).

Smith, M. L., Glass, G. V., & Miller, T. I. (1980). *The benefits of psychotherapy.* Baltimore: Johns Hopkins University Press.

Snow, C. E. (1999). Social perspectives on the emergence of language. In B. MaWhinney (Ed.), *The emergence of language* (pp. 257–276). Mahwah, NJ: Erlbaum.

Snyder, S. H. (1978). Neuroleptic drugs and neurotransmitter receptors. *Journal of Clinical and Experimental Psychiatry, 133*, 21–31.

Snyderman, M., & Rothman, S. (1987). Survey of expert opinion on intelligence and aptitude testing. *American Psychologist, 42*(2), 137–144.

Soccio, D. (2004). *Archetypes of wisdom. An introduction to philosophy* (5th ed.). Belmont, CA: Wadsworth/Thomson Learning.

Society for Neuroscience. (2008). *Society for neuroscience membership.* Retrieved March 10, 2008, from the Society for Neuroscience Web site, http://sfn.org/index.cfm?pagename=membership_Aboutmembership_statistics

Soderquist, D. R. (2002). *Sensory processes.* Thousand Oaks, CA: Sage Publications.

Solomon, G. F., & Moos, R. H. (1964). Emotions, immunity, and disease: A speculative theoretical integration. *Archives of General Psychiatry, 11*, 657–674.

Solso, R. (1991). *Cognitive psychology* (3rd ed.). Boston: Allyn & Bacon.

Somers, M. D. (1993). A comparison of voluntarily childfree adults and parents. *Journal of Marriage and the Family, 55*(3), 643–650.

South, S. J. (1991). Sociodemographic differentials in mate selection preference. *Journal of Marriage and Family, 53*(November), 928–940.

Spanos, N. P. (1978). Witchcraft in histories of psychiatry: A critical analysis and an alternative conceptualization. *Psychological Bulletin, 85*, 417–439.

Spanos, N. P. (1994). Multiple identity enactments and multiple personality disorder: A sociocognitive perspective. *Psychological Bulletin, 116*, 143–165.

Spanos, N. P., Weekes, J. R., & Bertrand, L. D. (1985). Multiple personality: A social psychological perspective. *Journal of Abnormal Psychology, 94*, 362–376.

Spear, L. P. (2000). The adolescent brain and age-related behavioral manifestations. *Neuroscience and Biobehavioral Reviews, 24*, 417–463.

Spearman, C. (1927). *The abilities of man.* London: Macmillan.

Spence, K. W., & Platt, J. R. (1966). UCS intensity and performance in eyelid conditioning. *Psychological Bulletin, 65*, 1–10.

Spencer, H. (1882). *Principles of psychology.* Ann Arbor, MI: D. Appleton and Company.

Spencer, S. J., Steele, C. M., & Quinn, D. M. (1999). Stereotype threat and women's math performance. *Journal of Experimental Social Psychology, 35*, 1–28.

Sperling, G. (1960). The information available in brief visual presentations. *Psychological Mechanisms, 74*, 277.

Spiegel, K., Leproult, R., & Van Cauter, E. (1999). Impact of sleep debt on metabolic and endocrine function. *Lancet, 354*, 1435–1439.

Spiers, H. J., Maguire, E. A., & Burgess, N. (2001). Hippocampal amnesia. *Neurocase, 7*(5), 357–382.

Spitz, R. A. (1965). *The first year of life: A psychoanalytic study of normal and deviant object relations.* New York: International Universities Press.

Sprecher, S. (2002). Sexual satisfaction in premarital relationships: Associations with satisfaction, love, commitment, and stability. *Journal of Sex Research, 39*(3), 190–196.

Steele, C. M. (1997). A threat in the air: How stereotypes shape intellectual identity and performance. *American Psychologist, 52,* 613–629.

Steffens, A. B., Scheurink, A. J., & Luiten, P. G. (1988). Hypothalamic food intake regulating areas are involved in the homeostasis of blood glucose and plasma FFA levels. *Physiology and Behavior, 44,* 581–589.

Steinberg, L., Dornbusch, S. M., & Brown, B. B. (1992). Ethnic differences in adolescent achievement: An ecological perspective. *American Psychologist, 47,* 723–729.

Steiner, I. D. (1972). *Group process and productivity.* New York: Academic Press.

Stephenson, T. (2005). Global HIV/AIDS report. *Journal of American Medical Association, 294,* 2961.

Stern, E., & Silbersweig, D. A. (2001). Advances in functional neuroimaging methodology of the study of brain system underlying human neuropsychological function and dysfunction. *Journal of Clinical & Experimental Neuropsychology, 23,* 3–18.

Sternberg, R. (1988a). *The triangle of love.* New York: Basic Books.

Sternberg, R. J. (1988b). *The triarchic mind.* New York: Cambridge Press.

Sternberg, R. J. (1995). For whom the bell curve tolls: A review of The Bell Curve. *Psychological Science, 6,* 257–261.

Sternberg, T. J. (1997). The triarchic theory of intelligence. In D. P. Flanagan, J. L. Genshaft, & P. L. Harrison (Eds.), *Contemporary intellectual assessment: Theories, tests, and issues* (pp. 92–104). New York: Guilford Press.

Stevenson, H. W. (1992). Learning from Asian schools. *Scientific American, 267,* pp. 6, 70–76.

Stine, G. J. (1995). *AIDS update 1994–1995.* Englewood Cliffs, NJ: Prentice Hall.

Strack, F., Martin, L. L., & Stepper, S. (1988). Inhibiting and facilitating conditions of the human smile: A nonobtrusive test of the facial feedback hypothesis. *Journal of Personality and Social Psychology, 54,* 768–777.

Straub, R. (2002). *Health psychology.* New York: Worth Publishers.

Strubbe, J. H., & Woods, S. C. (2004). The timing of meals. *Psychological Review, 111,* 128–141.

Sue, D. W., & Sue, D. (1990). *Counselling the culturally different: Theory and practice.* New York: Wiley.

Sue, D., Sue, D., & Sue, S. (1994). *Understanding abnormal behavior* (4th ed.). Boston: Houghton Mifflin.

Sue, S. (1998). In search of cultural competence in psychotherapy and counseling. *American Psychologist, 53*(4), 440–448.

Sue, S. (2003). In defense of cultural competency in psychotherapy and treatment. *American Psychologist, 58,* 964–970.

Sulloway, F. J. (1983). *Freud: Biologist of the mind.* New York: Basic Books.

Sulloway, F. J. (1995). Birth order and evolutionary psychology: A meta-analytic overview. *Psychological Inquiry, 6* (1), 75–80.

Summers-Feldman, S., & Pope, K. S. (1994). The experience of "forgetting" childhood abuse: A national survey of psychologists. *Journal of Consulting and Clinical Psychology, 62*(3), 636–639.

Suzuki, L. A., & Vraniak, D. A. (1994). Ethnicity, race, and measured intelligence. In R. J. Sternberg (Ed.), *Encyclopedia of human intelligence* (pp. 61–74). New York: Macmillan.

Swaab, D. F., & Hofman, M. A. (1990). An enlarged suprachiasmatic nucleus in homosexual men. *Brain Research, 537,* 141–148.

Sweeney, P. D., Anderson, K., & Bailey, S. (1986). Attributional style in depression: A meta-analytic review. *Journal of Personality and Social Psychology, 50,* 947–991.

Swihart, G., Yuille, J., & Porter, S. (1999). The role of state-dependent memory in "red-outs." *International Journal of Law and Psychiatry, 22*(3–4), 199–212.

Sykes, I. J., & Eden, D. (1985). Transitional stress, social support and psychological strain. *Journal of Occupational Behavior, 6*(4), 293–298.

T

Takai, T. (1989). An overview of international student adjustment in Japan. *Bulletin of the Faculty of Education, Nagoy University (Ed. Psy), 36,* 139–147.

Takakusaki, K., Saitoh, K., Harada, H., & Kashiwayanagi, M. (2004). Role of basal ganglia-brainstem pathways in the control of motor behaviors. *Neuroscience Research, 50*(2), 137–151.

Talarico, J. M., & Rubin, D. (2003). Confidence, not consistency, characterizes flashbulb memories. *Psychological Science, 14*(5), 455–461.

Talbot, N. L., Duberstein, P. R., King, D. A., Cox, C., & Giles, D. E. (2000). Personality traits of women with a history of childhood sexual abuse. *Comprehensive Psychiatry, 41,* 130–136.

Taylor, S., Thordarson, D. S., Maxfield, L., Fedoroff, I. C., Lovell, K., & Ogrodniczuk, J. (2003). Comparative efficacy, speed, and adverse effects of three PTSD treatments: Exposure therapy, EMDR, and relaxation training. *Journal of Consulting and Clinical Psychology, 71,* 330–338.

Taylor, S. E., & Armor, D. A. (1996). Positive illusions and coping with adversity. *Journal of Personality, 64,* 873–898.

Taylor, S. E., & Crocker, J. (1981). Schematic bases of social information processing. In E. T. Higgins, C. P. Herman, & M. P. Zanna (Eds.), *Social cognition: The Ontario Symposium* (Vol. 1, pp. 89–134). Hillsdale, NJ: Erlbaum.

Tellegen, A. (1985). Structures of mood and personality and their relevance to assessing anxiety with an emphasis on self-report. In A. H. Tuma & J. D. Maser (Eds.), *Anxiety and the anxiety disorders* (pp. 681–706). Hillsdale, NJ: Erlbaum.

Teng, E., Stefanacci, L., Squire, L. R., & Zola, S. M. (2000). Contrasting effects on discrimination learning after hippocampal lesions in monkeys. *Journal of Neuroscience, 20,* 3853–3863.

Terman, L. M. (1925). *Genetic studies of genius, Vol. 1: Mental and physical traits of a thousand gifted children.* Stanford, CA: Stanford University Press.

Terman, L. M., & Oden, M. H. (1947). *Genetic studies of genius, Vol 4: The gifted child grows up.* Stanford, CA: Stanford University Press.

Terr, L. C. (1991). Childhood traumas: An outline and overview. *The American Journal of Psychiatry, 148,* 10–20.

Terrace, H. S. (1979). *Nim.* New York: Knopf.

Thase, M. E., Frank, E., Mallinger, A. G., Hammer, T., & Kupfer, D. G. (1992). Treatment of imipramine-resistant recurrent depression, III: Efficacy of monoamine oxidase inhibitors. *Journal of Clinical Psychiatry, 53*(1, Suppl.), 5–11.

Thomas, A., & Chess, S. (1986). *Temperament in clinical practice.* New York: Guilford Press.

Thompson, J. (2000, July 18). I was certain, but I was wrong. *New York Times.* Retrieved August 24, 2005, from http://query.nytimes.com/search/restricted/article?res=F40A17FB3D550C7B8DDDAF089

Thompson, T. L., & Zebrinos, E. (1997). Television cartoons: Do children notice it's a boy's world? *Sex Roles: A Journal of Research, 37,* 415–428.

Thomson, E., & Colella, U. (1992). Cohabitation and marital stability: Quality or commitment? *Journal of Marriage and the Family, 54*(2), 259–267.

Thorndike, E. L. (1898). Animal intelligence: An experimental study of the associative processes in animals. *Psychological Review Monograph Supplements, 2*(Whole No. 8).

Thorne, B., & Henley, T. (2001). *Connections in the history and systems of psychology* (2nd ed.). Boston: Houghton Mifflin.

Thurman, P. J., Swaim, R., & Plested, B. (1995). Intervention and treatment of ethnic minority substance abusers. In J. F. Aponte, R. Y. Rivers, & J. Wohl (Eds.), *Psychological interventions and cultural diversity* (pp. 215–233). Boston: Allyn & Bacon.

Timmerman, I. G. H., & Emmelkamp, R. M. G. (2001). The prevalence and comorbidity of Axis I and Axis II pathology in a group of forensic patients. *International Journal of Offender Therapy and Comparative Criminology, 45,* 198–213.

Tincoff, R., & Jusczyk, P. (1999). Some beginnings of word comprehension in 6-month-olds. *Psychological Science, 10,* 172–175.

Tisch, S., Silberstein, P., Limousin-Dowsey, P., & Jahanshahi, M. (2004). The basal ganglia: Anatomy, physiology, and pharmacology. *Psychiatric Clinics of North America, 27*(4), 757–799.

Toates, F. (2007). *Biological psychology* (2nd ed.). Boston: Pearson/Prentice Hall.

Toland, K., Hoffman, H., & Loftus, E. F. (1991). How suggestibility plays tricks with memory. In J. F. Schumacher (Ed.), *Human suggestibility: Advances in theory, research and application* (pp. 235–253). New York: Routledge.

Tolman, E. C. (1932). *Purposive behavior in animals and men.* New York: Century.

Tolman, E. C., & Honzik, C. H. (1930). Introduction and removal of reward, and maze performance in rats. *University of California Publications in Psychology, 4,* 257–275.

Tomasello, M., Call, J., Nagell, K., Olguin, R., & Carpenter, M. (1994). The learning and use of gestural signals by young chimpanzees: A trans-generational study. *Primates, 35,* 137–154.

Tomkins, S. (1962). *Affect, imagery, and consciousness. The positive effects* (Vol. 1). New York: Springer.

Tomkins, S. (1963). *Affect, imagery, and consciousness. The positive effects* (Vol. 2). New York: Springer.

Tomkins, S. (1982). *Affect, imagery, and consciousness. The positive effects* (Vol. 3). New York: Springer.

Topel, H. (1988). Beta-endorphin genetics in the etiology of alcoholism. *Alcohol, 5*(2), 159–165.

Townsend, K. C., & McWhirter, B. T. (2005). Connectedness: A review of the literature with implications for counseling, assessment, and research. *Journal of Counseling and Development, 83,* 191–201.

Tramo, M. J., Cariani, P. A., Koh, C. K., Makris, N., & Braida, L. D. (2005). Neurophysiology and neuroanatomy of pitch perception: Auditory cortex. In G. Avanzini, L. Lopez, S. Koelsch, & M. Manjno (Eds.), *The neurosciences and music II: From perception to performance* (pp. 148–174). New York: New York Academy of Sciences.

Trapp, B. D. (2004). Pathogenesis of multiple sclerosis: The eyes only see what the mind is prepared to comprehend. *Annals of Neurology, 55*(4), 455–457.

Triandis, H. C., Marin, G., Lisansky, J., & Betancourt, H. (1984). Simpatia as a cultural scripts of Hispanics. *Journal of Personality and Social Psychology, 47,* 1363–1375.

Tugade, M. M., & Fredrickson, B. L. (2004). Resilient individuals use positive emotions to bounce back from negative emotional experiences. *Journal of Personality and Social Psychology, 86,* 320–333.

Tulving, E. (1995). Organization of memory: Quo vadis? In M. S. Gassaniga (Ed.), *The Cognitive Neurosciences* (p. 839). Cambridge, MA: MIT.

Tulving, E., & Thompson, D. M. (1973). Encoding specificity and retrieval processes in episodic memory. *Psychological Review, 80,* 352–373.

Turner, R. J., & Wagonfeld, M. O. (1967). Occupational mobility and schizophrenia. *American Sociological Review, 32,* 104–113.

Tyack, P. L. (2000). Dolphins whistle a signature tune. *Science, 289,* 1310–1313.

U Underwager, R., & Wakefield, H. (1998). Recovered memories in the court room. *False memories in the law, textbooks, and the media.*

U.S. Department of Health and Human Services (USDHHS). (1996). *Indian health services: Trends in Indian health—1996.* Rockville, MD: U.S Department of Health and Human Services, Indian Health Services, Office of Planning, Evaluation, and Legislation, Division of Program Statistics.

U.S. Department of Health and Human Services. (2005). *STDs today.*

U.S. Surgeon General. (1996). *Physical activity and health: A report of the Surgeon General.* U.S. Department of Health and Human Services, Centers for Disease Control and Prevention. http://ww.cdc.gov/nccdphp/sg.htm

V van der Kolk, B. A., & Fisher, R. (1995). Dissociation and the fragmentary nature of traumatic memories: Overview and exploratory study. *Journal of Traumatic Stress, 8,* 505–525.

Vicari, S., Bellucci, S., & Carlesimo, G. A. (2001). Procedural learning deficits in children with Williams syndrome. *Neuropsychologia, 39,* 665–677.

Vogt, B. A. (2005). Pain and emotion interactions in subregions of the cingulated gyrus. *Nature Reviews Neuroscience, 6*(7), 533–544.

von Gunten, A., Bouras, C., Kovari, E., Giannakopoulos, P., & Hof, P. R. (2006). Neural substrates of cognitive and behavioral deficits in atypical Alzheimer's disease. *Brain Research Reviews, 51*(2), 176–211.

W

Wade, C., & Tavris, C. (2002). *Invitation to psychology* (2nd ed.). Upper Saddle River, NJ: Prentice-Hall.

Wade, K. A., Garry, M., Read, J. D., & Lindsay, D. S. (2002). A picture is worth a thousand words. *Psychonomic Bulletin & Review, 9*, 597–603.

Wagatsuma, H., & Yamaguchi, Y. (2007). Neural dynamics of the cognitive map in the hippocampus. *Cognitive Neurodynamics, 1*(2), 119–141.

Wald, J., & Taylor, S. (2002). Efficacy of virtual reality exposure therapy to treat driving phobia. *Journal of Behavior Therapy & Experimentation Psychiatry, 31*(3–4), 249–257.

Walden, J., Normann, C., Langosch, J., Berger, M., & Grunze, H. (1998). Differential treatment of bipolar disorder with old and new antiepileptic drugs. *Neuropsychobiology, 38*, 181–184.

Waldman, I. D., Weinberg, R. A., & Scarr, S. (1994). Racial-group differences in IQ in the Minnesota Transracial Adoption Study: A reply to Levin and Lynn. *Intelligence, 19*, 29–44.

Walk, R. D. (1981). *Perceptual development.* Monterey, CA: Brooks/Cole.

Walk, R., & Gibson, E. (1961). A comparative and analytical study of visual depth perception. *Psychological Monographs, 75*, 44.

Wall, P. D., & Melzack, R. (1994). *Textbook of pain.* Edinburgh, Scotland: Churchill Livingstone.

Warren, R. M. (1984). Helmholtz and his continuing influence. *Music Perception, 1*(3), 253–275.

Watson, D. L., & Tharp, R. G. (2007). *Self-directed behavior* (9th ed.). Belmont, CA: Wadsworth.

Watson, J. B. (1924). *Behaviorism.* New York: W. W. Norton.

Watson, N. F., & Vaughn, B. V. (2006). *Clinician's guide to sleep disorders.* New York: Taylor & Francis.

Weber, E. H. (1846). Der Tastinn und das Gemeingefühl. In R. Wagner (Ed.), *Handwörterbuch der Physiologie.* Braunschweig: Bieweg.

Wechsler, D. (1944). *The measurement of adult intelligence* (3rd ed.). Baltimore: Williams & Wilkins.

Weinfield, N. S., Ogawa, J. R., & Stroufe, L. A. (1997). Early attachment as a pathway to adolescent peer competence. *Journal of Research on Adolescence, 7*, 241–265.

Weisenberger, J. M. (2001). Cutaneous perception. In E. B. Goldstein (Ed.), *Blackwell handbook of perception* (pp. 535–566). Oxford: Blackwell Publishers.

Wells, G. L., Small, M., Penrod, S., Malpass, R. S., Fulero, S. M., & Brimacombe, A. E. (1998). Eyewitness identification procedures: Recommendations for lineups and photospreads. *Law and Behavior, 22*(6), 1–39.

Wender, P. H., Kety, S. S., Posenthal, D., Schulsinger, F., Ortmann, J., & Lunde, I. (1986). Psychiatric disorders in the biological and adoptive families of adopted individuals with affective disorders. *Archives of General Psychiatry, 43*, 923–929.

Wentworth, P. A. (1999). The moral of her story: Exploring the philosophical and religious commitments in Mary Whiton Calkins's self-psychology. *History of Psychology, 2,* 119–131.

Werner, G., & Mountcastle, V. B. (1965). Neural activity in mechanoreceptive cutaneous afferents: Stimulus-response relations, Weber functions, and information transmission. *Journal of Neurophysiology, 28,* 369–397.

West, T. G. (1991). *In the mind's eye.* Buffalo, NY: Prometheus.

Whitaker-Azmitia, P. M. (2005). Behavioral and cellular consequences of increasing serotonergic activity during brain development: A role in autism? *International Journal of Developmental Neuroscience, 23*(1), 75–83.

White, H. (1997). Longitudinal perspective on alcohol and aggression during adolescence. In M. Galanter (Ed.), *Recent developments in alcoholism: Vol. 13. Alcohol and violence: Epidemiology, neurobiology, psychology, and family issues* (pp. 81–103). New York: Plenum.

Whitfield, P. (1993). *From so simple a beginning.* New York: Macmillan.

Whittington, C. J., Kendall, T., & Pilling, S. (2005). Are the SSRIs and atypical antidepressants safe and effective for children and adolescents? *Current Opinion in Psychiatry, 18*(1), 21–25.

Widiger, T., Frances, A., Warner, L., & Bluhm, C. (1986). Diagnostic criteria for the borderline and schizotypal personality disorders. *Journal of Abnormal Psychology, 95,* 43–51.

Williams, M. R. (1996). Suits by adults for child sexual abuse: Legal origins of the "repressed memory" controversy. *Journal of Psychiatry and the Law, 24,* 207–228.

Williams, W. M., & Ceci, S. J. (1997). Are Americans becoming more or less alike?: Trends in race, class, and ability differences in intelligence. *American Psychologist, 52,* 1226–1235.

Wilder, D. A. (1984). Intergroup contact: The typical member and the exception to the rule. *Journal of Experimental Psychology, 202,* 177–194.

Wilsnack, S. C., Vogeltanz, N. D., Klassen, A. D., & Harris, T. R. (1997). Childhood sexual abuse and women's substance abuse: National survey findings. *Journal of Studies on Alcohol, 58*(3), 264–271.

Wilson, J. D., & Foster, D. W. (1992). Hormones and hormone action: Introduction. In J. D. Wilson & D. W. Foster (Eds.), *Williams textbook of endocrinology* (8th ed., pp. 1–8). Philadelphia: W. B. Saunders.

Wilson, S., Becker, L. A., & Tinker, R. H. (1995). Eye movement desensitization and reprocessing (EMDR): Treatment for psychologically traumatized individuals. *Journal of Consulting and Clinical Psychology, 63,* 928–937.

Wilson, S., Becker, L. A., & Tinker, R. H. (1997). Fifteen-month follow-up of eye movement desensitization and reprocessing (EMDR) treatment of post-traumatic stress disorder and psychological trauma. *Journal of Consulting and Clinical Psychology, 65,* 1047–1056.

Winograd, E., Goldstein, F. C., Monarch, E. S., Peluso, J. P., & Goldman, W. P. (1999). The mere exposure effect in patients with Alzheimer's disease. *Neuropsychology, 13*(1), 41–46.

Winter, D. G. (1988). The power motive in women—and men. *Journal of Personality and Social Psychology, 54*, 510–519.

Wise, S. M. (2000). *Rattling the cage: Toward legal rights for animals.* Cambridge, MA: Perseus Books.

Wolberg, L. R. (1995). *The technique of psychotherapy* (4th ed.). Northvale, NJ: Jason Aronson.

Wolf, M. M., Braukmann, C. J., Ramp, K. A. (1987). Serious delinquent behavior as part of a significantly handicapping condition: Cures and supportive environments. *Journal of Applied Behavior Analysis, 20*, 347–359.

Wolitzky, D. L. (1995). The theory and practice of traditional psychoanalytic psychotherapy. In A. S. Gurman & S. B. Messer (Eds.), *Essential psychotherapies* (pp. 12–54). New York: Guilford.

Wolpe, J. (1958). *Psychotherapy by reciprocal inhibition.* Stanford, CA: Stanford University Press.

Wong, E. C., Kim, B. S. K., Zane, N. W. S., Kim, I. J., & Huang, J. S. (2003). Examining culturally based variables associated with ethnicity: Influences on credibility perceptions of empirically supported interventions. *Cultural Diversity and Ethnic Minority Psychology, 9*, 88–96.

Wood, S. E., Wood, E. G., & Boyd, D. (2005). *Mastering the world of psychology.* Boston: Allyn & Bacon.

Working Party of British Psychological Society. (1996). Working Party report—Recovered memories. In K. Pezdek & W. P. Banks (Eds.), *The Recovered Memory/False Memory Debate* (pp. 373–392). New York: Academic Press.

World Resource Institute. (1998–1999). *Environmental change and human health.* Washington, DC: United Nations World Resource Institute.

Wright, W. (1998). *Born that way: Genes, behavior, personality.* New York: Knopf.

Y

Yamaguchi, S. (1991). Basic properties of umami and effects on humans. *Physiology & Behavior, 49*(5), 833–841.

Yep, G. A. (1995). Communicating the HIV/AIDS risk to Hispanic populations. In A. Padilla (Ed.), *Hispanic psychology: Critical issues in theory and research* (pp. 196–212). Thousand Oaks, CA: Sage.

Yeung, R. R. (1996). The acute effects of exercise on mood state. *Journal of Psychosomatic Research, 40*(2), 123–141.

Yunker, G. W., & Yunker, B. D. (2002). Primal leadership (book). *Personnel Psychology, 55*, 1030–1033.

Z

Zajonc, R. B. (1968). Attitudinal effects of mere exposure. *Journal of Personality and Social Psychology, 9* (Monograph Suppl. 2 pt. 2), 1–27.

Zebrowitz, L. A., Hall, F. A., Murphy, N. A., & Rhodes, G. (2002). Looking smart and looking good: Facial cues to intelligence and their origins. *Personality & Social Psychology Bulletin, 28(2)*, 238–249.

Zhou, J. N., Hofman, M. A., Gooren, L. J., & Swaab, L. J. (1995). A sex difference in the human brain and its relation to transsexuality. *Nature, 378*, 68–70.

Zimbardo, P. G. (1970). The human choice: Individuation, reason, and order versus deindividuation, impulse, and chaos. In W. J. Arnold & D. Levine (Eds.), *Nebraska Symposium on Motivation, 1969* (Vol. 17, pp. 237–307). Lincoln: University of Nebraska Press.

Zimbardo, P. G. (2007). *The Lucifer effect: Understanding how good people turn to evil.* New York: Random House.

Zola, S. M., Squire, L. R., Teng, E., Stefanacci, L., Buffalo, E. A., & Clark, R. E. (2000). Impaired recognition memory in monkeys after damage limited to the hippocampal region. *Journal of Neuroscience, 20,* 451–463.

Zuckerman, M. (1994). *Behavioral expressions and biosocial bases for sensation seeking.* New York: Cambridge University Press.

Zwanzger, P., & Rupprecht, R. (2005). Selective GABAergic treatment for panic? Investigations in experimental panic induction and panic disorder. *Journal of Psychiatry & Neuroscience, 30*(3), 167–175.

Glossary

A **Abnormal behavior** a pattern of emotion, thought, and action considered pathological due to its statistical infrequency; it disrupts the person's ability to function, violates social norms, and causes significant personal distress.

Absolute threshold the lowest level of stimulation required for a sensory receptor to respond.

Abundancy motives motives that encourage the individual to attain greater satisfaction and stimulation.

Accommodate modifying existing mental frameworks to fit new experiences.

Accommodation the process of changing the shape of the lens so that the reflected light of both distant objects and nearby objects may be focused onto the retina.

Acetylcholine (ACH) a neurotransmitter important for muscle movement, attention, and memory.

Achievement motivation the drive to satisfy or complete a goal.

Achromatopsia a kind of color blindness resulting from damage to the brain.

Acquaintance (date) rape forced intercourse that occurs in the context of a voluntary encounter between the involved parties.

Acquired immunodeficiency syndrome (AIDS) a set of symptoms and infections resulting from damage to the human immune system caused by the human immunodeficiency virus (HIV).

Acquisition the stage of learning where a response is acquired.

Action potential the full-blown electrical signal that is generated in a neuron and sent through it, resulting in the release of neurotransmitter.

Actor/observer difference paying greater attention to the situation when explaining our own behavior but focusing on dispositional factors when explaining the behavior of others.

Acute stress disorder (ASD) an anxiety disorder in which fear and related symptoms are experienced soon after a traumatic event and last less than a month.

Adaptation a decline in responding to constant stimulus.

A-delta fibers fibers involved in the sensation and perception of pain; they are responsible for initial sharp pain and pain reduction from rubbing.

Adrenal glands endocrine glands located on top of the kidneys that are responsible for releasing hormones such as adrenaline (epinephrine) and glucocorticoids.

Adventitious reinforcement reinforcement that occurs when a behavior is, by chance, followed closely in time by a reinforcer.

Affective component of an attitude the emotional response associated with a person, place, or idea.

Affective flattening a reduced external expression of emotion.

Affectiveness-primacy theory *see* common-sense theory.

Afferent fibers nerves or fibers that travel to the brain.

Afterimages seeing a complementary colored image after staring at a colored object.

Aggression any behavior intended to cause either physical or emotional harm to another individual.

Agoraphobia an anxiety disorder in which a person is afraid to be in places or situations from which escape might be difficult (or embarrassing) or help might be unavailable if symptoms of panic were to occur.

Ah-ha experience a sudden insight about a solution to a problem.

Alcohol a legal, liquid mood-altering substance that falls into the depressants category of drugs.

Algorithm a step-by-step set of rules that, if followed correctly, will lead to a solution.

All-or-nothing law a rule of neuronal functioning stating that a neuron's response is not dependent on the strength of the signals it receives.

Alogia a poverty of speech or poverty in the content of the speech.

Alpha waves the movements our brain waves make while we are resting, meditating, under hypnosis, and before we fall into stage 1 sleep.

Altruism a helping behavior that is not motivated by self-interest and often incurs significant costs to the helper.

Alzheimer's disease a neurodegenerative disease often associated with aging and characterized by progressive memory loss and dementia.

Ambivalent/resistant attachment a style of attachment characterized by children who are overly clingy to their mother and anxious at the start of the stranger situation method. They become severely distressed (screaming, tantrums) by her leaving and alternate between pushing her away and clinging to her upon return.

Ames Room a room constructed to eliminate depth cues, making people on one side look huge when, actually, they are just closer.

Amphetamines (methamphetamine, for example) a drug of abuse that reduces GABA activity in the brain and is normally found in pill form.

Amplitude a physical property of sound defined as the height of a sound wave.

Amygdala a neurological structure found in the temporal lobe that is involved in fear and aggression.

Amyloid plaques abnormal protein developments in the extracellular space around neurons. They are frequently found in Alzheimer's disease.

Anal stage in this Freudian psychosexual stage (occurs 18 months to 3 years), children receive satisfaction through the anus by either having or retaining bowel movements.

Analgesia reduction of pain mediated by the central nervous system.

Analysis of variance (ANOVA) the statistical procedure used to evaluate differences among two or more treatment means by breaking the variability in the data into components that reflect the influence of error and error plus treatment effects.

Anima represents female aspects in men, according to Jungian theory.

Anima archetype a tendency to be feminine.

Animistic thought the belief that all objects possess qualities of living.

Animus represents male aspects in women, according to Jungian theory.

Anions negatively charged protein molecules found primarily inside neurons.

Antecedents stimuli that are present before a behavior occurs.

Anterior directional term used to indicate to the front.

Anterograde amnesia the inability to store any new memories in long-term memory.

Antidepressant drugs drugs used in the treatment of mood and anxiety disorders.

Antipsychotic drugs drugs used in the treatment of people with severe psychotic disorders.

Antisocial personality disorder a personality disorder characterized by a general pattern of disregard for and violation of other people's rights.

Apparent motion two flashing lights on a screen appear to be one light moving across a screen.

Approach-approach conflicts a conflict that develops when one needs to choose between two pleasurable goals that are equally desirable.

Approach-avoidance conflicts a conflict that arises when a person needs to choose an uncomfortable situation when the alternatives are equally unpleasant.

Archetypes in Jungian theory, archetypes are universal, inherited ideas present in all human beings. They represent a kind of person, a type of object, or a particular experience, and they reflect the common experiences of humanity in coping with nature, war, parenthood, love, and evil.

Arousal physiological activity in the nervous system and in muscles and glands.

Arousal theory a theory that states that we seek to maintain an optimal level of arousal at all times.

Asociality a lack of interest in social relations.

Assimilate applying existing mental frameworks to new things or situations.

Association a strengthened connection between neurons.

Associative learning learning that involves the formation of a neural connection.

Associative play a kind of play where children work using the same materials or on the same project but do not incorporate others in their task.

Asymptomatic no symptoms are visibly present.

Asymptotic level maximum level of learning or performance.

Atmospheric perspective more distant objects appear less sharp due to the amount of air and atmospheric particles between the object and the observer.

Attachment an emotional bond (i.e., love or affection) between an infant (animal or human) and another individual, such as a parent or a caregiver.

Attitude an enduring system of beliefs, feelings, and behavioral tendencies concerning people, objects, or ideas.

Auditory canal small tube leading into one's head through which sound waves travel into the auditory system.

Auditory nerve a cranial nerve responsible for carrying auditory signals from the cochlea into the brain.

Authoritarian a style of parenting where parents use threats and physical punishment to achieve strict obedience to their authority.

Authoritative a style of parenting where parents use more rewards, reasoning, and explanation to influence behavior.

Autoimmune disease a class of diseases in which the immune system mistakenly attacks one or more areas of the body.

Autonomic nervous system (ANS) a branch of the peripheral nervous system concerned with involuntary regulation of arousal and relaxation; it is divided into sympathetic and parasympathetic divisions.

Autoreceptors specialized receptors found on the synaptic terminal to which the neurotransmitter may bind and signal the cell to stop releasing neurotransmitter.

Aversive conditioning a behavioral treatment that repeatedly pairs an aversive stimulus with an undesirable habit.

Avoidance-avoidance conflicts a conflict that develops when one has the possibility of reaching a desired goal that also has an unpleasant outcome.

Avoidant attachment a style of attachment where children clearly avoid being close to and interacting with the mother/primary caregiver.

Avoidant conflict style a way of interacting in which couples avoid conflict and agree to disagree.

Avoidant personality disorder a personality disorder in which a person is consistently uncomfortable and restrained in social situations, overwhelmed by feelings of inadequacy, and extremely sensitive to negative evaluation.

Avolition a display of apathy or a lack of energy.

Axon long extension of a multipolar neuron through which a neural signal is conducted to the synaptic terminals.

Axon hillock the region of a neuron where the soma becomes the axon, and the area where an action potential is initially generated in the cell.

Axon terminal the bulbous endpoints of an axon from which neurotransmitter is released into the synaptic cleft.

Azimuth horizontal plane associated with sound localization.

B

Backward conditioning conditioning schedule where the unconditioned stimulus is presented first and then the conditioned and unconditioned stimuli coterminate.

Backward-working heuristics working backward from the goal state until the solution to the problem is reached.

Barbiturates (Seconal, Nembutal) drugs known to reduce anxiety, promote sleep (very deep, with reduced REM stage), increase sedation, and promote euphoria. They also depress breathing centers in the brain as well as centers for wakefulness and arousal.

Basal ganglia motor system a series of subcortical structures in the brain, responsible for motor function.

Basic anxiety Karen Horney's theory contends that anything that disturbs the security of children in relation to their parents produces basic anxiety. The insecure, anxious child develops various strategies by which to cope with feelings of isolation and helplessness, such as becoming overly submissive in order to win back the love that the child feels has been lost.

Basic level category the intermediate level in the category hierarchy.

Basilar membrane one of the membranes that make up the organ of corti, inside the cochlea. Hair cells are found rooted in this membrane.

Battery the administration of several tests with the idea that the drawbacks from one test instrument will be compensated for by the strengths of another test in the set.

Behavior modification changing behavior by using reinforcement to increase a desirable behavior and punishment to decrease an undesirable behavior.

Behavior therapy a type of treatment modality that employs action-oriented strategies to change behavior.

Behavioral component the aspect of emotion that is our outward expression of the emotion.

Behavioral component of an attitude how preexisting and preestablished ideas guide our actions.

Behavioral observation a method of personality and psychopathology assessment that involves direct observation of the person's actions and body language.

Behaviorism a view that psychology should study observable, measurable behavior.

Behaviorist one who adheres to the ideas central to the school of behaviorism, a school of psychology that emphasizes the study of overt, observable behavior.

Benzodiazepines a class of tranquilizers that are typically used to treat anxiety disorders.

Beta waves the brain waves associated with wakefulness and REM sleep.

Big Five model a way of describing individual similarities and differences in personality based on five dimensions: extroversion, conscientiousness, agreeableness, emotional stability, and openness to experience.

Bilateral both hemispheres.

Bilateral medial temporal lobe resection a silver straw is inserted into the middle of the brain and hippocampal tissue on both sides of the brain along with other surrounding tissue is sucked out.

Binding problem the question of how the sensory modalities or aspects within the sensory modalities combine to create a unified and coherent percept.

Binet-Simon Intelligence Scale an intelligence test designed to test a child's memory, attention, and ability to understand similarities and differences. The intelligence score compares the child's mental age with his or her chronological age.

Binocular cues depth cues that require both eyes.

Biofeedback a therapeutic technique that enables one to learn how to voluntarily change and thus control physiological functions that are normally automatic, such as heart rate, blood pressure, body temperature, muscle tone, and blood flow.

Biofeedback training treatment in which a person's physiological activity is displayed on a computer screen so that it becomes a source of feedback.

Biological perspective a view that behavior and mental processes result from genes, hormones, anatomical structures, and the physiological process of the body.

Biological preparedness assumption that organisms are more naturally inclined to associate certain types of stimuli.

Biopsychology a field of psychology dedicated to examining the biological substrates of behavior and mental processes.

Bipolar cells retinal cells responsible for opponent-process color vision.

Bipolar disorder a mood disorder marked by alternating or intermixed periods of mania and depression.

Birth defects physical and mental abnormalities apparent at birth.

Bisexual a person erotically attracted to both men and women.

Blastocyst the hollow ball of cells that forms from the division of the zygote.

Bobo doll an inflatable doll used to study observational learning in children.

Body dysmorphic disorder a somatoform disorder characterized by excessive worry that some aspect of one's physical appearance is defective.

Borderline personality disorder a personality disorder in which an individual displays repeated instability in interpersonal relationships, self-image, and mood, as well as extremely impulsive behavior.

Bottom-up processes reducing an object into parts, where their identification and combinations determine perception of the whole.

Breathing control a relaxation exercise that stimulates the release of endorphins by the process of inhaling, holding, and exhaling air slowly. This procedure gives one a feeling of peacefulness and relaxation and an increased tolerance to pain.

Broaden-and-build theory a theory that suggests that positive emotions create a more long-term payoff by broadening and building our potential by enhancing creativity, increasing motivation, and developing insights.

Burnout a physical and emotional exhaustion caused by chronic frustration that wears down the body's immunological system. Burnout also has a major pathological impact on one's cognitive and emotional state by causing a negative attitude, lack of motivation, and depression.

Bystander effect states that in an emergency situation, if no one else around us perceives the event as an emergency, then we, too, are not likely to perceive the event as an emergency and ultimately do not offer assistance to the person in need.

C **C fibers** fibers responsible for dull, throbbing pain.

Caffeine a stimulant found in coffee and soft drinks.

Calcium a positively charged ion that plays a role in synaptic transmission.

Cancellation a psychotherapeutic intervention that allows one to get rid of continuously intrusive and distressing thoughts through the process of distraction.

Cannon-Bard theory the theory of emotion that suggests that information from our senses is relayed simultaneously to the body and mind.

Case study an intensive examination of an individual with characteristics or abilities that the researcher wishes to study.

Catatonic schizophrenia a subtype of schizophrenia characterized by gross disturbances in motor activity, such as a catatonic stupor.

Catharsis an emotional release.

Causalgesia pain that follows the path of a partially damaged peripheral nerve during healing.

Central cues hunger triggers from the central nervous system, which consists of the brain and the spinal cord.

Central nervous system (CNS) branch of the nervous system including the brain and spinal cord.

Cephalo-caudal law one of the laws of developmental direction; it states that development begins at the head (cephalo) and proceeds to the tail (caudal).

Cerebellum part of the metencephalon that is important for motor coordination and some forms of learning.

Cerebral cortex thin, wrinkled surface of the telencephalon.

Change motive occurs because animals and people tend to prefer complex and changing stimuli.

Chloride a negatively charged ion found largely in the extracellular fluid.

Cholecystokinin (CCK) a hormone secreted when the food moves from the stomach into the intestinal tract, which signals the brain to stop eating.

Chronic pain pain existing for more than six months.

Chunking the process of combining several smaller units of information into one larger unit.

Ciliary muscles muscles in the eye that contract or release to change the shape of the lens for accommodation.

Cingulate cortex region of cortex that is part of the limbic system and is important for emotion.

Circadian rhythm a 24-hour sleep-wake cycle that our bodies cycle through.

Circumvallate papillae a type of bump found along the back surface of the tongue, associated with taste receptors.

Clang associations the stringing of words together because they rhyme or sound alike.

Classical conditioning the learning process that results in associations between stimuli and outcomes.

Classical theory states that a concept is formed by the defining features it shares with other items in that category.

Claustrophobia fear of closed spaces.

Client-centered therapy a treatment approach in which the client is guided to accept the self through self-reflection.

Clique close-knit, typically same sex, group of friends who share common interests.

Cocaine a highly addictive stimulant that is a drug of abuse. It can be snorted, smoked, or injected.

Cochlea a bony, snail shell–like structure that houses the organ of corti for the auditory system.

Cognition how we process, store, analyze, and use information mentally.

Cognitive approach an approach to the study of learning that emphasizes the role of covert mental processes.

Cognitive behavior therapy a form of therapy that focuses on changing irrational beliefs and modifying maladaptive behaviors.

Cognitive component an aspect of emotion that has to do with what we are thinking when we experience a particular emotion.

Cognitive component of an attitude the logic and rationale behind our attitudes.

Cognitive dissonance theory feeling of psychological discomfort that occurs when we engage in behaviors that are opposite to what we believe. This feeling motivates us to take some form of action to reduce the state of discomfort.

Cognitive economy reducing the amount of cognitive effort required for thinking, understanding, and learning.

Cognitive expectancies a person's expectations of future success based on past experiences.

Cognitive perspective suggests that behavior is motivated by mental processes such as thought, language, and problem solving.

Cognitive restructuring guiding the client through the identification of irrational and self-defeating thoughts and then altering the thoughts to eradicate the maladaptive feelings and behaviors.

Cognitive therapists assume that maladaptive behaviors stem from irrational thoughts, beliefs, and ideas.

Cognitive therapy a treatment method used to help clients replace their negative thoughts with more objective ones.

Cohort a generational group as defined in demographics, statistics, or market research.

Cold fibers fibers that carry information of cold-sensing thermoreceptors.

Collective unconscious in Jungian theory, a region of the mind possessed by all human beings that is a storehouse of experiences weathered by our ancestors. The collective unconscious was thought by Jung to contain archetypes, which are universal ideas present in everyone and allow people to have common fears and wishes.

Collectivist this term refers to cultures that place a low value on individual freedom and self-expression. What is seen as important is a furtherance of the needs of the group and a subjugation of individual desires to group welfare.

Color blindness inability to see certain colors.

Color constancy the perception that colors are the same in bright and dim conditions.

Commitment one of the three ingredients in the triangular theory of love that involves investments in the future of the relationship.

Common-sense theory (also called affectiveness-primacy theory) the early theory of emotion based on common sense, which suggests that an event or stimulus excites a mental process called emotion, and this mental state gives rise to the physiological arousal that occurs for each emotion.

Communication an exchanging of information using sounds, smells, or gestures.

Companionate love a positive feeling and attraction to someone that is characterized by feelings of trust, concern, warmth, and friendship.

Complementarity the idea that we like people who are different from us if they possess qualities that we personally lack but admire. We are also attracted to people who serve to complete what we perceive as missing in ourselves.

Complexity a physical quality of sound associated with the combination of multiple sound waves that results in the sound we hear.

Compliance a change in our behavior because someone makes a request of us.

Compound stimulus stimulus that involves multiple features.

Compulsions repetitive and rigid behaviors that a person feels driven to perform in order to prevent or reduce anxiety.

Concept an internal representation that may be abstract, and consists of a grouping of objects or events.

Concordance rate a statistical measure that indicates in how many pairs in a sample of twins that both twins have the disorder being studied.

Concrete operational stage the third of Piaget's stages of cognitive development; in this stage, children have the ability to think about the operation of concrete objects (objects that physically exist and are subject to the laws of physics).

Conditioned emotional reflex a conditioned reflex that develops when a conditioned stimulus becomes associated with an emotional state.

Conditioned inhibition learning that a conditioned stimulus predicts the absence of the unconditioned stimulus.

Conditioned response a reflexive response that is learned when a conditioned stimulus becomes associated with an unconditioned stimulus.

Conditioned stimulus a stimulus that elicits the conditioned response.

Conditioned taste aversion aversion to a flavor acquired through classical conditioning.

Conditions of worth according to Carl Rogers, a child perceives that the appreciation he or she can expect from significant others depends on the child's ability to meet certain conditions that these others have.

Conductive hearing losses hearing deficits associated with the transmission of auditory information to the inner ear. Often involves problems with the auditory canal, tympanic membrane, or middle ear.

Cones photoreceptors for sensing different wavelengths of light (color) and fine details.

Confabulation a person unwittingly invents information to fill in the gaps in his or her memory and comes to believe the invention to be a fact.

Confirmation bias the tendency to ignore information that disconfirms our existing belief and focus on information that supports our existing beliefs.

Conflict a stressor that causes distress when two or more motives clash with each other, making it difficult to decide on a course of action.

Conflict resolution a process where parties with shared and opposing interests join together in order to come to an agreement for the purpose of working out a settlement.

Conformity a change in behavior simply designed to match the behavior of others around us.

Confounding variable an extraneous variable that changes systematically along with the independent variable in an experiment.

Congruence in Rogersian theory, congruence refers to agreement among an individual's ideal self, which represents who the person wants to be; the true self, which is who the person really is; and the self-image, which reflects the way the person sees himself or herself as being. If these three aspects do not correspond with one another, inner conflicts arise within a person.

Connectedness theory a theory that states that we seek out and maintain relationships with others because it is a basic human need to feel connected to others.

Conscious in Freudian psychoanalysis, this term refers to thoughts a person is aware of recalling.

Consequences stimuli that follow a behavior.

Conservation the knowledge that an object retains all of its properties, even when placed in different contexts that may alter its appearance.

Contact comfort comfort that comes from touch that is more important for attachment than the nourishment.

Contact hypothesis proposes that levels of prejudice are reduced as people from different groups interact with one another.

Contempt engaging in behaviors that convey a lack of respect for one's partner, such as rolling the eyes, speaking with a condescending tone of voice, or intentionally saying things designed to psychologically wound the partner.

Context-dependent memory information is easier to recall when a person is in the same physical environment as when the information was learned.

Contiguity how closely two stimuli occur in time or space.

Contingency situation where one event is dependent on another.

Contrecoup injury traumatic injury to the brain on the opposite side from where the impact occurred.

Control group in a controlled experiment, the group of subjects exposed to all experimental conditions except the independent variable, in order to provide a comparison with the experimental group that is exposed to the independent variable.

Conventional level encompasses Stage 3 and Stage 4 of Kohlberg's moral reasoning, where moral decisions are determined by social rules.

Convergence a binocular depth cue that takes into account the amount by which the eyes point inward or are "crossed."

Convergent thinking the tendency to narrow down alternatives to one solution by using knowledge and logic.

Conversion disorder a somatoform disorder in which a psychosocial need or conflict is converted into a physical symptom that affects voluntary motor or sensory functions.

Cooperative play interactive play with others, including games, role playing, and construction.

Corpus callosum the primary connection between the two hemispheres of the brain.

Correlation coefficient a number ranging from -1.00 to $+1.00$ that is calculated using an inferential statistical procedure. The correlation coefficient provides two pieces of information concerning the degree of relationship between the variables: the magnitude of the relationship and the direction of the relationship.

Correlational study a nonexperimental strategy designed to measure the degree of relationship between two or more variables.

Coup injury traumatic injury to the brain, localized around the area of impact.

Covert behaviors internal responses such as thoughts and feelings.

Cranial nerves series of 12 motor and sensory nerves that are part of the peripheral nervous system.

Creativity the ability to think about something in original and useful ways.

Cribiform plate a flat piece of bone at the top of the nasal cavity through which olfactory receptor cells send their axons to the olfactory bulb in the brain.

Cross-cultural perspective a view that places an emphasis on the human mind and behavior as largely influenced by the culture in which an individual is raised.

Cross-sectional design a method in which different groups of subjects who are at different stages are measured at a single point in time; a method that looks for time-related changes.

Crowd a larger group of similarly stereotyped individuals who are defined by the actions, beliefs, and attitudes of the members, such as geeks, goths, stoners, preps, or jocks.

Cryotherapy therapy for pain by cooling the skin.

Culture-fair intelligence test an intelligence test that uses culture-neutral questions and therefore does not penalize someone who is not from the dominant culture.

Curiosity motive stimulates individuals to explore new places in order to gain new information.

Cutaneous of or pertaining to the skin.

Cybertherapy a style of treatment in which clients receive therapy from a licensed professional over the Internet.

D

Dark adaptation the ability to see in the dark following the replenishment of rhodopsin in the rods.

Debriefing a necessary follow-up when deception has been used in a research study, in which immediately following the conclusion of the study, participants are informed of the true nature and purpose of the study.

Decay the process by which a mental representation of a stimulus is gradually lost.

Decibels unit of measurement for the loudness of sounds.

Deep structure the underlying meaning of the sentence.

Defense mechanism in Freudian theory, this term refers to a collection of unconscious defensive tactics employed by the mind to protect the self from being overwhelmed by anxiety that would be experienced if the frightening idea were to reach conscious awareness.

Deficiency motives drives that attempt to meet a physiological deficit, such as the need for sleep or sex.

Deindividuation the presence of others makes us less noticeable. The decreased sense of inhibition increases the likelihood that people will engage in behaviors in which they wouldn't normally engage.

Delta waves the larger brain waves found in stages 3 and 4 of sleep.

Delusional disorder a disorder consisting of persistent, nonbizarre, false beliefs about reality that are not part of a schizophrenia disorder.

Delusions false beliefs about reality that are held against evidence to the contrary.

Delusions of grandeur a type of delusion in which one harbors unfounded beliefs that one has some great, unrecognized talent, knowledge, or insight; that one has a special relationship with an important person or with God; or that one is a prominent person.

Delusions of influence a type of delusion that involves the false belief that one's thoughts, feelings, or actions are being controlled by external agents; that one's private thoughts are being broadcast indiscriminately to others; that thoughts are being inserted involuntarily by alien forces; or that some mysterious agency has robbed one of one's thoughts.

Delusions of persecution a type of delusion marked by mistaken beliefs that one is being cheated, spied on, followed, poisoned, harassed, or plotted against.

Delusions of reference a form of delusion in which events unrelated to oneself are given personal significance, such as the belief that a newspaper article is directed solely to oneself.

Demyelination loss of myelin on axons in the nervous system.

Dendrites branchlike protrusions from the soma through which neural signals are brought into the cell.

Dendritic spines small regions all over the dendrites that are the points at which synaptic terminals interact with the cell.

Density the proximity of receptors to one another.

Dependent personality disorder a personality disorder marked by a pattern of clinging and obedience, fear of separation, and a persistent, excessive need to be taken care of.

Dependent variable the variable that is observed and measured for change in an experiment; it is the outcome of interest and is predicted to be affected by (or dependent on) the manipulation of the independent variable.

Depersonalization disorder a dissociative disorder marked by a persistent and recurrent feeling of being detached from one's own mental processes or body; that is, one feels unreal and alien.

Depolarization the process by which a cell becomes slightly more positive. *See also* excitatory post-synaptic potential.

Depressants drugs that lower the activity of the nervous system.

Depressive realism the observation that depressed people often have a more accurate perception of reality than do people who are not depressed, in that depressed people are not subject to optimistic or wishful thinking.

Dermis the under layer of the skin.

Development changes that occur over time, and relevant to psychology, development is change in behaviors, skills, and abilities, from conception to death.

Developmentally disabled classification for individuals who score below 70 on an IQ test and who have a severe deficiency in daily life functioning.

Difference threshold the minimal increase in intensity required to detect a difference.

Differentiation neurons are enlarged and form synapses with other neurons.

Diffusion of responsibility theory a theory that states that the greater the number of people present in a situation in which help is required, the less likely any single individual is to help. The responsibility to help becomes spread out, or "diffused," among all those present.

Directionality problem in correlational research, when two variables are correlated, it is not possible to know for sure which variable (if either) is the causal agent and which is the effect.

Discrimination (1) the unfair treatment of someone based on his or her group membership. (2) a process that occurs when a conditioned response can be elicited only by the conditioned stimulus.

Disorganized schizophrenia a subtype of schizophrenia characterized by disorganized behavior, bizarre delusions, and vivid hallucinations.

Displacement new information entering short-term memory pushes out old information that is forgotten.

Display rules culture-specific norms for how and when we express different emotions.

Dispositional attribution attributing others' behavior to personality traits.

Dissociative amnesia a dissociative disorder characterized by an inability to recall important personal events and information.

Dissociative disorders dissociative disorders are characterized by a splitting apart of significant aspects of experience from memory or consciousness. In dissociative states, people experience a disruption in the usually integrated functions of consciousness, memory, identity, or perception of reality.

Dissociative fugue a dissociative disorder in which a person travels to a new location and may assume a new identity, simultaneously forgetting his or her past.

Dissociative identity disorder (DID) a dissociative disorder in which a person develops two or more distinct personalities or personality states.

Distraction-conflict theory a theory that states that the presence of others diverts our attention from the task at hand and ultimately results in an impaired performance.

Divergent thinking the tendency to generate a number of useful and appropriate solutions to a problem.

Door-in-the-face approach a method to increase compliance. When an individual has previously denied a large request, he or she is more likely to yield to a small request at a later time.

Dopamine a neurotransmitter involved in movement and pleasure.

Dorsal directional term used to indicate the top.

Dorsal column pathway *see* Lemniscal pathway.

Dorsal horn cells where nerves or fibers from the periphery enter the spinal cord.

Dorsal lateral prefrontal cortex the area of the brain responsible for impulse control.

Double approach-avoidance conflict a type of conflict caused when one finds it difficult to decide between options that have both pleasant and unpleasant outcomes.

Downward drift hypothesis the theory that explains the link between low socioeconomic status and behavior problems by suggesting that problem behaviors lead people to drift downward in social status.

Dream analysis a technique used to interpret and apply meaning to the content of a person's dream.

Drive the motivation to restore homeostasis by reducing our needs.

Drive-reduction theory a theory that suggests we are motivated to behave in ways that help us fulfill our needs.

Drug dependence when a person becomes addicted to drugs and experiences tolerance and withdrawal symptoms when trying to quit.

Dysthymic disorder a less intense but relatively constant state of depression for a period of at least two years.

E

Ear drum *see* tympanic membrane.

Echoic memory information stored in our auditory sensory register. Auditory echoes occur in the sensory register, lasting about three seconds before fading away.

Ecstasy a designer drug made in a lab by altering the chemical structure of an already-existing drug. Ecstasy is chemically similar to amphetamines and mescaline (hallucinogenic drug). Effects of using ecstasy are enhanced mood and energy levels and a heightened sensory experience.

Ectoderm outer layer of the embryo; it becomes the skin, the hair, the nails, and the brain and spinal cord.

Ego in Freudian psychoanalysis, this term refers to a personality structure that develops as the child matures and is introduced to the norms of behavior expected by society. The ego's function is to decide on a plan of action in any given situation that will satisfy the desires of the id aspect of the psyche, the superego portion of the psyche, and the expectations of others in the situation.

Ego alien a state of being that is foreign and unwanted by the person. It is synonymous with the term "ego dystonic."

Ego dystonic a state of being that is foreign and unwanted by the person. It is synonymous with the term "ego alien."

Ego ideal in psychoanalytic theory, it is the portion of the superego that incorporates those actions for which the child has been rewarded.

Ego syntonic a state of being that is experienced by the person as compatible with his or her self-concept.

Egocentric thought the inability to think from another's point of view.

Elaborative rehearsal connecting new material to what you already know and have already stored in long-term memory.

Electroconvulsive therapy (ECT) a treatment for severe depression that involves passing an electrical current through the brain.

Electroencephalograph (EEG) a machine that displays the recording from the electrodes picking up the brain activity.

Elevation aspect of sound localization associated with one's ability to detect the source of a sound on a vertical plane.

Embryo a developing individual during the embryonic period, formerly embryoblast in the germinal period.

Embryoblast part of the blastocyst that becomes the embryo or child.

Embryonic period one of the three prenatal periods, the beginning of which is marked by tiny blood vessels from the trophoblast establishing a connection with the mother's blood system through the wall of the uterus, and lasts until the eighth week.

Emotional health a state of optimal feeling that results from a combination of effective stress management, good coping skills, and one's optimistic appraisal of the environment.

Emotional intelligence the ability to perceive and respond to others' emotions effectively, the ability to understand and express one's own emotions appropriately, the ability to control and regulate one's emotions, and the ability to use emotions to facilitate thinking and motivation.

Emotional labor the act of controlling one's emotions in workplace settings to conform to workplace-specific display rules.

Emotions feelings such as happiness, sadness, fear, excitement, dread, and disgust.

Empathy identification and understanding of the client's situation, feelings, and motives.

Empathy-altruism theory our ability to experience the emotions and feelings of another increases the likelihood that we will offer assistance when the situation is highly demanding of time, energy, or other resources.

Empirical evidence data gathered through direct sensory experience rather than through intuitive speculation.

Empiricism a philosophical school of thought from the seventeenth century that argues that human knowledge derives from our experience and observation.

Endocrine system system of glands in the body responsible for releasing hormones to regulate various bodily processes.

Endoderm the innermost layer of the embryo; it develops into inner organs such as the digestive tract, the respiratory system, the pancreas, and the circulatory system.

Endorphins a class of neurotransmitters that serve as natural painkillers and are associated with the pleasure of social contact.

Energy reservoir theory a theory that states that long-term weight regulation holds that our bodies' long-term storage levels dictate the levels at which we consume stored energy and store new energy.

Enzymatic degradation process by which the neurotransmitter is broken down in the synaptic cleft.

Epidermis top layer of the skin.

Epilepsy a disorder characterized by abnormal electrical discharge in the brain.

Epinephrine a neurotransmitter that triggers the release of stored glucose from muscle tissue for the purpose of providing energy for the body.

Episodic memory memories of the events of your life, such as your memory of going to a party last Friday night or your memory about the time you got the flu and couldn't go on the skiing trip with your friends.

Erotomanic type a subtype of delusional disorder characterized by the erroneous belief that one is loved by someone of high social status.

Estrogen any of a number of female sex hormones.

Evaluation apprehension theory the mere presence of other people does not affect our performance; rather, it is the knowledge that we are being watched that affects our performance.

Evolutionary perspective a view that mental processes and behaviors need to change to match new circumstances. Otherwise, the species may eventually become extinct.

Evolutionary theory of sexual differences a theory that explains behavioral and cognitive differences between men and women as being a result of their different survival tactics.

Exchange model the likelihood of helping others is a function of the costs of helping.

Excitatory post-synaptic potential (EPSP) a positive change in the membrane potential of a neuron. *See also* depolarization.

Exemplar theory states that concepts can be represented by individual examples that are stored in memory from personal experiences.

Experiment a formal procedure for testing a hypothesis and either confirming or disconfirming a causal relationship between two or more variables that is predicted by the hypothesis.

Experimental group in a controlled experiment, the group of participants that is exposed to the independent variable.

Experimenter bias the tendency of experimenters to influence the results of a research study in the expected direction. The experimenter's actions can have an unintended influence on subjects' behavior.

Explicit memory occurs when you are trying to memorize something and you are consciously aware that you are trying to remember.

Extension of waking life theory a theory that dreams contain our ongoing problems and recent events.

External cues triggers that are outside our body that are picked up by our senses and that stimulate eating, such as the taste and smell of food or the pleasure of other people's company.

External ear *see* pinna.

External locus of control an ongoing belief that one has no power in controlling what happens in one's life.

Exteroceptive originating from outside the body.

Extinction the stage of learning where a response is eliminated.

Extracellular thirst occurs when the fluid becomes depleted in the body's tissue.

Extraneous variable a variable in an experiment that needs to be controlled so that it doesn't interfere with the testing of the effect of the independent variable on the dependent variable.

Extrinsic motivations a drive to receive external rewards, such as the need to earn money or get a good grade on a test.

Eye movement desensitization and reprocessing (EMDR) a therapeutic process in which a client is asked to visualize a stressful event while the therapist slowly moves his finger back and forth in front of the client's eyes.

Eyeblink conditioning an aversive classical conditioning paradigm in which a conditioned stimulus signals an airpuff or shock to the eye.

Eyewitness testimony research shows that when witnesses to crimes testify in court they tend to be highly inaccurate.

F

Facial feedback hypothesis states that our emotions, which involve complex cognitive and physiological systems, are triggered by our interpretations of our facial muscles.

Factor analysis a statistical procedure that assesses the pattern of answers on a test instrument; a correlational procedure that allows us to see the degree of relationship among many traits or behaviors at the same time.

Familiarity the sense that one knows someone else increases the likelihood of interpersonal attraction.

Family archetype in Jungian theory, this term represents connection and belonging; the strengths one ideally gains from one's family.

Family therapy a special type of group therapy in which parents and children enter treatment as a unit in order to improve communication patterns and resolve interpersonal conflicts.

Father archetype in Jungian theory, this term refers to an unconscious conception common to all human beings that a father represents authority—facing challenges, tests of character, rationality, and self-discipline. It is the masculine principle that counterbalances the sympathy and comfortable containment of the mother archetype.

Feature detection theory a theory stating that letter and number recognition results from determining the type and combinations of elemental features.

Feature detectors specialized cells in the visual cortex that respond to particular features in the environment.

Fetal alcohol syndrome (FAS) a condition caused when a fetus is exposed to alcohol through the mother's blood, resulting in abnormal physical and mental development.

Fetal period the third prenatal period; it lasts from the ninth week until birth.

Fissures long, deep indentations in the cerebral cortex.

Fixation getting stuck in a particular stage of development during childhood. This concept is central to the psychodynamic perspective.

Fixed interval schedule schedule of reinforcement where the first response made after a constant period of time earns a reinforcer.

Fixed ratio schedule schedule of reinforcement where a constant number of responses must be completed before a reinforcer becomes available.

Flashbulb memories vivid, detailed memories caused by traumatic or memorable events that an individual remembers in great detail years later.

Flexor reflex the reflex of withdrawing a limb in response to pain or a harmful stimulation.

Flooding full exposure to the feared stimulus or situation.

Foliate papillae a type of bump found on the sides of the tongue, associated with taste buds.

Foot-in-the-door approach a method used to increase compliance. When an individual has previously yielded to a small request, he or she is significantly more likely to yield to a larger subsequent request.

Forgetting curve most forgetting happens within the first nine hours of learning, with the first hour being the most vulnerable.

Formal operational stage the fourth of Piaget's stages of cognitive development; in this stage the ability to think about and perform operations with abstract concepts emerges, as does hypothetical thinking.

Fornix a series of connections from the hippocampus to other regions of the limbic system.

Forward or **delayed conditioning** conditioning schedule where the conditioned stimulus is presented first and then the conditioned and unconditioned stimuli coterminate.

Fovea location on retina where most cones are located.

Free association a psychodynamic treatment in which the client reveals whatever feelings, thoughts, or experiences come to mind.

Frequency the physical dimension of sound waves associated with pitch.

Frequency theory theory of pitch perception arguing that the tones we hear result from the frequency of firing of the hair cells.

Freudian dream theory according to Freud, our dreams contain hidden messages that are often camouflaged in symbols.

Frontal lobe the largest region of the cerebral cortex, responsible for language, problem solving, short-term memory, and motor movement.

Frustration an unpleasant feeling of disappointment and anger that results when an obstacle blocks one from reaching a goal.

Functional fixedness the inability to view objects being used in any way other than their familiar functions.

Functionalism a view that the study of the mind should focus on the study of the functions of the mental processes.

Fundamental attribution error the tendency to attribute the behavior of others to internal causes, such as personality.

Fungiform papillae a type of bump found on the front tip of the tongue, associated with taste buds.

G **GABA** the major inhibitory neurotransmitter in the nervous system; it is known to play a role in anxiety and panic-related disorders.

Galanin a neurotransmitter that stimulates cravings for fat.

Gamma-aminobutyric acid *see* GABA.

Gamma-hydroxybutyric acid (GHB) an intoxicant and a date rape drug. GHB is naturally produced in the human body's cells and is structurally related to the ketone body beta-hydroxybutyrate. GHB has historically been used as a general anesthetic to treat conditions such as insomnia, clinical depression, narcolepsy, and alcoholism and to improve athletic performance. It is sold illegally as ecstasy.

Ganglion cell cell in retina whose axons form the optic nerve.

Gate control theory popular theory for pain that suggests the inhibition and excitation of particular cells in the spinal cord determine if a pain message is sent to the brain.

Gender identity a person's psychological feeling of being male or female.

Gender identity disorder psychological distress prompted by the experience of identifying with the gender that does not match one's genitalia.

Gender roles behaviors an individual exhibits because he or she thinks these are the expected behaviors of his or her gender.

General Adaptation Syndrome (GAS) the system Hans Selye used to describe the effect of long-term stress on the body; it has three stages: alarm, resistance, and exhaustion.

General intelligence an individual's cognition that underlies all intelligent performance.

Generalization a process that occurs when a conditioned response occurs to stimuli that resemble the conditioned stimulus.

Generalized anxiety disorder a disorder marked by persistent and excessive feelings of anxiety and worry about numerous events and activities.

Genes hereditary material located within the chromosomes found in each cell of the human body.

Genital stage in Freudian theory, this is the fifth and final stage of personality development through which all children pass, which begins at puberty. This stage is based on creating love relationships through which sexual desires can be appropriately expressed.

Genuineness the therapist is completely honest with the client and with himself or herself regarding his or her own feelings about the process.

Germinal period the first two weeks after conception.

Gestalt a view that the whole (or "Gestalt," in German) of experience is more than the mere sum of its parts.

Gestalt Psychologists a group of perceptual scientists from Germany who believe that perception begins with analysis of whole patterns.

Ghrelin a hormone secreted by an empty stomach that appears to serve to increase appetite.

Gifted a term used to describe individuals who have the following three qualities: exceptional ability, exceptional motivation, and exceptional creativity.

Glucocorticoids stress hormones released by the adrenal glands. One of their many effects is to increase blood glucose levels.

Glucose a simple sugar that serves as the major energy source in the body.

Glutamate a major excitatory neurotransmitter in the nervous system. It is known to be involved in epilepsy, schizophrenia, memory, and ischaemic stroke.

Goodness of fit the fit between the child's temperament and the parents' expectations and behavior toward the child.

Graded potential the variable rate of responding by receptors.

Gradual in-vivo exposure exposing the client slowly and gradually toward an anxiety-provoking stimulus or situation.

Grandiose type a subtype of delusional disorder characterized by an inflated sense of worth, power, knowledge, identity, or special relationship to a deity or famous person.

Graphemes written symbols used to express language.

Gray matter regions of central nervous system tissue made up mostly of cell bodies and unmyelinated axons that give it a gray appearance.

Gross-fine law one of the laws of developmental direction; it states that general, rudimentary parts/behaviors become specific, finely detailed parts/behaviors.

Grossly disorganized behavior actions that depart from normal functioning and are not appropriately responsive to the environment.

Group two or more people who interact and are interdependent upon one another.

Group behavior the many ways that our behavior is influenced when individuals are members of a specified group.

Group therapy a type of treatment setting in which a number of clients, usually 7 to 11, share and discuss similar issues.

Groupthink poor decision making that occurs when members of the group are overly concerned with maintaining group cohesiveness.

Gustatory system the sensory system for taste.

Gyri ridges of cerebral cortex found between sulci and/or fissures.

H

Habituation a nonassociative learning process that decreases the magnitude of an unconditioned response.

Hair cells sensory receptor cells for the auditory system.

Hallucinations perceptions in the absence of stimuli; an imaginary sensation, such as hearing voices when no one is speaking, or smelling things that don't exist in the immediate environment.

Halo effect the tendency to believe that a person has other positive characteristics when we perceive that he or she has a certain other positive trait.

Hardiness the ability to assume a great deal of responsibility and respond to a large number of stressors without experiencing ill health, due to a combination of three factors: viewing oneself as in control of one's life, feeling committed to what one is doing, and looking forward to the challenge of dealing with stressors.

Hassles everyday inconveniences or troublesome situations that are an annoying aspect of life and are generally experienced as stressful.

Health a state of physical, mental, and social well-being exhibited by one having energy, vitality, fitness, a sense of purpose, and an optimistic perception about life.

Heritability the proportion of observed variables in a particular trait that can be attributed to inherited genetic factors in contrast to environmental ones.

Hermaphroditism a child born with both sets of genitals.

Hertz a unit of measurement for the frequency of sound.

Heterosexuality sexual attraction to individuals of the opposite sex.

Heuristics a mental shortcut that may or may not lead to a solution.

Hierarchy of needs Abraham Maslow's ordering of human needs. Maslow categorized needs on the basis of their presumed strength or potency, from the most urgent physiological needs to the most uniquely human need for self-actualization.

Hippocampus region of the medial temporal lobe important for memory and spatial location.

History effects an extraneous variable(s) that may threaten internal validity when an outside event or occurrence might have produced effects on the dependent variable.

Histrionic personality disorder a personality disorder in which an individual displays a pattern of excessive emotionality and attention seeking.

Holophrase single words used to represent an entire phrase.

Homeostasis physiological balance.

Homophobia the irrational fear or strong negative feelings toward individuals who are homosexual.

Homosexuality sexual attraction to individuals of the same sex.

Homunculus somatotopic representation in cortex of skin sensitivity.

Hostile aggression/emotional aggression a type of aggression associated with feelings of anger.

Human immunodeficiency virus (HIV) a virus that attacks the immune system, causing it to be unable to fight off pathogens that enter the body.

Humanism a view that the exploration of humans, rather than God, should be the primary focus.

Humanistic perspective a view of a human being as someone who has the potential for the entire range of experience and behaviors (e.g., sadness, joy, good deeds, and bad deeds) and strives to fulfill his or her potential.

Humanistic theory this approach to personality emphasizes the positive nature of human beings and their inborn potential for goodness.

Hunger a drive to reduce the physiological need for food.

Huntington's disease a genetic neurological disorder affecting the basal ganglia motor system and causing a variety of motor and cognitive deficits.

Hypnogogic hallucinations unusual images, drifting thoughts, and feelings of floating that occur during stage 1 sleep.

Hypnopompic hallucinations vivid, dreamlike hallucinations that occur when one is waking up.

Hypnosis a technique used by a trained specialist to induce an altered state of consciousness called a hypnotic state. A person experiencing this state is very relaxed and highly suggestible.

Hypochondriasis a somatoform disorder in which people mistakenly fear that minor changes in their physical functioning indicate a serious disease.

Hypothalamus region of the diencephalons responsible for basic motivational behaviors such as feeding, fighting, fleeing, and sex.

Hypothesis a predictive, testable statement about the relationship between two or more variables that is then tested by conducting a experiment.

I

Iconic memory information stored in the visual sensory register. One hundred percent of the visual information is stored in iconic memory, but it is only momentarily available for recall.

Id one of three structures in Freud's model of the mind. The id is the original source of personality, present at birth. It consists of a collection of basic biological drives that provide the energy for the operation of the entire personality for the id itself, and for both the ego and the superego. The id and its motivations are unknown to the conscious self.

Ideal self the part of your self-concept that consists of the person you would like to be.

Identical twins develop from the divided sphere of cells during the germinal period.

Ideographic goals goals that are specific to individual people, such as finishing up a paper for class or keeping weekend plans with your friends.

Imaginal thought consists of images perceived in one's mind.

Imaginary audience the belief that one's behaviors are the focus of everyone else's thoughts.

Implantation when the blastocyst comes into contact with the uterine wall and sends tendrils into the lining of the wall.

Implicit memory formed when your previous experiences unconsciously influence your current memory or behavior.

Implicit motives those aspects of our motives of which we are not consciously aware.

Incandescent light light from a heat source.

Incongruence in Rogersian theory, incongruence is an uncomfortable discrepancy between the three aspects of self—the self-concept, the ideal self, and the true self—which leads to defensiveness due to the person's unrealistic sense of himself or herself.

Incus one of the three small bones of the middle ear.

Independent variable the variable in an experiment that is manipulated by the experimenter; that is, the independent variable is given in different amounts to the groups of subjects participating in the experiment to see what effect it has on the dependent variable.

Individualistic this term refers to cultures that place a high value on individual freedom and self-expression. It is generally contrasted with collectivist cultures.

Individuating maturation the idea that development proceeds in a prepro-grammed sequence determined genetically and well in advance of the individual's conception.

Induced movement the illusion that a stationary object is moving due to movement of surrounding objects or backgrounds.

Indulgences papers stating that one's sins were forgiven.

Inferiority complex in Alfred Adler's theory, each child's struggle to overcome feelings of inferiority is viewed as a core problem in life. Children experience feelings of inferiority mainly because they begin life as small and relatively powerless. They are surrounded by larger and more competent adults and react to this inferior position by striving for superiority and power.

Information processing model (also known as the three-stage memory model) developed by Atkinson and Shiffrin, this model divides the basic structure of memory into three parts: the sensory register, short-term memory, and long-term memory.

Informational social influence conformity to the group because we assume that the group has knowledge that we personally lack.

Inhibiting hormones hormones released by the hypothalamus that inhibit the release of hormones from the pituitary gland.

Inhibitory post-synaptic potential (IPSP) a negative change in the membrane potential of a neuron.

Innate motives motives we are born with, such as the biological drives of thirst and hunger.

Insanity a legal term that refers to the inability of some individuals to understand the consequences of their actions. People with a mental disorder may not be held legally responsible for their criminal behavior if they are determined to be insane.

Insight when a solution to a problem suddenly appears, with apparently little effort.

Insomnia inability to fall asleep or maintain a sleeping state.

Instincts reflexive responses that are involuntary and genetically programmed.

Instrumental aggression a type of aggression in which there is an intention to cause harm to another person as a means of achieving a goal or to obtain something of value.

Instrumental competence competence in sociability, such as friendliness, cooperation, independence, and achievement oriented.

Insulin a hormone secreted by the pancreas that converts glucose into energy. The role of insulin is to get glucose into the cells for energy.

Integration approach a conflict resolution approach that minimizes the gains of all involved through the use of creative procedures.

Intellectual health a part of health that focuses on education, achievement, and career development.

Intelligence an individual's problem-solving ability, capacity to acquire knowledge, abstract thinking or reasoning ability, memory, and adaptation to the environment.

Intelligence quotient (IQ) consists of a child's mental age divided by chronological age and multiplied by 100.

Interactionist approach this theory holds that personality can only be understood by considering the genetic heritage of the individual, the person's child-rearing experiences, the era in which the person grew up, the stage of life the individual is currently in, the significant relationships in the person's life, and other influential environmental factors.

Interaural differences differences in the time and sound pressure received by each ear.

Interdependence the behaviors of each group member influence and affect the others in a tangible way.

Interference occurs when the storage or retrieval of information is affected by other information entering the memory system.

Internal locus of control one feels in control of his or her behavior and consequences from the environment.

Interoceptive originating from within the body.

Interposition a monocular depth cue where objects perceived to be in front of other objects also appear closer.

Intersex a human being possessing both male and female genitalia; a modern term for "hermaphroditism."

Interview a face-to-face meeting in which the psychologist asks a series of questions and allows the interviewee to explain his or her situation; its purpose is to assess personality, often with the intention of determining if psychopathology is present.

Interviewer bias occurs when the interviewer thinks he or she already knows the answer to the question and uses subtle pressure, consciously or unconsciously, to get the interviewee to change his or her view of an event.

Intimacy one of the three ingredients in the triangular theory of love that involves feelings of closeness.

Intracellular thirst occurs when the body's cells have lost water and have departed from a state of equilibrium.

Intrinsic motivations a drive to participate in an activity because it provides an internal reward, such as pleasure.

Introspection looking inward.

Ions single molecules such as sodium, potassium, and calcium that maintain electrical charges and may influence the activity of neurons.

Iris two muscles in the eye responsible for constricting and dilating the pupils.

Ischaemic stroke deprivation of blood flow to a particular area of the brain as a result of a blockage in the circulatory system.

J

Jacobson's progressive relaxation technique an exercise that utilizes a physiological approach to managing stress by creating relaxation through the release of muscle tension.

James-Lange theory the theory of emotion that suggests that our bodies react to situational stimuli by creating physiological arousal, and then we arrive at the mental experience that we know as emotion based on our perceptions of the physiological changes that have occurred in our bodies.

Jealous type a subtype of delusional disorder in which the false beliefs center on the conviction that one's sexual partner is unfaithful.

K **Kanzi** a pygmy chimpanzee who demonstrated an elementary understanding of syntax.

K-complexes consist of a brief high-amplitude peak and occur longer than half a second. K-complexes are occasionally seen in stage 2 sleep and are associated with sleep spindle activity.

Keppler, Johannes discovered that objects reflect light.

Kin selection we seek to perpetuate our genetic material through those who are closely related to us.

Kinesthetic sense of body position and movement.

Korsakoff's syndrome a condition characterized by memory problems due to a thiamine deficiency caused by chronic alcoholism.

L **Language** a system of communication with a particular set of rules for combining symbols (sounds, written symbols, or hand signs), which can generate an infinite number of meaningful combinations.

Language-acquisition device (LAD) a neural structure in the brain that humans are born with that allows us to recognize and produce the sounds and grammatical rules of the language that we are exposed to in our environment.

Latency period in Freudian theory, this is sometimes referred to as the fourth stage of personality development through which all children pass, taking place from 6 years of age to puberty. In this stage, children develop socially and also repress sexual urges while engaging in socially acceptable activities.

Latent content of dreams the unconscious desires that our dreams symbolize.

Latent learning learning that is not expressed in behavior until the proper incentives are in place.

Lateral directional term used to indicate to the side.

Lateral geniculate nucleus (LGN) part of the thalamus that receives visual input from retinal ganglion cells.

Lateral hypothalamus (LH) stimulates hunger and causes us to start eating.

Law of effect behaviors followed by positive consequences are likely to be repeated, whereas behaviors followed by negative consequences are not likely to be repeated.

Law of specific nerve energies this law from Johannes Muller states that we are aware of objects only through signals or energies transmitted through our nerves, and that different kinds of nerves transmit different signals.

Laws of developmental direction laws of how anatomical and motor development proceeds.

Lazarus's cognitive theory this theory of emotion states that we cannot experience an emotion without first having some cognitive appraisal of the stimuli. Appraisal can be conscious or unconscious, meaning that we may be aware of our appraisal or it may occur outside our awareness.

Learned helplessness a negative mental state that results from finding that one's efforts to escape an unpleasant situation are ineffective; thus the person concludes that making further efforts to improve the situation is useless.

Learned motives motives that satisfy needs that are not directly tied to bodily requirements, such as the need for social approval.

Learning a set of processes that account for changes in behavior that result from experience.

Learning perspective views behavior as a product of consequence.

Lemniscal pathway pathway from the skin up the spinal cord that carries information about touch, vibration, and body position.

Lens part of the eye that focuses light onto the retina.

Leptin a hormone secreted by the fat cells that signals a person to stop eating.

Levels of processing model states that the information we remember best is that which has been processed most fully when we receive it.

Life change units (LCUs) the numerical value assigned to stressful life events by researchers Holmes and Rahe, in order to quantify the amount of current stress in a person's life.

Life-span development Erik Erikson's theory that suggests that changes in personality occur throughout the life span, with particular dilemmas occurring at each of the eight stages.

Limbic system series of brain structures involved in processing emotion and memory.

Linear perspective a monocular depth cue where straight lines converge toward an unseen point in the distance.

Linguists professionals who study the nature of language.

Lithium carbonate drug used for the treatment of bipolar disorder.

Little Albert a child who developed a conditioned fear in Watson's study of the conditioned emotional reflex.

Logos means "knowledge" in Greek.

Longitudinal design a research method that measures subjects over an extended period and provides information about age-related changes.

Long-term memory (LTM) where we store information in order to retrieve it later. Information tends to stay in long-term memory for a long time, and the capacity for storage is large—probably unlimited.

Loosening of associations (also called derailment) this symptom of schizophrenia involves jumping from one topic to another, making the person's conversation difficult or impossible to follow. The listener is left with the impression that what is being said would make sense if only he or she could listen just a little more closely.

Loudness the psychological property of sound associated with its amplitude.

Luminance perceived brightness.

Luminescent light light from colliding electrons returning to baseline rate.

Lysergic acid diethylamide (LSD) a hallucinogenic drug of abuse.

M **Maintenance rehearsal** repeating or reviewing information in your mind or even saying it out loud in order to store it in memory.

Major depressive disorder a severe occurrence of low mood that may cause a lack of pleasure in activities or things that generally provide the depressed person with enjoyment. The degree and pervasiveness of the sadness are such that they interfere with the person's ability to function in life.

Malleus one of the three small bones of the middle ear.

Malleus Malleficarum a religious text used by church authorities to identify and punish witches.

Manifest content of dreams the actual plot of our dreams.

Manipulation motive the desire to handle things in our environment.

Manual babbling rhythmic and repeated hand movements seen in deaf babies exposed to sign language.

Marijuana a drug extracted from the Cannabis sativa plant. Its leaves, seeds, and flowers are dried and crushed. The mixture of these is marijuana.

Maturational readiness individuals vary in the rate at which they develop motor behaviors, adaptive behaviors (e.g., alertness, intelligence), language, and social behaviors.

Mean a measure of central tendency calculated by adding a group of scores and then dividing by the total number of scores.

Means-end analysis a heuristic in which differences are identified between the present state and the goal state, and changes are made to reduce these differences.

Mechanoreceptors receptors in the skin responsible for touch.

Medial directional term used to indicate to the middle.

Median a measure of central tendency found by arranging scores from the highest to the lowest and selecting the score that falls in the middle. Half of the values in the group of scores lie above the median and the other half fall below.

Meditation a mildly altered state of consciousness.

Medulla region of the myelencephalon responsible for basic life functions such as respiration and heart rate.

Meissner's corpuscle mechanoreceptor in the skin that provides information about light touch.

Melatonin a hormone released by the pineal gland that plays a role in mood, particularly in some types of depression.

Meniere's disease a form of sensorineural hearing loss associated with a buildup of fluid in the inner ear.

Mental age to assess a child's intelligence, the child answers questions at the lowest age level first and continues until he or she can no longer perform the task. The age level at which the child can no longer answer the questions correctly is considered the child's mental age.

Mental disorder a significant impairment in psychological functioning that meets the *Diagnostic and Statistical Manual*'s criteria for a documented disorder.

Mental images representations that arise from stored information rather than from visual sensory input.

Mental maps mental representations of spatial relationships.

Mental rotation visually rotating objects in our mind in the same way that we rotate objects in the real world.

Mental set the tendency to use strategies that have worked in the past even though another strategy might work better.

Mental status exams tests to measure psychosis, which, in their simplest form, look at whether the person is oriented in terms of knowing who he or she is, where he or she is at the present moment, and what is the approximate date.

Mere exposure effect repeated exposure to a stimulus increases our attraction and positive feelings toward that stimulus.

Merkel's discs mechanoreceptors found in the skin that provide information about pressure and texture.

Mesmerism using the magnetic force of the body to restore the balance of another's force and cure him or her of an illness.

Mesoderm middle layer of the embryo; it becomes muscles, bones, the circulatory system, and the excretory system.

Meta-analysis a statistical procedure for combining and analyzing data from many studies.

Method of savings a method for measuring how much learning was "saved" from a previous learning attempt.

Miller's Magic Number the term used to describe that short-term memory has a capacity of about seven (plus or minus two) items, depending on the individual.

Minnesota Multiphasic Personality Inventory (MMPI-2) the most widely researched and clinically used self-reported objective personality test, which also yields information about potential mental disorders.

Minnesota Twin Study a study that found that intelligence had a heritability of .60 to .70.

Misinformation effect when a person is given new information after witnessing an event, and this new information changes what is remembered.

Mitosis the process of cell division.

Mnemonic device a way in which to organize or associate information you are learning in order to improve your capacity for recall.

Mode a measure of central tendency found by identifying the most frequently occurring score in a group of scores.

Modeling the imitation of the behavior of others.

Modern racism covert prejudice tied to one's race.

Modern sexism covert prejudice tied to one's sex.

Monoamine oxidase inhibitors (MAOIs) a category of antidepressant drugs that block the body's enzymes from destroying serotonin and norepinephrine.

Monocular cues depth cues that can be seen with only one eye.

Moon Illusion the illusion that the moon is bigger at the horizon than at its zenith, and their identical visual angles leads to the perception that the moon is also farther away at the horizon.

Moral treatment an approach that emphasizes moral guidance and respectful procedures to treat patients with mental disorders.

Morality principle in Freudian theory, this term refers to the overall moral guidance that the part of the psyche referred to as the superego provides the person to oversee his or her choice of behaviors. The superego gauges whether the person's behaviors are morally appropriate.

Morphemes the smallest units of meaning in language.

Mother archetype in Jungian theory, this term refers to an unconscious conception common to all human beings that a mother is caring, nurturing, and selfless with her offspring.

Motion parallex objects are passed more slowly as the distance between them and the observer increases.

Motivation the stimulation to behave in certain ways.

Motoric thought consists of mental representations of motor movements we perceive in our mind.

Movement detectors cortical cells that respond to motion or movement of an object.

Muller, Johannes described the law of specific nerve energies.

Multiple intelligences theory suggests that there are eight different forms of intelligence: linguistic, logical-mathematical, spatial, bodily-kinesthetic, musical, interpersonal, intrapersonal, and naturalistic.

Multiple sclerosis (MS) a degenerative disorder characterized by the loss of myelin in the nervous system. Some believe it to be an autoimmune disorder.

Multitasking engaging in more than one behavior simultaneously because one or more behaviors have become habitual.

Muscular paralysis loss of muscle tone.

Myelin sheath fatty substance that coats some axons in the nervous system.

Myelinated axons axons in the nervous system that are coated with myelin.

Myers-Briggs Type Indicator (MBTI) a personality assessment instrument designed to measure normal populations, such as college students, on four personality dimensions.

Myotonia muscle tension experienced during sexual excitement in multiple parts of the body such as the feet, the legs, the arms, and the face.

N

Narcissistic personality disorder a personality disorder marked by a broad pattern of grandiosity, a need for admiration, and a lack of empathy.

Narcolepsy an inappropriate attack of sleep and/or an inappropriate attack of behaviors associated with healthy/normal sleep.

Natural selection a process whereby some individuals in a species survive and reproduce more than others as a result of a particularly adaptive set of traits.

Naturalistic observation a strategy that involves going to the location where a behavior of interest occurs and observing it as it happens.

Needs the most basic necessities for human survival.

Negative punishment a desired stimulus is taken from the learner.

Negative reinforcement an undesirable stimulus is alleviated.

Negative symptoms [of schizophrenia] symptoms of schizophrenia that seem to be deficits of normal thought, emotion, or behavior, such as avolition, asociality, and affective flattening.

Neologisms made-up words that do not have a shared meaning with others.

Nervous system contains all the neural tissue in the body.

Neural conduction the process by which an electrical signal is sent through a neuron.

Neurofibrillary tangles abnormal mass of proteins found inside neurons in individuals with Alzheimer's disease.

Neuron functional cell of the nervous system.

Neuron proliferation extremely rapid rate of neuron generation.

Neuronal migration the movement of neurons to different locations in the brain during gestation.

Neurosis a large group of disorders characterized by unrealistic anxiety and other associated problems.

Neurotransmitter a class of chemicals commonly released by synaptic terminals that induce changes in the receiving neuron.

Neutral stimulus a stimulus that does not elicit the response under investigation.

Nicotine an addictive chemical found in cigarettes, tobacco, and other by-products. Often associated with smoking, nicotine addiction has recently been recognized as a serious problem among people of all ages.

Night terrors terrors occurring during stages 3 and 4 of sleep that are characterized by waking in a panic and are accompanied by screams, rapid breathing, and increased heart rate.

Nightmares frightening dreams that occur in REM sleep.

Nim Chimpsky a young chimpanzee to whom Herbert Terrace taught sign language. Nim learned about 125 signs and could string them together in two or three-word combinations.

Nociceptors pain receptors.

Node of Ranvier a gap between two sections of myelin on a myelinated axon where the axon membrane is exposed.

Nomothetic goals goals that are common to all people, such as trying to have a successful career or trying to get along with others.

Nonassociative learning learning that does not involve the formation of a neural connection.

Nonattachment when children have no opportunity to form an emotional bond with a caregiver.

Nonparticipant observation observing the behavior of animal or human subjects while being concealed from view, as, for example, behind a two-way mirror.

Non-REM sleep characterizes sleep stages 1–4, in which rapid eye movements do not occur.

Nonverbal behavior any behavior that does not involve pronunciation and/or writing of words (e.g., facial grimaces, posture, eye contact, and hand gestures).

Norepinephrine a neurotransmitter and stress hormone involved in attention, learning, and depression.

Normal curve a symmetrical, bell-shaped distribution, with a large number of scores in the middle, tapering to very few extremely high or low scores.

Normative conformity a change in our behavior caused by the desire to belong to and to meet the standards of a group.

Norms (1) rules for accepted and expected behavior. They are culturally based guidelines concerning what is appropriate or inappropriate action. Norms are developed through consensus, meaning that people living within a culture typically set and enforce the norms because they agree with them. (2) (in reference to testing) the group means by which individual scores are interpreted.

Nucleus accumbens a brain region largely associated with the pleasurable and reinforcing effects of the neurotransmitter dopamine.

O

Obedience a change in behavior by an individual that stems from receiving a direct command from a person in a position of authority.

Object agnosia a form of visual agnosia pertaining to the perception of objects.

Object permanence the knowledge that something or someone continues to exist, even if the individual cannot see, hear, touch, smell, or taste it.

Objective test tests that are free of the subjective judgments of the person doing the assessment.

Observational learning the learner watches a model behaving and notes the consequences of each action.

Obsessions persistent thoughts, ideas, impulses, or images that are experienced repeatedly, intrude into consciousness, and cause anxiety.

Obsessive-compulsive disorder (OCD) an anxiety disorder characterized by recurrent and unwanted thoughts and/or a need to perform rigidly repetitive physical or mental actions.

Obsessive-compulsive personality disorder a personality disorder in which an individual is so focused on orderliness, perfectionism, and control that he or she loses flexibility, openness, and efficiency.

Occipital lobe a region of the cerebral cortex containing tissue important for vision.

Occupational health a state of feeling satisfied with one's employment or career situation.

Odorants molecules that stimulate olfactory receptor cells.

Olfactory bulb a region of the brain that receives input from the olfactory receptor cells.

Olfactory cavity nasal cavity into which air containing odorants is pulled.

Olfactory epithelium thin band of tissue at the top of the olfactory cavity that contains the olfactory receptor cells.

Olfactory system the sensory system for smell.

Ontogeny the development of an animal from conception to death.

Operant conditioning learning by reinforcement.

Operational definition a measurable form of a variable.

Opiates (morphine, heroin, opium) sleep-inducing and pain-relieving drugs.

Opponent process theory theory of color vision where bipolar and ganglion cells respond in "on-off" or "center-surround" fashion to opponent colors.

Oral stage in Freudian theory, this is the first stage of personality development through which all children pass, taking place from birth to 18 months of age. In this stage, the infant receives gratification through using the mouth for sucking, eating, and biting.

Organ of corti an organ inside the cochlea that holds the sensory receptor cells for the auditory system.

Organic sense sensations from the internal organs.

Ossicles the set of three small bones in the middle ear, which are responsible for transmitting sound wave information from the tympanic membrane to the oval window.

Oval window a small membrane-covered opening in the cochlea that receives pressure from the ossicles to stimulate the organ of corti.

Ovaries female reproductive organs.

Overextension generalizing the meaning of a word beyond its true meaning.

Overlap overextending the use of a word to refer to different objects, but also underextending to refer to only some of the same objects.

Overlearning practicing beyond the point of mastery.

P

Pacinian corpuscle mechanoreceptor in the skin that provides information about deep pressure and vibration.

Pain disorder a somatoform disorder marked by pain, with psychosocial factors playing a central role in the onset, severity, or continuation of the pain.

Palinaesthesia an illusion of persistent touch following the removal of a stimulus in some patients with right parietal lobe damage.

Pancreas an endocrine gland responsible for regulating blood sugar levels.

Panic disorder an anxiety disorder marked by recurrent and unpredictable panic attacks.

Papillae the series of small bumps on the tongue, many of which are associated with taste perception.

Paradigm shift a major change in the standard way of thinking.

Paradoxical cold excess stimulation of cold fibers by a warm stimulus leads to a cold sensation.

Paradoxical warm excess stimulation of warm fibers by a cold stimulus leads to a warm sensation.

Parallel play children play next to each other but do not interact.

Paranoid personality disorder a personality disorder characterized by a pattern of extreme distrust and suspiciousness of others.

Paranoid schizophrenia schizophrenia marked by a preoccupation with delusions or by frequent auditory hallucinations related to a single theme, especially grandeur or persecution.

Paraphilia a compulsive and sometimes destructive deviation in sexual preference and behavior.

Parasympathetic division the division of the autonomic nervous system responsible for calming or relaxing the body and conserving energy.

Parenting style how parents interact with their children.

Parietal lobe a region of the cerebral cortex containing the somatosensory cortex and the association cortex.

Parkinson's disease a neurodegenerative disease caused by the selective loss of dopamine neurons in the substantia nigra.

Partial reinforcement extinction effect the finding that extinction is faster after continuous reinforcement than after partial reinforcement.

Participant observation a technique for observing people or animals in their natural environment, in which the observer becomes unobtrusive by participating in the scene.

Passion one of the three ingredients in the triangular theory of love associated with sexual desire and physiological arousal.

Passionate love an intense feeling for another with a sexual or erotic content. It is also accompanied by hope and expectation for the future and involves the idealization of the object of one's affection.

Passive-aggressiveness the expression of anger through covert behaviors that oppose another person's request. This form of anger expression tends to be resorted to when a person fears retaliation if he or she were to openly express anger.

Patterned speech production of words.

Penis envy in Freudian theory, the idea that all girls wish that they possessed a penis, the symbol of social rank and/or biological superiority.

Perception interpretation of sensation.

Peripheral cues hunger triggers that occur in areas of the body outside the brain and spinal cord.

Peripheral nervous system (PNS) branch of the nervous system containing the somatic nervous system, autonomic nervous system, and cranial nerves.

Permissive a parenting style where parents set few limits, and the children are permitted to dictate their own schedules for their daily rituals of play, meals, and bed.

Persecutory type a subtype of delusional disorder that involves a conviction that one is being malevolently treated in some way.

Persona the Latin word for "mask." The persona is that part of ourselves of which we are conscious and which we see when we look in a mirror. However, it is only the outer self; there is more that lies within us.

Personal fable the belief that one's thoughts are completely unique and that no other has experienced the same thoughts or can understand.

Personal unconscious in Jungian theory, a region of the mind to which traumatic personal experiences are relegated to enable the person to function without being overwhelmed by the anxiety that memory of the incident would elicit.

Personality a generally consistent set of thoughts, emotions, and behavior that endure over time and across situations. The term originates from the Latin word *persona*, which means "mask."

Personality types a collection of personality traits that tend to be found together in people.

Phallic stage in Freudian theory, this is the third stage of personality development through which all children pass, taking place from 3 to 6 years of age. In this stage, the child finds pleasure in the genitals.

Phantom limb continued sensation (usually of pain) in a missing limb.

Phencyclidine (PCP) a drug of abuse.

Pheromones chemical signals associated with stimulation of the vomeronasal organ and sexual behavior.

Phi phenomenon illusion of apparent motion where individuals perceive two flashing dots to be one dot that has moved to another location, but they admit not seeing the movement.

Phobia persistent and unreasonable fear of particular objects, activities, or situations.

Phoenix and Ake two bottle-nosed dolphins who rarely confuse subject-verb-object word order requests that are signed to them.

Phonemes the speech sounds that are particular to each language.

Phonetics the process of learning the respective sounds of the letters of the alphabet.

Photons molecules of light.

Photopigment chemical found in photoreceptors that breaks down in response to light, causing a photoreceptor response.

Photoreceptors visual receptors found in the retina that receive light.

Phrenology a theory by the nineteenth-century German physician Franz Gall that posited that skull shape corresponds to the over- or underdevelopment of parts of the brain that were thought to correspond to specific personality characteristics.

Phylogeny evolutionary development of a species.

Physical dependence a condition in which one's body needs the drug to function.

Physical health a state of having good health that results from a combination of proper nutrition, physical fitness, medical self-care, and lack of substance abuse.

Physiological component an aspect of emotion that involves immediate physiological reactions (changes in the body) that occur as a result of various situations or thoughts that we experience.

Physiological reactions bodily processes such as heart rate, breathing, sweating, reflexes, brain activity, and cellular activity.

Physiological zero the range of normal temperatures for the human body.

Pineal gland an endocrine gland responsible for the release of melatonin.

Pinna the external portion of our auditory system that first receives the auditory sound wave information. Helps to funnel sound waves into our auditory system and allows sounds waves to resonate.

Pitch the psychological dimension of sound waves associated with frequency.

Pituitary gland considered the "master gland" because the hormones it releases directly influence the release of hormones from other endocrine glands in the body.

Place theory a theory of auditory pitch perception arguing that the tone we hear is a result of the location along the basilar membrane that is stimulated.

Placebo an inactive substance given in place of the independent variable, to keep control group subjects from knowing that they are in the control group. This procedure controls for the effects of expectation.

Placental barrier allows nutrients from the mother's blood to pass through to the child and for waste to leave.

Plastic a term used to refer to the flexibility of the nervous system.

Plasticity new, unspecialized neurons can be flexible in their functioning, which is useful if brain injury or nerve damage occurs. Plasticity also refers to the formation of new synaptic connections.

Pleasure principle in Freudian psychoanalysis, this term describes how the id operates on instinct, seeking pleasurable experiences and avoiding painful ones, without regard to the consequences. The reality of the situation is not considered.

Plutchik's theory this theory of emotion states that the purpose of emotion is adaptation to the environment, and that emotions are activated to aid in survival.

Pons region of the metencephalon important for sleep.

Ponzo Illusion the illusion that two horizontally placed lines are unequal in length due to perception of depth.

Positive psychology a subfield in psychology that studies well-being and correlates of happiness.

Positive punishment an undesired stimulus is presented to the learner.

Positive reinforcement a desirable stimulus is provided to the learner.

Positive symptoms [of schizophrenia] symptoms of schizophrenia that seem to be thoughts, emotions, or behaviors that are not normally experienced, such as hallucinations and delusions.

Postconventional level encompasses stage 5 and stage 6 of Kohlberg's moral reasoning, where moral decisions are determined by internalized principles.

Posterior directional term used to indicate to the back.

Posthypnotic suggestion a suggestion during hypnosis that a person acts on after he or she is no longer hypnotized.

Postnatal neurogenesis the formation of new brain and nerve cells that occurs after birth.

Post-synaptic potential a positive or negative change in the membrane potential of a neuron.

Post-traumatic stress disorder (PTSD) a mental disorder that involves flashbacks, nightmares, hypervigilance, and other symptoms that show up more than a month after the sufferer experiences a life-threatening traumatic event.

Postural muscle paralysis occurs during REM sleep, when sleep muscles in the body are extremely relaxed/paralyzed.

Potassium a positively charged ion found mostly in the intracellular fluid of neurons.

Power motivation the need to achieve power over others. It is associated with various behaviors, including seeking positions of leadership and status.

Pragmatics the characteristics of spoken language that aid us in interpreting the social meaning of the communication.

Preconscious in Freudian psychoanalysis, this term refers to the level of thoughts not immediately within the conscious mind but easily accessible to it.

Preconventional level encompasses stage 1 and stage 2 of Kohlberg's moral reasoning, where moral decisions are determined by the consequences for the behavior.

Prejudice a negative attitude harbored by an individual toward a person, place, or thing.

Prenatal period runs from conception to birth and is divided into three periods: germinal, embryo, and fetus.

Preoperational stage the second of Piaget's stages of cognitive development; in this stage children have significant language increases and can represent things using symbols.

Presbycusis natural degeneration of auditory hair cells with aging.

Pressures a form of stress that may be experienced as having a relatively short time frame in which things must be accomplished, or having numerous responsibilities that are experienced as weighing on one's mind.

Primacy effect we remember the first words in a list more easily than the later words because these words get the most rehearsal and get into long-term memory.

Primacy versus recency effect an observation that we are most likely to remember information that was most recently presented to us as well as information that was presented to us first.

Primary auditory cortex cortex located in the temporal lobes, responsible for processing sound information.

Primary drives drives that are unlearned and serve to satisfy biological needs.

Primary hyperalgesia lower thresholds for experiencing pain once exposed to the painful stimulus.

Primary motor cortex cortex located in the frontal lobes, responsible for motor movement.

Primary visual cortex cortex located in the occipital lobes, responsible for processing visual information.

Priming an unconscious mental process by which something registers in your memory without your being aware of it.

Proactive interference information you already know interferes with learning or remembering new information.

Problem-focused coping dealing with a problem by generating alternative courses of action rather than by attending to the negative emotions prompted by the problem.

Problem solving an attempt to overcome obstacles in order to reach a goal.

Procedural memory the memory storage area that contains knowledge of how to perform certain tasks, like riding a bike or driving a car.

Process loss an aspect of group interaction that leads to poor decision making.

Projective tests personality and psychopathology assessment tools that are composed of ambiguous stimuli to which the examinee is asked to respond. The idea behind these tests is that examinees will "project" their unconscious wishes and conflicts onto the ambiguous stimuli.

Propositional thought consists of the internal silent verbal language we perceive in our mind.

Prosocial behavior any behavior that is intended to help or benefit another.

Prosopagnosia inability to recognize faces due to cortical damage.

Prototype theory states that a concept is formed on the basis of a mental example that embodies the most common and typical features of that set of objects.

Proximity a factor influencing interpersonal attraction in which we are more likely to develop positive feeling toward people we see the most.

Proximo-distal law one of the laws of developmental direction; it states that development begins in the center of the body and then proceeds to the extremities.

Psychedelic drugs hallucinogenic drugs of abuse.

Psychoactive drugs drugs that distort mood, sensations, perceptions, thinking, and/or consciousness.

Psychoanalysis the original Freudian therapy that emphasizes the use of free association and dream analysis to uncover unconscious conflicts that lead to psychopathology.

Psychodynamic model refers to the active interplay among personality structures, such as the id, the ego, and the superego in Freudian psychoanalysis, and is based on the idea that there are powerful mental processes that remain hidden from conscious awareness, which nevertheless influence a person's behavior.

Psychodynamic perspective a view that argues that mental processes are motivated by conflicting interactions among the id, the ego, and the superego.

Psycholinguistics the study of how language is acquired, processed, understood, produced, and used.

Psychological androgyny "androgyny" derives from words of Greek origin—*andro*, meaning "male," and *gyn*, meaning "female." Androgyny means having male and female organs. The term "psychological androgyny" is used to describe an individual who attributes to himself or herself characteristics that are traditionally masculine and feminine. The androgynous person integrates qualities of both sexes and is thus relatively free of gender constraints.

Psychological dependence a condition in which one needs a drug to function cognitively and emotionally.

Psychometrics the area of psychology that studies the measurement of intelligence.

Psychoneuroimmunology a science that studies how the combination of the central nervous system, the endocrine system, and psychosocial factors affects the immunological system.

Psychopathology the scientific study of mental, emotional, and behavioral disorders; also, abnormal or maladaptive behavior.

Psychosexual stages in psychoanalytic theory, these are the five developmental periods during which particular kinds of pleasures must be gratified if personality development is to proceed normally.

Psychosomatic disorders medical conditions caused or made worse by psychological factors such as stress.

Psychosurgery a medical procedure that involves operating on a part of the brain in an attempt to cure a mental illness.

Psychotic psychosis is a condition of a mental disorder in which the person has lost contact with reality. The withdrawal from reality tends to be marked by hallucinations and delusions, disturbed thoughts and emotions, and personality disorganization.

Punishers stimuli that decrease the likelihood that a behavior will be repeated under similar circumstances.

Punishment the learning process that weakens the underlying S-R-O association.

Pupil opening in the eye that lets in light.

Puzzle box a crate modified to be a box with a door on one side. An animal, such as a cat, is placed inside in order to observe the sequence of behaviors it learns to get out.

R

Racism the unfair treatment of someone based on his or her membership in a racial group.

Railroad Illusion *see* Ponzo Illusion.

Random activation synthesis theory a theory that states that dreams are meaningless.

Random assignment an experimental control procedure that gives each participant in an experiment an equal chance of being in the experimental or control group. This provides the best opportunity to begin the experiment with equal groups, so that if the groups end up being different after the experimental group receives the treatment, then the difference observed is likely due to the effect of the independent variable.

Random selection a control procedure that involves ensuring that every member of a population of interest to the researcher has an equal chance of being included in the sample.

Range the difference between the largest and smallest scores in a set of data; a rough index of the amount of variability in the data.

Rape a crime in which sexual activity is forced upon a nonconsenting partner.

Rational-emotive therapy (RET) a treatment strategy for those whose maladaptive behaviors and distressed feelings are derived from illogical and destructive beliefs.

Reality principle in Freudian psychoanalysis, this term refers to the manner in which the ego structure of the psyche is aware of reality and prevents the id aspect of the psyche from acting purely on the principle of seeking pleasurable experiences regardless of the consequences.

Recall retrieving information simply by searching memory without the aid of any retrieval cues.

Recapitulation theory the assertion that ontogeny recapitulates phylogeny.

Recency effect we recall the last words in a list because these are still in short-term memory.

Receptive field area of space or location on the body to which a receptor or other higher-order cell responds.

Receptor specialized cells in sensory organs that receive physical stimulation and transform it into a pattern of responding.

Receptor potential the rate at which a receptor responds to a stimulus.

Reciprocal liking one factor of interpersonal attraction that states that we are more likely to have positive feeling for those that we know have positive feelings for us.

Recognition requires you to match information presented to you to existing information in memory.

Recognition by components theory (RBC) theory proposed to account for object recognition, stating that objects are recognized by the basic geometric shapes of which they are composed and how those shapes are combined.

Reconstructive memory when we store only the highlights and piece together the event during retrieval using information that may or may not be accurate.

Recovered memory therapy any therapeutic procedure that attempts to uncover repressed memories, which may be interfering with current psychological functioning.

Reflex a simple form of behavior in which sensory information results in a rapid motor response, often without input from the brain.

Reframing a technique used in family therapy or in stress management that involves offering the client a different way of conceptualizing a problem so that it looks less threatening.

Reinforcement the learning process that strengthens the underlying S-R-O association.

Reinforcers stimuli that increase the likelihood that a behavior will reoccur under similar circumstances.

Relative motion depth cue of relative speed in passing different objects.

Relative size more distant objects have smaller visual angles.

Releasing hormones hormones released by the hypothalamus that cause the subsequent release of hormones from the pituitary gland.

Reliability a test consistently demonstrates the same score when the same person is tested and then retested on an alternative form of the test.

REM behavior disorder a sleep disorder that causes a person to act out his or her dreams.

REM sleep stage of sleep where our eyes move rapidly back and forth.

Renewal effect reappearance of an extinguished conditioned response following a change in context.

Repetitive transcranial magnetic stimulation (rTMS) a procedure in which an electromagnetic coil is pressed against the scalp of an awake and unsedated patient; the coil transmits high-intensity magnetism to the brain.

Representational thought the preoperational child's ability to understand that words can stand for objects.

Repress in Freudian theory, this term refers to an unconscious defensive maneuver that involves pushing anxiety-provoking thoughts into the unconscious region of the mind.

Repressed memories memories of which we are not consciously aware.

Resistance a psychodynamic approach in which the client is unwilling or unable to bring uncomfortable and unpleasant materials into the open.

Resting membrane potential the electrical potential of an inactive (resting) neuron.

Reticular formation a brain structure embedded within the brain stem and responsible for nervous system arousal.

Retina structure in the eye that contains the photoreceptors, bipolar cells, and ganglion cells.

Retinex theory theory of how color is processed by the cortex, which can account for color constancy.

Retinotopic the retina's visual representation of space, where adjacent points in space signal responses in adjacent cells in the retina and CNS structures.

Retrieval the process of getting information out of long-term memory storage into conscious awareness.

Retroactive interference the learning of new information interferes with recall of information you have already learned.

Retrograde amnesia the inability to retrieve old memories from long-term memory.

Reuptake process by which neurotransmitter is reabsorbed into the synaptic terminal from the synaptic cleft.

Rhodopsin photopigment of rods.

Riddle of induction the question of how the rapid acquisition of matching word to meanings occurs.

Rods photoreceptor that responds in dim light and is responsible for peripheral vision.

Rohypnol (flunitrazepam) this substance is most commonly known as a date-rape drug; it continues to be abused among teenagers and young adults, usually at raves and nightclubs.

Rooting reflex when a baby's cheek is touched, the baby reflexively turns his or her head to face the object.

Rorschach Inkblot Test a personality test that asks a person to project meaning onto meaningless inkblots. Its use is based on the projective hypothesis, which states that when shown ambiguous stimuli, people will project their unconscious wishes and conflicts onto the stimuli.

Rubber Hand Illusion the illusion that a viewed rubber hand is one's own.

Ruffini cylinders mechanoreceptors in the skin that provide information about stretch in the skin.

S

Salient attention-getting.

Satiety feelings of fullness that generally compel us to end our food intake.

Scatterplot a graph of data from a correlational study, created by plotting pairs of scores from each subject; the value of one variable is plotted on the x (horizontal) axis and the value of the other variable on the y (vertical) axis.

Schacter-Singer theory the theory of emotion that states that the emotions that we experience are based on our interpretations of physiological responses to situational stimuli.

Schedule of reinforcement a set of guidelines that determine when and how a reinforcer may be earned.

Scheduling worries a cognitive therapy technique that directs clients to worry about their problems only during a certain period of time. This intervention has the effect of showing clients that they can gain control over their anxiety.

Schema a mental framework for organizing concepts according to related themes or aspects of a particular situation.

Schizoid personality disorder a personality disorder in which a person persistently avoids social relationships and shows little emotional expression.

Schizophrenia an enduring psychotic disorder that involves disturbed behavior, thinking, emotion, and perception.

Schizotypal personality disorder a personality disorder in which a person displays a pattern of interpersonal problems marked by extreme discomfort in close relationships, odd forms of thinking and perceiving, and behavioral eccentricities.

Scientific method an approach to gaining a reliable body of knowledge about the world (and universe) by using controlled observation and careful measurement of phenomena, generating testable predictions to verify the truth of theories.

Seasonal affective disorder a type of depression induced by reduced exposure to natural light and alterations in melatonin.

Secondary sex characteristics traits other than genitalia that distinguish human beings as being male or female, such as a beard or breasts.

Securely attached infants identify the mother (or caregiver) as a source of comfort and enjoyment, perhaps trusting her or him to be there when needed.

Selection by consequences learned behaviors are selected for or against as a result of the consequences they produce.

Selective perception perceiving only certain stimuli among a larger array of possibilities.

Selective serotonin reuptake inhibitors (SSRIs) a class of drugs used heavily in the treatment of depression that block the reabsorption of serotonin from the synaptic cleft.

Self-actualization the fulfillment of one's human potential. In Abraham Maslow's hierarchy of needs theory, self-actualization encompasses the pinnacle of human experience, the top rung of the hierarchy.

Self archetype the most important archetype in Jungian theory, the self-archetype represents unity and balance between the conscious and the unconscious, the anima and the animus, thinking and feeling, sensing and intuiting, persona and ego, introversion and extroversion. Through this archetype, a person integrates the opposite sides of personality within the self.

Self-attributed motives those motives about which we are consciously aware.

Self-concept the sum of all information, thoughts, and beliefs that individuals have about themselves.

Self-efficacy a positive self-evaluation in which the person has the conviction that he or she is competent to handle the things that are likely to confront him or her in life.

Self-esteem possessing a sense of personal value and worth; a positive evaluation of oneself.

Self-help groups voluntary organizations created to help people with similar problems meet and support one another in overcoming a behavioral or mental problem.

Semantic memory the memory storage area that holds general knowledge about the world.

Semantics the study of meaning.

Sensation the process of receiving and transforming information from the environment through the sense organs.

Sensation seeking the tendency to seek novel, varied, complex, and intense sensations and experiences.

Sensitization a nonassociative learning process that increases the magnitude of an unconditioned response.

Sensorimotor stage the first of Piaget's stages of cognitive development; in this stage, behavior consists primarily of simple motor responses to sensory stimuli (such as reflexes).

Sensorineural hearing losses a group of hearing disorders associated with damage to the neurons in the auditory system and brain.

Sensory maps neural organization of the representation of physical stimuli received by senses.

Sensory modality any one of the five senses: touch, vision, hearing, taste, smell.

Sensory register memory buffers for the sensory systems.

Sensory specific satiety the phenomenon where one decreases food consumption primarily because that food has been repeatedly consumed.

Sensory threshold the minimal amount of stimulation required for a receptor response.

Separation anxiety distress over leaving the primary caregiver.

Sequential design a research method used by developmental psychologists that involves taking repeated measures of a cross-sectional sample of subjects after fixed intervals of time have passed.

Serial position phenomenon we are more likely to remember the items that come first in a list as well as those that come last, and least likely to remember items from the middle of the list.

Serotonin a neurotransmitter involved in the regulation of mood, sleep, and appetite. Boosting serotonin levels alleviates depressive symptoms in many depressed people.

Set point theory a theory that suggests that our body weight is set at a specific value; this value differs across individuals but remains constant for each individual over time.

Sex having either male or female genitalia.

Sexism the unfair or unethical treatment of someone because of his or her sex.

Sexual coercion the forcing of another person into a sexual behavior exists along a continuum, from forcible rape to nonphysical forms of pressure that compel girls and women to engage in sex against their will. The touchstone of coercion is that a woman lacks choice and faces severe physical or social consequences if she resists sexual advances.

Sexual orientation the sex that a given person is sexually attracted to.

Sexual response cycle the four phases of the human sexual response are excitement, plateau, orgasm, and resolution.

Sexually transmitted diseases (STDs) infections that are spread from person to person, primarily through sexual contact. There are three main categories of infections: viral, bacterial, and fungal.

Shadow archetype in Jungian theory, this term represents the things we fear about ourselves and don't want to think about due to their negative nature. Consequently, the elements of the shadow become denied aspects of the self.

Shaky-bridge study a study conducted by Dutton and Aron that supports the Schacter-Singer theory. Men crossed either a shaky bridge or a stable bridge and were met by an attractive female research assistant. When the participants had completed a questionnaire, the research assistant wrote down her phone number on a piece of paper and handed it to the participants, telling them to call her if they had any questions. Most of the men who crossed the shaky bridge called the female assistant because they attributed the physiological reaction due to fear as physical attraction.

Shape constancy shapes are perceived as constant, regardless of visual angle.

Short-term memory (STM) the part of memory that allows us to work on incoming information with strategies such as maintenance rehearsal and elaborative rehearsal.

Simultanagnosia inability to recognize more than one object simultaneously.

Simultaneous conditioning conditioning schedule where the conditioned and unconditioned stimuli begin and end at the same time.

Situational attribution attributing others' behavior to social circumstances.

Six primary emotions the basic emotions that are easily identified across cultures: joy, anger, fear, sadness, surprise, and disgust.

Size constancy the perception of the size of an object changes as it moves farther from the observer, even though the visual angle decreases and it appears smaller on the retina.

Sleep apnea a sleep disorder that normally affects overweight older men. The body stops breathing for a moment or two and then rouses itself to return to normal breathing.

Sleep deprivation not getting the amount of sleep needed to sustain our health.

Sleep paralysis a nonpathological experience that occurs when a person awakens while still in REM sleep. He or she is conscious that his or her body is paralyzed, which is normal during REM sleep.

Sleep spindles bursts of very high-frequency brain waves found in stage 2 sleep.

Sleep talking words a person says while asleep.

Sleepwalking a person who is asleep is able to walk around and appears to be awake.

Small *N* design a design in which just one or a few subjects are used; typically, the experimenter collects baseline data during an initial control condition, applies the experimental treatment, then reinstates the original control condition to verify that changes observed in behavior were caused by the experimental intervention.

Social cognition the way we mentally organize information and think about the social world.

Social-cognitive learning theory an explanation of personality that combines learning principles, cognition, and the effects of social relationships.

Social-facilitation theory a theory that states that the presence of others results in a state of physiological arousal and enhances performance on simple or well-learned tasks.

Social health having the desired number of social contacts and a social network consisting of family members, friends, and community members that one can turn to in times of need.

Social learning theory a branch of behaviorism that incorporates mental processes, considering thoughts to be covert behaviors.

Social norm of reciprocity helping others in a time of need because one believes it increases the likelihood that they will help us in the future when we are in need.

Social norms appropriate behaviors agreed upon within a group.

Social perception the way in which we individually view the social environment.

Social phobia people experiencing social phobia avoid certain social situations—such as eating or speaking in public, dating, talking with authority figures, or meeting new people—where they might encounter the scrutiny of others and be evaluated unfavorably.

Social psychology the branch of psychology that attempts to understand how individual behavior is affected by the social environment and the presence of other people.

Social Readjustment Rating Scale (SRRS) an evaluation tool developed by researchers Holmes and Rahe to assess a person's total life change units in order to predict the likelihood of developing a disease or illness in the near future.

Social roles shared expectations regarding how people behave when they are placed in certain positions.

Social skills training a technique that attempts to resolve deficits in social skills and shape suitable interactions through the use of modeling and reinforcement.

Sodium a positively charged ion found mostly in the extracellular fluid of neurons.

Soma neuronal cell body.

Somatic delusions false beliefs about one's body, such as that one's body is emitting foul odors when it is not.

Somatic nervous system (SNS) portion of the peripheral nervous system responsible for transmitting sensory and motor information to and from the central nervous system.

Somatic type a subtype of delusional disorder characterized by the belief that one has some physical defect or general medical condition.

Somatization disorder a somatoform disorder marked by numerous recurring physical ailments without an organic basis.

Somatosensation skin senses.

Somatosenses consist of the cutaneous, kinesthetic, and organic senses.

Somatosensory cortex the primary cortex for the skin senses, located in the parietal lobes.

Somatotopic spatial organization in the brain that mirrors the organization of the sensory organ.

Sound localization ability to locate the source of a sound in one's environment.

Sound shadow lower sound pressure in the ear on the opposite side of the head from the sound source.

Sound waves the form of energy detected by our auditory system.

Source monitoring the mental process of determining whether a memory is real or imagined.

Span of attention the extent of information that people can hold in their minds at any given time.

Specific intelligences specific cognitive abilities on which individuals may vary.

Specific phobias severe and persistent fears of a specific object or situation (other than social phobia and agoraphobia).

Spinal nerves nerves emanating from the spinal cord.

Spinothalamic pathway pathway that carries information about pain and temperature up the spinal cord to the brain.

Spiritual health a state of well-being that results from a predominance of positive feelings of love, hope, and contentment, which tends to result from a set of attitudes such as feelings of charity toward others.

Split-brain procedure where the corpus callosum is severed, separating the two hemispheres.

Spontaneous decay the disappearance of a sensitized unconditioned response following a rest period.

Spontaneous recovery the reappearance of a habituated unconditioned response following a rest period.

Stage theory of memory a theory that states that there are three stages of memory: the sensory register, short-term memory, and long-term memory.

Standard deviation an index of how much a typical score differs from the mean of a group of scores.

Standardization standard procedures for administering and scoring a test.

Stanford-Binet Intelligence Scale a revision of the Binet-Simon test by Lewis Terman of Stanford University that enabled the test to measure adults' intelligence.

Stapes one of the three small bones of the middle ear.

State-dependent memory people tend to recall information better if they are in the same emotional or psychological state as when the information was encoded.

Statistical significance the degree to which an event, such as the results of an experiment, is unlikely to have occurred by chance alone.

Stereopsis the comparison of the different retinal locations of images in the right vs. left eye, used for depth perception.

Stereotype a generalization about someone based on his or her group membership.

Stereotype threat the performance of a member of a group changes because he or she is influenced by a stereotype about his or her group.

Still face effect visible distress of an infant whose smile is ignored or unreciprocated.

Stimulus-outcome association the type of association that develops during classical conditioning.

Stimulus-response-outcome the type of association that develops during operant conditioning.

Stonewall a behavior that involves turning away from a person with whom one has a conflict and conveying the message through body language that one will not deal with the other person.

Strange situation method a method for investigating attachment styles that consists of exposing the infant to a series of situations with and without the presence of the mother.

Stranger anxiety fear of strangers by infants.

Stress the internal and external reactions to physical, chemical, environmental, and emotional factors that strain one's tolerance for adverse events and eventually destroy the capacity to cope.

Stressor situations, experiences, or events that produce physiological and emotional arousal in a person.

Striate cortex also known as primary visual cortex.

Striving for superiority according to Alfred Adler, this basic drive propels us toward competence and mastery.

Structuralism an interest in the basic structural elements of the consciousness (such as sensations, for example).

Structured interview a set number of questions is put to the interviewee, in the same order as the questions are given to all interviewees. These interviews may be conducted in person or via computer.

Subgoal analysis involves breaking the problem down into small intermediate steps that will lead toward a solution.

Subject mortality the loss of research subjects (not always literally due to death, but instead for *any* reason) in studies that are conducted over a period of time, so that subjects need to be communicated with more than once.

Subordinate category the most specific level in the category hierarchy.

Substitute term used by Watson in reference to the conditioned stimulus.

Sulci small indentations in the cerebral cortex.

Summation the addition of neural signals received by a neuron at its axon hillock, which will determine the likelihood of reaching the threshold of excitation and the generation of an action potential.

Superego in psychoanalytic theory, it refers to the seat of a person's moral self. The superego is the internalized representation of societal values, as taught to the child by parents and other members of society.

Superior colliculus structure in the brain that seems to integrate vision, touch, and hearing for attention and orientation responses.

Superior temporal gyrus the top of the temporal lobe important for integrating visual details with the overall shape of an object.

Superordinate category the highest, most general level in the category hierarchy.

Superstitions beliefs that two events are causally associated when, in fact, they occur together coincidentally or as a result of a third, unrecognized factor.

Surface structure the actual words that compose a sentence.

Survey method a series of questions designed to help understand attitudes, behaviors, or demographic variables of a particular group.

Sympathetic division division of the autonomic nervous system responsible for arousing the body for expending energy.

Synaptic cleft space between the synaptic terminal and the dendritic spine of the receiving cell.

Synaptic pruning connections between neurons are obliterated.

Synaptic transmission a biochemical process where a neural signal is passed from one neuron to another.

Synaptic vesicles small membrane-enclosed capsules containing neurotransmitter; they are primarily found in the synaptic terminal.

Synchrony the extent that the cells are active as a unit versus working independently from one another.

Synesthesia a rare form of imagery in which mental images extend beyond normal sensory associations.

Syntax the grammatical rules for combining words into sentences.

Synthetic heat the sensation of painful heat if close warm and cold spots are alternately stimulated.

T

Tardive dyskinesia a side effect of antipsychotic drugs that creates involuntary control of the lip and tongue and facial tics.

Taste buds small clusters of taste receptor cells found in the walls lining the taste pores around papillae on the tongue.

Taste pores small grooves in the tongue found around papillae.

Taste receptor cells sensory receptor cells for taste.

Tectorial membrane a membrane found in the organ of corti.

Temperament consistent individual difference in type and intensity of emotional reaction.

Temporal lobe lobe of cerebral cortex responsible for hearing, visual recognition, and memory.

Teratogens disease, chemicals, and/or radiation that can be harmful to the growth of the fetus.

Terminal branches branches of the axon that end with a synaptic terminal.

Test-retest reliability a high degree of correlation between two sets of scores; for example, a group of people who take an assessment instrument at one point in time and then retake the instrument later should have a high degree of correlation between their scores.

Testes male reproductive organs.

Testosterone a male sex hormone secreted mainly by the testes and responsible for the development of male sexual characteristics.

Thalamic pain pain in the body due to brain damage.

Thalamus region of the diencephalon and part of the limbic system considered the sensory relay station of the brain.

Thematic Apperception Test (TAT) a personality test that employs black-and-white pictures of ambiguous meaning. The test taker is asked to create a story explaining the picture, which is thought to require the examinee to project unconscious wishes and conflicts into the picture. These projections can then be interpreted by the examiner.

Theory of kin selection we are more likely to help blood relatives because helping them increases the likelihood that our own genes will be passed on to the next generation.

Thermoreceptors skin receptors for temperature.

Theta waves brain waves that are slower in frequency and can be found in stage 1 sleep.

Thinking involves using knowledge to form concepts, inspire creativity, solve problems, and communicate with others.

Thinning process of reducing neurons and synapses.

Third variable problem in a correlational study, two variables may be correlated not because either variable causes the other, but because both are caused by a third variable that is not included in the study.

Thirst a drive that arises when the body requires water.

Thought disorders disturbances in thinking characterized by the breakdown of logical associations between thoughts.

Thought stopping a cognitive therapy technique that helps decrease the frequency and intensity of stress-producing obsessive negative thoughts by having the client order himself or herself to stop dwelling on a particular train of thought.

Thought substitution a cognitive therapy technique that gets the client to think about positive, reassuring, self-accepting thoughts in place of negative, self-defeating ones as a means of reducing anxiety.

Threshold of excitation the threshold at which a cell becomes depolarized enough to generate an action potential.

Thymus a gland located in the upper area of the chest that plays a role in growth and metabolism.

Timbre the psychological dimension of sound associated with the complexity of the sound wave.

Tinnitus a constant ringing in the ears that results from repeated exposure to very loud sounds.

Token economy a system of compensation in which appropriate behaviors are rewarded with symbolic tokens that can be exchanged for items and/or privileges such as food, clothing, games, more time with an activity, or trips to various places.

Tolerance the point at which a person who consumes alcohol or drugs needs to consume more of the drug in order to feel the effect.

Top-down processes high-level information or knowledge processes that determine perception.

Trace conditioning conditioning schedule where the conditioned stimulus is presented first and is terminated before the unconditioned stimulus.

Trait theory a theory that considers personality to be made up of a collection of traits. Some traits tend to cluster to form personality types.

Traits personality characteristics or dimensions that are measured in people to help predict their future actions.

Tranquilizers (Xanax, Valium) drugs that are less powerful than barbiturates but have similar effects. Some effects of tranquilizers are increased muscle relaxation, increased sedation, reduced anxiety, and reduced likelihood of a seizure.

Transcendental meditation (TM) a technique that allows one to achieve relaxation by blocking out the negative thoughts and feelings that can cause stress.

Transference a psychodynamic treatment in which the client projects his or her feelings for another person onto the therapist.

Transsexual a person whose gender identity does not match his or her actual genitalia.

Trephination a form of surgery consisting of drilling a hole in the skull.

Trial-and-error learning involves trying a variety of methods and eliminating those that don't work.

Triangular theory of love a theory that suggests that seven kinds of love can be derived from the varying combination of three main ingredients: passion, intimacy, and commitment.

Triangulation in family therapy, this occurs when a third person (child, therapist, etc.) is unsuspectingly solicited in a conflict-ridden dyadic relationship, which results in his or her inadvertently "covering up" or "defusing" the problem of the actual people in conflict.

Triarchic theory of intelligence suggests that successful intelligence consists of three types of intelligence: analytic, creative, and practical.

Trichromatic theory suggests that colors are perceived by the relative activity among the three kinds of cones.

Tricyclics a category of antidepressant drugs that block the reuptake of serotonin and norepinephrine at neuronal synapse.

Trophoblast the part of the blastocyst that becomes the placenta, the umbilical cord, and other supporting structures.

True self the part of your self-concept that reflects you as you really are.

***t*-test** a type of inferential statistic that analyzes whether the difference between the means of two groups is likely to have occurred by chance alone.

Two point discrimination the closest distance between two points in which the individual can still tell they are two points.

Tympanic membrane thin membrane that covers the end of the auditory canal and that vibrates in response to sound waves.

U

Umami a fifth type of taste associated with monosodium glutamate.

Unconditional positive regard a sense of being valued for oneself regardless of the degree to which specific behaviors are approved or disapproved by parents or significant others.

Unconditioned response a reflexive response made to an unconditioned stimulus.

Unconditioned stimulus a stimulus that evokes an involuntary response every time it is presented.

Unconscious in Freudian psychoanalysis, this term refers to thoughts, feelings, and motivations that are not accessible during the normal state of awareness.

Underextension limiting the use of a particular word.

Undifferentiated schizophrenia a classification of schizophrenia reserved for those who meet the criteria for schizophrenia but don't fall neatly into one of the three classifications.

Uninvolved a style of parenting where parents are emotionally detached, being more interested in their own activities than in their child's.

Unmyelinated axons axons that do not have a myelin sheath.

Unstructured interview interviews that allow the interviewee to talk about the topic at hand in his or her own way. The interviewer also has the option to improvise relevant follow-up questions during the interview.

Uplifts the positive experiences in life that help buffer and eliminate the destructive effects of hassles.

Urbach-Wiethe disease a rare disorder causing bilateral damage to the amygdala.

V

Validating conflict style the type of relationship where the couple engages in active listening and the partners try to truly understand each other's feeling in order to reach a compromise.

Validation in family therapy, this is when the therapists convey their acceptance and understanding of the clients' feelings and wishes.

Validity a test accurately measures what it is intended to measure.

Variable any observable phenomenon that can take on more than one value.

Variable interval schedule schedule of reinforcement where the first response made after a variable period of time earns a reinforcer.

Variable ratio schedule schedule of reinforcement where a variable number of responses must be completed before a reinforcer becomes available.

Vasocongestion occurs when the tissues swell with blood during sexual excitement. It occurs in different parts of the body such as the penis, the testicles, the breasts, and the vulva area.

Ventral directional term used to indicate the bottom or base.

Ventromedial hypothalamus (VMH) signals fullness and tells us to stop eating.

Verbal behavior any behavior that involves pronunciation and/or writing of words.

Vertigo dizziness often associated with spinning, which may be caused by a variety of conditions.

Vestibular system the sensory system associated with balance and orientation.

Virtual reality exposure clients are exposed to the fear stimulus via a computer-generated, three-dimensional visage that appears in a head-mounted video display.

Visual acuity the ability to see fine details.

Visual agnosia inability to recognize objects due to cortical damage.

Visual angle the angle that results from a triangulation of the top and bottom of a viewed object and the eye of an observer.

Visual cliff a large glass table where just under the glass on one end (shallow end) is a solid surface with a checkerboard pattern. The same surface is placed a few feet below the glass at the other end (deep end) of the table, giving the appearance that there is a drop.

Volatile conflict style a conflict resolution style in which the couple has very passionate fights, which may include yelling, screaming, and even occasional name calling. When they are not fighting, the partners tend to be equally passionate about their positive feelings toward each other.

Volley principle a theory of auditory pitch perception arguing that the tones we hear result from the pattern of firing in a group of auditory hair cells.

Voltage-dependent calcium channels special ion channels for calcium that open when there is a specific change in the membrane potential of a neuron. This process frequently occurs at the synaptic terminal and causes neurotransmitter release.

Voltage-dependent potassium channels special ion channels for potassium that open when there is a specific change in the membrane potential of a neuron. This process frequently occurs along an axon as it returns to the resting membrane potential.

Voltage-dependent sodium channels special ion channels for sodium that open when there is a specific change in the membrane potential of a neuron. This process frequently occurs along an axon as it conducts the neural signal to the synaptic terminals.

Voluntarism a view that we can choose what we experience (Wundt saw attention as a process that we can direct at will to the stimuli that enter our experience).

Vomeronasal organ the sensory organ in the nasal cavity responsible for detecting pheromones. Its function in humans is debated.

W **War of the Ghosts** an Indian fable used by Bartlett to investigate reconstructive memory.

Warm fibers fibers that carry information from thermoreceptors responding to heat.

Washoe a chimpanzee who learned about 160 signs and demonstrated the ability to vary the meaning of a sentence by correctly arranging the words.

Wavelength the distance between peaks or troughs on a wave.

Wechsler Adult Intelligence Scale (WAIS) an intelligence test for adults that contains both verbal (VIQ) and nonverbal performance (PIQ) subtests, and produces an IQ score for each subtest and an overall IQ score.

Wechsler Intelligence Scale for Children (WISC) an intelligence test for children that contains both verbal (VIQ) and nonverbal performance (PIQ) subtests, and produces an IQ score for each subtest and an overall IQ score.

Wechsler Preschool and Primary Scale of Intelligence (WPPSI) an intelligence test for children 4–6½ years of age.

"What" system visual pathway for color, fine detail, and form.

"Where" system visual pathway for depth and movement.

White matter nervous system tissue made up primarily of myelinated axons that give it a white appearance.

Withdrawal physiological symptoms that our bodies experience when we stop using drugs. These may include vomiting, aches, pains, sweats, and tremors.

Womb envy a concept proposed by Karen Horney to counter Freud's idea that all girls experience penis envy. Horney suggested that men might well feel "womb envy" because of their inability to produce a child from their own bodies as women do.

Working memory the part of the short-term memory that allows us to work on incoming information.

Y

Yerkes-Dodson Law a law stating that task performance is at its peak for moderate levels of arousal.

Yoga a Hindu technique that achieves relaxation and peace of mind through concentration, deep meditation, controlled breathing, and various body posture positions. Practicing yoga activates the parasympathetic nervous system, which decreases heart rate, blood pressure, and respiratory rate.

Z

Zeitgeist the spirit of the time/a prevailing view.

Zygote the fertilized egg.

Index

Page numbers followed by *f* or *t* refer to figures or tables respectively.

A

abnormal behavior. *See also specific disorder*
  defined, 447–452
  diagnosing, 452–454
absolute threshold, 95
abstract symbols, 271
abstract thoughts, 271
abundancy motives, 166
accommodation, 104, 265
acetylcholine (ACH), 81
achievement motivation, 175–176
Achievement Place, 216–217
achromatopsia, 115
acquaintance rape, 327
acquired immunodeficiency
  syndrome (AIDS), 329, 331, 521
acquisition, 202
  of operant response, 212–213
action potential, 78, 79*f*
actor/observer difference, 344
acute stress disorder (ASD), 460
adaptation, 94
addiction, development of, 150–151
A-delta fibers, 102
Adler, Alfred, 413, 437
adrenal glands, 84
adrenaline, 84
adventitious reinforcement, 217
affective component of an
  attitude, 347
affective flattening, 469
affectiveness-primacy theory, of
  emotion, 178
afferent fibers, 97
African American psychologists, 13
African Americans, psychotherapy
  and, 499
afterimages, 108–109

aggression
  alcohol and, 361
  defined, 359
  discomfort and, 361
  social learning theory and, 360
  types of, 359–360
aging, forgetting and, 249
agnosia
  object, 115
  visual, 115
agoraphobia, 459
"ah-ha" experience, 219
AIDS. *See* acquired
  immunodeficiency syndrome
  (AIDS)
alarm stage, 520
alcohol, 151–152, 527
  aggression and, 361
Alda, Alan, 232–233
algorithms, 266
all-or-nothing law, 78–79
Allport, Gordon, 430–431
alogia, 469
altruism, 357
Alzheimer's disease (AD), 73–74
  forgetting and, 250
ambivalent/resistant attachment,
  infants with, 397
Ames Room, 113, 114*f*
amphetamines, 153
amplitude, 116
amygdala, 16, 71–72
amyloid plaques, 73
anal personality, 414
anal stage, 417
analgesia, 102
analysis of variance (ANOVA), 51
analytic intelligence, 275
androgyny, 312
angel dust, 157

anima archetype, 15, 421
animal communication, language
  vs., 270–271
animal studies, 44–45
animals, as research subjects, 52–53
animistic thought, 387
animus archetype, 421–422
ANOVA (analysis of variance), 51
antecedents, 196
anterior surface, of brain, 68
anterograde amnesia, 248
antianxiety drugs, 486
antidepressant drugs, 485–486
  monoamine oxidase inhibitors
    (MAOIs), 486
  selective serotonin reuptake
    inhibitors, 485–486
  tricyclics, 485
antipsychotic drugs, 485
antisocial personality disorder, 455
anxiety disorders, 457
  causes of, 460–461
  general characteristics of, 458
  types of, 458–460
apparent motion, 114
approach-approach conflicts, 517
approach-avoidance conflicts, 517
archetypes, 15, 420
Aristotle, 4–5
arousal theory of motivation, 168–169
Asch, Soloman, 355
Asian Americans, psychotherapy
  and, 498
asociality, 469
assimilation, 265
association, 197
associative learning processes, 197,
  200–209
  classical conditioning, 200–211
  operant conditioning, 211–215

associative play, 399
asylums, 484
asymptomatic STDs, 329
asymptotic level, 196
atmospheric perspective, 111
attachment, 396–398
attention, span of, 9
attitudes. *See also* prejudice
   changing, 350
   components of, 347–348
   defined, 347
   formation of, 348–349
   prejudice and, 349–350
auditory canal, 117
auditory pitch perception, theories
   of, 118
auditory system, 115–119
   anatomy of, 116–117
   disorders of, 119
authoritarian parents, 398
authoritative parents, 398–399
autistic savants, 284
autoimmune disease, 76
autonomic nervous system (ANS),
   66–67
autoreceptors, 81
aversive conditioning, 491–492
avoidance, 525–526
avoidance-avoidance conflicts, 517
avoidant attachment, infants
   with, 397
avoidant conflict style, of
   marriage, 315
avoidant personality disorder, 457
avolition, 469
axes, of *DSM-IV-TR*, 453
axon hillock, 76
axon terminal, 76
axons, 76
azimuth, 118

B

babbling, 269
   manual, 391
backward conditioning, 205
backward-working heuristic, 267
Bandura, Albert, 429–430, 523
barbiturates, 152
Bard, Philip, 178
Bartholow, Roberts, 8

Bartlett, Sir Francis, 245
basal ganglia motor system, 72
basic anxiety, 425
basic level categories, 264
basilar membranes, 117
battery of tests, 413
behavior modification, 491
behavioral component
   of an attitude, 347
behavioral component, of
   emotion, 177
behavioral observation, 412
behavioral therapy, 490
behaviorism, 11–12, 218
behaviors
   cultures and, 2–3
   involuntary, 2
   nonverbal, 2
   verbal, 2
   voluntary, 2
bell curve, 48, 48*f*
Bem, Sandra, 312
benzodiazepines, 486
Berkeley, George, 8
bias, experimenter, 42
Big Five model, 431–432
bilateral damage, 74
bilateral medial temporal lobe
   resection, 247
Binet, Alfred, 276
Binet-Simon Intelligence Scale, 276
binocular cues, 111
biofeedback, 101
   technique, 529–530
   training, 217–218
biological perspective, 16–17
biological preparedness, 203
biological treatments, 485–488
   antianxiety drugs, 486
   antidepressant drugs, 485–486
   antipsychotic drugs, 485
   mood stabilizers, 486
   psychosurgery, 486–488
biopsychology, 63–64
   research methods in, 44–46
bipolar cells, 105
bipolar disorder, 464–465
birth control options, 331–332
birth defects, 380
birth order, personality and, 424, 437
bisexual individuals, 318

blastocyst, 379
Bobo doll, 220, 360
bodily-kinesthetic intelligence, 275
body dysmorphic disorder, 462
borderline personality disorder,
   455–456
bottom-up processes, 109
brain
   development, 381–383
   personality and, 433–434
   surfaces of, 68–69, 68*f*, 69*f*
brain electrical activity mapping
   (BEAM), 46
brain freeze, 122
brain stem, 74–75
brain waves, sleep and, 136–137
brain-imaging techniques, 45–46
breathing control, 530
brief psychodynamic therapy, 489
broaden-and-build theory, of
   emotion, 182
Broca, Paul, 8
burnout, 513
Buss, David, 308
bystander effect, 359

C

C fibers, 102
caffeine, 154, 528
calcium ions, 77
Calkins, Mary Whiton, 12
cancellation technique, 528–529
Cannon, Walter, 178
Cannon-Bard theory, of emotion,
   178–180
case study, 37
cataplexy, 142
catatonic schizophrenia, 469
categories, 264–265
   basic level, 264
   subordinate, 264
   superordinate, 264
catharsis, 489
Cattell, Raymond, 431
causalgesia, 102–103
causation, correlation and, 50–51
central cues, to hunger, 171
central nervous system (CNS), 65
   navigating, 67–69
central tendency measures, 47–48

cephalo-caudal law, 379
cerebellum, 75
cerebral cortex, 70–71
change motives, 175
Chicano psychology, 13
child testimony, 235–236
chloride ions, 77
cholecystokinin (CCK), 172
Chomsky, Noam, 268, 270, 271
chronic pain, 103
chunking, 242
Churchill, Winston, 261
Cicero, 5
ciliary muscles, 104
cingulate cortex, 72
circadian rhythm, 135–145
circumvallate papillae, 121
clang associations, 468
Clark, Kenneth, 13
classical conditioning, 200–209, 268
    application of, 210–211
    discrimination and, 207–208
    extinction and, 208–209
    generalization and, 207
classical theory, 264
claustrophobia, 210
client-centered therapy, 428, 489
clinical psychologists, 18
cliques, 400
Clozaril, 485
cocaine, 153–154
    fetus and, 380–381
cochlea, 117
coercive paraphilia, 326
cognition
    defined, 262
    social, 346
cognition, learning and, 218–220
cognitive approach, 218
cognitive behavior therapy
    (CBT), 494
cognitive component
    of an attitude, 347–348
cognitive component, of
    emotion, 177
cognitive development, 386–393
    intellectual development, 393
    language development, 391–393
    memory development, 388–390
    perceptual development, 387–388
    Piaget's stages of, 386–387

cognitive dissonance theory, 351
cognitive economy, 264
cognitive expectancies, 430
cognitive perspective, 16
cognitive psychologists, 18
cognitive restructuring, 492
cognitive therapy, 492–494
cohort, 43
cold fibers, 98
cold receptors, 98
collective unconscious, 15, 420,
    421–422
collectivist cultures, 433
color, perception of, 108–109
color blindness, 115
color constancy, phenomenon of, 109
commitment, 365
common-sense theory, of
    emotion, 178
communication, 268
    animal, language vs., 270–271
    sexual, tips for, 322–323
companionate love, 365
complementarity, 363
compliance, 354
compound stimulus, 203
compulsions, 459–460
computed tomography (CT) scan, 45
concepts, 264
concordance rate, 466
concrete operational stage, 387
conditioned emotional reflex, 201
conditioned response (CR), 200
    acquisition of, 202
    extinction and, 208
    spontaneous recovery and
        renewal of, 208–209
conditioned stimulus (CS), 200
    characteristics of, 202–204
    timing of, 205–206
conditioned taste/odor aversions, 211
conditioning
    backward, 205
    delayed, 205
    forward, 205
    higher order, 206–207, 214
    operant, 269
    simultaneous, 205–206
    trace, 205
conditions of worth, 428
conductive hearing losses, 119

cones, 105
confabulation, 236
confirmation bias, 352
conflict, 515–518
    types of, 517
conflict resolution, 518
    integration approach to, 518
conformity, 354–356
    normative, 355–356
confounding variables, 40–41
Confucius, 5
congruence, 427, 428f
connectedness theory, 176
conscious level, 413
consciousness
    defined, 133
    drugs and, 149–157
    Freud's levels of, 413
    levels of, 134–135
    study of, 12, 133–134
consequences, 196
conservation, 387
contact comfort, 298
contact hypothesis, 351
contempt, defined, 316
context-dependent memory, 246
contiguity, 206
contingency, 196
contrecoup injury, 75
control, as goal of psychology, 33–34.
        See also experimental control
control group, 38
conventional level, 401
convergence, 111
convergent thinking, 284
conversion disorders, 451–462
cooperative play, 399
coping styles
    effective, 528–533
    ineffective, 525–528
corpus callosum, 69
correlation, 49–50
    causation and, 50–51
correlation coefficient, 49
counseling psychologists, 18
coup injury, 75
covert behaviors, 449
Cowper's gland, 321
CR. See conditioned response (CR)
cranial nerves, 65
creative arts, for reducing stress, 533

creative intelligence, 275
creativity
    defined, 283
    improving one's, 284–285
    IQ and, 283–284
    thought and, 284
cribiform plate, 120
cross-cultural perspective, 15
cross-sectional designs, 42–43
crowds, 400
cryotherapy, 102
CS. See conditioned stimulus (CS)
culture-fair intelligence test, 282
culture(s)
    behaviors and, 2–3
    emotion and, 184–185
    personality and, 433
    psychotherapy and, 497–500
curiosity motives, 175
cutaneous sense, 97
cybertherapy, 496

D

Dalí, Salvador, 138
dark adaptation, 105
Dark Ages, 6
Darwin, Charles, 17, 166, 182, 212
date rape, 327
date rape drugs, 327–328
death wish, 414
debriefing, 52
decay, 249
decibels (dB), 116
deep structure, 270
defense mechanisms, 415–416,
    416t, 526
deficiency motives, 165
deindividuation, 369
delayed conditioning, 205
delta waves, 138–139
delusional disorders
    general characteristics, 471
    types of, 471–472
delusions, 468
    of grandeur, 468
    of influence, 468
    of persecution, 468
    of reference, 468
    somatic, 468
demyelination, 76

dendritic spines, 75
dendrites, 75
density, 100
dependence
    physical, 150
    psychological, 150
dependent personality disorder, 457
dependent variable, 38
depersonalization disorder, 464
depolarization, 78–79
depressants, 151
depressed people, 450
depression, 465
    causes of, 466–467
depressive realism, 450
depth, perception of, 111–114
derailment, 467
dermis, 97
Descartes, René, 7
description, as goal of
    psychology, 33
descriptive statistics, 47–48
developmental direction, laws of, 379
developmental psychologists, 18–19
developmental psychology
    defined, 377
    Gesell's influence on, 377–379
    research methods in, 42–44
developmentally disabled, 279–280
Diagnostic and Statistical Manual of
    Mental Disorders, 4th edition
    (DSM-IV-TR), 452–453
    axes of, 453
    evaluating, 453
difference threshold, 95
differentiation, 382
diffusion of responsibility
    theory, 358
directionality problem, 51
discomfort, aggression and, 361
discrimination, 207–208, 350
disorganized schizophrenia, 469
displacement, 241
display rules, 185
dispositional attribution, 344
dissociative amnesia, 463
dissociative disorders
    causes of, 464
    general characteristics, 463
    types of, 463–464
dissociative fugue, 463

dissociative identity disorder
    (DID), 463
distraction-conflict theory, 369
divergent thinking, 284
divorce, 314–316
Dix, Dorothea, 484
Domjan, Michael, 44
door-in-the-face approach, 354
dopamine, 82, 526
dorsal column pathway, 99
dorsal horn cells, 99
dorsal lateral prefrontal cortex, 383
dorsal surface, of brain, 68, 68f, 69f
double depression, 465
double-approach-avoidance
    conflicts, 517
downward drift hypothesis, 471
dream analysis, 488–489
dreams, 144–145
drive-reduction theory, of
    motivation, 169, 169f
drives, 169
    hunger, 170–174
    primary, 170
    thirst, 170
drug dependence, 150
drug tolerance, 150
drugs
    consciousness and, 149–157
    types of, 151–157
DSM-IV-TR. See Diagnostic and
    Statistical Manual of Mental
    Disorders, 4th edition
    (DSM-IV-TR)
duality of structure, 270
Dunn, John, 361
dypaurenia (sexual pain
    disorder), 323
dysthymic disorder, 465

E

ear drum, 117
ears, 116–117
Ebbinghaus, Herman, 4, 9–10,
    248–249
echoic memory, 241
ecstasy, 155–156
educational psychologists, 19
effect, law of, 212
ego, 13, 415, 420, 526

ego alien, 457
ego dystonic, 457
ego syntonic, 454
egocentric thought, 386–387
egotistical, defined, 414
Egyptians, psychology and, 4
Einstein, Albert, 261
elaborative rehearsal, 240
Elavil, 485
electricity, 8
electroconvulsive therapy (ECT),
    487–488
electroencephalograph (EEG), 45, 136
elevation, 118
Ellis, Albert, 492
embryoblast, 379
embryonic period, 379–380
emotion
    affectiveness-primacy theory
        of, 178
    behavioral component of, 177
    broaden-and-build theory of, 182
    Cannon-Bard theory of, 178–180
    cognitive component of, 177
    common-sense theory of, 178
    culture and, 184–185
    defined, 166
    evolutionary aspects of, 182–184
    James-Lange theory of, 178
    Lazarus's cognitive theory of,
        181–182
    physiological component of, 177
    Schacter-Singer theory of,
        180–181
    social functions of, 184
    theories of, 176–185, 179t
    in workplace, 185
emotional aggression, 359
Emotional Competence
    Inventory, 275
emotional development. See social
    and emotional development
emotional flooding, 316
emotional health, 511
emotional intelligence, 275
emotional labor, 185
empathy-altruism theory, 357, 490
empirical evidence, 35
empiricism, 8
encoding, 240
endocrine system, 83–85

endoderm layer, 380
endorphins, 83, 521
energy reservoir theory, 173
engineering psychologists, 19
enzymatic degration, 81
epidermis, 97
epilepsy, 6, 69
epinephrine, 84, 527
episodic memory, 243
Erikson, Erik, 394–395, 413, 437
erotomanic type delusion, 471
estrogen, 307
ethics, in psychology, 52–53
ethnic diversity, in psychology,
    12–13
evaluation apprehension theory, 369
evolutionary perspective, 17
evolutionary theory of sexual
    differences, 308–309
exchange model, of prosocial
    behavior, 357
excitatory post-synaptic potential
    (EPSP), 78
exemplar theory, 264
exercise, to reduce stress, 531–532
exhaustion stage, 521
exhibitionism, 326
experimental control, 39–41
    confounding variables and, 40–41
    defined, 40
    extraneous variables and, 40
    nuisance variables and, 40
    strategies for, 41–42
experimental designs, 38–39
    examples of, 38–39
experimental group, 38
experimental psychologists, 19
experimenter bias, 42
experiments, 38
explanation, as goal of
    psychology, 33
explicit memory, 243
extension of waking life theory, 145
external cues, to eating, 173–174
external ear, 116–117
external locus of control, 430, 523
extinction, 208–209
extracellular thirst, 170
extraneous variables, 40
    confounding variables, 40–41
    nuisance variables, 40

extraversion, 431
extrinsic motivations, 168
eye, 104–107
eye movement desensitization and
    reprocessing (EMDR), 497
eyeblink conditioning paradigm,
    204–205
eyewitness testimony, 233–234
Eysenck, Hans, 400, 431

facial feedback hypothesis, 178
factor analysis, 430
false memories, 230–231, 390. See
    also memory
familiarity, 362–363
family archetype, 421
family therapy, 495
father archetype, 421
feature detection theory, 109
feature detectors, 108
Federal Emergency Management
    Association (FEMA), 367
female orgasmic disorder, 323
female sexual arousal disorder, 323
Festinger, Leon, 351
fetal alcohol syndrome (FAS),
    152, 380
fetal period, 380
fetishism, 326
fight-or-flight response, 519
first-letter technique, 251
fissures, 70
five-factor model (FFM), 431–432
fixation, 417
fixed interval (FI) schedules, 214, 215
fixed ratio (FR) schedules, 214
flashbulb memories, 238
flexor reflex, 99
flooding, 491
foliate papillae, 121
foot-in-the-door approach, 354
forensic psychologists, 19
forgetting, 248–250. See also
    memory
    aging and, 249
    Alzheimer's disease and, 250
    reasons for, 249
forgetting curve, 249
formal operational stage, 387

forms, perception of, 109–110
fornix, 72
forward conditioning, 205
four F behaviors, 73
fovea, 105
Franklin, Eileen, 230
free association, 488
frequency of sound wave, 116
frequency theory, 118
Freud, Sigmund, 11, 13–15, 244, 318, 488. *See also* neo-Freudians
    criticisms of theories of, 419–420
    defense mechanisms, 415–416, 416t
    importance of dreams and, 144–145
    levels of consciousness, 413
    pyschosexual stages of development, 416–419, 419t
    structure of personality, 414–415
Freudian, defined, 414
Freudian dream theory, 144
Freudian slips, 414
Fromm, Erich, 456
frontal lobes, 70
frotterism, 326
frustration, 513
Fry, Arthur, 283
functional fixedness, 267–268
functional magnetic resonance imaging (fMRI), 46
functional neuroanatomy, 69–75
functionalism, 11
fundamental attribution error, 344
fungiform papillae, 121

G

Gage, Phineas, case study of, 37, 434
Gall, Franz, 434
Galton, Sir Francis, 273
Galvani, Luigi, 8
gamma-aminobutyric acid (GABA), 81
gamma-hydroxybutyric acid (GHB), 327
ganglion cells, 104–105
Garcia, John, 203–204
Gardner, Howard, 274–275
gate control theory, 101–102

gender
    brain differences and, 301–302
    differences, 300–303
    intelligence and, 282
    in psychology, 12
gender identity, 306
gender identity disorder, 306
gender role behavior, 310–316
gender roles, 282, 299
General Adaptation Syndrome (GAS), 520–521, 527
general intelligence, 274
generalization, 207
generalized anxiety disorders, 458
genes, 303
genetics, personality and, 434–435
genital stage, 419
Genovese, Kitty, 358–359
genuineness, 490
germinal period, 379
Gesell, Arnold, 377–379, 395
Gestalt, 10–11
Gestalt Psychologists, 110
ghrelin, 172
Gibran, Kahlil, 361
giftedness ranges, 278–279
Gilbert, William, 7–8
glucocorticoids, 84
glucose, 85
glutamate, 81–82
goals
    ideographic, 175
    nomothetic, 175
Goleman, Daniel, 275
goodness of fit, 396
Gottman, John, 315
gradual in-vivo exposure, 490
grandiose type delusions, 471–472
graphemes, 270
gray matter, 69
gross-fine law, 379
grossly disorganized behavior, 468–469
group behavior, 366–369
    decisions and, 366–368
    task performance and, 368–369
group therapy, 494–495
groups
    control, 38
    defined, 366
    experimental, 38
groupthink, 367

gustatory system, 121–123
gyri, 70

H

habituation, 198
hair cells, 117
Haldol, 485
hallucinations, 468
halo effect, 363
handedness, 299–300, 300t, 305
happiness, study of, 5, 472, 523
hardiness, 523
Harlow, Harry, 398
hassles, 514
health
    defined, 511
    emotional, 511
    intellectual, 511
    occupational, 511–512
    physical, 511
    social, 511
    spiritual, 512
health psychologists, 19
Hebb, Donald, 16
help, reasons people don't, 358–359
Hering, Ewald, 109
heritability, 274, 434
Herman, Louis, 272–273
hermaphroditism, 305–306
hertz (Hz), 116
heterosexuality, 317
heuristics, 266–267
    backward-working, 267
hierarchy of needs, Maslow's, 169, 169f, 426–427
higher order conditioning, 206–207, 214
Hill, Barney and Betty, 236–237
hippocampus, 72
Hippocrates, 6, 483–484
history effects, 42–43
histrionic personality disorder, 456
HIV. *See* human immunodeficiency virus (HIV)
Holstege, Gert, 321
homeostasis, 66, 169
homophobia, 320
homosexuality, 317, 320
hormonal theory of sexual differences, 307

Horney, Karen, 413, 437
Horry, Robert, 368
hostile aggression, 359
human immunodeficiency virus
        (HIV), 329–330, 521–522
humanism, 7
humanistic perspective, 17
humanistic theories of personality,
        426–428
humanistic therapy, 489–490
Hume, David, 8
hunger, 170–174
    central cues to, 171
    external cues, 173–174
    peripheral cues to, 171–173
Huntington's disease, 71
hypnogogic hallucinations, 138
hypnopompic hallucination, 237
hypnosis, 145–148
    benefits and limitations of, 146–147
    memory and, 236
    process of, 147–148
    repressed memories and, 146
hypnotics, 150
hypoactive sexual desire
        disorder, 323
hypochondrias, 462
hypothalamus, 73, 84
hypothesis, 4, 32

ice cream headache, 122
iconic memory, 241
id, 13, 414, 526
ideal self, 427, 489
ideographic goals, 175
Ildefonso, case of, 262–263
imagery, 263–264
imaginal thought, 262
imaginary audience, 387
immune system, effects of stress on,
        521–522
implantation, 379
implicit memory, 244
implicit motives, 174
incandescent light, 103
Ince, L. P., 101
incus, 117
independent variable, 38
individualistic cultures, 433
individuating maturation, 378

induced movement, 114
indulgences, 7
industrial/organizational
        psychologists, 19–20
infections
    bacterial, 329, 330
    fungal, 329, 330
    viral, 329, 330
inferences, 2
inferiority complex, 423
infinite productivity, 271
information processing memory
        model, 240–243
informational social influence, 356
inhibiting hormones, 84
inhibitory post-synaptic potential
        (IPSP), 78
innate motives, 165
insanity, 452
insight, 266
insight learning, 219
insomnia, 143
instincts, 167
Institutional Review Boards
        (IRBs), 52
instrumental aggression, 359
instrumental competence, 399
instrumental conditioning, 211–215
insulin, 172
integration approach, to conflict
        resolution, 518
intellectual development, 393
intellectual health, 511
intelligence
    accuracy of testing for, 280
    analytic, 275
    bodily-kinesthetic, 275
    creative, 275
    cultural differences in, 280–282
    defined, 273
    emotional, 275
    gender differences in, 282
    general, 274
    interpersonal, 275
    intrapersonal, 275
    linguistic, 274
    logical-mathematical intelligence,
        274–275
    measuring, 276–282
    musical, 275
    naturalist, 275
    origins of, 273–274

practical, 275
spatial, 275
specific, 274
theories of, 274–275
intelligence quotient (IQ), 276
    creativity and, 283–284
interactionist approach, to
        personality, 435
interaural differences, 118
interdependence, 366
interference, 249
    proactive, 249
    retroactive, 249
internal locus of control, 430, 523
Internet resources. See Web sites
interpersonal attraction, 361–366
    familiarity and, 362–363
    physical attractiveness and,
        363–364
    proximity and, 362–363
    reciprocal liking, 363
interpersonal intelligence, 275
intersex, 305, 306
interviewer bias, 236
interviews, 410–411
    structured, 410
    unstructured, 410
intracellular thirst, 170
intrapersonal intelligence, 275
intrinsic motivations, 168
introspection, 9
involuntary behaviors, 2
ions, 77
iris, 104
ischaemic stroke, 81

Jacobson's progressive relaxation
        technique, 530
James, William, 11, 167, 178, 216, 347
James-Lange theory, of emotion, 178
jealous type delusions, 471
jet lag, 135
Johnson, Virginia, 320
Jung, Carl, 15, 413, 420–423, 437
    personality types, 422–423

Kaczynski, Ted, 452
kanji, 270

Kanzi, 272
Katrina, Hurricane, 341–342, 367–368
K-complexes, 138
Keppler, Johannes, 103
kin selection, 167
  theory of, 357
kinesthetic sense, 97
Kinsey, Alfred, 299
kinship studies, 435
Koelling, Robert, 203–204
Koffka, Kurt, 10
Kohlberg, Lawrence, 400–402
Kohler, Wolfgang, 10, 219
Korsakoff's syndrome, 152

L

Lange, Carl, 178
language
  acquisition of, 268–269
  animal communication vs., 270–271
  development of, 391–393, 392f
  early research on animals' use of, 271–272
  elements of, 269–270
  necessity of, for thought, 262–265
  recent research on animals' use of, 272–273
language-acquisition device (LAD), 268
Laozi, 5
Lashley, Karl, 16
latency stage, 418
latent content, of dreams, 144
latent learning, 218–219
lateral geniculate nucleus (LGN), 107
lateral hypothalamus (LH), 171
lateral surface, of brain, 68f, 69
Latino/a Americans, psychotherapy and, 499–500
Lazarus's cognitive theory, of emotion, 181–182
learned helplessness, 524
learned motives, 166
learning
  associative, 197
  cognition and, 218–220
  defined, 195
  insight, 219
  latent, 218–219
  nonassociative, 197, 198–200
  observational, 220, 269
  performance and, 196–197
  trial-and-error, 265
  types of, 197–218
learning perspective, 15–16
left-handedness, 300
lemniscal pathway, 99, 99f
lens, 104
Leonardo da Vinci, 7
leptin, 172–173
LeVay, Simon, 319
levels of processing model, of memory, 240
libido, 414
Librium, 486
life change units (LCUs), 514–515
life-span development theory, 425–426
light, defined, 103
limbic system, 71–74
linear perspective, 113
linguistic intelligence, 274
linguists, 269
listening, attentive, 250
lithium carbonate, 486
"Little Albert," 201–202
Locke, John, 8
locus of control
  external, 430
  internal, 430
Loftus, Elizabeth, 231–232, 234–235, 390
logical-mathematical intelligence, 274
longitudinal designs, 43
long-term memory (LTM), 242–243
  types of, 243
loosening of associations, 467
loudness, 116
love
  companionate, 365
  passionate, 365
  Sternberg's triangular theory of, 365–366
  theories of, 364–366
luminance, 111
luminescent light, 103
Luther, Martin, 7
lymphocytes, 521
lysergic acid diethylamide (LSD), 155

M

magnetic resonance imaging (MRI), 46
maintenance rehearsal, 240
major depressive disorder, 465
male erectile disorder, 323
male orgasmic disorder, 323
malleus, 117
Malleus Malleficarum, 6, 484
mania, 464–465
manifest content, of dreams, 144
manipulation motives, 175
manual babbling, 391
Marcus Aurelius, 5
marijuana, 156–157
marriage, 314–316
  styles of, 315
Maslow, Abraham, 17, 169, 426–427, 472
Masters, William, 320
maturational readiness, 378–379
McMartin Day Care scandal, 229–230
MDMA. See methylenedioxymethamphetamine (MDMA)
mean, 47
means-end analysis, 266
mechanoreceptors, 97
medial surface, of brain, 68f, 69
median, 47
medical model, of mental illness, 451–452
meditation, 148–149
medulla, 75
Meissner corpuscles, 97
melatonin, 84
memory. See also forgetting
  accuracy and, 229
  beginnings of debate on, 229–230
  biology of, 247–248
  context-dependent, 246
  echoic, 241
  episodic, 243
  explicit, 243
  false, 230–231, 390
  flashbulb, 238
  forgetting and, 248–250
  hypnosis and, 236
  iconic, 241

implicit, 244
information processing model of, 240–243
levels of processing model of, 240
long-term, 242–243
procedural, 243
processes of, 239–240
questioning accuracy of, 231–239
reconstructive, 245
repressed, research on, 238–239
semantic, 243
serial position phenomenon and, 247
short-term, 241
of space alien abduction, 236–237
stage theory of, 528–529
state-dependent, 246
stress and, 235
for trauma, 237
ways of improving, 250–253
working, 241
memory development, 388–390
Meniere's disease, 119
mental age, 276
mental disorder, diagnosis of, 452
mental health, 472
mental images, 263
mental maps, 219
mental processes, 2
mental set, 267
mental status exams, 450
mere exposure effect, 362
Merkel's discs, 97
Mesmer, Franz, 147
mesmerism, 147
Mestral, George de, 283
meta-analysis, of psychotherapy, 500–501
method of loci technique, 251
method of savings, 248
methylenedioxymethamphetamine (MDMA), 155–156
Milgram, Stanley, 352–354
Miller, George, 242
Miller's Magic Number, 242
mind, 2
Minnesota Multiphase Personality Inventory (MMPI-2), 411
Minnesota Twins Study, 274
misinformation effect, 234
mnemonic devices, 250

mode, 47
modeling, 269, 360
modern racism, 350
modern sexism, 350
Moniz, Antonio Egas, 486–487
monoamine oxidase inhibitors (MAOIs), 486
monocular cues, 111–112
mood disorders
    causes of, 466–467
    general characteristics, 464
    types of, 464–465
mood effects, retrieval and, 245–246
mood stabilizers, 486
Moon Illusion, 114
moral development, stages of, 400–402
    conventional level, 401
    postconventional level, 401
    preconventional level, 400
moral treatment, 484
morality principle, 415
morphemes, 269
mosaic, 104
mother archetype, 421
motion parallax, 111
motivation
    arousal theory of, 168–169
    cognitive theories of, 168
    defined, 165–166
    drive-reduction theory of, 169
    evolutionary theories of, 166–167
    incentive theories of, 168
    instinct theories of, 167
    Maslow's hierarchy of needs, 169
    power, 176
    theories of, 166–169
motives
    abundancy motives, 166
    change, 175
    curiosity, 175
    deficiency, 165
    implicit, 174
    innate, 165
    learned, 166
    manipulation, 175
    self-attributed, 174
motor skill development, 384–386
motoric thought, 262
movement, perception of, 114
movement detectors, 114

Muller, Johannes, 94
multiple intelligence theory, 274–275
multiple sclerosis (MS), 76
multipolar neurons, 75–76, 76f
multitasking, 216
Munstenberg, Hugo, 12
Murray, Henry, 412
muscular paralysis, 142–143
musical intelligence, 275
myelin sheath, 76, 80
myelinated axons, 76
Myers-Briggs Type Indicator (MBTI), 411
myotonia, 320

N

narcissism, 456
narcissistic personality disorder, 456
narcolepsy, 142–143
Native Americans, psychotherapy for, 497–498
natural selection, 212–213
naturalist intelligence, 275
naturalistic observational techniques, 36
nature vs. nurture, 343–344
needs, 17
negative punishment, 213
negative reinforcement, 213
neo-Freudians
    Alfred Adler, 423–424
    Erik Erikson, 425–426
    Karen Horney, 425
    Carl Jung, 420–423
neologisms, 468
nervous system, 8, 64–69, 64f
    autonomic, 66–67
    central, 65
    peripheral, 64–65
    somatic, 65–66
neural conduction, 78
neurofibrillary tangles, 73
neuronal differentiation, 382
neurons, 75–77
neuropsychologists, 20
neurosis, 425
neuroticism, 431
neurotransmitter systems, 80–83
neurotransmitters, 76
neutral stimulus (NS), 200

nicotine, 154, 527–528
night terrors, 142
nightmares, 142
Nim Chimpsky, 271
Nin, Anais, 345
nine-dot problem, 267
nociceptors, 98–99
nodes of Ranvier, 76, 77f, 80
nomothetic goals, 175
nonassociative learning processes, 197, 198–200
nonattachment, 397
noncoercive paraphilia, 326–327
nonconformity, social, 448–449
nonexperimental research techniques, limitations of, 37
nonparticipant techniques, 36
non-REM sleep, 138
nonverbal behaviors, 2
norepinephrine, 83, 171, 527
normal curve, 48
normative conformity, 355–356
norms, 280, 448–449
nuclei, 73
nucleus accumbens, 82
nuisance variables, 40
nurture vs. nature, 343–344
nutrition, to reduce stress, 532

O

obedience, 352–354
object agnosia, 115
object permanence, 386, 389
objective tests, 411
objects, perception of, 109–110
observational learning, 220, 269
observational techniques, 35–37
    naturalistic, 36
    nonparticipant, 36
    participant, 36
    survey method, 36–37
obsessions, 459–460
obsessive-compulsive disorder (OCD), 457, 459
obsessive-compulsive personality disorder, 457
occipital lobes, 71
occupational health, 511–512
odorants, 120
Oedipus complex, 414

olfaction, properties of, 120
olfactory bulb, 120
olfactory cavity, 120
olfactory epithelium, 120
olfactory system, 119–121
    anatomy of, 120
ontogeny, 378
operant conditioning, 211–215, 269
    applications of, 216–218
operational definitions, 34
opiates, 102, 155
opponent process theory, 109
optimism, 523
oral stage, 417
organ of corti, 117
organic sense, 97
ossicles, 117
oval window, 117
ovaries, 84
overextension, 391
overlap, 391
overlearning, 252

P

Pacinian corpuscles, 97
Pagocytes, 521
pain, perception of, 101–103
pain disorder, 462
palinaesthesia, 100
pancreas, 84–85
panic disorders, 458
papillae, 121
paradigm shift, 7
paradoxical cold, 100
paradoxical sleep, 139
paradoxical warm, 100
parallel play, 399
paranoid personality disorder, 454
paranoid schizophrenia, 469
paraphilia, 326
    coercive, 326
    noncoercive, 326–327
parasympathetic division, 66
parenting style, 396
parents
    authoritarian, 398
    authoritative, 398–399
    permissive, 398
    uninvolved, 399

parietal lobes, 70
Parkinson's disease, 71
participant techniques, 36
passionate love, 365
patterned speech, 391
Pavlov, Ivan P., 16, 200
Paxil, 486
pedophilia, 326
perception, 93, 96
    of color, 108–109
    of depth and size, 111–114
    of movement, 114
    of objects and forms, 109–110
    of pain, 101–103
    of temperature, 100–101
    of touch, 100
perceptual development, 387–388
peripheral cues, to hunger, 171–173
peripheral nervous system (PNS), 64–66
permissive parents, 398
persecutory type delusions, 472
personal distress (subjective discomfort), 450–451
personal fable, 387
personal unconscious, 420
personality
    assessment of, 410–413
    behavioral theories, 428–430
    biological theories, 433–435
    birth order and, 424
    brain and, 433–434
    culture and, 433
    defined, 409
    Freud's structure of personality, 414–415
    genetics and, 434–435
    humanistic theories, 426–428
    interactionist approach to, 435
    neo-Freudians, 420–426
    psychoanalytic model of, 413–426
    theories of, 436t
    trait theories, 430–433
personality disorders
    causes of, 457–458
    general characteristics, 454
    types of, 454–457
personality factors, of stress, 522–524
personality inventories, 411
personality types, 430–431

perspectives in psychology
  biological, 16–17
  cognitive, 16
  cross-cultural, 15
  evolutionary, 17
  humanistic, 17
  learning, 15–16
  psychodynamic, 13–15
pessimism, 523
phallic stage, 417–418
phantom limb pain, 101
phencyclidine (PCP), 157
pheromones, 121
phi phenomenon, 10–11, 114
Phillips, Elery, 216
phobias, 210, 458–459
  agoraphobia, 459
  social, 459
  specific, 459
Phoenix and Ake, 272–273
phonemes, 269
phonetics, 269
photons, 103
photopigments, 105
photoreceptors, 104–105
phrenology, 434
phylogeny, 378
physical dependence, 150
physical development, 377–386
  brain development, 381–383
  motor skill development, 384–386
  prenatal, 379–381
  sensory development, 383–384
physical health, 511
physiological component, of
    emotion, 177
physiological reactions, 3–4
physiological zero, 98
physiology, 5–6
Piaget, Jean, 265, 386–387
pineal gland, 84
Pinel, Philippe, 484
pinna, 116–117
pitch, 116
  perception of, 118
pituitary gland, 84
place theory, 118
placebo, 38
placental barrier, 380
plasticity, 381
Plato, 5

Platt, John, 204
play
  associative, 399
  cooperative, 399
  parallel, 399
pleasure principle, 414
Plutchik's functional theory of
    emotion, 183–184, 183f
pons, 74
Ponzo Illusion, 113, 114f
positive psychologists, 18
positive psychology, 472, 523
positive punishment, 213
positive reinforcement, 213
positron emission tomography
    (PET) scan, 45, 233
postconventional level, 401
posterior surface, of brain, 68
posthypnotic suggestion, 147
post-synaptic potential, 78
post-traumatic stress disorder
    (PTSD), 72, 460, 518–519
  memory and, 237
postural muscle paralysis, 139
potassium ions, 77
power motivation, 176
practical intelligence, 275
pragmatics, 270
preconscious level, 413
preconventional level, 400
prediction, as goal of psychology, 33
preformation, 379
prefrontal lobotomy, 487
pregnancy, unplanned, 331–332
prejudice, 347, 349. See also
    attitudes
  attitudes and, 349–350
  contemporary, 350
  reducing, 350, 351–352
premature ejaculation
    disorder, 323
prenatal period, 379
preoperational stage, 386
presbycusis, 119
pressures, 514
primacy effect, 247, 252
primacy versus recency effect, 12
primary auditory cortex, 71,
    117, 117f
primary hyperalgesia, 102
primary motor cortex, 70

primary visual cortex, 71, 107
printing, 6–7
proactive interference, 249
problem solving, 265–268
  obstacles to, 267–268
  strategies for, 266–267
problem-focused coping, 532–533
procedural memory, 243
process loss, 367
projective tests, 411–412
propositional thought, 262
prosocial behavior, 356–359
  defined, 356
  exchange model of, 357
  factors influencing, 357–358
prosopagnosia, 115
Prossor, Beverly, 13
prototype theory, 264
proximity, 362–363
proximo-distal law, 379
Prozac, 486
psychedelic drugs, 155
psychoactive drugs, 149–150, 526–528
psychoanalysis, 11, 488–489
psychoanalytic theory, 413–426
psychodynamic perspective, 13–15
psycholinguistics, 269
psychological androgyny, 312
psychological dependence, 150
psychology
  ancient views on, 4–6
  careers in, 18–21
  defined, 1–2
  ethics in, 52–53
  ethnic diversity in, 12–13
  gender in, 12
  goals of, 33–34
  historical approaches to, 9–11
  history of, 4–12
  important individuals who
    influenced, 14t
  modern age and, 8
  modern contributions to, 11–12
  modern perspectives in, 13–17
  positive, 472, 523
  Renaissance and, 6–8
  research in, 31–32
psychometrics, 276
psychometrists, 20
psychoneuroimmunology, 522
psychopathology, 447

psychosexual stages of development,
    Freud's, 416–419, 419*t*
  anal stage, 417
  genital stage, 419
  latency stage, 418
  oral stage, 417
  phallic stage, 417–418
psychosis, measuring, 450
psychosomatic disorders, 514
psychosurgery, 247, 486–488
psychotherapies
  aversive conditioning, 491–492
  behavioral therapy, 490
  cognitive behavior therapy, 494
  cognitive therapy, 492–494
  cultures and, 497–500
  cybertherapy, 496
  effectiveness of, 500–501
  eye movement desensitization and
      reprocessing, 497
  family therapy, 495
  group therapy, 494–495
  humanistic therapy, 489–490
  psychoanalysis, 488–489
  self-help groups, 495–496
  social skills training, 492
  systematic desensitization,
      490–491
psychotic, defined, 450
psychoticism, 431
psychotomimetics, 155
punishment, 213–214
  negative, 213
  positive, 213
pupil, 104
puzzle box, 212, 212*f*

Q

quantitative/measurement
    psychologists, 20

R

racism, 350
Railroad Illusion, 113, 114*f*
random activation synthesis
    theory, 145
random assignment, 42
random selection, 41
range, 48

rape, 327–328
rational-emotive behavior therapy
    (REBT), 492–493
rational-emotive therapy (RET),
    492–493
Rayner, Rosalie, 201
reality principle, 415
recall, 244–245
recapitulation theory, 378
recency effect, 247, 252
receptive fields, 100
receptor potentials, 94
receptors, sensory, 93–94
reciprocal determinism, theory
    of, 429
reciprocal liking, 363
recognition, 245
recognition by components (RBC)
    theory, 110
reconstructive memory, 245
recovered memory therapy, 230–231
red-outs, 72
reflexes, 66
reframing, 514
reinforcement, 213
  adventitious, 217
  negative, 213
  positive, 213
  schedules of, 214–215
relationships, myths about, 312–314
relative motion, 114
relative size, 114
releasing hormones, 84
reliability, 280, 410
REM behavior disorder, 143
REM sleep, 139
  deprivation, 140
Renaissance, psychology and, 6–8
repetitive transcranial magnetic
    stimulation (rTMS), 488
representational thought, 386
repressed memory, research on,
    238–239
research
  beginning process of, 34–35
  in psychology, 31–32
  techniques, 35–37
research methods
  in biopsychology, 44–46
  in developmental psychology,
      42–44

resistance, 489
resistance stage, 520–521
resting membrane potential, 77
reticular activating system (RAS),
    74–75
reticular formation, 74–75
retina, 104, 106*f*
retinex theory, 109
retinotropic manner, 107
retrieval, 240, 244–245
  context effects on, 245–246
  mood effects on, 245–246
retroactive interference, 249
retrograde amnesia, 247
reuptake, 81
rhodopsin, 105
rhyming, 251
riddle of induction, 392–393
Risperdal, 485
rods, 105
Rogers, Carl, 17, 427–428, 489
Rohypnol, 327
rooting reflex, 384
Rorschach, Hermann, 412
Rorschach Inkblot Test, 412
Rotter, Julian, 430
Rovee-Collier, Carolyn, 389
Rubber Hand Illusion, 100
Ruffini cylinders, 97

S

Sacks, Oliver, 115
saliency, 202–203
Sanchez, George, 12–13
satiety, 172
Savage-Rumbaugh, Sue, 272
scatterplots, 40*f*, 50
Schacter, Dan, 232–233
Schacter-Singer theory, of emotion,
    180–181
schedules of reinforcement
  defined, 214
  fixed interval, 214, 215
  fixed-ratio, 214
  variable interval, 214, 215
  variable ratio, 214–215
scheduling worries, 529
schema, 265, 346, 386
schizoid personality
    disorder, 454

schizophrenia
    causes of, 470–471
    general characteristics, 467
    negative symptoms of, 469
    positive symptoms of, 467–469
    types of, 469–470
schizotypal personality disorder, 455
school psychologists, 19
scientific method, 31, 32–33
seasonal affective disorder, 84
secondary sex characteristics, 304
securely attached infants, 397
sedative drugs, 150
selection by consequences, 213
selective forces, 212–213
selective serotonin reuptake
        inhibitors (SSRIs), 82, 485–486
self archetype, 422
self-actualization, 169, 426–427
self-attributed motives, 174
self-concept, 427
self-efficacy, 430, 523
self-esteem, 427
self-help groups, 495–496
Seligman, Martin, 501, 523, 524
Selye, Hans, 519–520
semantic memory, 243
semantics, 270
Seneca, 5
sensation, 93
sensation-seeking motivation, 175
sensitization, 198–200
sensorimotor stage, 386
sensorineural hearing losses, 119
sensory development, 383–384
sensory maps, 95
sensory modalities, 93
sensory receptors, 93–94
sensory register, 240–241
sensory specific satiety, 122
sensory threshold, 95
separation anxiety, 396
sequential design, 43
serial position phenomenon,
        246–247
serotonin, 82, 526–527
set point theory, 173
sexism, 350
sexual aversion disorder, 323
sexual behaviors, problematic,
        326–328

sexual coercion, 328
sexual communication, tips for,
        322–323
sexual development, 303–310
sexual differences
    evolutionary theory of, 308–309
    hormonal theory of, 307
    social psychological theories of,
        309–310
sexual dysfunctions, 323–324
    treatment of, 324–325
sexual masochism, 326
sexual orientation, 317–320, 318t
    continuum, 318
sexual pain disorder
        (dypaurenia), 323
sexual response cycle, 320
    excitement phase, 320–321
    orgasm phase, 321
    plateau phase, 321
    resolution phase, 322
sexual sadism, 326
sexually transmitted diseases
        (STDs), 329–331
shadow, 15
shadow archetype, 422
shaky-bridge study, 180–181
shape constancy, 113
Shapiro, Francine, 497
short-term memory (STM), 241
    Miller's Magic Number and, 242
sibling relationships, social
        development and, 399
Simon, Benjamin, 236–237
Simon, Theodore, 276
simultanagnosia, 115
simultaneous conditioning, 205–206
single-unit recordings, 46
situational attribution, 344
six primary emotions, 184f, 185
Sixteen Personality Factors (16PF)
        Test, 431
size, perception of, 111–114
size constancy, 113
skin receptors, 97–99
Skinner, B. F., 15, 35, 196, 196f, 212,
        214, 268–269, 269f, 429
sleep, 135–145
    bodily changes during stages of,
        137–138
    brain waves and, 136–137

    cycles, 139
    deprivation, 140
    disorders, 141–145
    non-REM, 138
    non-REM deprivation, 141
    reasons for, 139–140
    REM, 138
    REM deprivation, 140–141
    researching stages of, 136
    stages of, 136–137, 138–139
    triggers for, 135–136
sleep apnea, 143–144
sleep paralysis, 143
sleep spindles, 138
sleep talking, 142
sleepwalking, 141–142
slice preparation, 46
small N designs, 46–47
smoking, 527–528
social and emotional development
    attachment and, 396–398
    Erikson's stages of, 394–395
    moral development, 400–402
    sibling relationships and, 399
    social interactions, 398–400
    temperament and, 395–396
social cognition, 346
social factors, of stress, 524–525
social health, 511
social interactions, of infants,
        398–400
social learning theory, 360
social motivation, 147–176
social norm of reciprocity, 357
social norms, 356
social perception, 345–346
social phobias, 459
social psychologists, 20
social psychology
    defining, 342–343
    nature vs. nurture issue, 343–344
    reasons for importance of,
        344–345
    sociology vs., 343
Social Readjustment Rating Scale
        (SRRS), 515, 516t
social roles, defined, 369
social skills training, 492
social-cognitive learning theory,
        429–430
social-facilitation theory, 369

sociology, social psychology *vs.*, 343
sodium ions, 77
Solomon, George, 522
soma, 75
somatic nervous system (SNS), 65–66
somatic type delusions, 471
somatization disorder, 462
somatoform disorders
  causes of, 462
  general characteristics, 461
  types of, 461–462
somatosensation, 65
somatosenses, 97
somatosensory cortex, 70, 99
somatotopic manner, 99
sound, properties of, 116
sound localization, 118
sound shadow, 118
sound waves, 116
  complexity of, 116
source monitoring, 390
space alien abduction, memory of, 236–237
span of attention, 9
spatial intelligence, 275
specific intelligences, 274
specific nerve energies, law of, 94
specific phobias, 459
speed of light, 103
Spence, Kenneth, 204
Spencer, Herbert, 167
Sperling, George, 241
Sperry, Roger, 16, 69
spinal nerves, 65
spinothalamic pathway, 99, 99*f*
spiritual health, 512
split-brain procedure, 69
spontaneous decay, 198
spontaneous recovery, 198
sports psychologists, 20
St. Mary's of Bethlehem Hospital, London, 484
stage theory of memory, 528–529
standard deviation, 47–48
standardization, 280
Stanford Prison experiment, 369
Stanford-Binet Intelligence Scale, 276–277
stapes, 117
star-tracing task, 248

state-dependent memory, 246
statistics, 47–51
  descriptive, 47–48
  inferential, 49–51
stereopsis, 111
stereotype threat, 282
stereotypes, 350
stereotyping, 301
Stern, William, 276
Sternberg, Robert, 275, 365
still face effect, 398
stimulants, 153–154
stimulus-outcome association, 211
stimulus-response outcome association, 211
stonewalling, 316
storage, 240
strange situation method, 397
stranger anxiety, 296
stress
  body's physiological response to, 519–521
  defined, 512
  effects of, on immune system, 521–522
  ineffective coping styles for, 525–528
  personality factors of, 522–524
  social factors of, 524–525
stress management, 528–533
stressors, types of, 512–519
striate cortex, 107
striving for superiority, 423
structuralism, 10
structured interviews, 410
subgoal analysis, 267
subject mortality, 43
subjective discomfort (personal distress), 450–451
subordinate categories, 264
sulci, 70
summation, 78
Sumner, Francis, 13
superego, 13, 415, 526
superior colliculus, 96
superior temporal gyrus, 96
superordinate categories, 264
superstitions, 217
surface structure, 270
survey method, 36–37
sympathetic division, 66–67

synaptic cleft, 76
synaptic transmission, 80
synaptic vesicles, 76
synchrony, 136
synethesia, 263
syntax, 270, 271
synthetic heat, 100
systematic desensitization, 490–491

T

tabula rasa, 5
tardive dyskinesia, 485
taste buds, 121
taste pores, 121
taste receptor cells, 121
tastes, basic, 121–122
T-cells, 521
techniques of research
  case study, 37
  limitations of nonexperimental, 37
  observational, 35–37
tectorial membranes, 117
temperament, 395–396
temperature, perception of, 100–101
temporal lobes, 71
teratogens, 380
Terman, Lewis, 276, 278
terminal branches, 76
Terrance, Herbert, 271
testes, 84
testimony. *See also* memory
  child, 235–236
  eyewitness, 233–234
testosterone, 307
test-retest reliability, 410
thalamic pain, 103
thalamus, 73, 95–96
Thematic Apperception Test (TAT), 174, 412
theories, 32
therapies. *See* biological treatments; psychotherapies
therapists
  degrees for, 502*t*
  specialties of, 502*t*
  suggesting for seeking, 501–503
  types, 502*t*
thermoreceptors, 98
theta waves, 138

thinking. *See also* thought
  convergent, 284
  defined, 262
  divergent, 284
  language and, 262–265
thinking distortions, 493*t*
third variable problem, 51
thirst, 170
Thompson, Jennifer, 234
Thorazine, 485
Thorndike, Edward L., 15, 211–212, 212*f*, 265
thought. *See also* thinking
  animistic, 387
  creativity and, 284
  egocentric, 386–387
  imaginal, 262
  mental representations and, 262–263
  motoric, 262
  propositional, 262
  representational, 386
thought disorders, 467
thought stopping, 529
threshold of excitation, 78
thymus glands, 84
timbre, 116
tinnitus, 119
Titchener, Edward, 10, 12
Tofranil, 485
token economies, 216–217, 491–492
Tolman, Edward Chase, 218–219
top-down processes, 110
touch, 97–103
  perception of, 100
trace conditioning, 205
trait theories, 430–433
  "Big Five" model, 431–432
  universality of, 432
tranquilizers, 152, 486
transcendental meditation (TM), 531
transference, 489
transsexuals, 306–307
transvestic fetishisms, 326
trauma, memory for, 237
traumatic events, 518–519
trephination, 483
trial-and-error learning, 265
triangular theory of love, Sternberg's, 365–366
triangulation, 495

triarchic theory of intelligence, 275
trichromatic theory, 108–109
tricyclics, 485
trophoblast, 379
true self, 427, 489
t-test, 51
twin studies, 434–435
two point discrimination, 100
tympanic membrane, 117
Type A personality, 524

umami, 122
unconditional positive regard, 428, 489–490
unconditioned response (UR), 200
unconditioned stimulus (US), 200
  characteristics of, 204–205
  timing of, 205–206
underextension, 391
undifferentiated schizophrenia, 469–470
uninvolved parents, 399
unmyelinated axons, 76
unplanned pregnancy, 331–332
unstructured interviews, 410
uplifts, 514
Urbach-Wieth disease, 72

vaginismus, 323
validating conflict style, of marriage, 315
validity, 280, 410
Valium, 486
variable interval (VI) schedules, 214–215
variable ratio (VR) schedules, 214–215
variables
  confounding, 40–41
  defining, 34–35
  dependent, 38
  extraneous, 40
  independent, 38
  nuisance, 40
vasocongestion, 320
ventral surface, of brain, 68, 68*f*

ventromedia hypothalamus (VMH), 171
verbal behaviors, 2
Verougstraete, Wendy, 283
vertigo, 119
vestibular system, 119
vicarious trial-and-error (VTE), 220
virtual reality exposure, 491
vision, 103–115
  anatomy of, 104–107
  central nervous system pathway for, 107
  disorders, 115
visual acuity, 105
visual agnosia, 115
visual angle, 111–112, 113*f*
visual cliff, 388
volatile conflict style, of marriage, 315
volley principle, 118
voltage-dependent calcium channels, 80
voltage-dependent potassium channels, 79
voltage-dependent sodium channels, 79
voluntarism, 9
voluntary behaviors, 2
vomeronasal organ, 121
voyeurism, 326

Wallace, Alfred Russell, 212
War of the Ghosts, 245
warm fibers, 98
warm receptors, 98
Washburn, Margaret, 12, 35
Washoe, 272
Watson, John B., 11–12, 16, 35, 201, 428–429
Web sites, 29, 61, 91, 131, 163, 193, 227–228, 259, 295, 339, 375, 407, 445–446, 481, 511, 539
Wechsler, David, 277
Wechsler Adult Intelligence Scale (WAIS), 277
Wechsler Intelligence Scale for Children (WISC), 277
Wechsler Preschool and Primary Scale of Intelligence (WPPSI), 277

weight regulation, theories on
    energy reservoir theory, 173
    set point theory, 173
Wernicke, Carl, 8
Wertheimer, Max, 10
"What" system, 107–108
"Where" system, 107–108
white matter, 69
Williams syndrome, 283
witch hunting, 484
withdrawal symptoms, 150
withdrawing, 525–526

Wolpe, Joseph, 490
womb envy, 425
women. *See* gender
word salads, 467–468
working memory, 241
Wundt, Wilhelm, 4, 6, 8–9

X chromosomes, 303
Xanax, 486

Y chromosomes, 303
Yerkes-Dodson Law, 168–169, 168*f*
yoga, 531

Zajonc, Robert, 368–369
zeitgeist, 6
Zimbardo, Philip, 354
Zoloft, 486